Pacific Medical Journal

by David Wooster

Address:
HardPress
8345 NW 66TH ST #2561
MIAMI FL 33166-2626
USA
Email: info@hardpress.net

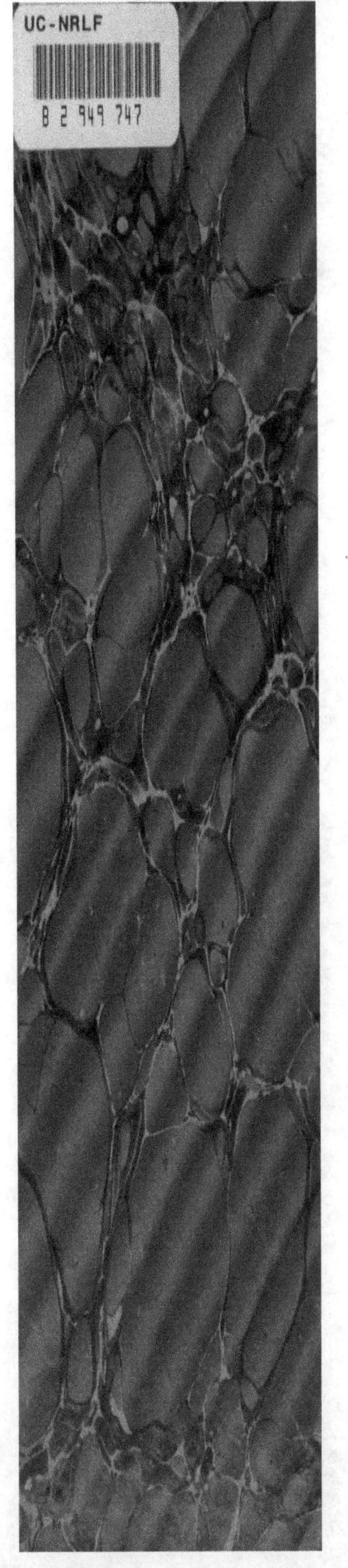
UC-NRLF
B 2 949 747

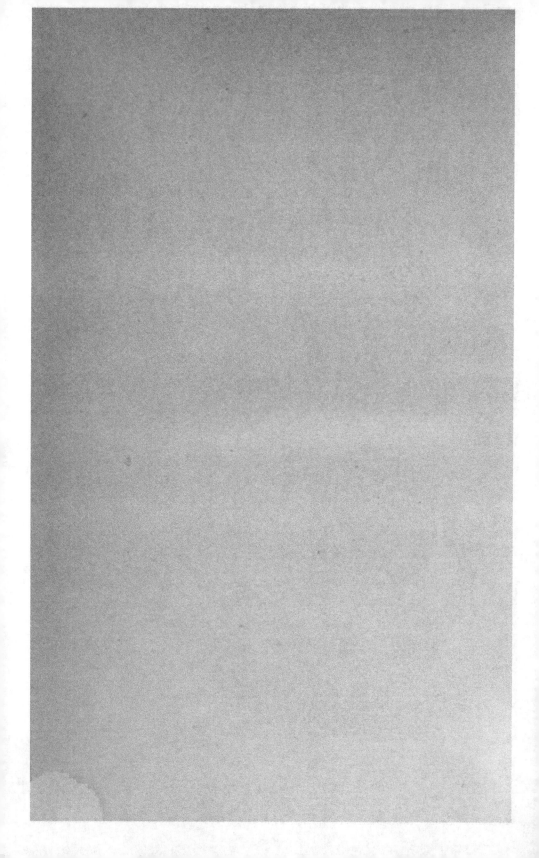

PACIFIC

Medical and Surgical Journal.

Editors and Proprietors:

HENRY GIBBONS, M.D. HENRY GIBBONS, Jr., M.D.

Vol. V.—JUNE, 1870.—MAY, 1872.

New Series.

SAN FRANCISCO:

J. F. BROWN, BOOK AND JOB PRINTER,

No. 534 Commercial Street.

TERMS: Published monthly at $5.00 a year, payable in advance. Postage prepaid by the Publishers.

INDEX TO VOL. V.

PAGE

Accidents at Dr. Squibb's Laboratory... 232
Address, Annual, before the San Francisco Medical Society. By J. F. Morse, M.D... 344
" before the San Francisco Medical Society. By B. D. Dean, M.D... 447
" Valedictory. By L. C. Lane, M.D... 321
A Defense of Physic, with Special Reference to the Fair Trial. By C. F. Buckley, M.D,... 145
Adulteration of Drugs... 280
Albuminuria, Metallic... 474
" Strychnia in... 316
Alcohol and Tobacco, An Indictment against... 185
" " " Effects on the Sight of... 45
" Medicinal Use of... 429
Alcoholism and Absinthism... 475
Alder, Tag, as a Hemostatic... 282
Amyl, Nitrite of, and Chinese Samshu... 582
Ammonia, Vapor of, in Pelvic Pains... 282
" " " " the Treatment of Whooping Cough 301
Amputations after Gunshot Wounds... 86
Anesthesia, Local... 231
" by Hypodermic Injections... 312
Anesthetic Vapors, Treatment of Chorea by... 375
" A New—Hydramyle... 232
Aneurism, Femoral, Digital Compression in... 281
" The Compression Treatment of... 377
" of the Splenic Artery, Death from... 313
" Traumatic, from Dislocation of the Shoulder... 432
Apothecaries, Liquor Dealers' Licenses for 279
A Repulsive Association... 222
Arseniate of Strychnia: New Antidote to the Poison of Snakes. By Louis Lanszweert, M.D... 108
Asthmatics, Colorado for... 138
Ataxia, Locomotor, Two Cases of. By F. H. Engels, M.D... 337
A Very Mean Trick... 463
Bacteria in the Blood... 526
Barber, E. T., M.D. Case of Recurrent Measles... 65
Bath, Warm, in Insanity and in Burns... 576
" " " Fracture of the Neck of the Femur in a Child Seven years of age—Suit for Malpractice.. 61
Bates, C. B., M.D., Bromide of Potassium in Poisoning by Strychnia... 551
Bed-Sores, Galvanic Treatment of... 472
Belladonna, Action of, on the Heart and Arteries. By David Wooster, M.D... 398
Benjamin Rush and Henry Holland—A Contrast... 580
Bentley, E., M.D., Diagnosis of Pericardial Adhesions: Rejection of Concentric Hypertrophy... 553

PAGE

Bentley, E., M. D. Rapid Development of Mortification in the Crittenden Case 219
Bitters, Label for... 315
Black-Book called for... 184
Bladder, Irritable, Gelseminum in... 525
Blake, James, M.D., On a New form of Pessary... 410
Blisters in the Pneumonia of Infants. By G. G. Tyrrell, L. R. C. S. I., &c... 401
Blood, Effects of Loss of. By H. Gibbons, M.D... 1
Bloodletting in Puerperal Convulsions.. 424
Board of Health of California... 522, 575
Boards of Health, State, Recommended... 576
Boiling out the Stomach... 225
Bowel Obstructions and their Treatment. By C. B. Holbrook, M.D... 491
Brain, Case of Concussion of. By H. Gibbons, M.D... 485
Breasts, A Woman with four... 140
Bright's Disease Detected by the Ophthalmoscope... 279
Bromide of Calcium... 518
Bromide of Iron in Spermatorrhea....90, 532
" of Potassium, Effects of... 477
" " " in Uremic Convulsions... 432
" " " in Poisoning by Strychnia. By C. B. Bates, M.D... 551
Bronchitis, Atomised Turpentine-Water in... 582
Bubo, Opening of, with Caustic Potash. 474
Buckley, C. F., M.D. A Defense of Physic with Special Reference to the Fair Trial... 145
Buckley, C. F., M.D. The Fair-Crittenden Case... 267
Burns, Tea Leaves in... 92
" Warm Bath in... 576

BOOK NOTICES.
Acton on the Reproductive Organs.. 270
Anstie: Neuralgia and Diseases which resemble it... 511
Ashurst, Jr.'s Surgery... 510
Atfield's Chemistry... 42
Bancroft's Tourists' Guide... 72
Beale: The Mystery of Life... 42
Beasley's Druggists' General Receipt Book... 362
Bennett on Pulmonary Consumption 509
Blanding: Insanity and its Treatment 42
Both on Small-Pox... 575
Browne: Medical Jurisprudence of Insanity... 420
Butler's Physicians' Annual for 1872 419
Calkins: The Opium Habit... 133
Chambers: Restorative Medicine... 221
Combe: The Management of Infancy 270
Dalton's Physiology... 419
Dillnberger: Diseases of Women and Children... 180
Flint, Jr.. Physiological Effects of Severe and Protracted Exercise.. 131

PAGE
Fox on Skin Disease 303
Green's Pathology and Morbid Anatomy 419
Hamilton on Fractures and Dislocations 270
Hammond on Diseases of the Nervous System 132
Hartshorne's Essentials of Practice.. 302
Holbrook: Parturition Without Pain. 363
Hood on Bone-Setting 574
Hope: Till the Doctor Comes and How to Help Him 134
Ingham: Plain Talk About Insanity. 574
Jeffries on the Eye 132
Jeffries: Parasites of the Skin 574
Map of Central California 72
Meadows' Manual of Midwifery 180
Medical Communications to the Mass. Medical Society 303
Meredith on the Teeth 269
Neumann: Text Book of Skin Diseases 364
Ogle: St. George's Hospital Reports.. 302
Physicians' Visiting List 364
Radcliffe: Dynamics of Nerve and Muscle 71
Report of Surgical Cases Treated in the U. S. Army 363
Rindfleisch's Pathology 572
Ringer's Therapeutics 572
Simpson: Anesthesia, Hospitalism and Hermaphroditism 510
Stewart on Bright's Disease 573
Storer: Insanity in Women 72
Tanner: Diseases of Infancy and Childhood 71
Taylor: Movement Cure in Paralysis 133
The American Practitioner 362
The Book of Travel of a Doctor of Physic 133
The Human Feet, their Dress and Care 72
The Physician's Prescription Book.. 180
The Three Half Yearly's 511
Thomas: Diseases of Women 573
Transactions of the American Medical Association..364, 419
" " Otological " 362
" " Med. Society of Penn. 364
" " Ohio Medical Society 363
Turnbull on Diseases of the Ear 509
Tyndall: Light and Electricity 134
Waring's Therapeutics 362
West: Disorders of the Nervous System in Childhood 222
Wilkins: Report on Insanity and Asylums 575
Williams on Pulmonary Consumption 508
Wright on Headaches 269
Wunderlich's Medical Thermometry. 511
Wunderlich, Med. Therm. 574
Wythes' Dose and Symptom Book 303, 363
Calabar Bean, Failure of, in Tetanus 375
Calculi, Formation of, under the Prepuce, By H. W. Nelson, M. D. 175
Camphor in Hospital Gangrene 91
Camphor Inhalations, Physiological Action of 81
Cancer, Tannic Acid in 476
Carbolic Acid, Black Urine from 581
" " Paper 379
" " Pills of 430

PAGE
Castor Oil in Pregnancy and Child-bed.. 517
" " to Disguise 240
Cataract, Extraction of 193
Caustic Potassa, Opening of Bubo by.... 474
Cesarean Operation, Statistics of 379
Chemicals on Exhibition 282
Chemistry of Food, So Called 310
Cheney, W. Fitch. M. D. Cases of Mushroom Poisoning 119
Chicago Medical Journals 425
Chloral Hydrate, Action of 473
" " in Cod-oil 189
" " Coma after 15 grains of. 144
" " in Enuresis 92
" " Experiences with, By G. W. Graves, M. D... 7
" " Liebreich on 373
" " by J. W. B. Reynolds M. D. 121
" " Peculiar effects of 83
" " in Sea Sickness 91
" " in Snake Poisoning 234
" " in Tetanus 82, 84
" " Toxemia from Persistent use of 378
" " Value and Safety of 527
Chloralm, Chloride of Aluminium 81
Chlorate of Potassa in Chronic Dysentery 476
Chloroform, Can it be used to Facilitate Robbery 366
" Deaths from 274
" vs. Ether 283
" Suicide by Swallowing 278
Cholera, Contagion of 240
" Cure, Reward for a 273
Chorea, Treatment of, by Anesthetic Vapors 375
Chromic Acid, Violent Action of 315
Cigar Stumps, Value of 526
Circumcision in Utero 281
Climate and Disease 420
Cod Liver Oil, Pepsine, Pancreatine 369
" " " Saponified 231
Cocoanut Milk, Medical Properties of... 240
Collusion between Physicians and Apothecaries 422
Commune, Atrocities of, in a Medico-Psychological Aspect 134
Compression Digital, in Femoral Aneurism 281
" Treatment of Aneurism by... 377
Concussion as a Sanitary Agent 278
Confederate Army Medical and Surgical Memoirs 80
Conium in Mastitis 274
Consumption, Atomized Turpentine-Water in 582
" Cure for 228
" Mortality of 432
" New Volume on 422
Convulsions, Puerperal, Bloodletting in.. 424
" " Veratrum Viride in 472
" Uremic, Bromide of Potassium in 432
" Veratrum in Large Doses in 78
Cord, Two Ligatures on the 295
Corrosive Sublimate Externally Applied, Death from 380
Cox, J. B. M. D. Case of Insertion of the Placenta in the Lower Segment of the Uterus 458
Cox, J. B., M.D., Hypertrophy of the Heart and Pericardial Adhesions... 537

PAGE

Creasote, Pills of.......... 430
Croup, Glycerine Inhalations in.......... 90
" Hot Air in.......... 91
Cundurango and Dr. Bliss, A Warning... 366
" Excelsior.......... 280
" Failure of..........138, 313, 358
" Reported Cure by.......... 470
" Speculation, The.......... 274
Cushing, C., M. D. Case of Traumatic Tetanus: Recovery.......... 444
Cyano-Pancreatine.......... 282
Davison, H. B., M.D., New Mode of Operating for Radical Cure of Varicocele 543
Dean, B. D., M. D., Address before the San Francisco Medical Society.... 447
Death of Mrs. Dr. Price.......... 580
Departed Heroes.......... 577
Diabetes, Treatment of.......... 477
Dietetics of Disease; Beef-tea.......... 468
Differences between Doctors and Lawyers 227
Digitalis, Action of.......... 252
Dislocation of the Elbow, By A. S. Hudson M. D..........52, 394
" Inward, of Radius and Ulna, By C. R. Thorne, M. D.......... 289
" Partial, of Head of Radius.......... 475
Diplomas, Sale of.......... 516
Dirt, Poverty and Drunkenness among the Working classes in London.... 275
Dissecting Poisons, Clinical Lecture on, By James Paget, M. D.......... 207
Doctors, Thirty-two in one Family...... 431
Druggists' Bill, The New York.......... 227
" Examination of, in New York.. 526
Drugs, Adulteration of.......... 90
Dynamics of Nerve and Muscle.......... 360
Dysentery, Enema of Ipecac in.......... 520
" Ergot in.......... 468
" Chronic, Chlorate of Potassa in.......... 476
Ear, a Tick in, for Three Weeks.......... 269
Eczema Cured by Vaccination.......... 581
Egg, Dried White of, in Commerce...... 283
Ellinwood, C. N., M. D. Clinical Lecture on Lupus.......... 413
Embalming, Process of.......... 477
Engels, F. H., M. D. Attempted Suicide by Taking 15 grains of Strychnia...... 460
" " " " " Two Cases of Locomotor Ataxia and one of (probably) Cerebral Sclerosis. 337
Epilepsy, Treatment of.......... 432
Epistaxis, Ipecac in.......... 477
Ergot, Action of.......... 249
" in Dysentary.......... 468
" Quinia as a Substitute for.......... 576
Ergotin, Hypodermic Use of in Hemoptysis 576
Ethics, a Point in.......... 578
Eucalyptus: Its Medical Virtues. By D. Wooster, M. D.......... 550
Erysipelas, Traumatic, Turpentine in.. 274
Ether, Chloroform vs.......... 283
Ethics, Medical.......... 183
" of the Medical Profession By J. F. Montgomery, M.D.......... 97
Eucalyptus Gobulus.......... 457
" Leaves.......... 89
Examinations, Professional.......... 187
Experts, Medical. Reform Needed.......... 423
Expulsion of Dr. Ruppanner.......... 366

AAGE

Exsection of Os Calcis for Necrosis, By E. B. Robertson M.D.......... 49
" Sub Periosteal, of Joints...... 282
Fee-Bill Adopted by the San Francisco Medical Society..........425, 426
Female Medical Students in Moscow..... 314
" Physicians, A Point Gained for.. 87
Ferris, A. S., M.D. Sulphite of Soda, in Acute Laryngitis.......... 115
Foreign-Body, Cases of Removal of....11, 66
Forensic Medicine—Dr. Buckley's paper.. 181
Fracture of Neck of Femur, in Young Child; Suit for Malpractice. By E. T. Barber, M D.......... 61
Fractures, Glue Bandages for.......... 427
Galvanic Treatment of Bed-Sores and Indolent Ulcers.......... 472
Gangrene, Hospital, Camphor in.......... 91
Gelseminum in Irritable Bladder.......... 525
" Therapeutic value of...... 79
Gibbons, H., M.D. Cases of Intussusception and Concussion of the Brain. 485
" " " " Effects of the Loss of Blood.......... 1
" " " " Insanity and disease in California...... 496
" " " " The American Medical Association and Dr. Martin.......... 67
" Jr. Henry, M.D. Report of two Cases of Placenta Previa.......... 453
" " " " " Mortality Statistics of San Francisco for 1871.......... 385
" " " " " Remarks on the Monthly Mortality of San Francisco, 47, 95, 143, 190, 238, 287, 319, 383, 435, 483, 534, 584
Gleet, Astringent Injections in.......... 240
Glue Bandage for Fractures.......... 427
Glycerine in Croup.......... 90
" Leucorrhea.......... 312
Gonorrhea, Treatment by water Injections..........281 478
Gordon, Chas. H. M.D. Tartrate of Iron and Potassa in Typhoid Fever.... 418
Graduates in Medicine in California...... 306
Graduation, Requirements of Candidates for.......... 464
Graves, G. W., M.D. Experience with Chloral Hydrate.......... 7
Gynecological Instruments, New.......... 521
Harvard, Falling off at.......... 521
Health, Extraordinary State of, in India. 90
Heart, Pistol-Ball in, for Four Days..... 88
Hemiplegia, Two Cases of; Necropsy. By F. A. White, M.D.......... 561
Hemoptysis, Hypodermic Use of Ergotin in.......... 576
" in Consumptive Patients.... 517
Hemostatic Cotton-Wool.......... 284
" Tag-Alder as a.......... 282
Hernia, Hydrocele of the Round Ligament Mistaken for.......... 89
" Strangulated, Reduced while Standing.......... 527
Hernial Sac, Puncture of.......... 431
Hiccough, Cases of Persistent, By E. L. Willard, M.D.......... 507
High-Heeled Boots, Chinese Feet and Crooked Shins.......... 43

PAGE
Holbrook, C. B., M.D., Bowel Obstructions and their Treatment 491
" " " Formation of Urea.. 397
Homeopathy in an Economic Light....... 470
Homeopathic Remedies.................. 230
" Surgery, What is it?....... 135
Homer on Physic, Doctress Thetis........ 376
Hospital, Central Pacific R. Road........ 371
How to Choose a Doctor.................. 479
Hubbard, L., M.D. Dime Ejected from the Trachea by Vomiting.............. 11
Hudson, A. S., M.D. The Luxated Elbow 52, 394
Hydrocele, New Treatment of............ 368
" of Round Ligament Mistaken for Hernia........................ 89
Hydrochloric Acid as an Antiseptic...... 233
Hydropathy in Typhoid Fever........... 477
Hydrophobia, Reported Cure of.......... 521
Hypertrophy of the Heart and Pericardial Adhesions. By J. B. Cox, M.D.... 537
Hypertrophy, Concentric, Rejection of. By E. Bentley, M.D............... 553
Hypodermic Injections, Stimulant, in Typhoid Fever............ 183
" Use of Morphia, Death After 306
Hyoscyamus, On the Preparation of Tincture of.......................... 45
Ice in Acute Rheumatism............... 582
Infinitesimal Science.................. 273
Infirmary or Hospital.................. 230
Innovation not Always Improvement..... 469
Iodide of Potassium in Lupus Exedens.. 583
Insanity, Warm Bath in................ 576
Insanity and Disease in California, By H. Gibbons, M.D......... 496
" Physical and Moral Causes of.. 80
Intussusception, Case of, By H. Gibbons M.D.............................. 485
Iodine for Wens of the Scalp............ 430
Ipecac in Epistaxis.................... 477
" Enema of in Dysentery............ 520
Iron, Pills of Sulphate of, and Carbonate of Potassa.... ....281, 430
" Tartrate of, and Potassa in Typhoid Fever. By Chas. H. Gordon M.D. 418
Irrigation—Effects on Health............ 139
Items—Editorial, 44, 82, 83, 91, 92, 186,. 129, 234, 313, 469, 470
" of News &c. 92, 96, 192, 284, 303, 316, 375, 376, 380, 384, 436, 446 480, 536
Journal Contents: End of Volume....... 575
Journal, The......43, 225, 365, 371 426, 427
Journals, Pamphlets &c. received........ 72
Kidney, Abscess of, By E. L. Willard M.D. 12
King, E. W., M.D. Necrosis of Tibia... 552
Lane. L. C., M.D. Valedictory Address... 321
Lanszweert, L., M.D. Arseniate of Strychnia—New Antidote to the Poison of Snakes............................. 108
Laryngitis, Acute, Sulphite of Soda in, By A. S. Ferris M.D.............. 115
Lectures, Intermediate Course of......... 306
Legislation on Medicine................. 304
Leucorrhea, Glycerine in................. 312
Libel, Suit for.......................... 271
Ligature, Antiseptic..................... 284
Lithotomy, Success or Failure of........ 476
Logan, T. M., M.D. Mortality Reports of State Board of Health, with Remarks 46, 93, 141, 189, 236, 286, 317, 381, 433, 481, 533
Lupus, Clinical Lecture on, By C. N. Ellinwood, M.D......................... 413
Lupus Exedens Cured by Iodide of Potassium.................................. 583
Lying-in and Foundling Asylums of Austria................................ 182
" " Hospital and Foundling Asylum of San Francisco..................77, 463
Malaria, What is it?..................... 283
Malformation............................ 280
Malingerer in Bed Twenty-five Years... 316
Malpractice, Protection from Suits for... 512
" Suit for........................ 528
" Suit for, in Case of Fracture of Femur in Young Child, By E. T, Barber M.D..... 61
Mammary Abscess, To Prevent........... 82
Martinache, M. J., M.D. On Extraction of Cataract........................ 193
Mastitis, Conium in..................... 274
Maternal Impression on the Offspring.... 83
McNutt, Wm. F., M.D. Mrs. Winslow's Soothing Syrup..................... 504
Measles, Case of Recurring, By E. T. Barber M.D............................ 65
Medical Association, American, Annual Meeting of........................ 18
Medical Association, American, and Dr. Martin, By H. Gibbons M.D....... 67
Medical Association, American, The Late Meeting of......................... 75
Medical Association, American, Fare of Delegates.......................... 522
" Editors' Association, Annual Meeting of................... 15
" Instruction, St. Paul's School of.......................... 309
" School, The Cheapest.......... 351
" " Gradation of Studies in 79
" Society of Alameda County, Proceedings of 70, 179, 300, 357
" " of California, Meeting of 271
" " of California, Proceedings of.........31, 257, 471
" " of California, Standing Committees of........ 374
" " District................ 522
" " of Sacramento, Proceedings of....130, 255, 416, 563
" " San Francisco, Officers of, for 1872........... 426
" " San Francisco, Proceedings of, 122, 249, 295, 461, 564
Medicine, A New History of............. 520
Membrana Tympani, Reproduction of.... 380
Meningitis, Cerebro-Spinal, By D. Stewart Smith, L. M. C. S. &c............. 293
Mercury, Action of, on the Liver......... 186
" Danger from the Vapor of...... 514
Montgomery, J. F., M.D. Ethics of the Medical Profession................ 97
Mortality, Monthly, of San Francisco, with Remarks, By H. Gibbons, Jr. M.D. 47, 95, 143, 190, 238, 287, 319, 383, 435, 483, 534, 583
" Report of State Board of Health, By T. M. Logan, M.D., 46, 93, 141, 189, 236, 286, 317, 381, 433 481, 533
" Statistics of San Francisco for 1871, By H Gibbons, Jr. M.D.... . 385

PAGE
Mortification, Rapid Development of in the Crittenden Case. By E. Bentley M.D. 219
" Rapid Development of, By C. F. Buckley M.D. 267
Morse, J. F., M.D. Annual Address before the S. F. Medical Society 344
Mucilage of Gum Tragacanth 301
Mushroom Poisoning, Cases of. By W. Fitch Cheney, M.D. 119
Nail, on the Growth of, as a Prognostic in Cerebral Paralysis 88
" Ingrowing, Dr. Pancoast's Treatment of 232
Navy Medical Offices on the Pacific Coast 307
Necrology, 76, 80, 92, 229, 235, 284, 311, 316, 443, 470, 530
Necrosis of Os Calcis: Exsection. By E.B. Robertson, M.D. 49
" of the Tibia. By E.W. King, M.D. 552
Nelson, H. W., M.D. Formation of Calculi under the Prepuce 175
Nerve-Centres, Influence of Tobacco in Diseases of 284
Nutrition of the Human Body in Relation to Disease. By A. Trafton, M.D. 545
Nitrous Oxide Gas, Death from 45
Nostrums, Composition of 88
Oatman, Ira E., M.D. Inflammation and Ulceration of Os and Cervix Uteri 24
Obituary, see Necrology
Office, What a Physician's should be 229
One Hundred and Fifteen Years Old 226
Opium. Poppy Culture 467
Ovariotomy, Bone and Teeth in Cyst. By J. H. Wythe, M.D. 117
" in a Child 379
" Following Puerperal Peritonitis By G. G. Tyrrell, L. R. C. S.I. &c. 195
" Removal of Cancerous Tumors, By J. W. B. Reynolds M.D. 437
Oxygen Gas in Pulmonary Diseases 367
Paralysis, Cerebral, on the Growth of the Nail as a Prognostic in 88
Pedantic Composition 312
Pelvic Pains, Vapor of Ammonia in 282
Pericardial Adhesions, Can they be Diagnosticated? 462, 565, 567
Pericardial Adhesions and Hypertrophy of the Heart, Diagnosis of. By J. B. Cox, M.D. 537
Pericardial Adhesions, Diagnosis of, and Rejection of Concentric Hypertrophy. By E. Bentley, M.D. 553
Perineal Section for Removal of Foreign Body from Bladder, By E. B. Robertson, M.D. 66
Personal 74, 76
Pessary, On a New Form of, By J. Blake, M.D. 410
Pharmaceutical Society, California 178
Phlebitis, Inguinal, from Digital Compression 283
Phosphates in Pregnancy 188
Physician Senators 581
Physicians, American and European, compared 307
" Duration of Life of 316
Physiological Experimentation 276
Pills, New Excipient for 431
Pinus Canadensis, Extract of 279
Piracy, Literary 471
Placenta, Case of Insertion of, on Lower Segment of Uterus, By J. Bradford Cox, M.D. 458
" Delivery of 296
" Previa, Report of Two Cases of, By H. Gibbons Jr. M.D. 453
" Previa, Successfully Treated by Digital Compression, By R. H. Plummer, M.D. 204
Plummer, R. H. M.D. Placenta Previa, Case of 204
Pneumonia of Children, Blisters in, By G. G. Tyrrell, F, R. C. S. I. &c. 401
" Discussion on Treatment of 416
Poison and Antidote 372
" of Snakes, New Antidote to, By L. Lanszweert, M.D. 108
Poisoning, Cases of Mushroom, By W. Fitch Cheney, M.D. 119
" Protection against in England. 139
" by Quinia 228
Pregnancy, Early 376
Pregnancy, Tubal 237
Prescriptions, Bungling 478
" Write in Plain English 44
Profession, Our Poor 277
Professional Incidents in Australia 523
Pruritus of Face a Precursor of Small-Pox 581
Puberty, Infantile 85
Puerperal Peritonitis, Subsequent Ovariotomy, By G. G. Tyrrell, F. R. C. S. I. &c. 195
" Temperatures 318
Pulse, Counting the 310
Pus, Injections of, into the Medulla 320
Pus, Test Solution for 142
Quack, a Villainous 311
Quack Stoned to Death 275
Quacks, Ancient and Modern 466
Quackery, An Act against Empiricism 530
Quassia for Surgical Dressings 188
Retention of Urine, Ice in the Rectum for 377
Reynolds, J. W. B., M.D. Abdominal Section. Removal of Cancerous Tumors 437
" " " Hydrate of Chloral 121
Rheumatism. A Speedy Cure for 479
Rheumatism, Acute, Ice in 582
Robertson, E. B., M.D. Exsection of Os Calcis for Necrosis 49
" " " Removal of Foreign Body from the Bladder by Perineal Section. 66
Rupture of Rectus Femoris Muscle, Recovery 475
Scabies. Presence of, in Paris 517
Scarlatina, Origin of the Poison of 223
Sclerosis, Cerebral, Probable case of, By F. H. Engels M.D. 337
Scott, J., M.D. On the Treatment of Uterine Affections 163
Sea-Sickness, Chloral Hydrate in 91
Sight, Effect of Alcohol and Tobacco on 45
Skin Transplantation or Grafting 232
" " Mr. Pollack's case of 85
Sleep Walking in Childhood 226
Small Pox—A Fearful Responsibility 136
Small-Pox, Pruritus of the Face a Precursor of 581

PAGE

Small-Pox on the Railroad.............. 579
" " in London.................... 90
" " in Paris and Philadelphia 315, 380
" " Sulphur vs............... 315
" " in Utero.................... 478
Smith. D. Stewart, L. M. C. S. Case of Cerebro-Spinal Meningitis.............. 293
Snake-Poisoning. Chloral Hydrate in..... 234
Soap-Bubbles, To Produce Large and Long Lasting.................. 86
Social Evil, The......78, 185, 225, 305, 365 426
" " Dr. Holland's Bill........... 465
" " By W. E. Whitehead. M.D., U. S. Army.................... 55
Solar Eclipse, Danger from............... 314
Speculum, Abuse of; Tinkering the Uterus.................. 137
Spermatorrhea, Bromide of Iron in....90, 532
Spleen, Function of.................... 525
Statistics, Medical, Remarks on.......... 122
Student, A Hospital, of the Olden time.. 137
Students, Rebellion among European.... 142
Strychnia, Bromide of Potassium in Poisoning by. By C. B. Bates, M.D. 551
" in Albuminuria............ 316
" Attempted Suicide by taking 15 Grains of. By F. H. Engels. M.D. 460
" Poisoning by................... 479
Strychnos Potatorum: Clearing nut of India.................. 224
Suicide, the Fashions of................ 84
Sulphite of Soda in Acute Laryngitis, By A. S. Ferris M.D.................. 115
Sulphur vs. Small-Pox.................. 315
Surgeon, The Oldest.................... 315
Sunstroke in the German Army.......... 284
" How to Cure.................. 233
Syphilis, Clinical Lecture on Primary, By F. F. Maury, M.D.............. 352
" Iodides of Ammonium and Sodium in.................. 524
Syphilitic Corpuscles in the Blood....... 515
Tannic Acid, Concentrated Solution of... 528
" " in Cancer.............. 476
Taraxacum, Value of; Dandelion Coffee. 519
Tea-Spoon as a Measure.................. 224
Teeth: The Perkins-Hyatt Base for Artificial.................. 87
Tenia in a New Born Infant 368
Tetanus, Chloral in....................82, 84
" Failure of Calibar Bean in........ 375
" and its Remedies............. 467
" Traumatic, Case of, with Recovery, By C. Cushing, M.D............ 444
The Gazette Hebdomadaire and French Physicians.................. 184
The Percentage System...............272, 367
The Prince of Wales and his Doctors..... 468
The Winter in Paris..................... 421
Thorne, C. R., M.D. Inward Dislocation of the Radius and Ulna.............. 289
Tobacco and Alcohol, Effect on the Sight of.................. 45
Tobacco, Influence of, in Disease of the Nerve-Centres.................. 284
Trachea, Dime Ejected from, by Vomiting, By L. Hubbard, M.D.............. 11
Trafton, A., M.D., Nutrition of the Human Body in Relation to Disease... 545
Traveling in Europe...................... 311

PAGE

Trismus Nascentium, Its Cause and Treatment.................. 476
Turpentine in Traumatic Erysipelas...... 274
Turpentine-Water, Atomized, in Bronchitis and Consumption.............. 582
Typhoid Fever, Hydropathy in........... 477
" " Stimulant Hypodermic Injections in.............. 183
" " Tartrate of Iron and Potassa in, By C. H. Gordon, M.D........ 418
Tyrrell, G. G., F. R. C. S. I. &c. Case of Puerperal Peritonitis with Subsequent Ovariotomy: Recovery........ 195
Tyrrell, G. G., F. R. C. S. I. &c. Blisters in the Pneumonia of Children......... 401
Ulcers, Indolent, Galvanic Treatment of 472
Urea, Formation of..................... 374
" " " By C. B. Holbrook, M.D.............. 397
Urine, Black, from Carbolic Acid........ 581
Uteri, Inflammation and Ulceration of Os and Cervix, By I. E. Oatman M.D. 241
Uterine Affections, On the Treatment of, By J. Scott, M.D.............. 163
Uterine Disease, Treatment of.......... 256
Uterine Os, Ulcers of.................. 227
Vaccination Papers..................... 524
" Value of Re-..............81, 228
Vaccine Lymph Preserved in Glycerine.. 205
Value of a Hospital Patient............. 517
Varicocele, New Mode of Operating for Radical Cure of. By H. B. Davison, M.D.................. 543
Veratrum Viride in Large Doses in Convulsions.................. 472
" " in Puerperal Convulsions.................. 472
Vesico-Vaginal Fistula: An Enthusiastic Surgeon.................. 379
Veterinary Surgeon, A Learned.......... 140
Vital Statistics of Australia............ 430
" " See Mortality Statistics....
Vomiting of Pregnancy, Raw Beef in the.. 233
Wanted: A Rara Avis..................... 185
Water, Soft, for Horses.................. 89
Weight, Discarding the, in the Pharmacopeia.................. 520
Wens of Scalp, Iodine for............... 430
White, F. A., M.D. Two Cases of Hemiplegia: Necropsy.............. 561
Whitehead, W. E., M.D. The Social Evil.. 55
Whooping Cough: Vapor of Ammonia in the Treatment of.................. 301
Wythe, J. H., M.D. Ovariotomy: Bone and Teeth in the Cyst.............. 117
Willard, E. L., M.D. Case of Abscess of the Kidney.............. 12
" " " Cases of Persistent Hiccough.............. 507
Winslow's Soothing Syrup, By W. F. Mc Nutt, M.D.................. 504
Witness A Medical, Answers Back........ 424
Witness on Insanity, A Sensible......... 309
Wooster, D., M.D. Action of Belladonna on Heart and Arteries.............. 398
Wooster, D., M.D., Eucalyptus: Its Medical Virtues.................. 550
Wounds, A New Plan for Dressing........ 277
Wounded, Proportion of, in Battle........ 89

PACIFIC

MEDICAL AND SURGICAL JOURNAL.

VOL. V.—JUNE, 1871.—No. 49.

ORIGINAL COMMUNICATIONS.

On the Effects of the Loss of Blood.

Read before the San Francisco Medical Society, by HENRY GIBBONS, M.D.

Less than fifty years ago, blood-letting was employed empirically, in conformity with custom, often without reason. Since that time, it has been discarded in obedience to popular prejudice, and with as little reason as formerly sustained its general use. The rising generation of doctors scarcely know the meaning of the word *venesection;* and they would take off a leg or ligate the subclavian with less perplexity than open a vein. Indorsing the popular clamor, they denounce their ancestry as professional butchers of the school of Sangrado, who bled indiscriminately for every ailment.

But the subject begins to assume a new phase. Marvelous as it may appear, the discovery is made that bleeding has its uses—that it is not uniformly destructive—that it may be made a valuable therapeutic agent. Richardson, in England, and Fordyce Barker, in America, among others, discuss the subject elaborately, defending the practice by fact and argument, and condemning its entire abandonment as an abuse on a level with its indiscriminate use. Practitioners in remote districts are whetting up their rusty lancets, and proclaiming through the journals the pre-eminent value of the abstraction of blood in certain dangerous forms of disease.

That a vulgar prejudice against blood-letting has taken possession of the public mind—that charlatans have found this a convenient weapon for defense and for aggression—that certain medical sects have sought and acquired popularity by fomenting the same prejudice—have had more to do with molding the prevailing sentiment of medical men and driving the lancet out of use, than it would be agreeable to professional pride to acknowledge. As the case now stands, it requires some nerve to stem the popular current; and he who ventures to do so must expect to be pronounced an old fogy, if not something worse. At whatever risk, I propose to state a few facts bearing on the question, which may pass for what they are worth.

Miss N., aged sixteen, had suffered for more than a year from irregular menstruation, the discharge being occasionally suspended for two or three months. This was complicated with a troublesome cough, with vicarious hemorrhage from the lungs. Her appetite was poor, and there was a tendency to anemia and debility. These conditions were such as to awaken serious apprehension of the development of pulmonary disease. She was placed under a tonic and invigorating course, with out-door exercise.

About a week prior to the monthly period, being out, very imprudently, at an evening party, she was caught on the way home in a sudden storm and completely drenched with a cold rain. The cough was much aggravated in consequence; but as the menstrual period approached, it failed to provoke the pulmonary hemorrhage. Instead, however, there came on epistaxis, so profuse as to cause much prostration. With perfect rest this soon ceased. Then came the regular uterine flow, but of a hemorrhagic character. The hemorrhagic tendency next developed itself in the bowels, and large quantities of half-digested blood were discharged. The patient was greatly prostrated, her appearance conforming to the bloodless condition of the system.

By the ordinary hemostatics, with extreme quiescence, the flow was arrested, and reaction promptly ensued. The tendency to repair was so active as to leave no call for stimulants, nor even for tonics. Convalescence was rapid. The cough had almost disappeared when the body became exsanguine, and what remained of it vanished rapidly, so that in a month from the hemorrhagic depletion, she was restored to a condition of health better than she had enjoyed for more than a year.

Mrs. B., in labor with her fifth child; had cough, with thoracic oppression, which she informed me had been growing upon her for several months, and which she would like me to attend to particularly after confinement. The labor was natural, but followed by profuse hemorrhage, requiring close attention for twenty-four hours. She was much prostrated by loss of blood, but the reaction was prompt and recovery rapid. With no special treatment for the pulmonary symptoms, except small quantities of onion syrup, the cough and oppression rapidly diminished, and at the end of a month had entirely disappeared, so that her health became better than for a long time previously.

It may be said in regard to this case, that the disturbance of the respiratory organs was the result of sympathy, or reflex irritation originating in the gravid uterus, and that it would have vanished spontaneously at the end of gestation. Possibly so; but is there not good reason for believing that the cure was accelerated by the hemorrhage? The disappearance of those pulmonic developments which arise during gestation is by no means a uniform result of delivery. It is much more common for disease to be arrested by pregnancy, and revived after confinement.

I would ask my professional brethren to call to mind the cases within their recollection, of persons losing a great part of their blood by spontaneous hemorrhage or by wounds, and to inquire what permanent mischief has resulted. I think they will find that, in most cases, not only has the blood been reproduced without serious trouble, but the vital forces have been invigorated, so that the individual has risen after the hemorrhage to a higher point of nutrition, if not of health, than before. The cry for blood to supply the emptied vessels calls forth every latent energy of the body; the functions of digestion, assimilation, and nutrition are stimulated to their highest power, and the organism is lifted even above the level of ordinary health. How does this fact accord with the prevailing idea, which associates loss and weakness, directly and indirectly, with the abstraction of the vital fluid?

About the year 1848, while I resided in Philadelphia, an incident took place at Bristol, some miles distant, the particulars of which I verified by careful inquiry, as follows: A man, who labored under an attack of delirium tremens, took a sharp carving-knife, and cut off his genital organs close to the pubic bone. When an attempt was made to seize him, he stood brandishing the knife, and repelling all approach; and it was not till he sank to the ground from loss of blood that he could be secured. The loss of blood, to the extent of nearly emptying the blood-vessels, instead of aggravating the morbid condition of the brain, promptly restored the normal function of that organ, and he recovered rapidly and perfectly.

According to the received pathology of delirium tremens, the brain in this case was suffering from deficient nutrition. And yet the abstraction of the vital fluid, through which nutrition must be performed, had the effect of restoring the organ to its natural action.

Many years ago, I was summoned hastily to a man who had attempted to destroy himself with a shoemaker's knife. He was a shoemaker, about twenty-seven years of age, of German parentage, with the rather singular name of Adam Dady. He had had a quarrel with his wife, and it was said had been drinking. I found him nearly lifeless from loss of blood, with superficial wounds of the throat, arm, fore-arm, and leg, evincing a very resolute attempt at self-destruction. While I dressed the wounds he remained unconscious, and I left him in that condition. Another message, however, soon recalled me, for the purpose of attending to another wound, which had not been discovered at first. He had attempted to amputate the genitals, and, in doing so, had completely severed the spermatic cord of one side, so that the testicle was exposed and almost detached. I removed the testicle, dressed the wound, and again left him. Next morning, he was perfectly rational, and anxious to recover. His first inquiry was whether he could be a father with only one testicle. Recovery was rapid and complete, and he lived to be, not only a good husband and a good citizen, but the father of a large family of children.

I was once called into the country several miles, to see a young man who was attacked with mental derangement. He had enlisted in the army, and deserted; and the fear of arrest, coupled with religious excitement, had overcome his reason. I found him raving wildly, and trying to escape from the hands of his friends. In accordance with the general practice of the day in such cases (for it was forty years ago), I sought to bleed him; but neither persuasion nor threats could induce him to submit to treatment. He proposed finally, by way of compromise, to take a glass of wine with me. I went down-stairs, and ordered a glass of wine to be sent up, and a glass of water for myself, as I did not drink wine; and I left a few grains of tartrate of antimony to be put in the wine. The madman swallowed his draught, not, however, till I had set him the example by swallowing mine, the dusk of twilight concealing the difference in color of the two draughts. I then renewed the proposition to bleed him; and when he persisted in his refusal, as I supposed he would, I warned him that he would be a very sick man before morning if he did not submit. Soon after my departure he became very sick, and, remembering my prediction, he sent for a carpenter residing in the neighborhood, who was in the practice of bleeding, and desired to be bled immediately. The carpenter, elated with the importance of his position, opened a vein, and took all the blood he could get. The poor fellow fainted, and spent the night vomiting and purging, and when I saw him in the morning, he was perfectly exhausted, and also perfectly submissive and perfectly sane. He recovered rapidly from that moment, and had no return of insanity.

I will cite a case, illustrating the influence of blood-letting on labor, which also occurred under the old *régime*. I was in attendance on a lady who had been several times confined under the care of my father. Labor advanced favorably till the child's head was in the inferior strait, when there was a complete arrest of progress, though not of pain. The patient declared that she required bleeding—that she could not be delivered without it—that my father had always bled her before her children could be born. She was a small woman, with lax fibre, presenting no indication whatever which pointed to the necessity, or even the propriety, of the operation. I ridiculed the idea for awhile, but after waiting half an hour, and observing not the slightest progress, I yielded to her entreaties, and opened a vein. As soon as the pulse began to give way, I closed the vein, and proceeded to tie up the arm. Before I had done this, though acting with all reasonable expedition, she cried out that the child was coming, and I had barely time to receive it as it emerged into the world.

It was formerly the general practice to bleed robust women in cases of tardy labor. We often observe a suspension of progress, without a suspension of painful effort—a want of that consentaneous and almost intelligent action of the muscular fibres of the uterus, which constitutes a model labor. There is pain enough, there is contraction enough, but it is misdirected. All the older obstetricians must have lively recollections of the confidence with which blood-letting was resorted to in such cases; how we tied up the arm, and opened a vein, and let the blood flow till the bounding pulse began to flag; and then closed the orifice, applied the "figure of eight," and sat down at the bedside, with "Now it will come;" and how it *did* come.

In every energetic labor there arrives a period of excitement, when the accoucheur feels that his patient could very well spare a portion of the circulatory fluid. Pain and muscular effort force the heart into vigorous action, the pulse becomes full and bounding, the skin hot, the face suffused and turgid, sometimes even livid; the superficial veins are full, almost to bursting. In these conditions, the idea of unloading the distended vessels must have forced itself on the mind of every practitioner. Should headache, or muscular startings, or delirium, be superadded, what remedy so safe and so effectual as the lancet?

Besides the direct benefit resulting under these circumstances from the abstraction of blood, it prepares the way for the safe action of anesthetics and opiates, and guards against convulsions, hemorrhage, fever, and other incidents of parturition. The spontaneous discharge from the uterus, which very generally follows the birth of the child in such cases, appears to be a measure of safety instituted by nature. There can be little doubt that a moderate hemorrhage attending childbirth, in a robust woman, is salutary.

But I will refrain from further comment, as my design was merely to offer a few facts as matter for thought. In the inquiry into the merits of blood-letting, which is now beginning to awaken the attention of medical observers everywhere, the old ground, trodden centuries ago, will be gone over again, as if new.

Experience with Hydrate of Chloral.

By G. W. GRAVES, M.D., of Petaluma, Cal.

The use of chloral hydrate as a therapeutical agent being comparatively of recent date, it may be of interest to some of our professional brethren to give the results of a careful, though limited, experience with this powerful drug.

Our object being simply to contribute something to our present knowledge of the remedy, we omit giving nativity of patients, particular date, etc., of administration.

I first commenced the use of chloral hydrate during the summer of 1870, and while I have given it and seen it given to quite a number of patients, I shall only notice here ten of the most interesting cases. Of the ten, it was highly satisfactory in six cases, the other four being very slightly, if at all, relieved.

In September last, I gave it in fifteen-grain doses, four times a day, to a boy of fifteen years, suffering from severe attacks of chorea, and, though it quieted him temporarily, it was not satisfactory. After a week it was abandoned, and bromide of potassium, tincture of castor, and fluid extract cimicifuga proved much more satisfactory in this case.

In October, I gave it to a married lady of forty years of age, who had been afflicted with spasms two or three consecutive days in every month for nine months. She took twenty grains every four hours for two days before the attack was expected, and, though it produced considerable stupor, the attack came on, but was somewhat modified. It was abandoned, and after trying many antispasmodics, the continued use of bromide of potassium has proved to be of more benefit in this case than any other remedy used.

During the same month (October), I prescribed it for a gentleman of thirty-eight years, who was suffering—and often suffered—from hemicrania. He had often taken quinine and morphine, but getting tired of their use, I advised him to take fifteen grains of chloral hydrate, and repeat the dose in an hour if necessary. He has generally been relieved by the first dose, which causes him to take a short nap of sleep, after which he gets up well. In this case its action is highly satisfactory.

On the 16th of October, I commenced giving chloral hydrate to a lady of twenty-one years, who had been suffering several days with very severe pain in the knee, caused by synovial inflammation of the joint. This lady's suffering being unendurable, and opiates by the stomach causing much nausea and vomiting, I used hypodermic injections of morphia with very good success in relieving the pain; but the local inflammation caused by the use of the instrument becoming troublesome in her case, I resorted to hydrate of chloral, giving fifteen grains at a dose, to be repeated in half an hour if necessary. She seldom had to repeat the dose, and said it "acted like a charm;" and so it did, for it enabled her to control the pain and sleep at will, the dose having to be increased at times to twenty-five or thirty grains when she desired to sleep soundly. The latter doses would insure her five or six hours' sleep, from which she would awake feeling comfortable, without any nausea. I afterward operated on this patient for caries of the tibia, and during the reparative process, which was perfected after about five weeks, she was relieved of frequent pains, and made quite comfortable, by taking ten grains of hydrate of chloral whenever she needed it, which was never more than three or four times in twenty-four hours. In this case its action was always speedy and highly satisfactory.

On the 15th of November, I was called to see a man about twenty-eight years of age, who had compound comminuted fracture of the tibia and fibula. The soft parts were terribly lacerated, and the wound extremely painful. This man positively refused to accept the advice of myself and a consulting physician (Dr. J. H. Crane, of this city) to have amputation performed, declaring that he would prefer to die. As we were far in the country and could not well withdraw after his refusing to let us operate, we yielded to the entreaties of the patient to "do the next best" we could, and after removing the spiculæ and sawing off the broken ends of the bone that had been deprived of its periosteum, we dressed the wound and placed the limb in as comfortable a position as possible, but informed him and his friends that we could not expect him to recover without amputation. The large doses of morphia found necessary to keep him from suffering caused so much nausea and constipation that I sent him a solution of chloral hydrate and morphia, and directed him to take a dose containing ten grains of the former and the sixth of a grain of the latter whenever an anodyne was indicated, and repeat in an hour if necessary. This combination was highly satisfactory, one dose giving him more ease and comfort than half or two-thirds of a grain of morphia by itself, and not causing any nausea. It had to be repeated four or five times in twenty-four hours, and by this course the patient was kept from suffering until his death. On the tenth day, I amputated just above the knee—the joint having become involved, and the patient consenting—but it was too late, and he died on the twelfth day. Notwithstanding the patient died, the chloral hydrate was of immense benefit in keeping him from suffering when opium disturbed his stomach too much and caused constipation.

During the months of November and December, I gave it a faithful trial in a case of epilepsy of five years' standing. It proved to be of very little, if any, benefit, and I have found the bromides of potassium and ammonium, in large doses, the most efficient remedies that I used in this case. The patient was a delicate girl of nineteen years.

During the same months (November and December), I gave chloral hydrate to a gentleman about forty years of age, for asthma ; and I believe it has effected a cure. This patient had been suffering with repeated attacks at night for more than two months, and the usual remedies only partially relieved the paroxysms, to return again. Not being able to detect any disease of the heart to contra-indicate its use, I directed him to take twenty grains when he felt the attacks approaching. He was able to relieve himself at all times, but occasionally had to repeat the dose in twenty or thirty minutes. The attacks grew less frequent and less violent, and have not troubled him for two months past. I consider it highly satisfactory in this case.

During the month of January, I used it with perfect success and satisfaction in a case of angina pectoris, with a girl fifteen years of age, after other remedies had been tried without satisfaction. I gave it in twenty-grain doses, and occasionally had to repeat it in thirty minutes. I was highly pleased with it in this case, and the patient recovered rapidly and well, while kept from suffering.

During the month of February, I administered it twice to a man thirty-one years of age, who had been dissipating until he was showing symptoms of delirium tremens, not being able to sleep. Thirty grains acted nicely, and caused him to sleep seven hours. This patient renewed his spree, and, after a few days, I gave him forty grains, which caused him to sleep eight hours, and he got well without other treatment.

During the month of March, I gave thirty-grain doses to a man of forty years of age, in a case of neuralgia, without any appreciable benefit. Quinine and morphine relieved him.

I have used chloral hydrate and seen it used in many other cases, which I have not noticed here, and my conclusions are, that it is a most valuable anodyne and hypnotic, and can often be administered when opium produces nausea and other bad effects. I have never tried it in large doses to produce anesthesia, but would not hesitate to do so if chloroform was contra-indicated.

Like all other new remedies, it has been overrated by some and abused by others; but skilled physicians will soon be able to judge in what cases it can be beneficially used.

We will be badly mistaken in our opinion of chloral hydrate if a few years' use by the profession does not demonstrate it to be a most valuable remedy in many complaints.

A Dime Ejected from the Trachea by Vomiting.

A Letter from LORENZO HUBBARD, M.D., A. Assist.-Surgeon U. S. A., read before the San Francisco Medical Society.

Professor Henry Gibbons: I send you the following case more for its novelty than any important practical application:

Carpenter Simes, a private in Company A, First U. S. Cavalry, while playing with a *dime*, by tossing it into his mouth, accidentally threw it far back into the pharynx, where, coming in contact with the posterior nasal orifices, it excited a strong disposition to sneeze. The spasmodic inspiration which followed drew the piece through the glottis into the trachea, and subsequent inspirations lodged it at the point of the bifurcation of the right bronchus. By inflating the lungs, and then making a strong effort at expiration, the "piece" would rise into the trachea, but when it reached the glottis suffocation was so imminent he was forced to allow it to descend. When he first made his situation known to me, three hours after the occurrence of the accident, he said he could feel the "bit" resting directly under the right nipple, and that the parts at this point had become quite sore.

While the piece was yet movable, and had not really found a lodgment, I determined to try the experiment of vomiting, with the hope that in the spasmodic effort of retching and coughing it might be ejected. In this I was not disappointed, for in the very first effort it was thrown out to the distance of several feet, with considerable force. I also send you the "bit" with which this strange experiment was made, supposing that possibly the case might interest our Society.

CAMP BIDWELL, March 17, 1871.

Abscess of Kidney—Discharge through the Urethra.

BY EMORY L. WILLARD, M.D., of Eureka, Lander County, Nevada.

The following case occurred recently in the course of my practice: Marcelius Aberdy, aged 43, by trade a butcher, came under treatment February 10th; had been sick twenty days, being taken ill about January 16th, 1871; disease, nephritis—abscess of kidney being the result. On the 10th of February I found him with the following symptoms: much pain in the lower part of the groin and back; much debility and hectic flush, with indications of sinking; general torpidity of the entire emunctory system; suppression of urine; constipation of the bowels; low grade of fever; deranged stomach; nausea almost constant. All the symptoms were acute, attended with pain, sleeplessness, and nervousness, which yielded readily to the subcutaneous injection of morphia, with soporifics, tonics, mucilaginous drinks, and wine. On the fourth day of treatment, an abscess, evidently of the kidney, broke through, and discharged copiously pure pus by the urethra. Immediately he showed decided signs of recovery, and is convalescent and fast improving.

California State Medical Society.

An adjourned meeting was held in Pacific Hall, San Francisco, May 1st, 1871.

The Censors reported that one hundred and one names of candidates for membership had been laid before them; of whom seventy-three presented the requisite vouchers, and were recommended by them for election. They were accordingly elected, and the remainder of the list was laid over for future action. Following is a list of the new members, with residence, and school, and date of graduation:

Name.	*Residence.*	*School.*	*Date.*
Alemby Jump	Downieville	Western Reserve Medical College	1849
Erastus W. Foote	Lockeford	Vermont Medical College	1840
H. M. Biggs	Santa Barbara	University of California	1870
Chas. B. Bates	Santa Barbara	Toland Medical College	1868
Henry M. Fiske	Sutter Creek	St. Charles University, Medical Department	1843
		University of Pacific	1870
Wm. Reiley Fox	San Leandro	Chicago Medical College	1863
E. B. Harris	North San Juan	New York Medical University	1846
E. B. Robertson	San Andreas	Medical Department, University of Pacific	1864
J. E. Pelham	Shasta	Transylvania Medical College	1839
John P. Reiley	Marysville	Medical College of City of New York	1846
George C. Chase	Downieville	Dartmouth Medical College	1848
Robert M. Hunt	Nevada	Castleton Medical College	1850
		Albany Medical College	1869
Thomas C. Hanson	Oakland	Toland Medical College	1867
Wm. W. Hays	San Luis Obispo	Medical Department, Georgetown College	1861
J. R. Bradway	Red Bluff	Rush Medical College	1847
J. S. Adams	St. Helena	Albany Medical College	1855
G. W. Graves	Petaluma	University of Virginia	1868
Eustace Trenor	Oakland	College Physicians and Surgeons, New York	1856
J. N. Brown	San José	Ohio Medical College	1860
H. H. Warburton	Santa Clara		

Name.	Residence.	School.	Date.
H. L. Nichols	Sacramento	Bowdoin Medical College	1845
Gerrard G. Tyrrell	Sacramento	F.R.C.S. and King's and Queen's Col., Ireland	1850
E. R. Taylor	Sacramento	Toland Medical College	1865
C. S. Haswell	Sacramento	Toland Medical College	1866
W. T. Wythe	Sacramento	Med. Dept., Willamette University, Oregon	1867
R. H. Plummer	Silveyville	Toland Medical College	1866
L. McGuire	Folsom	Toland Medical College	1868
Thomas C. Stockton	San Diego	Bellevue Hospital Medical College	1868
A. Trafton	Sacramento	Louisiana Medical College	1848
B. H. Pierson	Woodland	University of Missouri	1846
W. S. Thorne	San José	Bellevue Hospital Medical College	1869
R. W. Murphy	Sacramento	Bellevue Hospital Medical College	1871
T. T. Cabanis	Siskiyou	University of Maryland	1849
George H. Evans	Dixon	Nashville Medical College	1869
J. D. Callaghan	Monterey	University of Louisiana	1851
C. S. Coleman	San Leandro	Geneva Medical College	1850
H. H. Toland	San Francisco		
Wm. C. Jones	Forest Hill	Bellevue Hospital Medical College	1871
Samuel F. Sproul	Chico	Jefferson Medical College	1855
Jos. F. Wayland	Chico	University of Louisville	1855
W. Fitch Cheney	Chico	University of New York	1862
C. M. Bates	San Francisco	University of Pennsylvania	1855
J. C. Tucker	San Francisco	University of New York	1848
V. Bruce Gates	San Francisco	Jefferson Medical College	1871
H. S. Gates	San Francisco	Geneva Medical College	1836
N. R. Davis	San Francisco	College Physicians and Surgeons, New York	1848
E. T. Barber	Eureka	Toland Medical College	1866
A. Thorndike	Stockton	Jefferson Medical College	1850
E. H. Bryan	San Francisco	University of Missouri	1852
E. Kelley	San Francisco	University of New York	1857
James A. Brown	Sutter Creek	University of Louisville	1844
C. E. Holbrook	Benicia	University of Pacific	1863
A. A. O'Neil	San Francisco	Toland Medical College	1867
C. A. Toland	San Francisco	Toland Medical College	1869
H. B. Davison	Colusa	Jefferson Medical College	1871
H. Neal	San Juan South	Jefferson Medical College	1859
C. T. Sage	San Francisco	University of California	1870
N. Williams		Geneva Medical College	1841
A. J. Cory	San José	Ohio Medical College	1860
Benj. Cory	San José	Ohio Medical College	1845
Benj. Shurtleff	Shasta	Harvard Medical College	1848
C. N. Kirkpatrick	Redwood City	Ohio Medical College	1848
G. W. Dutton	Tomales	University of Pennsylvania	1869
S. H. Rupe	Healdsburg	Toland Medical College	1866
L. Seawell		University of California	1870
Laurent Lasvignes		University of Montpellier, France	1847
M. C. Parkinson	Ione City	Starling Medical College, Ohio	1857
Charles Boreman	Jackson	William and Mary Medical College	18—
H. G. Pike	Sanel	Vermont Medical College	1856
E. A. Stockton	Stockton	Ohio Medical College	1853
David Wooster	San Francisco	Western Reserve Medical College	1849
D. Ray	Woodland	College Physicians and Surgeons, Iowa	1871

The following named physicians were elected honorary members: J. H. Wythe, M.D., D.D.; P. Landsdale, Med. Inspector U. S. N.; J. M. Brown, Surgeon U. S. N.; David

Kindelberger, do.; W. E. Taylor, do.; S. F. Shaw, Passed Assistant do.; W. M. Nickerson, Assistant do.; C. McCormick, Surgeon U. S. A.; R. Murray, do; C. C. Keeney, do.; E. Bentley, Assistant do.; P. W. Randle, late do.

The permanent members being one hundred and fifty-six in number, the Society was entitled to sixteen delegates to the National Association. The appointment was made as follows: T. M. Logan, President; J. J. Franklin, Sonora; S. D. Campbell, Suisun; A. B. Mehring, Woodland; F. W. Todd, Stockton; Luke Robinson, Colusa; A. B. Stout, Geo. Hewston, R. Beverly Cole, Henry Gibbons, Jr., J. D. Whitney, San Francisco; G. L. Simmons, W. R. Cluness, Sacramento; D. B. Hoffman, San Diego; W. W. Ross, Watsonville; A. Thorndike, Stockton.

The thanks of the Society were presented to the proprietors of the Pacific Hall, for the free use of the hall.

The delegates to the National Association from east of the Rocky Mountains were, on motion, elected honorary members of the Society.

A vote of thanks was bestowed on the President, Dr. Logan, for his untiring attention and devotion to the interests of the Society.

Adjourned.

Association of Medical Editors.

The stated annual meeting of this Association was held in San Francisco, May 1, 1871. Dr. H. R. Storer, of the *Gynæcological Journal*, President, and Dr. Henry Gibbons, Jr., of the *Pacific Med. and Surg. Journal*, Secretary *pro tem.*

Dr. N. S. Davis, Committee on Revision of By-laws, read the following report, which was adopted:

Your Committee respectfully recommends the following alterations and additions in the organization of the Association. In place of the present article relating to officers, substitute the following:

"OFFICERS.—The officers of the Association shall be a President, Vice-President, Secretary, Assistant-Secretary, and Treasurer; all, except the Assistant-Secretary, to be elected annually by ballot, and shall commence their term of service at the opening of the next annual meeting after their election. The Assistant-Secretary shall be appointed annually by the President, and shall be resident at the place of the next succeeding meeting.

"It shall be the duty of the Secretary to procure a suitable book, and keep in it a permanent record of the organization, list of members, and proceedings of the Association; and in case of his inability to attend any particular meeting, he shall, prior to such meeting, transmit the book of records to the Assistant-Secretary.

"It shall be the duty of the Assistant-Secretary to procure suitable accommodations for the annual meetings of the Association, and to assist the Secretary in the performance of his duties."

Committee on Registry of Physicians; no report. On motion, this committee was discharged.

The President announced that he had had extended correspondence with Prof. Henry, of the Smithsonian Institution, who stated that he would be pleased to forward any medical journals to foreign countries, which might be sent for that purpose to the Institution. The only prerequisite was that they be prepaid to Washington. Further information on the subject could be obtained by addressing Prof. Henry.

The President also announced that at the meeting in 1870 the Association represented thirteen journals; one of which, the *St. Louis Medical and Surgical Reporter*, had since been discontinued. He had addressed a circular letter to forty-one journals, the editors of all but three of which had responded favorably, and had signed the Articles of Association. These three were the *Philadelphia Medical and Surgical Reporter*, the illness of whose editor had probably prevented a reply; the *American Journal of Medical Sciences*, whose editor declined because unable to take active part by reason of age and sickness; and the *Boston Medical and Surgical Journal*, the editor of the latter alleging as a reason, that the Association might at some future time impose rules which he would not be inclined to obey.

Dr. N. S. Davis presented the following resolutions, which he desired to lie over until after the President's address in the evening:

Resolved, That the social, educational, and scientific interests of the Profession, would be greatly promoted by a more complete organization in every State and district in our country; such organization being calculated not only to elicit and diffuse knowledge, but also to afford the most effectual means for procuring concerted and efficient action on all important questions of medical education and progress.

Resolved, That deficiency in the general education of young men entering upon the study of medicine in this country is an evil of great magnitude; not only constituting a barrier to individual progress in professional life, but greatly lessening the general reputation and usefulness of the Profession.

Resolved, That the members of this Association be requested to use their respective medical periodicals as agencies for calling the special attention of the Profession to the topics mentioned in the foregoing resolutions, until such a professional sentiment is created, that no regular practitioner will feel at liberty to receive a student into his office, who does not present testimonials from some competent source that he has, at least, a competent knowledge of the ordinary branches of education, including the lower mathematics and the natural sciences; and until the social organizations are so far complete, that the several State Societies become the real and authoritative representatives of the Profession in each State.

The President read a letter from Dr. T. M. Logan, President of the California State Medical Society, inviting the members of the Association to seats on the platform during the session of the State Society in the afternoon.

On motion, the invitation was accepted, and the members of the State Society were invited to be present at the adjourned meeting in the evening, to listen to the President's address.

The Association then adjourned to eight o'clock in the evening.

On assembling in the evening, the President delivered, to a large audience of physicians and others, an instructive and interesting address on the "Reciprocal Relations of the Medical Profession, its Press, and the Community." At its conclusion, the Association was called to order, Dr. B. F. Dawson, of the *American Journal of Obstetrics*, being present, in addition to those already named.

The resolutions of Dr. N. S. Davis were re-read, and, on motion, were unanimously adopted.

The officers for the ensuing year were unanimously elected, as follows: President, Dr. B. F. Dawson; Vice-President, Dr. H. Gibbons, Jr.; Secretary, Dr. F. H. Davis.

Dr. J. M. Toner having announced that his list of physicians already comprised fifty thousand names, and that it was at the service of medical journals, a resolution of thanks for his kind offer, and requesting the co-operation of all the editors of medical journals to assist him in making his complete index of the medical literature of the United States, was proposed and carried.

The Committee on Foreign Exchanges was enlarged, so as to consist of Drs. T. Parvin of Louisville, W. S. Mitchell of New Orleans, B. F. Dawson of New York, and Joseph Jones of New Orleans.

Adjourned. H. GIBBONS, JR., Sec'y *pro tem.*

Annual Meeting of the American Medical Association.

The twenty-second annual session of the American Medical Association convened on Tuesday, May 2d, at twelve M., at Pacific Hall, San Francisco.

The Convention was called to order by Dr. A. B. Stout, of San Francisco, Chairman of the Committee of Arrangements, who introduced Dr. Alfred Stillé, of Pennsylvania, President of the Association. Dr. Stillé took the chair, assisted by Dr. J. S. Weatherly of Alabama, and Dr. Henry Gibbons of California, as Vice-Presidents.

The meeting was opened with prayer by Rt. Rev. Bishop Kip.

Dr. Stout made an address of welcome.

The President delivered the annual address, which was listened to with marked attention. In the course of the address, he canvassed pretty fully the question of *Women Doctors*, and administered to the sex a merciless castigation for their attempts to rise to a level with man in intellectual pursuits. He proved conclusively that the female mind was vastly inferior to that of man, and that women are incapable of studying and practicing medicine with success, or of attaining to distinction in any pursuit which requires mental force. His strictures on this topic were highly relished by a portion of the audience, while others were perplexed to comprehend how such an inferior animal could be the mother of man.

A note was read from Professor S. D. Gross, of Philadelphia, regretting that he was unable to be present in the body, on account of an injury lately received, but that he would attend in spirit.

Invitations were extended to the members of the Association, from the Pioneers, Academy of Sciences, Hospitals, and various public bodies, to visit their several institutions.

The Standing Committees, being called on for reports, exhibited the usual alacrity in the performance of their duties, and the usual interest in the welfare of the Association, by making no answer to the call, with some honorable exceptions, as follow:

On Cultivation of the Cinchona Tree—Dr. Lemuel J. Deal, of Pennsylvania. The report of this Committee was continued until next year.

On the Structure of the White Blood Corpuscles—Dr. J. G. Richardson, of Pennsylvania. Continued by request.

On Vaccination—Dr. Henry A. Martin, of Massachusetts. The Secretary said that Dr. Martin had intended to be present, and bring with him a heifer, from which the members could obtain fresh vaccine matter, but business prevented him from attending. On motion, the subject of Dr. Martin and his heifer was continued.

On Protest of Naval Surgeons—Dr. W. S. W. Ruschenberger, U. S. N. The Secretary read the report of the Committee, recommending that the former report of Dr. Pinkney be not published. Dr. Pinkney read a letter, defending himself against the charges made. After considerable discussion, the matter was made the special order for eleven o'clock, to-morrow.

On National Medical School—Dr. Francis Gurney Smith, of Pennsylvania. Partial report read, and referred to Committee on Publication.

On Criminal Abortion—Dr. D. A. O'Donnell, Maryland. Report referred to the Committee on Obstetrics.

On Nomenclature of Diseases—Dr. Francis Gurney Smith, of Pennsylvania. Partial report submitted, and the Committee continued.

On what, if any, legislative means are expedient and advisable to prevent the spread of contagious diseases—Dr. M. H. Henry, of New York. Continued by request.

On American Medical Necrology—Dr. C. C. Cox, D. C., reported progress, and was continued.

On Medical Education—Dr. E. Geddings, South Carolina. Made the special order for eleven o'clock, to-morrow.

On Prize Essays—Dr. T. M. Logan, of California. Will be called to-morrow.

On Climatology and Epidemics, it was understood that some reports were on hand, and would be presented through the appropriate Section.

In the evening, the hall was thrown open to the members, and their families and friends, for social intercourse. A large number of the physicians from different parts of California were present, and had an opportunity of renewing acquaintance with former preceptors and rriends from the East, whom they had not met for many years. There was much interest and enjoyment in these revivals of old friendships.

WEDNESDAY, May 3.

The Committee of Arrangements and Credentials reported the list of accredited members, from which it appeared that twenty-five States were represented. On the motion to receive the report, Dr. Toner raised the question whether Dr. Thomas, who was connected with the Female Medical College of Philadelphia, was in harmony with the County Medical Society.

Dr. Gibbons, Sr., questioned the propriety of arraigning members in that way. Such matters should be referred to the Committee on Ethics, and not agitated in the Society. He moved the appointment of a Committee on Ethics for that purpose. Adopted.

The Chair appointed Drs. Gibbons of California, Davis of Illinois, F. Gurney Smith of Pennsylvania, Toner of District of Columbia, and Parsons of New Hampshire.

Dr. T. M. Logan submitted a list of members of the California State Medical Society not delegates, and moved that they be elected members by invitation.

The Chairman read the section of the law of the Association, which provides that members by invitation can only be elected when they are from districts unrepresented by delegates in the Association.

Dr. Stout said that, notwithstanding the statute, he hoped some indulgence would be extended to the physicians of California.

Dr. Davis, of Chicago, strongly urged that the laws be not violated; that they had been carefully prepared to cover that very point. He moved that the members of the California State Medical Society be invited to seats on the floor of the Convention, and to mingle with the members of this Association.

Dr. Logan then withdrew his motion, and the one proposed by Dr. Davis was put to vote and carried.

At the request of the Secretary, Dr. Yandell came on the stage to read the report of the Committee on Medical Education, signed by Dr. E. Geddings, of South Carolina.

Dr. Toner objected to the report, on the ground that it was signed only by one member of the Committee.

The Chair decided the point not well taken.

An appeal was taken, and the decision of the Chair sustained.

Dr. Yandell proceeded to read the report, which is a pamphlet of thirty-nine printed pages, but before he had concluded its reading, Dr. Gibbons moved that the further reading be dispensed with.

Dr. Davis asked what would be done with the report.

Dr. J. B. Johnson, of Missouri, thought the report ought not to come before the Association, as it was only signed by one member of the Committee, and therefore in violation of the constitution, which requires that reports be signed by all the members of the Committee.

Dr. Ayres said that he was on the Committee to prepare that report, but that their views were entirely opposite in the matter, and hoped that the further reading of the report would be dispensed with.

Dr. Yandell urged, in favor of the report, that it was customary to leave the labor in such cases in the hands of a single member, and that when any one member had attended to his duty, his labors should be thankfully acknowledged.

Finally, the report was referred to the Committee on Publication.

Dr. Gibbons said he held in his hand *The New England Homeopathic Journal*, containing an article on "Vaccination," furnished by Dr. Henry Martin, and signed by him as "Chairman of the Committee on Vaccination of the American Medical Association." Yesterday, Dr. Martin was continued as Chairman of that Committee. Dr. Gibbons now moved that the vote so continuing him be reconsidered, and that he be removed, and another member appointed in his place.

Dr. Storer said Dr. Martin stood high in the regular Profession, and had no leaning toward homeopathy. He was an active and useful member.

Dr. Gibbons had nothing to say against Dr. Martin. He might, if he chose, write for homeopathic journals; but when he did so in his official capacity, taking pains openly to compromise this Association, it was time to displace him as our representative.

Dr. Storer proposed to refer the case of Dr. Martin to the local Society of which he was a member.

Dr. Johnson, of St. Louis, thought that would be useless, as the Massachusetts Society allowed irregular practitioners to be members.

Dr. Dawson, of New York, regarded Dr. Martin's conduct and the tenor of his article as insulting to the Association, and moved that he be expelled.

It was finally agreed to remove Dr. Martin as Chairman of the Committee, and refer his case to the Censors for further action.

A motion was adopted to the effect that all matters coming properly before the Committee on Medical Ethics be referred directly to them, and not read before the Association.

Dr. Logan presented a report from the Committee on Prize Essays, who state that they had received five essays, and that they award one prize to E. R. Taylor, M.D., of Sacramento city, for his essay on the "Chemical Constitution of the Bile," bearing the motto, "*Divide et impera.*"

The other prize was awarded to B. M. Howard, M.D., of New York (winner of the first prize last year), for his essay on "The direct method of artificial respiration for the treatment of persons apparently dead from suffocation by drowning, or from other causes." Motto, "*Festina lente.*"

The report was adopted, and the Committee requested to hold all other essays at the disposition of the authors.

Dr. N. S. Davis, on behalf of the Committee on Medical Education, submitted an elaborate report, closing with the following resolutions:

Resolved, That each State and local Medical Society be requested to provide, as a permanent part of its organization, a

Board of Censors for determining the educational qualifications of such young men as propose to commence the study of medicine, and that no member of such societies be permitted to receive a student into his office until such student presents a certificate of proper preliminary education from the Censors appointed for that purpose, or a degree from some literary college of known good standing.

Resolved, That a more complete organization of the Profession in each State is greatly needed, for the purpose of affording a more efficient basis, both for educational and scientific purposes.

Resolved, That a Committee of three be appointed for the purpose of continuing the correspondence with the State Medical Societies, and of asking their earnest attention to the foregoing resolutions, in addition to those submitted for their action in 1869.

Dr. J. S. Moore moved that an entrance fee of $100 to all colleges be fixed upon.

Dr. Russell spoke against the resolution, and said that this would exclude the poor boy from receiving a medical education.

Dr. J. S. Moore thought that was just the reason why a certain amount should be fixed upon. The Profession was overcrowded now, and when qualified men could not get respectable fees they would forsake the Profession. Young men of ability would not enter a profession where every one could obtain entrance by the payment of fifteen or twenty dollars. The Profession should be protected.

Dr. Yandell said that his learned friend from Missouri signified his intention of bringing this matter before the Association three years ago, and had not done so until now. He had three years to collect his ideas, and there was not one presented which would hold water. The fact is that cheap instruction had not increased the numerical strength of the Profession. A certain number of students graduated every year, and that number would not be, and had not been, increased. He did not believe in aristocracy. The brain is the aristocrat.

Dr. Weatherly, of Alabama, did not agree with the last

speaker. You could not compare cheap common education to cheap professional education.

Dr. Stout, of California, believed in universal education —without price, if it were possible. He favored the idea of establishing a National Medical School, but thought the health of the medical profession should not be swayed down to the level of the poor boy. He honored a poor young man, but did not believe in bringing down the standard of the Profession to that level.

Dr. Davis said the less the Association had to do with these details, the better it would be for it. He thought each college should be allowed to fix the rate, as they knew best what their course was worth.

The matter was finally laid on the table.

THURSDAY, May 4.

In the absence of the President, Dr. Gibbons, Vice-President, took the chair.

Professor Carr, of Oakland, desired to know at what hour on Friday the Association would adjourn, for the purpose of taking the boat for Oakland, according to the programme. The Mayor and citizens were greatly interested, in connection with the medical men of Oakland, in the contemplated visit, and would convey the members to the University grounds and buildings, and other interesting localities. It was agreed to adjourn at eleven A.M.

The Committee on Publication reported that the copy of Vol. XXI. was put into the hands of the printer on May 26th, 1870, but in consequence of the necessity of ascertaining definitely, by means of circulars distributed to the members of the Association, how many copies it would be necessary or safe to print, the volume was not fairly started until the first of July. They then went to press, and six hundred and fifty copies were printed. The report is accompanied by a table, exhibiting the number of copies of each volume, and the number disposed of since the last report. Submitted by F. G. Smith, Chairman, and referred to the Committee on Publication.

The Treasurer's report was read by the Secretary, from which we learn that the balance on hand is $704.32. The Treasurer reiterates the hope that the Association will not refer any matter to the Committee on Publication not of real value, as all matter thus referred must be published, at times causing the volume of Transactions to cost more than the sum fixed for its purchase by members. Referred to the Committee on Publication.

The report of the Librarian, F. A. Ashford, M.D., of Washington, was received and read. He reported that the books intrusted to his custody by his predecessors had been well preserved at the Smithsonian Institution, through the kindness of Prof. Henry and its Regents. Three hundred and thirty-nine volumes, including pamphlets, monographs, etc., composed the collection at the date of the last report, and the additional matter received during the past year has been chiefly a continuation of the medical and surgical journals. Referred to the Committee on Publication.

John C. Atlee, M.D., delegate to the Association of Medical Superintendents of American Institutions for the Insane, reported that he had attended the twenty-fourth annual meeting, at Hartford, Conn., in June last, and was cordially received. The Association, formed in 1844, by thirteen Superintendents, has been steadily increasing in the number of its members, and now embraces more than sixty, representing institutions in almost every State in the Union. Reports embracing a variety of subjects relating to insanity were read and ably discussed, and four days were profitably occupied. Referred to the Committee on Publication.

Dr. Kerwan, delegate from the Association above mentioned to the American Medical Association, addressed the meeting at some length, urging closer relations between the Associations. His remarks came in the form of a report, and were referred to the Committee on Publication.

Dr. Storer said that at a previous meeting the question of having the Association devoted specially to the treatment of the insane, meet in closer relations with the American Medical Association, was discussed, and the sense of the meeting always favored the "close relations." He would then offer the following resolution:

Resolved, That the Association of Superintendents of Institutions for the Treatment of the Insane and the American Medical Association should be more closely united, and that the meetings of the two Associations should be held at about the same time and at the same place.

Adopted.

Dr. Yandell, of the Special Committee to whom was referred the report of Dr. Pinkney on Foreign Naval Medical Affairs, submitted at the session of the Association in 1870, presented the said report, and moved its reference to the Committee on Education. Adopted.

The Chairman of the Section on Materia Medica and Chemistry, Dr. Yandell, reported having received a valuable paper from Dr. W. P. Gibbons, of Alameda, entitled "The Botany of the Pacific Coast." The paper was accompanied by one hundred and eighty specimens of indigenous plants, etc., and would certainly be considered a valuable contribution to the science of medicine.

The Committee moved that the paper be referred to the Committee on Publication.

Dr. Gibbons requested that the recommendation of the Committee be withdrawn. The paper was not complete—not as perfect as he could make it by additional work.

On motion, a vote of thanks was passed, and the paper returned to its author for completion.

Dr. H. R. Storer, delegate from the American Medical Association to the Canadian Medical Association, submitted a verbal report in behalf of himself and associates—Dr. Sullivan, of Boston, and Dr. Gerrish, of New York. He eulogizes the Canadian Association. Its members were accomplished in point of medical education, almost all of them having graduated from European Colleges of note.

The Committee on Nominations made the following report: We recommend for President, Dr. D. W. Yandell, of Kentucky; First Vice-President, Thomas M. Logan, of California; Second Vice-President, C. L. Ives, of Connecticut; Third Vice-President, R. F. Michel, of Alabama; Fourth Vice-President, J. K. Bartlett, of Wisconsin; Assistant-Secretary, D. Murray Cheston, of Philadelphia; Librarian, F. A. Ashford, of D. C.; Treasurer, C. Wister, of Philadelphia. Next place of meeting, Philadelphia.

On motion of Dr. Davis, the report was accepted, and the officers unanimously elected.

The Committee on Ethics reported, in regard to the protest of the Councilors of the Massachusetts State Society against the action of the Association, which had been referred to them, that the Association knew of no such body as the Councilors of that Society, and that the constitution of the Massachusetts State Society contained nothing to prevent this Association from recognizing delegates appointed by it.

In regard to Dr. Martin, they reported that, the Association having removed him from his official position on the Committee on Vaccination, further action was inexpedient, and that his case be left with his local Society.

In regard to Dr. Thomas, they reported that, inasmuch as a proposed amendment to the constitution bearing on his case was on the minutes from last year, and would come up for consideration, they had concluded to leave the subject to the action of the Association on that amendment. Report adopted.

The amendment referred to, proposed by Dr. Hartshorne, was read, as follows:

Resolved, That the constitution shall be so construed as not to exclude delegates from Female Colleges.

Dr. Harding, of Indiana, advocated the amendment. The question ought to be settled. It was a bone of contention, year after year, and nothing was wanted but a decision by this body to harmonize the action of State and local Societies. We can not ignore the question any longer. Female physicians exist, and many of them are well educated. They have succeeded against all opposition, and all they ask is to be recognized when they are worthy of it, and not be treated as quacks and interlopers. By refusing this, we only drive them into irregular practice, and make enemies of them, instead of friends.

Dr. N. R. Davis—I hope the members will scan the full drift of this amendment. It means that delegates from female colleges, whether male or female, shall be admitted to this floor. Hitherto they have sent only male representatives; but if we adopt this amendment, we shall witness the spectacle of women coming among us as delegates. The question is associated with other movements of women to usurp the sphere belonging to man—to exercise suffrage, etc. I have nothing to say of the capacities of women to study and practice medicine. I have taught them, lectured to them, stripped my patients at the clinic before mixed classes. But let women labor within their sphere, and not claim seats on this floor.

Dr. Donahue, of Ohio, moved to lay on the table, but withdrew the motion, amid cries of remonstrance.

Dr. King, of Pennsylvania—I can not see why an educated and competent woman should be refused the same professional courtesies that we bestow on men. The sphere of woman is an old and hackneyed topic. Every nation has its own sphere for her. Let us judge her by her merits, and not by her sex. There is nothing in our Code of Ethics to exclude her. But the code is construed differently in different localities. In Pennsylvania, as the case now stood, a member of the Medical Association could not recognize a female as a member of the Profession—could not consult with her. If he was summoned, and found a woman had charge of the case, what could he do? According to the law of the Association, he must say to her, "Walk out of this house, and let me take exclusive charge of this case." As the case now stands, he could not consult with the President of the Association, the eminent Dr. Stillé, and this because the Doctor was consulting physician in the Philadelphia Female Medical College.

Dr. Gibbons, of California—I am surprised at so good a logician as Dr. Davis resorting to the *ad captandum* bugbear of female suffrage. The question is not, Shall women study and practice medicine? We can not settle that question. They are doing it in spite of us, and the more we oppose them, the greater their determination and their success, and the stronger the public sympathy for them. The question is, When a woman has had a regular medical education, and has received a well-earned diploma, shall we treat her with the same courtesy as a man, or shall we trample her under foot merely because she is a woman? I don't understand why the idea of a female delegate in this body is so terrifying. We have ladies here now, as spectators, by special invitation, and the members appear satisfied. This is the first time I ever spoke publicly on this question. But standing here on the verge of the continent, outside of the vortex of excitement, and surveying dispassionately the course of events in America and in Europe, I am satisfied that, in our opposition to female doctors, we are only damming up the stream to increase its power. Public sentiment is more and more against us. Our best policy is to accept the situation. In view of the future, I wish to place myself on the record in favor of the amendment. Let women study and practice medicine if they will. It is a matter of taste. We can not help it. But I protest against the mixed classes and mixed clinics of Dr. Davis. If a woman is smart enough to compete with me in practice, let her do it. I will show her fair play, just as I do to a man.

Dr. Johnson, of Missouri—I am opposed to the amendment, not because I object to female physicians, but I think they should keep to themselves, and have their own schools and their own societies. There are subjects brought before us in our meetings which are not suitable for discussion in mixed bodies.

After an animated discussion of about two hours, a motion to indefinitely postpone was carried: yeas, 85; nays, 25.

At one o'clock, the Association adjourned, and the members proceeded, by invitation, to Toland Medical College, where they enjoyed a sumptuous collation, sandwiched with speeches from Drs. Toland, Yandell, Davis, and others.

FRIDAY, May 5.

Met at nine o'clock A.M. President Stillé in the chair.

A communication was read from Dr. Hewston, Corresponding Secretary California State Medical Society, expressing, on behalf of the physicians of the State, the cordial feeling with which the Association was welcomed by them, and their thanks for the opportunity thus afforded to mingle with their Eastern friends, in the social and fraternal intercourse which had been interrupted for so many years. Ordered to be entered on the minutes.

CHAIR OF HYGIENE, AND NATIONAL HEALTH COUNCIL.

Dr. Logan, of California, presented the following resolutions:

WHEREAS, The science of hygiene, and its corollary, Preventive and State medicine, are subjects eminently congenial with the purposes of this Association, inasmuch as they have for their objects the preservation of human life, and the removal of those causes of disease and death which it is in the power of legislation to ameliorate, if not eradicate; and, *whereas*, the great fundamental idea that was made the prominent element for medical association, and that led eventually to our national organization, was a higher standard of medical education; and, *whereas*, the present system adopted by our colleges provides more and more satisfactorily for the thorough qualification of the graduate, as regards the principles and practice of his art, but does not provide at all adequately for the special study and cultivation of questions of State medicine; therefore, be it

Resolved, That this Association recommends a distinct and separate chair of Hygiene, independent of Physiology, to be established in all our medical schools, and constituted a requisite curriculum preliminary to that diploma which confers one of the highest honors of the Profession.

Resolved, That the inauguration of the enlarged philanthropic policy of State medicine in Massachusetts and California is worthy of our special approbation, and commends itself to other States for imitation: and, therefore, the President of this Association is hereby authorized to nominate, at this session, a committee, consisting of one physician from each State in the Union, to memorialize the Legislatures of all the other States to follow the example of one of the oldest, most enlightened, and conservative, as well as of one of the youngest, most progressive, and enterprising members of our glorious confederacy, who have led off in the right way, and at the right time, for the prevention of disease, and the correction of "those multitudinous agencies, whether physical, whether moral, whether born of earth, of air, or of society, which are, either openly or insidiously, degenerating the human race."

Resolved, That this Association further recommends that initiative steps be taken, as soon as six States shall engraft State medicine upon their statute books, for the formation of a "National Health Council," whose objects shall be the prosecution of the comparative study of international hygienic statistics, and the diffusion and utilizing of sanitary knowledge; and that said Council shall be aided and assisted by this Association, in using whatever influence may legitimately lie in their power, with foreign States, as well as with the medical profession and the people generally, in securing co-operation in the ends and objects of public hygiene.

Resolved, That said National Health Council, although thus organized as a branch *per se*, shall be auxiliary to this Association, and shall constitute a special Section on Hygiene, to which all questions germane to this department of medicine shall be referred. "Only," to use the language of the great Virchow, "by thus working harmoniously together, by thus mutually enlightening each other, will the State gain an organ to which may be safely intrusted the solution of the great question of our time, viz.: bodily and mental health, and development of future generations."

The resolutions were accepted and adopted.

Dr. Logan then moved that the President be placed upon the Committee for Pennsylvania. The motion was carried.

COMMITTEE NOMINATIONS.

The Chairman of the Committee on Nominations submitted their final report, as follows:

Time of meeting, first Tuesday in May, 1872. Place, Philadelphia.

Committee on Publication.—F. Gurney Smith, of Pennsylvania, Chairman; W. B. Atkinson, Pennsylvania; D. Murray Cheston, Pennsylvania; F. A. Ashford, District of Columbia; Caspar Wister, Pennsylvania; H. F. Askew, Delaware; J. Aitken Meigs, Pennsylvania.

Committee on Prize Essays.—Alfred Stillé, Chairman, Philadelphia; F. G. Smith, Philadelphia; D. A. O'Donnell, Baltimore; B. F. Dawson, New York; L. P. Bush, Delaware.

Committee on Medical Education.—J. S. Weatherly, Alabama, Chairman; L. Cooper Lane, San Francisco; J. M. Toner, Washington; Samuel Willey, Minnesota; W. O. Baldwin, Alabama.

Committee on Medical Literature.—T. Parvin, Indiana, Chairman; H. Carpenter, Oregon; J. P. Whitney, San Francisco; G. Mendenhall, Cincinnati; L. P. Garvin, Rhode Island.

Committee on American Medical Necrology.—J. D. Jackson, Kentucky, Chairman; Charles W. Parsons, Rhode Island; E. A. Hildreth, West Virginia; William Lee, Washington, D. C.; T. M. Logan, California; W. C. Warrener, Oregon; H. D. Holton, Vermont; W. J. Scott, Ohio; W. D. Buck, New Hampshire; A. Sager, Michigan; V. Karsey, Indiana; A. E. Ames, Minnesota; H. K. Steele, Colorado; —— Mason, Wisconsin; S. D. Gross, Philadelphia; D. W. Stormont, Kansas; J. B. Johnson, Missouri; H. R. Storer, Massachusetts; W. S. W. Ruschenberger, U. S. N.; J. W. H. Baker, Iowa; O. J. Hamilton, Illinois; J. H. Peabody, Nebraska; L. P. Bush, Delaware; G. W. Russell, Connecticut; Paul C. Chew, Maryland.

Committee of Arrangements.—E. Hartshorne, Chairman; S. W. Gross, Murray Cheston, J. F. Maury, James Tyson, W. S. Mitchell, John H. Packard, William Pepper, Richard Townsend.

OFFICERS FOR THE SECTIONS.

Chemistry and Materia Medica.—Professor R. E. Rogers, Philadelphia, President; E. Cutter, Massachusetts, Secretary.

Practical Medicine and Obstetrics.—D. A. O'Donnell, Baltimore, President; B. F. Dawson, New York, Secretary.

Surgery.—John T. Hodgen, Missouri, President; W. F. Peck, Davenport (Iowa), Secretary.

Meteorology and Epidemic Diseases.—George Sutton, Indiana, President; Elisha Harris, New York, Secretary.

Medical Jurisprudence.—S. C Busby, Washington, President; E. L. Howard, Baltimore, Secretary.

Physiology.—J. C. Dalton, New York, President; D. Payton, Oregon, Secretary.

Psychology.—Isaac Ray, Philadelphia, President; John W. Kerwan, Pennsylvania, Secretary.

Library Committee at Washington.—J. M. Toner.

On the Climatology and Epidemics of—Maine, Dr. Wood, Portland; New Hampshire, A. B. Crosby; Massachusetts, E. Cutter; Rhode Island, Edward T. Caswell; Connecticut, J. C. Jackson; New York, W. F. Thoms; New Jersey, E. M. Hunt; Pennsylvania, W. S. Wells; Maryland, C. H. Ohr; Georgia, A. J. Semmes; Missouri, W. S. Edgar; Alabama, R. F. Michel; Texas, S. M. Welch; Illinois, D. Prince; Indiana, D. Clark; District of Columbia, J. W. H. Lovejoy; Iowa, I. Williamson; Michigan, S. H. Douglass; Ohio, J. A. Murphy; California, F. W. Hatch; Tennessee, B. K. Bowling; West Virginia, E. A. Hildreth; Minnesota, Charles N. Hewitt; Virginia, A. G. Wortham; Delaware, L. P. Bush; Arkansas, T. Sinks; Mississippi, J. P. Moore; Louisiana, S. M. Bemiss; Wisconsin, J. K. Rantell; Kentucky, S. P. Yandell, Sr.; Oregon, E. R. Fisk; North Carolina, F. J. Haywood; Colorado, R. G. Buckingham; South Carolina, M. Simmons.

Special Committees.—A. L. McArthur, Chicago, Illinois. On the nature and process of the restoration of the bone.

George Sutton, Indiana. Comparative Pathology, and the effects which diseases of inferior animals have upon the human system.

T. Antisell, Chairman of the Committee on the cultivation of the Cinchona-tree.

Vaccination.—Chairman, T. M. Wise, Kentucky.

Anatomy and Disease of the Retina.—R. F. Michel, Alabama.

Some Diseases Peculiar to Colorado.—John Elsner, Denver, Colorado.

Skin Transplantation.—J. Ford Thompson, Washington, D. C.

J. K. BARTLETT, Secretary.

The report was received and adopted.

The Secretary read the minutes of the Sections on Obstetrics and Medical Jurisprudence. Referred to the Committee on Publication.

Dr. O'Donnell offered a resolution condemning criminal abortion, and urging stringent measures for its prevention. Adopted.

THE LINE AND STAFF IMBROGLIO.

Surgeon J. M. Browne, of the United States Navy, returned the thanks of the medical gentlemen of that department of the public service for the hearty co-operation of the Association in the recent contest between line and staff; a contest to define the position and rights of the latter, and acknowledge the dignity of the Profession. The law now recognized the usefulness of the staff and regulated the rank of staff officers; it did not give them all they were entitled to, but enough on which to make an honorable concession and fair compromise. Dr. Browne then read a document, containing the acknowledgments of medical gentlemen in the Navy for the assistance received from the American Medical Association.

Referred to the Committee on Publication.

DISSEMINATION OF ETHICAL KNOWLEDGE.

Dr. Montgomery, of Sacramento, offered a resolution to the effect that a Chair of Ethics should be established in all the Medical Colleges in the United States, either as an Independent Chair or in connection with some other department.

A brief discussion ensued, from which it appeared that the object of the resolution was not clearly understood; whereupon it was withdrawn by the mover.

NUMBER OF LICENSED PHYSICIANS IN THE UNITED STATES.

Dr. McArthur, of Illinois, referred to the physicians who had taken out licenses in accordance with law, the roll having been prepared by Dr. Toner. It showed sixty thousand physicians in the United States, of whom only three thousand professed to be homeopaths. He moved that Dr. Toner's list be referred to the Committee on Publication, with instructions to publish in the Transactions such a summary of it as they may deem proper. Adopted.

A MEMORIAL TO SIR JAMES Y. SIMPSON, THE DISCOVERER OF CHLOROFORM AS AN ANESTHETIC,

Having been inaugurated by the physicians of Europe and Canada, and in view of the fact that the co-operation of the American Medical Association was desired, Dr. Storer moved that the members be recommended to take the necessary steps in the matter as an evidence of their appreciation of the deceased. Carried.

Dr. Gibbons, of the Committee on Ethics, read some extracts from letters written by Professor Sayre of New York, and Professor Gross of Philadelphia, in regard to a suit for malpractice, which had been instituted against the latter for the evident purpose of extorting money. Professor Gross determined to submit to trial rather than pay black-mail. The result was, that when the case for the prosecution was presented, the Judge refused a trial and dismissed it—so utterly groundless was the suit. The prosecution was mainly got up by a scaly lawyer, who is partial to such dirty work. The Committee on Ethics did not deem it expedient to propose any action on the subject.

THE FEMALE QUESTION AGAIN.

Dr. Atlee, of Philadelphia, offered the following resolution:

Resolved, That the American Medical Association acknowledges the right of its members to meet in consultation the graduates and teachers of Women's Medical Colleges, provided the Code of Ethics of the Association is observed.

Dr. Storer—I hope that no action will be taken on the resolution. Inasmuch as the question was discussed fully yesterday, I protest against its coming up again. The sense of the Association was fully ascertained by the votes already taken.

Dr. Johnson, of Missouri—It is not the same resolution. I voted against that of yesterday, but I am in favor of this. It has nothing to do with the admission of women to this Association, but it is simply a declaration that our laws do not prohibit the members from consulting with properly qualified female physicians, if they see proper.

Dr. Atlee—I introduced this resolution at the suggestion of several gentlemen who voted against delegates from female schools, but who believe with me that it is illiberal and proscriptive to forbid consultations with female physicians. Our code is silent on the question, and yet our County Society in Philadelphia construes it to prohibit such consultations. If this Association pronounce on it, the question will be settled. The County Society will yield.

Dr. McArthur, of Illinois—Let the question come up in the form of an appeal from the local Society, and then it will be regularly before us. There is nothing in the code to prohibit consultations with females—not a word.

Dr. Gibbons—Then why not say so?

Dr. McArthur—Because it is a work of supererogation. The code is plain enough, and it can do no good to interpret what does not need interpretation.

Dr. Gibbons—We are told by Dr. Atlee that the proposed declaration will settle the difficulty in Pennsylvania. If there is no other objection than its superfluity, we can certainly afford to do a merely superfluous act for the sake of peace and harmony in our ranks.

Dr. Toner—I move an amendment: "*Provided*, such graduates and teachers are recognized by the local and State Societies."

The amendment was lost on a rising vote: 53 to 51.

The hour for adjournment to the Oakland boat being at hand, and the resolution being likely to prevail, its opponents resorted to strategy to prevent a final vote. Motions for the yeas and nays, to postpone, to lay on the table, etc., were offered, and a motion was finally made and carried to hold an evening session for the settlement of the question.

The members then departed in a body for Oakland, where they made a tour of inspection of the public grounds and buildings, and performed a variety of gastronomic exercises.

EVENING SESSION.

The Secretary not having succeeded in finding his way back from Oakland, Dr. J. C. Tucker was chosen Secretary *pro tem.* Dr. Atlee's resolution was read.

Dr. Storer—This is a question of great moment. Women are disqualified by nature for successful practice. They do not inspire their female patients with the confidence which is given by our sex. They may carry out directions and act as nurses, but in difficult cases they can not make a diagnosis. They are subject to a monthly perturbation, which affects their judgment, and renders them unfit for practice. Some advocates for female doctors have gone so far as to say that it was impossible for a male physician to enter the chamber of a female patient without exciting improper feelings in her.

Dr. Gibbons—What if women do have mental perturbations at stated periods? It is well known that a majority of male practitioners are liable to diurnal perturbations from the popular custom of drinking. [Hisses.] We have an Academy of Sciences in this city, and are collecting specimens of all kinds. I would thank some one to catch one of those hissing animals for the collection. [Renewed hisses.] I must have been misunderstood. I am not aware of having said anything to call for such a demonstration. What I mean to say is, that in accordance with the custom of society, a majority of physicians are in the habit of taking more or less wine every day, and that, as a physiological fact, the alcohol of the wine finds its way to the brain. But the resolution before us has nothing to do with the question whether women should be doctors. The question is as to the construction of our Code of Ethics. It is the duty of this Association to define its code, so that it shall not be construed differently in different places. It is construed one way in Illinois, according to Dr. McArthur, and another way in Pennsylvania. Let us, for the sake of peace and harmony, settle its meaning.

Dr. Atlee—I appeal to this Association to take action on the subject. I believe that its judgment will settle the question in Pennsylvania, and put an end to the unhappy difference among us. Those of us who are disposed to adhere to our organization are not only prevented from consulting with female physicians, but are liable to censure for consulting with such of our brethren as consult with females, or represent female colleges. For instance, I dare not consult with your President, Dr. Stillé, without risk of impeachment. We are not willing to violate the sentiment of the Society, and therefore we submit for the present, hoping for relief. There are others who do not submit, but who consult openly with females, and defy the Society to expel them, threatening to sue for damages if they are expelled; and the Society dares not expel them. It is a bad state of affairs, and I think the passage of the resolution would cure the evil.

Dr. Johnson—Common humanity, if nothing else, would require us to render assistance in a case of emergency when called on by a female physician. Am I to refuse to assist in saving the life of a woman in convulsions, or who is bleeding to death, because her medical attendant is a female? Though I am averse to admitting female delegates or their representatives on this floor, yet on the point involved in the resolution before us, the common sense of mankind, and the common sympathies of humanity, are against proscription.

Dr. Stillé, calling Dr. Gibbons to the Chair—I wish to correct some misapprehensions. The College of Physicians of Philadelphia, the oldest medical society on the continent, and comprising the *élite* of the Profession, has never prohibited consultations with females. The County Society, of recent formation, and with fewer members, has taken a different course.

Dr. Atlee—Is the College of Physicians represented here?

Dr. Stillé—No; it is not. But I am a member of the Board of Censors of the County Society, and also Consulting Physician of the Female College, and I have never been arraigned for an offense. There are no such difficulties as has been represented.

Dr. Atlee—Nevertheless, a majority of the County Society insist on construing the Code of Ethics so as to regard females as irregular practitioners, and to forbid consultation with them. If no formal arraignment is made, it is from policy. Some of us feel bound to conform to the will of the majority, though we might not be indicted for setting it at defiance. All we ask is that this Association define its own code, so that it shall have a uniform construction by different societies.

Dr. Weatherly—I think this body has no authority for meddling in local quarrels, and therefore move an indefinite postponement.

The motion was carried by a decided majority, and so the question goes over to enliven the next session.

Dr. Storer submitted the following resolution, which was also postponed indefinitely:

Resolved, That this Association views with dissatisfaction the course of gentlemen who, in setting at defiance their local and State Societies, have contemplated the establishment of a precedent that, admitted in other matters, would at once destroy the authority of this Association.

The thanks of the Association were voted to the various transportation companies and public bodies, and to private individuals, who had accommodated and entertained the members and facilitated the purposes of the meeting.

Before the final adjournment, Dr. N. S. Davis made a brief and fervent address, felicitating the members on the success which had attended the meeting in California, the social enjoyments of the occasion, and the fraternal feeling with which the members were about to separate. Then adjourned *sine die*.

The following day (Saturday) was appropriated to an excursion around the Bay, on the steamer *Antelope*, in which the members, with their families and friends, very generally participated. Under the skillful management of Captain E. A. Poole, the party was conducted toward the Golden Gate, far enough to obtain a glimpse of the great Pacific Ocean, and to rock gently on the margin of its billows. Then, returning through Raccoon Straits, the vessel skirted the western shore of the Bay, passing doleful San Quentin and beautiful San Rafael, and, rounding to before the thriving city of Vallejo, landed at the Government works on Mare Island. Here the excursionists were handsomely received by Commandant Parrott, and the other officers, and by Surgeons Browne, Taylor, and Woods. The gardens, compact with roses and gorgeous flowers, were thrown open, and the gifts of Flora lavishly distributed. A large number of the medical delegates visited the hospital, which they pronounced a model of construction and management.

Returning, the vessel was conducted along the city front to the Dry Dock at Hunter's Point, giving a view of the southern expanse of the Bay, as it was lost in the horizon in the direction of San José. Late in the afternoon, the company disembarked at Vallejo-street wharf, saturated with the sweets of nature, which the surroundings of the great Bay had supplied, and with certain other supplementary sweets provided on the boat. The physicians of California, who were present in large numbers, will not soon forget the enjoyment derived by them on that occasion from the cordial and unrestrained social intercourse with their brethren from abroad.

REVIEWS AND NOTICES OF BOOKS.

Chemistry: General, Medical, and Pharmaceutical, including the Chemistry of the U. S. Pharmacopeia. A manual on the general principles of the Science, and their application to Medicine and Pharmacy. By John Attfield, Ph.D., F.C.S., Professor of Practical Chemistry to the Pharmaceutical Society of Great Britain; formerly Demonstrator of Chemistry at St. Bartholomew's Hospital; Honorary Member of the Colleges of Pharmacy of Philadelphia, New York, and Chicago, etc., etc., etc. From the second and enlarged English edition. Revised by the author. Philadelphia: Henry C. Lea. 1871. Pp. 552. San Francisco: A. L. Bancroft & Co.

A cursory inspection of this volume gives us a most favorable impression of its value, and convinces us that it is what the author says in his preface he intended—"A Systematic Exponent of the general Truths of Chemistry," "written solely for the Pupils, Assistants, and Principals engaged in Medicine and Pharmacy." It is comprehensive and terse, yet perspicuous, and, if we mistake not, will take the first place as a text-book in Colleges.

The Mystery of Life: An Essay in Reply to Dr. Gull's Attack on the Theory of Vitality in his Harveian Oration for 1870. By Lionel S. Beale, M.B., F.R.S., Fellow of the Royal College of Physicians; Physician to King's College Hospital, etc. With two colored plates. Philadelphia: Lindsay & Blakiston. 1871. San Francisco: A. L. Bancroft & Co.

A pleasing little book of 70 pages, on the old and still unsettled question of the origin of life. The name of the author is sufficient to insure the reading of it by all philosophic inquirers, on both sides of the controversy, more particularly as most men have formed opinions on the subject with a positiveness and a confidence proportionate to its mysteries and incomprehensibilities.

Insanity and its Treatment: Lectures on the Treatment, Medical and Legal, of Insane Patients. By G. Fielding Blandford, M.D., Oxon., Fellow of the Royal College of Physicians in London; Lecturer on Psychological Medicine at the School of St. George's Hospital, London. With a Summary of the Laws in Force in the United States on the Confinement of the Insane. By Isaac Ray, M.D. Philadelphia: H. C. Lea. 1871. Pp. 471. San Francisco: A. L. Bancroft & Co.

The student or miscellaneous reader, who would pick up with

little labor a clear and general idea of the subject of insanity in nearly all its bearings, will find this book better adapted to his purpose than any other that we know of. It is as lively as a novel in its style, and at the same time eminently practical. We hail it as a valuable acquisition to a department of medical science, the interest and magnitude of which increase every day.

EDITORIAL.

About the "Journal" for this Month.

It is scarcely necessary to refer to the obvious fact that we have given up the present number of the JOURNAL almost entirely to the proceedings of the National Association. Meantime, a large number of valuable contributions are laid over, which will appear in turn. Among them are the following: "Phthisis Pulmonalis," by Dr. Graettinger; "Abscess of Ankle," by Dr. E. B. Robertson; "Recurring Measles," by Dr. E. T. Barber; "The Social Evil," by Dr. W. E. Whitehead; "Luxated Elbow," by Dr. A. S. Hudson; "Suit for Malpractice," by Dr. E. T. Barber; "Antidote to Snake-poisoning," by Dr. L. Lanszweert; "Removal of Foreign Body from Bladder," by Dr. E. B. Robertson; "Medical Ethics," by Dr. J. F. Montgomery. Sundry notices of books and pamphlets received are also necessarily deferred.

High-heeled Boots, Chinese Feet, and Crooked Shins.

It is worthy of note that while a malignant hatred of Chinese, individually, is fomented under cover of hostility to their immigration, our females have fallen in love with Chinese costumes and customs, in some respects, and accepted them as models. The pictures of Chinese ladies, to which one has been accustomed for many years, bear a close resemblance to the American belle of the present day. The repulsive hump, the crippled feet, and the mincing gait of our women, if they do not fortify the Darwinian theory of the origin of the species from monkeys, at least give the appearance of retrograding monkey-wards. The dress, uncouth and deforming as it is, would not of itself deserve notice; but the high heels, crippling the feet and distorting the limbs, are an outrage on grace, on anatomy, on humanity, entitling the authors, could they be detected, to criminal responsibility. A convention of corn-doctors, in the interest of their trade, could not devise a better scheme for good times. Women whose pedals are solidified, may escape with only corns, of which we hope and pray they may have a full and a tender crop. But that a whole generation of little girls should have their toes jammed into the points of their boots, to do the work of heels, and that their legs should be thrown out of the natural balance, and the pliant bones bent into semicircles, is a sacrifice to fashion which would disgrace a nation of Hottentots. Should the wicked custom hold a few years, there will not be a decent foot or an esthetic leg in our female population, except among washerwomen and the like. And all this is a trifle compared with the mischief done to the pelvis, spine, and chest, by the constrained attitude which the abnormal elevation of the heel must of necessity induce. Fashion is at best a cruel tyrant; but the whole history of her capricious rule does not exhibit a grosser violation of natural laws, and a more unpardonable assault on the beauty and health of woman, than the invention of HIGH-HEELED BOOTS.

Write your Prescriptions in Plain English.

The best commentary we have seen on the popular outcry against the use of Latin, or scientific names for medicines, is contained in a current newspaper article, attributing extraordinary virtues to the *hydrastis canadensis* as a cure for small-pox. As to the plant, it is probably as good as the *sarracenia*. But the point of the article is the statement that "the plant is popularly called orange root, and sometimes yellow puccoon, but it must not be confounded with another plant commonly called puccoon."

Something Good from New York.

It is gratifying to find that the public authorities of the city of New York are credited at last with *one* good mark, though the credit belongs entirely to the medical department. The *London Med. Press and Circular* says: "The city of New York and the State of Massachusetts give forth the fullest and best government documents on public health which appear in print."

GENERAL SUMMARY.

Effects of Alcohol and Tobacco on the Sight.

On the subject of color-blindness and amblyopia, Dr. Richard H. Derby (*N. Y. Med. Journal*) says: "Almost always both eyes are affected. This form of amblyopia occurs almost solely in men; out of fifty-six cases only three were women. It is a disease of adults; its frequency increasing from the twentieth to the fortieth year. In a portion of the cases abuse of alcohol was certainly the cause of the affection, and in others the excessive use of tobacco undoubtedly contributed to produce the disease. Forster, in a paper on the injurious action of tobacco on the vision, attaches still greater importance to this agent as a cause of amblyopia, supporting the views of Mackenzie, Sichel, Hutchinson, Lureiro, and others. The author cites twenty cases, in which there was a central scotoma, with a horizontal diameter of 18° to 25°, within which large letters could still be recognized. All of these patients suffered from some affection of the digestive and nervous system. Loss of appetite, constipation, loss of sleep, were common symptoms. Each one of the twenty patients was a strong smoker, and in eleven of these cases a very marked improvement was observed when the use of tobacco was given up."

On the Preparation of Tinct. Hyoscyamus.

Dr. Donovan, in the *Medical Press and Circular*, says that this preparation is inert when made from the plant in the first year of its growth. He has taken one ounce of the tincture, prepared according to the *Dublin Pharmacopœia*, with no other effect than dryness of the fauces and throat. The active properties of the plant are developed in the second year, and the tincture prepared from it becomes milky on the addition of water—a good, but simple test of its medicinal activity.

Death from Nitrous Oxide Gas.

A case is reported in the *Dental Cosmos*, of a young lady in Philadelphia, who inhaled nitrous oxide gas, for the purpose of having a tooth extracted, and died in a few minutes. She had hypertrophy of the heart.

STATE BOARD OF HEALTH.

Abstract from the Reports of Deaths and their Causes, in the following cities and towns in California, during April, 1871 :

[illegible]

Abstract from Reports of Births :

CITIES AND TOWNS.	Total Births.	Males.	Females.	Still-born.	Live-born.	AUTHORITIES.
San Francisco...	120	72	48	22	98	S. F. Board of Health.
Sacramento.....	55	28	27	10	45	Sac. Board of Health.
All other places.	183	99	84	10	173	Various sources.
TOTAL......	358	199	159	42	316	

Remarks.—Our table, as far as it goes, shows the sanitary condition of the State to be all that can be desired, affording no occasion for comment. While returning our best thanks to our correspondents for their continued favors, we would renew the request that, if they wish us to make use of their contributions (which are to be further used in our general report to the Legislature) for such abstracts as the above, they must be more regular hereafter. This journal, we are informed, goes to press about the 20th of every month, and the many blank spaces, which render our table imperfect, show how many fail to come up to time. This is to be regretted, the more at this particular juncture, when we would otherwise have been enabled to demonstrate, without a doubt, the important fact that the salubrity of the climate of California is without a parallel.

THOMAS M. LOGAN, M.D.,
Permanent Secretary State Board of Health.

Mortality in San Francisco during April, 1871.

By H. Gibbons, Jr., M.D.

CAUSES OF DEATH.

Alcoholism	4	Diphtheria	4	Meningitis	11
Aneurism of Aorta	3	Disease of Brain	1	Old Age	2
Angina Pectoris	1	Diseases of Heart	13	Ossification of Arteries	1
Apoplexy	3	Dropsy	2	Ovarian Tumor	1
Ascites	1	Drowning	1	Paralysis	4
Asthma	1	Emphysema	1	Peritonitis	1
Atrophia	4	Empyema	1	Phthisis	54
Brain, Injury to, by fall	1	Enteritis	3	Pleuritis	1
Bright's Disease	1	Erysipelas	3	Pneumonitis	13
Burns	2	Fever, Remittent	1	Premature Birth	7
Cancer of Breast	1	" Scarlet	2	Pyemia	2
" of Uterus	1	" Typhoid	6	Rheumatic Gout	1
Cerebritis	1	Fracture of Thigh	1	Rheumatism	2
Cholera Infantum	2	Gangrene	1	Stabbing	1
Cirrhosis	1	Gun-shot Wound	2	Suicide	3
Concussion of Brain	1	Hematemesis	1	Syphilis	1
Congestion of Brain	4	Hemoptysis	1	Trismus Nascentium	1
" of Lungs	4	Hemorrhage	1	Unknown	9
Convulsions	11	Hepatitis	1	Uremia	1
Croup	1	Hip-joint Disease	1	Uterine Tumor	1
Debility, General	3	Hydrocephalus	5	Whooping Cough	3
Dentition	1	Ileus	1		
Diabetes	1	Inanition	3	Total	232
Diarrhea	2	Kidney Disease	1	Still-births	22

AGES.

Under 1 year	43	From 15 to 20 years	3	From 60 to 70 years	14
From 1 to 2 years	13	From 20 to 30 years	29	From 70 to 80 years	5
From 2 to 5 years	12	From 30 to 40 years	46	From 80 to 90 years	0
From 5 to 10 years	4	From 40 to 50 years	45	From 90 to 100 years	0
From 10 to 15 years	3	From 50 to 60 years	15	Unknown	0

NATIVITIES.

California	72	Wales	1	Portugal	1
Other parts of U. S.	41	France	6	China	21
British Amer'n Prov.	1	Germany	23	Western Isles	2
Mexico	2	Austria	1	Australia	1
England	9	Sweden	4	At Sea	1
Ireland	39	Russia	1	Cape de Verde Island.	1
Scotland	3	Switzerland	2		

SEX. — Male, 151; Female, 81. Total, 232.
COLOR. — White, 201; Copper, 21; Black, 10.

RECAPITULATION.

Died in City Wards	185	St. Vincent de Paul Asylum	2
City and County Hospital	11	Alms House	2
U. S. Marine Hospital	3	Industrial School	1
French Hospital	4	Mount St. Joseph's Infirmary	2
German Hospital	2	Casualties	9
St. Mary's Hospital	8	Suicides	3

REMARKS.—We are still able to claim for our city unusual immunity from fatal disease. The low mortality rate existing in March was unchanged in April, and the prospects are as favorable for May. For six years past the number of deaths in April has been as follows: In 1866, two hundred and three; in 1867, one hundred and seventy-seven; in 1868, one hundred and ninety-three; in 1869, two hundred and eighty-six; in 1870, two hundred and sixty-one, and in 1871, two hundred and thirty-two—an increase for the present year over the first three years, but showing a progressive diminution since the epidemic period inaugurated in June, 1868. The total mortality from disease in March and April was almost identical; among many individual diseases, as aneurism, congestion of the brain and of the lungs, debility, pneumonia, and pyemia, it was precisely the same. In March more deaths occurred from atrophia, cancer, convulsions, enteritis, inanition, softening of the brain, etc.; on the other hand, in April the deaths were more numerous from diseases of the heart, meningitis, alcoholism, and notably so from consumption and casualties. While there were but thirty-nine in March from the former cause, there were fifty-four in April, and from casualties there were nine deaths in April to but two in March. The number of American-born decedents remains about the same; among the Irish there was a large increase of mortality. It is noticeable that only eleven deaths occurred in the City and County Hospital, the usual number varying from fifteen to twenty.

PACIFIC

MEDICAL AND SURGICAL JOURNAL.

Vol. V.—JULY, 1871.—No. 50.

ORIGINAL COMMUNICATIONS.

Necrosis of Os Calcis—Exsection.

By E. B. ROBERTSON, M.D., County Physician of Calaveras County.

Alice B., born in this county, of healthy parents; age, nine years; was attacked with acute pain in the posterior and inferior part of the os calcis, on the 8th day of August, 1867. I was called to see her on the tenth, and was informed by her parents that she had been in the habit of jumping a rope at school—an amusement by no means uncommon among children.

There was no very distinct swelling at the time of my first visit. I ordered elevation of the part, and cold applications and saline aperients. On the 15th, I was again called to see her. Found distinct redness and swelling about the heel and beneath the malleoli of either side. Ordered warm poultices to be continually applied, so as to envelop the heel and ankle; gave an aperient, and left a few doses of Dover powders, one of which was to be taken at night, to secure rest. On the 20th, I again visited her. and found that an abscess had pointed immediately beneath the internal malleolus, which was lanced, letting out a considerable quantity of pus. I continued to visit the patient for some months, from time to time; and here allow me to digress, to say that the family resided some five miles from town, and it was not convenient for me to see my patient so frequently as I should have done had she been nearer at hand.

Pus continued to form, and burrow and point in different directions, sometimes being lanced, and at others bursting of itself, until about the sixth month after the attack, when small pieces of bone became detached and escaped. About the first of April, 1868, her health was failing; hectic symptoms were present, which, by the way, does not contra-indicate an operation for the removal of its cause. It was thought unsafe to trust to nature alone any further.

The patient was brought to town by her mother, for the operation, and to be where I could attend to the after-treatment. The operation I performed April 4, 1868, assisted by Drs. Hœrchner and Marcel. Complete anesthesia was effected by a mixture of ether and chloroform—four parts of the former to one of the latter—the patient being laid on an ordinary table. A horizontal incision was made, commencing at the inner edge of the os calcis, severing the tendo-achillis at about its insertion, and continued along the outer side of the foot to a point near the calcaneo-cuboidal articulation. Opened the sheath of the tendon of the peroneus longus, though not intentionally. All the soft parts were divided to the bone as advance was made with the incision; the knife was then turned downward to the sole of the foot, making another incision at right angles with the first. The bone, when exposed, presented three apertures corresponding to as many openings through the soft parts, through which the portions of necrosed bone had escaped. The entirety of the original bone was found to be disorganized, and the apertures before mentioned communicated with a cavity toward the interior of the substance, but it was connected with the periosteum by a thin lamina of osseous matter recently deposited. The bone was so much disorganized that it was an easy matter to divide it with a pair of cutting bone-plyers, part adhering to the inferior flap and part to its superior connections, from which its several portions were peeled off from the periosteum until it was entirely removed, or what was remaining of it.

Upon further examination, the cartilages next the astragalus, and also the cuboid, were found to be disorganized; so much so that a portion of each was carious, and, of necessity, gouged or scraped off. The cavity was then washed out with simple water, and filled with wet lint; the inferior flap brought up to place, and retained by silver wire and quilled suture; a piece of wet lint laid over the wound, and a roller loosely applied; directions given the mother to keep the dressings constantly wet with cool water. The inflammatory fever following the operation was inconsiderable.

On the second day after the operation, the bowels not having moved, she was given three drachms of sulphate of magnesia. Returned in the evening, and was informed that the medicine acted; patient as comfortable as could be expected. April 7th, third day after the operation, patient comfortable; no reason to interfere with dressing other than to continue the water to keep moist.

April 8th. Removed outside dressings; found union of the edges of the wound as far as desirable; lint inside still adherent.

April 9th. Removed inside lint, washed out the cavity with tepid water, and refilled the cavity as before, through an opening left for that purpose along the outer side.

The water dressing was continued until April 13th, after which the cavity was washed out daily with a weak solution of iodine—half-ounce of the compound tincture to a pint of water—then filled to its full capacity with lint cut in strips and saturated with glycerin. This dressing was continued without interruption until the cure was completed. As the cavity was filled by granulation, the lint was necessarily cut smaller, until it would not admit any; the external opening being guarded until it entirely healed from the bottom, which was completed at the expiration of about three months. The constitutional treatment and regimen were about as follows:

℞. Potass. iodidi, ℨiss.
Syr. sarsap. comp.
Aquæ font., āā ℥viij.

M. Sig. Take one table-spoonful three times a day. Fresh beef or mutton, milk, raw eggs, freely allowed; other common articles, such as fruit and vegetables, used sparingly.

I examined the foot about one year after the operation, and it presented the following appearance: The ankle-joint completely anchylosed; the heel a little shorter than the opposite, as if not quite filled out posteriorly, and at the point where it was kept open, remained a considerable fissure or depression, owing to cicatrization advancing inwardly during treatment. In fact, we did not try to prevent it.

She is now (two years after the operation) an active, healthy girl; the lameness is very trifling. The bone is apparently well reproduced. The anchylosis remains, and probably always will, as there appears to have been, and still is, adhesion of the bones.

A New Observation—The Luxated Elbow.

BY A. S. HUDSON, M.D., of Stockton. Read before the Section on Surgery of the American Medical Association, and recommended for publication.

Error leads to failure; the lesson of failure is to correct the error. In February, 1870, a child of Mr. J., between two and three years old, was brought to our notice, five weeks after it had fallen from a few steps and injured the left elbow. Careful inquiry—the patient under chloroform—decided a dislocation of the ulna and radius inward. A strong and persistent effort at reduction, by the methods taught by Prof. Gross and others, failed to reduce it. What was the reason of failure? Prof. Gross, in speaking of this injury, says, "It is easily reduced." But the study of the subject and its literature, leads us to question the correctness of his statement. "Malgaigne totally failed in a recent case. Triquet, after several failures, succeeded on the fifteenth day; but the joint never recovered its motions. Dubruyn succeeded on the fifth day, with *difficulty*." These facts controvert the statement, "It is easily reduced."

The written and illustrated pathology of this injury is simply fallacious and incomprehensible. Cooper employs this remarkable language: "In the dislocation inward, the greater sigmoid cavity of the ulna is entirely separated from the internal condyle of the humerus." Yet he calls it an "incomplete dislocation." Dr. Gross says, "The head of the radius hitches against the inner condyle;" and at the same time figures it occupying the trochlea, which is quite remote from the condyle, and innocent of obstruction toward reposition. Prof. Hamilton says, "The ridge which divides antero-posteriorly the greater sigmoid cavity of the ulna, having been driven over the elevated inner margin of the trochlea, falls down upon the epitrochlea so as in some sense to embrace it, instead of the trochlea." This language is no less remarkable than that of the authors above quoted. Prof. Hamilton may have written the pathology of this mischief with the wood-cut illustrating it before him, instead of the displaced bones; which cut is obviously a copy of one in Gross or Furgusson, and that one quite imaginary and erroneous. When carefully studied, this belief becomes overbearing: namely, that for the coronoid process of the ulna to rest in the trochlea, and the point of the olecranon on the inner condyle of the humerus, with the lower arm pointing away from the body, as figured and described by Hamilton, is an *anatomical impossibility*.

PATHOLOGY.

As witnessed in the child above-mentioned, and subsequently demonstrated on the cadaver, the typical form of dislocation of radius and ulna inward on the humerus, is that in which both bones of the elbow are wholly removed from their respective articulations. The sigmoid cavity of the ulna embraces the inner condyle of the humerus, on which it freely moves. The head of the radius felt in the bend of the arm occupies the trochlea, separated from the ulna. Therefore, it can be none other than a *complete dislocation.* Now, if the head of the radius be not separated from the ulna in the displacement, a slight motion at straightening the arm will at once return the bones into position with a sudden jolt. But if, by the force of accident, or the scalpel on the dead subject, the orbicular ligament becomes stretched or severed, then the epitrochlea wedges in between the ulna and radius, and the coronoid of the ulna drops down past or over the abrupt wall of the epitrochlea, and makes the case no more complete, but adds a bold and effectual opposition to the usual plans of reduction. Herein lies the great obstacle the surgeon must encounter.

SIGNS.

The signs of this dislocation, as presented in our case, and in the dead subject under manipulation, were: First, unusual prominence of the outer condyle of the humerus; second, obscuration of the inner condyle; third, pointing of the fore-arm inward diagonally across the body; fourth, head of the radius felt in the bend of the arm, with the olecranon prominence removed from the centre to near the inner margin of the arm.

REDRESS.

The anatomy of the parts, with the position of the displaced bones, indicates the plan of reduction to be this: To forcibly bend the fore-arm backward on the elbow, with or without extension, which lifts the coronoid process of the ulna over the abrupt side of the epitrochlea into its place. This unlocks the hook, and the joint is restored.

The sequence of this case is one of interest and surprise. Its record deserves perpetuity. Eight months or more after the accident, Dr. S., who administered to the child immediately after it occurred, was prosecuted on a charge of malpractice. He was justly acquitted of the charge, on the ground that it could not be proved the child had sustained any appreciable damage, either through the accident, or at the alleged neglectful hands of Dr. S. The limb exhibited all the natural strength and motions of the joint. The naked arm alone showed the characteristic deformity.

The Social Evil!

BY W. E. WHITEHEAD, M.D., U. S. A.

This subject has agitated the world since the earliest periods, as shown by the records of history; for do we not read, that Sodom and Gomorrah were destroyed in consequence? And do not nearly all the Jewish laws point to the great prevalence of this evil? Where large numbers of people live together, as in our large cities, or, in fact, so long as we are created with animal instinct, as we have been since the fall of man in the Garden, the "social evil" will exist.

The question arises, If this evil will and must exist, how can we best counteract it by proper legislation and proper moral restrictions? But, more especially, what legal measures can be adopted to check it, or at least modify the effects of prostitution?

I would propose, that a law be passed imposing a tax upon every housekeeper where a prostitute lives, whether she carried on her trade in that house or not; this tax to go toward the support of infirmaries or hospitals wherein the unfortunates might at all and any time receive treatment and professional medical advice. Let these infirmaries be located in the neighborhoods where the largest number of prostitutes congregate. For it would be soon found, that, provided the police, or a certain number of trusty members of the police force, detailed especially to find out the habitats of prostitutes, notified the housekeepers that they must pay the fine, in many instances the women would have to seek other quarters, and thus it would not be very long before certain streets and localities would become the only proper places for them; for, as in all other matters of trade, "birds of a feather would flock together;" and thereby one of the greatest evils of the present condition of things would be materially improved; for then those trade localities being known, respectable persons might avoid them. But, as things now exist in many of the larger cities, you often find a house of prostitution next door to a church building, to the residence of a minister of the Gospel, and in the most respectable portion of the town, thereby subjecting respectable families residing in their vicinity to suspicion, often to insult, the young to temptation, and, worse, familiarity with this great social evil.

We will not stop to estimate the depreciation of house property or rentals in the heretofore respectable neighborhood where one or more houses supported in the manner spoken of happen to open their portals.

To show that great benefits may be derived from having the social evil under legal restraint, I take the liberty to introduce at this point a brief abstract of an elaborate report of a committee appointed by the Board of Health of St. Louis, to examine into the effects of regulating the "Social Evil and the Workings of the Social Evil Law:"

"Whole number of prostitutes registered when the law went into operation, 718; number now registered, 480. Decrease, 238. Number of houses of ill-fame in the city when the law went into effect, 119; number now in the city, 90; number of inmates diseased at first, 58; number now, 18. Since the registration 229 women have been added to the registry list, making the total registry 947; actual decrease of this class of women, 468."

The report further states that the general sanitary condition of these women has been greatly improved under the operation of the law. Of the total number of women registered, it has been ascertained that 702 of them became prostitutes from choice; 101 because they had been seduced; 87 because their husbands treated them badly, and 57 from necessity. The number of men seeking the society of these women has decreased since the law went into effect, notwithstanding the increased chances of immunity from disease. This is attributed, however, mainly to the fact that the men seeking such society are taken more notice of by the officers of the law. The report also states that the whole number of cases of private diseases (venereal) treated at the hospital and charitable institutions of the city, for eight months previous to the passage of the "Social Evil Law," was 539, and the number treated in the same institutions for the eight months the law has been in operation was only 174, showing a decrease of 70 per cent.

From the above brief abstract, it is plainly to be seen, that for the short season that the law has been in effect in St. Louis, and notwithstanding the difficulty arising from carrying out the requirements of such a law in the outset, great benefits have grown out of it; not alone in a material reduction in the number of cases of venereal diseases, but in the appreciable reduction in the number of prostitutes; and last, but not least, in the reduced number of men seeking the society of prostitutes. This latter is a most important feature of the good working of such a law; for when the demand is cut off, the supply necessarily diminishes. This is a fixed law of trade, aside from the higher moral effect upon the young men of a city, or more particularly of strangers visiting the same, and who are generally anxious to be shown the "elephant," as a tour of the bawdy-houses of a city is called. This more particularly is the case with men from the rural districts, who, on entering a city, are very desirous of visiting houses of prostitution; and frequently their city friends are equally desirous of taking them around town; but, judging from the report above, such entertainment is not so much sought after at present in St. Louis as in former times. How often has this custom of visiting houses of prostitution brought ruin—physical, moral, and pecuniary ruin—upon families and men from rural burgs and districts, who, after a visit to some large city upon business, having made a tour of the houses of ill-fame, become diseased, and, through shame, ignorance, or other causes, upon reaching their homes become victims to loathsome diseases.

Fortunate are they if they do not spread this vile pestilence; for should they happen to be married men, how easily virtuous, pure wives may become tainted, and innocent children born into the world a shame and deplorable objects of loathsome pity to all beholders, thus entailing misery upon generations yet unborn.

All these truths have too often been forced upon the attention of my professional readers in their experiences as medical practitioners.

Now it seems to me that some law might be enacted to govern the "social evil." We have the statistics showing the effects of laws to govern prostitution in various foreign countries, and now in some of our own cities. Why can not those learned in the law unite with our profession to frame a law suited to our system of Government, culling what is evil, and taking the good that has proved by experience to work well, from the laws of other countries, and upon such a basis frame a general law, which might be easily modified and adapted to suit local interests and prejudices?

Without ever having read *any* laws upon this subject, I shall be glad to contribute a few general ideas or principles upon which to base a law to govern the "social evil." In our country it is very essential to have our laws so framed and executed that they may not be irksome or interfere with the proper exercise of the rights of the citizen—"life, liberty, and the pursuit of happiness." A law to govern the social evil would prolong life by preventing disease, and would promote happiness for the same reason, and from higher moral points. The only thing, then, is to guard against any infringements upon the liberty of individuals. But, as all trades and professions are subject to laws—moral, social, or otherwise—why not subject those living by prostitution to rigid laws? Moral or social laws exercise but little restraint upon this vile trade; therefore we must have rigid legal restraint imposed, to prevent its moral inroads and the dissemination of vile diseases, sapping the health and vigor of our people, and consequently destroying the wealth, energy, and power of our country. This is no figure of speech, nor picture of the imagination. We have only to look around us to see the mischief arising from unrestrained social evil.

All houses of prostitution, assignation, bed or boarding-houses where prostitutes live; saloons, bar-rooms, cigar stores, dance halls, or other places where prostitutes are kept or employed during certain hours of the day or night, whether they carry on their trade in such places or not, should be licensed, registered, and compelled to pay a heavy license fee. All prostitutes, or all women who trade in their charms indiscriminately for lust, for love, or for money, should be compelled to register their names, residences, and places where they carry on their trade at the police station or precinct in which they board or live. Infirmaries, dispensaries, or hospitals should be established in every police precinct, or in certain districts, where all cases of venereal diseases could receive proper treatment, and where all prostitutes should be compelled to report once a week or fortnight, to be examined, to receive a clean bill of health, or, if diseased, to be sent to an infirmary or hospital for treatment. Fines for violations of the above rules to be imposed at fixed rates, said fines and the license fees to be appropriated to the liquidation of the expenses of the infirmaries, dispensaries, or hospitals. No person suffering under any form of venereal disease should be refused treatment at the above-named institutions; but all strangers and non-registered prostitutes should be compelled to pay a fee for such treatment, and, if placed in the hospital, to pay a certain sum per week for board, medical attendance, and medicine.

All prostitutes to be compelled to show, at all times, to any person seeking their society, or to any officer of the law having proper authority, their certificates of health or freedom from disease at the date of the last weekly or fortnightly examination, or otherwise to be subjected to arrest or fine, or to both, when deemed necessary.

None other than venereal diseases to be treated in the infirmaries or dispensaries, and none others to be admitted into the hospitals.

The infirmaries, dispensaries, and hospitals to be under charge of resident physicians, who shall receive appointments upon successful competitive examination; and visiting physicians to be appointed by the Mayor and Common Council, or by the Mayor and Judges of the higher county or city courts, to hold office for two years or more, and to be selected from the city or county physicians of professional reputation and worth. The resident physicians to receive, as remuneration, their board and washing, and to be retained for two or more years; the visiting physicians to receive salaries of not more than one thousand dollars per year. Either of the above offices to be filled by re-appointment upon the same conditions as above specified.

Registered certificates to be given to each prostitute; these certificates to be signed by the Mayor, Chief of Police, and ranking police officer of the precinct on duty where the certificate is issued; copies to be kept of all certificates issued at the station-house of the precinct or district, and at the Police Head-quarters, open to any or all persons who may desire to see them for any purpose other than for publication.

All certificates of health or freedom from venereal diseases to be signed by the resident and visiting physicians of one of the dispensaries, infirmaries, or hospitals. A certain number of policemen in each precinct to be detailed to report all houses of ill-fame, and to see that all prostitutes are registered; these duties to be performed by policemen of the "Sanitary Squad" in cities or towns where such police organizations exist.

The above suggestions are proposed merely to open proper discussion upon the subject; for it is only by discussion and mutual interchange of ideas that proper, just, and efficient laws were ever or can ever be framed. Laws hastily framed, the provisions of which have not been thoroughly ventilated, are sure to be irksome, if not unjust, to some parties, thereby rendering them inoperative, and soon to become obsolete.

Fracture of the Neck of the Femur in a Child Seven Years of Age—Suit for Malpractice, etc.

Reported by Dr. E. T. BARBER, of Eureka, Humboldt County, Cal.

Was called, on the 16th of June, 1869, to see a boy, seven years old, who had been run over the day before by one wheel of a logging-truck, weighing about 4,500 pounds. I found the child upon his back, the right leg straight, the left one flexed at the knee, with an apparent shortening of three or three and a half inches; the left heel rested upon the right leg in the space just above the internal malleolus, the foot and knee turned outward, and the whole limb seemed rigid and fixed; the hip was flattened, and the head of the femur could not be felt; a red mark ran diagonally across the back of the pelvis and thigh, and there was marked tumefaction of the parts. The position of the limb indicated a fracture, but the immobility a dislocation; and I was much perplexed as to the exact nature of the injury. The wheel was three feet in diameter, and one foot in thickness; and the child had been shoved along five or six feet, and accumulated considerable dust in front of the body, before it passed over.

After the child had been chloroformed, I proceeded, with the intelligent assistance of Capt. F. Wilkinson, to manipulate to reduce what I supposed to be a dislocation and an impaction of the head and neck of the femur into the sciatic notch. Extension was made, and the limb flexed and carried across its fellow and upward over the abdomen, using the crest of the ilium as a fulcrum to raise the head of the bone from its impacted position within the pelvis. The limb at once lost all rigidity, and could be abducted, adducted, everted, or inverted at pleasure; and by slight extension and counter-extension, it could be extended to the same length of the other, and all deformity would be effaced. If, when extended, rotation was made, feeble crepitus could be felt; and, if extension and counter-extension were removed, muscular contraction would soon shorten the limb from one-half to one full inch. There was no longer any room for doubt as to the nature of the accident, and the case was treated for fracture of the neck of the femur.

It was found necessary to keep up extension and counter-extension for about eleven weeks; for the first four, Hodge's apparatus (modified by attaching a screw to the foot to regulate the extension) was used; after that time, extension was maintained by adjusting the pulley and weight, and using the weight of the body to get counter-extension. When extension was removed, no difference in the length of the limbs could be detected, even by the most careful measurement. The child was instructed in the use of crutches, and occasionally seen until four months after the accident, when the father brought the child in town and exhibited him to numerous persons, including the editors of our two local papers. The child, when requested to do so, would lay aside all support and walk without deformity or lameness, planting both feet alike upon the ground, with the toes turned out naturally.

The case was now discharged, and lost sight of for nearly one year and a half, when notice was received from an attorney to settle damages for malpractice, or stand suit for $5,000. An examination of the boy revealed the following condition, viz.: When standing upon his feet at rest, there was shortening of the injured limb of nearly one inch, with the foot turned out like its fellow; but the limb could be shoved upward till it was shortened about three inches. The head of the bone could not be felt; in fact, the distance intervening between the great trochanter and the crest of the ilium, excluded the idea that the head of the bone remained attached to the femur. The boy could voluntarily evert or invert the foot. It was evident, from the examination, that there had been refracture, and the lameness was but a result of it.

Suit was brought, and the case came before the Eighth Judicial Court of the Third District of California, in December, 1870, Judge Haynes presiding. The prosecution claimed that there had been no fracture, but a simple dislocation upon the dorsum ilii; and that the defendant, who is a surgeon, was employed to reduce said dislocation, but through "carelessness, negligence, and want of skill" failed to reduce the same, whereby the plaintiff suffered bodily pain, and became permanently a cripple, etc., etc. The material allegations of the complaint were denied by the defendant, in his answer. Upon the trial of the case, Drs. D. U. Lindsey, —— Parsons, C. M. Neilson, Wm. Todd, and I. Parry testified, that, in their judgment, the case presented was one of unreduced dislocation of the femur upon the dorsum ilii, and that there never had been a fracture of the bone. In addition to this, Drs. Lindsey and Neilson gave, as reasons why, in their belief, no fracture ever existed, that the *London Lancet* had never reported a case of fracture of the neck of the femur in a case so young, and that Dr. Cooper, in his work upon fractures, did not speak of such a case. While Drs. Lindsey, Neilson, and Parsons agreed, that, upon the facts in the case as given above, a fracture was indicated, they also testified that they would not believe the testimony of any man who would say that in the case of a child of seven years of age such indications could be present; that it was contrary to nature that such things could be, owing to the structure of the femur at this point in the young.

The defendant denied that the injury was dislocation of the hip, and asserted that it was a fracture of the femur, and proceeded to prove it by showing a state of facts existing at and immediately succeeding the injury, which, in the opinion of experts, were conclusive indications of fracture;

also, by the testimony of a number of surgeons of learning and experience, who had recently examined the injured limb, and gave positive opinions that it was not a dislocation, but a fracture of the head or neck of the femur; and, lastly, by the depositions of Drs. Toland, Lane, and Gibbons, Sen., of San Francisco, who, after reading the statement of facts, as stated above and proven during the trial, gave their unqualified opinion that it was a fracture. Drs. O. B. Payne, M. Spencer, Fitch, and Church, of Humboldt County, California, examined the child, and testified that they could not feel the head of the femur upon the dorsum ilii; and from their examination of the case, as well as from its history, they believed it to have been a fracture of the head or neck of the femur, and that the bone had been subsequently refractured, producing the shortening and consequent lameness complained of.

The learned Judge, in his decision, remarked that "about four months after the injury, according to the testimony, the father took the child to town and was pleased with the result, and called the particular attention of numerous parties to the child, and exhibited him as evidence of the defendant's skill as a surgeon. These witnesses were unanimous that, without crutch or cane, he walked well and naturally; no perceivable difference in the length of his legs; in stepping, placing his left foot squarely and firmly on the ground, heel first; no limping, or deformity whatever; and the fact that he was thus able to walk about at that time, is incompatible with unreduced dislocation or fracture then existing. It is true, that either dislocation or fracture must have occurred at the time of the accident; but the injury, whatever it was, had been so treated that the plaintiff was recovering as fast as could have been expected. This necessarily leads to the conclusion that some injury, either sudden or gradual, must have intervened since that time. This change seems to have been gradual. How it was brought about does not seem clear from the evidence. It is shown that he commenced riding horseback between four and five months after the accident, and that on two occasions he complained of his hip hurting him, and he cried to be taken from the horse. It is further shown, that the father, on one occasion, in accounting for his lameness, said it was not the Doctor's fault, but his own, in allowing him to go about too soon. In these facts we find at least a plausible theory of the unfortunate change which has taken place. After impartial review of all the evidence, and giving due weight to the testimony, the conclusion is that the plaintiff has failed to sustain the allegations of his complaint. He has not shown that defendant was careless, negligent, or unskillful in his treatment of the case. Judgment must be entered for defendant."

A Case of Recurring Measles.

Reported by E. T. BARBER, M.D., of Eureka, Humboldt County, Cal.

Was called, in January, 1871, to see Mrs. H., aged 60 years, sanguine temperament, weight 170 pounds, and a woman of more than average intelligence and culture. She suffered from chilliness, pains over the body, sneezing, suffused eyes, headache, and severe fever, with some delirium. In a few days, an eruption, characteristic of measles, showed itself upon her face and neck, and soon over the whole body. In seven to ten days, the eruption had disappeared, and the patient was restored to her usual health. She then gave the following remarkable history of herself, which was confirmed by her husband and relatives:

When she was but six years old, all of her father's family, including herself, were sick with the measles. The eruption showed itself upon each of the others, but every effort failed to bring it out in her case, and she was quite sick, but soon recovered. After a few months, she was again attacked by the same train of symptoms, and the family physician failed, as before, to bring out the eruption, though he claimed that she had the measles again. From that time up to her thirtieth year, these symptoms, characteristic of measles, recurred as often, on the average, as twice a year; and sometimes the fever ran very high, and the skin would be dark purple in color.

During an attack in the thirtieth year of her age, she was very sick, and was subjected to what she termed the "hot treatment," viz.: hot drinks, hot baths, etc., and the eruption came out and completely covered the body. In due time, it subsided and disappeared, and she was well again, but for a few months only, as the disease has continued to recur as often as before; but from that time to the present the eruption has never failed to show itself at the proper time, or if not, a hot draught and a hot bath always brought it out. The last attack preceding the one in January, was eight months before, and she and her friends aver that she has had the measles not less than 108 times. She has had as many as five attacks in one year, and had two intervals of two years between attacks, and one interval of five years. Her general health has been good, with this exception, as she affirms that she never was sick in her life, except when she had the measles.

Her menses showed themselves in her fifteenth year, and were regular till her pregnancy, in her thirty-second year. She had one attack while carrying the child. Two years after, she gave birth to another child; and from that time she was not very regular, and the menses ceased in her fortieth year.

Foreign Body in the Bladder Removed by Syme's Operation, or Perineal Section.

By E. B. ROBERTSON, M.D., of San Andreas, Cal.

On the 23d of January, 1871, I was requested by Dr. Hœrchner, to see and operate on a patient of his, from whom I obtained the following history:

He had been troubled with a stricture about the bulbous portion of the urethra for many years, and had been in the habit of introducing a bougie for the purpose of dilating the canal, in order to pass urine. On the 20th of January, he found his bougie so broken that he could not use it. He lived sixteen miles from town, the nearest place where a new instrument could be had; and, feeling an urgent desire to pass urine, he sought to improvise some means of relief. He took an ordinary wooden pen-holder, dressed it to his mind, oiled it, and introduced it and pressed back the organ to reach the stricture, when the instrument slipped from his fingers, the organ advanced forward, covering the pen-holder, and in his manipulations to get it out, he worked it into the bladder.

Upon inserting the index-finger into the rectum, I readily detected one end of the stick, yet in the membranous portion of the canal. At the request of Dr. Hœrchner, I made the perineal section, as follows:

The patient was placed on an ordinary table, with the nates near the edge, and the feet drawn up; the wrists were fastened to the ankles by a few turns of a roller; chloroform was administered, and the limbs steadied by assistants. The index-finger of the left hand was inserted into the rectum, to steady the pen-holder, by pressing it toward the symphisis pubis; a free incision was made in the raphe of the perineum, the thumb of the left hand following and directing the knife, until the end of the pen-holder was reached, when it was seized with a pair of forceps and removed. No other dressing was used than lint wet with water, and so kept. The cure was complete in a short time, without any unfavorable symptom. I can not say whether the strictured portion was cut through in the operation or not. He had no further trouble from the accident or operation.

[COMMUNICATED.]

The American Medical Association and Dr. Martin.

A pamphlet has come to hand, issued by Henry A. Martin, M.D., "member of the American Medical Association, and late Chairman of the Committee on Vaccination," purporting to give a statement of the action of the Association at its recent meeting in San Francisco, in reference to the author of the pamphlet. The action of the Association in that case is greatly misrepresented by Dr. Martin. The "full report" of the proceedings which he relies on, was taken from the newspapers, and is not correct. No correct version of the matter has been published, as far as I have seen, except that contained in the June No. of the Pacific Med. and Surg. Journal. As the case of Dr. Martin was presented to the Association by me, I deem it a duty that I owe to that body, as well as to him and to myself, to place the subject in its true light.

The offense charged against Dr. Martin was not that he had written for a homeopathic journal, but that he had written as an officer of the National Association, affixing to his signature the official title of "Chairman of the Committee on Vaccination," etc. Nor was it proposed to expel him from the Association, but only to depose him as Chairman of the Committee. If Dr. Martin can see no impropriety in thus speaking for the committee without consulting any of them, and in committing the Association in some degree to the support of a periodical openly at war with the regular profession, his views of propriety must differ widely from those of his professional brethren in general.

Before the vote was taken on the motion to remove Dr. M. from the position of Chairman of the Committee, the reading of his communication was called for. It begins thus:

"Mr. Editor:—I am not one of your household of medical faith, in fact quite the reverse; but whatever I may have done in the past, I shall not now write a line that can ruffle the temper of the most sensitive believer in Hahnemann and his famous dogma."

At this point the reading was interrupted by members who felt indignant that the Association should be made responsible, through its representative, for such truckling and abasement, as they regarded it. In the discussion that ensued, it was distinctly stated that the right of Dr. Martin to publish his productions in a homeopathic journal, under his proper signature, was not denied; that if he chose, in doing so, to fall on his knees and eat humble pie, he was responsible only to his local society; but when the American Association was placed in this humiliating attitude through him, as its avowed representative, he should at least be removed from the official position which he had abused. This view was concurred in, and the resolution of removal adopted, I believe unanimously. A motion was made to bring charges against him, but his case was promptly referred to the Committee on Ethics. That committee subsequently reported against any further action, except to refer the subject to the local society. The report was adopted unanimously, without discussion; and so the matter ended.

Had Dr. Martin taken pains to acquire a correct knowledge of the action of the Association in his case, he would probably have omitted from his pamphlet the "hisses and groans," "howling anathemas," and "lying telegrams." A little reflection might have taught him not to charge on his professional brethren the errors of the telegraph, or of newspaper reporters. He refers to the journal in which he published his communication as "a perfectly respectable homeopathic journal, *edited by a distinguished Fellow of the Massachusetts Medical Society*"—the italics being his own. On another page he refers to the same journal as edited by Dr. I. T. Talbot (FELLOW OF THE MASSACHUSETTS MEDICAL SOCIETY)—the capitals being his also. Is not this rather hard on the Massachusetts Medical Society?

I have no unkind feeling toward Dr. Martin—quite the reverse. His earnest labors in connection with the subject of kine-pock challenge my respect and admiration. But, like the rest of us, he can make mistakes.

H. GIBBONS, M.D.

Proceedings of the Alameda County Medical Association,

Held in Oakland, June 5, 1871.

Present: Drs. Babcock, Fox, Hanson, John Le Conte, Joseph Le Conte, Pinkerton, Sherman, Van Wyck. Dr. John Le Conte in the Chair.

Dr. C. S. Kittredge, of Oakland, was proposed for membership.

Dr. VAN WYCK reported a case of extensive cranial tumor occurring to a child four years of age, the result of injury received from a runaway team. Compression and evaporating lotions having failed to reduce it, incision was proposed. A lengthy discussion on such lesions arose, in which the prevailing impression appeared to be against opening. He also reported a case of craniotomy, *primipara*, aged 37; in labor forty hours; antero-posterior diameter, 2½ inches.

Dr. PINKERTON reported a case of suppurative parotitis following intussusception, occurring in a child six years old. There was extensive discharge and partial paralysis of the face. The doctor had been unable to find reported cases of this complication with intussusception, but Flint reported its frequency after typhoid fever.

Dr. SHERMAN called attention to the article on the proper application of forceps, by Dr. Clark, in the last number of the *New York Journal of Obstetrics*. The laws laid down were three in number, and much more simple and practical than those generally given in the books.

Dr. JOSEPH LE CONTE presented the results of recent discoveries in regard to the determination of sex: First, in insects; then in lower animals, and, lastly, in man—to the effect that early impregnation produced females; late impregnation, males. The case of the Jews was cited, in which a delay of a week after menstruation, by their laws, gave a preponderance of males.

Drs. Carr and Trenor were appointed to prepare papers for the next meeting.

Adjourned. H. P. BABCOCK, Secretary.

REVIEWS AND NOTICES OF BOOKS.

Dynamics of Nerve and Muscle. By Charles Bland Radcliffe, M.D., F.R.C.P., Physician to the Westminster Hospital, and to the National Hospital for the Paralyzed and Epileptic. London: Macmillan & Co. 1871. San Francisco: A. L. Bancroft & Co.

This work, in some respects remarkable, is substantially a philosophical inquiry into the relations of electricity to animal life. An important point which the author believes he has established, is, that spasm and muscular contraction in general, so far from being caused by stimulation or irritation, result from the want of normal electrical excitation; and that the muscle is in a state of repose when normally electrified. "Every thing," he says, "is in opposition to that dogma which ascribes to nerve and muscle a life of which the state of action is the expression. Every thing, indeed, points to a solution of the problem of which the effect is to bring phenomena which have been regarded as exclusively vital under the dominion of physical law." We are not prepared to dispute the facts or criticise the logic on which the conclusions are based. But we confess to a repugnance—it may be only a prejudice—against the doctrine which excludes from physiology a vital principle, and which attributes the phenomena of animate existence to chemical and mechanical action.

A Practical Treatise on the Diseases of Infancy and Childhood. By Thomas Hawkes Tanner, M.D., F.L.S. Author of "The Practice of Medicine," "Index of Diseases and their Treatment," etc. Third American edition from the last London edition, revised and enlarged, by Alfred Meadows, M.D., London; Member of the Royal College of Physicians; Physician to the Hospital for Women, and to the General Lying-in Hospital; Honorary Fellow of the Obstetrical Society of Berlin. Pp. 559. Philadelphia: Lindsay & Blakiston. 1871. San Francisco: A. L. Bancroft & Co.

The author of this volume is well known to the profession in England and America as a straightforward, practical writer, in whose judgment the reader learns to confide almost by instinct whilst perusing his works. Whilst there is nothing in the present work remarkably novel or original, it will be found by the practitioner none the less valuable, by reason of the wide field which it covers in a small compass, and the great amount of practical knowledge it communicates.

The Human Feet: their Dress and Care. Showing their natural, perfect shape and construction; their present deformed condition; and how flat feet, distorted toes, and other defects are to be prevented or corrected, with directions for dressing them elegantly, yet comfortably, and hints upon various matters relating to the whole subject. With illustrations. 12mo. Pp. 202. Price, $1 25. New York: S. R. Wells. San Francisco: A. L. Bancroft & Co.

This little book may be made valuable by every reader. It will have special attraction for that large class of individuals who use their feet more, and derive more pleasure from the use of their feet, than their head.

Bancroft's Tourists' Guide. The Geysers, San Francisco, and around the Bay, north. San Francisco: A. L. Bancroft & Co.

Every one traveling in California, stranger or denizen, wants this book, or *will* want it, should he set out without it. In conjunction with it, is the map, entitled

New Map of Central California. Published by A. L. Bancroft & Co.

This will save the trouble of asking a thousand questions, one-half of which will not be answered at all, and three-fourths of the other half not answered correctly.

The Causation, Course, and Treatment of Reflex Insanity in Women. By Horatio R. Storer, M.D. For sale by A. L. Bancroft & Co., San Francisco.

Before noticed.

JOURNALS, PAMPHLETS, Etc., RECEIVED.

The Kansas City Medical Journal, a new candidate for public favor, is published bi-monthly at Kansas City, Mo. The number before us, for April, is highly creditable to the editor, A. P. Lankford, M.D.

Effects of Increased Atmospheric Pressure upon the Human Body, with a report of thirty-five cases brought to City Hospital from the caisson of the St. Louis and Illinois Bridge. By E. A. Clark, M.D.

Uterine Catarrh frequently the Cause of Sterility. New Treatment. By H. E. Gantillon, M.D. Boston, 1871.

THE NEW YORK MEDICAL JOURNAL has changed editors. Dr. E. S. Dunster, who has conducted it with much ability for five years, leaves it in charge of Drs. William T. Lusk and James B. Hunter.

REPORT OF A SPECIAL COMMITTEE of the Medical Society of the District of Columbia, upon the claims of Homeopath and other Irregular Practitioners for Professional Recognition.

ATLANTA MEDICAL AND SURGICAL JOURNAL. The first and second numbers of this journal—just revived—have been received. It is edited by Drs. W. F. and J. G. Westmoreland.

ARCHIVES OF SCIENCE AND TRANSACTIONS OF THE ORLEANS COUNTY SOCIETY OF NATURAL SCIENCES. Vermont. Edited by Drs. J. M. Currier and Geo. A. Hinman.

A REPORT ON THE PROGRESS OF SURGERY, made to the St. Louis Medical Society. By E. A. Clark, M.D., Professor of Surgery in Missouri Medical College.

LETTERS TO "THE TIMES," on Small-pox Encampments, and a Word on the Contagious Diseases Act. By Surgeon-Major T. Atchison. London, 1871.

MODERN SPIRITUALISM: its Scientific and Moral Aspects. By I. S. Douglas, A.M., M.D., Ph. D., Milwaukee. A very sensible and well-reasoned tract.

THE DETECTION OF CRIMINAL ABORTION. By Ely Van de Walker, M.D., Syracuse, N. Y. Reprinted from the *Journal of the Gynæcological Society*, Boston.

THE VIRGINIA CLINICAL RECORD is the title of a new monthly journal, which comes to us from Richmond, Virginia, stored with valuable reading.

THE AMERICAN JOURNAL OF OBSTETRICS has changed publishers. It is issued by W. Baldwin & Co., New York, quarterly, $5 a year.

THE AMERICAN JOURNAL OF MICROSCOPY—E. M. Hale, M.D., editor, Chicago— is published monthly at $2 per annum.

THE SEMI-MONTHLY MEDICAL AND SURGICAL REPERTORY. Griffin, Georgia. Edited by Drs. E. F. and J. J. Knott.

THE GEORGIA MEDICAL COMPANION, monthly. Edited by Drs. T. S. Powell and W. T. Goldsmith.

PROCEEDINGS OF THE STATE MEDICAL ASSOCIATION OF ARKANSAS. 1870.

WOMAN AS A PHYSICIAN. By J. P. Chesney, M.D.

EDITORIAL.

Something Personal.

Some months ago we complimented the editor of the *Richmond and Louisville Medical Journal*, on his good taste in copying fourteen articles from one of our issues, reminding him, however, not uncourteously, that he had not given us credit in a single instance. The editor, Dr. E. S. Gaillard, makes this the occasion of a coarse and vulgar attack, in his June number, upon our senior editor personally, replete with statements so shamelessly false as to demonstrate on their face that he knew them to be so, and that he designed to say what he knew to be untrue. So palpable is the outrage as to warrant the inference that the writer is the subject of a constitutional infirmity—a vice of organization, which relieves him in a measure from responsibility for his conduct. Were it not that we have better material for our columns, we would insert his article entire, without a word of comment, as the severest punishment that could be inflicted on him.

In the same number of his journal, Dr. Gaillard devotes *nineteen pages* to abuse of Dr. Yandell, President elect of the American Medical Association, applying to him such epithets as "infamously treacherous," "base and notorious coward," "card-player, cock-fighter," and so forth. Drs. Yandell and Gaillard were both prominent as surgeons in the Confederate service; and Gaillard having lost an arm in the service, can afford, with little risk, to be brave with his pen. Dr. Yandell is able to take care of himself. He has done so through the press, at greater length than appears to us necessary, for the reason that every reader will see at a glance the *animus* of Dr. Gaillard's assault, and pronounce sentence on the writer rather than on the object of attack.

The introduction of personal matters in medical journals should be avoided if possible, and we have seldom admitted them. But since we have been dragged into this explanation and defense, we shall not dismiss the subject without ventilating it in another point. The *Richmond and Louisville Medical Journal* flaunts on its front, under the head of "ASSOCIATE EDITORS," the names of twenty distinguished members of the Profession, scattered from New York to New Orleans. Of course, this is all a sham, as the "associate editors" contribute nothing to the *Journal* but their names, as indorsers. It is probable most of them do not even read it. If they knew its contents, they would scarcely be willing to submit to this responsibility. We should like to know if Professors Frank H. Hamilton, L. A. Sayre, W. H. Van Buren, Paul F. Eve, S. H. Dickson, and others, are really willing to act as godfathers to the *Journal* and to indorse its personalities, as they are made to do. We are pleased to observe that Professor Stillé has withdrawn his name from the roll of "associate editors." The sooner his example is followed by the others, the better for the interests of the Profession, for the character of medical journalism, and for their own reputation.

The late Meeting of the National Association.

We have noticed with regret that a few of our exchanges—only a few—have referred to disorder and want of harmony as a feature of the sessions of the Association lately held in San Francisco. There can be nothing farther from the truth. With the exception of one of the sessions, less personal feeling was exhibited, and less acrimony in debate, than attend the average assemblages of clergymen and church organizations. The exception occurred at the only session which was held at night, and was manifestly due to California champagne, which some of the delegates had been sampling at the Oakland entertainment, supposing it to be as tame and inanimate as the champagne to which they had been accustomed elsewhere. But the effervescence from this source was as transitory as the chemistry of the occasion would allow. We do not recollect that a solitary hiss was emitted at any other time than this; and as the present writer enjoyed a complete monopoly of the sibillation, and has no grief therefor, it would seem that others should not complain. All the circumstances of the occasion, the renewal of old acquaintances and old friendships, the revival of youthful memories, were well calculated to warm the heart and develop the kindlier feelings. And we venture to say, that at no time since its organization, twenty-five years ago, has an annual session of the Association developed as great a degree of fraternal regard, and disbanded with a feeling of professional accord and brotherhood so universal.

Outside of the Association, there were a few members of the

Profession in this city who refused to co-operate in the reception. Of this, our friends from abroad were in some way made cognizant. One of the delegates, writing to the *Baltimore Medical Journal,* mentions the dissension among the physicians here, which were made painfully apparent to the Association. What the writer means we can not divine. Assuredly no public exhibition of the kind took place. The physicians of the city and State vied with each other in perfect harmony of feeling and action, for the purpose of honoring and entertaining their guests. Possibly the impression arose from a publication made in a disreputable sheet, denouncing the Association, and asserting that a large number of the most eminent medical men were hostile to it and refused to acknowledge it, and naming some twenty individuals of this description. But the statement was as mendacious as it was malignant; for a number of those so named were members of the Committee of Arrangements. A few professional eunuchs refused the hand of fellowship to their brethren from abroad, but their opposition was silent and negative. On this subject, the late President, Dr. Stillé, in a letter addressed to the senior editor, makes the following pertinent remarks: "I sincerely trust that the late meeting may have some influence in promoting union among the members of the Profession in your city, and at the same time in showing those of them who kept aloof that their conduct has done more to lower them in the opinion of their visitors than they can readily estimate. The people of San Francisco have lived so isolated a life until the railroad was opened, that some of them seem to have forgotten that they belong to the family of civilized man, and are expected to conform to the usages and courtesies of older communities."

Personal Items, Etc.

Our friend, Dr. Storer, still remains in California, enjoying "otium," and other good things, including exemption from the *hay asthma*, which has heretofore been a regular summer tormentor in his eastern home. Should his health continue to improve, he will remain through the summer.

Dr. P. M. O'Brien died at his home in Santa Clara, on the 20th of June, at the age of fifty-six. He was one of the first settlers, having commenced practice in San Francisco more than twenty-one years ago. His death was the result of exposure to the hot sun in a long ride in an open vehicle. Cerebral congestion ensued—in fact, *sun-stroke*, which is very rare in California, notwithstanding the intense heat of the interior. Dr. O'Brien will be remembered as a most worthy man, and a highly honorable physician.

Dr. Barstow, of this city, in a paroxysm of mental alienation, a few days ago, attempted suicide by shooting himself near the ear, with a pistol. It was at first supposed the ball had entered the brain, but the impression now is that it glanced from the bone and passed down into the neck. If this be the case, he is likely to recover. His father-in-law, Dr. Rogers, late Physician of the Port, was thrown from his vehicle while hastening to the relief of his relative, and severely injured on the head, while his son, who was riding with him, had his ankle sprained. The report that Dr. R. had his skull fractured was erroneous. He is recovering. Dr. Barstow was formerly connected with the army on this coast, and studied medicine with Dr. Davis, of Chicago.

San Francisco Lying-in Hospital and Foundling Asylum.

We have received from Dr. Hardy, Attending Physician to this excellent institution, the First Annual Report, from which we gather the following statements:

47 mothers have been delivered of 50 children; 41 were primiparas; 38 were unmarried—8 have since married respectably; 19 were Irish, 14 American, 6 English, 6 European; 26 were Protestants, 18 Catholics, 2 Hebrews. 45 of the 47 were natural labors, one forceps case, one turning. All were discharged in good health. Of the 50 infants, 3 pairs twins; 28 males, 22 females. 4 still-born, one from a knot in the cord.

Dr. Hardy adds: "I am anxious to have every physician throughout the State, and, indeed, throughout the Coast, fully informed of the designs of the institution, and urged to use their influence in sending unfortunate seduced (but otherwise respectable) girls to it, that they may escape the abortionist, and be screened and protected from exposure, so as to keep themselves thereafter respectable. Their first step for relief is always an application to some physician, to have the germ destroyed. Therefore, it is in the power of the physician to save them from the criminal abortionist. Please do what you can to aid us in our efforts."

The Social Evil.

The well-written communication under this head presents a highly plausible argument in favor of the system of licensing prostitution. But the experiment referred to has not been long enough in operation to test its efficiency. In other parts of the world where the system has had a fair trial, it does not appear to have restrained either prostitution or disease, but simply turned them into hidden channels. During a detention in Panama, twenty-one years ago, the writer had an opportunity of witnessing a common mode of "cleaning up" around the back doors of houses, where all manner of filth was habitually deposited. Instead of removing the offal, the adroit scavenger brought sand in a wheelbarrow and covered it so as to give the appearance of perfect cleanliness. Such, we apprehend, will be the result of all movements against prostitution which involve its legal sanction.

Veratrum in Large Doses in Convulsions.

Dr. Herbert Hearn, of Brooklyn (*Amer. Jour. Obstetrics*, for May), treats puerperal convulsions with veratrum viride in doses ordinarily regarded as poisonous. He uses it as a substitute for the lancet, and in such cases as would seem to require blood-letting; giving from half a drachm to a drachm of the tincture every five, ten, or fifteen minutes, till a decided impression is made on the pulse, and keeping the pulse down to near fifty, until the tendency to convulsion has passed away. Four drachms in twelve hours was given in one case; five drachms in ten hours in another; five drachms in four hours in a third, with uniform success. Vomiting sometimes results, but not commonly. Convalescence is rapid and perfect, without prolonged feebleness. He uses it also in convulsions of children, using from five to ten drops for a child of two years. In the instance of a child of that age, to whom he gave, by mistake, ten drops fluid extract, the convulsion ceased in ten minutes, and the patient made a good recovery. In most of the cases detailed, bromide of potassium, chloroform, and other sedatives were also employed before or after the veratrum, and sometimes with it; but it is evident, from his statements, that the curative results were derived mainly from the veratrum. He believes that the medicine has a direct effect on the spinal cord, but that its primary influence is on the ganglionic or sympathetic nervous centres.

Gradation of Studies in Medical Schools.

For a number of years, the attempt has been in hand to change the system of teaching in our medical colleges, so as to graduate the lectures according to the *status* of the class: or, in other words, to *grade* the schools: and thus avoid the absurd practice of giving the same lessons to novices and advanced students. It is but justice to the managers of the Female Medical Colleges in Philadelphia and New York, to credit them with leading off in this reform. Their classes are divided into three grades, corresponding respectively to three years of study, and an examination for promotion is held at the close of each term. Perhaps the frown and scoff from without incited them to place their institutions on an advanced basis, which, in the absence of much competition, they could better afford to do than the male colleges. Whatever their motive may have been, it would be exceedingly mean to refuse them the public acknowledgment which is their due. More recently, the Harvard School has adopted a similar course, requiring three years of study in accordance with the following programme: First year—Anatomy, Physiology, and General Chemistry. Second—Medical Chemistry, Materia Medica, Pathological Anatomy, Theory and Practice, Clinical Medicine, Surgery, and Clinical Surgery. Third—Pathology, Anatomy, Therapeutics, Obstetrics, Theory and Practice, Clinical Medicine, Surgery, and Clinical Surgery. We may expect before many years to see this system, or a modification of it, adopted universally.

Therapeutic Value of Gelseminum.

Gelseminum (or, as it is sometimes written, gelsemium) is of late attracting considerable attention. It is highly lauded by some practitioners as a nervous sedative, in cerebral congestion, mania, and a great variety of disturbances resulting from disorder of the nerve-centres. We know of one physician who regards it as invaluable in nervous or sick headaches: ten or fifteen drops of the tincture to be given three times daily. The physiological effects of the agent are very remarkable. Even moderate doses will sometimes produce a peculiar, heavy sensation in the forehead, with partial paralysis of the levator muscles of the eyelid, so that it is difficult to keep the eyes open. We have employed it frequently for a number of years, often with benefit, but certainly not with such happy results as some others ascribe to it. The following formula will be found valuable in hysterical and functional disturbances of the nervous system:

R. Tinc. valerianæ ammon., oz. i;
Tinc. gelsemini, dr. i.
M. Sig. A tea-spoonful p. r. n.

Some of our druggists prepare an ammoniated "elixir" of valerian, which is better than the officinal tincture, in being much less disagreeable.

Medical and Surgical Memoirs of the Confederate Army.

Professor Joseph Jones, of the University of Louisiana, is engaged in preparing an elaborate treatise on the Diseases of the Southern States, the result of fifteen years' assiduous labor, including the experiences of the recent civil war. There will be two volumes of one thousand pages each, which will be issued as soon as a sufficient number of subscribers shall have been secured to defray expenses, and furnished at actual cost. Dr. Jones, it is well known, is capable of making this a highly valuable work. He writes to us as follows: "At present I am engaged in preparing for the press, the labors of the past fifteen years. These investigations were undertaken for the advancement of the Medical Profession, and they have been prosecuted at heavy cost of time, money, and health; and I hope that the Profession will sustain me in the effort to place them in a living form. You will oblige me by directing the attention of your medical friends to the subject."

Physical and Moral Causes of Insanity.

A few years ago, insanity was very generally ascribed to moral causes, but of late physical causes are mainly sought for. The change of opinion in this regard is well illustrated by a fact stated by Dr. John P. Gray, Superintendent of the New York State Lunatic Asylum at Utica. In 1843, 128 cases were set down to moral causes, and 93 to physical; while in 1866, 12 cases only were attributed to moral, and 263 to physical causes.

Fatality in the Profession.

One of our exchanges mentions the death of Dr. Miller, in Rockingham County, Virginia, aged 60, who was killed by lightning, June 2d, whilst holding a hatchet in his hand; Dr. I. Burton Mustin, of Philadelphia, May 31st, aged 26, from a dissecting wound, and Dr. C. R. Parvin, of Philadelphia, June 3d, aged 21, from a slight wound of the thumb, caused by the slipping of the knife while amputating the fingers of a patient. It is said of the last case, that, "taking cold in the wound, pleurisy set in with fatal result"—rather an awkward account to come from a professional source.

Chloralum: Chloride of Aluminium.

This preparation appears to be growing into favor as a disinfectant of the most valuable character. It is declared to be safe, odorless, and non-poisonous—harmless as common salt. It may be applied by sponging to the bodies of the sick, and it may be sprinkled over floors and poured over the evacuations of patients. It is free from the objections to carbolic acid, that the latter has an offensive and persistent odor, and may prove poisonous. Cloths wet with the solution and hung in the air, it is said, will speedily remove all offensive odors. The name, *chloralum*, is unfortunate, being liable to translation into *chloral*, and associating it with hydrate of chloral, to which it has no sort of affinity.

Physiological Action of Camphor Inhalations.

We have lately met with a lady, aged sixty-five years, who exhibits a sensibility to the action of camphor, which is worthy of note. She is subject to spasmodic twitchings and distressing nervous paroxysms, which prevent sleep. Under these circumstances, she pours some spirits of camphor on a napkin and snuffs the vapor, which acts with the promptness of chloroform as a sedative. That a powerful impression may be made on the nervous system by the inhalation of camphor in alcoholic solution, is very easily demonstrated by experiment on one's own person. The etherial solution is worthy of trial.

Value of Revaccination.

Dr. Grieve, of the Hampstead (Eng.) Small-pox Hospital, gives an analysis, in the *London Lancet* for June, of eight hundred cases of small-pox treated in that hospital during the present epidemic. He refers to the disease as possessing an intensity almost unprecedented, with many deaths from the hemorrhagic form, which was always fatal. Of the eight hundred cases, not one could prove that he had been revaccinated. There were sixty officials connected with the hospital, all of whom were revaccinated; and although they were in constant contact with the disease for three months, not one of them contracted it.

To Prevent Mammary Abscess.

Dr. Joseph R. Beck, of Lancaster, Ohio (*Phil. Med. Times*), makes a paste of ext. belladonna and glycerin, and spreads it over the breasts with a spatula "from the sternum to the axilla. Cover with a cloth dipped in olive oil, and this in turn with oiled silk. Allow the dressing to remain undisturbed during a variable period of from two to three or four weeks, inasmuch as it can be worn by the patient for any length of time without inconvenience." He has never known this treatment to fail, when used in time. Fortunate Dr. Beck!

"Contagious Mental Alienation."

Such is the term employed by some "learned physician" to explain the atrocities of the Parisian insurrection. The idea may be admissible in an abstract psychological study of the subject; but when science endeavors to cover such crimes with the cloak of insanity, and so to lessen the accountability of the perpetrators, she teaches unsound and dangerous morality. Let murder be called murder.

> "Murder, most foul, as at the best it is,
> But this most foul, brutal, and unnatural."

In Love with Small-Pox.

A man was imprisoned fourteen days in Derby, England, for refusing to comply with the Act requiring vaccination. On his release he was paraded through the streets, with bands of music and a procession of several thousand people, carrying a red flag. The *British Medical Journal* thinks it a pity that the processionists can not have the luxury of an isolated encampment, where they might enjoy the most intimate association with small-pox.

Chloral Hydrate in Tetanus.

A case is recorded of a boy in Florence who suffered from tetanus, caused by running a nail in his foot, and who was cured after thirty-five days of treatment and the use of five ounces of hydrate.—Very gentle tetanus, we should say, to dally five weeks with its victim.

So Much for a Name.

It is announced that a dealer in patent medicines, etc., in an Eastern city, has purchased the exclusive right to a certain preparation for the hair, at the price of $100,000. The composition of the article is of minor importance. There is more money to be made by buying a worthless article for $100,000, than a valuable one for $1,000.

Peculiar Effects of Chloral Hydrate.

At a meeting of the Medical and Chirurgical Faculty of Maryland (*Med. and Surg. Reporter*), Dr. Dunbar mentioned two cases in which the prolonged use of chloral hydrate was followed by ulceration of the fingers, particularly about the nails. One was an elderly man, who died not long afterward from acute bronchitis; the other, a young lady, who recovered.

Health of San Francisco.

The mortality report for May exhibits some points of interest, and that for June promises to be equally favorable. The death-rate for the last six months has been remarkably small. Our summer influenza, which generally appears in June, has not yet come to hand.

Can not supply Back Numbers.

Owing to accessions of subscribers who have taken the back numbers, our stock is exhausted, and we regret to say that we shall not be able to supply back numbers to new subscribers.

GENERAL SUMMARY.

Maternal Impressions on the Offspring.

It may be mentioned, in connection with the subject of the relation of bodily deformities in the offspring to maternal mental impressions, that Dr. William Hunter investigated this subject, at the Lying-in Hospital to which he was attached, and that in two thousand cases there did not occur a single instance in which there was any coincidence between the fright, or accident, or longings of the mother, and the deformity of the child. There are certainly many curious cases recorded, which we can not venture to explain ; the following case for instance : An old patient inquired one day if the writer had ever seen an infant with two tongues; being answered in the negative, she undertook to show one, and accordingly a child was brought, when the following story was related : three or four months before her labor she went into a builder's yard, and was much alarmed by seeing a large dog with its tongue hanging out of its mouth. Some days after her confinement she looked in her child's mouth and saw that it had two tongues ; she showed it to her medical man, and he confirmed her opinion. On examination, however, it was found that the *sublingual gland* was remarkably developed, and that this had been mistaken for a second tongue !—*Tanner on Infancy and Childhood.*

Tetanus Neonatorum treated with Chloral Hydrate.

Dr. Widerhofer, of Vienna, showed lately to his class a child three months old, which was attacked by tetanus neonatorum at the end of the first week after birth, and was treated with chloral hydrate in doses of one and two grains at the time of each onset of convulsions. It was in danger for a fortnight. During the intermission of the spasms it was fed from the breast by its mother. It is now a fine, healthy-looking child. This is the sixth case (out of ten or twelve) that Dr. Widerhofer has had of recovery under treatment by chloral. Under all other methods all his previous cases died. Considering that Vogel, and other great German authorities on children's diseases, had quite recently never seen a case of this affection recover, such a success must be taken to indicate a real advance in therapeutics. Dr. Widerhofer gives from two to four-grain doses of chloral by the rectum, if the infant can not take it by the mouth.—*Lond. Lancet.*

The Fashions of Suicide.

Dr. Lankester's annual report of inquests held in 1868–69, contains some particularly interesting observations on suicide and the means by which it is effected. During the year there were seventy-five suicides in Central Middlesex, and 1,552 in England and Wales. The proportion is about one in 12,000 of the population. The proportion of males to females is pretty constantly as five to two. Nine-tenths of the whole occur between the ages of twenty and forty. Drink is a common, but not an exclusive cause. Sleeplessness almost invariably precedes suicide; a fact, therefore, to which too much importance can scarcely be attributed by medical men. Considerable change has taken place in the selection of poisons. That most frequently used during the last seven years is *cyanide of potassium*. It is purchased without difficulty. It is used in enormous quantities by photographers, and its action is most deadly. The next most frequent agent is oxalic acid, which is employed by shoemakers, saddlers, and harness-makers. The use of opium for purposes of suicide is on the decline, owing to the difficulty of obtaining a sufficient quantity. It is used by druggists, medical men, and members of their families. The same remark applies to the employment of hydrocyanic acid.—*Med. Press and Circular.*

Mr. Pollock's Case of Skin-Transplantation.

Those who have been awaiting with interest the result of Mr. Pollock's experiment of transferring portions of skin from a negro to a granulating surface in a white subject will read with regret, in one of our hospital reports of this week, that both the pieces of pigmented skin have been lost in consequence of some unexpected and unaccountable sloughing which attacked the cicatrix of the wound. By this unfortunate accident Mr. Pollock is compelled to postpone until another opportunity presents a histological investigation, which promises results of great physiological interest. The experiment had, however, already demonstrated the power of black skin to reproduce itself in a white subject by the development of pigment in the new skin which it propagated. Mr. Pollock thinks it just possible that the sloughing may have spared a few living pigmented epithelial cells; if so, they may be expected shortly to give evidence of their presence.—*Lancet.*

Infantile Puberty.

Robt. P. Harris, M.D., Phila. *(Am. Jour. Obstetrics)*, in an interesting article on "Early Puberty," observes that, from an examination of numerous reported cases of infantile puberty, the following conclusions may be drawn: 1st—With very rare exceptions, no matter how young the infant may be in whom the menses have made their first appearance, the mammæ are found unusually developed, and the pubes shaded with hair; 2d—The subjects have, in almost all instances, menstruated regularly, grown rapidly and vigorously, been somewhat inclined to obesity, and have not presented any signs of weakness resulting from the menstrual loss; 3d—This form of precocity appears to be little, if at all, dependent upon any climatic influence; the latter variety is undoubtedly accelerated by heat; 4th—The maturity of the uterine system is generally independent of any marked precocity of development in the mental faculties; 5th—Sexual passion, so general with precociously developed male infants, is seldom a marked characteristic in females of corresponding years; 6th—The first appearance of the menses is more common during the first, second, and third years of infantile life than it is in the fourth, fifth, and sixth; 7th—Infantile puberty is more common in the female than in the male sex, although in the latter there are cases which are quite as remarkable as any in the former.—*N. Y. Med. Record.*

To Produce Large and Long-lasting Soap-bubbles.

For the production of unusually large soap-bubbles that will last for hours, and exhibit splendidly the beautiful colors of the rainbow, a fluid may be employed that can easily be prepared in the following way: Fine shavings of palm-oil soap are shaken in a large bottle with distilled water, until a concentrated solution of the soap is obtained; this is filtered through gray filtering paper, and mixed then with about one-third of pure glycerin. The fluid is to be shaken up before use. By means of a small glass funnel, of two inches' diameter, connected with a tube of india-rubber, soap-bubbles may be prepared with this fluid that will vie in the beauty of the display of color with the rainbow itself, and which may be kept for a long while by putting them carefully upon an iron ring which is slightly rusty and thoroughly wet with the soap solution. Bubbles of one foot and more in diameter will keep from five to ten minutes; those of two to three inches in diameter, for hours—often for ten to twelve.—*Druggists' Circular.*

Amputations after Gun-shot Wounds.

Dr. Sédillot, of Lyons, who, during the course of the recent French war, has observed over fifteen hundred cases of gun-shot wounds, and has himself performed fifteen amputations in a single day, has written a paper calling attention to the extensive mutilation of the parts caused by the projectiles of the present day. According to Dr. Sédillot, the best rule is to amputate on the second or third day after the infliction of the wound, before the period of inflammation has set in. In consequence of the extensive suppuration caused by the projectiles now in use, the following rules are recommended to be observed : first, that the wound should be reduced to the smallest diameter; second, a free exit of pus should be favored; and third, a radical reform in the method of amputation should be adopted, to wit : that the extremity of the bone, instead of being inclosed in the flesh, should be left sticking out.—*Phil. Med. and Surg. Reporter.*

The "Perkins-Hyatt Base" for Artificial Teeth.

A new base as a substitute for rubber is announced by the "Albany Dental Plate Company," with the following claims for superiority :

1. It is lighter and at the same time stronger than dental vulcanite or hard rubber.
2. Its color is very near that of the natural gum, and will not change in the mouth.
3. It is entirely free from all unpleasant taste.
4. It is not in the least affected by the acids of the mouth.
5. It is not injurious to any mouth, even the most sensitive, which is not true of rubber plates containing a large amount of mercury.
6. It can be manufactured and fitted to the mouth easier, quicker, and more satisfactorily to the operator, than can be done with any other known base for artificial teeth, saving enough time and trouble to the operator to pay for the plate.
7. It is more pleasant and comfortable to the wearer than plates made of any other material whatever.

A Point Gained for Female Physicians.

WILLIAMSPORT, June 16th.—The Pennsylvania State Medical Society, now in session here, yesterday formally rescinded their notorious rule against women physicians, after an animated discussion and a determined opposition—yeas, 50; nays, 40. The obnoxious rule prohibited, on pain of expulsion from the society, consultation with women physicians, or with those men who consulted with them or taught them medicine. Among the active champions of the ladies were Doctors Joseph Parrish, of Media;

Wilmer Worthington, of West Chester; Washington L. Atlee, of Philadelphia; Hiram Corson, of Montgomery County, and Traill Green, of Easton. The only organized opposition to women physicians now existing in the State is to be found in the Philadelphia County Medical Society.—*Philadelphia Evening Bulletin.*

Pistol Ball in the Heart Four Days.

Dr. G. F. Dudley, of St. Louis, Mo. (*Med. Archives*), reports the following interesting case: A male, aged thirty-eight, was wounded by a bullet from a small four-barreled pistol, the ball entering the left chest, about an inch to the left of the nipple. Four days after the accident the patient died. A post-mortem revealed that the bullet had passed between the fifth and sixth ribs through the lower lobe of the left lung, through the pericardium, and penetrating the left ventricle of the heart at about two-thirds way from the base to the apex, had passed through the cavity of the ventricle and lodged in the base of the heart at the junction of the ventricle with the auricle. There had been a small amount of hemorrhage into the pericardial sac.—*N. Y. Med. Record.*

Composition of Nostrums.

Brandreth's Pills.—Resin of podophyllum, inspissated juice of pokeberries, saffron, cloves, oil of mint.

Holloway's Pills.—Aloes, myrrh, saffron, sometimes calomel.

Radway's Ready Relief.—Etherial tincture of capsicum with camphor.

Radway's Renovating Resolvent.—A vinous tincture of ginger and cardamom, with sugar.

Morison's Pills.—Aloes, colocynth, cream of tartar, sometimes gamboge.

Granular Effervescent Citrate of Magnesia.—Bi-carb. of soda, carb. of magnesia, and tartaric acid.

Hamburg Tea.—Senna, 8 parts; manna, 3 parts; coriander, 1 part.

On the Growth of the Nail as a Prognostic in Cerebral Paralysis.

Dr. S. Weir Mitchell, of Philadelphia, related before the College of Physicians, as reported in the *Am. Jour. of Med. Sciences*, that he had observed in several cases of palsy that the nails of the limbs of the affected side cease, on the occurrence of the accident, to grow. This he assured himself of by staining the nails at the roots with nitric acid. He was able to predict, on seeing after a time a white line of nail making its appearance, and before there were any other signs of improvement, that power was about to return to the limb, and that voluntary motion would shortly be restored.—*Druggists' Circular.*

Proportion of Wounded in Battles.

At the battle of Konigsgratz the percentage of wounded in the Prussian army was 4.90, and in the Austrian army 9.28; at the battle of Magenta the percentage of wounded French was 6.07, and of Austrians 7.05; at the battle of Waterloo the number of wounded in the British force was 17.76; during the late civil war in America the number of wounded in the Federal army at Shiloh was 12.51; at Chattanooga, 18.22; at Gettysburg, 11.68, and at Wilderness, 19.29; while the reports respecting the Confederate armies gave much larger proportions. The mean of all this was 15.70 per cent. of the whole strength.

Soft Water for Horses.

Youatt, in his book entitled "The Horse," says this animal will never drink hard water if soft water is in reach; that he will leave transparent hard water for a pool of soft, even though the latter be discolored with mud. Very cold water from the well will make the hair rise up and not unfrequently cause an attack of the gripes. Give soft water, if practicable, especially if the animal is ailing.

Hydrocele of Round Ligament Mistaken for Hernia.

A case is reported in the *American Journal of Obstetrics*, in which the surgeon cut down extensively upon a supposed femoral hernia, in a female, which proved to be a hydrocele of the round ligament. The operator failed to recognize the nature of the tumor until, having exposed it fully and made divers efforts to reduce it, an exploring needle occasioned a jet of dropsical fluid, and the swelling vanished.

Eucalyptus - Leaves.

The Rev. M. J. Berkeley mentions in the *Gardeners' Chronicle*, on the authority of a letter received from Cannes, that Dr. Gimbert has introduced a new method of dressing wounds by using eucalyptus-leaves in the place of lint. The leaves, which have a "catty" smell, are merely laid on the wounds. The balsamic nature of them not only cures, but after a few hours all the unpleasant odor of the matter ceases.

Glycerin Inhalations in Croup.

Dr. Stehberger, of Mannheim (*American Practitioner*), recommends in the treatment of croup the inhalation of glycerin by atomization. It increases the secretions of the mucous membrane, and softens the cough. The inhalation is to be continued for fifteen minutes, and repeated in half an hour, or whenever necessary. It is of no service in the advanced stage.

Small-pox in London.

Nearly two hundred deaths per week from small-pox continue to occur in London. The *Lancet* mentions as a fact that should carry conviction to the factious opponents of vaccination, that not a single re-vaccinated person has been admitted to the Small-pox Hospital at Homerton, and no death of a vaccinated person has occurred under seventeen years of age.

Bromide of Iron in Spermatorrhea.

Dr. Norris, of Beloit, Wis., recommends bromide of iron as a specific in this disease. He gives from three to five grains, three times a day, and a fourth dose of ten grains at night—sometimes as much as twenty grains. It procures a good, refreshing sleep, free from lascivious dreams. He administers it rubbed up with syrup.—*North-Western Med. and Sur. Journal.*

Extraordinary State of Health in India.

The *London Lancet* for June, states that during the last three months there has not been any death from cholera, small-pox, or other epidemic disease among the European troops stationed in the Madras Presidency; and with the exception of the death of a soldier from cholera, there has been no fatal case among the troops from those diseases in the last five months.

Adulteration of Drugs.

A New York drug firm purchased a lot of asafetida to arrive, as a fair article. It proved to be adulterated, and was refused. The importer sued for the purchase money, and it was proved on the trial that some specimens contained 60 per cent. of gypsum. The importer did not get the money either for the asafetida or the gypsum.

The Speculum in Dyspepsia.

A writer in the *Leavenworth Med. Herald* says: "Dyspepsia, according to our judgment and to our experience, is always symptomatic, and does not constitute a disease. If you ever meet with a very rebellious case of dyspepsia among females, take your speculum and look carefully," etc. We would suggest the same course of investigation in females who are troubled with toothache or corns.

Coryaria Thymifolia — Ink-plant.

The juice of this plant is an excellent ink, red at first, but turning to black in a few hours. Its superiority over other inks has induced the Spanish Government to order it used for all public documents in New Granada, where the plant is found. So says the *Pall Mall Gazette.*

Merited Tribute to an Editor.

At the recent semi-centennial anniversary of the Philadelphia College of Pharmacy, William Procter, Jr., the retiring editor of the *American Journal of Pharmacy*, was taken by surprise by the presentation of a valuable gold watch.

Camphor in Hospital Gangrene.

In the military hospital of Rennes, France (*New York Medical Gazette*), camphor has been found very efficacious in hospital gangrene, after the failure of iron, carbolic acid, etc. It is sprinkled abundantly over the wound, in powder.

Hot Air in Croup.

In addition to the inhalation of various vapors, it is advised to keep the air in the apartment of a patient with croup at a temperature of between ninety and one hundred degrees.

Chloral Hydrate in Sea-Sickness.

The testimony in favor of chloral hydrate in sea-sickness is almost conclusive. It is given for this purpose in doses of from twenty-five to fifty grains.

Chloral Hydrate in Enuresis.

A writer in the *British Medical Journal* recommends this article in the highest terms for the cure of incontinence of urine. A girl who had suffered nightly for weeks took fifteen grains every night before retiring, and not a single return of incontinence took place.

Tea-Leaves for Burns.

Dr. W. H. Searles (*Chicago Medical Examiner*) prefers a poultice of tea-leaves to all other applications for burns and scalds in the first stage. He applies it warm, spread on cotton-wool. It soothes pain, conduces to sleep, and *tans* the surface.

To Preserve Lemons.

At a meeting of the Phil. Col. of Pharmacy, two lemons were produced which had been kept covered with tin foil for three months. One of them was spoiled, and the other fresh and good.

ITEMS OF NEWS, ETC.

THE DEATHS IN PARIS during the last week of the siege were 4,670, against 1,350, the ordinary average mortality.

SALICINE IN TYPHOID FEVER is highly recommended by some German practitioners. It is said to do good as an antiseptic.

PERMANGANATE OF POTASSA in solution, applied by means of gun cotton, is recommended as a disinfectant. Ordinary cotton is decomposed by the salt, and will not answer.

SOMETHING WRONG.—A late number of the London *Lancet* announces the marriage of "Louisa F. Lundy, M.R.C.S.E., to Margaret Caroline, daughter of Robert Miller, Esq."

THE TEMPERATURE OF THE BODY, in males, is taken in some of the Prussian hospitals by introducing the bulb of the thermometer in the anus. It saves time. The axilla is used in females.

DR. JOSHUA STEVENS, father of the editor of the *Cincinnati Lancet and Observer*, died at his home in Ohio, in May, aged seventy-eight. He was a student of Dr. Joseph Parrish, of Philadelphia.

Microscopists, who are constantly telling us wonderful stories, say that a cubic inch of tartar, such as collects on people's teeth, contains two hundred and fifty millions of animalcules. Bring us a tooth-brush!

Oppolzer, the famous surgeon and professor in the University of Vienna, died in May, at the age of 63.

STATE BOARD OF HEALTH.

Abstract from the Reports of Deaths and their Causes, in the following cities and towns in California, during May, 1871:

CITIES AND TOWNS.	Total No. Deaths	Prevalent Diseases. Consumption	Inflam. of Lungs	Inf. Stom. and Bowels	Diphtheria	Scarlatina	Typhoid Fever	Names of Reporters
San Francisco	226	38	6	17	1	0	4	S. F. B'd of Health.
Sacramento	39	7	0	5	0	3	0	Sac. B'd of Health.
Petaluma	3	1	0	0	0	0	0	Dr. G. W. Graves.
Dixon	3	0	0	0	0	0	0	Dr. R. H. Plummer.
Santa Clara	7	1	0	1	0	0	1	Dr. H. H. Warburton
Stockton	12	1	1	4	0	0	0	Stockton B'd Health
Marysville	5	1	1	1	0	0	0	Dr. C. E. Stone.
Placerville	4	0	0	0	0	0	0	Dr. E. A. Kunkler.
Auburn								Dr. A. S. Du Bois.
San Diego	1	0	0	0	0	0	1	Co. Med. Society.
San Luis Obispo								Dr. W. W. Hays.
Oroville								Dr. J. M. Vance.
Woodland	0	0	0	0	0	0	0	Dr. A. B. [illegible]
Oakland	10	2	0	1	1	0	0	Dr. T. H. Pinkerton.
Los Angeles	8	1	1	0	0	0	1	Dr. R. T. Hayes.
Nevada City	2	0	0	1	0	0	1	Drs. [illegible]
Truckee	2	0	0	0	0	0	0	Dr. W. [illegible]
St. Helena	2	0	0	0	0	0	0	Dr. J. S. [illegible]
San José								Dr. J. N. Brown.
Napa City	0	0	0	0	0	0	0	Dr. M. B. Pond.
Cacheville	1	0	0	1	0	0	0	Dr. [illegible]
Siskiyou								Dr. [illegible]
Watsonville	0	0	0	0	0	0	0	Dr. [illegible] E. Cleveland.
Folsom	2	0	2	0	0	0	0	Dr. [illegible]
North San Juan	3	0	0	1	0	0	0	Dr. [illegible]
Sut'r C'k & Amador	3	0	1	0	0	0	0	Dr. [illegible]
Monterey	1	0	1	0	0	0	0	Dr. [illegible]
Santa Cruz	5	1	2	1	0	1	0	Dr. [illegible]
Vallejo	3	0	0	0	0	1	0	Dr. [illegible]
Suisun & Fairfield	1	0	1	0	0	0	0	Dr. [illegible]
Colusa								Dr. [illegible]
Weaverville	1	0	0	0	1	0	0	Dr. [illegible]
Santa Barbara	6	2	0	0	0	0	0	Dr. [illegible]
Redwood City	2	1	0	0	0	0	0	Dr. C. [illegible]

Abstract from Reports of Births:

CITIES AND TOWNS.	Total Births.	Males.	Fe-males.	Still-born.	Live-born.	AUTHORITIES.
San Francisco...	88	47	41	21	67	S. F. Board of Health.
Sacramento.....	34	18	16	3	31	Sac. Board of Health.
All other places.	224	116	108	20	204	Various sources.
TOTAL......	346	181	165	44	302	

REMARKS.—With the exception of Sacramento and Stockton, our table for May everywhere exhibits even a less degree of mortality than that of April, which, as was remarked, showed the sanitary condition of the State to be all that could be desired. The increased mortality of the above-named localities—being for Sacramento fifteen, and for Stockton eight, more than that of the previous month—appears to be due chiefly to diseases of the digestive organs, and which are attributable to the atmospherical vicissitudes peculiar to the spring months. We would observe, in this connection, that, under our usual heading of inflammation of the stomach and bowels, we have this month included all diarrheal and choleraic affections, whether of a zymotic or sporadic character, believing that by so doing we will afford a better idea of the nature of the prevailing and preventable forms of morbid action that are now terminating fatally. Doubtless the same cause to which our correspondents in the southern parts of the State attribute, and justly, too, their augmented mortality, obtains also in our great railroad centres, viz.: the influx of a floating population in quest of health. These, bringing with them the causes of death contracted elsewhere, and dying in our cities and towns, give a false impression as to the real sanitary condition.

THOMAS M. LOGAN, M.D.,
Permanent Secretary State Board of Health.

PROFESSOR D. HAYES AGNEW succeeds to the chair of surgery in the University of Pennsylvania, made vacant by the resignation of Professor H. H. Smith.

CHOLERA IN ST. PETERSBURG has been very fatal during the spring months.

Mortality in San Francisco during May, 1871.

By H. Gibbons, Jr., M.D.

CAUSES OF DEATH.

Abscess	2	Diseases of Heart	6	Measles	1
Alcoholism	1	Dropsy	3	Meningitis	11
Aneurism of Aorta	2	Drowning	1	Metrorrhagia	1
Apoplexy	6	Dysentery	4	Nephritis	1
Ascites	6	Enteritis	3	Old Age	2
Atrophia	8	Erysipelas	1	Ossification of Aortic Valves	1
Bright's Disease	2	Epilepsy	1	Peritonitis	1
Bronchitis	2	Fever, Congestive	1	Phthisis	38
Burns	1	" Remittent	1	Pleuritis	1
Cancer	2	" Typhoid	4	Pneumonitis	6
" of Breast	1	Fracture of Skull	2	Poisoning	1
" of Uterus	4	Gastritis	3	Premature Birth	6
Childbirth	1	Gun-shot Wound	1	Purpura	1
Cholera Infantum	3	Hemoptysis	3	Rheumatism	1
Congestion of Brain	3	Hemorrhage	1	Softening of Brain	3
" of Lungs	5	Hepatitis	1	Suicide	6
Convulsions	6	Hydrocephalus	5	Syphilis	4
Croup	2	Hydrothorax	1	Throat-cut	1
Cyanosis	3	Inanition	7	Unknown	10
Debility, General	6	Injuries, unspecified	1	Whooping Cough	1
Delirium Tremens	1	Jaundice	1	Wound of Jaw	1
Dentition	1	Liver and Spleen, Laceration of	1		
Diarrhea	4	Liver, Disease of	3	Total	226
Diphtheria	1				

AGES.

Under 1 year	48	From 15 to 20 years	4	From 60 to 70 years	7
From 1 to 2 years	12	From 20 to 30 years	29	From 70 to 80 years	5
From 2 to 5 years	6	From 30 to 40 years	43	From 80 to 90 years	3
From 5 to 10 years	10	From 40 to 50 years	35	From 90 to 100 years	0
From 10 to 15 years	5	From 50 to 60 years	19	Unknown	0

Sex. — Male, 154; Female, 72. Total, 226.
Color. — White, 198; Copper, 24; Black, 4.

NATIVITIES.

California	81	France	2	Australia	2
Other parts of U. S.	37	Germany	14	Holland	1
British Amer'n Prov.	2	Austria	1	South America	4
Mexico	1	Sweden	1	Dalmatia	1
England	4	Switzerland	3	Isle of Jersey	1
Ireland	39	Italy	4	Unknown	1
Scotland	1	China	22		
Wales	2	West Indies	2	Total	226

RECAPITULATION.

Died in City Wards	176	St. Vincent de Paul Asylum	1
City and County Hospital	17	Alms House	1
U. S. Marine Hospital	1	Italian Hospital	1
French Hospital	2	Mount St. Joseph's Infirmary	4
German Hospital	2	Magdalen Asylum	1
St. Mary's Hospital	3	Casualties	10
Orphan Asylum	1	Suicides	6

Remarks.—The health of the city still continues remarkable; a similar mortality for each month of the year would give a yearly rate of but fifteen per thousand, and when it is considered that this extraordinary diminution in the number of deaths has continued for four months, it is still more worthy of comment. The deaths in May for six years past have been, in 1866, one hundred and ninety-nine; in 1867, two hundred and eight; in 1868, two hundred and eighteen; in 1869, three hundred and nine; in 1870, two hundred and seventy-one; in 1871, two hundred and twenty-six. There are few unusual features in the record of deaths from individual diseases. No deaths from scarlet fever are reported, and there have been but two since January, and they were in April. The mortality from consumption was thirty-eight—fourteen less than for April. The number of suicides (six) and of casualties (ten) was unusually large. Perhaps the most gratifying exhibit is in relation to the mortality of children under five years of age. This has never been less in any one year (1866) than thirty-six per cent. of the total, thirty-nine per cent. being the usual proportion. In one month in 1870 it reached forty-eight per cent., and in one it was as low as thirty-one per cent., but in May last it was but twenty-nine per cent.; and more remarkable still, it has averaged for the first five months of this year, but twenty-nine per cent. This, in face of the fact that children undoubtedly form a larger proportion of the population than ever before. The number of deaths (nineteen) between the ages of five and twenty years is unusual.

A MODEL ADVERTISEMENT.—"Marshall L. Brown, M.D., Physician and Surgeon, Winchendon, Mass. Especial attention paid to all diseases flesh is heir to. Also, attention paid to diseases of horses."

A MEDICAL STUDENT in the University College Hospital of London was arrested for stealing instruments, etc., from his colleagues. He confessed to the crime, and alleged billiards and bad company as the cause.

CAMMANN'S STETHOSCOPE is mentioned as a novelty in a volume lately issued in London, purporting to record the recent progress in medicine in various parts of the world.

IN SCOTLAND the proportion of male illegitimate births is greater than the legitimate. In other countries the reverse is true.

PACIFIC

MEDICAL AND SURGICAL JOURNAL.

Vol. V.—AUGUST, 1871.—No. 51.

ORIGINAL COMMUNICATIONS.

The Ethics of the Medical Profession.

Read before the Sacramento Society for Medical Improvement, by JOSEPH F. MONTGOMERY, M.D.

Medicine, or the healing art, or the medical profession, however we may term it, regarded in its most liberal and comprehensive significance, whether contemplated as it presented itself in its feeblest infancy when human pain first demanded and human sympathy first administered relief, or as we see it in its present ample proportions, embracing the science and the art, or the principles and practice, of its various departments, has ever been recognized by all people, whether civilized or savage, in all ages of the world, as an agency of the highest importance to the human race, as evinced by their actions, whether their belief were founded in reason or superstition; and, as its votaries at the present day, it behooves us to consider well how best to enlarge and perfect its usefulness, to exalt its dignity and amplify its power, that of a truth we may enforce a more decided and generous recognition of its worth, and thereby multiply our opportunities and increase our ability to do good, each in his day and generation, according to his capacity.

Commencing, as intimated, with the origin of man: As far as we can learn from the traditional history or the dim records of the past, obscured by fable and mythology, or as related in the pages of the sacred Scriptures, we find it was earliest practiced by heads of families, of tribes, and of nations; and then chiefly by priests, who were deified in the popular mind, and who resorted to divinations and incantations, as best calculated to inspire confidence, by operating upon the superstitious imagination of those upon whom they exercised their influence. In succeeding centuries the art was pursued also by those whose origin was regarded as doubtful or enshrouded in mystery, and who claimed to be possessed of preternatural powers, or of sacred and exclusive knowledge derived from the gods; among such being Æsculapius and his pretended descendants, and their followers and ministers, the Asclepiades. These collected in their temples, from observation and experience, materials and facts that were subsequently made useful.

Until a recent period, facts regarding the ancient history of medicine have been sought for only in the classical authors of Greece and Rome; but late investigations show satisfactorily that to the Hindoos probably belongs the honor of producing the first systematic works on medicine, dating back to from the fifth to the ninth or tenth century before Christ. Those works give evidence of considerable medical information at that early day, exceeding that then possessed by any other people. This knowledge of remote Asiatic antiquity is derived mainly from the sacred books of India, as we are informed by late writings of several distinguished European authors.

Egypt first profited by this Eastern learning, and subsequently Greece and Rome. Moderns have supposed that, with some hints from the Egyptians, the Grecians were the originators of the medical science and art in Europe. A more extended knowledge of history, as mentioned, shows this not to be correct, their own most ancient records proving that they obtained much of their knowledge from a mysterious nation in the East, which was very probably the Hindoo, among whom the arts and sciences were successfully cultivated, and whose great progress in medicine attracted attention, and was communicated through the Egyptian priesthood to the philosophers of Greece. With the assistance in general literature thus obtained, the Greeks arrived at the most elevated period of their history.

It was at this enlightened age that medicine assumed most certainly the form of a science, under the genius of Hippocrates, born 450 B. C., who has been styled the "Father of Medicine." He, like the mythical heroes of antiquity, was regarded—by the ignorant, at least—as descended from gods and princes; owing to which hypothesis, they explained the extent of his improvements and the accuracy of his supposed productions. But the value of his labors may be explained more rationally. Medicine was then, and for some time immediately antecedent thereto, more than ever before, appreciated as a science of the greatest importance to man, and facts concerning it were then accumulated by the thoughtful priest, the observant physician, and the skillful surgeon, who left to their successors their legacy of thought and skill. These were the sources of the knowledge that immortalized Hippocrates. Medicine was first cultivated in Greece by a succession of able men, placed in favorable circumstances for accumulating knowledge, assisted materially by physicians of other nations. Such an accumulation of facts enabled them to arrive at principles, which were systematized by Hippocrates and formed into text-books for the Western world. Thus, to the recorded experience of his predecessors in all accessible countries, he added the knowledge acquired during a long life of study and observation, at home and abroad; and, by condensing experience and generalizing facts, to suit the people and country, he attained great credit as an original author.

Yet medicine made but little progress for many centuries following, owing much to the speculative, theorizing character given to it by its successive teachers and practitioners. Indeed, forgetting or disregarding the doctrines of the reputed founder of the science, as laid down in his various works, the theories and the practice promulgated through an extended lapse of time were of the most absurd and irrational character, even among those esteemed the most enlightened nations of the earth, as the Egyptians, Greeks, and Romans, already alluded to. Even Galen, in the second century before the Christian era, a pupil of the Alexandrian school, who paid more heed than others to the doctrines of Hippocrates, which were founded upon facts derived from observation and experience, and who, by his learning, industry, and talents, contributed much to the records of medicine, was yet too much imbued with the speculative spirit of the age to accomplish the good he might otherwise have achieved. As it was, his doctrines, though founded simply in reasoning, and that radically erroneous, were comparatively absolute for fourteen centuries; those who followed him servilely adopting his teachings as true, without daring to investigate or think for themselves, or to question the authority of their master.

During a part of this time, extending from about the year 620 A.D. to the end of the fourteenth century, the Arabs, under the influence of Islamism, became powerful and made extensive conquests, including therein India, Syria, Egypt, Spain, and Persia. In the last-named country the Nestorians dwelling there, possessing a knowledge of Grecian and Roman literature, had founded schools; and there, and elsewhere, under the power of the Arabs, learning, including medicine, was fostered and preserved during the Middle Ages. Thus, through them, a link was established and maintained, but for which much of the ancient knowledge we now possess would have been lost. Their instruction, example, and labors hastened much the revival of letters in the West.

Early in the fifteenth century the art of printing was discovered, and that, added to other causes, contributed to a general awakening of the human mind, after long ages of torpor, and a taste for books, libraries, and sound erudition was rapidly diffused throughout Europe. At the beginning of this period the Arabic literature was still predominant in the schools of medicine, and the only authorities then invoked and explained were Rhazes and Avicenna. But the monuments of Greek and Latin antiquity were soon hunted up and published, and letters became fully revived. During the two succeeding centuries the separation of medicine from the priesthood was effected, celibacy ceased to be obligatory on physicians, and they no longer obtained ecclesiastic benefices; surgery was reunited to medicine; schools, hospitals, and dispensaries followed the upward march, and governments turned more of their solicitude to the regulation of medical police and hygiene, and then commenced a notable amelioration in the sanitary condition of the people.

This sketch is presented to show the indispensable need of the Profession to the human race, and to prove its vitality and indestructibility under the most adverse circumstances, where society has any existence — to show that where man is there must be also in some form, or to some degree, the healing art; for, in the darkest period of the world's history, when barbarism and vandalism swept over the best portions of the earth, demolishing governments and dynasties, and destroying libraries and temples, and every thing sacred and beautiful and pure, as though they would blot out the last vestige of literature and learning, even then medicine survived, and quickly enforced the regard and patronage of the rulers of the rude races who had themselves wrought the deplorable destruction. And when, at last, man recovered his reason, and civilization and learning revived and advanced apace, medicine was ready for the bound, and thence made steady and enduring progress in the road to greater perfection.

During the two succeeding centuries — the seventeenth and eighteenth — still further advances were made in the science, and its various departments were established and given specific form. Some of the most noticeable discoveries in the century are, the circulation of the blood, in 1628; the virtues of cinchona, in 1638; the lymphatic system, in 1647, and the true nature of respiration, in 1668. Steady and striking progress was made in the several departments in the eighteenth century, but we have no time to allude to them, except to the discovery of vaccination, as published to the world in 1798.

Nor is the nineteenth century behind, if it be not in advance of, any of its predecessors, in its solid additions to the science and the art of our noble vocation. It is distinguished for many discoveries, foremost among which is the anesthetic, that so effectually shields against pain as to divest operative surgery of its terrors, and next, chloral, the new remedy that promises, with due caution and discrimination in its use, great benefits to the race, as an agent whose special action on the nervous system tends to induce sleep when much needed, and to allay and arrest that fearful class of diseases attended with spasms or convulsions, especially eclampsia gravidarum and tetanus, and which, hitherto, have often, if not generally, defied all means at our command.

But the most striking feature in the contributions to the science in this century is the extent and variety of the means devised and employed to insure a clearer diagnosis of the multitudinous disorders of the human system. First among these we will place the methods or means designed to develop or convey the physical signs of disease, as mensuration, palpation, percussion, succussion, and auscultation; and then the implements that serve as aids in the same direction, as the thermometer, the specula for the several outlets, the sounds, the ophthalmoscope, the laryngoscope, and the microscope. Then, again, the beautiful instruments, of wonderful contrivance and mechanism, that have been added to the case of the surgeon, to enhance much his ability to employ his skill with gratifying success. And yet again, the augmented facilities for acquiring a thorough knowledge of the Profession, as afforded in the munificent increase and diversification of the means for imparting instruction in the schools. The advancement and the achievements of the Profession have been striking and grand indeed, and we should all much the more, in consequence, love and honor it, and be proud of our affiliation with it.

But in view of all this, in the midst of these congratulations, we fear an important constituent or adjunct of our honored calling has been too much overlooked or slighted. We mean, as you may anticipate, the Ethics of the Profession, without which, all else is comparatively "as sounding brass or a tinkling cymbal." It is to the Profession as the vital spark to the previously inanimate body; for, as the perfect physical or material man, formed after God's own image, was as any inert, worthless matter, until the breath of life had been breathed into him, so the medical profession — it matters not what may be its genius, its learning, its science, its splendid achievements — will lack true dignity and power, the charm to animate and delight its followers, the grateful, soothing assurances of mutual good-will to cheer and sustain its members in their trying work, unless there exist and be diffused among them, the genuine *esprit de corps* of a confiding, undoubting, harmonious brotherhood, composed of high-toned gentlemen, scrupulously governed in all their conduct by the purest principles of morality and honor.

We have a comprehensive and admirable Code of Ethics, the offspring of the American Medical Association, that does it credit, apparently providing for every relation, contingency, and occasion, as relates to the Profession and the public, and which, if fully obeyed, it would seem, should accomplish all aimed at in its preparation, and should forbid and provide against all cause for serious discord or strife or enmities among our members; but how far it has fallen short in fulfilling its laudable design is made sadly manifest all over the land. In every city, town, and village in the country there are lamentable instances of unpleasant rivalries between physicians, leading to disturbances varying in degree from formal coolness, instead of cordiality, to bickerings, mutual detraction, and open rupture, highly discreditable to the parties immediately involved in them, while they soil the reputation and impair the usefulness of the Profession generally. Why is this? and how shall it be remedied? are important questions that should awaken inquiry, and employ the talents of the best men in the Profession to devise means to remove the disgrace and repair the damage shared, more or less, by all its members.

It may be safely assumed that the fundamental cause of this trouble is, in the main, the innate selfishness of man, which leads him, too often, to resort to many questionable, if not disreputable, expedients to subserve his own interest, without duly regarding the feelings or the rights of his professional brother. Such a selfish and mercenary disposition may tempt him to make a display of diplomas; to advertise himself in the secular press, either in pretentious cards, or in notices of his connection with cases arising out of accidents, or with others of unusual local interest, particularly those involving operations; to court the rich or the distinguished to secure their recognition and favor, while adroitly turning the poor over to his more conscientious fellows; by exacting notoriety by fast driving with a showy turn-out; to allude, on occasions deemed auspicious, to his successes, while, possibly, adverting to the misfortunes or maladroitness of his rivals; to employ, or encourage, or allow, agents or too partial friends to sound his praises among the patients and patrons of others and encourage them to summon him in their place, instead of defending his brother and sternly refusing to supplant him; to indicate by a shrug, a frown, or a word that his predecessor or competitor had erred; to agree to a fee-bill and then unwarrantably disregard its conditions, or to arrange with apothecaries for percentages on prescriptions, or with others, particularly with associations or corporations, to share the benefits of their business by mutual encouragement and aid. Then, the same spirit or disposition leads to the formation of cliques, rings, or factions, who league or co-operate together for mutual benefit, to the exclusion, mainly, of all others. And, further still, the same craving spirit has led some to so far forget their true dignity and a just regard for the honor of their profession, as to consult with irregulars or homeopathists, simply to put money in their purse, thus, to their shame, yielding to the promptings of a sordid and debasing desire.

These, and many other like deviations from the true line of professional propriety and duty, necessarily—inevitably, indeed—tend to the unpleasant condition of things we deplore; for, to insure general good feeling and harmony, a catholic and unselfish spirit must prevail, and reciprocal courtesies and impartial fairness must be extended alike to all. The aim should be assimilation and homogeneity in the ranks, as far as practicable; that while the most gifted shall not be depressed, the less favored may be assisted and urged upward to a higher grade of excellence.

The only legitimate hope for success or aspiration for distinction, rests upon a thorough knowledge of the Profession and an active, vigilant, considerate, and faithful performance of its responsible and delicate duties. The arts of the shopkeeper or the charlatan to acquire pelf, should be despised and spurned, and any who could be so base as to resort to means so degrading, should find neither favor nor recognition with honorable members. No one should seek or desire an advantage of another, but, on the contrary, he should scorn to profit by any injustice done his fellow by the public. Physicians should stand by and defend each other in every thing that is reasonable and just, and, above all, they should determinedly oppose the brutal custom of dismissing one medical man, while in charge of a case, and employing another in his stead. This often perpetrates a wrong that nothing can atone for, in the wounds inflicted upon the feelings of sensitive and honorable gentlemen that the vulgar can have no conception of. Each should defend and sustain his brother under such circumstances, and insist upon consultation in lieu of dismissal. The public must be made to respect the Profession, and to do justice to every individual member of it, or else no one knows how soon he may be the victim of detraction and ostracism. We would hope that the harsh indictment herein presented, or the unsightly picture drawn of the vicious conduct and unseemly short-comings of some, is suited to but few comparatively; yet, still, those few may be sufficient, unhappily, to disturb the harmony of the entire body.

The remedy for the evils complained of must lie chiefly with the ruling spirits, the master-minds of the Profession, the professors and teachers, and those whose purity of character and distinguished talents and attainments, as well as their great labors and successes in practice, command for them universal respect, and give them vast influence among their fellows. All these, we humbly submit, should, for the honor of our calling, earnestly direct their best efforts to correct the vicious state of things unfortunately existing, and which we have endeavored, though feebly and imperfectly, to present and detail in this paper. The reform must begin in the schools, and be rigidly enforced in every community by those of our number who have a just appreciation of the sacredness and dignity of our mission, and of its high importance to the welfare of our fellow-men, until our name shall have been completely divested of the cruel reproach now resting upon it.

The more surely and thoroughly to effect this, a Chair of Ethics should be added to all medical schools, where the true principles that should ever actuate a gentleman in every position of life, particularly in his confidential and sacred character of physician, should be so continually and forcibly impressed upon the mind, presented in every form applicable to the many conditions and circumstances liable to arise in the multifarious and delicate relations he must sustain in the discharge of his duties, that he could not well be at fault, or do aught unworthy his high office.

It may be contended that the reformation proposed is impracticable, and, therefore, should not be undertaken — that it presupposes a capacity for perfection in man at variance with nature, and, consequently, that the improvement and elevation suggested are not attainable; but we can perceive nothing in this view that should discourage the aim at greater perfection than that now existing. Great advances have been and are continually and steadily being made in medicine as a science, and its *morale* also has already much improved, although, in both respects, we will concede, it falls far short of what it may become under the persevering labors of its zealous disciples. We should be encouraged, therefore, to give the Ethics of the Profession greater consideration and more prominence, realizing that it has hitherto been too much neglected in the earnest search after strictly scientific truth, or the eager pursuit of sordid gain. While we may not be able to make gentlemen and blameless and honorable men of all who may enter the ranks of the Profession, we maintain that the plan or course indicated must needs result in much good, and virtually accomplish the grand consummation we so ardently crave and hope for. But few young men, however unfavorable or unpropitious may have been their early associations and training, taken through the ordeal proposed — taught by men of great learning, exalted character, and refined tastes; brought in daily contact and intimate association with a body collected mainly from amongst the best youths in the country, and breathing, as it were, an atmosphere pervaded by every manly and ennobling sentiment — could well fail to be rendered worthy disciples of a Profession, even as noble and honorable as we could hope ours to become in the improved character contemplated. All would be taught to regard it as a Profession, and not a trade; and so refining and elevating would be their instruction that few, if any, could do aught to cast a shadow or affix a stain upon it. And, then, in all places, where even a few members could congregate, societies would be formed, the code would be strictly enforced, and if any member could be so base, after enjoying such advantages, as to violate its obligations, he would be expelled from their association, and branded before the world as one unworthy the recognition of his fellows, or the respect and confidence of the public.

If we attempt so much, we will surely accomplish striking and enduring good, even if we do fall short of our highest aims.

Arseniate of Strychnia: New Antidote to the Poison of Snakes.

BY LOUIS LANSZWEERT, M.D.

[Read before the Section on Practice of Medicine of the American Medical Association, and recommended for publication.]

As no single author has yet undertaken the study of the so-called antidotes for the cure of the bite of venomous snakes, under all its varied phases, I can not accept the sweeping assertion of Dr. S. Weir Mitchell, of Philadelphia, in his able report upon this interesting subject, that there is no antidote to snake-poison, the remedies usually applied for such purpose being, in his opinion, nearly, if not entirely, useless. To attempt to controvert an opinion emanating from such high authority, might be regarded as temerity on the part of one, who, although comparatively unknown, has devoted years of conscientious study to the investigation of this interesting and important matter.

In a theoretical point of view, with its practical application, this subject of antidote is comprised in the single word, "Therapeutics," and its aim is to effect a cure, or alleviate pain, through hygienic agents, chirurgical processes, and proper pharmacological preparations. These are the means employed. In view of the numberless and highly important researches of professional contemporaries, it would be gross ignorance and rank injustice not to admit the incontestable progress of medical science. But in the face of this important fact, it is painfully apparent that a simple and more rational theory, a more natural and consistent systematization of diseases, and a more exact appreciation of their nature, origin, and seat, with attendant details, and correlative circumstances, are demanded in this enlightened age. While the astonishing conquests of surgery, and the wonderful and beautiful discoveries in chemistry have contributed to the rapid advancement and success of therapeutic means, a more *practical* and *philosophic* direction should be given to public hygiene. Although possessing curative means, more numerous and perfect, through the discovery and successful application of a host of new remedial agents, why is the practitioner so often impotent and powerless in the treatment of certain affections which should not be beyond the reach of the resources of the Profession? Mainly because he has not sufficiently noted the *indications* to be taken into consideration in connection with the character and constitution of the malady, and the consequent modifications of treatment, according to the prevalence of such or such morbid elements, manifested at divers periods in the progress of the malady. Such, in my opinion, is the reason of the perplexed and comparatively unsolved problem of the few cures effected by the numerous so-called antidotes for the bite of snakes and snakes and other venomous reptiles.

In order to make the results of my researches applicable to practical cases, it was necessary to institute a variety of comparative experiments, in order to fully test the utility of the agents employed. By this means, I am enabled to offer for your consideration a new therapeutic agent (arseniate of strychnia), as an antidote to the bite of the rattlesnake. I make no pretensions to any wonderful discovery in medical science; but having, in the carrying out of the ideas I have long entertained upon this subject, through a protracted series of experiments, become possessed of certain important facts, I consider it a duty I owe to myself and your honorable body to make known the results.

The *Bibliothèque Impériale* (now *Républicaine*), of France, contains, I believe, the first treatise ever written on the cure of poison by venomous animals. This treatise is known as the "Treatise of Fahdiliteth," and consists of three manuscripts, written in the year 1198, by Maimonides, a native of Cordova, who was proscribed, with many other Christians and Jews, and banished from Spain in 1164, on account of a refusal to adopt the Islam religion. He emigrated to Cairo, where he opened a school of philosophy, and was afterward appointed physician to Saladin, then King of Egypt. He was intimate with the Cadi Fahdil, a high functionary, who, "one day in the month of Ramadham, in the year 1198," remarked: "I was thinking, yesterday, that when a person has been bitten by a venomous animal, before finding the doctor, he can succumb from the effects of poison. I command you then to compose a treatise, small in volume, concise in expression, and indicating what a person should do, immediately when bitten by a venomous animal—what treatment he shall follow," etc. Maimonides, at that time sixty-three years of age, wrote the aforesaid treatise comprised in the manuscripts I have mentioned, which have been translated by Rabbinowiz, for the use of the Profession, as an interesting portion of the history of medicine. This treatise is divided into two distinct parts: First, the treatment of the bites in general; second, treatment in cases of poisons taken internally.

Maimonides adopted the same general medication which is practiced to-day: a strong ligature above the wound—cutting out the parts—sucking the part thoroughly, having previously rinsed the mouth, which should not contain either a wound or a carious tooth, with olive oil. The oil, in this case, was not considered in the light of an antidote, but was merely used as a coating for the mucous membrane, in the same manner that jugglers and mountebanks use mucilaginous substances in the trick of fire-eating. Far too much stress has been laid on the use of sweet-oil as an antidote. Under the head of *An Antidote to Poison*, we find the following, in a paper published in Los Angeles, California, and though I doubt the efficacy of the remedy so strongly recommended—it having entirely failed in three experiments made by myself, the subjects of which were two rabbits and a dog—I present it for what it is worth :

"It is now over twenty years since I learned that sweet-oil would cure the bite of a rattlesnake—not knowing it would cure any other kind of poison. Practice, observation, and experience have taught me that it will cure poison of any kind, both on man and beast. I think no farmer should be without a bottle of it in his house. The patient must take a spoonful of it internally, and bathe the wound, for a cure. To cure a horse, it requires eight times as much as for a man. Here let me say, of one of the most extreme cases of snake-bite in this neighborhood—eleven years ago this summer, the case being of thirty years' standing [!] and the patient having been given up by his physician—I took the oil and gave him one table-spoonful, which effected a cure. It is an antidote for arsenic and strychnine. It will cure bloat on cattle, caused by eating too freely of fresh clover; it will also cure stings of bees, spiders, and other insects; and will also cure persons who have been poisoned by a low, running vine, growing in the meadows, called 'ivy.'"

In cases of poison by the bite or sting of venomous animals, the first effort at medication is to be directed against the absorption of the venom. This is effected by ligature above the wound, cauterization by fire, hot iron, nitrate of mercury, butter of antimony, chloride of potassium, and by cupping over the wound; the employment of ammoniated and acidulated lotions, chlorine washings, oily embrocations, etc. Sometimes emollient poultices, spread with ammonia, are used with good effect. In the way of internal applications, sudorific mixtures, Eau de Luce, diffusible stimulants, tincture of Peruvian bark, liquid ammonia, acetate of ammonia, etc. As to the specific agents recommended, we find Eau de Luce, an alcoholic solution of succinate of ammonia, as different in its composition as the pharmacopeia, iodine and iodide of potassium; Biberon's antidote, or specific, composed of iodide of potassium, gr. xij, bichloride of mercury, gr. ij, bromine, ℥v; arsenic, Cedron bean, and Yerba de la Kibora (Daucus pusillus), the favorite of our native Californians; also. guaco, and some one or two more plants, unknown to botanists, but used by the Indians in Arizona, and by the natives of Mexico. Here is certainly a host of—so to speak—remedies to select from, various authors having written more or less in praise of their efficacy. As it was extremely difficult to test the merits of the entire list, my attention has been only directed to Eau de Luce, aqua ammonia, arsenic, Cedron bean, and the California Yerba de Kibora.

Highly interesting as it might be to give, in this connection, the details of the experiments with these remedies, as applied to dogs, rabbits, rats, and other animals, they would occupy far too great a space, and trespass too largely upon your valuable time and attention. Allow me, then, to state, that so far as my experiments have been made, I have invariably obtained good results, and, in many cases, effected positive cures by the use of liquid ammonia, the Cedron bean, and the California Yerba de Kibora. In some cases where I confidently expected a cure, however, these remedies did not meet my expectations. There are certainly a great variety of antagonistic elements to contend with in the treatment of this venom—the nature of the animals experimented upon differing materially in their wild state in their native haunts, or in a captive and domesticated condition. From his extended observation, Dr. Guyon concludes that the intensity or power of the venom is less owing to difference of season, than to the length of time it had been accumulating in the reservoir or receptacle of the reptile, and that its secretion is greatest during the winter season, when it is in a torpid condition, and does not take any food. This is the case, however, in a still greater degree during the shedding and rutting seasons. Dissatisfied with the results of my experiments in search of a universal remedy, and noticing the resemblance in bitter taste of the

Cedron bean and nux vomica, the same being the striking characteristic of our Yerba de Kibora, I was induced to institute a series of experiments with strychnia.

In 1852, through the agency of a particular friend who had resided for many years in India, and who, at my instance, made liberal donations of money for the purpose, I became possessed of one of the most important secrets of the celebrated snake-charmers of that country, to whom the venom of the most poisonous of these reptiles seems to be almost, if not entirely, innocuous. The substance was nothing more nor less than arsenic, which kept the system in a condition to successfully resist the action of the poison of the venomous reptiles he was accustomed to handle. When accidentally bitten, and fearful of the effects, the charmer would take four or five grains of this antidote. To any other person such a dose would, under ordinary circumstances, prove fatal; but, to an habitual arsenic-eater, this is nothing uncommon, and in this case, the action of one poison in the system is materially modified, if not entirely neutralized and rendered innocuous, by its contact with another.

We find reported in Braithwaite (xxviii. p. 423), that five cases of snake-bite occurring in the island of St. Lucia, were successfully treated by Mr. Ireland, by the use of grain-doses of arsenious acid, in the form of Fowler's solution, given every half-hour until the patient began to revive. The number of doses varied from six to eight, which always produced copious vomiting and purging — results of the highest importance to the success of the treatment.

In order to obtain a more readily soluble substance than arsenious acid, I made the following preparation, as an arseniate of strychnia: Dissolve thirty grains of pure strychnia in four ounces of distilled water, containing seventy-five grains of arsenic acid, and evaporate the solution until crystallization takes place, draining the crystals, and reserving the liquid, with the addition of eight ounces of alcohol, for external application. For internal use, one grain of this arseniate of strychnia was mixed with ten grains of sugar and twenty-five grains of turmeric, and divided into twelve powders—one powder administered dry, or mixed with a table-spoonful or two of wine or brandy, at the time of the bite; the same to be repeated every fifteen or twenty minutes after the first dose, and in cases of the recurrence of the swelling, accompanied with pain and throbbing, the dose may be repeated in an hour. Not only in my own case, but in four others in this city, has this preparation proved in the highest degree efficacious. In order to effect a cure, in one case only have I administered more than six powders in twenty-four hours.

So many deceptions have been practiced by the so-called snake-charmers, that in order to place my discovery beyond any imputation of charlatanism, during my late sojourn in Paris I submitted it to the world-renowned physiological chemist, M. Claude Bernard, whose investigation of curarin is well known. Through his kindness the laboratory of Physiologie Comparée of the Jardin des Plantes was placed at my disposal, where a series of experiments were made and repeated with the Professor's able assistant, M. Grehant, Professor Dumeril kindly allowing me the use of a number of venomous reptiles then at the Garden. The experiments were made principally upon rabbits, by subcutaneous injection. The quantity injected at the time as a dose, with an aqueous solution of arseniate of strychnia, was about a centimetre cube (twenty drops); said cubic centimetre of solution containing one milligramme of arsenic acid and half a milligramme of strychnia. In ten cases the result proved entirely satisfactory as regards the efficacy of the antidote. The snakes, having been so long kept in confinement, were, after a few bites, rendered comparatively harmless. It was accordingly necessary to let them remain quiet for some time before repeating the experiments. Professor Bernard promised me his co-operation and personal assistance in investigating the subject, but the unsettled condition of affairs in France has prevented this.

With your kind permission, I take this opportunity of communicating to you this discovery, and the results of my investigations, in the hope that some of your body may further investigate the matter, and by actual experiment prove the efficacy and value of this antidote to the poison of snakes, and also test its application in cases of hydrophobia.

Sulphite of Soda in Acute Laryngitis.

BY A. S. FERRIS, M.D., San Francisco.

As this is one of the most distressing and rapidly fatal diseases that the physician is called upon to treat, I will give, for the readers of the PACIFIC MEDICAL JOURNAL, a report of two cases successfully treated with the above, in conjunction with other remedies.

CASE I.—On the morning of the 27th of August, 1870, I was called to see Mrs. B., aged about forty years, living on Welch street. I found her gasping for breath; countenance purple; could not speak above a whisper. What little air was inhaled entered with a whistling sound. Diagnosis: acute laryngitis.

℞. Sulphitis sodæ, ʒij.
Opii pulv., gr. vi.
Sulph. quiniæ, ʒss.

M. Ft. chart., No. vi. Give one every hour until breathing relieved.

6 P.M. Visited her again; found the breathing much better, but a good deal of mucous rattling in the throat; diaphoresis well established; skin much less purple; a harsh, croupy cough; but slightly under the influence of the opium.

Continue the powders every fourth hour.

28th. Found her much improved; still much laryngeal irritation. Gave the following:

℞. Sulphitis sodæ, gr. clx.
Aquæ menthæ, ℥iv.

M. Sig. Take a table-spoonful every fourth hour. Also,

℞. Hyd. chlor. mitis., gr. xx.
Sig. Take immediately.

29th. The calomel had operated well, and my patient was convalescing. Continued the sulphite of soda. The recovery was rapid.

CASE II.—June 17th, 1871, was called early in the morning to see the little son of Mr. McL., on Shipley Street, aged three and a half years. Found him in a very critical condition, almost suffocated, grasping at any thing within his reach, and often in the air; face purple, nose pinched, cry hardly a whisper, and unable to cough. His parents had given every domestic remedy known to them, by the advice of a druggist living near by; had vomited thoroughly with ipecac, and rubbed his neck and chest with camphorated oil. Still he was becoming more and more asphyxiated. Diagnosis: true inflammatory croup.

℞. Sulphitis sodæ, ʒi.
Sulph. quiniæ, gr. xv.
Sulph. morphiæ, gr. i.
M. Ft. chart., No. vi. One every fourth hour.

℞. Sulphitis sodæ, gr. clx.
Syrup. simp., gr. lx.
Aquæ menthæ, dr. i.
M. Sig. Give a tea-spoonful every hour.
Leeches, No. iv. Apply over the larynx and trachea.

Visited him three times and before night found him breathing much easier, and countenance changing for the better.

18th. Found him somewhat improving, still he could only speak in a whisper. Gave

℞. Hyd. chlor. mitis, gr. x.
Cretæ preparatæ, gr. vi.
M. Sig. To be taken immediately

4 P.M. Calomel had operated, both as an emetic and cathartic. Vomited up tough membranous patches. Continue the sulphite of soda.

19th. Much better; still had croupy cough. Gave

℞. Syrup. scillæ comp., ℥iss.
Tinct. opii camph., ℥ss.

M. Sig. Give half a tea-spoonful every fourth hour.

20th. Called and found him playing on the floor.

Ovariotomy — Bone and Teeth in Cyst.

BY J. H. WYTHE, M.D., late Surgeon U. S. V.

Mrs. King, of Sacramento, about twenty-five years of age, and the mother of four children, had been for some years a patient of Dr. Haswell, who attended her in two confinements, the last one in February, 1871. In March I received a letter from my son, a partner of Dr. Haswell's, desiring a consultation with me for what had been diagnosed as an ovarian tumor. I found the patient very pale and emaciated, with an enormous abdominal enlargement. The case was further complicated by symptoms of pneumonia in the right lung, which, however, seemed to be somewhat yielding to treatment.

The abdominal enlargement was uniform, with distinct fluctuation, but on one side a bony substance could be distinctly felt through the parietes, which suggested the idea of extra-uterine pregnancy. A vaginal examination showed the uterus to be healthy, admitting the sound two inches, and quite mobile.

So unpromising was her case that it was doubtful whether she could survive the tapping needful for full diagnosis; but on consultation, in which Drs. Simmons and Hatch participated, it was deemed best. About five gallons of partially decomposed pus was drawn off, weighing thirty pounds, and the tumor decided to be ovarian and unilocular. It was agreed to defer operating for a week or two, hoping she might gain strength under the influence of quin. et ferri citras, and the watchful care of her attendants, Drs. Haswell and Wythe Jr.

On April 13th I performed ovariotomy, assisted by Drs.

Haswell, Wythe Jr., Hatch, Simmons, Logan, Cluness, Tyrrell, Taylor, Murphy, and Messrs. Fisher and Hatch, medical students. After complete anesthesia was attained by a mixture of chloroform and ether, an incision about four inches long was made in the linea alba, and each successive layer of the abdominal wall divided on a director, until the tumor was reached. On inserting the hand, the anterior surface of the tumor was found to be adherent, but the adhesions were readily broken, excepting on the right side, where a slight degree of force ruptured the wall of the cyst, whose contents escaped into the cavity of the abdomen faster than it could be removed by the sponges of the attendants. After peeling away the cyst from the peritoneum, it was lifted from the pelvic cavity, secured with a stout double linen ligature, and removed. The external wound was secured with the twisted suture, adhesive strips, and bandage, and the patient placed in bed. As in my former cases, the pedicle was returned to the abdominal cavity, with the ligature left out at the lower angle of the wound. The ligature in this case came away May 1st.

An examination of the removed tumor, showed it to be a cutaneous proliferous cyst of the ovary, having its lining membrane studded with numerous follicles, giving rise to the pulp of numerous teeth, thirteen of which were well and fully formed. In addition, five or six small, irregular pieces of bone were imbedded just below the lining tissue. Two or three smaller cysts, also, had begun to form from the inner surface, which would, doubtless, have finally rendered the cyst multilocular.

Symptoms of pyemia occurred after the operation, with abdominal abscesses, one of which broke into the bladder. Careful medical attention and nursing, however, with the use of stimulants—sulphite of soda, and the injection, now and then, of a solution of carbolic acid—has resulted in a very fair recovery.

On July 1st I again visited Sacramento, and assisted Dr. Tyrrell to perform a similar operation on a patient of his, a Mrs. English. This has also been a perfect success, and I doubt not will be reported in full by the doctor. At that date, Mrs. King was able to walk about the garden, and was daily gaining strength.

Cases of Mushroom Poisoning.

By W. FITCH CHENEY, M.D., Chico, California.

Called Monday, March 27th, 1871, to visit family of Mr. B. Found his wife and three children suffering from constant retching and vomiting, with some purging, and intense pain in the epigastrium.

On the day previous (Sunday), all those affected had partaken freely of supposed mushroom, at dinner. Upon examination I found them under the influence of a kind of stupor, with pupils largely dilated, pulse weak, and ranging from fifty to sixty; skin cool — unnaturally so — with a mottled appearance, making the derangement of the circulation a marked symptom. Arranging the cases in order of age, Charles was aged seven, Ella nine, Flora fourteen, and Mrs. B. thirty-two. Their symptoms seemed to be alike. In the view that the poison had been taken twenty-four hours before, and for the last sixteen or eighteen hours they had all been vomiting, and after each paroxysm had taken freely of water, I considered that the stomach, in each case, had been emptied of any poison remaining unabsorbed. I administered a solution of morphia and soda, with a minute amount of ipecac, which resulted in quiet, when I ordered each a full dose of ol. ricini, which promptly acted on Tuesday morning. I then prescribed quin. sulph. in comp. tr. cinchona; also, as much whisky as I thought they would bear. At this time the pupils were still dilated, and other symptoms (pulse, skin, etc.), unchanged. This was still the condition of things until toward night, when they all were sleeping quietly — skin moist and natural, while there was but little change in the pulse.

About eleven o'clock P.M. of the same day, the boy awoke with a loud cry, and immediately went into almost a cataleptic state, which lasted fifteen or twenty minutes. I got to the bedside just as he came out of it. I found him nearly pulseless, skin cool and clammy, with breathing labored—almost stertorous. With stimulants and frictions he rallied, only to have another seizure, in which he died. A moment before death, the respirations being labored, I put my ear to the chest, and while I so held it, the heart *suddenly* ceased pulsation—a moment later, he was dead.

The history of the death of the little girl, aged nine, which I was told occurred two or three hours after, was in every particular like that of the boy, although, after the death of the boy, she was still sleeping tranquilly, and promised well.

The mother, on Wednesday morning, under the treatment, seemed very little, if any, changed for the better. She complained still of the burning sensation in stomach, pupils still in some measure dilated, pulse feeble—perhaps not quite so slow. Wishing counsel, my friend, Dr. Thomas W. Tilden, became, at this time, associated with me in the case, and, at his suggestion, we added to the previous treatment, the solution of chlorinated soda; and having previously given bismuth, we added to it about one-fourth grain powdered opium, to relieve tenesmus and check the bowels, which were now somewhat inclined to run off. The stimulus was also increased.

In the evening the symptoms were much the same, except an appreciable lowering of the pulse, and a corresponding increase in frequency. Treatment continued, and stimulus ordered to any extent the head would bear. Thursday morning, patient almost comatose—rapidly sinking, pulseless, and with thoracic respiration. As a last resort, an enema was injected, of turpentine one ounce, with about one pint of water; also, one drachm of the oil given by the mouth, with no effect, and about eleven A.M. she died.

The girl, Flora, gradually came out of this condition,

under the same general treatment, although for some time she retained the dilated pupil, etc. Hearing every year, through the public press, of more or less of poisoning from this cause, I was surprised to find next to nothing in our authorities upon the subject, and was left to watch symptoms, and treat on general principles.

It will be observed that in symptoms, the effect is like that of digitalis and belladonna — the infrequent pulse and condition of the pupil, as well as the mottled appearance of the skin, showing a disordered capillary circulation. The appearance of the boy when *in articulo mortis* was strikingly like death from hemorrhage.

The amount of stimulus given the woman was extraordinary, yet the effect was *nil*, not even checking the sinking heart, to say nothing of increasing its force.

I report the above cases in the hope that attention may be drawn to them, and that we may stimulate others who may have had more fortunate experiences with similar cases, to suggest such a course to the Profession as may qualify us to combat these poisons more successfully than I did.

It did not seem to me a question of clearing the digestive organs. When I saw the cases, the poison had full time to be absorbed into the circulation, and was then master of the situation; and the only thing to do, after clearing the bowels, was to support the patients, for, as far as I can learn, we have no knowledge of an antidote.

Hydrate of Chloral.

By J. W. B. REYNOLDS, M.D., of Yountville, Napa County.

I have been in the habit of prescribing this medicine dissolved in the syrup of orange-peel, as in the following formula:

℞. Chloral hydratis, ʒij.
Syr. cort. aurant. ℥i.

M. S. A tea-spoonful, in three or four table-spoonfuls water, every half-hour, till sleep is produced.

I have never observed any decomposition to take place, when prepared in this way. In fact, I have taken it myself for six weeks, from the same solution, having kept the bottle on my office-table, with nothing to protect it from the light, and nothing but a common cork to keep out the air. There are still three or four tea-spoonfuls left, of four ounces I dissolved in the syrup nine months ago, and the solution looks as pure now as it did the day I made it. It is certainly more palatable in this form than in any other way I have used it, and, if it is as liable to decompose in solution with water as some writers seem to think, the syrup is greatly to be preferred in this respect, for I am satisfied that a genuine article of chloral, dissolved in syrup of orange-peel, will not decompose in any reasonable length of time.

Proceedings of the San Francisco Medical Society.

MARCH 14, 1871.

The subject for discussion being "Medical Statistics," Dr. J. P. WHITNEY desired to say a few words in regard to the previous question, particularly with reference to blood-letting. He related the following case: A lady, but a few months past the climacteric, had, since that time, suffered more or less numbness, and even pain, which, however, she had not thought of sufficient importance to mention. While out of town a week ago, she was attacked with hemiplegia of the left side, involving sensation, but not motion. A well-known physician residing in the vicinity was called in, and ordered stimulants. There was no improvement; and on my return, the patient being left in my charge, I said she would be benefited by the loss of blood. It seemed she had mentioned the subject to the other physician, as I had before suggested bleeding, if head-symptoms, flushing of the face, etc., arose; but he said it would make her worse, and prescribed the opposite course—he would not dare to bleed. The patient, however, was growing worse; there was now some paralysis of motion as well as sensation, and I bled her liberally, from which time she began to improve, and has now nearly recovered sensibility.

In commenting on the case, Dr. WHITNEY said he was not vain enough to suppose that this result was due to superior sagacity on his part. In his view the other physician had allowed himself to be educated to believe that bleeding is harmful. A multitude of cases of frequent occurrence indicated the value of blood-letting. A patient with apoplexy is attacked with hemorrhage from the nose, and is relieved. In these cases it is wise to adopt nature's suggestions, but not to generalize too hastily.

Taking up the subject of "Medical Statistics," Dr. WHITNEY said it was well known that he considered it foolish to attempt to apply the numerical method to pathology and therapeutics. He was as well aware as any one to what extent statistics might be applied to knowledge. Newton and Kepler studied the subject of eclipses by knowing accurately all the elements entering into the calculation. In chemistry, with its laws of definite proportion, it is known that certain elements brought into contact will unite in definite proportion. If more than this proportion exist, there will be a residuum. In such cases the numerical method is available. He would challenge any one to name a solitary disease which ever had its treatment improved by the application of this method. Abercrombie, in his chapter on Medical Science, said that no reliance could be placed on statistics. It was advisable to make terminology as definite as possible, so as to have records of disease better understood. The best received definition of pathological conditions was that nomenclature of diseases which the Committee of the London College of Physicians had been two years in arranging. The advantages of registration were not in applying statistics to disease, but in the discussion of questions of sociology. A few years ago an attempt was made by two individuals — both writers of elaborate articles on the social evil—to estimate the number of prostitutes in London. One made the number less than seven thousand; the other, over eighty thousand. Statistics, as applied to pathological questions, were quite as wide of the mark. Again, were statistics reliable, there are many cases in which the law does not allow facts to be stated. Dr. WHITNEY concluded by reading an extract from Copeland, strongly condemning the application of statistics to pathology and therapeutics.

Dr. GIBBONS replied that there was a great deal of truth in what Dr. Whitney had said and read. If the remarks were made with a view to prove that statistics might be erroneously collated, he would agree with them. But they were made to oppose statistics in the abstract. What are statistics, but the record of facts and observations? It is only because they do not give results with mathematical precision, that the objections to them are sustained. The whole science of medicine is identified with statistics. Our professional lives begin with them. We treat a case of scarlatina; it dies. We treat six successive cases in the same way; they also die. We are not satisfied to continue this treatment, and abandon it. Adopting another course, the patients recover. Thus we go on from year to year accumulating statistics—comparing the past with the present. Are we to repudiate all this experience and these records, because we can not arrive at mathematical precision? The accumulated experiences of others are but statistics. In regard to the enumeration of prostitutes, the conclusion seems to be, that as the estimates are so different, no one must ever attempt to find out the truth. Such reasoning would prevent even an approximation from being made. Objections have been urged to reporting causes of deaths, on account of the impossibility of making accurate mortuary statistics. The reports can not be mathematically correct; possibly, there is no single disease in which the report is correct, but as a general thing, the causes of error are constant, and the reports are valuable for purposes of comparison. Though a particular barometer may range too high or too low, it is just as good for comparison of one day with another. But in many cases the result is very near exact. Is it possible that any great error exists in the number of deaths from small-pox, reported during the epidemic here? Is it not of value to have an approximation to the number of *cases* of the disease, even though this number be very imperfect? The same causes of error operate everywhere, so that these statistics will serve purposes of comparison with other cities, or with this city at some future time. Will any one say it is useless to make them? In the same way we may determine the fatality of pulmonary diseases with reference to locality, and the protective power of vaccination. Formerly, and for a series of years, small-pox carried off about ten thousand to every one million inhabitants. Inoculation was introduced; it prevented small-pox in the individual, but increased the amount of disease. We know that vaccination has greatly diminished the mortality, which would amount to one hundred and thirty thousand per annum in the United States, but for vaccination. We can not be accurate, yet we know the mortality is much less. Is it not important to know that ninety out of every one hundred deaths from scarlet fever are in children under five years of age? Dr. Copeland may talk about the fallacy of statistics, yet he never wrote ten pages in his life without depending on them. The census is never perfect, but we refer to it for medical knowledge. Questions of sex are determined by it. We learn that in nine months after a cholera epidemic, the proportion of females born is larger than usual. Instead of discarding all statistics, our business is to correct and improve them.

Dr. Whitney expressed himself as much astonished at the line of argument just presented. He thought he had defined his meaning. The worthlessness of medical statistics was due to the uncertainty of the data on which they are based. One calls a certain class of things facts; another thinks them of so little value as to be useless. It was equivalent to confounding the doctrine of probability with a mathematical certainty. He would defy Dr. Gibbons to point to any part of Dr. Copeland's works in which he had availed himself of statistics, if they were not legitimate. He did not object to mortuary reports, but he objected to their being made in accordance with a certain nomenclature which could not be enforced. He spoke of syphilis in the higher walks of life, which might have been contracted innocently; of the advisability, and even necessity of concealment in these cases, and of the publicity of the records. In further general remarks on the fallibility of statistics, he alluded to the statements by Dr. Gibbons in reference to small-pox, which contained interesting facts, yet none that threw light on the disease. These sources of fallacy in regard to pneumonia were so numerous as to make it utterly useless to attempt to apply statistics to improvement in its therapeutics.

Dr. GIBBONS thought it difficult to find out what Dr. Whitney meant, unless the last sentence would throw light on the matter. No one wished to make statistics the *foundation* of improvement in therapeutics. Statistics were but the results of experience, and only when undue importance was placed upon them did they mislead us in practice. We continually apply statistics, if not by studying records, yet mentally. They are almost at the foundation of surgery—at least, at the foundation of statistical inquiry, as in the operation of ovariotomy, for instance.

Further remarks were made by Dr. GIBBONS, to whom Dr. WHITNEY, in closing the discussion, replied, that the whole point of difference seemed to hinge on the definition of historical and statistical facts, which were not synonymous. Facts can be of historical, but not of statistical value. Let Los Angeles be spoken of as a good climate for consumptives, and in five years (because of the influx of consumptives) statistics will show a very great mortality from this disease.

May 23, 1871.

The Secretary presented to the Society, on behalf of Dr. H. Neal, of South San Juan, a double-bodied lamb, preserved in alcohol. The thanks of the Society were directed to be returned to Dr. Neal.

Dr. Soule mentioned a case occurring in his practice, of a child born with two teeth—the lower central incisors.

Dr. Horatio R. Storer, of Boston, being present, was invited to address the meeting. In response, Dr. Storer said there were many questions which were of great interest to him, and he would like to suggest them, and hear the views of the members upon them. It had been said years ago, that a great amount of uterine disease existed in California, in consequence of over-indulgence. He would like to hear the views of members on this point; also, on the Chinese question, as regards prostitution. He would ask for the expression of opinion on one point in reference to contagion. While in Sacramento, he had been asked by Dr. Donaldson whether it was advisable to establish a maternity in connection with the hospital. He considered it a great mistake to do so. He had also visited Dr. Deane's hospital, in this city, where both lying-in cases and cases of pelvic disease were received. Puerperal disease was often induced by physicians who attended both obstetrical and surgical cases. The subject had received great attention in England, many leading members of the Profession being decidedly opposed to the establishment of maternities in connection with general hospitals. In many cases, where this connection exists, Dr. Storer believed he had seen more puerperal fever and erysipelas than where separate. There was always puerperal fever in Bellevue Hospital.

Dr. Favor related two cases occurring in his practice, as follows: 1st. *Urethro-vaginal fistula.*—Was consulted by a lady, in good general health, and aged about forty-four years, for a difficulty in passing water. She was obliged to urinate from eight to ten, and even twenty times during the night. An examination showed the orifice of the urethra obliterated, and a cicatrix. Under the pubic arch, high up near the bladder, was an aperture through which the sound entered the bladder. The orifice must be in the urethra, as the patient has some control of urination. When did this occur? She did not know. Had borne children. Ten years ago she was run over by a wagon. An abscess formed in the right hypochondriac region, and broke in the vagina, discharging pus. What was the nature of this abscess? Did it originate in the kidney, and extend to the bladder? or, in the peritoneum, and extend to the anterior cul-de-sac? Nitrate of silver (thirty grains to the ounce) had been applied to the orifice, and the citrate of iron and strychnia ordered. The frequency of urinating had diminished to four times a night.

Case 2. *Supposed pregnancy.*—Was consulted by a woman who had all the palpable symptoms of pregnancy. The womb was enlarged, presenting a globular tumor, as high as the umbilicus. There was a little obscure fluctuation. A slight sanguineous discharge, continuing a week, occurred every two weeks. Patient dropsical; lower limbs having been swollen for years, but the abdominal enlargement was of but three months' duration, and had been gradual. There was no nausea; os uteri felt as it does during pregnancy—it was not open. The sound was not used, fearing that pregnancy existed. The specific gravity of the urine was 1,018; not albuminous. Liver torpid, no apparent enlargement; appearance cachectic; appetite tolerably good; bowels always constipated. Had given cit. iron and strychnia, with tr. digitalis; and there had been diminution of anasarca, but no change in the tumor. Was the woman pregnant?

Dr. STORER remarked, in regard to the second case, that the diagnosis must remain obscure until sufficient time had elapsed to give presumptive evidence of pregnancy. Soon the fetal heart may be heard; there will be motion or quickening. But cases occur in which these signs never appear.

Dr. Scott asked if ballottement had been performed, or if the vagina was of a violet color, or the cervix was shortened.

Dr. Favor answered that he had not performed ballottement, and could not reply to the other questions.

The absence of these signs, added Dr. Scott, would militate against the theory of pregnancy.

Dr. Storer, resuming, made some remarks upon the diagnosis, if it were decided that pregnancy did not exist, and upon the treatment; referring, under the latter head, to the recent successful removal of a uterine fibroid, by Dr. Scott.

Dr. Gibbons followed with some remarks upon uterine disease in California, and concluded by referring to the comparative immunity of American women in California from the accidents of childbirth.

Dr. Storer thought this immunity was not confined to California. The prevalence of accident among the lower classes was, perhaps, because the ignorant were not inclined to submit to instrumental interference. He had been enabled to overcome this difficulty when in obstetric practice, by obtaining the sanction of Bishop Fitzpatrick, of Boston, to baptize with the finger, or a syringe.

Dr. Storer, having put the question, "Is your climate particularly favorable for surgical operations?"

Dr. J. P. Whitney said that he did not think there was any question that the results of operations were favorable to California. Some drawbacks existed, such as the inactivity of the skin, and consequent tendency to kidney disease. Uremic difficulties were prevalent. For the same reason, in his experience, uremic convulsions attendant upon puerperal cases, were inordinately frequent.

Dr. Scott said, that when about to come to California, he had been told that he would find a large amount of uterine disease, and that its prevalence was attributable to the hills. His experience had extended to hilly cities elsewhere, and to India, England, Dublin, and New York, but he found no excess of uterine disease here. Uterine disease was quite as prevalent among the natives of India as others. Their labors were easier, but getting up was attended with the same dangers. Procidentia and prolapsus, erosions, and other misplacements were just as frequent. He did not think the hills caused uterine disease, but if it existed, they would aggravate it.

Proceedings of the Sacramento Society for Medical Improvement.

The Society met at the office of Dr. Montgomery, April 25th, 1871, with the President, Dr. Hatch, in the chair.

Present: Drs. Hatch, Nelson, Cluness, White, Tyrrell, Trafton, Oatman, Logan, Simmons, Nichols, Montgomery, and Nixon.

Drs. Donaldson, White, and Curtis were unanimously elected to membership.

Dr. MONTGOMERY read the regular paper of the evening, entitled "The Ethics of the Medical Profession." [See page 97.]

Dr. NELSON was very well pleased with the paper, but did not agree altogether with the author in regard to Medical Ethics.

Dr. TRAFTON was highly pleased with the paper, and thought it would be for the general interest of the Profession for medical men to act strictly in accordance with the views of Dr. Montgomery as regards Medical Ethics.

Dr. OATMAN thought we were fortunate in having the subject of Medical Ethics brought before the Society in the shape of a paper, and wished to commend the author by saying that he thought Dr. Montgomery had done the subject ample justice. He desired here to allude to the habits of the public in regard to their duties to the Profession. Most of the differences which occur among physicians originate in the conduct of patrons, and upon that subject the public mind needed education. The Code was ample for honorable members of the Profession — its teachings were pure. He thought that medical men should be very slow in taking each other's patients. He had known some instances where, in consultations, the counsel had taken the cases of the attending physician. *This should never occur.* Remembered having a case of typhoid fever, with torpid bowels at the commencement. Administered a small dose of cit. magnesia. Counsel was called soon after, and when he (Dr. O.) arrived, found the consulting physician there before the appointed time. Told him that he had moved the bowels of the patient with a light dose of cit. magnesia; and his immediate reply was, in the hearing of the patient and others of the family, "that it was the most abominable physic that could be given in such a case," or words to that effect. The result of that consultation was, that the consulting physician was afterward retained by the family, and that he (Dr. O.) was supplanted.

Dr. Tyrrell remarked that the paper was a most excellent one; however, he thought it could not be intended in any way to apply to members of this Society, but that it must have been more particularly meant for the benefit of the *San Francisco doctors*.

On motion of Dr. Trafton, Dr. Montgomery's paper was ordered to be printed in the San Francisco Pacific Medical and Surgical Journal, for the *benefit of the San Francisco medical fraternity*.

A. B. Nixon, Secretary.

REVIEWS AND NOTICES OF BOOKS.

On the Physiological Effects of Severe and Protracted Exercise; with Special Reference to its Influence on the Excretion of Nitrogen. By Austin Flint, Jr., M.D., Professor of Physiology in the Bellevue Hospital Medical College, etc. (Reprinted from the *New York Medical Journal*, June, 1871.) New York: D. Appleton & Co. San Francisco: A. L. Bancroft & Co., and A. Roman & Co.

Our readers are cognizant of the silly feat performed by the pedestrian, Weston, who walked one hundred miles in less than twenty-two consecutive hours, with the aid of flagellation and other torture worthy of an ancient gladiator. Professor Flint used the opportunity thus afforded to make a series of observations and experiments, on the effects of muscular exertion on the action of the kidneys and other organs, the results of which are embodied in this volume, and which are deemed of great value in determining certain physiological problems.

THE EYE IN HEALTH AND DISEASE: Being a Series of Articles on the Anatomy and Physiology of the Human Eye, and its Surgical and Medical Treatment. By B. Joy Jeffries, A.M., M.D., Fellow of the Massachusetts Medical Society, Member of the American Ophthalmological Society, etc. Boston: Alexander Moore. 1871. San Francisco: A. Roman & Co., and A. L. Bancroft & Co.

This is a beautifully executed volume of one hundred and twenty pages, intended in great part for non-professional readers. It refers to a variety of defects and disorders of the organ of vision which are very common, and of which the outside world know too little for their own good. In regard to the use of spectacles, the author gives this sensible advice: "Every person whose eyes are not normal had better consult some scientific oculist, avoiding all traveling quacks, and every doctor who advertises in any shape whatever."

A TREATISE ON DISEASES OF THE NERVOUS SYSTEM. By William A. Hammond, M.D., Professor of Diseases of the Mind and Nervous System, and of Clinical Medicine, in the Bellevue Hospital Medical College; Physician-in-Chief to the New York State Hospital for Diseases of the Nervous System, etc. With 45 Illustrations. New York: D. Appleton & Co. 1871. Pp. 754. San Francisco: A. Roman & Co., A. L. Bancroft & Co.

To form a solid judgment of a work like this requires more time than a journalist has at his disposal, while performing his monthly tour, at railroad speed, through the field of medical literature. But knowing with what industry and success Dr. Hammond has pursued the study of the nervous system, and judging from the table of contents and occasional glimpses at the text of the volume before us, we are disposed to place it in the foremost rank among the many excellent works in its department which have been published in the last twenty years. That the author has given it the deliberate thought which the magnitude of the theme and the responsibility of authorship alike required, may be inferred from the statement in the preface, that the fourth volume of Prof. Austin Flint, Jr.'s "Physiology of Man," which will be published during the coming season, will, with the present treatise, constitute a complete work on "The Physiology and Pathology of the Nervous System."

Opium and the Opium Appetite: With Notices of Alcoholic Beverages, Cannabis Indica, Tobacco and Cocoa, and Tea and Coffee, in their hygienic aspects and pathologic relations. By Alonzo Calkins, M.D. Philadelphia: J. B. Lippincott & Co. 1871. San Francisco: A. Roman & Co.

With much industry the author of this volume has collected from a great variety of sources, statistics, statements, and assertions, good, bad, and indifferent, touching the subjects of his inquiry, and has thrown them together into a readable book; readable especially by such persons as understand French, Latin and irregular English. We should be sorry to indorse some of his deductions, which appear to us as the result of preconceived opinions. But despite of its flippant and pedantic style and its faulty logic, it will be read with interest and benefit by all classes.

The Book of Travels of a Doctor of Physic: Containing his observations made in certain portions of the two continents. Philadelphia: J. B. Lippincott & Co. 1871. San Francisco: A. L. Bancroft & Co.

The very title of this book puts you in good humor with the writer, for you know you have a sensible fellow to deal with. But any one who would infer that he is a dry, commonplace wayfayer, will find himself greatly mistaken when he comes to peruse the record. Our traveling Doctor tells his story with zest, and carries you with him on a very pleasant and edifying journey.

Paralysis, and other Affections of the Nerves: their Cure by Vibratory and Special Movements. By Geo. H. Taylor, M.D. Author of Diseases of Women, Exposition of the Swedish Movement-Cure, etc., etc. New York: Samuel R. Wells. 1871. San Francisco: A. L. Bancroft & Co.

There are some very curious things connected with the so-called movement-cure well deserving the attention of the medical inquirer. Dr. Taylor writes upon it with much learning and ingenuity, and the present volume will be read with much interest by all persons interested in the subject.

LIGHT AND ELECTRICITY: Notes of two Courses of Lectures before the Royal Institution of Great Britain. By John Tyndall, L.L.D., F.R.S. Author of "Heat as a Mode of Motion," etc., etc. New York: D. Appleton & Co. 1871. San Francisco: A. L. Bancroft & Co.

Sixteen lectures in all, nine on Light, and seven on Electricity, are condensed in this volume within the limits of 200 pages, forming a concentrated extract of inestimable value to the student of science.

TILL THE DOCTOR COMES, AND HOW TO HELP HIM. By George H. Hope, M.D., M.R.C.S.E. Revised, with additions by a New York Physician. New York: G. P. Putnam & Sons. San Francisco: A. L. Bancroft & Co.

Just what the title says — no more and no less. A hundred pages, in pamphlet form, for popular use. Parents and nurses all should read it.

EDITORIAL.

Atrocities of the Commune in a Medico - Psychological Aspect.

In view of the prevailing disposition to attribute crime to other than moral causes, it is by no means surprising that medical philosophers should seek to explain the atrocities of the Paris Commune by ascribing them to physical or cerebro-physical influences. Referring to this topic, a French writer, in the *Gazette Hebdomadaire*, remarks that "all who speak or write of the events of Paris from the 18th of March to the 28th of May, employ such terms as *moral malady*, *mental aberration*, *dementia*, *convulsions*, *epilepsy*, *alcoholism*, *delirium*, *frenzy*, *rage*, *furious madness*, *monomania*," etc. The *London Times* speaks of *delirium tremens*, and the Germans of the *morbus democraticus*. These expressions, borrowed from the medical vocabulary, are on all lips, and at the end of all pens; and it is notable that they are mostly used in a literal sense rather than figuratively. In fact, the deeds of the Commune, especially the last ones, are so extraordinary, so monstrous, so far in excess of any thing that ever preceded them, that they appear to pass beyond the limits of sound reason, and into the domain of maniacal fury. In a professional, still more than a popular view, these events seem like a vast exhibition of collective madness—like the confused explosion of an outbreak of epidemic insanity. The mind naturally refers to the great mental aberrations of the Middle Ages, which burst forth upon the entire population, everywhere spreading terror, desolation, murder, and incendiarism. We are also made to think of the transports of savage fury which are provoked by epilepsy and alcoholism, and which can only be appeased by blood, carnage, and destruction.

"Alcoholism! Ah, that is one of the direst social maladies of the present time. Who can describe the extensive *role* performed in our early disasters, and afterwards in our civil discords, by the abuse of alcohol, that redoubtable poison which dethrones the reason, destroys the conscience, extinguishes the noble sentiments, stimulates the evil instincts, and converts man into an ignoble brute or a beast! We have not forgotten the severe orders by which the unfortunate General Thomas, during the siege, scourged the shameful and obscene debaucheries, the drunkenness, the want of discipline, and the cowardly desertion, to which certain battalions of the national guard abandoned themselves in the trenches, in the very face of the enemy. It is also notorious that intoxication was one of the most efficient means employed by the Commune to inflame the zeal of its adepts, to excite the enthusiasm of its faithful servants, to sharpen the ardor of its combatants. We remember in what a pitiful condition the troops of Versailles found the defenders of the forts of Issy and Vauvres! In fine, all the evidence goes to prove that most of the incendiaries were a prey to alcoholic excitement, which rendered them deaf to the voice of humanity and insensible to every idea of compassion."

Homeopathic Surgery — What is it?

Can any one tell what is meant by homeopathic surgery?—how the law [?] of "similia similibus" can apply to the use of the scalpel, the ecraseur, the ligature? If a man is stabbed, can he be cured by a little more stabbing, in a small way? If he have a ball fired into his corpus, can he be saved by shooting him with diminutive bullets, dynamic or potentized, or what not? If one be bleeding to death from a wounded artery, can similia similibus save his life by cutting another artery? The expression, "homeopathic surgery," is absurd in itself. You may as well talk of homeopathic farming, or homeopathic mining. A homeopathist may practice surgery, but in doing so he must tread in the footsteps of the regular schools. He can strike out no new course. He can not apply his favorite "law" to surgical art. On the contrary, it comes in to balk him at every step; to shake his confidence in himself, and to make his hand tremble. In attempting to practice surgery he enters the camp of his enemies, whom he has always denounced as murderers, and accepts their guidance and employs their weapons. His puny straw of *like to like*, he has left outside.

A "homeopathic surgeon" is a fabulous animal, having no real existence. "Homeopathic blacksmith," "homeopathic cobbler," "homeopathic shoe-black," would be just as appropriate—the last indeed more so, because shoe-blacks do apply the law of similia similibus. Hahnemann had no knowledge of surgery. He ignored it. He scarcely ever mentioned the word; nor did his early followers. They were ashamed to follow the teachings and the practice of the men whom they denounced. They have had half a century of existence, with much increase and success, say they. But not a man among them has ever done any thing for surgery. Not a single homeopathist in Europe or America has ever identified himself with it. Not a single name have they given to the history of surgery, in a period effulgent with the splendid achievements of the regular schools.

Small-pox — A fearful Responsibility.

"In London alone, let it be distinctly observed that as many as one thousand lives a month are now sacrificed to a perfectly preventible disease." So says the *London Times* of a late issue, in regard to small-pox. If not literally true that small-pox is a preventible disease, under all circumstances, it is true that it can be shorn of its fatality, and that death from small-pox amounts to *homicide*, for which *somebody* is responsible. Who is that somebody? It may be the subject himself, who neglects or refuses the preventive. It may be the parent or guardian, who has done the same. It may be the custodians of the public health, officially created, or commissioned by the laws of humanity. But above all, the responsibility and the *crime* must lie at the door of those individuals who teach hostility to vaccination—who denounce the practice, and use positive means to deter from it. The motive may not be bad. But what signifies the motive? Women murder their offspring from good motives. Men have been burned at the stake from good motives. In all but motive, the anti-vaccinators are murderers. If their motives were bad, it would be a comparative blessing to society. Then they could do less harm. There would be fewer deaths from small-pox.

Abuse of the Speculum — Tinkering the Uterus.

On several occasions we have entered on the pages of this *Journal* our protest against the habitual or empirical use of the speculum, and the reckless and indiscriminate cauterizing, scarification and slitting of the os uteri. For this we have been criticized, if not censured, by individuals who failed to appreciate our objections as applicable to the abuse of certain means, and not the proper use. All that we have ever said on this point is more than sustained by Dr. Storer and other members of the Gynæcological Society of Boston. In the course of discussion (see *Journal* for July), Dr. Storer remarked upon patients constantly falling into his hands with more or less complete obliteration of the vagina — from the careless employment of nitrate of silver—the constant and indiscriminate use of vaginal pessaries—the mangling of the cervix by surgical procedures in displacements with sterility or dysmenorrhea. Dr. Blake went even further, in declaring that he had never seen any benefit from incising the cervix for dysmenorrhea, even when dilatation was subsequently kept up. Dr. Warren had repeatedly incised the cervix for mechanical dysmenorrhea, but had never seen any benefit, even when the canal remained very patulous. This is even further than we have ever gone, and further than we are prepared to go.

A Hospital Student of the Olden Time.

A century ago medical students were admitted into the Philadelphia Hospital on terms which the present generation would not consider attractive. A limited number of students then resided in the Hospital and discharged the duties since imposed on resident physicians. The *Phila. Med. Times*, in an interesting sketch of the Hospital and its Library, thus describes some of the conditions on which a student was admitted to this desirable position. He was to bring with him a single feather bed, which he was to leave in the house; to serve five years; to give two sufficient securities to pay at the rate of a hundred pounds per annum for every day that he absented himself without leave from the Managers; to fill up his time of study; "to look for no indulgence, by leave to attend parties of pleasure or places of amusement, nor to be abroad in the evening; nor will it be considered for his benefit to receive visits at home. None of these things making any part of the views of careful parents or friends in placing him, nor the Managers in receiving him, as apprentice." He was allowed two seasons, selected by the Managers, out of the five, to attend medical lectures, "always observing to return home as soon as each lecture shall be over."

Colorado for Asthmatics.

Dr. Crane, of Detroit, long a sufferer from asthma, having removed to Colorado, was cured in a few months. Therefore, "the pure, rarified atmosphere of that elevated, non-malarious region is a positive antidote for asthma in all its forms." A most remarkable deduction for a medical philosopher. Why, there are asthmatics who will be entirely cured by moving into a malarious district. Some are cured by removing from the hill-top to the valley, and some by removing from the valley to the hill-top.

Cundurango — "Died after being Cured."

There is nothing novel in the claim of a cancer-cure. The world has had sovereign cures for cancer by the score. The testimony of a few, or indeed of many, is worth little on the promulgation of a new remedy. All new remedies work miracles. One of our exchanges records several cures by cundurango, and a foot-note attached to one of the reports reads thus, in small type: "* This case has since died."

Time is required to establish the reputation of a remedy—to separate the *post hoc* from the *propter hoc*. Men who are acquainted with the history of the healing art are slow of faith when it comes to famous cures. They remember the sarracenia for small-pox, chestnut-leaf tea for whooping-cough, and so forth. They remember Joanna Stephens' remedy for stone, so potent and so certain as to warrant the English Parliament in giving her twenty-five thousand dollars for the secret. They remember Perkins' tractors, and the Perkinian Institution of London. The cancer problem is the perpetual motion of medicine. It has been solved a thousand times, and yet remains to torture the wits of men. We have no objection to the trial of new remedies. Let them be tried, by all means. But let the evidence in their favor be weighed with judgment, and in the light of past experience.

Irrigation — Effect on Health.

In view of the extensive irrigation of the San Joaquin country, it becomes an inquiry of much interest, What will be the effect, if any, on the health of the population? We should be glad to find reasons for an opinion not unfavorable. But the reasons and the precedents are unfortunately on the other side. In Solano County, we have the experience of the people living near the canal by which, a few years ago, the waters of Cache Creek were let in upon the lands for irrigation. The result has been disastrous in the development of malarious disease. It will probably be the same in the San Joaquin Valley. But we must take the evil with the good in mundane affairs. Perhaps prolonged cultivation, and the planting of trees and gardens, will tend to correct the mischief. Habits of life, too, may be made protective by subjecting them to hygienic principles.

GENERAL SUMMARY.

Protection against Poisoning in England.

The Council of the Pharmaceutical Society of England has promulgated, in the following form, its recommendations for precautions in the storing of poisons:

"1. That in the keeping of poisons, each bottle, vessel, box, or package, containing a poison, be labeled with the name of the article, and also with some distinctive mark indicating that it contains poison.

"2. Also, that in the keeping of poisons, each poison be kept on one or other of the following systems, viz:

"(*a.*) In a bottle or vessel tied over, capped, locked, or otherwise secured, in a manner different from that in which bottles or vessels containing ordinary articles are kept in the same warehouse, shop, or dispensary; or,

"(*b.*) In a bottle or vessel rendered distinguishable by touch from the bottles or vessels in which ordinary articles are kept in the same warehouse, shop, or dispensary; or,

"(*c.*) In a bottle, vessel, box, or package, kept in a room or cupboard set apart for dangerous articles.

"3. That all liniments, embrocations, and lotions containing poison, be sent out in bottles rendered distinguishable by touch from ordinary medicine bottles; and that there also be affixed to each bottle (in addition to the name of the article, and to any particular instructions for its use) a label giving notice that the contents of the bottle are not to be taken internally."—*Medical Press and Circular.*

A Learned Veterinary Surgeon.

The *N. Y. Med. Gazette* gives Dr. Burr, of Binghamton, as authority for the following colloquy, which occurred during a recent trial in that city. It appears that a Mr. A. sold to Mr. B. a colt as a gelding, which colt had had but one testicle removed, the other remaining within the cavity of the abdomen. The veterinary surgeon who had castrated the animal was sworn, and, on his cross-examination, stated the following interesting features in the anatomy of the horse: Attorney—"What are, and where are varicose veins to be found?" Witness—"I don't know, but I know where the bellicose veins are." Attorney—"Where are they?" Witness—"Close to the belly?" Attorney—"Where is the scrotum?" Witness—"I am not quite certain, but I think that it is the film that covers the teeth during infancy." Attorney—"Have you ever made any examinations in the abdominal region?" Witness—"No; all my examinations have been made in the Broome County region." Attorney—"That is sufficient."

A Woman with Four Breasts.

The *Medical News and Library* for April contains an account of a woman who was possessed of four breasts, two in the normal position and two in the axillary region. The latter two had attained about the size of an orange. She was delivered of a dead premature child, and, in spite of an attack of fever, the secretion of milk was regularly established in all the breasts; but, when examined microscopically, the milk of the supplementary breasts was found to be of a much purer quality.

STATE BOARD OF HEALTH.

Abstract from the Reports of Deaths and their Causes, in the following cities and towns in California, during June, **1871:**

CITIES AND TOWNS.	Total No. Deaths.	[illegible]	[illegible]	[illegible]	[illegible]	[illegible]	[illegible]	AUTHORITIES.
San Francisco	221	50	[illegible]	11	1	2	7	S. F. Board of Health.
Sacramento	26	5	1	6	1	0	0	Sac. Board of Health.
Petaluma	1	1	0	0	0	0	0	Dr. G. W. [illegible]
Dixon	0	0	0	0	0	0	0	Dr. R. H. Plummer.
Santa Clara	7	1	0	0	0	0	1	Dr. H. H. W[illegible]
Stockton	20	3	2	7	0	0	0	Stockton Bd. Health.
Marysville	5	0	0	[illegible]	0	0	0	Dr. C. E. Stone.
[illegible]	1	0	0	0	0	0	0	Dr. F. A. [illegible]
[illegible]								Dr. [illegible]
San Diego	4	2	0	0	0	0	0	Co. Med. Society.
San Luis Obispo	3	1	0	0	0	0	0	Dr. W. W. Hays.
[illegible]								Dr. [illegible]
Woodland	1	0	0	0	0	0	1	Dr. A. B. M[illegible]
Oakland	8	1	1	1	0	0	[illegible]	Dr. T. H. [illegible]
Los Angeles	10	3	1	2	0	0	0	Dr. H. S. Orme.
Nevada City								[illegible]
[illegible]	1	0	0	0	0	0	0	Dr. W[illegible]
St. Helena	1	0	0	1	0	0	0	Dr. J. S. A[illegible]
San Jose	13	3	1	2	0	0	1	Dr. J. N. Br[illegible]
Napa City	5	1	0	0	0	0	2	Dr. M. B. Pond.
[illegible]								Dr. [illegible]
[illegible]	2	0	0	0	0	1	[illegible]	[illegible]
Watsonville	2	[illegible]	0	1	0	0	[illegible]	Dr. [illegible]
[illegible]	[illegible]	[illegible]	[illegible]	[illegible]	0	[illegible]	1	Dr. [illegible]
Bridgeport [illegible]	[illegible]	[illegible]	[illegible]	[illegible]	0	1	[illegible]	Dr. [illegible]
[illegible] & [illegible]	3	0	0	1	0	0	0	Dr. [illegible]
Monterey	3	0	1	0	[illegible]	[illegible]	0	[illegible]
Santa Cruz	6	2	0	0	[illegible]		0	Dr. [illegible]
Vallejo	3	0	0	2	0		[illegible]	[illegible]
Suisun & Fairfield	2	0	0	[illegible]	0	[illegible]		[illegible]
Colusa	1	0	0	0	0	[illegible]	[illegible]	Dr. [illegible]
Trinity County	1	0	1	0	0	[illegible]	[illegible]	[illegible]
Santa Barbara	1	1	0	0	0	0	[illegible]	[illegible]
Redwood City	1	0	[illegible]	0	[illegible]	[illegible]	[illegible]	[illegible]

Abstract from Reports of Births:

CITIES AND TOWNS.	Total Births.	Males.	Females.	Still-born.	Live-born.	AUTHORITIES.
San Francisco....	111	54	57	17	94	S. F. Board of Health.
Sacramento.....	34	19	15	3	31	Sac. Board of Health.
All other places.	132	69	63	13	129	Various sources.
TOTAL......	277	142	135	33	244	

Remarks.—The effects of the past comparatively dry season upon the public health continue, thus far, to show the same favorable results noticed last month. It is yet, however, too soon to expect the febrile and choleraic affections, attributable in all parts of the world to hot and dry summers. In some parts, especially the interior valleys of the State, the heat has been at times excessive; and too much caution cannot be impressed upon the minds of the people, in preventing the temperature of the head becoming raised so high, from exposure to the sun's rays, as to endanger the due circulation of the constituents of the blood, or the action of the nerve currents. Dr. Hays, of San Luis Obispo, reports a fatal case of idiopathic tetanus, caused by bathing, while heated, in cold water. He states that he had a similar case last summer, brought on from exposure, with like result; the patient dying in one week from the time of attack. He also had two cases of sun-stroke the same day, which, however, recovered. Considerable alarm has been created by a reported death from small-pox in San Francisco, and the demand for vaccine virus, from all parts of the State, has been consequently greater than the supply. An experience of twenty-one years with this disease in California, warrants me in giving assurance that there need not be the slightest apprehension during the dry season. In all parts of the world, dry weather is found to suppress the development of small-pox, and for this reason it cannot be inoculated in some portions of the west coast of Africa.

THOMAS M. LOGAN, M.D.,
Permanent Secretary State Board of Health.

Rebellion among European Students.

Karsten, Professor of Botany in Vienna, examined a class of one hundred and six candidates, who had passed all the other Chairs, and rejected all but four. Whereupon, the indignant students assaulted the professor and forced him to take refuge in his carriage, and to suspend his lectures.

Test Solution for Pus.

A saturated alcoholic solution of guaiacum exposed to the air until it acquires the property of giving a green color with iodide of potassium, is said, by Dr. Day, of Geelong, to be a good test for pus. When added to liquid pus, or dried pus moistened, it gives a clear blue color.—*Michigan Med. Journal.*

Mortality in San Francisco during June, 1871.

By H. Gibbons, Jr., M.D.

CAUSES OF DEATH.

Abscess	1	Dentition	3	Inanition	10
Anemia	1	Diarrhea	2	Injuries, unspecified	1
Aneurism of Aorta	4	Diphtheria	1	Liver, Disease of	1
Apoplexy	1	Diseases of Heart	5	Meningitis	6
" of Lungs	1	Dropsy	2	Metrorrhagia	1
Asthma	1	Empyema	1	Old Age	2
Atrophia	10	Enteritis	2	Paralysis	4
Bright's Disease	2	Erysipelas	1	Peritonitis	7
Bronchitis	3	Epilepsy	2	Phthisis	39
Burns	1	Fever, Catarrhal	2	Pneumonitis	9
Cancer	1	" Puerperal	1	Premature Birth	3
" of Neck	1	" Scarlet	2	Pyemia	3
" of Stomach	1	" Typhoid	7	Softening of Brain	1
Cerebritis	3	Fracture of Skull	1	Suicide	3
Cholera Infantum	6	" of Atlas	1	Syphilis	1
Congestion of Brain	5	Gastritis	1	Tetanus	4
" of Lungs	1	Gunshot Wound	3	Unknown	9
Convulsions, Infantile	13	Hemorrhage, Bowels	1	Uremia	1
" Puerpural	1	Hepatitis	2	Whooping Cough	1
Croup	2	Hernia	1		
Cyanosis	2	Hydrocephalus	7	Total	221
Debility, General	5	Hydrothorax	1	Still-births	17

AGES.

Under 1 year	62	From 15 to 20 years	4	From 60 to 70 years	8
From 1 to 2 years	8	From 20 to 30 years	32	From 70 to 80 years	5
From 2 to 5 years	9	From 30 to 40 years	32	From 80 to 90 years	1
From 5 to 10 years	9	From 40 to 50 years	34	From 90 to 100 years	1
From 10 to 15 years	3	From 50 to 60 years	13		

Sex.—Male, 149; Female, 72. Total, 221.
Color.—White, 192; Copper, 27; Black, 2.

NATIVITIES.

California	87	Scotland	1	China	26
Other parts of U. S.	26	Wales	1	West Indies	1
British Amer'n Prov.	4	France	8	Australia	2
Mexico	3	Germany	17	Isle of Wight	1
England	8	Sweden	1	Norway	1
Ireland	33	Italy	1		

RECAPITULATION.

Died in City Wards	167	Mount St. Joseph's Infirmary	8
City and County Hospital	16	Alms House	2
U. S. Marine Hospital	3	Italian Hospital	1
French Hospital	5	Casualties	6
German Hospital	3	Suicides	3
St. Mary's Hospital	7		

Remarks.—We are glad to be able to chronicle a continuance of the unusual healthfulness of the city which has prevailed for several months past. June is no exception to what has been said of the months immediately preceding it. The deaths in June since 1866 were, in 1866, 211; in 1867, 201; in 1868, 275; in 1869, 293; in 1870, 282; in 1871, 221. The year promises to contrast most markedly with 1869 and 1870. One-half of it is already gone, and the mortality has reached only 1,449, against 1,586 in 1870, 1,834 in 1869, and 1,318 in 1868. The sanitary condition of the city is well illustrated by reference to the records of mortality from consumption, which generally bears a more or less constant ratio to the population. The deaths from this disease were, in the first half of 1866, 180; of 1867, 183; of 1868, 172; of 1869, 239; of 1870, 250; of 1871, 273. In round numbers, nearly one-fifth of the mortality for the past six months was from consumption; while in 1866 and 1867, it amounted to but little more than one-seventh. By comparison with the population at these two periods, however, it will be seen that in the earlier years there were about 14½ deaths per 10,000, and in 1871 about 15 per 10,000. Thus the death-rate of this disease keeps pace with the population, while the diminution of mortality from other causes is greater than at first appears. In the first half of 1866, the population being 125,000, there were, exclusive of consumption, 1,021 deaths; in the first half of 1871, the population having increased 44 per cent., or to 180,000, the deaths, exclusive of consumption, were but 1,176. As was to be expected, infantile diseases were more fatal in June than in previous months, there being 79 deaths under five years of age, principally from atrophia, convulsions, inanition, cholera infantum, and brain diseases. The number of deaths from tetanus (4), peritonitis (7), and gunshot wounds (3), is unusually large.

Coma from fifteen grains Chloral Hydrate.

Dr. Shaw, in the Phila. *Med. and Surg. Reporter*, describes the effect of a fifteen-grain dose of this substance, given to a paralytic patient for severe abdominal pain. The man soon lapsed into deep coma, with spasmodic and occasionally suspended respiration, which continued eight hours, during which time his life was despaired of. He then recovered.

Mushroom Poisoning.

Our correspondent, Dr. Cheney, to whom we are under obligation for the article in this number of the JOURNAL on "Mushroom Poisoning," will find an elaborate and valuable paper on the subject, written by Dr. T. M. Logan, in the number of our journal for May, 1868.

PACIFIC

MEDICAL AND SURGICAL JOURNAL.

VOL. V.—SEPTEMBER, 1871.—No. 52.

ORIGINAL COMMUNICATIONS.

A Defense of Physic, with Special Reference to the Fair Trial.

BY C. F. BUCKLEY, B.A., M.D., San Francisco.

From a variety of unusual circumstances, and the many strange, if not startling, developments that transpired during it, the *cause célèbre*, which has recently so preoccupied the public mind of California and the United States generally—the trial of Laura D. Fair for the murder of A. P. Crittenden—bids fair to be regarded as one of the most important public prosecutions in the criminal annals of the civilized world; and it must be admitted, that the more closely we examine its details, the more fully do we become convinced of its legitimate claims to all the importance attached to it by the community. Apart from a few well-known trials for political conspiracies, we believe there is no other trial on record which has raked up, for serious consideration, more of the novel and embarrassing social problems of its time. The questions, How far the science of the Troubadours—the recitation of verses—may be made available for *charming* juries into verdicts, in "practical America?"—How far the ideas and habits of thought of a class of the community which, if not large or influential, is certainly clamorous and obtrusive, by no means scouted as criminal by society at large, and in many cases may, and actually does, assume the garb of respectability, should be allowed to take practical shape in our midst, and what measures, if any, society should adopt to protect itself against its aggressions?—To what extent medical testimony should be accepted and utilized in unraveling some medico-legal difficulties in courts of justice?—all clearly forced upon us by this trial—are, of themselves, sufficient to establish its fame.

Of these problems, the first is yet scarcely ripe for discussion; but from the *success* here attendant on it, it may be well worth the consideration of our friends of the junior bar. The second, though of the very first importance to social reformers and every well-meaning member of society, is, happily, alien to our present object; but, having lived for some time in other lands, we may be permitted to state, that the labors of the advocates of "Free Love"—notoriously the odious and repulsive sheet of Woodhull and Claflin—have brought more discredit on American society, have degraded us more in the eyes of Europe, than all the excesses our roughs and rowdies and desperadoes can accomplish.

The third problem—the only one with which we are at present concerned—though of somewhat less scope than the preceding, will nevertheless be found to have very extensive ramifications throughout the social system, affecting the happiness and *status* of numberless families, as well as the direct issue of life or death to a great many individuals. The Courts of Probate and Chancery, as well as the Criminal Courts, are deeply concerned as to the legitimate sphere and value of medical testimony coming constantly before them; and the community, as well as the Courts, have a right to know wherein they may be benefited, or the contrary, by it. The question is clearly too comprehensive for discussion in a single article; but, while only drawing attention to the particular manifestations of it in the above case, we hesitate not to indorse, to the full, the remark of a recent writer in the *American Law Review:* "That it is not the expert medical testimony which is so faulty, as the manner of obtaining it." It may be safely added, that, in many instances of doctors in the Law Courts, there is no expert knowledge at all; and this is notoriously the case in questions involving insanity, for unless they have been specially attending maladies of this class, doctors know just as much about it as other men.

Before proceeding directly to the medical testimony in the Fair case, we may be excused for referring to some remarks bearing severely on the profession of Medicine in general. Of course, the members of our profession know too well their own power and usefulness; they feel too deeply the shortcomings of their resources, and have too much of the every-day practical sense of intelligent mankind, to feel aggrieved at the declamations of an advocate, however able. But when a man is so silly as to step out of his way to denounce a whole profession commanding the respect of the civilized world, because a few persons coming before him stultify themselves; is so profound in the ways of logic, and so conversant with modern research, as to claim that medical testimony is valueless in insanity, because physicians *did not study Metaphysics in the Middle Ages;* so excessively careful of his assertions, as to tell an intelligent jury, the public, the world, that so well-known a character as John Locke was not a physician, while all his biographers tell us to the contrary; and in face of the discoveries of Lavoisier, and Volta, and Wollaston, and Graham, and Liebig, with which the average school-boy is acquainted, asserts that there is no science in Medicine, we ought to feel about as much disturbed by his efforts, as the eagle in his flight by the chirping of a cock-sparrow. When, however, we remember that, with the masses, the aphorism, "Doctors differ," is still solely confined to members of the medical profession; when Mr. Lecky, with all his wonderful research, and profound logic, and general impartiality, tells the world in his "History of Morals," that, if Medicine were cultivated with quarter the assiduity and talent devoted to Engineering, the triumphs of the former would be tenfold what they now are; when a man of the intellectual calibre of the late Lord Brougham expresses an opinion which has been construed into a total want of confidence in medical testimony in Law Courts; and, above all, when we observe that here in our midst, *twelve* of our most intelligent and respectable citizens, against whom the suspicion of bias was rendered an utter impossibility, deliver a verdict diametrically opposed to the *verdict* of *four* physicians, it becomes us to inquire a little into causes—to see if no misapprehensions leading to misstatements exist; for we know that the latter, persistently reiterated, pass current for truth.

That "doctors differ," is a proposition which it would be simple folly to seek to controvert, and that medical doctors are ridiculously prone to dissension, we freely admit; but why the general assertion should be so long and so extensively regarded as applicable only to medical doctors, is to us incomprehensible. Is it not approaching the libelous, not to accord to our fellow-doctors of the theological stripe a fair average amount of propensity in this direction? and is it not perfectly open to question whether Law herself can completely abolish the predilection of her doctors for an occasional ramble into the domains of "Difference?" It is unnecessary to say that we have no reference whatever to the exhilarating quarrels and laudable efforts of our advocates, whose duty it is to differ. Here diversity of opinions and diversity of arguments to maintain them, are exactly what we look for, what we pay for, and, according to the extent of resource, in which we calculate ability. But when we glance at the grave and learned men who preside over the legal tribunals of the civilized world—the great, shining lights of the legal system—whose decisions are as the torches that must guide their less pretentious brethren through its dark labyrinths, and whose duty it is emphatically to agree, what do we find? Perfect unanimity of opinion? Alas for human frailty!—nothing of the kind. Like all ordinary doctors, they differ, too, and this in matters that apparently dwarf into utter insignificance before the short-comings of Physic and Divinity. If any of our readers doubt the fact, we beg to remind them of the celebrated Yelverton trial, a few years ago, in England, where, in a simple compact of matrimony, two of the Law Lords declared the proceeding valid, while three others held the contrary opinion; and of the still more recent Legal-tender case in the Supreme Court of the United States, where seven (we believe that is the number) of the highest legal authorities in the land were opposed in opinion to four of their peers, and thus set aside a decision which had a majority on a former occasion. The most curious feature, however, is, that the laws which those gentlemen are called upon to study and propound, and in which they so commonly hold opinions diametrically opposed, are simply the handiwork of man—the trivial emanations of his brain—commensurate with his finite power and littleness; while those which we are so rudely stigmatized for holding different views upon, are the delicate, intricate fashionings of the Almighty, and proportionate to his Omnipotence, Infinity, and Universality.

On reading over Mr. Lecky's remarks, the thought then uppermost in my mind was the futility of human efforts to grasp all knowledge. Some writer (we believe Mr. Lecky himself somewhere advances the same idea) has said, that the works of the greatest men are merely the reflex of the popular sentiment of their time; and certainly, if the general proposition be correct, and if Mr. Lecky, earnest and painstaking inquirer as he is, so thoroughly conversant with every subject which he undertakes to discuss, so little given to assertions without the ablest arguments in their support, has in other matters as faithfully followed the current of popular opinion as in this, his claims to a high place among the great are eminently secure. We are, however, far from being convinced of the correctness of the popular opinion on this subject, and, consequently, with extreme deference, question the soundness of Mr. Lecky's view. The nature of the subject necessarily forbids its discussion in a general article; but before any candid and impartial tribunal, that contrasts the labors that have led to the highest triumphs of engineering, with those involved in the discoveries of our Hunter and Bichat and Bernhard and Beale and Richardson and Virchow, and legions of others nowise inferior, we fear not a favorable decision; and if, for a moment, our censor had ever reflected on the fact, that there is scarcely, throughout the varied ramifications of engineering, a single principle of action, whether in mechanics, hydraulics, pneumatics, or optics, which has not been successfully adapted to the requirements of the healing art, and had also duly weighed the difficulties surrounding the study of medicine (above all of which peers the sacredness of human life), it is to us unintelligible how so strange and partial an opinion could have been delivered to the world.

Of the quality and extent of the labor involved in the cultivation of medicine, we may be permitted to cite one or two examples of men who devoted some time to other pursuits as well. We shall take Cuvier, in the last century, and Virchow, in this. Every person familiar with his biography knows that the great labor of Cuvier's life was the cultivation of one branch of medical science, namely: Comparative anatomy; yet in his "hours of idleness"—in the mere intervals of relaxation from his favorite pursuit—he planned and executed, in France, public works of a character which, up to that time, were admitted on all hands to be unequaled in his country as monuments of engineering skill. Virchow—a man well known throughout the civilized world as an able investigator of disease, but better known in Prussia as one of her most laborious statesmen, and one of the best informed and most powerful debaters in her Senate—a short time since assured his medical brethren, that to him the labors of State—his well-considered and able efforts for his country's weal, in the most critical period of her history—were "a source of complete relaxation, as compared with the more onerous and more exhausting demands of Science."

But it is really a work of the veriest supererogation to seek to defend the medical profession against such charges as that advanced by Mr. Lecky, while two of the three chief blessings of modern civilization—telegraphy and photography, whose history is so intimately connected with the incidental labors of physic—are everywhere shedding their benign influences around, to repel it.

Before receiving the opinion of the late Lord Brougham as adverse to medical testimony in general, two considerations of more or less importance should influence our decision: 1st, the character of Lord Brougham himself, and, 2d, the character of the medical testimony then coming before the Courts over which his Lordship presided. It is true that Lord Brougham held an unusually pre-eminent position among the great intellects of Europe for many years previous to his death, but it should not be forgotten that it was much more owing to his general acquirement and cultivation than to any legal ability or originality of any character. Indeed, he never was regarded as a great lawyer, and his countrymen universally recognize the fact that he was particularly addicted to what are technically known as "crotchets;" so much so, indeed, that it would be impossible to find in the biographies of this century a character who so closely resembles that of Dr. Johnson, whose views on questions of public policy or social dynamics have long since become a by-word, and only remain as a standing admonition against our placing too much reliance on the utterances of even the acknowledged "leaders of thought."

The second consideration, however, viz.: the condition of the medical profession in England at the time this opinion was delivered, is of much more importance; and after duly examining the position, it will be found that it would be just as erroneous in a Judge to deduce any inference of a general character from the medical testimony of a half-dozen "great" doctors, taken at random from the pages of the local press, as to generalize on the intrinsic value of such testimony from the so-called "medical experts" coming commonly before the British Courts in Lord Brougham's time. Up to 1858, matters relating to the medical profession were precisely what they are here now. Any young or old man of sufficient enterprise, whose inclination so led him, could "hang out his shingle" without at all undergoing the fatigues or incurring the expenses attendant on special study. There was no such thing as a door-way of entry: the "smart" man could drive in his "coach-and-four." Up to that time, in the United Kingdom, "success"—not in investigating or staying the ravages of disease, not in acquiring and applying what science and educated experience have side by side taught us for the preservation of human life, but in noisy self-assertion, and the consequent accumulation of wealth—was regarded as the sole standard of skill, the chief guarantee of knowledge; and consequently against the opinions of Sir Astley Cooper, or Addison, or Bright, that of the most ignorant and clamorous charlatan in the realm might have been paraded with success before juries. So here, now, with the "discerning public," what value would the testimony of the quiet, unknown student of medical science, whose paraphernalia consisted of a scalpel and a book, no matter how deeply learned in the mysteries of his craft, be held at, when compared with that of the *illustrious* individual who has accumulated a fortune by a little petty legerdemain, either in the wonderful beauties of embalming, or peddling bottles of physic all through the State at a dollar each, while nominally assuming the benevolent character of giving "advice *gratis*," or in manipulating corrupt Legislatures to obtain grants for special hospitals for private ends? That the medical testimony generally coming before the Courts in this country is deplorably inferior to that which obtains in Europe at the present time, few will dispute; yet even there it is by no means what it should be. For many years past the physicians of the United Kingdom, humiliated by the ignorance and presumption of many of its members from time to time in the Law Courts, have been almost unanimously demanding legislative reform in this respect. They are, thus far, ineffectually beseeching of the law-makers to create the special degree of "Doctor in Jurisprudence and Public Health," to be conferred only on persons who showed a competent knowledge of both those subjects to entitle them to it; men who would be "medical experts" not in mere name, but in reality; whose opinions would inevitably be fair exponents of the medical knowledge of their time, and solvers of many difficulties alike embarrassing to Judges, juries, and the public.

Turning now to the medical testimony in the trial of Mrs. Fair, our first feeling is the impossibility of referring to it without being severe. The "logic of events" has fully decided its merits; the public voice has long since doomed it; the decision of the jury directly killed it, and the reputed beauties of embalming, even with the sacrifice of $2,100, have not been able to preserve its purity or prevent its offending the public nostril. But as it has been extensively paraded as "expert medical testimony," and so regarded as a standard of value for medical testimony in general, it becomes us to allude to it a little more in detail. We might premise, that every medical man of our acquaintance had no other feeling at the time, than one of extreme humiliation and disgust at the shameless ignorance, or, still more inexcusable, prostitution of medical science which was exhibited throughout the whole proceeding,* and undoubted relief at the just, proper, and correct conclusion arrived at by the jury.

We omit altogether comment on that part of the testimony which threw actual doubt on the cause of death, viz.: that the *mortification* of the bowels, found on *post-mortem* examination, might *have existed while Mr. Crittenden was yet pleading in Court* during the day of the fatal shooting. The idea is so preposterous, so opposed to the universal, unexceptional experience of medical men, who invariably find persons laboring under this form of trouble "doubled up,"

* We except with great pleasure the evidence of Drs. Douglass and Sawyer.

dying in bed, that we can only attribute its utterance to some general form of mental disturbance, which seemed to have been epidemic during this trial. Probably the most attractive and refreshing piece of medical evidence in the whole proceeding, is that of a gentleman who calls himself a "specialist," as it assuredly is that containing most *new light.* From him, who, it appears, has devoted much time, and, as we are assured, no little of the public money—both of which, it is only fair to state, might have been expended otherwise with more advantage to the community—we learn that diseases of the womb are the "only functional diseases that *produce anemia.*" To our brethren elsewhere, and to ourselves, who have been in the habit of regarding anemia as the most common predisposing cause of womb complaint, this will certainly be a rude shock; yet we have no doubt this oracle, who stated on oath that "one-third of the females who suffer from uterine complaint are mad"—which would give at least THREE THOUSAND female lunatics to Stockton from this cause alone—will one day favor the world with a satisfactory explanation. All physiologists, up to the present, are agreed that the lungs, liver, kidneys, and spleen, are the blood-making, blood-modifying organs, and that the womb has a special function to perform in procreation; but, no doubt, their ideas are antiquated and exploded! The diseases of the blood-making, blood-changing organs have now no influence in producing that profound *change* of the blood known as anemia; uterine disease alone effects the change! So saith the oracle on oath!

To this it would be no unnatural sequence, and our friends elsewhere may at any time learn the *fact* from a California specialist, that the liver is the organ chiefly concerned in the procreation of the species! But the *grotesquerie* of this gentleman's evidence does not stop here. We love to linger with specialism of this character; but we fear the general reader can not duly appreciate the causes of our "affinity" until he is informed that we, too, have been at one time devoted to the study of insanity, and have taken no little interest in its peculiar features; and we, consequently, feel constrained to admit, that when we observe an individual ascending the witness' stand, gazing around and stating, that from Mrs. Fair's appearance he should conclude "she was just the sort of person likely to have such spells," *i. e.*, hysterical insanity, we are afflicted with an ardent curiosity to follow him a little more closely, for much, indeed, may be learned by the student here. The belief in the insanity of our neighbors is, at all times, a symptom of evil omen, and *special* study is a dangerous toil.

It is with extreme reluctance we touch on the evidence of Drs. Lyford and Trask. Our only feeling on reading it was one of profound astonishment, that they did not more thoroughly *prepare* their subject, considering the importance of the issue at stake. That before and after the trial they were deplorably ignorant of insanity and every thing therewith connected, needs not the slightest proof on our part. They have themselves proved it beyond all question. But that, with such time as they had to devote to the subject, apart altogether from any inducement, and with their undisguised efforts to establish insanity in the case, they should have, as far as in them lay, established the very contrary—which fact the prosecution was apparently too independent to notice—is to our mind bordering very closely on the marvelous. Of course, their testimony related chiefly to the culprit's condition during her sojourn in the jail-cell, and to prove their "insane" theory herein, they dwell specifically on these facts only: First, her biting the tumbler; second, the contraction of the pupil; third, her constantly lying down, doing nothing, but occasionally reading the newspaper.

The first and second of these became at one time almost the levers of deliverance, and from both sides of the house received an importance which only a complete ignorance of their value could inspire; for, so far from all three going to prove the presence of insanity, as far as any three symptoms could go, they establish the very contrary. We know of only one form of insanity in which a lunatic would be at all likely to bite glasses presented to him—viz., suicidal mania—and none of the attending gentlemen pretend to assert that this was present. If they dared to assert it, the facts would contradict them. To the uninitiated, it may now seem wonderful to learn that the "contraction of the pupil," so constantly set forth as *the* index of insanity, is really a most forcible argument against it; yet such is the fact, laid down by all the eminent authorities on the subject, the common daily experience of alienist physicians, and supported by the general observation of mankind, with whom the "wild, steady gaze of the lunatic" is almost proverbial—which "wild gaze" is due to no other cause than the *dilatation* of the pupil. The "lying down" is also strong corroborative proof of the absence of insanity; for the victim of acute mania—which is the only form of insanity from which there could be so rapid a recovery as occurred in this case—is emphatically never "lying down," unless completely overcome by exhaustion and sleep. On the contrary, he is invariably found "standing up," groping and fidgeting round his apartment, busily in search of some imaginary object. *Reading* the paper in *acute mania* is simply out of the question; it is as near an impossibility as any thing in medicine.

But apart altogether from what "retained" physicians or specialists have said on this subject, it is but simple justice to examine dispassionately the broad facts of the case, and see what grounds it legitimately presents for the plea of Mrs. Fair's insanity.

Monomania on the subject of matrimony was advanced, and dwelt on with some slight plausibility, by the defense, as an evidence of a "mind diseased." It is a theory which, though apparently not affecting the issue, should by no means be lost sight of, for reasons hereafter to be alluded to. It is very unfortunate for the sustaining of it that Mrs. Fair herself should have been examined, for her testimony is completely subversive of it. She says in one moment that she *is* Mr. C.'s wife, and in the next that "she *considered* herself so, and he *considered* her so, too." To the *monomaniac*, there would be no second thought about the matter—no "*considering*" of the subject whatsoever; it would be an absolute, fixed reality of the altered reason, explicable, if at all, on reasons summoned up from the phantom world of the deranged imagination, and totally beyond the reach of our common ken. But Mrs. Fair further *explains* why she *considered* herself the wife of Mr. C.: "because she believed God created only one person for another." The reason may not appear perfectly satisfactory to Mr. Brigham Young, or several of our less pretentious Gentile friends, but it is unquestionably a natural, though a fearfully corrupt, explanation for endeavoring to justify an unrecognized state of existence, and one to which many a profligate spirit has recourse, and seeks to derive consolation from in his abandonment.

It is well known that no two persons are ever afflicted with insanity of a precisely similar character. True, a dozen different persons in an asylum may be all kings or queens at the same time, yet all from widely different causes; but this *one* interpretation of the Divine will, this constant effort to reconcile our vicious habits with factitious laws of Providence, is so prevalent among the abandoned and criminal classes, that, if insanity at all, it must be regarded as epidemic insanity (hitherto unknown). It would be quite as just to attribute all forms of crime to monomania—a theory, too, not wanting advocates, but which civilized communities must yet discard—as accuse Mrs. Fair of it in this instance. Her reasoning is clearly the reasoning of viciousness, not madness, throughout; and her whole conduct, in endeavoring to have a divorce effected between Mr. Crittenden and his wife, demonstrates most clearly that she herself did *not* really believe in the "celestial marriage," which, if arising from monomania, would be a fixed, unaltered idea—a belief that no reasoning could subvert—a belief that would have caused her actually to reject, with scorn and indignation, any other form of matrimony if proposed to her. We dwell on this the more, because, if monomania of any kind had been established, it should beyond all question rid her of all responsibility for the crime committed, though the crime may be in no wise connected with the special phase of insanity previously manifested; for, at the present time, monomania is almost universally regarded as only a particular expression, intensified in this particular direction, of a general mental disturbance—a condition in which any morbid impulse, suicidal and homicidal especially, is very liable to supervene at any moment.

Hysteric and impulsive, or moral, insanity are jumbled together in almost hopeless confusion by the medical testimony; yet all the authorities on the subject divide them, and there can scarcely be a difference of opinion as to the judiciousness of the practice. Let us, then, first take the theory of hysteric mania, and we find it, also, on all sides surrounded by insuperable difficulties of its own. There is no history of any previous attack, which should naturally be expected under the circumstances; the periodic monthly change was *not* present at the time, though it is the rule that it should be when the paroxysm of hysterical mania is directly connected with menstruation. We are, however, told that in this case it was suppressed for "eleven days," of which, unfortunately, there is no evidence whatever, save the dictum of a man who does not profess to keep a record of the lady's menstruation—the best way of ascertaining to a certainty that such did exist—but establishes an undying fame by pointing out the identity of *suppressed menstruation* and *retrocedent gout!* But granting, for a moment, that this suppressed menstruation really existed—which it is quite unreasonable from the evidence to assume—we are singularly curious to discern its bearing on the subject, and we can really see none, save the efforts of a benighted mind to explain a diabolical act. If the so-called suppressed menstruation, supposing it to exist, really gave rise to hysteric mania, surely we ought to find this hysteric mania; but in vain do we look for the traces of its manifestation. It is usually, indeed, a singularly innocent form of insanity. Mere rambling, incoherent absurdity (so to speak), a greater desire to display mischief than actual injury to any body, its invasion and departure are never instantaneous, and a history of one violent, without any previous, attack, is utterly unknown. We do not wish to assert that such is an impossibility, but it is decidedly contrary to the published experience of the matter, as well as our own.

The ground of hysteric insanity is further rendered totally untenable by the preparation for the event, proven in this case, and by the reason advanced immediately after the perpetration of the act. We believe few alienist physicians will doubt that, if Mrs. Fair had labored under an outbreak of hysteric mania at the moment of the shooting, the shot would never have been fired, because it is almost a certainty that in her altered mental condition, at that exact moment, she would have totally forgotten that she had a pistol on her person. If suffering at all from this form of excitement, the probability is infinitely greater that she would have jumped up and seized either Mr. C. or his wife by the hair, and would unquestionably never have given so coherent and natural a cause, as that of "her child's and her own ruin," for the commission of the deed, immediately after.

We are, then, finally reduced to the theory of impulsive insanity ; and it is certainly the only one that bears at all on it the impress of plausibility — the only one advanced that can bear a single moment's rational investigation. No matter what the relations existing between Mr. Crittenden and Mrs. Fair were — call it infatuation, lust, or love — it is quite sufficient for us to know that such did exist, apparently, in their usual warmth and strength of character, a few hours, at furthest, before the fatal moment, as evidenced by the kissing and embracing on Mrs. Marillier's stairs, before his departure for the ferry-boat, although she knew then quite well that he was going to see his wife; and it certainly does seem — without regarding the subject very closely — nothing else than morbid impulse in her to openly and deliberately shoot down the man whom, an hour before, she so tenderly embraced.

Nor, in order to explode this theory, is it sufficent to show that she had previously made violent threats, and bought a pistol to give force to her threats. It is quite evident, from her character, that simple braggadocio alone, without any ulterior object, is amply sufficient to explain those facts, and moreover there are many cases on record where persons, while laboring under morbid impulse, have perpetrated crimes of a similar character, with all the semblance of the maturest deliberation. A case occurred in England, some two years ago, where two men traveled together a good deal on foot, always sleeping together in various inns at night. One night, however, they both happened to lie down by the roadside, and during the night one dashed out the other's brains. Here was, to all appearances, most distinct premeditation: a manifest watching for an opportunity. The murderer was accordingly tried, found guilty, and sentenced to death. Happily, while lodged in prison awaiting the time of execution, the prisoner suffered from a genuine fit of epilepsy, which was succeeded by unmistakable mental derangement; and, from this fact, it was very justly concluded by the medical officer in charge, that the same condition may have existed at the time of the murder, which, taken in connection with the absence of any satisfactory motive, induced the Home Secretary to commute the sentence.

Numbers of other cases may be cited, wherein the most matured deliberation appeared to exist; and one of peculiar interest to the writer may not be unworthy of mention. From time to time, he was a good deal solicited by a young gentleman under his care in an asylum, to be allowed to sit next to him at dinner. When this request was complied with, on the very first occasion, while engaged in carving, he happened to observe his patient grasp his knife very firmly, and change color several times. Accordingly, he called his name, "Alfred," pretty audibly, and the knife literally dropped from the latter's hand, as though he were galvanized, and he immediately burst into tears. On being questioned, after dinner, as to the meaning of his demeanor, at that particular time, he replied: "I wanted to kill you, just at that moment, and probably would have done so, only that your voice recalled me to my senses. My God! what should I do, if I had done you any harm!" Here again, was apparently premeditation, of the most cunning character: an effort to obtain a suitable position, with suitable means, for accomplishing his purpose. But, in reality, there was nothing of the kind, for this poor imbecile bore no trace of animosity against the writer, never exhibited aught else than the most childish affection for him, and could have satisfied no fixed desire whatsoever by the accomplishment of his purpose.

Apparent preparation and premeditation, then, are clearly not at all conclusive of the absence of the homicidal impulse; neither would the threats by Mrs. Fair, nor her purchasing a pistol previously, convince us that she did not suffer from such a condition at the time. There are, however, other circumstances connected with her whole conduct which, beyond the least doubt, satisfy us that no morbid or insane impulse existed at the time, not even the "semi-consciousness" of one medical witness. 1st. There is no history whatever of any form of mental derangement—with some form of which homicidal impulse is most commonly associated—prior to the exact moment of the fatal occurrence; but there *is* a very decided history of unusual willfulness and boldness. 2d. She gives a perfectly sane, intelligible, and coherent, if not satisfactory, reason for the perpetration of the act, which would be an utter impossibility in case a merely homicidal impulse dictated her action: she would have completely forgotten what impelled her thereto, and instead of justifying the deed, she would be, in all probability, overwhelmed with the deepest remorse instantaneously. 3d. Above all, had this morbid impulse existed, as claimed, there certainly would have been no continuance of the insanity for a lengthened period afterward—there would have been none; not a *scintilla* of the "glass-biting;" none of those wild expressions of desire to "go to *his* funeral;" and, in this latter fact, which was proven by the defense, it is utterly impossible not to see a perfectly connected train of thought, from beginning to end, totally incompatible with the theory of insanity.

We have already shown that the physical symptoms in jail, as sworn to by the defense, were of themselves opposed to the existence of mania. Taking, then, the three points just referred to in relation to the homicidal impulse, together with the evident proven preparations, stern justice compels us to say that nowhere can we find a *scintilla* of evidence to support the theory of Mrs. Fair's insanity in any direction. While, on the other hand, we remember her fierce, unwomanly nature, which all the evidence prominently displayed; with what uncontrolled, unbridled violence she ever gave loose rein to her passions; and, also, bear in mind that insanity, in any person who has ever been sane, is essentially a *change of character*, it is impossible to forego the conclusion, with Hamlet—if we may be excused for a brief quotation on a subject whereon so much poetry has already been lavished—that "she was but mad north-northwest; when the wind was southerly, she knew a hawk from a hand-saw." Still more accurately does Mark Antony describe the situation, when he says to his favorite:

> "You have been a-boggler ever.
> But when we in our viciousness grow hard
> (Oh, misery on't!) the wise gods seal our eyes,
> In our own filth drop our clear judgments, make us
> Adore our errors, laugh at us while we strut to our confusion."

In conclusion, though we are fully aware of the defects of medical science, and the inadequacy of its resources to supply positive and definite evidence in many of the cases involving it before the Courts, yet we are perfectly fearless in asserting that in many other cases it can distinctly do so; and, further, that in all cases of medico-legal difficulties, the services of physicians may be rendered infinitely more valuable than they are now reputed to be. "It is not," we repeat, "medical testimony that is so much at fault as the manner of obtaining it;" and it is the bounden duty of the makers and administrators of the law to look squarely at the defects of the present system and correct them, instead of eternally caviling about "doctors in Courts." For example, in a case of doubtful insanity, is it just that the opinion of yesterday's purchaser of a diploma should be paraded before juries as an "expert opinion," against that of a man who has spent a life-time engaged in its special study? And yet, what legal provision is there to prevent such a course?

Again, we ask, is it just to the community or to the medical profession, that such men as the two leading medical witnesses, neither of whom, avowedly, had ever been connected with the management of the insane, and who were consequently unable, even if willing, to detect a case of dexterous "shamming," should be the sole observers of a prisoner arraigned for the highest crime known to the law, whose only defense was insanity, and in whom insanity appeared for the first time *after* the crime was committed? We can only add, that, if greater medical ability were combined in this case with the willingness displayed to effect it, even despite the astounding eloquence of our local legal Troubadour, the result of the trial would, in all probability, have been alike discreditable to the jurisprudence of the State and country, and dangerous to the morals and safety of society.

On the Treatment of Uterine Affections.

Read before the San Francisco Medical Society, by JOHN SCOTT, M.D., F.R.C.S. Ireland, Surgeon to the California Women's Hospital.

I think it must be generally admitted, that while gynecology has made great advances, of late years, in the diagnosis of special lesions and the reflex disturbances they occasion, it has accomplished comparatively little toward the establishment of such a system of "uterine therapeutics" as will enable us to treat successfully the majority of the cases which daily come before us. For a long time the only armament deemed necessary in the treatment of uterine diseases consisted of a speculum, a stick of caustic, and a pessary. Even at the present day, they constitute almost the entire "stock in trade" of a large number of practitioners; and if, unfortunately, they are found not quite so efficient as they were deemed, either the patient is considered incapable of judging when she is cured, or the disease itself is regarded as totally incurable. This style of practice has come to be considered empirical, and justly so; but have we, in reality, got much beyond the idea which was uppermost in the minds of those who resorted to it?

Our instrumentation may have become more elegant and our appliances more varied, but when we come to estimate solid results, in the shape of unmistakable cures, are we not forced to confess that in too many instances our expectations are very far from being realized? Putting aside cystic or other degenerations of the ovaries, fibroid and malignant disease of the uterus, what is the character of five-sixths of the female ailments which demand the exercise of our skill for their removal? Roughly summed up, they come under the head of erosions, endometritis, peri-metritis and para-metritis, cellulitis, induration, hypertrophy, prolapsus, and flexions. Looking back over a past experience, how many of these cases have we absolutely cured? how many, after the exercise of all our skill and patience, have settled down into a state of chronic invalidism for life? and, alas, how many have we not only not benefited, but actually injured, by the use of remedies daily vaunted as both safe and judicious, while in fact they are really neither?

The truth must be told, and the sooner the better: we have no system of uterine therapeutics, built on a rational or scientific basis, to guide us, and our attempts at medication are, at best, but the embodiment of the dictates of a rational empiricism. Clearly, our pathology must be grievously at fault, or our practice would not be so varied and contradictory. Take, for instance, a simple erosion of the os, attended with a discharge of a benign, or an irritating, character, and the chief indication seems to be, the arrest of the discharge and the healing of the so-called ulceration. Having accomplished this result by persistent local applications to the abraded surface, have we restored our patient to health? Let extensive cicatrices of the os, indurations and hypertrophies, with perhaps pelvic inflammations, local pains, and general ill health tell their own tale; and we shall too often find, that for a comparatively simple affection, one much more serious and vastly more intractable has been substituted.

Endometritis—whether acute or chronic—ranks next in frequency; and as a tough, stringy discharge, proceeding from the uterine canal, is considered pathognomic of the affection, we have the term applied to a numerous class of cases of greatly differing importance. Looked upon by some as simple catarrh of the uterus, and considered as amenable to treatment as a similar affection of the throat and nasal passages, by others it is regarded as one of the most formidable and unmanageable of uterine maladies, and justifying a resort to the use of the most radical means for its removal. The removal of the obnoxious discharges being considered the *sine qua non* of success, astringents, caustics, escharotics, and injections into the cavity are in turn resorted to or abandoned, praised or condemned, equally without reason or discrimination, and with much the same result. Happy the man who, having simply failed to meet the reward of his well-meant efforts to cure, is not obliged to charge himself with the production of pelvic complications of the gravest nature: the too frequent consequences of a reckless tampering with an organ, the absolute integrity of which is so essential to woman's well-being, both physically and mentally.

Flexions—the *opprobia medicinæ* of the present day—next demand our attention, not only from the frequency with which they are met, but from the now acknowledged fact that, if not actually causing, they are found in connection with untold bodily and mental suffering, and that a large number of them (especially retroversions) are found irremovable during the entire menstrual life of the sufferer. The frequency and the importance of these lesions being so apparent, is it creditable to us, in this latter half of the nineteenth century, that we are forced to confess our utter inability successfully to cope with them? and that *relief*, only, in the shape of mechanical support to a diseased and weakened organ, in the form of a pessary, is all we have to offer? That relief from prominent symptoms is occasionally afforded in cases where the uterus is free from adhesions, and that an occasional conception may so alter the nutrition of the organ as to restore its integrity, I freely admit; but at what a cost are these very rare results obtained! How often does it happen that, parturition over, the displacement recurs, more markedly than before; how numerous the cases where pelvic inflammation, abscess, or perforation is the result of continued mechanical pressure; how indefinite the period during which a pessary must be worn; and, after all, how utterly incapable of effecting by it the restoration of the organ to its natural position, and retaining it there, while it leaves untouched the cause of the displacement itself!

A word now as to prolapsus, the treatment of which, as laid down by systematic writers, is both uncertain and unsatisfactory. A ruptured perineum, a capacious pelvis, relaxation of the ligaments, are, one and all, assigned as the great predisposing causes of prolapsus; and, in consonance with these views, the perineum is restored or the vagina narrowed by plastic operations, for the purpose of relegating the organ to its normal position and retaining it there. At first, all goes well, and the object seems accomplished; but time — which proves all things — eventually demonstrates that we have only substituted a retroflexion for a prolapsus, thus proving the unsoundness of the reasoning on which the practice was based.

Of indurations and hypertrophies, I need say nothing more than that the treatment laid down for them is as varied as it is inefficacious and disappointing.

In thus hastily glancing at the present unsatisfactory condition of uterine therapeutics, and the perplexities which beset the humble inquirer after truth, I have for my object the attempt to indicate, that, in the majority of female ailments, it is possible to trace the existence of a common pathology, and, as a logical deduction, to found on it a simpler, more uniform, and more successful method of treatment. However we may differ as to the causation of the different affections I have enumerated, I think the profession will be unanimous in admitting that congestion is a marked feature in all, and that the removal of this congestion—or accompanying inflammation—must form an essential feature in any treatment which is to prove successful.

How best to effect the removal of uterine congestion—or chronic inflammation—is, I believe, the problem to solve; and hoping to contribute something toward the accomplishment of this object, I venture to lay before my brethren a mode of treatment which, while it has not the charm of novelty to recommend it, has in my hands given me the most gratifying results. We are all familiar with the good effects produced by the judicious application of leeches to a congested or inflamed uterus; and, but a short time ago, Dr. A. Meadows, of London, detailed a case of retroversion, in which a single application, resulting in a smart hemorrhage, not only removed the displacement, but cured the patient. The result was as fortunate as it was unexpected; but we are aware, at the same time, that it is impossible to circumscribe or control the effects of leeching, and that its repeated use is often attended with the most unpleasant consequences. To prove effectual in the removal of long-standing or obstinate disease, repeated applications would be required; but while in one application the amount of blood drawn may be trifling, in another it is so profuse as to seriously weaken and alarm the patient; and it too frequently happens that the congestion, which seems to succeed their application, renders nugatory their beneficial effect. This has been my experience, but, believing that the principle was a sound one, I resorted, subsequently, to free scarification of the os, with marked, but only temporary benefit. Proceeding farther, I found that in cases of engorgement, by hypertrophy and subinvolution, the cautious scarification of the cervical canal to a depth of about two lines, and followed by the immediate application of tincture of iodine to the track of the incisions, was productive of the happiest effects; and I can now point to many cases where the absorption of hypertrophied tissue and complete recovery was the result. The practice has, however, its drawbacks and its limits. A smart hemorrhage occasionally takes place some days afterward; and when such complications as pelvic adhesions exist, the use of the knife is precluded. Under these circumstances, I felt as if I had got, in common parlance, "to the length of my tether," when the following case occurred, to illustrate the benefit and the safety of the practice I have since so extensively adopted. Some twelve months ago I was consulted by an unmarried woman, aged thirty-five years, for frequent suppression of the catamenia, attended with local pains, occasional edema of one leg, severe headaches, and frequent vomitings, with loss of appetite and general ill-health. When I first saw her, she had not menstruated for seven weeks, and, on examination, I found the uterus partially anteflexed and hypertrophied, but perfectly movable in all directions. Desirous of bringing on the catamenia before instituting further treatment, I inserted, without the slightest difficulty, a medium-sized sponge-tent, and, as she had no pain whatever during its application, I allowed it to remain in till the following day. Its withdrawal was followed by a hemorrhagic discharge; but on my visit next day, I learned that she had had a severe rigor, followed by fever, and intense pain over the hypogastric region, with retention of urine. Acute metritis had set in, and, on examination, I found the uterus greatly enlarged and intensely tender to the touch, especially the front wall, which was very prominent. Chagrined beyond measure at such an untoward result, and anxious to prevent, if possible, the extension of the inflammation to the peritoneum and cellular tissue, I ventured, on the spur of the moment, to plunge a small exploratory trocar into the parenchyma of the front wall of the cervix obliquely upward. A gush of serum followed it, and the patient declared herself instantly free from pain. A second puncture the following day, and a few doses of opium, effected the complete resolution of the attack, which would otherwise have clearly entailed the most serious consequences and a prolonged illness.

Encouraged by these results, I determined to try the effects of puncture in well-marked chronic engorgements. I adopted a similar practice, but substituted for the trocar a small lancet which I had inserted in a handle for the purpose. I at first used a blade which was much too narrow to enable me to deplete the organ effectually, but I afterward changed it for the one which I now show you, and which resembles a bleeding-lancet, but is only half the breadth, has a well tempered point, and a fine cutting edge. I am fully aware that in puncturing the cervix with a lancet, for the purpose of reducing engorgement by local depletion, I can lay no claim to originality, for it has been done by several before me; but what I do lay claim to is the carrying out this treatment persistently and consecutively, and with results for which I was totally unprepared by previous reading or experience, and which I have since verified to a degree which leaves on my mind no doubt whatever of the exceeding value of the treatment. From the first the benefit has been most marked, both locally and generally, and my two colleagues in the Woman's Hospital can bear testimony to the truth of my statements. The diminution of engorgement, the absortion of hypertrophied tissue, and the healing of erosions, with relief to local pains and the improvement of the general health, are so marked as to be indubitable; and if steadily and judiciously persisted in, complete and perfect recovery is the almost certain result. But the greatest triumph which the treatment has achieved in my hands has been the removal of flexions which had hitherto baffled all my efforts, and with them the absorption of adhesions which had existed for years, and which had firmly tied down the uterus in its false position. I do not myself think that the local depletion occasioned by the puncture can alone account for the results I have witnessed, for while the quantity of blood drawn is at one time free and another time limited, the relief is the same, and the absorption of redundant tissue is progressive. The capillaries are not merely divided, but the parenchyma itself is punctured, and explain it how we may, it is, I believe, the puncture of the parenchyma which stimulates absorption, and which is not merely confined to the spot punctured, but extends to the entire uterus. The depth of the puncture is a matter of the highest importance; for if too deep it will not only cause pain, but will absolutely increase the mischief it is intended to remedy; while if too shallow, the mucous membrane and capillaries only are divided, and the beneficial effects are but transitory. One-sixth of an inch is the utmost extent to which I penetrate, and in cases of flexion, I chiefly direct my attention to the posterior or anterior lip of the cervix, as it happens to be a retroversion or an anteversion. Having punctured, I apply, by the sponge-holder, warm sponges, to increase the bleeding, and if the latter should continue longer than is desired, it can be easily controlled by a little prolonged pressure of the sponge to the bleeding point, subsequently brushing it with a little solution of perchloride of iron and glycerine. In this way I arrest any undue bleeding from the occasional division of a small arterial branch, but I commonly allow it to cease of itself. The punctures are made every four or five days, as the state of the organ may demand, beginning about the third day after the cessation of the catamenia, and ending about three or four days before its commencement. I do not mean to say that puncture constitutes the sole treatment in all the cases I have alluded to, but it constitutes the main treatment, and for its entire safety and its great efficiency, I can honestly vouch. I have now a record of a number of really typical cases, some of which I shall briefly detail to the Society.

In the latter end of December, 1870, I was consulted by Mrs. ——, æt. twenty-eight; married nine years; no children; had a six months' miscarriage eight years ago, which was followed by severe pelvic inflammation, and has never been well since. Has naturally a good constitution, and is pretty strong, but easily tired; is nervous, sleeps badly, suffers from constant flatulence, indigestion, and headaches; complains of constant pain in the left ovarian region, which is slightly enlarged and very tender on pressure; pain extends down left leg, and troubles her very much; pain in back, but not constant; a sense of dragging in the uterine region, and frequent pain on sitting down; constant vesical irritation, obliging her to get up frequently at night, and troubling her during the day; thirst, low fever, pulse 100; says she had a pelvic abscess about two years after her miscarriage, produced by cold and temporary suppression of the catamenia; has been much worse since. On examination, the uterus was found very low down, completely retroverted, drawn to the left side, and perfectly tied down by adhesions; very tender to touch; left lateral ligaments thickened, and an obscure but painful enlargement in left ovarian region, apparently the remains of the abscess she spoke of; no leucorrhœa, but a tough endometritic discharge from the os; cervix red and swollen. The treatment was mainly local, and consisted in the persistent use of puncture of the cervix, particularly the posterior lip; daily warm hip-baths, warm vaginal injections, and careful regulation of the diet, with rest in the recumbent posture for the first six weeks. The amendment began soon after the institution of treatment, and was first seen in the diminution of the vesical irritation, relief to pain, gradual disappearance of fever, and improvement of the general health. Some two months had elapsed before the uterus became partly movable and the adhesions began to soften, but exactly three months and a half from the time I first saw her, the uterus suddenly, and without any aid from me, resumed its perfectly normal position in the pelvis — became, in fact, slightly anteverted — and has retained it ever since. I never was more astonished in my life, for on my previous visit the uterus, though mobile to a considerable extent, was still retroverted and partly adherent, and when I next visited her—a menstrual period having intervened—the metamorphosis had completely and effectually taken place. I have only to add that this lady is in the enjoyment of the most perfect health, and that I have selected this case as one which, more than any other, places the value of the treatment beyond doubt or cavil.

The next case was one of marked and exceptional severity, and has been under treatment for six months, with the most gratifying results.

Mrs. ——, æt. twenty-nine; married; two children; no miscarriages; admitted into the California Woman's Hospital, January 9, 1871.

History.—Was confined of her second child six years ago; confinement a laborious one, and was succeeded by what she considered inflammation of the bowels, but which was evidently pelvic peritonitis. This was followed by slight enlargement in left iliac region, with pain there and extending down left leg. Her medical attendant, some time afterward, discovered a tumor in left ovarian region, and applied leeches and blisters, with temporary relief. Two years ago she had a severe access of inflammation, and has been very ill since. Her catamenia were irregular and painful, occurring every two or three weeks, and she had constant low fever, with frequent and painful micturition.

Present State.—Patient emaciated; face florid; constant, most severe headache; insomnia; thirst; loss of appetite and low fever, with very frequent and painful micturition;

urine sometimes pale and at other times depositing lithates; pain over the hypogastric region, but particularly in left groin; pain down left leg and in both hips; constant bearing down; great mental depression.

On examination the uterus was found very low down; cervix enormously hypertrophied and indurated; uterus completely fixed, and surrounded by a mass of indurated tissue filling three-fourths of the pelvis, leaving only the right side free; a tumor occupying the left side, but unable to define its nature particularly; tenderness on pressing over the uterus externally, and an enlargement felt over the seat of the right cornua; canal three inches and a half long. Treatment consisted mainly of local depletion of cervix by puncture every four or five days; hot hip-baths, hot poultices, hot douche, and opiates. By the end of two months matters had vastly improved: the cervix had diminished in size (it had measured about three inches across), and had become softer, and a considerable amount of the organized effusion into the cellular tissue had been absorbed. I was then able to define distinctly a tumor occupying the left ovarian region, about the size of the fist, which was connected, and seemed continuous with the left side of the uterus; it was movable and solid to the touch. The fever and vesical irritation had also greatly lessened; appetite had returned, and the patient had gained four pounds. On consultation, it was deemed advisable to pass an exploratory needle into the tumor, to determine its contents. No fluid followed, and the effect of the puncture was unfavorable, as the tumor enlarged considerably after it, and became painful, and the fever returned, but not to the same extent. I then resumed the treatment by puncture, with the happiest effect. All inflammatory symptoms gradually subsided, the tumor steadily decreased in size, and absorption of hypertrophied tissue took place. At the present date her condition is this: She has lost her headaches, micturition natural, no thirst or fever, appetite good, and she has gained fourteen pounds in weight without the aid of a single tonic but that of good food. The uterus is high up in the pelvis, and mobile; cervix of natural size and soft, and canal two inches and a half long. The tumor has become very small, and is evidently disappearing by absorption; and the patient is now returning home, with every prospect of enjoying excellent health. What the nature of the tumor is, I can not undertake to say, but it is apparently fibroid; but whether its growth excited the uterine hypertrophy and cellulitis, I know not. I believe the uterine tissue has undergone fibroid degeneration, and that the enlargement at the seat of the right cornua (since disappeared) was distinctly of the same character. I would here remark that if it should be found possible, by this treatment, to control the growth of uterine fibroids, an immense boon will henceforth be conferred on humanity.

The next case I shall notice is one of puerperal mania, succeeding parturition, and found in connection with subinvolution of the uterus.

Mrs. ——, æt. twenty-six; married at sixteen; mother of two fine children; had one miscarriage, two years ago, and has a history of uterine disease for many years. She is a small woman, weighing only about ninety-five pounds, and was confined on the 6th of March of a child weighing twelve pounds. The labor was a severe one, and the soft parts were extensively bruised. Paralysis of the bladder continued for a fortnight afterward, and she was unable to use the lower extremities for some time. Five weeks after parturition, she became suddenly insane; face flushed; pulse, 120; talked incessantly; imagined herself suddenly possessed of great wealth, and became altogether most unmanageable. A lochial discharge had continued ever since her confinement, and the abdomen felt larger than natural. I made a vaginal examination, and found the uterus large and low down, with great congestion of the vagina; os eroded. I made four punctures, which bled very freely, and I kept up the discharge by hot sponging. That night the patient slept calmly, without any opiate, and the next day all incoherence had disappeared; she was still talkative, however, but easily controlled. The second day, I again punctured, drawing blood freely; and the day following perfect sanity was established. The treatment was continued at longer intervals for some time afterward, and she is now fat, strong, and in most excellent health. In this case the patient had been absolutely insane for several days before I saw her, and would unquestionably have continued so but for the treatment.

If space permitted, I might cite many other cases of an equally satisfactory nature, but the above will, I think, suffice. In attempting to estimate the value of the treatment, I have been strongly impressed with the belief that medication is too exclusively directed to the lining membrane of the uterine cavity, while the pathological condition of the parenchyma is entirely overlooked. That uterine disease may, and does, in many cases, originate in a congestion of the mucous lining—uterine catarrh and endometritis, for instance—I fully believe; but when we consider the very intimate union which exists between the mucous membrane and the parenchyma, and which makes it impossible to dissect the former from the latter, I think we may reasonably infer that disease can not long exist in one without involving the other. Hence we have altered nutrition and circulation, leading to plastic effusions, hypertrophies, indurations, and flexions, plainly irremovable by astringents and caustics applied to the cavity, which can only aggravate and perpetuate the mischief they are intended to remedy.

Formation of Calculi under the Prepuce.

Read before the Sacramento Society for Medical Improvement, May 16th, 1871,
By H. W. NELSON, M.D.

I call the attention of the Society, this evening, in a few remarks, to a rather novel, and at the same time interesting, case of the formation of calculi under the prepuce, in a traumatic phymosis, which came under my care in 1869, that may be of some value to the surgeon.

Calculi are found, as we all know, in various organs in the body—such as the kidneys, bladder, prostate gland, and salivary glands. Those, of course, that are found in the kidneys and bladder are the results of a morbid condition of the urine; those in the salivary glands being deposits from the saliva. I shall not dwell on the causes leading to these formations, as we are familiar with them, but will proceed at once to the case under consideration. The formation in this case, as if in the bladder, must have been a deposit from the urine, in consequence of distention of the prepuce at each time of urination, the opening in the foreskin being so small, that after the expulsive efforts of the bladder were over, there always remained a quantity of urine in the sac, that could not be expelled for want of voluntary contractile power over that part of the organ.

On the 29th of August, 1868, a Chinaman, aged about thirty-five, and to all appearance quite healthy, called on me for advice, and to inquire if I could cure him of his deformity. He could not speak English very well, and it was with some difficulty that I could get at even a partial history of his case; but I gleaned sufficient to make out the true state of things. When a boy, and while playing, he fell from a height, and alighted astride of some hard substance —perhaps a rail or picket, I could not learn which—cutting and lacerating the end of the prepuce extensively, as I could see by the cicatrix. It healed up after their method of treatment, leaving an opening for the urine to pass, surrounded by dense tissue on the upper surface and close to the corona of the gland. The opening was so small that it was with difficulty that I could introduce the point of the smallest silver probe. The foreskin was elongated to the extent of about four inches, and seemed quite thick. Underneath and throughout the whole length, the frœnum was large and thickened, measuring nearly three-fourths of an inch in diameter. He told me that when he urinated, the skin would distend like a bladder to the size of a man's fist, which caused great suffering. He would endeavor to urinate slowly, in order to relieve him of the pain. The stream of urine through the opening in the foreskin was probably the size of a common pin, and ejected perpendicularly. When the bladder was emptied, there remained nearly a gill of urine in the sac, which gradually dribbled away, but not to empty it.

With the assistance of a friend, a dentist, I placed the patient under the influence of chloroform, and made a thorough examination of the parts, but did not detect the calculi then; in fact, did not suspect the existence of any. I proceeded to remove the whole of the foreskin. I made an incision on the anterior surface, extending from the end to the corona of the gland, laying the gland exposed; and, to my surprise, discovered a number of calculi, and removed thirty-eight, in size varying from a No. 6 shot to a buckshot. I then cut away the prepuce with a straight bistoury, commencing at the upper point of first incision; carried the knife downward, cutting through the frœnum; and then upward, on the opposite side, to the point of commencement. Then, with a pair of scissors, I removed a strip of the mucous lining, so that the edges could be easily drawn together. Eight or nine fine sutures were then passed through. The after-treatment consisted merely of water-dressing, with loose bandage. In two or three days the parts swelled greatly, and became painful, so that I was obliged to remove some of the sutures where tension was the greatest. About the eighth day, the swelling subsided, and the cut edges commenced to cicatrize, and in a little over two weeks the parts were perfectly healed.

The urethra was very large, and would admit the introduction of the end of my little finger. The distension of the urethra I conceive to be caused by the severe pressure of the urine against its walls at the time of urinating, as the discharge from the small opening in the prepuce was not sufficiently rapid to keep up with the contractile power of the bladder.

Another singular feature in this case was a depression, or small, smooth cavity, in the gland on the right side. I suppose that at the time of each passage of water, the calculi were kept in constant motion, or stirred up as it were, thereby grinding or wearing away this cavity, one of them being kept at that spot by some means.

In three months afterward I saw the man, when he pronounced himself quite well. He experienced no difficulty in passing his urine, nor had he any symptoms of gravel or stone in the bladder. I have no doubt that these stones were formed in the sac, from a sedimentary deposit in the urine, which could not escape.

California Pharmaceutical Society.

The Secretary of this Society, James G. Steele, has kindly furnished us with a copy of the proceedings, which we have not space to admit in full. It appears that a number of questions of much interest and importance are under consideration, among which are a proposed course of lectures, a registration of qualified apothecaries, the training of apprentices, etc. Much discussion ensued on the subject of the examination and registration of apothecaries, and it was determined that any bill to be considered in the Legislature should be drawn and presented by a joint committee of the California Medical Society and the California Pharmaceutical Society. The Executive Committee reported in favor of asking an appropriation from the next Legislature, to establish a College of Pharmacy. Mr. Parks presented a sample of opium produced in this State, assaying over nine per cent. of morphia. Mr. Steele exhibited samples of elixirs, syrups, etc., made from the formulas of the Newark Pharmaceutical Society. Provision was made for a representation in the National Association, to meet this month in St. Louis. Charles A. Tufts, of Dover, N. H.; Dr. Squibb, of Brooklyn; Prof. E. Parrish, of Philadelphia; S. M. Colcord and T. W. Metcalf, of Boston, were elected honorary members.

We are pleased to note that the Society is in a flourishing condition as to finances and membership, one hundred members being on its roll. Its library is increasing, and thirteen periodicals on pharmacy are received.

Proceedings of the Alameda County Medical Association,

Held in Oakland, August 7, 1871.

Dr. Carr read a lengthy paper on the "Genesis of Crime," taking for his text a conversation between a lady of San Francisco and her minister. The clergyman visited her just prior to her confinement, and protested against the use of chloroform on that interesting occasion, as an attempt to outwit Deity—hence, sinful! The lady's reply was, "If I could outwit God, I would have so little respect for Him as not to call sinful anything I might do." A copy of this paper was requested for publication, but declined by the Doctor.

Dr. Pinkerton reported a fatal case of carbuncle, in which carbolic acid had been freely used, and there had been no suppuration from first to last. The question arose if such free use of the antiseptic were beneficial. Dr. Cushing had been quite successful, in early cases, with sol. potass. permang. It did not prevent suppuration, but there was no extensive sloughing.

The resignations of Drs. Trenor and Babcock as members of the Board of Censors were accepted, and Drs. Pinkerton and Bolton appointed to the vacancies.

REVIEWS AND NOTICES OF BOOKS.

Handy-book of the Treatment of Women's and Children's Diseases according to the Vienna Medical School: With Prescriptions. By Dr. Emil Dillnberger. Translated from the second German edition, by Patrick Nicol, M.B. Philadelphia: Lindsay & Blakiston. 1871. San Francisco: A. L. Bancroft & Co.

It is plainly impossible to cover, in less than two hundred and fifty pages, so much ground as the title of this volume implies, without sacrificing utility to brevity. Accordingly, the American practitioner will derive little benefit from it, further than to get some idea of the difference of practice between two distant regions. In this point of view, the comparison is by no means unfavorable to our own country. Taking the "Handy-book" as a criterion, there can be no doubt that our countrymen have better resources at command in the management of many diseases; for instance, bronchitis, croup, pertussis, and chorea. Nevertheless, there are useful hints scattered through its pages, which will more than compensate the reader for the small cost of the volume.

A Manual of Midwifery: Including the Signs and Symptoms of Pregnancy, Obstetric Operations, Diseases of the Puerperal State, etc., etc. By Alfred Meadows, M.D., Lond., Member of the Royal College of Physicians, Physician to the Hospital for Women and to the General Lying-in Hospital, Honorary Fellow of the Obstetrical Society of Berlin. First American from the second London edition, revised and enlarged, with illustrations. Philadelphia: Lindsay & Blakiston. 1871. Pp. 487. San Francisco: A. L. Bancroft & Co.

A work which embodies a larger amount of practical information on its subject in a smaller compass than any other book in the library. It has received high commendation in England. The plates, which are numerous, are admirably perspicuous, and the mechanical execution of the volume is in the first style of art.

Braithwaite's Retrospect of Practical Medicine and Surgery. Part 63. July, 1871. New York: W. A. Townsend. San Francisco: A. Roman & Co.

A work well known by the profession everywhere. The present number contains one hundred and twenty-six articles, comprising the cream of medical periodical literature, mostly British, for the last six months.

THE PHYSICIANS' PRESCRIPTION BOOK: Containing Lists of the Terms, Phrases, Contractions, and Abbreviations used in Prescriptions, etc., etc. By Jonathan Pereira, M.D., F.R.S. Fifteenth edition. Philadelphia: Lindsay & Blakiston. 1871. San Francisco: A. L. Bancroft & Co.

Every physician is familiar with this book: so small that it can be hid in one's watch-fob, and so comprehensive that, if properly used, it will qualify the practitioner who is unskilled in the classics, to write prescriptions with the adroitness of an expert.

MINUTES OF THE TWENTY-SECOND ANNUAL MEETING OF THE AMERICAN MEDICAL ASSOCIATION, held in the City of San Francisco, May 2d, 3d, 4th, and 5th, 1871. Published by W. B Atkinson, M.D., Permanent Secretary, 1400 Pine Street, Philadelphia. Price, twenty-five cents.

EDITORIAL.

Forensic Medicine — Dr. Buckley's Paper.

Our professional brethren will read with much satisfaction the "Defense," by Dr. Buckley, to which we allot much of the space in our present issue. His comparison between the medical and other professions, on the score of difference in opinion and judgment, is eminently just. So are his strictures on the incompetency of witnesses who are called on as medical experts, and the recklessness with which advocates select such witnesses for the purpose of bolstering up their cases. In his criticisms on the testimony in the "Fair" case, Dr. Buckley may have erred in accepting as absolutely correct the published reports of the statements made by some of the medical witnesses, though we have no doubt that he is correct in the main, and that the witnesses deserve the castigation inflicted by him. If medical experts were appointed by the Court, or by some impartial tribunal, and selected on the ground of capacity and merit, the profession would not be scandalized by the public exhibition of ignorance and contradiction, and the ends of justice would be served much better. As the case now stands, it is the interest of counsel in a bad cause to avoid selecting skilled and conscientious physicians as witnesses, and to take pliant tools which they can bend to their purposes. So long as this practice exists, the profession will be liable to discredit and disgrace, whenever its members appear as witnesses before legal tribunals; instead of bringing its science and judgment to the aid of law, it will continue, as heretofore, to furnish skillful advocates with the means of obscuring the truth and defeating the ends of justice.

Lying-in and Foundling Asylums of Austria.

We are indebted to the kindness of Dr. B. F. Hardy, of the San Francisco Lying-in Hospital, for an account of the Lying-in and Foundling asylums of Austria, principally of Vienna, furnished by Dr. P. S. Post, of the city last named. A few of the most important features in the organization and management of these institutions may possess some interest for our readers. Each province is required to maintain at least one hospital of each kind. They are supported in part from the provincial treasuries, and in part from the pay of patients. In Vienna, a further income is derived from the medical students, who have the clinical privileges of the wards allotted to non-paying patients. The estimate placed by the public on the Lying-in Hospital of Vienna, may be inferred from the fact that not far from 10,000 births take place annually in that institution, or a little over one-third of all the children born in the capital. Women are admitted a month or two before confinement, or sooner if they pay; and remain nine days after, or longer, if sick, or if they pay. Children not paid for remain four months, the mothers nursing them for that time; after which they are sent to the Foundling Hospital. The mortality of mothers in childbed is 1.5 per cent. A woman not paying must give her name and residence. All who desire are admitted for confinement.

Children of any description are admitted in the Foundling Hospital, besides those from the Lying-in establishment. When the expenses are paid, the infant is given back to its mother after a term of years. As soon as convenient after admission, they are given out to nurses, outside, who are paid for the service. The enormous proportion of 80 per cent. die in the first year, the rate of mortality in Vienna, in general, being 33 per cent. For children without parents to take care of them, a guardian is appointed by the authorities, his duty being to look to the interest of his ward, without, however, incurring any responsibility. The terrible mortality is ascribed to neglect and abuses of various kinds; but it scarcely exceeds the mortality among foundlings in other countries, which is always distressingly large among children deprived of the care of the real mother.

Medical Ethics.

In the paper on this subject published in our August number, Dr. Montgomery proposes that the ethics of the profession should be taught systematically in our medical schools. We have no doubt that benefit would result from this course, by impressing the minds of students with the importance of honorable deportment in their subsequent relations with their *confreres*. It is true that laws will not make gentlemen; that ill-bred selfishness will disregard all codes; that our profession will always be harassed and dishonored by, here and there, a boorish disciple of piratical tendencies, who breeds mischief in his daily path and becomes notorious as a pest in the camp. But it is equally true that much annoyance and discord are introduced in professional circles by men holding a fair position, who habitually overlook the little amenities of professional intercourse, perhaps without intending wrong, and without appreciating the error of their conduct. Much of this irregularity would be avoided if care were taken to instill in the minds of students a high sense of professional honor, and a firm resolution to observe sacredly the code which governs, or which should govern, the guild of their choice. The subject is one that may well claim the serious attention of medical men. It certainly augurs favorably for the future harmony of the profession, that so great an interest has been awakened within a few years past in regard to the obligations of practitioners toward one another, and that an increasing disposition is manifest from year to year to observe and enforce the code of ethics.

Stimulating Hypodermic Injections in Typhoid Fever.

We find in the *Gazette Hebdomadaire* of June 16th, some account of a novel mode of treatment adopted by a German physician in the collapse of typhoid fever. The subjects were Prussian soldiers, who, during the siege of Paris, suffered from typhoid of extremely ataxic type, with feeble heart-movement, small and irregular pulse, cyanosis, cold extremities, and general collapse. Dr. Zuelzer, observing the resemblance to the choleraic condition, in which he had derived good results from stimulating hypodermic injections, determined to try the same method, and accordingly injected into each of the four extremities ten drops sulphuric ether, with five drops "anisated ammoniacal solution." "The results were remarkable. The pulse, before small and irregular, became full and strong; the contractions of the heart, which had been feeble and irregular, became energetic and regular; its impulse, before imperceptible, was now well marked. Frequently, after one or two injections, the cyanosis and collapse vanished. This plan has the additional advantage of gaining time for other treatment. Small abscesses are formed at the places of puncture, but they are of no importance."

The "Gazette Hebdomadaire" and the French Physicians.

Most cordially do we greet the renewal of acquaintance with our old, familiar friend, the *Gazette Hebdomadaire*, after the interruption of its visits by the "two sieges of Paris"—an interruption due, not to want of industry or of devotion to duty on the part of the editor, Dr. Dechambre, but to the insurmountable cordon of war. We gather from its well stored pages that the medical scientists of Paris are laboring with increased assiduity in the service of the profession and of humanity, in their "concours," and clinics, and lectures, and in their numerous associations. The fidelity and zeal with which they adhered to their proper work during troubles and dangers never before surpassed, reflect unbounded honor both on themselves and on the profession at large. The only bright and stainless page in the history of the French metropolis for the year 1871, is that which records the deeds of the medical profession.

A Black Book Called For.

The Alameda County Medical Society has determined on keeping a record of the names of individuals who refuse to pay their physician for his services. It is not designed, we need scarcely say, for those who are really necessitous, but only for such as are able to pay, and who habitually defraud their medical attendant by a variety of tricks which are common everywhere. We see no reason why such a register may not be kept with advantage by every local medical association. A "Black Book" was ordered to be procured, for the purpose of recording the names of persons who make a practice of defrauding their physicians, by evading the payment of their medical bills. Dr. Babcock proposed to amend the Constitution so as to prohibit withdrawal from membership, except on account of removal from the county; the prohibition being based on the ground, that it is the duty of every regular practitioner to unite himself with the local society.

The Social Evil—Proposed Legislation.

The Board of Health of San Francisco have drawn up a bill to license prostitution, under certain restrictions such as have been adopted in some parts of the old world and in one or two American cities. The San Francisco Medical Society have made this the subject of discussion at their next meeting, to be held September 12th. We may as well say for ourselves, as the editors of this Journal, that, after due attention to the working of the system elsewhere, and after deliberate consideration of the subject, our convictions are firmly established in hostility to any legislation which will sanction prostitution by licensing it. Want of space prevents us from enlarging on this occasion.

Wanted—A Rara Avis.

A physician is wanted in a desirable location in the northern section of the State. The application calls for "a graduate of some respectable college, of good common sense and urbane manner—one not too airy or technical, or in the habit of boasting of the great practice he has had elsewhere, and of his cases and cures—a man of temperate habits, and disposed to observe the recognized code of professional ethics." In drawing this picture, we fear that the writer has unwittingly described such rare attainments as are seldom united in one individual.

An Indictment Against Alcohol and Tobacco.

The report of the British Factory Inspector, contains a statement made by the certifying surgeon at Bolton-le-Moors, that the children of the mill population are year by year getting smaller, and physically less capable of doing their work. He attributes this partly to their being the children of intemperate parents, partly to their being brought up on tea and coffee, instead of more substantial food, and partly to the circumstance that many young children, of about 12 years old, begin to smoke, acquiring the habit from their fathers, and possibly from their mothers.

California State Medical Society.

Let every physician in the State who can attend the meeting in October, do so. The Committee of Arrangements have taken much pains to secure reports from the various standing committees, and there can be no reasonable doubt that the meeting will be one of interest and edification. It will be held in Sacramento on Wednesday, October 11th.

Crowded Out.

We have on hand for next number a report of a case of ovariotomy, by Dr. Tyrrell; a case of cerebro-spinal meningitis, by Dr. Stewart, with several other communications. The proceedings of the Alameda County Society we have had to curtail, and those of the San Francisco Society to omit altogether.

Erratum.

An important error occurred in printing one of the formulas contained in the article in our last issue contributed by Dr. Ferris. It occurs on page 116, the third formula, which directs sixty grains of syrup and one drachm of mint water. It should read, *half an ounce of each.*

GENERAL SUMMARY.

Action of Mercury on the Liver.

In the *Edinburgh Medical Journal* for April, Dr. T. R. Frazer presents the ablest and most exhaustive paper on the action of mercury on the liver that we have ever seen. He takes up and discusses *seriatim* the various doctrines in regard to the influence of mercury on the liver, viz.: "1. Mercury simply increases the flow of bile into the intestines. 2. It causes an increased formation of the bile by removing abnormal conditions that interfere with the secreting function of the liver. 3. It causes an increased formation of bile by an indirect action on the liver. 4. It causes an increased formation of bile by a direct and primary action on the liver. 5. Mercury has no cholagogue action whatever." After reviewing these propositions he concludes that we are entitled to maintain the *first* as true. The second, third, and fourth propositions may be regarded as elaborations of the first, advanced to explain the obvious effects on which it is founded. But in the present state of our knowledge of pathology and physiology it is impossible to prove that any one of these three is true. The fifth proposition maintained by Thudicum, Scott, and Bennett has not been proved by them. In their experiments various disturbing agencies were present. Lesion of nerves, absorption of bile unmodified by digestion, the presence of inflammation and suppuration in the immediate vicinity of the liver, and imperfect digestion were all present, and must have exerted a modifying influence. The most important of these was the disturbance of digestion caused by interrupting the flow of the bile into the intestines. This alone would be sufficient to render inconclusive the experiments of these gentlemen.—*Michigan Med. Journal.*

Professional Examinations.

The following were the questions in Surgical Anatomy and the Principles and Practice of Surgery submitted to the candidates for the diploma of Membership of the Royal College of Surgeons, London, at the last examination : 1. Describe the inguinal canal, its boundaries and relations to other structures, including hernial protrusions. 2. What are the causes and the immediate and remote consequences of sudden extravasation of urine? What treatment would you adopt in such a case? 3. Give the pathology of non-traumatic aneurism, from its commencement to its termination. 4. Describe the operation known as Chopart's, and the relative position of the various parts cut through in this amputation. 5. How are scirrhus and medullary cancer distinguished in the living subject? What organs does each form specially affect, and at what ages do they respectively occur? 6. By what form of accident is dislocation of the head of the femur backward usually caused? Describe the two dislocations in this direction, the deformity existing in each, and the proper method of reducing them. The following were the questions on the Principles and Practice of Medicine, viz.: 1. Describe a case of tubercular meningitis in a child, from the appearance of premonitory symptoms to the termination in death. 2. Give the symptoms of diabetes mellitus, with the methods of analyzing the urine; also, the treatment by medicines and diet. 3. Write a prescription in full for hemoptysis, gastrodynia, and dysentery; also, a prescription for an aperient draught and a sleeping draught. There were fifty-four candidates, of which number five were rejected on the first day, and twelve on the second.—*Phil. Med. and Surg. Reporter.*

Phosphates in Pregnancy.

Mr. Metcalfe Johnson, of Lancaster, recommends, in the *Med. Times,* the hydrated phosphate of lime of the "British Pharmacopœia" as a remedy for the sickness of pregnancy. He gives it in doses of three to ten grains each, three times daily, suspended in water and flavored according to the patient's taste. In some cases the relief has been so striking that patients have sent to ask for "some of that medicine that relieves the sickness." Mr. Johnson thinks the drug may supply phosphates to the nervous system and also to the embryo, and that if phosphates be not supplied, the child may grow at the expense of the mother's osseous and nervous tissue.—*The Doctor.*

Quassia for Surgical Dressings.

"Flies cannot bear the smell of the wood, maggots are therefore entirely avoided," says Mr. C. C. Mitchinson, in the *Lancet.* The use of an infusion of quassia as a dressing for open wounds and ulcers in hot climates and during the prevalence of hot weather, he recommends, and states that in the United States army, after one of the James River engagements, 500 wounded men under the care of a friend of his were treated in the above manner.—*The Doctor.*

Commendable Conduct of French Physicians.

When the great Cathedral of Notre Dame was fired by the Communists, the resident physicians and surgeons of the Hotel Dieu, adjoining, at the risk of their lives, and with the aid of some other persons, succeeded in extinguishing the flames. But for this, the Hotel Dieu would have been burnt, with frightful loss of life to the helpless invalids within its walls.

Chloral Hydrate in Cod Oil.

This combination is reported to be much less nauseous than the pure oil, and to prevent the night sweats of phthisis, to induce sleep, and to create appetite. It is prepared by digesting in a sand-bath with gentle heat, one part, by weight, of the hydrate, with twenty of oil.

STATE BOARD OF HEALTH.

Abstract from the Reports of Deaths and their Causes, in the following cities and towns in California, during July, 1871 :

CITIES AND TOWNS.	Total No. Deaths.	PREVALENT DISEASES.						AUTHORITIES.
		Consumption.	Inflam. of Lungs.	Infl. Stomach and Bowels.	Diphtheria.	Scarlatina.	Typhus & Typhoid Fevers.	
San Francisco	230	32	6	7	1	0	10	S. F. B'rd of Health
Sacramento	29	2	1	0	0	0	0	Sac. B'rd of Health
Petaluma	2	0	0	1	0	0	0	Dr. G. W. Graves.
Dixon	1	1	0	0	0	0	0	Dr. R. H. Plummer.
Santa Clara	..	..	..	..	..	..	..	Dr. H. H. Warburton
Stockton	11	1	0	1	1	0	0	Stockton B'd Health.
Marysville	10	1	1	1	0	0	1	Dr. C. E. Stone.
Placerville	5	0	0	1	0	0	0	Dr. E. A. Kunkler.
Auburn	..	..	..	..	..	..	..	Dr. A. S. Du Bois.
San Diego	2	0	0	1	0	0	0	Co. Med. Society.
San Luis Obispo	..	..	..	..	..	..	..	Dr. W. W. Hays.
Oroville	..	..	..	..	..	..	..	Dr. J. M. Vance.
Woodland	1	0	0	0	0	0	1	Dr. A. B. Mehring.
Oakland	5	1	0	0	0	0	0	Dr. T. H. Pinkerton.
Los Angeles	12	2	2	0	0	0	0	Dr. H. S. Orme.
Nevada City	6	1	0	0	0	0	0	Dr. J. A. Guffin.
Truckee	4	0	1	2	0	0	1	Dr. Wm. Curless.
St. Helena	1	0	0	1	0	0	0	Dr. J. S. Adams.
San José	18	2	0	3	0	1	1	Dr. J. N. Brown.
Napa City	6	1	0	0	0	0	1	Dr. M. B. Pond.
Cacheville	0	0	0	0	0	0	0	Dr. E. L. Parramore.
Siskiyou	..	..	..	..	..	..	..	Dr. T. T. Cabanis.
Watsonville	1	0	0	0	0	0	0	Dr. C. E. Cleveland.
Folsom	0	0	0	0	0	0	0	Dr. L. McGuire.
Bridgeport Town'p	2	0	0	0	0	0	0	Dr. J. L. Asay.
Sut'r C'k & Amador	2	0	0	0	0	0	0	Dr. H. M. Fiske.
Monterey	1	0	0	0	0	0	0	Dr. C. A. Canfield.
Santa Cruz	5	2	0	1	0	0	0	Dr. Benj. Knight.
Vallejo	1	0	0	1	0	0	0	Dr. J. M. Brown.
Suisun & Fairfield	5	1	1	0	0	0	0	Dr. S. D. Campbell.
Colusa	3	0	0	1	0	1	1	Dr. Luke Robinson.
Trinity County	1	0	0	0	0	0	1	Dr. J. C. Montague.
Santa Barbara	6	2	1	1	0	0	0	Dr. C. B. Bates.
Redwood City	6	1	0	1	0	0	1	Dr. C. A. Kirkpatrick.

Abstract from Reports of Births:

Cities and Towns.	Total Births.	Males.	Females.	Still-born.	Live-born.	Authorities.
San Francisco...	78	46	32	25	53	S. F. Board of Health.
Sacramento.....	53	28	25	4	49	Sac. Board of Health.
All other places.	208	119	89	22	186	Various sources.
Total......	339	193	146	51	288	

Remarks.—Our table exhibits such a favorable condition of the health of the State as to render comment unnecessary.

THOMAS M. LOGAN, M.D.,
Permanent Secretary State Board of Health.

Mortality in San Francisco during July, 1871.

By H. Gibbons, Jr., M.D.

CAUSES OF DEATH.

Anemia	1	Diphtheria	1	Jaundice	1
Aneurism of Aorta...	2	Diseases of Heart....	11	Kidney, Diseases of ..	6
" of Pulm'ry		Drowning	1	Liver, Disease of.....	2
Artery.....	1	Dysentery	1	Lungs, Apoplexy of..	1
Apoplexy	4	Enteritis	3	Meningitis	12
Ascites.............	1	Fever, Congestive....	1	Old Age............	4
Atrophia	10	" Continued	2	Paralysis	1
Bowels, Obstruction of	1	" Remittent	1	Peritonitis..........	4
Bronchitis..........	1	" Typhoid	8	Phthisis	32
Burns..............	2	Fracture of Skull	4	Pneumonitis........	6
Cancer.............	2	Gangrene	1	Premature Birth.....	4
" on Head......	1	Gastritis	2	Scrofula............	1
" of Breast.....	1	Gunshot Wound	2	Sore Throat	1
" of Stomach...	1	Hemoptysis	1	Stomach, Ulceration .	1
" of Uterus.....	2	Hemorrhage, Internal.	1	Suffocation.........	1
Cholera Infantum....	11	Hemor'ge, Umbilical.	1	Suicide	4
Cirrhosis of Liver....	2	Hepatitis............	2	Syphilis	4
Congestion of Brain..	5	Hip-joint Disease	1	Tabes Mesenterica ...	1
" of Lungs.	4	Hydrocephalus.......	1	Unknown	7
Convulsions, Infantile	12	Hydrothorax.........	1	Variola............	2
Cyanosis	2	Hysteria	1	Whooping Cough....	2
Debility, General.....	4	Inanition	8		
Diarrhea	5	Injury to Pelvis.....	1	Total	230
Difficult Parturition..	1	" to Spine.....	1	Still-births	25

AGES.

Under 1 year	68	From 15 to 20 years..	3	From 60 to 70 years..	11
From 1 to 2 years....	16	From 20 to 30 years..	25	From 70 to 80 years..	9
From 2 to 5 years....	7	From 30 to 40 years..	42	From 80 to 90 years..	1
From 5 to 10 years...	2	From 40 to 50 years..	27		
From 10 to 15 years..	3	From 50 to 60 years..	16	Total	230

Sex. — Male, 149; Female, 81. Total, 230.

Color. — White, 203; Copper, 22; Black, 5.

NATIVITIES.

California	93	Scotland	4	China	21
Other parts of U. S.	33	France	6	West Indies	1
British Amer'n Prov.	4	Germany	18	Holland	1
Mexico	3	Sweden	4	Poland	1
Central America	1	Russia	1	Unknown	1
England	5	Switzerland	2		
Ireland	29	Italy	2		

RECAPITULATION.

Died in City Wards	175	Mount St. Joseph's Infirmary	6
City and County Hospital	15	Alms House	2
U. S. Marine Hospital	2	Home for Inebriates	1
French Hospital	3	Small-pox Hospital	1
German Hospital	3	Casualties	12
St. Mary's Hospital	6	Suicides	4

Remarks.—The sanitary condition of San Francisco is still excellent, if such statement may be based on the report for July. No increase in the monthly mortality has taken place, no epidemic disorders prevail, and the number of deaths from individual diseases is, in general, at its minimum. As an exception to this conclusion may be mentioned cholera infantum, which caused 11 deaths, a greater number than in any other month in this year; indeed there were no deaths from this cause in the first quarter of the year, and but 11 in the second quarter. Three deaths from aneurism are reported, the location of the aneurism in one case being most unusual, *i. e.*, the pulmonary artery. Infantile convulsions caused 12 deaths; inflammation of the brain, 12; atrophia, 10; inanition, 8. The same number in the aggregate resulted from these diseases in June, and yet the mortality in children under five years of age increased from 79 in June to 91 (nearly 40 per cent. of the total deaths) in July. The number of suicides in July (4) was unusually large; the same may be said of the deaths from violence (12). It is certainly unusual to report 4 deaths from fracture of the skull and 2 from gunshot wounds in one month. Typhoid fever is increasing somewhat, and we learn from the Health Officer that nearly all the deaths from this cause have occurred in the level portions of the city, where drainage is necessarily least perfect. Early in the month it was reported that there was a case of small-pox at the hospital—an arrival from Nevada. Two deaths from this cause are noted. We have heard of no other cases occurring, and presume there is little danger to be apprehended of a spread of the disease. Although cholera is quite prevalent in the East and in Russia, and has even reached

London, and is likely to become epidemic there, and possibly in our own country, we have little to fear from its ravages in San Francisco. It has never prevailed here to any extent, and California escaped altogether a visitation when it last occurred in the United States. While San Francisco has many natural advantages in a sanitary point of view, it behooves us, nevertheless, to keep our city in as cleanly a state as possible. The gods help them that help themselves. During the month of July no deaths were recorded from asphyxia, asthma, Bright's disease, croup, delirium tremens, dentition, dropsy, epilepsy, scarlet fever, softening of the brain, measles and tetanus, which diseases caused 21 deaths in July, 14 in June, 9 in April, 16 in March, 12 in February, and 19 in January. The mortality in July for the past six years has been as follows: 1866, 214; 1867, 248; 1868, 346; 1869, 296; 1870, 298; 1871, 230. It will be seen that in every year but 1866 the mortality has exceeded that of 1871.

Billroth's Pathology is in high favor everywhere. The American publishers have received from England an order for three hundred copies.

Cholera in Russia.—In St. Petersburg, from August 29, 1870, to June 12, 1871, there were 4,622 cases of cholera, with 1,848 deaths.

Women have been admitted to study medicine in the University of Helsingfors, Finland, by consent of the Russian Emperor.

PACIFIC

MEDICAL AND SURGICAL JOURNAL.

Vol. V.—OCTOBER, 1871.—No. 53.

ORIGINAL COMMUNICATIONS.

On Extraction of Cataract—Benefit of the Extraction of the Lens in the Capsule.

By Dr. N. J. MARTINACHE, late Master of Clinic of Sichel and Wecker, Paris.

It is not my intention to give a complete description of the operation for cataract, but simply to call the attention of physicians to a particular *modus operandi* for the extraction of the crystalline lens in the capsule. Every physician knows perfectly that the methods of operating for cataract were very numerous—too numerous, indeed; but little by little, all these methods have almost entirely disappeared, and the only operation now performed on adults is the extraction. This is certainly a great progress, and it is out of my design to commence any discussion as to the comparative merits of the ordinary method and Græfe's linear extraction.

It is enough to mention the name of Von Hasner, who is absolutely in favor of the ordinary extraction, to prove its merits. But putting the merits aside, let us speak of the inconveniences. By these two methods we leave certainly in the eye some crystalline elements, impossible to be removed; and then, acting as extraneous bodies, they are a permanent cause of irritation. A simple comparison, drawn from common practice, will plainly illustrate this fact. I mean the delivery of the placenta after accouchement.

Every one understands the importance of it, and foresees the danger of a placenta remaining in the uterus. So it is with the operation for cataract. When crystalline elements are left in the eye, the eye is in danger, more or less, according to the quantity of the retained elements ; and, cautious as he may be, the surgeon is bound to leave some cortical masses, when the extraction is performed by opening the capsule.

In my opinion, the true operation for cataract is the extraction of the lens in the capsule. By doing so, no irritating spur is left in the eye, and no danger is to be feared after the operation ; the healing process is more rapid, and the power of the sight is greater than in any other method.

Some weeks ago, I saw a patient who had been blind for ten years. In the right eye the sight was annihilated, and in the left eye there was a very peculiar form of cataract. Looking at this left eye, it was impossible to see any opacity of the lens in the pupil ; but by looking through the pupil with a plan ophthalmoscope, a black spot was to be seen. This spot was a cataract, situated in the posterior cortical masses of the lens; it was round, and about three lines in diameter. The perception of light was good, and the patient having been for ten years in the same condition, I proposed the operation, and it was agreed to. Owing to the fact that the anterior part of the lens was *transparent*, it was a very difficult one to perform, As it was impossible to see the opacity in the pupil, it was to be feared that, after lacerating the capsule, the surgeon would be at a loss and unable to finish the operation, as I had observed in a former case. So I decided to remove the lens with the capsule.

The patient having been placed under the influence of chloroform, I made a large incision, upward and in the sclerotic, as in Græfe's operation. Then, without any iridectomy, I proceeded to the removal of the lens, by exerting pressure with the india-rubber scoop on the inferior part of the eye-ball. When the lens was engaged between the edges of the wound, I depressed the iris downward and backward with another scoop, and removed the lens with the capsule. About the fifth part of the vitreous humor escaped. I reduced the iris, and put the bandage on. Two days after, the iris was protruding; I made the excision, and in five days the cicatrix was complete. The patient never had any pain during the healing process, and four weeks after the operation the sharpness of the sight was number one.

In conclusion, I will venture this remark: It is to be hoped, and I feel confident of it, that in the future, and before a long time, the only operation performed will be the extraction in the capsule, without any iridectomy.

A Case of Puerperal Peritonitis—Subsequent Ovariotomy, with Successful Result.

By GERRARD GEORGE TYRRELL, L.R.C.S.I. and K. and Q.C.P.I., of Sacramento.

As the subject of ovarian disease and its removal by the operation of ovariotomy is just now occupying much of the attention of many of our best surgeons upon the Pacific Coast, no doubt stimulated by the advent to our shores of one of the most skillful and brilliant ovariotomists in America, H. R. Storer, I am induced to offer the record of the following case as a contribution to the statistics of the subject, and one not devoid of many points of interest both to the physician and the practical surgeon.

Mrs. English, residing in Sacramento; æt. thirty; a fine, tall, stout, and hitherto remarkably healthy young woman, was confined of her fourth child upon the 29th of November, 1870, after an apparently easy labor of four hours' duration, attended by a neighboring woman. She says that she was unusually large after the child was born, which necessitated the procuring of a larger abdominal bandage than the one usually worn upon these occasions. During the night, the abdominal distension increased so much as to burst the bandage, when one of those omnipresent "old women," so familiar to us all, suggested some medicine "to take down the wind," which she had procured from an "irregular" practitioner of this city. The medicine proving any thing but salutary, the "irregular" was himself called in next day, who confirmed the old woman's diagnosis, and prescribed some nostrum which excited vomiting, pain in bowels, etc.; the bowels remained constipated, and tenderness began to be experienced over the abdomen.

December 2d, all the symptoms having become much aggravated, "irregular" No. 1 called in "irregular" No. 2, who declared that there was another child in the womb, and thereupon proceeded to introduce his hand into the uterus, and removed therefrom what was, I presume, a clot, but which he called an aborted fetus. As soon as the woman had recovered from the shock of this proceeding, she had a rigor, followed by intense uterine pain, alarming vomiting and prostration, inability to move from the dorsal position; in fact, acute metro-peritonitis set in. Next day, 3d of December, all the symptoms were aggravated, and on the 4th of December, these irregular gentlemen abandoned the case to die, and I was sent for. I found her lying on her back, perfectly sensible; knees drawn up, extremities cold, face pinched and clammy, countenance expressive of great anxiety and pain, eyes sunken, skin moist and cool, tongue slimy and coated with white fur, vomiting constant, bowels constipated, breathing hurried, with frequent sighing, pulse 140, thready, intellect clear. Further examination disclosed an abdomen enormously distended, and so very tender that palpation or percussion could not be satisfactorily practiced; enough was, however, elicited to determine perfect dullness all over the abdominal region, with the exception of a small space in the epigastrium, which was resonant; the lochia were not quite suppressed, but very fetid; milk still remained in the breasts; urine very scanty, painful in urinating, and lateritious. Ordered flannels wrung out of hot water, saturated again with tr. opii, applied to abdomen, and covered with oiled silk, to be renewed constantly, and two grs. gum opium to be taken every three hours; vagina to be injected with warm water, to which was added some Labarraque's solution.

5th.—Is improved; vomiting ceased after the second pill was swallowed; slept at intervals during the night; pulse 120, and much fuller than yesterday; skin and extremities moist and warm; tenderness still very great over abdomen; lochia increased in quantity; thirst urgent. Ordered lemonade with cream of tartar as drink. Continue medicaments.

6th.—Slept better last night; no return of vomiting; pulse, 100; tongue cleaning; face has lost its pinched expression; countenance cheerful; breathing natural; tenderness of abdomen subsiding, and tension decreasing; fluctuation is now apparent to palpation, giving a distinct wave on percussion; lochia abundant, and devoid of fetid odor; thirst is abating; urine scanty, and high-colored. Continue applications to abdomen, and give one pill every four hours, together with diuretic mixture three times a day.

7th.—Is much better this morning; slept well last night; can now stretch out her limbs without pain, and turn upon her side with a little help; pulse, 98, full and regular; tongue clear; skin moist and warm; abdominal distention decreasing; fluid apparently very thin; no resonance anywhere, except beneath epigastrium. Ordered a liniment of iodine, glycerin, and camph. oil, to be applied to abdomen and covered with oiled silk; a dose of senna and rhubarb as a purgative, after the action of which continue the opium pills.

8th.—Had a copious evacuation from the medicine, and feels in good spirits this morning; the abdomen has in a great measure lost its tenderness, and can be freely handled, except over the uterus, where percussion gives pain; no tumor can be discovered in abdomen; uterus moves freely; the fluid in cavity of abdomen seems thin, and is not encysted; no resonance can be discovered anywhere, except in epigastric region, neither does position alter its relation;

abdomen measures forty-six inches round umbilicus. From this date she daily gained strength, but the dropsy did not decrease in proportion as tenderness vanished, so I employed various drastic cathartics; iodine was persistently used by inunction; diaphoretics and diuretics alike were disappointing in their results, and on December 21st, the abdomen measured forty-four inches, having decreased just two inches in two weeks. She complained much of the weight of the fluid, and begged that some relief be afforded. I accordingly called in my friend, Dr. Nelson, to see the case. After careful manipulation, we could discover no tumor in abdominal cavity; the fluid could by wavelets be seen all over the abdomen, and was evidently free in the cavity. We agreed that if the fluid did not continue to decrease, to tap the abdomen.

On the 8th of January we again met, and as the symptoms were no better, and the fluid continued without increase or decrease, we agreed to tap. Accordingly, I introduced a trocar into the linea alba, between umbilicus and pubes, and drew off over eight gallons of fluid, which, in flowing, had the color of a weak infusion of senna, very thin, but in the vessel looked as dark as porter. The specific gravity of this fluid was 1.019, highly albuminous, and under the microscope exhibited blood corpuscles, fibrin threads, and cholesterin. I sent a specimen of the fluid to Dr. James Blake, of San Francisco, who most kindly examined it under his microscope, but says he failed to find either pus or exudation corpuscles, but confirmed my own examination in finding both blood, cholesterin, and fibrin shreds. His opinion was that the fluid was probably ovarian. Immediately after we removed the canula, Dr. Nelson and myself carefully examined the now flaccid abdomen, but utterly failed in finding any trace of a tumor or its remains. We ordered gr. i. opium every two hours. Six hours after the operation, she was seized with a most profuse watery diarrhea, which subsided spontaneously. No inflammatory symptoms ensued, and in three days she was about the house. The abdomen is now resonant where such is normal; no trace of tumor; is passing a quantity of pale, limpid urine. Says she feels as well as ever.

From this date she progressed favorably, became able to resume her household duties, had no sign of any return of the ascites, and, in fact, was well until about the middle of March, or over two months from the date of tapping, when she discovered a tumor growing in the left side. This increased rapidly, and on the 28th March she called my attention to it. I at once discovered a unilocular ovarian tumor, about the size of a cocoa-nut, occupying a position midway between umbilicus and pubes, rather more to the left side. It was tense, smooth, perfectly movable, and apparently filled with a thick fluid. On April 16th it had increased to the size of the uterus at term. Its weight was now so distressing, that, in the presence of Dr. Wythe, of Santa Clara, I tapped it, and drew off three gallons of thick, brown, gelatinous, and stringy fluid, mingled with shreds like boiled fat, one of which remained in the track of the canula as it was withdrawn. The operation gave considerable relief until the 1st of May, two weeks after the operation, when a large abdominal abscess formed round the seat of the puncture, which opened spontaneously on the 6th of May, giving exit to a large quantity of thin pus.

The tumor, in the meantime, was refilling rapidly, and now presented evidences of a multilocular character in its irregularity of outline. Adhesions had also taken place between it and the abdominal parietes, no doubt owing to the peripheral inflammation induced by the abdominal abscess, and this abscess was undoubtedly the result of the decomposition of the shred of lymph, or gelatiniform matter, which was engaged in the track of the canula as it was withdrawn. The patient's health is beginning to fail, is getting emaciated, anemic and despondent; prefers death to a constant pain, and inability to work. Ordered cit. ferri et quiniæ, and one grain opium at bedtime.

May 28.—Tumor is discharging through the abscess in

abdominal parietes a very thin, purulent fluid. Some days it will flow a gallon or more; then it will cease for a week, and flow again. Cyst is now adherent throughout. Uterus freely movable; uterine sound reaches to two and a half inches. Since, patient gradually growing weaker; emaciation progressing rapidly; begs for a removal of tumor. Having explained to her the very great risk she ran of a fatal termination, if an operation was performed, she made up her mind to take the chances; and, accordingly, upon July 1, at 10 A.M.—assisted by Drs. Wythe, of Santa Clara, Simmons, Cluness, Hatch, Wythe, Jr., Nelson, Haswell, and Oatman, of this city—I performed the operation for ovariotomy. Dr. Hatch, having kindly undertaken the anesthetic, in a few moments had the patient under the combined influence of ether and chloroform. I commenced the operation by making an incision, about five inches long, a little to the right of the median line, between the umbilicus and pubes; not, I must confess, in deference to the opinion of Dr. Storer, who is an advocate for that line of incision, but rather that I might avoid the track of the abscess, which lay midway between these points. In this incision, I divided the right rectus muscle, drawing it to either side. I continued the dissection through the tissues, until I reached the tumor, and found it adherent to the abdominal walls, as I expected. By introducing my hand carefully, I gradually broke down the adhesions, which were very firm in the region of the liver and transverse colon. The omentum was adherent throughout. It was carefully separated, and the tumor tapped, giving exit to several gallons of purulent fluid. Adhesions were now discovered to exist in the pelvic cavity; they were carefully ruptured, and the tumor withdrawn. It was attached by a broad but thin pedicle, which I inclosed in a Simpson's clamp, and then removed the tumor. There was little or no hemorrhage, but some bloody serum escaped out of the cavity of the abdomen. The wound was now closed by six silver pins, the clamp adjusted, a bandage firmly pinned, and the patient removed to bed, in just twenty-two minutes from the commencement of the operation. No sponging out of abdomen was permitted, and carbolized oil was used as a dressing to the wound; a grain of morphia was also administered. 1 P.M.—Complains of the pain and soreness of the wound; pulse, 80; respiration, 18. 6 P.M.—Very comfortable; still complains of pain; pulse, 80. Ordered urine to be drawn off by catheter, and gr. i. morph. every three hours, until pain ceases.

July 2.—Passed a very comfortable night; has not required morph. since 3 A.M.; has no pain, but some tympanitic distension of abdomen; pulse, 100; respiration, 20; skin, moist; tongue, dry from morph.; is very cheerful. 2 P.M. —Nurse says that at 11 A.M., her pulse fell to 80; it is now 98; temperature, 100 2-5. 7 P.M. — Pulse, 100; temperature, 100; respiration, 20.

July 3.—Slept well last night; very cheerful this morning; tympanites decreasing; pulse, 96; temperature, 96; has no pain. Continue morph., night and morning; barley-water for drink. Urine is drawn off as required.

July 4.—Slept well last night; very cheerful and full of hope this morning; no tenderness over bowels; tympanites abating; tongue, clear and moist; pulse, 84. Removed the dressing from wound. The line of incision, as far as the clamp, is healed by first intention; pedicle suppurating beneath the clamp. Redressed the stump with carbolized oil.

July 5.—Urinates without use of catheter; passed an excellent night. An induration of abdominal walls is noticed, extending anteriorly from the ensiform cartilage to the clamp, and laterally as far as the region of liver on one side, and the spleen on the other, indicating the region of adhesion, where, I presume, inflammatory exudation is taking place.

July 6.—Removed all the sutures and the clamp. The pedicle is firmly adherent to the abdominal walls, and suppurating where the clamp had constricted it; incision quite firmly united.

July 7.—Bowels moved, for the first time, this morning, and without medicine; no tenderness of abdomen; pedicle suppurating slightly; thickening of abdominal walls well marked.

July 8.—Is sitting up in bed to-day, and wishes to get out.

July 9.—Pedicle healing over, and is gradually retracting within the walls of abdomen.

July 10.—Was out of bed for a short time to-day; pedicle healing very fast; appetite, good; bowels, regular.

July 11.—Doing well. From this date, I need not record the daily progress of the case; suffice it to say, that recovery was uninterrupted. On the twenty-first day from operation, she walked four blocks. Five weeks after, no trace of the thickening in abdominal wall could be discovered. The pedicle was quite healed a little below the level of abdomen. Her strength was improving daily. In fact, she had quite recovered.

This case presents many features of interest in its early history. In the first place, here was a young woman, always stout, strong, and healthy; never had a day's illness, to her knowledge, except in childbed. Had children very rapidly; in fact, her third child was not fourteen months old, when the fourth and last was born. When carrying this child, she did not notice that she was any larger than usual, or that the abdominal weight was increased; neither was she conscious of any tumor existing in her abdomen, except the uterine one. She carried the child its full term; was then confined, after a very easy labor of four hours' duration. The placenta came away spontaneously, and every thing promised a speedy restoration to health. A few hours after confinement, for the first time, she makes the discovery that she is larger than usual, and that only when her bandage burst from the abdominal tension. This enlargement she and her attendants attributed to "wind." Was it, or was there then an immense ovarian tumor that had existed undiscovered? The midwife said that it was wind;

charlatan No. 1 said that it was wind; but charlatan No. 2 said that there was another child in the womb, and, upon the strength of this supposition, five days after the woman's confinement, thrust his hand into the uterus, and found—*nothing*. May he not have discovered some tumor that he mistook for an enlarged uterus? Three days after this occurrence, when summoned, I found an abdomen enormously distended, tense, inflamed, and full of fluid. The question naturally arises, What caused this peritonitis, and what gave rise to the rapid accumulation of fluid? Was it simple peritoneal effusion, encysted ovarian dropsy, or a combination of both, the result of a ruptured cyst? Time did not clear up the diagnosis; for, as the inflammation subsided, and the abdomen lost its tenderness and its tension, the physical signs were those of ascites. The abdomen was uniform, without any projection forward in assuming the dorsal position, as is the case in ovarian dropsy. No resonance was elicited anywhere, except in the epigastrium; change of posture caused change of shape; palpation caused wavelets to be seen all over the abdomen, and the most careful manipulation failed to discover any cystic inclosure. Had the enlargement been owing to an ovarian tumor, it must have existed during pregnancy, and yet its size was hardly compatible with a pregnant uterus at full term.

When paracentesis was performed, six weeks after confinement, the fluid evacuated was, in Dr. Blake's opinion, ovarian. Yet, neither Dr. Nelson nor myself could detect any remains of a cyst, although we explored the cavity of the pelvis and the abdomen carefully, as the tapping completely emptied it. Had there been a large cyst, it could scarcely have escaped observation, as the peritonitis, which had taken place, must have caused adhesion of the sac to some portion of the abdomen, and there we would have found it. From these facts, then, I think we can come to no other conclusion than that there was probably an ovarian cyst, which existed during pregnancy, and that it became suddenly ruptured, either during the throes of labor, or by the rough and ill-advised manipulation afterward used; that its contents, being poured into the abdominal cavity, excited peritoneal inflammation, and the forcible thrusting of the hand into the uterus, set up metritis. But whatever the lesion was that caused such a quantity of fluid to be poured out, after she recovered from the operation of paracentesis she remained perfectly well for over two months, and then noticed a small tumor in her left side. It grew apace, and was easily diagnosed as ovarian. This was the tumor that was removed by operation. It was unilocular, bosselated, and irregular in outline; its lining membrane covered with purulent deposit, through which four or five smaller cysts were making their appearance. The tumor, with its contents, was estimated to weigh between forty and fifty pounds. The only point in the operation that might, perhaps, be thought worthy of imitation, was the absence of any interference with the cavity of the abdomen, after the tumor was removed. No sponge or other material was used to wipe up the blood and serosity that were effused. Nature was trusted to do this work, and, as the result proved, she did it well.

Medical history is full of cases where ovarian disease was co-existent with pregnancy, and also cases where the tumor had burst before and after labor, but in all of them either signs or symptoms gave a clue to a correct reading of the lesion. In the present case, a difficulty of diagnosis was experienced, which adds an interest to the case, which will, I trust, compensate for the length of its narration.

Placenta Prævia Successfully Treated by Digital Compression.

By R. H. PLUMMER, M.D., of Dixon.

[Read before the Yolo County Medical Society.]

I was called at half-past five on the morning of January 19th, 1871, to see Mrs. L. The messenger said he feared she was dying; she was flowing profusely, had fainted several times, and couldn't speak. In a few moments, I was by her side, and the spectacle there presented was truly appalling. There lay a woman of stout physique, as white as the sheets that enshroud the pulseless form of the corpse; while pools of blood lay upon the floor, having trickled through the bed and run over its side.

By inquiry, I learned she was twenty-eight years of age, a native of Ireland, and had previously borne four living, healthy children, with no abortions. During the last month of her present pregnancy, she had complained of feeling unwell — occasional pains in the left side, with, at times, a half-benumbed sensation of the same lateral region. To use her language: "I had a very queer sort of feeling, such as I never before experienced, yet not ill enough to call a physician, though I often thought I ought to."

She had retired, the evening previous, ordinarily well; slept soundly till about four o'clock in the morning, when she awoke with a feeling of giddiness, and of numbness of one side, but without any pain, and discovered she was flowing freely—supposing, however, it was the "waters coming away." She called her husband, and said, "I believe I am going to be sick." The lamp was lighted. The flow continuing, the giddiness and numbness increasing, she put her hand down, and, upon raising it, exclaimed, with some difficulty of speech, that she was bleeding profusely, and bade him call a neighbor lady. Syncope followed immediately, from which it was several moments before she rallied, to find herself unable to utter an intelligible word. The lady desired was called, and then I was sent for, and before my arrival, she suffered repeated attacks of syncope.

I found her almost pulseless, and speechless, with cold extremities. Upon vaginal examination, I discovered I had to deal with a case of placenta prævia—the head presenting, the os dilated to about the size of a twenty-five-cent piece. The placenta was principally attached to the left side of the uterus, only a small portion overlying the os. Through the process of dilatation, it had been detached, severing the utero-placental vessels, whence the blood was still flowing.

In ordinary cases of placenta prævia, with ante-partem hemorrhage, the rule is to "turn and deliver;" but here was an extraordinary case. The fetus, in all probability (from previous history), already dead; the current of life had almost run out; the last flame of the wick was flickering in the socket. Should the flood-gates be not immediately closed—should the ebbing of that life-current be not stayed without delay—that soul would surely wing its flight to Him who gave it. I forcibly dilated the os sufficiently to enable me to discover the exact source of the hemorrhage, when, by digital compression, I was enabled to "stay further proceedings." I had brandy administered *ad lib.*, with hot applications to the extremities, frictions, etc., as hurriedly as possible. In the course of an hour or more, I had the gratifying evidence of a renewed life, in an improving pulse and returning power of speech. I also discovered the patient had an attack of hemiplegia, the left side, from the cervical region down, including the tongue (though the facial muscles were unaffected), being completely paralyzed. She was powerless to move either the thoracic or abdominal limbs of that side; while she experienced the sensation of the "pricking of a thousand needles." Yet there was neither hyperesthesia on the affected side, nor anesthesia on the opposite side, as portrayed by Brown-Sequard, in his "Lectures on Organic Affections and Injuries of the Spinal Cord," published in the *London Lancet;* and subsequent examination gave no evidence of tenderness or pain in any portion of the cord. Having no thermometer at hand, I could not ascertain the comparative temperature of the two sides, though, to the hand, there was no perceptible change.

In the course of a few hours, my patient rallied very much, when I administered the fl. ext. of ergot. "Pains" gradually came on, the os dilated, the head advanced, and, in a short time, much to my relief, took the place of my fingers in producing the necessary compression. About one o'clock P.M.—nine hours from the attack of hemorrhage—I delivered her of a dead male child.

I did not succeed in getting my patient to sleep any until the second night, about thirty-six hours after delivery, during which time she had taken gr. xx. of Dover powder, and gr. xl. of chloral-hydrate, and then it was only at intervals, to start up in horrible dreams of "doctors and other hobgoblins." During the third day, however, she had a refreshing sleep, from which she made a rapid recovery, the power of motion gradually returning, until, in eight days, the paralysis had entirely passed away. In sixteen days, the patient was able to sit up; and in a short time, having entirely recovered, moved away, since when I have heard nothing of her.

SELECTED.

Clinical Lecture on Dissection Poisons.

BY JAMES PAGET, D.C.L., F.R.S.

[From the London Lancet.]

The subject of dissection wounds has, of late years, seemed less important than it was thought to be some thirty years ago. When I was a student, it was believed that such wounds were not rarely fatal, and that frequently they led to severe disease. Now, they are made light of. My recent illness disposes me to think this levity misplaced. It is very improbable that there should be any change in the virulence of poisons generated in the dead body; and if there be any change in the consequences of inoculation with them, I should think it due to the changes in the manner of treating them. In my student-days the first signs of inflammation following such wounds were generally treated with leeches, purgatives, spare diet, and other depressing means; now, as for many years past, the prescription is good food, wine, rest, and, above all, fresh air. You may be certain that this is the better prescription; and I believe that if I could have availed myself of the whole of it, especially of the last two ingredients, I should have averted most of the troubles that I have lately suffered.

Let me now speak to you about these troubles. And, first, as to their source and the conditions on which they depend. The material with which I was infected was in the dead body of the patient on whose case I last lectured. He died after lithotomy, with acute cellulitis at the back of the pelvis, and with acute pleurisy; both of which, I believe, were of pyæmial origin. The grounds for this belief I stated to you when, at the last lecture, I showed you the morbid structures removed after death. I refer to it now only that I may remind you of the probability that the inflammatory products of pyæmial disease are especially virulent after death. The most dangerous examinations appear to be those of women who have died with puerperal peritonitis; and most of the cases thus named are pyæmial. I can only suspect that the material which poisoned me was in the pleuritic fluid, in which my hands were long soaked; but what the poisonous material—the virus—was, neither this, nor any record of similar cases, enables me to tell.

Whatever the virus was, it soaked through my skin; I had no wound or crack of any kind. Mr. Young, who began the examination, cut himself and suffered no harm. I had a sound skin, but one not impenetrable, and through it the virus worked its way. Mr. Young did what I advise you to do in any similar case. He washed his hands, sucked the cut part, made it bleed freely, and then took care of himself, and did not rub the cut part with nitrate of silver. He thus reduced his risk to less than that of the absorption of virus through sound skin.

This absorption is generally spoken of as if it were a strange and rare fact. Rare it may be, but strange it is not; for thus it is, that most commonly the poison of chancre passes through skin, and that of gonorrhœa through mucous membrane, and thus that the irritant matter of cantharides and other skin-irritants passes to the cutis, and from it may be absorbed. A wound or a crack that exposes a vascular surface is doubtless very favorable to infection by any virus; but it is not essential; I wish it had been and were still so.

Thus, then, this virus passed into me; and I will tell you presently some of the mischief that it did. But first let me say that this mischief would not have happened but that there was in me something that made my blood, or some of my textures, susceptible of such diseased processes as the virus could excite. For not all men can be made ill by a virus from a dead body, nor can the same man be made ill at all times; but there must be what is called a fitting soil for the virus to work in. We know no more what this soil is than we do what the virus is; we have to use figurative expressions; but we need not doubt that they imply facts, and that, for any living body to be made diseased by a dead one, there must be certain living materials which can be diverted by the dead ones from their normal relations and turned into a morbid course.

A chief interest in reference to these various susceptibilities of the influence of virus from dead bodies is, that one may become insusceptible. They who are day after day engaged in dissections, or in *post mortem* examinations, usually acquire a complete immunity from the worse influences of the virus. They may suffer local troubles from it, and some among them may get that curious warty affection of the skin of the hands or fingers which Dr. Wilks described in the Guy's Hospital Reports; or they may lose health through the influence of bad air or over-work; but they do not suffer with any infection of the lymph or blood.

Such an immunity as this I enjoyed when I was demonstrator of morbid anatomy, and made almost daily *post mortem* examinations. It mattered not what was the disease of which the examined body died, or what was the state of my skin, sound or cracked or wounded: nothing hurt me; and this immunity lasted many years.

A similar immunity in the case of many fevers is possessed by those who have passed through one attack. It is, as you know, very rare to have a second attack of scarlet fever or of typhus; and it is, perhaps, more rare to have a second indurated chancre, or a second complete series of secondary symptoms. In these cases we believe that the first attack alters the blood or tissues in such a manner that they are no longer susceptible of the same morbid changes as they were, even though in all other respects they appear unaltered. But I think it is not in this way that the immunity from the infections of dead bodies is obtained; for though few demonstrators or others constantly engaged in morbid anatomy escape quite unscathed, yet some do so; and these may be enough to prove that the immunity is acquired by what we may call custom. Just as a man, beginning with small quantities of strong drink, and gradually increasing them, may never get drunk, even though he may at last drink hugely too much; or as a Styrian (if the stories be true), may take arsenic till he can hardly be poisoned with it, so may any one by custom become insusceptible of the evil effects of the corpse-poisons. It may be that his blood and tissues become less alterable by alien matters, or that the living parts acquire more power of assimilating or excreting the dead materials that are introduced among them; how it comes to pass, we can not surely tell, but the fact of an acquired immunity seems certain.

I wish some of you would study these immunities more closely than any one has yet done. They are of infinite interest in physiology, for they show a striking contrast between dead and living things. *Gutta cavat lapidem* is a pattern of many proverbs that express the popular knowledge that all dead things yield to the repeated application of small forces; yet living things rather strengthen themselves against such forces. Not that this or any other contrast between dead and living things is absolute or constant; yet this, like all the rest, is worth most careful study. And of still more interest in pathology are these acquired immunities; for as yet we know scarcely more than the bare fact. Some immunities are local—such as that of which any one will tell you who has had a long succession of blisters on the same place. He finds at last he can be blistered there no more; yet you may blister him on some other part. And such, I suspect, is the immunity from the virus of soft chancre, which may be obtained through frequent inoculations; but of this I have no experimental knowledge. I think, however, that I have had personal knowledge of acquired immunity from another kind of inserted poisons—that, namely, of fleas, bugs, and the like pests of vacation life. Let me commend this subject of study to any of you who are not unwilling to be martyrs to science. I think you will find, as I have found in some continental tours, that for the first nights you will be driven half wild by the vermin of the bed or of the air, but that after a time you care less for them, and that at last you become indifferent to them; not because they leave you alone, but because their virus no longer irritates the blood or the textures that at first fiercely resented them.

This instance may seem a trivial one; yet I believe that in it you may find illustrations of much more serious things, even of that doctrine of syphilization of which you have heard so much.

But now observe: this immunity, it seems, may be gradually lost, just as that after vaccination may be; the influence, as the expression is, gradually wears out. My case is evidence of this. Years ago no virus of a dead body could hurt me; but then came a time in which I made few or no examinations after death. I stood by and watched others making them; and I became again susceptible to poisons that were once innocuous. My blood and textures regained the state they had before ever virus was introduced into them, and I became again more poisonable.

Think how curious a fact this, which is only one of a large class, is. Being more susceptible of morbid influences, one seems less healthy; but, in truth, one has become more healthy. Just as in vaccination, or in scarlet fever, one's blood or textures, or both, being so altered that the same poison will no longer act on them, they seem the better for the change; yet they are morbidly altered. And then, for years afterward, by the exact assimilation of the nutritive process, they are maintained in the same morbid state; like a scar which, useful as it is, is yet a morbid structure. And as a scar, if not too deep, gradually wears out — that is, gradually reverts to the healthy skin-structure—so is it with the blood and textures of the once infected person. Recovering their natural condition, they become again susceptible of infection; becoming again healthy, they become what may seem weaker, and are more liable to disease.

Think, again, of the long time during which facts like these prove that a process of recovery from disease may continue before it is perfect. The years through which a man must pass before he becomes liable to a second attack of these diseases tell the time that is required for his complete recovery from the first. Let the fact teach you both patience and hope in your treatment of the consequences of disease. It makes me believe that I might now, with perfect safety, examine any dead body whatever.

Now let me tell you, with commentaries, what the virus did in me. The examination was made on the 4th of February, and after it I finished a long day's work, feeling unharmed. On the 5th, which was a Sunday, I felt, not ill, but tired, and I spent the greater part of the day idly, falling asleep over good books. On the 6th I lectured, in the morning, on the morbid structures obtained from the examination, and the theatre was, as usual on Mondays in the winter, very cold. I was chilled and very tired; but a heavy day's work had to be done, and I did it. I had observed three or four small pustules on my hands, especially one on the back of my left hand, but they caused no discomfort, and I had no suspicion of being hurt till about five o'clock, when I felt my left axillary glands tender, and could not press my arm against my side. At half-past eight, when I got home, I was cold and ill; the mischief was begun.

I mention these things that I may illustrate, as I have so often done, the influence of fatigue in developing disease, or at least in making one susceptible of it. I can be as sure of this as of any thing which has not occurred, that if I could have rested for two or three days after the insertion of the virus, it would have done me little or no harm. I can not tell you whether it is by mere diminution of a normal power of resisting changes, or (as Dr. Carpenter has shown to be much more probable) by the production in the fatigued organs of some material on which morbid poisons may multiply or flourish; but you will find in every day's practice that fatigue has a large share in the promotion or permission of diseases than any other single casual condition you can name.

Thus, then, I was prepared for receiving injury, and the injury was supplied in some material of this dead body. And I would repeat that this material was probably something special enough to be called a virus or poison; for although any decomposing organic matter may in some persons give rise to the worst forms of blood-poisoning, yet I have no reason to think they would have done so in me. Not a day has passed for many months without my hands being in contact with pus and other decaying or decomposed organic matters; yet none of these poisoned me, though I was often enough as much fatigued as when I fell ill.

I wish that I could tell exactly all the signs of illness that I so anxiously watched; but during acute disease one can not record, and after recovery one can not well remember, the daily progress of a case. I can only tell the general consequences of this poisoning.

The first thing observed was a few small pustules on the hands, very trivial-looking things, which appeared on the day after the examination, and in the next week or ten days dried without discharging or causing any local trouble. I think they were only local effects of the simply irritant fluids of the body, or of the carbolic acid oil, with which I had uselessly though thoroughly rubbed my hands before beginning my part of the examination. I see no reason for supposing that the material which poisoned me was from any of these pustules.

The first sign of the general poisoning was (as I have said) the pain in the axillary lymph-glands. No lymph-vessels could be seen or felt up the arm at any time; the absorbed material traversed them, but did not irritate them; but the glands enlarged, and became painful to a degree far surpassing the swelling or any other sign of inflammation in them. I do not know whether this exceeding painfulness was due to something in the poison, or was dependent on some peculiarity in my nervous system. I have seen it in one other case of poisoned wound, in which, as in mine, it indicated no great severity of inflammation in the glands. With me it slowly diminished, but did not quite cease till I was nearly well again, although no considerable morbid changes took place in the glands. They were painful, nothing else.

Next after this affection of the axillary lymph-glands came wide-spread inflammation of cellular tissue. But before saying more of this I ought to tell what may have had some influence in determining the course of my case—namely, that my axillary glands were already damaged, and may have been less penetrable by fluid than they should be. More than thirty years ago, when I was a student, I was infected while dissecting (I had not yet acquired the immunity which I afterward gained and lost); and this infection was followed by one of the lesser and slower consequences of dissection injuries, the suppuration of lymph-glands. At that time my left axillary glands slowly suppurated, and, after discharging for many weeks, healed with a deep scar, and shriveling and partial calcification. Thus damaged they may have too much hindered the course of the absorbed fluid; but I doubt their doing so, for I have never been conscious of any obstruction in them; and in other cases of patients with healthy lymph-glands the same inflammation of cellular tissue as I had occurs.

This inflammation, which became evident four or five days after the infection, extended quickly from the axilla up the left side of my neck, over and below the clavicle, and down the back nearly as far as the ilium. Observe the range within which the inflammation was limited, for in this, as in other cases, it was in the range of lymphatics connected directly, or not far from directly, with the lymph-glands first affected. A frequent site for such cellular inflammation is down the side of the chest, or over or beneath the pectoral muscles. Thus it was with Mr. Bloxam, who was poisoned about a fortnight after me, and in whom acute pleurisy with effusion occurred on the same side. But, so far as I know, cases do not occur of similar inflammation on the opposite side, or separated far from the lymph-glands corresponding with the poisoned part, unless it be at a later period of illness, when pyæmia is established. This seems to be a point of distinction between these dissection-poisonings and pyæmia; their effects are at first, however severe, comparatively limited to the part poisoned, and to the lymphatic vessels and glands, or to the cellular tissue, nearly in relation with it. They may lead to pyæmia, but they do this only by secondary changes, or, as it were, by some accident.

The range of cellular inflammation in these cases, following as they do on the affection of the axillary glands, seems to indicate that they are due to arrest of lymph in the affected parts, and to its being poisoned by reflux from the glands. Thus poisoned it would at once infect the cellular tissue in contact or close proximity, and hence would be derived the spreading inflammation, much like phlegmonous erysipelas, with sloughing or diffuse suppuration.

In my case the inflammation, at first widely diffused, gradually concentrated its effects in two places — first at the back, nearly over the angle of the sixth rib, where suppuration was evident about a fortnight after the first appearance of the swelling, and, about a week later, under the edge of the trapezius, just above the level of the clavicle. Both these abscesses were freely opened. The first was seated in the deepest part of the subcutaneous cellular tissue, and the second under the cervical fascia. The first suppurated very freely; the second scantily. Both healed soundly in five or six weeks from the time of opening them.

The position of this second abscess deserves notice, for it was probably due in part to the old damage of the axillary glands, of which I have already spoken. It was such an abscess as might have pointed in the axilla, and I always felt as if it would do so, for hardness and pain could always be detected there. But it seemed as if the axillary tissues would not yield, and therefore the abscess extended upward, above the apex of the axilla, to the subfascial tissue beneath the edge of the trapezius. Both these abscesses were opened early—that is, so soon as fluid was clearly discovered in them. And I felt the comfort and utility of this practice; for though they had given me very little pain, and had been soothed with poultices, yet they seemed to keep alive my fever, and especially before the pointing of the second I had chills and exhaustion, which were evidently remedied by its being opened. In the opening of it I enjoyed the safety which I have often conferred on others by the adoption of Mr. Hilton's plan. The abscess lay very deep, and was very small, under the edge of the muscle, and with integuments and cellular tissue so thickened over it that all the landmarks for incisions were lost, and the district was one in the depths of which a knife, however skillfully used, might have given me serious trouble. The director penetrated the abscess safely, and the forceps sufficiently dilated the opening, and I had self-evidence on which to urge you to use Mr. Hilton's plan in all operations on abscesses in dangerous regions.

After the opening of the abscesses the infiltration of the cellular tissue about them cleared up slowly; and, more than once, patches of thick edema appeared over the left ilium, as if suppuration would take place there; and when erysipelas came on there was much more than usual edema with it, as if there were still some hinderance to the free movement of the lymph.

The general illness that attended these suppurations was not severe. When it was evident that abscesses would form—that is, a fortnight after infection—I was sent to Norwood, and, with the fresh air and quiet of the place, I gained strength, and could eat and drink well, and digest pretty well, and seemed floating into convalescence. But just before the evident suppuration of the second abscess, I had chills every day, and after them heat; and with these great loss of power and general distress—distress so keen that it seems hardly possible that I should now be unable to describe it, or even clearly to remember it.

This general illness, this constitutional disturbance, was, I believe, the beginning of erysipelas. But before speaking of this, let me tell that the pus from my abscess appeared to have irritant properties above those of ordinary pus. For my children's nurse, who made and put on my poultices, pricked her finger; and this was followed by very acute inflammation and suppuration, extending from the puncture over all the hand and forearm. The same thing happened through a similar accident, to Mr. Bloxam's nurse, one who was habituated to pus of all ordinary kinds, and had not suffered from them.

Of the erysipelas that affected me after these abscesses, beginning about a month from the time of infection, I need not say much; for it had no remarkable feature, unless it were in the degree of subcutaneous edema which predominated over the inflammation of the skin and remained very long. Beginning near the wound in the neck, the erysipelas spread slowly over the chest and back, down the left arm, and over the nates and parts of the thighs. The eruption was much more extensive on the left side than on the right; it slowly cleared up, and after desquamation no trace of it remained, unless it be in a weakness of the minute blood-vessels of my arm; for even now, after my bath, the affected part of this arm appears dusky and mottled.

It was during the erysipelas that my general health suffered most; but my recollection is not clear about any thing but the feelings of intolerable restlessness, which nothing but wine or morphia would tranquilize, and of the interest with which for many days I watched the progress of my own case, fancying myself an intelligent observer. At last, after the erysipelas had been extending for about ten days, and at the end of nearly six weeks from the infection, there came what seemed to me like a crisis. During the night in which my pulse and temperature were at their highest, I had a profuse sweating and a profuse flow of urine, such as I never had in my life before; and next day my pulse and temperature had come down to what might be deemed safety-points, and I was conscious of returning health.

In the treatment that I received during the erysipelas, I am sure that quinine was very useful. I generally took three or four grains of the hydrochlorate three times a day, and it always (I think) lowered my pulse and diminished my restlessness and (I believe) my temperature. And I wish I could tell the comfort that morphia gave me—whether in bringing sleep, or in changing the unrest that always increased toward night into a happy and complacent wakefulness, almost as refreshing as sleep. It was well that pleasure unnaturally obtained should have a penalty; and this was in the dryness of mouth, which seemed due to a total suspension of the secretion of saliva, and which became at last even less tolerable than restlessness. Locally, collodion, freely applied as soon as an erysipelatous redness appeared, gave great comfort. It did not hinder the spreading of the erysipelas; but it relieved the itching and heat of the eruption, and it prevented the horrid itching of the desquamation, which was intense, and renewed for many days on exposure to air at every place to which the collodion was not applied. These things were certainly beneficial; but I suppose that those which most helped me to a safe passage through the illness were, a judicious moderate use of food and wine, and very wise and gentle nursing.

This erysipelas, it may be believed, was part of the effects of the poison of the dead body—an issue of the blood-poisoning. Not such, I think, was a pneumonia with which I suffered twice, and which added greatly to the risk and length of my illness. This was, probably, personal, due only indirectly, if at all, to the poison—due rather to a susceptibility of my lungs to the inflammatory process : for I have had acute pneumonia five times during the eighteen years before this illness. All these attacks have occurred after severe over-work, with deficient food, and exposure to cold ; and the manner in which they have cleared off, leaving my lungs unimpaired in structure, has made it nearly certain that they were rheumatic or gouty. But, however this may be, the pneumonia, of which one attack commenced only two days after the infection, and the other a week after the disappearance of the erysipelas, must be ascribed to me rather than to the poison. They passed through their usual course, and left my lungs sound again; but I ask your attention to them as an illustration of one of the ways in which a specific disease may be complicated or modified by the personal constitution of the patient. Here was an instance of what one may call a specific poisoning; and one of the first things following it was pneumonia. Associated as this was with evidence of poison in the lymph-glands, it might have been thought pyæmial, or in some way due to the specific poison in the blood. Yet it was only such a pneumonia as I might have had without having been poisoned, or such as might occur in me in any feverish illness from whatever source.

Keep such facts as this in mind. They show that there is no disease so specific but that its signs may be confused or complicated with the things that are peculiar to the patient. Syphilis is a specific disease as sharply defined as any, but its course and appearance in a scrofulous man and in a gouty one are very different. Vaccination produces a well-marked specific disease; but in one patient it may be followed by inflammation of lymphatics, in another by eczema, in another by any thing you please; but all these are due in only a minor degree to the vaccination; they come out from the personal constitutions of the several patients disturbed by the vaccination, as they might have been by any thing else producing some slight fever.

This is not a mere question of doctrinal pathology. It is among the first necessities for success in practice, that in the total phenomena of disease observed in any patient, you should be able to estimate what belongs to the disease and what to the man. A farmer may as well expect success if he sows his fields without regard to their soils or to the weeds that may of themselves come up in them, as one of us may expect it if we treat diseases without exactly studying the constitutions of those in whom they occur.

Thus I have given a sketch of my three months' illness, and some of the thoughts which it suggested to me. But I ought to say that my case showed only one of many forms of disease that may be produced by the poisons of dead bodies. The suppuration of lymph-glands, which I had many years ago, is another. But besides such as these, you may find cases in trivial local inflammation; of direct and simple erysipelas; of spreading, suppurating, or sloughing inflammation of the cellular tissue of the hand and arm; of pyæmia; and of the fiercest septicæmia. And it is remarkable that different effects may be produced by the same poison acting on different persons. Mr. Erichsen mentions a case in which six students were infected by the same body: two had suppuration of the areolar tissue under the pectoral muscles and in the axilla; one, a kind of maniacal delirium; a fourth had typhoid fever; and the other two were seriously indisposed. I advise you to read up the subject in his "Art and Science of Surgery." He has given an excellent account of it; and so has Billroth in his and v. Pitha's "Handbuch der Chirurgie."

Sir William Lawrence used to say that he had not known any one recover on whose case more than seven had consulted. Our art has improved. I had the happiness of being attended by nine: Dr. Burrows, Sir Wm. Jenner, Dr. Gull, Dr. Andrew, Dr. Gee, Mr. Cæsar Hawkins, Mr. Savory, Mr. Thomas Smith, and Mr. Karkeek. In this multitude of counselors was safety. The gratitude I owe to them is more than I can tell — more than all the evidences of my esteem can ever prove.

Rapid Development of Mortification — An Explanation of the Morbid Condition in the Case of A. P. Crittenden.

[Editorial Note.—The following communication came to hand too late for insertion in its proper place; but as it is supplementary in some degree to the paper of Dr. Buckley in the last No. of the Journal, we make room for it here, so that it may come in as near to that paper as possible.]

By EDWIN BENTLEY, M.D., U.S.A.

The last number of the Journal contained an elaborate article, by Dr. C. F. Buckley, of this city, in which he says: "We omit altogether comment on that part of the testimony which threw actual doubt on the cause of death, viz.: that the mortification of the bowels, found on post mortem examination, might have existed while Mr. Crittenden was yet pleading in court during the day of the fatal shooting." The author, having thus failed in any way to elucidate the "morbid conditions" found at the post mortem examination, which must be regarded by all as a matter of the most vital importance, and not at all understood either by the court or the public, or, as far as any explanation has appeared in print, even by the medical witnesses, I propose to state the natural and simple pathological fact, which alone can account for the mortification found, without involving the necessity of its presence previous to the wound. This is the more important, as Dr. Buckley dismisses it without giving any explanation whatever of this natural and simple pathological fact; and I do it the more willingly, as the medical testimony has been so often arraigned, not alone during the trial of the accused, but since, so that the medical fraternity have been so divided among themselves that the legal profession has taken advantage of this lack of harmony to assail not only individuals, but the mass of the fraternity.

In the examination of the body of Mr. Crittenden, two important lesions were found, which were brought out on the examination of medical witnesses for the prosecution. First, a pistol-ball had passed through the cavities of the heart, opening up a communication between the right and left sides, as in fetal life, inflicting a wound necessarily and inevitably fatal, although life was prolonged some twenty-eight hours or more by the foreign matter which followed and was lodged in the track of the missile. This temporarily so repaired the openings in the walls of the heart that a partial circulation was allowed to go on. Had this wound alone been found, the inquiry into the cause of death might have rested here very properly. But a second condition was observed, scarcely less imposing in its fatal result than the pistol-wound itself, viz.: mortification of a portion of the intestines. As the deceased was in full health twenty-four hours before death, and in the active pursuit of his profession, the presence of this condition appeared almost incredible; and honest men seemed almost ready to doubt the evidence of their senses. The question arose, How is it possible for a man to be in court to-day, and mortification of the bowels to be found to-morrow? As well might it be asked, Can a man be in the active pursuit of his occupation to-day, and dead to-morrow? What practical surgeon has not seen a wound, or an amputation, made to-day, gangrenous to-morrow? The doctrine of thrombi or emboli, introduced by Virchow, in 1847, to every intelligent pathologist will explain the mortification found in the intestines, in the most ready and satisfactory manner. It is conceded that the foreign matter which followed the ball closed up the orifices in the heart, thus permitting a partial circulation of the blood to go on, and to perpetuate the degree of animal life which continued for twenty-eight hours after receiving the wound. Hence, detached fragments were not only liable to be, but could not help being, carried away by the continued course of the blood, and, lodging in the inferior mesenteric artery, so completely occluded it as to produce the condition of sphacelus which was found; it being well understood that the supply of blood may be as completely cut off by blocking up the interior of a vessel as by putting a ligature around it. Examples of coma and sudden death, brought on by occlusion of the cerebral vessels from emboli, are quite common. Many instances of this kind, within the last ten years, have come under observation.

Thus, a simple application of the most common principles of morbid action, gives a complete solution of the problem. The explanation can not fail to be intelligible to all who are capable of comprehending so much of the anatomy of the system and the laws of disease as to know that when a bandage is tied so tightly around a limb that the blood can not circulate through it, gangrene or mortification may result in a single day; and if the vessels are stopped up by a foreign substance within them, the course of the blood is as completely obstructed as if they were included in a ligature, and when the supply of blood is cut off, mortification is the inevitable result. Is it not much better for the profession and for society, that we insist, in court as elsewhere, on the application of these simple principles, to the elucidation of morbid action, rather than withhold our knowledge, and produce an impression on the public mind unfavorable to the capabilities of science, and the intelligence of our profession?

REVIEWS AND NOTICES OF BOOKS.

Restorative Medicine: An Harveian Annual Oration, delivered at the Royal College of Physicians, London, on June 21, 1871. (The 210th Anniversary). By Thomas King Chambers, M.D., etc. With two sequels. Philadelphia: Henry C. Lea. 1871. San Francisco: A. Roman & Co.

For upward of two centuries, the author tells us in the preface, the London College of Physicians complied with the letter of Harvey's wishes as expressed in his deed of gift, by causing an annual oration to be delivered in Latin. During the last few years it has been deemed advisable to substitute English. In compliment to America and American physicians, the oration of this year, though delivered in England, is printed and published in America first. "The offering is a poor one," says the author, modestly, "then, let it be repaid by a richer." The profession in our country will appreciate the compliment, particularly as the "Oration" has much intrinsic value, and will be read with instruction and pleasure.

On Some Disorders of the Nervous System in Childhood: Being the Lumleian Lectures delivered at the Royal College of Physicians in London, in March, 1871. By Charles West, M.D., Fellow and Senior Censor of the College, Physician to the Hospital for Sick Children. Philadelphia: Henry C. Lea. 1871. Pp. 131.

There are three lectures in this series: 1. Neuralgia and Epilepsy; 2. Chorea and Paralysis; 3. Disorder and Loss of Power of Speech, etc. Perhaps no living writer is more familiar with the phenomena of young life, both in health and disease, than Dr. West. His reputation will not suffer from these lectures. They are made much the more interesting by the multitudes of "side issues" which he introduces.

EDITORIAL.

A Repulsive Association.

Notwithstanding the repeated exposures of the trick referred to in the subjoined letter, the editors of this Journal are still frequently confounded with the individual therein mentioned, and often subjected to embarrassment and mortification in consequence. As an affair of business merely, involving the question of money, we have much less complaint to make than in regard to the bad reputation which reflects on a professional man from being confounded with an advertising charlatan, and associated with the traffic in "French safes," and the means of criminal abortion, and other filth. The following letter, which explains itself, is only one of many which we have written under similar circumstances:

San Francisco, September 20, 1871.

To A. R.—Sir: I have received from you, by mail, a letter asking my advice in your case. Your letter is addressed to "Dr. Gibbons," and refers to my "advertisement." My son and myself are the only persons of that name in San Francisco, but we do not belong to the advertising breed. Regular and honorable physicians never puff themselves in the newspapers.

That practice is left to impostors and charlatans, whose knowledge and skill would never be discovered if they were not to advertise themselves. There is an individual in this city, who, some years ago, came here from the mines, knowing no more of medicine than my horse, and perpetrated a fraud on me and on the public by changing his name so as to counterfeit mine, and advertising "patent French safes," etc. Perhaps your letter was intended for him. Yours, etc.,

H. Gibbons, M.D.

Origin of the Poison of Scarlatina.

An English writer, Dr. Carpenter, attributes the production of the poison of scarlet fever to the decomposition of the blood of animals. He details cases of the outbreak of the disease near slaughter-houses, and in localities where manure from slaughter-houses had been used. Though he does not deny its contagiousness, yet he believes it capable of arising *de novo* from the assigned source. So far, so good. We have long regarded the doctrine as fallacious which attributes scarlatina, and a number of other maladies, exclusively to a specific, self-generated poison. All such diseases must have started up at some period in the history of man, and their specific virus must have originated in the human body, as it were, without inheritance. And though the condition of things has changed in the long ages, yet it appears plausible in theory, and also consistent with fact, that specific poisons of the same nature continue to be developed or created by the original process. We believe it is universally conceded that erysipelas, while it springs up spontaneously, is capable of developing a specific virus which will reproduce the disease. What is there unreasonable in placing many other "zymotic" affections in the same category? How shall we account for the origin of chicken-pox, mumps, whooping-cough, and a variety of like affections, which often break forth in localities remote from their previous existence, unless the doctrine be admitted that the specific virus of many, if not of all, contagious disorders, may be generated in the human body under certain conditions hitherto inappreciable, without the presence of any pre-existing germinal poison *sui generis?* True, the hypothesis of *organic* germs is opposed to this view, unless we adopt the doctrine of the spontaneous generation of life. But that hypothesis, in regard to most diseases, is a mere conjecture. It is far more probable that the virus of specific diseases is mostly chemical, and developed in the fluids of the body in a similar manner to the poison which inoculates a dissecting wound.

Strychnos Potatorum—Clearing-nut of India.

The tree above named presents one instance among a multitude which might be recounted, of the opposite qualities possessed by different species of plants of the same genus. The fruit, when young, is made into a preserve and eaten. When mature it is used as an emetic, half a tea-spoonful of the powder being required. The dried seeds are used for the purpose of clearing muddy water, one of them being rubbed up for a short time in the earthen vessel, and the water being then poured in and left to settle. The impurities soon subside, and the water becomes clear, tasteless, and wholesome. The seeds are carried about by the officers and soldiers in India in time of war, for the purpose described. They are more easily obtained than alum, and more wholesome. The emetic and medicinal properties reside in the rind, and not properly in the seed, the latter having no active qualities, and in this respect presenting a striking contrast to its congener (strychnos nux vomica), which is the common source of strychnia. The tree grows in the woods and mountains of India, and is not so common as the nux vomica. The berry contains but one seed, while the latter has a number. We glean these facts from an article in the *Amer. Jour. of Pharmacy*, taken from the *London Pharm. Jour.*

The Tea-spoon as a Measure.

A writer in the *Canadian Pharmaceutical Journal*, who has examined the subject critically, says that tea-spoons have been gradually growing larger of late years, the spoon of the last century having been only about two-thirds of the size of that now in common use. He adds, however, that three sizes are made at the present time—large, medium, and small, containing 95, 85, and 60 minims respectively. Table-spoons, also, have increased, and vary from 4.5 to 6 fluid drachms in capacity. He infers that the dose of certain articles may be unsafe, if a tea-spoonful or a table-spoonful be ordered, and proposes to abolish the dessert-spoon as a measure, substituting two tea-spoonfuls. It is rarely, we apprehend, that more than a drachm is administered as a tea-spoonful, or more than half an ounce as a table-spoonful. On the contrary, nine times in ten, according to our experience, an ounce mixture, when ordered in tea-spoonful doses, will afford more than eight doses, and an eight-ounce mixture more than sixteen table-spoonfuls. Nurses seldom fill the spoon to its utmost capacity.

Contents of the Journal.

We are sure that our readers will not find fault with the space allotted to the Clinical Lecture on Dissection Wounds, by Sir James Paget. A view of the subject so complete and practical has not been produced hitherto.

The mortification of the intestines revealed by the necropsy in the case of the late Mr. Crittenden, the suddenness of which was a source of great perplexity during the legal investigation, receives an explanation highly ingenious and rational in the communication of Dr. Bentley. As a practical pathologist, Dr. B. is not excelled, if equaled, on this coast; and we have great confidence in his judgment on the question.

Dr. Tyrrell's case of ovarian disease, presents some features of novelty. The result is gratifying, more especially as the operation of ovariotomy has not been generally successful in California.

The paper of Dr. Plummer presents a useful hint as to a means of arresting uterine hemorrhage in certain cases.

The Social Evil — Proposed Legislation.

This subject was the theme of discussion at the meeting of the San Francisco Medical Society, September 26th. The minutes of the discussion will appear in our next issue. There appeared to be but one sentiment among the members, and it found expression in the unanimous adoption of the following resolution:

Resolved, As the sense of this Society, that all laws which license, and therefore sanction, prostitution, with the design of restraining disease or licentiousness, are unsound in principle, derogatory to private and public morals, and incapable of accomplishing what they attempt.

"Boiling Out" the Stomach.

At a meeting of the Atlanta Academy of Medicine (*Atlanta Med. and Surg. Jour.*), a member gave an account of his favorite method of emptying the stomach when other means had failed, by taking advantage of the effervescence of acid and alkali. A negro boy, æt. 14, was insensible from supposed poisoning by stramonium, and it was found impossible to induce emesis by any ordinary process. "An ash-hopper close by suggested the idea of acids and alkalies to *boil out* the supposed poison. With no time to lose, gave a tea-cupful of lye and the little tartaric acid he had, drenched down, followed by another tea-cupful of lye and a little soda—all he could get—and rolled him over a few times, when he boiled out several quarts of half-masticated, raw, red yam-potatoes. The boy remained insensible twenty-four hours longer, deaf the same length of time, and blind for about eight hours, had some fever on reaction, but made good his recovery." A great boy that!

One Hundred and Fifteen Years Old.

Dr. Bowling, of the *Nashville Journal of Medicine*, has been visiting "Aunt Vick," at Harpeth Hills, Tennessee. She was born, so he has ascertained, in August, 1756, in Camden, N. C. He found her standing in the middle of the floor, supporting herself by a crooked stick longer than herself, which she grasped near the top. She was bare-headed and bare-footed, and dressed in a strong, clean, white, home-made, cotton garment, that reached from her neck to the floor. She spoke with clearness, though very hard of hearing; has never been sick, and boasts that a doctor never gave her any "stuff;" has a good appetite and good digestion, and would sleep very well every night but for prurigo. She has two children, the younger of whom is seventy-five years of age.

Sleep-Walking in Childhood.

Dr. West, in his *Lumleian Lectures*, attributes somnambulism, in its most marked forms, to undue mental work, not always, indeed, on account of the tasks being excessive, but sometimes on the over-anxiety of the child to make progress. He adds, "I have not yet known a poor person's child a somnambulist." The inference is, that the children of the poor are not subjected to intellectual exercise and excitement, which may hold good in England, but certainly does not in America. A much better explanation, in our belief, is that somnambulism depends mainly on a nervous organization of peculiar sensitiveness, which is stimulated to morbid and extravagant development in the children of the rich, but repressed and blunted by the attrition of humble life.

Ulcers of the Os Uteri — Uterine Plug.

M. Després, Surgeon to the Paris Venereal Hospital for Females, has published a work, which is referred to in the *London Lancet*, recommending local treatment almost exclusively for ulcerations of the cervix uteri, and attaching equal value to different caustics, such as the red-hot iron and nitrate of silver. He says they all cure in about the same time. He also extols the *plug*, made as follows: Take a small piece of coarse gauze, in which a pledget of cotton-wool is placed, after it has been filled with about fifteen grains of powdered alum. Fold the gauze over the wool, and tie the ends of the former with a thread five or six inches long, which is allowed to hang out of the vagina, to facilitate the removal of the plug. The latter should remain twenty-four hours.

Differences among Doctors and Lawyers.

A good illustration of the propriety with which lawyers can taunt the medical profession with their differences in legal testimony, is contained in the following statement: The decisions of Lord Giffard, Chief Justice of England, in appeals from the lower Courts, for the first six months of the year 1870, cover forty-one cases. The judgment of the lower Courts was affirmed in only seventeen, modified in five, and positively reversed in nineteen. The *Phil. Med. Times*, in commenting on the matter, remarks that a physician who is called into Court will see in six hours more quarreling by lawyers over points of difference of opinion than among his brother practitioners in six months.

The New York Druggist Bill.

Our readers have been informed of the passage of a law by the New York Legislature, requiring every druggist and his assistants to undergo an examination by a Board of Commissioners, and to procure a license from them, if found qualified, at a cost of $30. The law ignores entirely the diplomas issued by colleges of pharmacy at home and abroad. Whereupon the druggists of New York city are justly indignant, deeming the whole affair a scheme to put money in the pockets of hungry commissioners. Steps have been taken to resist the law, and to set it aside by a judicial decision.

Cure for Consumption.

The following prescription was furnished to the *London Medical Press and Circular*, coming from a clergyman in the West of England, reputed of great skill in diseases of the chest: Isinglass, 1 oz.; eringo root, 1 oz.; garden snails, ½ pint; hartshorn shavings, ½ oz.; three dried vipers from Butler's, Covent Garden; 1½ pints water. Boil down to a pint. We suspect it was stolen by the clergyman from Li-po-tai, who was once ardently patronized by a distinguished clergyman of San Francisco.

Efficacy of Revaccination.

It is stated in the *Edinburgh Medical Journal* that at a recent meeting of the Glasgow Medico-Chirurgical Society, "not one member was able to adduce one single instance of a revaccinated person having taken small-pox." The sentiment maintained that when small-pox prevails, every individual above five years of age, in an infected locality, ought to be revaccinated. We believe this is the universal conviction of impartial medical observers in all parts of the world.

A Quarrel Ended.

For many months the profession in Georgia have been agitated by a bitter quarrel, in which the State Medical Society and the Atlanta Medical College were parties. We are pleased to learn from the *Atlanta Medical Journal* that the difficulties have all been settled, so as to secure "permanent fraternal relations," and that, in the words of the editor, "the medical profession of Georgia are now in peace, and are determined no longer to be a reproach to science and to humanity."

Poisoning by Quinia.

Dr. A. Brayton Ball, in the *N. Y. Med. Gazette*, describes the case of a patient in whom the use of sulphate of quinia, in ordinary doses, was followed by an erythematous rash resembling scarlatina, accompanied by edema, and extending over the whole body, followed by desquamation. The eruption was attended by intense burning and itching. He cites three other cases of like character, related in the *British Medical Journal*.

The California State Medical Society

Meets in Sacramento, on Wednesday, 11th inst., at 10 A.M. All physicians in the State are eligible to membership, on exhibiting to the Censors their Diploma, or furnishing satisfactory evidence of being regular graduates.

Death of Dr. Hyde Salter.

Dr. Salter, the well-known author, died very recently, at his home in London, at the age of 47. He fell a victim to the disease on which he wrote so ably, and to which he had long been subject—asthma.

Varicella in San Francisco.

Chicken-pox has prevailed lately in this city in an aggravated form, some cases so near to small-pox in character as to have been reported as such to the Board of Health.

GENERAL SUMMARY.

What a Physician's Office Should Be.

Professor McGraw, of the Detroit Medical College, in an address to the graduating class *(Detroit Review of Medicine)*, raps certain practitioners over the knuckles in the following style: "I have been in doctors' offices where a skull grinned from one corner, ghastly anatomical plates hung from the walls, and splints, suggestive of broken bones, were placed conspicuously in every corner. What a delightful resting-place for a sick woman, visions of death, disease, and injury, greeting her on every side! Now, gentlemen, make your offices pictures of comfort and cheerfulness. Banish from them every sign of your professional occupation, so that your patients may enter them not only without disgust, but with actual elevation of heart. I think, I need hardly say, that your apartments should be scrupulously clean, although I can recollect too many rooms occupied by physicians, whose windows were festooned with cobwebs and dead flies, and whose floors were stained with tobacco spit. I have been pleased sometimes to hear the occupants of such offices groan about the lack of custom, for if it is the duty of a physician to preach the virtues of cleanliness, he should himself be a living example of his own doctrine. Filthiness in a physician is, like dishonesty in a merchant, the very worst of sins."

Infirmary or Hospital?

A singularly common error is pointed out in the use of the terms *infirmary* and *hospital*, by the editor of the *British Medical Journal* (May 27, 1871), which is, however, mainly confined to England and this country. A *hospital* is defined as a place for shelter or entertainment, for the exercise of "hospitality," while an *infirmary* is a place for the reception of the sick. The error is traceable in London to St. Bartholomew's and St. Thomas', which were founded as priories, afterwards became hospitals, and have now become infirmaries, though still called hospitals. They might with equal propriety be called priories. In Scotland and Ireland, however, the term infirmary is correctly used. Thus, there is the Edinburgh Royal Infirmary, with 565 beds; the Glasgow Royal Infirmary, 547 beds; Aberdeen Royal Infirmary, 300 beds. The same journal suggests the change of name of St. Thomas' to that of "The Victoria Infirmary." Would it not be well for Philadelphians to remember this correct application of the terms in naming the new infirmaries proposed, as "The Infirmary of the Presbyterian Church," and "The University Infirmary," or "The Infirmary of the University of Pennsylvania."
—*Philadelphia Medical Times.*

Homeopathic Remedies.

In a paper read before the Chicago Medical Society (see *Med. Examiner*, September, 1871), Dr. C. W. Earle makes the following allusion to certain remedies employed by homeopaths: "Homeopathy came, and with one mighty bound went *back* five hundred years. Its advocates invaded the *loathsome* for remedies with which to humbug the people. Take Jahr's Pharmacopeia, and look at their remedies. On page 96 you will find an account of the American pole-cat, or skunk. The learned author of the advance school says: 'Near the *anus* there is a pouch where the follicular glands secrete an odorous matter; the animal squirts his liquor, etc. We make the three first attenuations by trituration.' The black spider (see page 83) is prepared for homeopathic medication by putting the whole animal in alcohol; 'macerating it for weeks, and even months, and then decanting the clear liquor, which is the mother tincture.' 'The three first attenuations of the common wood-louse' are prepared by trituration; the tincture, by twenty parts of alcohol. 'Lachesis (snake poison) is procured from the poison bags which are found in the upper jaw of these reptiles.'"

Saponified Cod-Liver Oil.

Dr. Van den Corput, of the St. John's Hospital, Brussels, has advocated for some time a combination of hydrate of lime with cod-liver oil in tuberculosis. He directs the preparation of boluses wrapped in gum and sugar in the following manner: Pure cod-liver oil, thirty drachms; make a soap with hydrate of lime of the consistence of pills, and flavor with essential oil of bitter almonds, or oil of aniseed, fifteen minims. Let the boluses weigh from four to five grains, and protect them with a mixture of one part of powdered iris root and three parts of powdered sugar. The boluses may also be wrapped in etherial tincture of tolu. The patient may take from six to eight per diem, two at a time, immediately *after* meals. To this calcareous soap a salt of morphine, or extract of aconite, or extract of henbane, may be added, as well as any other substance which the medical man may think indicated in a particular case.—*London Lancet.*

Local Anesthesia.

Dr. Spessa states, in the *Bulletin des Sc. Med.* (Italy), that he has succeeded in preventing pain, during the slitting of a fistulous tract, by injecting a solution of morphia into the tract before the use of the knife. The same author had occasion to touch the vulvar vegetations of a girl with butter of antimony: the pain was very acute, but disappeared on the part being brushed over with a solution of morphia. A boy of fifteen, suffering from hip-joint disease, required an issue over and behind the great trochanter. An injection of morphia was first made over the region, and Vienna paste applied, which latter remained about eight minutes. The paste did not give any pain. Dr. Spessa states that he would be glad to hear that a fair trial has been given to this mode of using morphia.—*London Lancet.*

Dr. Pancoast's Treatment of Inverted Toe-Nail.

Dr. Pancoast never removes the nail, nor any portion of it; but, as the trouble arises from the edge of the nail dipping down into the flesh at the side of the toe, he cuts away the soft parts, and leaves the nail in a position where it can do no harm; then raising up its free edge, and separating it thoroughly from the parts below it with a thin handle of a scalpel, he slips beneath it a strip or two of adhesive plaster, and carries the ends beneath the ball of the toe and round upon the metatarsus, so as to force the soft parts down and the nail up. When the parts heal, the side of the nail will be free from any covering. One great advantage of this operation is that the patient is almost immediately enabled to attend to his business. He keeps the parts covered for several days with a strong aqueous solution of sub-acetate of lead and laudanum.—*Medical Archives.*

Hydramyle—A New Anesthetic.

Dr. Richardson, in continuing his researches on the physiological action of the light hydrides, has recently succeeded in rendering one of the series applicable for the production of general anesthesia, and has administered the vapor of it to the human subject, for short operations, twice during the present week, and with marked success. He proposes to call the substance hydramyle. The vapor is so rapid in its action, that, in a case of extraction of a molar tooth, the patient was rendered insensible, the operation was performed, and recovery was completed in fifty seconds.—*Med. Times and Gazette.*—*Med. News and Library.*

Accidents at Dr. Squibb's Laboratory.

While handling a flask of hot carbolic acid in the laboratory of Dr. E. R. Squibb, at Brooklyn, on the 10th of August, a workman let it fall and inhaled the vapor which was disengaged by the breaking of it. For ten minutes he felt no effects, but then he staggered and fell, and in half an hour was dead. Two days afterward another flask of acid was broken, and the laboratory set on fire, destroying $800 worth of chloral hydrate and much other chemical material.

Skin Grafting.

At the late meeting of the Illinois State Medical Society *(Chicago Med. Journal)*, Dr. D. Prince stated that he had made several experiments in the transplantation of cuticle to the surface of chronic ulcers. In all of his cases the ulcers were suppurative, and the experiments failed. He had been informed by Dr. Hodgen, of St. Louis, that his trials in ulcers of a similar kind had also failed; but when the transplantation had been to the surface of ulcers that were dry or non-suppurative, it had been followed by a satisfactory degree of success.

How to Cure Sun-stroke.

Nine men were struck down in India by the heat, and lay insensible, breathing stertorously. Dr. Lethbridge laid them out in a row on the cool floor of the hospital, and then watered them copiously and continuously for five hours, by means of "bheesties with mussacks," before much improvement was perceptible. Every man recovered. So says the *London Med. Press and Circular*. Will our much esteemed contemporary send us a supply of "bheesties and mussacks," that we may try the remedy in these diggings?

Raw Beef in the Vomiting of Pregnancy.

Dr. James T. Bailey *(N. Y. Med. Record)* succeeded in the treatment of a case of this kind by giving raw beef for food. The beef was chopped fine, and sprinkled with salt and cayenne pepper, and a tea-spoonful taken every three hours. After the second tea-spoonful the vomiting ceased, and during the day the nausea disappeared. The patient soon acquired a taste for the food, and improved rapidly in flesh and appearance, and had no return of sickness.

Inguinal Phlebitis from Digital Compression.

At a meeting of the Surgical Society of Paris *(Gaz. Hebdomadaire)*, several cases of inguinal phlebitis following amputation of the leg were reported as resulting from the pressure of the fingers, which was employed instead of the tourniquet, during the operation. The cases, however, were not regarded as conclusive on this point by all the members.

Hydrochloric Acid as an Antiseptic.

A piece of meat, immersed for fifteen minutes in a mixture of one part of the acid to three of water, remained entirely free from putrefactive change after nearly a fortnight, though the action of the acid was not sufficiently powerful to prevent the appearance of a small quantity of mold. The meat was then immersed in a dilute solution of carbonate of soda, and the superficially absorbed acid thus converted into common salt.—*Amer. Jour. Pharmacy.—British Med. Journal.*

Chloral Hydrate in Snake Poisoning.

A case is reported in the *N. Y. Med. Record* of a young man in New Jersey, who had been bitten on the finger by a rattlesnake, and who was seized soon afterward with convulsions and other alarming symptoms. Whisky, and morphia by hypodermic injection were employed in vain, but he recovered rapidly under the use of twenty-grain doses of chloral hydrate, given every ten minutes till one hundred grains were taken.

Preparation of Aquæ Medicatæ.

The editor of the *Amer. Jour. of Pharmacy* condemns the method of preparing medicated waters as directed by the *American Pharmacopeia,* because the carbonate of magnesia they contain precipitates a portion of the insoluble alkaloid basis, the salts of which may have been dissolved in them. He prefers the old method of distillation, which is still retained by the *British Pharmacopeia.* So, we will take a step backward in this regard.

ITEMS OF NEWS, Etc.

Cats and dogs are proved to be insusceptible of the vaccine disease.

More than 300 dead Children are found in the streets of London every year.

The Liebig Extract of Meat Company slaughtered 88,869 head of cattle last year.

Gun-cotton is manufactured in England to the amount of one hundred tons per annum.

The Deaths from Yellow Fever in Buenos Ayres, during the recent epidemic, are estimated at 26,000.

The sale of Carbonated Waters, to be drank in the shop of the pharmacist, is strictly forbidden in Prussia.

Starvation in London.—Within the last three years, 140 persons have been registered in London as dying from starvation.

MAMMARY ABSCESS.—Out of 7,860 women delivered in the Vienna Lying-in Hospital, in 1867, fourteen only had abscess of the breast.

THE DEATHS IN NEW YORK, during the second quarter of 1871, were 28 per 1000, and in Bombay only 20. Small-pox prevailed in both cities.

GERMAN PHARMACOPEIA.—Arrangements have been made for framing a Pharmacopeia for the whole German Empire. Heretofore nearly every State has had one of its own, different from all the others.

DEATH FROM CHLORAL HYDRATE.—At a meeting of the Boston Gynæcological Society, Dr. Granger stated that a physician of Boston had died in August of last year from the effect of an overdose of chloral.

AMONG THE NOTABLE DEATHS which have taken place within the last few months are those of Dr. Liegeois, Vice-Professor of the Paris Faculty, Dr. Thomas Hawkes Tanner of England, the well known author, Dr. George C. Blackman, Professor of Surgery in the Medical College of Ohio, also well known as an eminent teacher and writer.

THE POETRY OF PHYSIC.—In the French edition of Hahnemann's Materia Medica, no less than forty-five octavo pages are devoted to the statement of nine hundred and twenty symptoms produced by the one-millionth of a grain of charcoal. Among the symptoms are, itching of the internal angle of the left eye, itching in a wart on the finger, repugnance for butter, obstruction of the left nostril for an hour, speedy loss of appetite by eating, etc., etc.—*Med. Press and Circular*.

TENSION OF NERVES.—The *Detroit Homeopathic Observer* refers to Dr. Hill, who recently died in Marysville, as having been Professor in the Eclectic College of Cincinnati, founder of the Homeopathic College of Cleveland, in which he held two professorships at once, Professor in the Homeopathic College of St. Louis, author of "Eclectic Surgery," "Homeopathic Surgery," and other works, "a member of the Legislature of Ohio, U. S. Consul at Nicaragua, a practitioner of surgery, a speculator in lands, a manufacturer or trader in lumber, etc., etc.—nerves always at a high rate of tension." To all this, the biographer adds that after leaving Ohio, "he pursued other avocations."

STATE BOARD OF HEALTH.

Abstract from the Reports of Deaths and their Causes, in the following cities and towns in California, during August, 1871 :

Cities and Towns.	Total No. Deaths.	Prevalent Diseases.						Authorities.
		Consumption.	Inflam. of Lungs.	Infl. Stomach and Bowels.	Diphtheria.	Scarlatina.	Typhus & Typhoid Fevers.	
San Francisco	247	11	11	11	1	2	10	S. F. B'rd of Health
Sacramento	23	1	1	0	1	0	2	Sac. B'rd of Health
Petaluma	5	0	0	2	0	0	0	Dr. G. W. Graves.
Dixon	1	0	0	1	0	0	0	Dr. R. H. Plummer.
Santa Clara	...	...	...		...	...	.	Dr. H. H. Warburton
Stockton	10	2	1	1	0	0	1	Stockton B'd Health.
Marysville	7	0	0	0	0	0	2	Dr. C. E. Stone.
Placerville	2	0	0	0	0	0	1	Dr. E. A. Kunkler.
Auburn	0	0	0	0	0	0	0	Dr. A. S. Du Bois.
San Diego	5	2	0	2	0	0	0	Co. Med. Society.
San Luis Obispo	...		...	.	...	...		Dr. W. W. Hays.
Oroville	...				...	...	.	Dr. J. M. Vance.
Woodland	0	0	0	0	0	0	0	Dr. A. B. Mehring.
Oakland	8	0	1	2	0	0	0	Dr. T. H. Pinkerton.
Los Angeles	17	1	1	2	0	0	1	Dr. H. S. Orme.
Nevada City	.				.	.	.	Dr. J. A. Gatlin.
Truckee	2	0	0	1	0	0	0	Dr. Wm. Curless.
St. Helena	2	1	0	0	0	0	0	Dr. J. S. Adams.
San José	..		.		.			Dr. J. N. Brown.
Napa City	1	0	0	2	0	0	0	Dr. M. B. Pond.
Cacheville	0	0	0	0	0	0	0	Dr. E. L. Parramore.
Siskiyou	..	..					.	Dr. T. T. Cabanis.
Watsonville	1	0	0	0	0	0	0	Dr. C. E. Cleveland.
Folsom	0	0	0	0	0	0	0	Dr. L. McGuire.
Bridgeport Town'p	0	0	0	0	0	0	0	Dr. J. L. Asay.
Sut'r C'k & Amador	1	0	0	0	0	0	0	Dr. H. M. Fiske.
Monterey	1	0	0	0	0	0	0	Dr. C. A. Canfield.
Santa Cruz			.	..				Dr. Benj. Knight.
Vallejo	2	0	0	0	0	0	0	Dr. J. M. Brown.
Suisun & Fairfield	1	1	0	0	0	0	0	Dr. S. D. Campbell.
Colusa	3	1	0	0	0	0	1	Dr. Luke Robinson.
Trinity County	2	0	1	1	0	0	0	Dr. J. C. Montague.
Santa Barbara	1	1	0	0	0	0	0	Dr. C. B. Bates.
Redwood City	0	0	0	0	0	0	0	Dr. C. A. Kirkpatrick.

Abstract from Reports of Births :

Cities and Towns.	Total Births.	Males.	Females.	Still-born.	Live-born.	Authorities.
San Francisco...	**93**	**51**	**42**	**20**	**73**	**S. F. Board of Health.**
Sacramento.....	**44**	**24**	**20**	**2**	**42**	**Sac. Board of Health.**
All other places.	**187**	**112**	**75**	**10**	**177**	**Various sources.**
Total......	**324**	**187**	**137**	**32**	**292**	

REMARKS.—With a smaller increase of deaths from zymotic diseases than is usual at this season of the year, the general health continues remarkably good. The public mind has been somewhat excited of late about the Asiatic cholera, but from what we know of the antecedents of this disease—that sudden outbreaks seldom or never occur, and that it is communicable by a specific poison emitted from a patient already attacked, and therefore follows the lines of human intercourse for the most part—it is not probable, seeing that it has not yet reached our eastern border, that we will be visited by it this fall. It will be time enough when the disease shows itself in any of the Atlantic States, to devise some means of quarantining or expurgating such railroad cars as may be found transporting passengers already attacked. We have another, if not more formidable, disease to provide against this winter, and that is small-pox. There is so much of this disease in other places with which we are in constant intercourse, that it is more than probable that, with the advent of the rainy season, small-pox will again make its appearance. As this loathsome disease spreads more rapidly in cold, damp weather, so its preventive, vaccination, produces its specific effects with more certainty at the same season. It is important, therefore, that all persons should see to it that they are protected, both from small-pox and varioloid, by vaccination, and which should be renewed as often as possible, in order to make the protection from both still more perfect.

THOMAS M. LOGAN, M.D.,
Permanent Secretary State Board of Health.

Tubal Pregnancy.

In the *Phila. Med. Times*, reference is made to a case of tubal pregnancy described in a German journal. The patient was forty-four years old, pregnant for the fourth time, and had reached the end of gestation without any abnormal symptoms, when fugitive labor pains were soon followed by convulsions, coma, rapid prostration, and death. A post mortem examination disclosed a fully developed dead fetus inclosed in membranes, and lying in a musculo-membranous sac, which was formed by the distended fallopian tube, the placenta being attached anteriorly.

Mortality in San Francisco during August, 1871.

By H. Gibbons, Jr., M.D.

Causes of Death.

Abscess of Lungs	1	Diarrhea	3	Laryngitis	1
Anemia	1	Diphtheria	1	Malarial Fever	1
Aneurism of Aorta	4	Disease of Brain	1	Meningitis	8
Apoplexy	8	Diseases of Heart	10	Old Age	3
Asphyxia	1	Dropsy	6	Ovarian Dropsy	1
Asthma	2	Drowning	1	Peritonitis	3
Atrophia	9	Dysentery	3	Phthisis	41
Bowels, Obstruction of	1	Enteritis	4	Pneumonitis	11
Bronchitis	2	Erysipelas	1	Premature Birth	4
Cancer	1	Fever, Remittent	2	Rheumatism	1
" of Liver	3	" Scarlet	2	Scrofula	1
" of Stomach	4	" Typhoid	10	Stomatitis	1
Cholera Infantum	6	Fracture of Skull	1	Suffocation	1
Congestion of Brain	3	" of Spine	1	Suicide	4
" of Lungs	4	Gastritis	3	Syphilis	2
Congestive Chill	1	Gastro-Enteritis	1	Tabes Dorsalis	1
Convulsions, Infantile	9	Hemoptysis	2	Tetanus	1
" Puerperal	1	Hepatitis	1	Unknown	15
Croup	5	Hospital Gangrene	1	Whooping Cough	3
Cyanosis	2	Hydrocephalus	3		
Cystitis	1	Inanition	10	Total	247
Debility, General	2	Intemperance	2	Still-births	20
Dentition	2	Injuries, unspecified	2		

Ages.

Under 1 year	54	From 15 to 20 years	3	From 60 to 70 years	6
From 1 to 2 years	12	From 20 to 30 years	30	From 70 to 80 years	8
From 2 to 5 years	14	From 30 to 40 years	48	From 80 to 90 years	1
From 5 to 10 years	3	From 40 to 50 years	37	Unknown	1
From 10 to 15 years	3	From 50 to 60 years	27		

Sex. — Male, 163; Female, 84. Total, 247.
Color. — White, 203; Copper, 40; Black, 4.

Nativities.

California	79	France	7	Western Isles	1
Other parts of U. S.	42	Germany	21	Australia	1
British Amer'n Prov.	5	Denmark	1	Belgium	2
Mexico	1	Russia	1	Norway	1
England	7	Switzerland	3	Finland	2
Ireland	29	Italy	2	Hindostan	1
Scotland	2	China	36	Unknown	3

Recapitulation.

Died in City Wards	191	Mount St. Joseph's Infirmary	11
City and County Hospital	13	Alms House	2
U. S. Marine Hospital	4	Small-pox Hospital	1
French Hospital	4	Casualties	6
German Hospital	4	Suicides	4
St. Mary's Hospital	7		

Remarks.—The deaths in August, for the last six years, have numbered: In 1866, 219; in 1867, 193; in 1868, 317; in 1869, 268; in 1870, 281, and in 1871, 247. It will be seen, that the mortality for 1871 is much less than for four years past, or since 1867. For the present year, up to September, a period of eight months, there were but 1,926 deaths; during a like period in 1870, the number reached 2,165. The mortality, in August, among children under five years of age, continues proportionally small, being less than a third of the total. In no infantile disorder has there been any decided increase of fatality; indeed, the statement for the month exhibits but one fact worthy of special comment. We refer to the unusual preponderance of deaths of foreign-born over those of native-born inhabitants. This has occurred in but one other month of the year, although there has been a near approach to it in several. Up to September of the present year, there were 984 deaths of native born, to 942 of foreign born — a difference in favor of the former of but 42, or a little over two per cent. During the same period of 1870, there were 1,223 native born decedents, and 942 foreign-born decedents—precisely the same number of the latter as in the present year. The diminution in the mortality (239) is then entirely among our native-born population. To present this subject more clearly, we have prepared the following table:

COMPARATIVE MORTALITY OF NATIVE AND FOREIGN BORN, FOR THE FIRST EIGHT MONTHS OF EACH YEAR.

	Native.	Foreign.	Excess of native.	Per cent. of excess.
1866	956	678	278	17.00
1867	993	681	312	18.64
1868	1,214	767	447	22.56
1869	1,462	936	526	21.93
1870	1,223	942	281	12.98
1871	984	942	42	2.17

This, certainly, is a remarkable showing. In 1866 and 1867, when the health of the city was excellent, the deaths of native born outnumbered those of foreign born, 17 to 18 per cent. During the two years of small-pox (1868–69), the per cent. increased to 22; in last year (1870), it fell to about 13, and now it is but little over 2. At first view, this great difference might appear to be due *entirely* to a large immigration; but this can account for only a small part of the difference. It must, indeed, be a large foreign immigration that would explain the large proportionate increase of foreign-born decedents, when it is remembered that the births—even those of foreign parentage—are all included in the native born. The explanation is mainly found in the fact of the greatly diminished infantile mortality. This accounts for nearly the entire decrease in the mortality of 1871 from that of 1870; for while this decrease amounted to 239, and was confined entirely to the native born, there were, also, fewer deaths of children under five years of age, by 209, in 1871. The subject might be pursued further, with advantage; but, for the present, we will merely subjoin the following statement of the comparative mortality of children under five years of age and of native born, for the first eight months of the years named:

	1866.	1867.	1868.	1869.	1870.	1871.
Mortality under five years	606	669	794	948	819	610
Mortality of native born...........	956	993	1,214	1,462	1,223	984
Ratio of infantile deaths to total mortality........................	37.09	39.98	40.07	41.03	37.98	31.67

Contagiousness of Cholera.

The Privy Council of Great Britain have issued a circular relating to the threatened invasion of cholera (*Med. Press and Circular*), in which they use this language: "Happily for mankind, cholera is so little contagious, in the sense in which small-pox and scarlatina are commonly called contagious, that if reasonable care be taken where it is present, there is scarcely any risk that the disease will spread to persons who nurse and otherwise closely attend upon the sick."

Medicinal Properties of Cocoa-nut Milk.

In India, according to a writer in the *London Pharmaceutical Journal*, the milk of the cocoa-nut is employed in debility and incipient phthisis, as a substitute for cod oil, with excellent results. It is also used, instead of cow's milk, in tea and coffee. In large doses, it acts as a substitute for castor oil.

Astringent Injection in Gleet.

A writer in the *London Med. Press and Circular* recommends, as an effectual remedy in gleet, an injection composed of tinct. opii, dr. j.; tinct. catechu, dr. jss.; mist. acaciæ, oz., ij.; to be used twice daily.

To Disguise Castor Oil.

Rub up two drops oil of cinnamon with an ounce of glycerin, and add an ounce of castor oil. Children will take it as a luxury, and ask for more.

PACIFIC

MEDICAL AND SURGICAL JOURNAL.

Vol. V.—NOVEMBER, 1871.—No. 54.

ORIGINAL COMMUNICATIONS.

Inflammation and Ulceration of the Os and Cervix Uteri.

By IRA E. OATMAN, M.D.

[Read before the Sacramento Society for Medical Improvement.]

Inasmuch as the affections to which I ask your attention are among the most common with which mothers are afflicted, and since the evidences of their existence are always obscure, and manifested sympathetically by reflex action through other, and often remote, portions of the organism, I think the subject is worthy of your deliberations on this occasion.

That inflammation and ulceration of the os and cervix uteri were examined with the speculum, were practically understood, and tolerably well treated by the ancients, is more than probable; it is well established. Yet the practice in such cases went into disuse by the custodians of medical science for many centuries subsequent to the overthrow of the Roman Empire. The Greek and Roman medical classics were preserved by the Arabs, until they went into the hands of the Roman Catholic priesthood. The close seclusion of the Mohammedan females on the one hand, and the canonical requirement of celibacy of the priesthood on the other, forbade that intimacy of the sexes necessary to the cultivation of this branch of medical science. Hence, gynæcology and midwifery were necessarily ignored by the profession during this long period—uneducated midwives doing all that was done.

These relations of society continued so long, that to investigate uterine diseases by medical men, as was done anciently, and give to them the attention and treatment which their importance clearly demands, was about as difficult to accomplish as to eradicate an erroneous religious dogma, universally believed in and practiced for a thousand years. In either case the error is thoroughly inbred from infancy, and becomes well-nigh constitutional.

The neglect of uterine pathology during those dark centuries extends its influence to this day, affecting the people generally, in all enlightened countries, with every form and variety of irregular practice. Nor is it too much to say that the writings of many of our contemporaries, until a recent period, show a less degree of attention to the pathology of uterine diseases than to that of any other class of cases of equal importance in medical science. What is true of authors has been, and is still, true to some extent of many regular physicians in good standing in the profession.

I need not detail the revival of uterine pathology, nor the slow progress which it made for three or four hundred years. Suffice for the present, that the use of the vaginal speculum in diagnosis did not become general until many years of the present century had expired. Now that some of the profounder minds in the profession in Europe and in this country are devoting their best energies to diseases of females, is it too much to claim and believe that we of less distinction may understand them as well, and treat them as successfully as they?

I do not propose to treat of cancer, in any of its varieties or stages; nor of traumatic inflammation from surgical wounds, nor yet from injuries frequently inflicted by whalebones, quills, etc., in the hands of the ignorant; nor of syphilis or gonorrhea; but of those inflammations, ulcerations, and abrasions commonly met with in practice. These are seldom acute when first observed; generally chronic, sometimes only hyperemia, or congestion, producing displacements, with reflex and other symptoms requirıng treatment. As most of the cases met with are in women who have borne children, I regard the passage of the child through the os uteri as the most fruitful cause of these affections. It is not uncommon for the attenuated edge of the os uteri to give way in one or more places at the instant the greatest diameter of the fetal head passes through. The depending position, the peculiar structure, and the hyperemia of the organ lubricated with muco-pus, as the os and cervix are in this case, seem to prevent the healing of the injuries to the os. Chronic inflammation ensues, and the epithelium gives way, leaving abraded, and in some persons ulcerated, surface, more commonly occupying the anterior lip, but frequently surrounding the os, varying in width from one to eight or ten lines. Ante and retroflexions, caused by constipation, copulation, tumors, etc., by obstructing the return of blood from the os and cervix, may produce hyperemia and inflammation, or engorgement and ulceration. The versions, from various causes, maintaining undue pressure upon the os, may produce ulceration. Besides these, pregnancy, abortion, over exertion, exposure to cold and dampness, sexual intercourse, pessaries, and other causes, may produce inflammation of those parts. The cases I have seen in young unmarried women have been without assignable cause, other than constitutional, for they have all been in feeble or scrofulous persons.

Congestion of the liver, or spleen, or even lungs; obstruction to the circulation in the right side of the heart; tumors, or constipation, or whatever would obstruct the return of blood to the heart through the hypogastric veins, or even the ascending cava, would produce hyperemia of the uterus, and aggravate existing ulceration or inflammation, if, indeed, they do not sometimes produce those conditions. We seldom observe acute inflammation here, with tumefaction, heat, redness, pain and tenderness upon pressure—the cases having become chronic, if they ever were acute, before we see them.

The peculiar structure of the uterus is such, and its usual vitality so low, that the hyperemia and tumefaction, with or without ulceration or abrasion, may continue until interstitial deposit produces induration, without increased redness, save at the point of ulceration or erosion, with no elevation of temperature, and in most cases little or no tenderness upon pressure. In some cases there is only indolent tumefaction, with hyperemia of the cavity of the os and cervix. But in the great majority of the cases we find added to these, erosion of and around the os, sometimes extending into the cervix; or granulating ulceration, occupying the same situations. These conditions are inseparable from chronic inflammation, or hyperemia, and tumefaction of the cervix uteri.

I need not say that versions and flexions are common accompaniments of these affections. The cervix is quite obliterated in some cases, even in youngish women.

The discharges from these surfaces vary with the condition of the parts. From the cavity of the cervix, if inflamed, we find it resemble the raw white of egg; if ulcerated, purulent; and if both affect the cavity, we find tenacious mucopus, translucent and yellowish. From ulcers on the vaginal cervix there is, of course, pus; and from congested or inflamed surfaces, aqueous or milk-like fluid. These are generally abundant, and the more so as the cases are recent and active; while in old cases there is often no visible discharge externally, which fact frequently misleads the patient as to the nature of the case; for in the normal state there should be no discharge, except the menses. I need not detail the signs and symptoms further, for some of the late authors are so systematic, concise, and replete on this head, that we have but to refer to them to be satisfied. But, that they may not be omitted entirely, I will state briefly that there is scarcely a portion of the organism that may not be the seat of some abnormal sensation, reflected from the disease under consideration. Some of the following symptoms, and often many of them, are in every case, viz.:

pains or achings in the thighs, hips, groins, and pelvis; bearing down and weight in the pelvis and abdomen; pains in back, sides, spine, and different portions of the chest; nausea, irregular appetite, constipation, and tenderness in the bowels; palpitation of the heart; sense of suffocation, and *serious fears* of heart disease.

Some feel melancholy and suicidal; others are nervous, impatient, intolerant, and generally "ill at ease;" while not a few become infatuated with illusions, hallucinations, and monomania, and a few go mad. Scarcely ever nymphomania; but, on the contrary, the sexual molimen is generally impaired, and sometimes entirely suspended. They fancy themselves the subjects of any disease but the one they have, and cannot be comforted. Hence they resort to numerous remedies, and all kinds of empiricism, with no permanent relief, and so lose confidence in all treatment, and sometimes in all medical science and men. At this time I am treating a case from a distance, who had been under medical advice for some time. When she came to me it was for the relief of a severe and constant globus hystericus of two weeks standing.

Although alarmed for her own safety, she ventured to suggest for her relief an *anthelmintic*. I kindly assured her that I thought she would recover under a different treatment. After the second application to an ulcerated os uteri, she felt no more of the globus; and without the fetid gum or ether, chloroform or chloral, she is happily recovering.

Sterility is almost invariable where the os uteri is occluded with the white of egg discharge. Asphyxia, convulsions, paralysis, and that interminable category of symptoms once conveniently included by the term *hysteria*, are all occasional symptoms in these cases. When the leucorrhea is great, the menses are frequently scant. Menorrhagia is not uncommon.

These conditions of the os and cervix are among the most fruitful causes of abortion; whilst recovery after parturition is protracted, and the liability to consecutive affections greatly increased. That acrid discharges from intra-uterine diseases often produce the affection under consideration is not in accordance with my observations.

The *diagnosis* is included in what I have just read, bearing in mind that the constitutional symptoms of acute, or even chronic, inflammation are seldom met with.

Attention to the brain and nervous system, the respiratory, the circulatory, the digestive, and the secretory systems, is necessary to a correct diagnosis. The same is true of a digital examination, which should be with one or two fingers in the vagina, with the other hand over the hypogastric region. This is of the first importance, as by this means we detect procidentia uteri, the versions and flexions, hypertrophy and tumors, cystic and rectal complications, humidity and tenderness; also, density and intra-pelvic cellulitis—a knowledge of all of which, with other complications, is necessary to a correct diagnosis of the pathology in the case.

I need not say that the speculum is indispensable to perfect the diagnosis, and in the use of local remedies.

In deciding upon the *constitutional treatment*, it is as difficult as it is important to determine the causative relations between the disease of the womb and the affections of the organs with which it is found to be in sympathy. For it may be caused by incurable disease of the lungs, heart, liver, or kidneys, for which palliative treatment alone would be indicated; but congestion or inflammation of these organs would require appropriate attention. *Constipation especially* should be relieved, and, with all the other causes, be avoided. In plethoric women, particularly if the case be acute, saline laxatives and a low diet, with rest and tepid baths, would be proper; while those of opposite habit may use the gentlest laxatives, anodynes, or tonics pro re nata. The anemic, feeble and nervous, should use the most invigorating tonics, with such anodynes as best agree with them. Four grains of quinine, and one or two each of ext. hyosciamus and citrate of iron, given in pill three or four times a day, generally answer well.

The same would be especially indicated in all the varieties of malarious disease or neuralgia, which often afflict all classes of women affected in this way. The most nutritious diet is indicated for the anemic or feeble, with good air and gentle exercise. It may be borne in mind, however, that in a large proportion of the cases *little or no constitutional treatment is required*—a gentle laxative only being occasionally useful. Where there is no local disease of other organs continuing the cause, the chief, and in many cases the only, reliance is upon local treatment. In all cases, expect in anemic persons, where there are *tumefaction*, *heat*, *diffuse redness*, and tenderness, leeches are useful, and in some cases give immediate relief to urgent symptoms, combined with rest, laxatives, and low diet. *But in the great majority of the cases they are not indicated;* in many persons they are *positively hurtful.* This is true in most of the chronic cases, and that class embraces nearly all of those we are called upon to treat. It is especially so in the anemic, in whose treatment it is a cardinal principle to enrich the blood and invigorate the general system as rapidly as possible to promote recovery.

The blood drawn by the leeches, and that which oozes away from their bites after their removal, depletes the already exhausted circulation, and in that proportion impairs the recuperative powers of the general system, on which we depend after all for recovery. In some such persons the loss of a small quantity of blood produces faintness and extreme exhaustion, from which they recover slowly. In almost all the cases there is ulceration, erosion, or abrasion of some part of the vaginal cervix and the os, and frequently extending into the cervical cavity, and generally of an indolent character. There may be a purplish hue, caused by congestion from pregnancy, or from versions, flexions, tumors, or constipation, or other organic changes, all of which should be removed as far as practicable. In pregnancy the case may be treated safely with due care, but it usually requires a longer time.

In all the cases just described, active stimulant, caustic or escharotic, is required to destroy the superabundant and enfeebled capillary, and it may be fungoid, surface, leaving the disease diminished in size, and far more healthy in appearance. This must be repeated at intervals of from three to seven days, the intervals being longer as the substance used is more destructive.

Of all the agents employed or recommended, the *nitrate of silver* stands pre-eminent. Applied in substance, where the inflammation is acute, it exerts a peculiar sedative influence upon the surrounding inflammation, as well as the ulceration. In the indolent cases it destroys the exuberant surface, and promotes a far healthier action beneath. The same is true of the abrasions. In these last, one, or at most two, applications in substance will suffice; the same being used in solution, varying in strength from saturation to a drachm to the ounce. When used in substance, a short piece of the rounded end of the stick in a thin quill, secured in the porte-caustique, is efficient, and avoids the danger of leaving a piece of the solid nitrate in the cervical cavity.

It is generally unnecessary to use it in substance more than two or three times, although after using the solution for an indefinite period the ulcer may become inactive, and require the solid form again. It must be witnessed to appreciate the salutary effects of this treatment, in not only removing the disease, but in promoting the absorption of the interstitial deposits and hypertrophy, upon which a large proportion of the displacements of the uterus depend. So long as any ulcer or abrasion is visible, astringent injections should be used three times a day. These may be made of carbolic or tannic acid, sulphate, acetate, or chloride of zinc, acetate or nitrate of lead, or some combination of these, of strength not sufficient to produce burning pain. Warm, tepid, or cold water, injected for several minutes twice daily, is not only agreeable, but palliative and adjuvant to the other treatment. The stronger escharotics are seldom required if due attention be paid to existing causes of the disease. Acid nitrate of mercury, potassa fusa and cum calce, chromic acid, and the actual cautery, with numerous other therapeutic means and substances, including the vegetable and mineral astringents, may sometimes be used with benefit; but the *nitrate of silver* and carbolic acid, in substance and in solution, will be all that is required in most cases.

I need not say that in the use of the speculum the utmost caution should be used to protect the modesty of the patient, and to avoid giving pain, as well as to prevent hemorrhage by the use of the instrument. This last is not only unnecessary, but positively hurtful. It is important to place the discharges under the microscope when malignant disease is suspected. I am aware that some of the sentiments herein expressed are not in accordance with those of some of the late authors. They are my own views on the subject, resulting chiefly from observations in practice.

Proceedings of the San Francisco Medical Society.

ACTION OF ERGOT.

At one of the late meetings of the Society, the subject of ergot was introduced by Dr. Gibbons, Sr., who referred to the difficulty in procuring active preparations of the drug, and the uncertainty attendant even on a good article. Recently, in two cases, he had known the administration of ergot to be followed by complete cessation of the pain of labor. Prior to its exhibition there had been considerable pain, but no progress, although the os was fully dilated. The want of progress in such cases seemed to be due to the absence of *rhythmical* or clonic contraction, the existence of muscular action and of pain being evident without expulsive effort. Perhaps there was tonic contraction of all the muscular fibres simultaneously.

Dr. J. D. Whitney suggested morphia in such cases, its action being very similar to its effect in some forms of constipation caused by spasm. Morphia allays spasm, permits rhythmical muscular action, and the bowels are moved.

Dr. Haine had entire faith in the action of ergot on the uterus, if the specimen were fresh. He had often gathered it, and experimented with it.

Dr. Favor said, in his experience, ergot scarcely ever failed to increase labor pains. He had never heard of its stopping uterine contractions until a short time ago. He had given it in two cases of flooding, the hemorrhage and pain both ceasing. From the effects of ergot in spermatorrhea, he supposed it to have similar action upon the ejaculatory ducts as upon the uterus. He related the case of a lady who took an ounce of the fluid extract early in gestation, to induce abortion. She, however, went to term. Either the preparation was poor, or ergot has no effect in the early stage of pregnancy. In ulceration of the os uteri, ergot seemed to contract the ulceration, and to render the granulations less red.

Dr. Soule said he had always had the impression that ergot was very unsafe, unless in the very last stage of labor. It was beneficial after labor to prevent flooding, and some made a practice of giving it under such circumstances. In regard to chloral, he thought it might be substituted for chloroform with advantage.

Dr. Holbrook remarked that his impressions of ergot coincided with Dr. Soule. Earlier in life he had used ergot to expedite labor, and in at least two cases the child was born dead. Ergot was excellent to tighten the parenchyma of the uterus in hemorrhage, especially in conjunction with quinia.

Dr. Haine was accustomed to give the ergot in powder, ten grains every ten minutes, placed on the tongue, and washed down with water. Its use had never been followed by death to the child. He was afraid of chloroform, but had used it only once. Hemorrhage was apt to follow from relaxation of the muscular fibre. The same might be said of chloral.

Dr. J. P. Whitney said he had used ergot many times, and had great confidence in it, and in our preparations of it. When the os was the size of a crown, and thin and soft, he had never known it to tighten up the circular fibres. It had saved life by preventing hemorrhage from post-partum relaxation of the uterus, and should be given in anticipation of such relaxation. A case was mentioned to illustrate this proposition. Ergot had of late been given, with astonishing success, in insanity. It seemed to have power to contract non-striated muscular fibre, with which blood vessels are supplied.

Dr. Holbrook explained the cause of death in utero, in the two cases he had before mentioned; said it was from tonic spasm of the uterus, which was made to replace rhythmical action, and not from blood poisoning.

Dr. J. P. Whitney mentioned a case in which he assented, after much urging by a consulting physician, to the administration of ergot, the result being a ruptured uterus.

Dr. Gibbons thought it almost impossible to kill a child by giving ergot to the mother. Possibly prolonged spasm might do so, but the pressure was uniform, and there was no poisoning of the blood. Poisoning could only result from the long continued use. Two or three doses were generally sufficient, and he believed there was not much danger from large doses. He believed with Dr. Haine, that much of the diversity of opinion as to the effects of the drug was due to its quality. As a hemostatic, ergot was of value, having a constringing power over the vessels. It had been used with advantage, not only in insanity, as stated by Dr. Whitney, but in a variety of brain diseases, and had some reputation in the treatment of aneurism. In referring to the latter uses, Dr. Gibbons mentioned two cases in his practice in which beneficial results had followed its exhibition.

Dr. J. P. Whitney thought that Dr. Gibbons taught a dangerous doctrine if he said that the compression of a child in utero will not stop its circulation. Compression for fifteen or twenty minutes will stop the placental souffle. It was not the intermittent pressure which was injurious, but the unremitting tonic pressure produced by ergot. This was illustrated by the case of a lady whose labors were short, consisting of one long pain, but in two labors the children were both born dead. Conceiving that death resulted from long pressure interfering with the circulation, at the third labor the exit of the child was facilitated by use of the forceps, and it was born alive.

Dr. Gibbons said that if there were no impediment to the exit of the child—if the os were fully dilated—he thought there could be very little danger to the child from tonic compression by ergot.

ACTION OF DIGITALIS.

Dr. J. P. Whitney introduced the discussion upon digitalis, by remarking that when he studied, it was considered by most a cardiac sedative, by some a depressant. Within two or three years Dr. Garrod had considered it to have the effect to diminish the force of the heart's contraction. Large doses of the tincture, an ounce or an ounce and a half, had been given without dangerous effects. This fact had shaken his belief, for a time, in the poisonous effects of the drug. He believed, however, that it was poisonous, by inducing forcible contraction of the heart—it was a tetanizer of the heart. He had formerly given it with a view to diminish the action of the heart; he now gave it in the opposite class of cases. While using it formerly in hypertrophy, he now gave it in atrophy and dilatation of the heart, and with the best effects. He did not recollect ever to have benefited a case of palpitation with hypertrophy with digitalis, while he believed hundreds had been injured by it. An explanation of the toleration of large doses might be that absorption did not take place, or that there existed some constitutional peculiarity. He knew two physicians of this city who gave large doses—two ounces of the tincture in three hours—in delirium tremens with apparent benefit. In a case of this disease, in which there was reason to believe that absorption was active, a large dose was followed by death in three quarters of an hour. He thought death was due to the digitalis. But digitalis acted in other ways than that considered. It was one of the most reliable agents in menorrhagia. It acted on the fibre of the unimpregnated uterus with as much certainty as ergot will upon the impregnated uterus. He had given it in a number of cases of hemorrhage following abortion, but not with satisfactory results. He preferred the infusion in half-ounce doses every three or four hours.

Dr. Scott remarked that he had seen digitalis given in large doses with impunity. Several circumstances appeared to corroborate the views held by Dr. Whitney. When at University College Hospital, he had found Wilson Fox's view to be that digitalis was a stimulant to weakened hearts. Again, in a case of hemorrhage from the uterus, he had given a drachm of the tincture, and nearly lost his patient. In half an hour she had ceased to breathe, and the heart had ceased to act. She, however, recovered. He was disappointed with the effects of digitalis in menorrhagia, but had found twenty drops of fld. ext. ergot every hour and a half more effectual.

Dr. Favor referred to Handfield Jones, who considered digitalis a cardiac tonic, acting on the cardiac nerves, and increasing the force of the heart, but diminishing its frequency. A writer in Rankin's Abstract claimed benefit from the use of the drug in those cases of delirium tremens attended with albuminuria, but not in others. Digitalis was claimed to have anaphrodisiac properties. If it acted on the involuntary muscular fibre, it might be of advantage in relieving congestion of the ovaries.

Dr. Baldwin mentioned a case of heart disease given up to die, which he had greatly relieved by giving a grain of powdered digitalis with half a grain of opium every four hours. Succeeding attacks of dyspnea and diminution of urinary discharge were relieved by the same means. The patient lived four years.

Dr. Gibbons remarked that the profession generally united in the belief that digitalis was a cardiac tonic, but this by no means determined its place in therapeutics. What hypertrophy and dilatation depended upon was an important question. The drug in hypertrophy from one cause might be injurious; from another cause, not objectionable. This lesion resulted from aortic contraction, aortic regurgitation, or mitral regurgitation. Digitalis had two or three distinct actions on the heart. It diminishes its frequency, increases its power, and establishes rhythmical action. It would appear that digitalis has no good effect when the hypertrophy is the result of aortic contraction or aortic regurgitation, while in mitral regurgitation it may benefit. These and other organic troubles, however, generally affect the rhythm of the heart movements, so as to produce great irregularity and fluttering, which digitalis relieves. This was well illustrated in a case now under treatment. When he was a student it was said that digitalis produced its best effects after the system was reduced, and accordingly patients were bled before exhibiting the drug. Physicians acted, without knowing it, on the principle that digitalis is a heart tonic. Digitalis is of much value in cardiac dropsy, but was very seldom beneficial in dropsy from any other cause. It had also an action on the lungs. In former times it was considered of great benefit in pulmonary affections. When obstinate and distressing cough was a prominent symptom, it might be added to expectorant mixtures with advantage. The great advantage of a combination of digitalis, squills, and calomel, or blue mass, was illustrated by two cases, one of cardiac and hepatic disease, with great orthopnea, allayed partially only by morphia injections, and which improved as soon as the mercury began to affect the gums; the other of cardiac hypertrophy, with entire absence of rhythm, edema of lower extremities, orthopnea, etc., which also improved as soon as the mouth became sore. The former patient, after being sick for many months, having been tapped fourteen times, was able to go out, and pay some attention to business, but died suddenly some time after.

Dr. Soule remarked that he had used digitalis considerably, and in the class of cases spoken of. His views of its action corresponded with those already expressed—that it was a heart tonic, applicable to cases in which the frequency of the action of the heart was increased at the expense of power and force.

Dr. Holbrook thought that fatty degeneration of the heart was just the case for digitalis, and that muscular hypertrophy was not. In hypertrophy with dilatation, such as attends mitral or aortic regurgitation, heart tonics were serviceable, hypertrophy in this case being only conservative. He added his experience of the value of digitalis, squills, and calomel as a diuretic, and remarked that early in practice it was his custom to bleed before giving digitalis, which he combined with antimony.

Dr. Haine made some remarks in favor of uniformity of preparation, advocating the use exclusively for a time of the infusion, tincture, powder, etc., until it could be determined which was the best.

H. Gibbons, Jr. Secretary.

Proceedings of the Sacramento Society for Medical Improvement.

Met pursuant to adjournment at the office of Dr. Oatman, July 18, 1871, with Dr. Hatch, the President, in the chair.

Present: Drs. Hatch, Cluness, Tyrrell, Montgomery, Trafton, Simmons, Urick, Nelson, Murphy, Oatman, and Nixon.

Dr. Oatman read the regular paper of the evening, "Inflammation and Ulceration of the Os and Cervix Uteri."

Dr. Cluness thought that sufficient importance had not been given to the use of the syringe. For the last year had ordered his patients to use Davidson's syringe, and in many cases had cured inflammation and ulceration by irrigation.

Sometimes used cold water, and in some cases used warm water. In very indolent cases of ulceration, used caustics as well as irrigation. Did not use leeches of late years at all. Thought the great majority of cases could be cured by local treatment, but in some cases resorted to constitutional remedies. In relaxed and anemic cases, resorted to constitutional as well as local treatment. In some cases, however, had used the remedies recommended by the author of the paper, and with good success.

Dr. Tyrrell agreed in the main with the views of Dr. Oatman. Thought glycerine was a valuable remedy not mentioned by the author of the paper.

Dr. Nelson had not much experience in the treatment of of uterine diseases, but was very much pleased with the paper. Had read in some journal that glycerine was almost a sure cure for any case. Thought, however, that many women were so broken down by the disease that they required constitutional treatment to restore strength to the system, after the local disease appeared to be cured.

Dr. Montgomery agreed with the general views of the author of the paper. Used leeches in plethoric cases, and tonics in anemic and weakly cases. Was partial to the local use of nit. argent. in cases of ulceration of the os and cervix. For the last four or five years had resorted to irrigation in most cases, as recommended by Dr. Cluness. Had not used glycerine. Thought that all cases, of course, could not be treated alike. Believed in the free use of the speculum.

Dr. Simmons had nothing new to suggest in the treatment of uterine diseases. Had used dry powdered tannin, pushed up against the os in a pledget of lint, with very good effect. Also recommended the use of a wet girdle around the body.

Dr. Trafton thought that one very important matter had not been mentioned by the author of the paper, and that was *non-sexual intercourse.* With that exception, the author of the paper had covered the whole ground of uterine diseases very effectually.

Dr. Hatch was of opinion that practitioners too frequently overlooked the inflammatory stage of the disease which preceded ulceration. The inflammation is seldom found to be acute. In regard to local treatment preferred irrigation with warm water, not with cold. Usually directed about one gallon of warm as an injection two or three times a day. As an escharotic preferred the nit. argent., but seldom used it of late. Thought that its use sometimes contracted the os. Used in some cases the sulph. zinc, especially where there were granulations.

Dr. Nixon said he generally tried to get along with such cases without resorting to the use of escharotics. Liked the method spoken of by Dr. Cluness—that of irrigation. Thought that the free use of warm water, with castile soap rubbed down in it, would cure a great majority of cases, if persevered in for a reasonable length of time. Believed that hyperemia of the uterine organ always preceded ulceration. In pale, chlorotic persons used quinia combined with iron as a tonic, and kept the bowels in a laxative state with mild aperients. Was pleased with the able and concise manner with which the author of the paper treated his subject.

A. B. Nixon, Secretary.

Proceedings of the California State Medical Society.

The first annual meeting of the State Society, after the reorganization, convened in the Senate Chamber of the Capitol at Sacramento, on Wednesday, October 11th, 1871, at 1 P.M. The President, Dr. T. M. Logan, in the chair.

Dr. A. B. Nixon, Chairman of the Committee of Arrangements, opened the meeting by an address of welcome, in which he referred to the eminent success which had attended the reorganization of the Society, upward of 150 members being already enrolled on the list, representing nearly every county in the State. He presented a brief view of the benefits that had accrued, and that would accrue, from the Association; and after sketching the programme of business, invited the members to a collation and a social entertainment, to be provided by the Sacramento Society at the conclusion of the exercises.

Dr. F. W. Hatch, Chairman of the Board of Censors, reported the names of the following gentlemen for election: W. H. Wells, of Dixon, Rush Medical College, 1849; Ed. M. Curtis, Sacramento, University of Vermont, 1862; Matthew Gardner, Davisville, McGill University, 1871; O. Harvey, Galt, Rock Island Medical College, 1844; S. B. Brinkerhoff, Santa Barbara, Buffalo University, 1850; E. B. Harris, San Juan North, University of New York, 1846; J. H. Urich, Michigan Bar, Ohio Medical College, 1849; T. T. Cabanis, Siskiyou, University of Maryland, 1848; H. W. Nelson, Sacramento, Canada School of Medicine and Surgery, 1848; John F. Morse, San Francisco, New York Medical College, 1848. The above-named gentlemen were elected.

It was moved that election of officers be postponed until October 12th. Lost.

The roll was called, and Drs. H. Gibbons, Sr., Franklin, Simpson, Nixon, Grover, Stout, Ferris, Logan, F. W. Hatch, Simmons, Todd, Hardy, Montgomery, Cluness, Dubois, Oatman, Nichols, Tyrrell, Taylor, W. T. Wythe, Plummer, Trafton, Murphy, Cabanis, J. H. Wythe, Curtis, Gardner, Haswell, Harvey, Brinkerhoff, Harris, Urich, Nelson, Cheney, Morse, and Cushing were present.

The annual election being in order, the following officers were duly chosen: President, Henry Gibbons, Sr., M.D., of San Francisco. Vice-Presidents, G. A. Shurtleff, M.D., of Stockton; F. W. Hatch, M.D., of Sacramento; F. W. Todd, M.D., of Stockton; J. F. Montgomery, M.D., of Sacramento. Corresponding Secretary, W. T. Wythe, M.D., of Sacramento. Recording Secretaries, Clinton Cushing, M.D., of Oakland; W. T. Grover, M.D., of San Francisco. Treasurer, Arthur B. Stout, M.D., of San Francisco.

Dr. Logan, the retiring President, introduced Dr. Gibbons, who, on taking the chair, made a few appropriate remarks.

The Board of Censors reporting favorably, Dr. Anderson Strong, St. Louis Medical College, 1860, and Dr. Thos. Ross, of Woodland, McGill University, 1863, were unanimously elected members of the Society.

On motion, the election of Board of Censors was postponed until the place of next meeting is selected.

The minutes of the adjourned meeting in May last were read and adopted.

Dr. H. Gibbons, Sr., Chairman of the Committee, read a report on Practical Medicine.

Adjourned until 7 o'clock P M.

EVENING MEETING.

The Society reassembled at 7:30 P.M., a large number of ladies and gentlemen being present.

The President introduced Dr. Logan, the retiring President, who delivered the annual address, as required by the constitution. The address was an elaborate and carefully prepared document, replete with valuable and interesting facts and suggestions.

An invitation was received from Dr. Nixon, Surgeon of the Central Pacific Railroad Hospital, to visit that institution. Accepted.

Dr. Cheney offered an amendment to the Constitution, providing that no physician be elected a member of this Society from a county having a local society, unless he be a member of the same, or unless there be some special reason for his election. Laid over to next meeting, according to law.

SECOND DAY.

The Society met at 10 A.M. In the absence of the President, Dr. Hatch, Vice-President, took the chair.

Dr. Simmons, of Sacramento, Chairman of the Committee on Surgery, read a report on "Practical Surgery."

Dr. Lane, of San Francisco, from the same committee, read a paper on "Coxalgia."

Both papers were referred to the Publication Committee.

Dr. CHENEY, of Chico, read a paper on "Skin Grafting." Referred to the same committee.

An invitation from the Johnston Brandy and Wine Manufacturing Company, to inspect their works during the noon recess, was received, and a number of the members visited the establishment accordingly.

Professor CARR, of the State University, read a paper on the "Genesis of Crime." On motion of Dr. Cole, a vote of thanks was tendered to the author, and a copy requested for publication.

Adjourned to 2 P.M.

AFTERNOON SESSION.

At 2 P.M. the Society met. Dr. Hatch in the chair.

The Board of Censors reporting favorably, the following gentlemen were elected members: Drs. Stillwagon of Napa, Pardee of Oakland, Roberts of ——, Rule of Napa.

On motion of Dr. LANE, the rules were suspended for the purpose of electing a Legislative Committee, who should represent the Society before the Legislature, for the purpose of accomplishing any legislation which might be advised. Drs. Stillwagon of Napa, Harvey of Sacramento, Pardee of Oakland, Brinkerhoff of Santa Barbara, and Logan of Sacramento, were elected.

Papers were read, and referred to the Committee of Publication, as follows:

Dr. Hoffman, of San Diego, on the "Medical Topography of San Diego County."

Dr. M. H. Biggs, of Santa Barbara, on "Climatology."

Dr. J. H. Wythe, of Santa Clara, on "Ovariotomy."

Dr. R. H. Plummer, of Solano, on the "Treatment of Typhoid Fever."

Dr. W. T. Wythe, of Sacramento, on "Quarantine."

On motion, it was determined to elect forthwith a Committee on Publication, and the following gentlemen were chosen: Drs. Logan of Sacramento, Chairman; Cluness of Sacramento, Grover of San Francisco, Cushing of Oakland, Wythe of Sacramento.

A committee, composed of Drs. Cabanis of Siskiyou, Franklin of Sonora, and Oatman of Sacramento, was appointed to nominate a Board of Censors. The Committee subsequently reported the following named gentlemen, who were duly elected, viz.: Drs. Carr, Pinkerton, and Van Wyck, of Oakland; Dr. Cheney, of Butte; and Dr. Franklin, of Tuolumne.

The subject of the next place of meeting was then taken up, and Oakland, Stockton, San Jose, and Marysville were put in nomination. The vote was taken by ballot, and Oakland was designated by a decided majority.

Dr. MURPHY, of Sacramento, exhibited an instrument which he had contrived for reducing fracture of the lower jaw, accompanying the exhibition with some explanatory remarks. The subject was referred to the Committee on Publication.

Dr. STOUT, of San Francisco, from the committee previously appointed, made the following report on the raising of cinchona, which was accepted, and referred to the Committee on Publication:

The committee on this subject report that during the year no facilities have offered which could be used to promote the cultivation of the cinchona tree in California. The committee, however, report progress, and ask for further time. The project is entertained that this well approved subject may be availed of to obtain, through legislative action, the appropriation of lands, not only to try the cultivation of the cinchona tree, but for the experimental culture of any other desirable plant—or, in other words, the foundation of a State botanical and zoological farm. Such an appropriation would render a permanent service and honor to the State, while the care and expense devoted to the one single object might be lost by the failure of the experiment. From such an appropriation, a magnificent botanical garden might be created. Associated with a State sanitary institution and thermal resort for chronic diseases, it would form a new and superb institution. Forming, as it would, the permanent residence of several competent physicians, botanists, and naturalists, this would secure for it efficient superintendence, while oftentimes the voluntary labor of many grateful convalescents, or of persons infirm from various causes, would diminish the expenses. In this prospect, your Committee respectfully ask to be continued.

ARTHUR B. STOUT.
THOS. M. LOGAN.

The committee was continued accordingly.

Dr. TODD, Chairman of the Committee on the Registration Law, made a report, recommending, among other things, that the records of marriages, births, and deaths be collected by the County Assessors. The report was referred to the Committee on Legislation, with a recommendation that they prepare a proper law on the subject, and that the duty of Registrar be connected with the State Board of Health.

Dr. HARVEY, of Galt, gave notice of an alteration of the Constitution of the Society, which was laid over by rule until the next annual meeting. It is in substance that Section 1, of Article 4, be amended by striking out in the second line the words "second Wednesday in October," and inserting "second Wednesday in April," as the time for the annual meeting.

Adjourned until 7½ P.M.

EVENING SESSION.

The Society was called to order by Vice-President HATCH.

The rules were, on motion, suspended on a suggestion to appoint a committee in the matter of the formation of a Mutual Aid Society, for the relief of indigent members and their families.

The Chair appointed on the committee Drs. Todd of Stockton, Cole of San Francisco, and Logan of Sacramento.

Dr. E. M. CURTIS, of Sacramento, read a fine paper on the subject "Why do we wear spectacles?" illustrating his ideas with a series of diagrams.

Dr. SMITH, of San Francisco, read a paper upon "Diseases of the Eye and Ear, and the Proper Treatment of the same."

Dr. Cushing, from the Committee on the Relations of Apothecaries and Physicians, presented a report, including the following resolution:

Resolved, That the fact of a doctor of medicine being engaged in the manufacture and sale of any secret or patent medicine, or in any way promoting the use of them, shall render him ineligible as a member of this Society.

Report received and adopted.

Certain objections, which had been urged against the admission of Dr. Jackson, of Yolo County, having been withdrawn, and the Board of Censors having reported favorably upon his nomination, he was duly elected.

On motion, Dr. H. L. Nichols, Secretary of State, was tendered a vote of thanks for procuring the use of the Senate Chamber.

The following resolution, offered by Dr. Montgomery, of Sacramento, was adopted:

Resolved, As the sense of this Society, that the subject of medical ethics should receive a larger share of attention in the medical universities and colleges of the country, to the end that the true principles inculcated therein may be more thoroughly impressed upon the minds of students, and, in consequence, more faithfully and scrupulously observed by them in their subsequent professional career.

The following resolution, offered by Dr. Cole, of San Francisco, was adopted:

Resolved, That the Board of Censors shall recommend no candidate for membership until he shall have presented his diploma, or other evidence of being a graduate of a recognized school, and of good standing; and that no voucher of a single member shall be considered sufficient evidence of his qualifications.

The Committee on Certificate of Membership reported one which they thought appropriate, and the report was adopted.

The Society then adjourned *sine die*.

Clinton Cushing,
W. T. Grover,
Secretaries.

[Note.—The Standing Committees will be announced in the next Journal.]

THE BANQUET.

After the adjournment, the members repaired to Armory Hall, for the purpose of enjoying an entertainment provided by the Sacramento Medical Society. Dr. Hatch presided at the table, and when the guests had gone through the extensive range of gastronomic exercises common to such occasions, and were capable of rising to intellectual effort, he announced a number of toasts or sentiments, and called for responses from individuals designated by him.

The first toast was "*The California State Medical Society.*"

Dr. Gibbons, the President elect, being called on, gave a brief outline of the history of the Society, and the benefits accruing from it. He pointed out the duty of the older members toward their junior and humbler associates, exhorting them to take such by the hand, and make them feel that they were improved and benefited by the association. He urged the cultivation of an *esprit du corps*, which would not only do good to members individually, but elevate the profession, and give it more influence and dignity in the community.

The next sentiment was "*The California Doctor in Europe.*"

Dr. Morse, who had just returned from two years' residence in Europe, being called upon to respond, gave some highly interesting reminiscences of his experiences in the Old World. He had visited many of the schools on the continent, and in Great Britain, and heard many of the most eminent professors. He described the arduous round of study required, especially by the German schools; and while he extolled the learning of European physicians, he expressed his firm conviction that American practitioners were decidedly superior in tact and practical knowledge, and more successful in the management of disease. When in London, he visited St. George's Hospital, the scene of the exploits of Hunter, and where that great man had died suddenly from cardiac disease, excited by a paroxysm of anger. Wishing to see the room in which the fatal quarrel had occurred, he requested the venerable janitor to point out the apartment formerly occupied by John Hunter. "John Hunter!" said the old gentleman; "I do not recollect any such name among our students, but I will make inquiry." At that juncture, the doctor saw over a doorway the inscription "Long Room," and he at once knew it was what he sought. In that hospital he had the pleasure of meeting with the distinguished Barclay, author of "Diagnosis," etc., to whom he introduced himself, and with whom he went the round of the wards. Everywhere he had been treated with gratifying attention by medical men. It was enough to announce himself as an American physician to secure to him access to medical institutions, and to the friendly regard of members of the profession.

"*The American Doctor at the Pyramids,*" called forth Dr. Harkness, who had lately made the tour of Egypt. Dr. H. gave some account of the present status of medical science in that land, which he thought had not advanced much since Mark Antony applied to his physician for some medicine to enable him to cope with the "terrific woman" whom he had married. At the great pyramid Dr. H. had found an Egyptian doctor, to whom women resorted from great distances to be cured of sterility. He was seated on the ground, invested with a solitary scanty robe, and, like Diogenes, requested visitors not to shade him from the warmth of the sun.

"*The Doctor in the Sierras*" was responded to by Dr. Cabanis, of Siskiyou, who referred to the enjoyments of practice among the mountains of the distant North, where his professional excursions sometimes took him one hundred miles from home. The speech of Dr. C. was not such as to induce young doctors to "locate" in Siskiyou.

"*Bob Sawyer in Court*" called up Dr. E. R. Taylor, who was understood to be veering somewhere betwixt medicine and law. He made a very witty and amusing speech on neither subject, and yet on both.

"*The Sacramento Society for Medical Improvement*" was responded to by Dr. Oatman, who alluded, among other matters, to the very large proportion of great men and scientists in all departments of knowledge, who had entered through the portals of medicine. The study of medicine had a remarkable influence on the mind, qualifying it admirably for other intellectual pursuits.

"*Luke, the Beloved Physician,*" was a sentiment which very naturally fell to the lot of Rev. Dr. WYTHE, who dwelt on the influence of the study of medicine in enlarging and liberalizing the mind, and qualifying it for the ministry of religion. He expatiated somewhat on the philanthropic and devotional relations of medical studies when rightly conducted.

"*Take a little wine for thy stomach's sake.*" This biblical quotation was aimed directly at Dr. HASWELL, the Head of the Good Templars, and an inveterate disciple of Rechab. The doctor took it coolly, as it did not apply to him, for his name was not Timothy, and he had no stomach ache. Though he drank only water, he enjoyed the better health on that account, and was quite as capable as any one in the room of appreciating the present exercises, and his head would be quite as clear when morning should come.

Dr. BEVERLY COLE was called out by a professional toast, having some personal allusion to rigidity of the spinal column. The doctor complained that he was unable to stand up without preparation, but he managed, nevertheless, to make a very entertaining speech.

Drs. STOUT, CUSHING, TODD, and others, were disturbed from their modest retirement by the Chairman, who called on them to respond to certain sentiments, which they did, briefly though pertinently. The occasion passed off most happily, leaving the best impression on the minds of the company, both as to the personal and fraternal relations of the members of the Society, and the professional and scientific advantages derived from the meetings. Great credit is due to the physicians of Sacramento for their excellent management of affairs from beginning to end.

The Fair-Crittenden Case — Letter from Dr. Buckley.

Audi alteram partem.

To me it is a very painful reflection, that a gentleman of my friend Dr. Bentley's varied attainments and uncommonly high order of intelligence, should so far misapprehend the very commonplace remarks in my paper, entitled "A Defense of Physic," as to attribute to me a "*failure* to elucidate the morbid conditions" in the case of Mr. Crittenden. I feel perfectly convinced that a little reflection on his part should have placed me in a juster light, both with Dr. Bentley and his readers. It is now scarcely necessary—if it is, I must only deplore the obscurity with which I express myself—to say that the object of my paper was not to discuss pathological problems, nor to infringe in any way on what may be fairly deemed legitimate differences of professional opinion; but to expose what I may be permitted to call the "enormities" of professional ignorance or corruption, or both, displayed during the "Fair trial," and, as a moral, to point out to those concerned the absurdity of denouncing medical testimony in general, when clearly the manner of obtaining it is the "*fons et origo mali.*"

It is to me, however, a source of unqualified pleasure to see that as regards one of those "enormities" Dr. Bentley and I are in perfect accord, so far as the chief feature of the case is concerned. One gentleman, it will be remembered, swore that the mortification of the bowels, found on post mortem examination, might have existed while Mr. Crittenden was pleading in Court previous to the shooting, thus throwing some doubt on the cause of death. This opinion I characterized pretty strongly as only to be accounted for "by some form of insanity, which appeared to be epidemic during this trial." Now, Dr. Bentley accounts for its appearance as the *result* of the wound, thus showing that it could not have existed beforehand, as sworn to, and consequently agreeing perfectly with me as to the utter untenableness of this opinion.

Now, with the greatest possible deference, I must take issue with Dr. Bentley when he says that, "so far as any explanation has appeared in print, this matter (alluding to the 'morbid condition') was not at all understood even by the medical witnesses;" and assures us that his theory of embolism "can *alone* account for it without involving its existence before the injury." To my mind, Drs. Douglass and Sawyer not only understood the matter thoroughly, but gave a very sound and satisfactory explanation of it when they stated "that with such marked impairment of the central circulatory organ, and such violent shock as must have occurred in the case, mortification of this nature would be no unnatural sequence of the injury." As to Dr. Bentley's own theory of embolism (and, by the way, I may remind him that this pathological condition was not first brought under the notice of the profession by Virchow in '47, but by Legroux in '37, and afterward more thoroughly elaborated, by Kirkes especially), it seems to me to admit of two very cogent *prima facie* objections. First, the collateral circulation in the mesenteric region is so perfectly free that the effects of embolism would be very readily repaired, and, consequently, mortification prevented; and, secondly, if embolism did actually exist, a man of Dr. Bentley's experience and industry ought to have been able to point out definitely and conclusively, to ocular demonstration, its existence and whereabouts—for, of course, it is so demonstrable. As some slight corroboration of the views of Drs. Douglass and Sawyer, I think I may safely remind Dr. Bentley of the somewhat analogous condition of ulceration of the duodenum after burns, one instance of which I myself have seen exceedingly well marked, although the victim of the injury had only survived it some six hours. I may also urge the possibility of the vasomotor nerves of the mortified region being either directly severed, or paralyzed by the injury.

C. F. Buckley, B.A., M.D.

A Tick in the Ear for Three Weeks.

Dr. Jacob Allen, San Diego, writes us as follows:

Aug. 3, 1871.—A Mr. H——, a healthy young man of about twenty-five, came into my office, and said he thought he had something in his ear. Said it had felt unpleasantly for the last two or three weeks. I placed him in a strong light, and with an ordinary bivalve ear speculum I could see into the ear distinctly, and saw something sticking close to the bottom of the cavity. I took a pair of crooked blunt-pointed forceps, and very readily grasped the substance. On bringing it to the light, what should I see but a large-sized wood-tick kicking and scrabbling as though he had left his home very unwillingly. The wonder is, how any live man could comfortably endure such an insect of so large size in his ear so long.

REVIEWS AND NOTICES OF BOOKS.

The Teeth, and How to Save Them. By L. P. Meredith, M.D., D.D.S. Philadelphia: J. B. Lippincott & Co. 1871. Pp. 271. San Francisco: A. L. Bancroft & Co.

The author of this work, a practitioner of dentistry in Cincinnati, issues it in the endeavor "to bridge over the stream of ignorance that lies between the profession and the masses." It is something novel of its kind, and appears well adapted to the purpose. Though it opens many secrets of the art to the outside world, yet honest and educated dentists will not fear it on that account.

Headaches: Their Causes and Their Cure. By Henry G. Wright, M.D., M.R.C.S.L., L.S.A., Member of the Royal College of Physicians of England, etc. From the fourth London edition. Philadelphia: Lindsay & Blakiston. 1871. Pp. 154. San Francisco: A. L. Bancroft & Co.

We have before expressed our favorable opinion of this little work, and the present revised and improved edition increases our estimate of its value. The subject is treated with method and science, and, withal, in a manner eminently practical.

THE MANAGEMENT OF INFANCY, PHYSIOLOGICAL AND MORAL: Intended chiefly for the use of Parents. By Andrew Combe, M.D. Revised and edited by Sir James Clark, Bart., K.C.B., M.D., F.R.S., Physician in ordinary to the Queen. First American, from the tenth London edition. New York: D. Appleton & Co. 1871. Pp. 302. San Francisco: A. Roman & Co.

A volume embracing a wider scope than its title indicates, forasmuch as it takes in the duties of parents to their unborn offspring. It is the most complete and sensible work of its kind that we know of, and the wonder is that half a century has elapsed since the issue of the original in England, before its republication in America. A copy of the book should go with every marriage license.

THE FUNCTIONS AND DISORDERS OF THE REPRODUCTIVE ORGANS, in Childhood, Youth, Adult Age, and Advanced Life, considered in their Physiological, Social, and Moral Relations. By Wm. Acton, M.R.C.S., Late Surgeon to the Islington Dispensary, etc. Third American, from the fifth London edition. Philadelphia: Lindsay & Blakiston. 1871. Pp. 348. San Francisco: A. L. Bancroft & Co.

This is a new edition of a well-known work, which has been for years a standard authority in its department. Whatever question there may be in regard to the public and unrestricted discussion of many of the topics involved, there can be no doubt of the propriety and the necessity of their investigation by the profession. To this task Dr. Acton addresses himself with great industry and ability.

A PRACTICAL TREATISE ON FRACTURES AND DISLOCATIONS. By Frank Hastings Hamilton, A.M., M.D., LL.D., Professor of the Practice of Surgery with Operations in Bellevue Medical College, Surgeon to Bellevue Hospital, Consulting Surgeon to Hospital for Ruptured and Crippled, etc. Fourth edition, revised and improved. Illustrated with 322 wood cuts. Philadelphia: Henry C. Lea. 1871. Pp. 789. San Francisco: A. L. Bancroft & Co.

Writing of a former edition of this work, the *London Lancet* credited the author with "giving to the world the only complete practical treatise on fractures and dislocations in our language during the present century." At home and abroad the work has fully sustained the reputation thus implied. The present edition is considerably improved by the exclusion of matter deemed effete, and the introduction of much that is new and fresh.

EDITORIAL.

The Meeting of the State Medical Society.

There never was a meeting of scientific or professional men more satisfactory and gratifying to all in attendance than the late annual session of the California State Medical Society at Sacramento. The number in attendance was not large, though there was a fair representation from most sections of the State. At a different season of the year the attendance would have been larger. Entire harmony and concert of action marked the proceedings. Of the Standing Committees on the several departments, a larger proportion than is usual on such occasions made reports. In number and in character, the papers which were read would compare favorably with those presented to the National Association at its recent meeting in San Francisco. The moments of the sessions were industriously employed, and no precious time was lost in idle debates on points of order, and other trivial matters, which are so prone to intrude themselves at such convocations. One single question of difference was introduced, in the form of a protest against the admission of a candidate for membership. But the good judgment of the Censors settled the affair amicably, so that the opposition to admission was withdrawn. We congratulate the Society and the profession throughout the State, on the results of the reorganization of this body, the membership of which in one short year embraces, in all probability, as large a proportion of the physicians within its jurisdiction as any other State Society in the Union.

The full proceedings, embracing the papers which were presented, will be published in pamphlet form. It will be noted, from the abstract in the Journal, that Oakland was selected as the place of meeting next year, and that a proposition was offered to change the time of meeting to April, that being the most healthful period in the State at large, and therefore permitting the attendance of many practitioners in the rural districts, who can not leave their business in the autumn.

Suit for Libel.

Our readers will recollect the suit instituted against Dr. John Scott for malpractice, which was withdrawn by the prosecution without trial, and of which some account was published in this

Journal. Subsequent to the publication, the prosecuting party instituted a second suit for libel, the alleged libel being contained in Dr. Scott's account as published by us, and consisting in the expression "constitutional syphilis" applied to the female whose case was described. The suit for libel was brought against Dr. Scott and the editors of the Journal jointly, but before trial the editors were exempted. The trial came off in October, against Dr. Scott alone. He claimed that, having been arraigned before the public for malpractice, and refused the opportunity to justify himself by trial, it was his right to make his defense through the press; and that an intelligent statement of the case of his patient required the disease to be mentioned, in order to show cause for the treatment which was adopted. The prosecution denied this right, and sued for defamation of character, and damages set at $20,000.

On the trial testimony was adduced to prove the existence of constitutional syphilis. A number of medical witnesses testified unqualifiedly on this point. It was also maintained that constitutional syphilis did not necessarily imply moral impurity, as the disease might have been inherited, or contracted by accident, or without criminal intercourse. These points being established by the defense, the counsel for the prosecution virtually abandoned the suit. The jury returned a verdict without delay favorable to the defendant.

The business of sueing for malpractice and for libel has not hitherto been very successful in California. We do not call to mind a single instance of the conviction of a regular practitioner for malpractice, though a number of suits have been instituted at different times during the last fifteen or twenty years.

The Per-centage System.

Can any thing be said in defense of the system which prevails among apothecaries, of allowing to physicians a per-centage on prescriptions sent to them? How far the practice maintains elsewhere, we can not say. But we can say that some practitioners in San Francisco—a small proportion of the whole number, we are glad to believe—take pains to send their prescriptions to certain apothecaries, often inconveniently remote, for the purpose of getting a share of the price; and we do not hesitate to pronounce the practice unjust to patients, if not positively dishonest. The journals sometimes condemn it, but not often. A writer in the October number of the *Canadian Pharmaceutical Journal* reprobates the practice severely, as it is carried on in Toronto. Would it not be well for all pharmaceutical journals and associations to take up the subject, and unite in an effort to eradicate the evil?

Reward for a Cholera Cure.

The newspapers say that the French Academy has offered a reward of 100,000 francs for a remedy for the cholera. It may be so—we hope not. In the first place, the idea of *a cure for a disease* is not in keeping with medical science. It has a vulgar, empirical flavor. It implies the existence of some one article or remedy adapted to various conditions and circumstances of disease; in fact, a specific. But the chief objection to such a proceeding, is the implied necessity of hiring professional men to perform a duty—the inference that franc-pieces are a stronger incentive to medical inquiries than the inspiration of science and philanthropy. Have not hundreds—aye, thousands—of medical men labored with all their might to work out the problem of a remedial treatment for cholera? Are not their best energies still directed in that channel? And will they do more from the sordid impulse of a golden bribe than the honorable ambition with which they are now inspired? A premium for the best treatise on the whole subject of cholera would be better. This would stimulate to the investigation of a wide field of inquiry, and crown the successful competitor with a wreath of fame. But the mere discovery of a cure for any disease, especially if made under the impulse of venal motives, can not elevate the discoverer above the level of the charlatan. Coming from a body holding such a high position as the French Academy, the mistake is the more deserving of notice and rebuke.

Infinitesimal Science.

A homeopathic doctor in New Jersey writes to the *New England Gazette* that after taking a few pellets of sulphur, 200th potency, he perceived a distinct smell of sulphur, which continued several days. He is willing to swear to it. The 200th potency is one grain of sulphur divided into the number of parts represented by a unit followed by 400 cyphers In other words, take the millionth part of one grain of sulphur, and divide it into a million of parts, and divide each of these parts into a million, and so on for sixty-six consecutive operations. A grain of the final quotient will represent the quantity of sulphur swallowed by our philosopher, and which perfumed his nostrils for several days.

Deaths from Chloroform.

The profession have ceased to be disquieted by reports of death under the influence of chloroform. Ether is held to severe account for an occasional death, occurring from one to twenty-four hours after its exhibition. But chloroform has an indulgence to clip the thread in a twinkling, at the rate of twenty-five to fifty per annum. The *British Med. Journal* reports three of these fatalities, two of which occurred in one week. A case is reported recently in Brooklyn, N. Y., happening in a dentist's office, from the inhalation of only (!) half an ounce. A death from nitrous oxide gas is also reported.

The Cundurango Speculation.

Cundurango has already gone to the tomb, with ten thousand other cancer cures. It would probably have had a longer run, but for the speculation of which it was the subject. Dr. Bliss, its distinguished champion, imported and monopolized all the *genuine* article, appointed agencies for its sale, and wrote up the cures with dispatch, which was highly necessary, for the reason that the patients got into a habit of dying soon after they were cured.

Turpentine in Traumatic Erysipelas.

An Italian physician quoted in *The Doctor* treats erysipelas from wounds by dressing the inflamed part with oil of turpentine. In a few hours the edema disappears, the color diminishes, and the fever abates. Two or three days generally suffice to conquer all the symptoms. He explains the cure on the supposition that erysipelas results from an organic germ, to which the oil is poisonous.

Conium in Mastitis.

A German obstetrician *(Practitioner)* highly recommends extract of conium, in small doses repeated several times daily, for the resolution of inflammation of the breast, from stasis of the milk. He reports several cases of cure. Care should be used in procuring an active article. We have used the preparations of conium more or less in a variety of diseases for upward of forty years, and we do not recollect to have derived any well marked benefit from them in a single case.

A Quack Stoned to Death.

A celebrated quack, known as "Indian Joe," was lately stoned to death by his stupid brethren of the Piute tribe, in Inyo County, because he failed to redeem his promise to cure two sick Indians. He should have been sent to San Francisco, where he could have made a fortune by practising on gentlemen and ladies of white blood, as a partner of Li-po-tai or Darrin. The poor fellow had not learned the virtues of *advertising*.

GENERAL SUMMARY.

Dirt, Poverty, and Drunkenness among the Working Classes in England.

In an interview of the Commissioners who conducted the recent inquiry into the mortality of Liverpool with the Land and House Owners' Association, some of the members of the association expressed an opinion than the habits of the people were much dirtier than before 1847. At that time the cleanly poor insisted on a dirty person removing from a court, and the owners were obliged to compel them to leave for fear of losing their other tenants; but now that sense of cleanliness seemed lost, even by the English, who were formerly very clean. This increasing dirtiness was attributed, to a great extent, to increasing poverty and intemperance; but, in addition to these, other causes were assigned. The epidemic of relapsing fever probably led to the enforced cleaning of the houses; but, in spite of this enforced cleanliness, nothing could exceed the dirt of the people, and the fetid condition of the atmosphere at night. How human beings could tolerate such a state of things would be incredible if they did not know the deadening influence of custom. With regard to the people and furniture of these houses, the Commissioners were not at all prepared either for the wretched appearance of the people, or for the aspect of the poverty disclosed. They could not have believed that in any town in this country they could have gone into room after room, and house after house, and have found in so many cases literally almost nothing but the bare walls, a heap of straw covered by dirty rags, and possibly the remains of a broken chair or table. In some houses there were no cooking utensils of any kind, or only an old saucepan. Another point was, that many people seemed to have no change of clothes. Inquiry from some people extracted the fact that they occasionally washed their hands and faces at the tap, but they seldom remove their clothes. The inquiry of the Commissioners led them to the conclusion that intemperance played a very large part in bringing about the poverty—with all its attendant evils—that existed. After giving instances with which they had met of constant employment and good wages associated with utter poverty, the Commissioners state that instances of this kind so frequently occur in all the poor districts of Liverpool that they questioned whether 20 per cent. of the laboring class in these streets were leading lives of ordinary restraint and decency.—*Med. Press and Circular.*

Physiological Experimentation.

A committee, consisting of ten individuals, having been appointed at the last meeting of the British Association, held at Liverpool, to consider the subject of physiological experimentation, in accordance with a resolution of the General Committee, the following report was drawn up, and signed by seven members of the committee: "1. No experiment which can be performed under the influence of an anesthetic ought to be done without it. 2. No painful experiment is justifiable for the mere purpose of illustrating a law or fact already demonstrated. In other words, experimentation without the employment of anesthetics is not a fitting exhibition for teaching purposes. 3. Whenever, for the investigation of new truth, it is necessary to make a painful experiment, every effort should be made to insure success in order that the suffering inflicted may not be wasted. For this reason, no painful experiment ought to be performed by an unskilled person with insufficient instruments and assistance, or in places not suitable for the purpose—that is to say, anywhere except in physiological and pathological laboratories under proper regulations. 4. In the scientific preparation for veterinary practice, operations ought not to be performed upon living animals for the mere purpose of obtaining greater operative dexterity.—*Med. Press and Circular.*

New Plan of Dressing Wounds.

The Paris correspondent of the *Lancet* observes that the surgical novelty of the day in Paris is M. Alphonse Guérin's new plan of dressing wounds. It consists in introducing a quantity of cotton wool into the stump immediately after amputation, or on any wound whatever, surgical or accidental. The amputated limb—to take this case—is then wrapped round and round with cotton wool, quite dry and alone; a bandage is then applied, and that is all. The bandage is pressed a little tighter on following days, if necessary, so that there may be a mild compression, but the dressing remains undisturbed till the twentieth or twenty-fifth day, when, on removing the packet of wadding, a glassful of pus is found in the folds of the cotton, and the wound is discovered quite healed. M. Guérin, amidst the extraordinary mortality which has attended all the amputations done since the beginning of the German siege, has already obtained by this means six successful cases of amputation of the thigh out of nine, whilst all his amputations of the leg are doing well. This has created quite a sensation in Paris in the surgical wards of the hospitals, and Professor Gosselin of La Charité, and M. Guyon of Necker, are already experimenting with this method of their colleague at St. Louis.—*London Lancet.*

Our Poor Profession!

Our "Obituary" gives the name of Samuel H. Cornish—as kindly a spirit as could be conceived, a real friend of the poor; he will be sadly missed by many a family in the locality in which he resided. Twelve months since he was in possession of a large general practice, and the confidence of all with whom he came in contact. A few months later he was a raging madman, confined within the walls of an asylum, and now kind death has come to put an end to his sufferings. This is a sad but true picture, and the subject of it, both publicly and privately, was a man *sans peur et sans reproche;* yet possessed of a highly sensitive nature, he was charged by a patient in childbed—probably suffering from puerperal mania—with being her murderer! The very thought—although, we believe, the woman afterward recovered—preyed so heavily upon his mind, that reason soon gave way, and the poor fellow died, as before mentioned, on Wednesday last—a helpless maniac. There is no other profession against a member of which such a charge could be made; no other where an innocent man may so easily forfeit his reputation, and even his very life! 'Tis a sad, sad reflection.—*Med. Press and Circular, Sept.* 27, 1871.

Suicide by Swallowing Chloroform.

A case of suicide by swallowing an ounce of chloroform is reported in Australia, which presents some points of interest. The deceased man was suffering from delirium tremens, brought on by a long course of drinking, and in this state procured and swallowed the chloroform. He immediately became insensible. His eyelids could be opened and pupils touched without the slightest proof of sensibility being manifested. When things were at the worst, and the man apparently dying, Mr. Gilbee and Dr. Neild, the medical men in attendance, determined to try the injection of ammonia, according to Professor Halford's plan of treating snake bites. Ammonia, in the proportion of one part to two parts of water, was injected four times into the veins of the arms. Two drachms were injected altogether. The effects were most promising: sensibility returned, and after five hours the patient could sit up and talk. He died, however, suddenly next day, apparently from syncope. The brain was found to be highly congested, and smelt of alcohol. The liver was diseased.—*Med. Times and Gazette.*

Concussion as a Sanitary Agent.

Col. Hardee, who was a Confederate soldier during the rebellion, recently addressed a meeting of farmers at the Florida Land Agency, and claimed "to have utilized concussion in the perfect annihilation of the horticultural pest known as curculio." He first noticed that the blowing of a whistle by a locomotive on a railway passing near by had driven the curculio to the extreme end of his orchard. He concluded that the insects didn't like the jarring, and, by way of confirming his opinion, he ignited two pounds of powder placed in the hollow of a live-oak stump. The result was that not only the curculio, but every winged insect in the orchard was destroyed. He adds that concussion is "a great fertilizer"—that it destroys "animalcules," and renders sickly places perfectly healthy. When there is little or no thunder, he argues, there is a great deal of yellow fever. How concussion affects air, soil, or trees he doesn't know; he only knows the facts. "I claim," he says, "that the Yanks were indebted to King Gunpowder for their healthfulness during the late wicked war."

Bright's Disease Detected by the Ophthalmoscope.

Professor Noyes, of the Detroit Medical College (*Western Medical Advance*), referring to the well-known connection between certain diseases of the kidneys and impaired vision, recites a case which presented the following symptoms: On examination of the right eye with the ophthalmoscope, the pupil dilated with atropine revealed the optic disc injected (hyperemia), swollen and edematous; arteries barely perceptible; veins swollen and tortuous; near the papilla optica there was a well defined white deposit or patch, and another still larger near the macula lutea, on the upper and outer side, irregular in shape. From these objective symptoms alone my diagnosis was at once made out, viz., retinitis albuminurica in the acute stage from Bright's disease of the kidneys. An examination of the urine, made subsequently, confirmed the diagnosis, it being found to be very heavily charged with albumen.

Liquor Dealers' License for Apothecaries.

The American Pharmaceutical Association, at its late meeting in St. Louis, adopted the following propositions on this subject: 1st. That apothecaries should not be taxed as liquor dealers if they confine the sale of liquors to the sick, and require a prescription, or other written evidence, of its need for medicinal use. 2d. That such sales shall be limited in quantity to half a pint or a pint. 3d. That when apothecaries prefer to enter the business of selling liquors with a view to supplying general demand, they should undoubtedly be required to take a liquor dealer's license. 4th. That in either case, we are of the opinion that the right of sale should not be construed to permit the drinking of liquors on the apothecary's premises, unless for relief in emergencies of illness.

Extract of Pinus Canadensis.

This article appears to be making its way into use in the Atlantic States. Dr. Marion Sims says of it: "I have used it for about eight months in some affections of the rectum, vagina, and cervix uteri; I have used it, considerably diluted, as a vaginal wash with great success; but I prefer to apply it to the os tincæ on cotton wool, either pure or mixed with glycerine, or glycerine and rose water. Thus applied, it should remain intact for two or three, or even four, days, and then be renewed. In this way I have seen chronic granular vaginitis remedied in a few days that had resisted the ordinary remedies for weeks; and I have seen granular erosions, with leucorrhea, disappear very readily under its use."

Adulteration of Drugs.

At the meeting of the American Pharmaceutical Association, held in St. Louis, a report on drugs was presented, which contained a number of curious statements in regard to the adulteration practiced by the trade. It is stated that several wholesale drug houses in New York have rooms set apart for the purpose of adulterating powdered drugs. One establishment employs a foreman to take special charge of this department, all sorts of cheap substances being mixed with the more precious powders. Some dealers, in sending opium to the grinders, always send a certain proportion of licorice to be powdered with it.

Malformation.

Mrs. F., æt. 32, mother of six well-formed children, gave birth, July 21st, at full term, to a child with all the intestinal canal, except the rectum, external to the abdomen. There was an aperture a little to the right of the umbilicus large enough to admit two fingers, through which the bowels protruded. In every other respect the child was well formed and healthy. It lived three days, during which time it nursed freely, and had several passages from the rectum.—*Med. News and Library.*

Cundurango! Excelsior!

The *Leavenworth Medical Herald* has a poem inspired by the great cancer-cure, which winds up with the following stanza:

"The evening sun went down in red—
The maid and matron both were dead;
And yet through all the realms around,
This worthless shrub of mighty sound
Will serve to fill the purse forlorn,
And cancer succumb—'in a horn'—
To Cundurango!"

Circumcision in Utero.

A member of the Philadelphia Obstetrical Society, having witnessed the circumcision of a Jewish child, described this operation to his wife, who was in the early period of pregnancy. A strong impression was made on her mind, and the event was the subject of constant thought for several days. Seven months afterward, she gave birth to a child whose glans penis was found exposed, "while the retracted prepuce actually showed the yet granulating cicatrix of what looked like a very recent circumcision!" This extraordinary circumstance, which is related in a first-class medical journal, under the head of "Birth-mark from maternal impressions," suggests a ready method by which our fellow-citizens of the Israelitish faith may do away with the sanguinary mode of performing circumcision in common use.

Pills of Sulph. Iron and Carb. Potass.

A pharmacist of Brussels (*Amer. Journal of Pharmacy*) proposes the following manipulation: 500 parts sulphate of iron, and the same of carbonate of potassa, are to be powdered separately, and then intimately mixed. A hot mixture of 100 parts clarified honey and 20 of white wax, is now added, and the whole beaten to a pasty mass, and set aside for twenty-four hours. A brown-green mass is produced, to which a sufficient quantity of powdered marshmallow is added to make into pills.

Digital Compression in Femoral Aneurism.

Prof. A. P. Reid, of the Halifax Medical College, reports in the *Canada Medical Journal* a case of femoral aneurism cured by compression with the thumb, kept up sixty-eight hours. The tumor was as large as a hen's egg, and situated six inches below Poupart's ligament. The pulsation stopped suddenly on the accession of a paroxysm of pain which caused the patient to jump out of bed with a loud scream. In four weeks there had been no indication of the disease returning.

Treatment of Gonorrhea with Water Alone.

A surgeon in the Royal Artillery writes to the *London Lancet* that he has for some time successfully treated cases of gonorrhea with water only. Beginning with injections of lukewarm water, he continues them hourly until chordee and scalding cease, and then uses cold water in the same way, until the case is cured. He uses no internal treatment, unless an occasional saline aperient, and says he has not had a single failure.

Cyano-Pancreatine.

This is a new preparation of animal fats and pancreatine, prepared by the Sisters of the Grey Nunnery in Montreal. It appears to be a pleasant preparation, and, we believe, will agree well with the stomach. We have not had an opportunity of trying its efficacy with any very decided results, but purpose doing so in the course of the next month or two, when we will again refer to its usefulness.—*Canada Med. Journal.*

Subperiosteal Exsection of Joints.

At a recent meeting of the Medical Society of Vienna, there was exhibited the elbow-joint of a girl just deceased, upon whom periosteal exsection had been performed three years before. The form of the joint had been reproduced, the cartilaginous covering and synovial membrane being clearly apparent, though the shape of the articular surfaces was somewhat modified. The *London Lancet*, in quoting the case, urges the introduction of the plan into British surgery.

Vapor of Ammonia in Pelvic Pains.

Dr. Bowling, editor of the *Nashville Medical Journal*, has made what he deems a valuable discovery in the treatment of the pain of dysmenorrhea, colic, strangury, etc. He pours a drachm of aqua ammonia in a chamber, and seats the patient on it. The smarting of the remedy must be borne for a few minutes, when the relief comes with great certainty.

Tag-Alder as a Hemostatic.

Dr. Dupuis, of Kingston *(Canada Lancet)*, recommends as a hemostatic the *alnus incana*, known as tag-alder, speckled, spotted, or hoary alder, a shrub common in Canada, growing to the height of ten to twenty feet. A decoction of the bark is applied to the wound or bleeding part, by means of cotton or sponge. It probably contains a large quantity of gallic or tannic acid.

Chemicals on Exhibition.

At the annual session of the National Pharmaceutical Association, lately held in St. Louis, there was exhibited a block of alum, beautifully crystallized, weighing seven hundred pounds. Also, a glass globe containing $600 worth of sulph. quiniæ, another with $700 worth of sulph. morphiæ, and a third containing one hundred ounces sulphate of cinchona.

Chloroform vs. Ether.

The last phase of this interminable controversy appears in the October number of the *American Journal of Medical Science*, presented by Dr. W. J. Morton, of Boston. After searching the recent authorities, and collating all accessible statistics, this writer comes to the conclusion that death from chloroform occurs in about one case in every three thousand in which it is administered. In the majority of cases it produces death by paralyzing the heart, through its action on the par vagum nerves of the pulmonary surfaces. He considers the two following propositions to be well established : 1. Death from chloroform is necessary and unavoidable in a certain per-centage of cases. 2. Death from ether is possible, not probable, and need never occur. He anticipates from the feeling of insecurity and danger which pervades the profession in Europe and America, that a large diminution of the popular use of chloroform must ensue, and a far more universal resort to ether.

What is Malaria?

Dr. Oldham, a British surgeon, has written a work in answer to this question, which is made the subject of a brief review in the last number of the *American Medical Journal.* He denies entirely the common idea of a poison in the atmosphere, and finds in changes of temperature and other atmospheric conditions, causes of sufficient potency, in his estimation, to explain all the phenomena imputed to malaria. Dr. Oldham is far from being singular in his unbelief; and it would not surprise us if his doctrine should become the popular theory of the professional world before the expiration of the present century.

Dried White of Egg in Commerce.

The dried white of egg is an important article of importation from the continent to England. How to prepare it in the most economical and perfect manner, is a question not yet settled. A French writer *(Gazette Hebdomadaire)* proposes to mix it with clean sand in cakes. When thus dried it may be transported with facility, and when required for use the albumen may be dissolved in water and separated from the sand.

Influence of Tobacco in Diseases of Nerve-Centres.

In the *Bulletin de l'Association Franc. cont. l'Abus de Tabac.* M. Tamisier states that out of fifty-nine grave affections of the nerve-centres observed from 1860 to 1869 among men, forty occurred in smokers. In fifteen cases of hemiplegia, nine abused tobacco, and two used it moderately; four did not smoke. Of eighteen cases of paraplegia, five were great smokers, three moderate smokers, and ten abstained from tobacco. Out of twenty cases of locomotor ataxia, fourteen were great smokers, five moderate, and one abstainer.—*The Doctor.*

Hemostatic Cotton Wool.

The cotton is soaked in a solution containing four per cent. of soda, then washed and dried. It is then dipped one, two, or three times in a diluted solution of perchloride of iron, dried, and pulled apart by the fingers. It absorbs moisture, and hence should be kept in a close jar or box.

The Tramp of Death.

A correspondent of the *British Medical Journal* states, that there occurred to the German troops, on the occasion of their recent triumphal entry into Berlin, twelve cases of sunstroke, three cases of which were immediately fatal, and recovery in the remaining cases is not prognosticated.—*The Doctor.*

Antiseptic Ligatures.

The antiseptic ligatures recently introduced by Professor Lister are prepared by steeping silk or cat gut in carbolated oil, for at least forty-eight hours.

ITEMS OF NEWS, Etc.

Sir Roderick Murchison is dead—aged 79.

Of twenty deaths of physicians recorded in a British journal, one was aged 90, and one 95.

The Cinchona Plantations in the north of India do not thrive. The climate seems to be too moist.

THE NUMBER OF PHYSICIANS in good standing in New York City, Brooklyn, and the vicinity, is 1,550.

QUINIA is now so extensively manufactured in the United States that only a small quantity is imported.

AMBROSE SMITH, having served the Philadelphia Collêge of Pharmacy as Treasurer for twenty-one consecutive years, declines a re-election.

SASSAFRAS OIL is manufactured in Richmond, Va., at the rate of forty gallons a week. Fifty pounds of the root furnishes one pound of oil.

DR. TEWKSBURY, of Maine, lately performed vesico-vaginal lithotomy in a girl seven years of age. Recovery was complete in fifteen days.

DR. HEADLAND, author of the prize essay on the "Action of Medicines," has been elected to the chair made vacant by the death of Dr. Hyde Salter.

A PRIZE of $400 is offered by Dr. Jacobi, President of the Medical Society of New York, for the best essay on the "Diseases of Infancy and Childhood in the United States."

WATSON'S PRACTICE is about to appear in a new edition, revised by the industrious author. Probably no work in our tongue on the practice of medicine has done so much service since Cullen's.

PROFESSOR LISTER, of Edinburgh, was recently summoned to Balmoral, to open a small abscess near the arm of Her Majesty the Queen. This event will immortalize him more than all his other exploits combined.

THE AMERICAN PHARMACEUTICAL ASSOCIATION had a very satisfactory annual session at St. Louis. Seven new organizations were represented, and 108 new members elected. Enno Sander, of St. Louis, was elected President. An invitation was extended to the International Pharmaceutical Congress to meet in this country in 1876.

THE CHICAGO MEDICAL EXAMINER, conducted by Drs. Davis, father and son, was burnt out by the great fire, and the October number, just ready for distribution, was destroyed. The books were saved, and the *Examiner* will be speedily resurrected, and the back numbers supplied. We suppose the *Chicago Medical Journal* shared the same disastrous fate.

STATE BOARD OF HEALTH.

Abstract from the Reports of Deaths and their Causes, in the following cities and towns in California, during September, 1871:

Cities and Towns.	Total Deaths.	Prevalent Diseases. Consumption.	Other diseases of Lungs.	Dis. Stomach and Bowels.	Diphtheria	Scarlatina	[illegible] Fevers.	Authorities.
San Francisco	248	15	6	35	3	1	11	S. F. B'rd of Health
Sacramento	33	4	1	3	0	0	3	Sac. B'rd of Health
Petaluma	1	0	0	0	0	0	1	Dr. G. W. Graves.
Dixon	0	0	0	0	0	0	0	Dr. R. H. Plummer.
Santa Clara	6	0	0	2	0	0	0	Dr. H. H. Warburton
Stockton	11	0	0	5	0	0	0	Stockton B'd Health
Marysville	[illegible]	0	0	0	0	0	5	Dr. C. E. Stone.
Placerville	2	0	0	0	0	0	0	Dr. E. A. Kunkler.
Auburn	1	0	0	0	0	0	1	Dr. A. S. Du Bois
San Diego	4	1	0	0	0	0	0	Co. Med. Society.
San Luis Obispo								Dr. W. W. Hays.
Oroville	0	0	0	0	0	0	0	Dr. J. M. Vance.
Woodland	6	0	0	0	0	0	0	Dr. A. B. Mehring.
Oakland	10	1	0	1	0	0	0	Dr. T. H. Pinkerton.
Los Angeles	21	3	3	0	0	0	3	Dr. H. S. Orme.
Nevada City	0	0	0	0	0	0	0	Dr. J. A. Gutlin.
Truckee	1	1	0	0	0	0	0	Dr. Wm. Curless.
St. Helena	2	0	0	0	0	0	0	Dr. J. S. Adams.
San José								Dr. J. N. Brown.
Napa City	3	0	1	0	0	0	0	Dr. M. B. Pond.
Cacheville								Dr. E. L. Parramore
Siskiyou	0	0	0	0	0	0	0	Dr. T. T. Cabanis.
Watsonville								Dr. C. E. Cleveland.
Folsom	0	0	0	0	0	0	0	Dr. L. McGuire.
Bridgeport Towns'p	0	0	0	0	0	0	0	Dr. J. L. Asay.
Sut'r C'k & Amador	3	1	0	0	0	0	0	Dr. H. M. Fiske.
Monterey	2	1	0	0	0	0	0	Dr. C. A. Canfield.
Santa Cruz								Dr. Benj. Knight.
Vallejo								Dr. J. M. Brown.
Suisun & Fairfield	[illegible]	0	0	0	0	0	0	Dr. S. D. Campbell
Colusa	0	0	0	0	0	0	0	Dr. Luke Robinson
Trinity County	3	1	1	0	0	0	0	Dr. J. C. Montague.
Santa Barbara	1	1	0	0	0	0	0	Dr. C. B. Bates.
Redwood City	2	0	0	0	0	0	0	Dr. C. A. Kirkpatrick.
Totals	371	30	12	46	3	1	24	

Abstract from Reports of Births:

Cities and Towns.	Total Births.	Male.	Female.	Still-born.	Live-born.	Authorities.
San Francisco	101	56	45	22	79	S. F. Board of Health.
Sacramento	47	30	17	4	43	Sac. Board of Health.
All other places	200	103	97	14	186	Various sources.
Total	348	189	159	40	308	

Remarks.—An excess of only 17 deaths this month over those of the previous month, notwithstanding we are approaching the season of greatest mortality, goes to confirm the fact, commented upon last month, of the highly favorable condition of the public health, which has obtained during the entire year.

In the corresponding month of 1870, which may be put down also as a healthy year, the rate of mortality, as shown by our table, was 400. This year we have the returns from eleven more localities, and yet we find the total mortality for the same month to be only 371—being minus 29 deaths.

THOMAS M. LOGAN, M.D.,
Permanent Secretary State Board of Health.

Mortality in San Francisco during September, 1871.

By H. GIBBONS, Jr., M.D.

CAUSES OF DEATH.

Abscess, Thoracic	1	Diseases of Heart	9	Meningitis	11
Anemia	1	Dropsy	2	Metrorrhagia	1
Aneurism of Aorta	2	Drowning	2	Morbus Coxaris	1
Apoplexy	6	Dysentery	4	Nervous Prostration	1
Atrophia	12	Eclampsia	1	Old Age	2
Bladder, Inflam. of	1	Enteritis	6	Ovarian Tumor	1
Bright's Disease	1	Fever, Remittent	2	Paralysis	7
Cancer	2	" Scarlet	1	Peritonitis	2
" of Intestines	1	" Typhoid	9	Phthisis	45
Cancrum Oris	1	Gastritis	6	Pneumonitis	3
Cholera Infantum	14	Gastro-Enteritis	1	Premature Birth	1
Congestion of Brain	6	Gunshot Wound	2	Softening of Brain	3
" of Lungs	2	Hemoptysis	6	Suicide	3
Convulsions	10	Hospital Gangrene	1	Syncope	1
Croup	3	Hydrocephalus	6	Syphilis	1
Cyanosis	1	Inanition	6	Unknown	9
Debility, General	5	Injuries, unspecified	1	Uremic Poisoning	1
Delirium Tremens	1	Intestines, Disease of	1	Wound of Heart	1
Dentition	4	Intussusception	2		
Diabetes	1	Laryngitis	2	Total	248
Diarrhea	3	Liver, Abscess of	1	Still-births	22
Diphtheria	3	" Disease of	2		

AGES.

Under 1 year	59	From 15 to 20 years	3	From 60 to 70 years	8
From 1 to 2 years	19	From 20 to 30 years	29	From 70 to 80 years	2
From 2 to 5 years	10	From 30 to 40 years	44	From 80 to 90 years	1
From 5 to 10 years	13	From 40 to 50 years	36	Unknown	0
From 10 to 15 years	1	From 50 to 60 years	23		

Sex.—Male, 164; Female, 84. Total, 248.

Color.—White, 213; Copper, 31; Black, 4.

NATIVITIES.

California	100	Germany	12	Italy	1
Other parts of U. S.	36	Prussia	4	China	29
British Amer'n Prov.	4	Austria	2	Australia	1
England	6	Denmark	1	Belgium	1
Ireland	36	Sweden	3	Greece	1
Scotland	4	Switzerland	2	Poland	1
France	1	Spain	1	Unknown	2

RECAPITULATION.

Died in City Wards	197	Mount St. Joseph's Infirmary	3
City and County Hospital	15	Alms House	8
U. S. Marine Hospital	2	Magdalen Asylum	1
French Hospital	3	Orphan Asylum	1
German Hospital	3	Casualties	6
St. Mary's Hospital	4	Suicides	3
Italian Hospital	2		

REMARKS.—As yet there has been no increase of mortality, such as was feared might occur in the autumn months. In September—a day shorter than August—there was but one more death. The number of deaths in this month for six years past is as follows: 1866, 186; 1867, 187; 1868, 350; 1869, 266; 1870, 264; 1871, 248. Though the aggregate remains about the same, there are a number of changes in the individual causes of death, such as aneurism, apoplexy, cancer, dropsy, inanition, pneumonia, of which there were fewer, and atrophia, cholera infantum, enteritis, gastritis, hydrocephalus, paralysis, softening of the brain, etc., of which there were more deaths in September. It will be observed that the latter list consists mostly of disorders of early life; and, indeed the table shows an increased mortality among children, as well as of natives of California. It will be seen that a death is reported from syncope, one from nervous prostration, and another from cancrum oris. The former is so palpably an *effect*—simply a *mode* of dying—that it is surprising that any one should give it as a cause. Beyond a few points of this character, the table presents nothing of marked interest.

PACIFIC MEDICAL AND SURGICAL JOURNAL.

VOL. V.—DECEMBER, 1871.—No. 55.

ORIGINAL COMMUNICATIONS.

Inward Dislocation of the Radius and Ulna.

BY W. S. THORNE, M.D., San Jose.

THE PACIFIC MEDICAL AND SURGICAL JOURNAL for July contains an article, entitled "A New Observation—The Luxated Elbow," by Dr. A. S. Hudson, of Stockton, which was read before the Section on Surgery of the American Medical Association, and recommended for publication. Having seen neither comment nor criticism upon the article in question, in this or contemporaneous journals, I venture to briefly review what I deem to be certain peculiarities, if not questionable features, of this "New Observation," and the conclusions deduced therefrom.

First, that the typical form of dislocation of the radius and ulna inward is of *necessity* a *complete dislocation.*

Second, that Professor Hamilton "has written and illustrated a fallacious and incomprehensible pathology of this lesion."

Third, that Dr. Hudson's description of this lesion, as he observed it in one case (typical ?), is, in the main, essentially identical with that given by Professor Hamilton, being only less elaborate and specific than the latter.

Fourth, that Dr. Hudson's case, from his own pathological history of it, was an example of incomplete dislocation, in the strict, surgical interpretation of terms.

Fifth, that a dislocation is of necessity complete, because the bones concerned in the joint are wholly removed from their *respective* articulations.

It seems to me illogical, and very unusual, for Dr. Hudson to assume the construction of a typical surgical lesion by observing a solitary example. Were this extraordinary latitude admissible, typical lesions might be multiplied indefinitely, limited only by the number of observers. It would seem that, in order to establish a typical form of the lesion in question, it would be necessary to record its aggregate and most constant features, extending through a series of cases, by various and reliable observers. Dr. Hudson, by the observation of a single case, five weeks after the receipt of the injury, is able to pronounce the harmonious authority and multiplied experience of distinguished surgeons for half a century as *erroneous*, *fallacious* and *incomprehensible.* In his "New Observation," Dr. Hudson says of the pathology of the injury, "as witnessed in the child, and subsequently *demonstrated* on the cadaver, the typical form of dislocation of radius and ulna inward on the humerus, is that in which both bones are wholly removed from their *respective* articulations; therefore, can be none other than a complete dislocation." Herein, I think Dr. Hudson fails to agree with the accepted interpretation of a complete dislocation. He admits that "the head of the radius felt in the bend of the arm occupies the trochlea." Hence, there are two articular surfaces, at least, in contact, although they have lost their *respective articular* relations. Hamilton defines a complete dislocation thus: "One in which no portions of the articular surfaces remain in contact." Dunglison says, "Luxation is *complete* when the bones have entirely lost their natural connection." Cooper's definition is yet more specific: "With the extent of the dislocation luxations are either complete or incomplete; the latter is applied when the articular surfaces still remain partially in contact. Incomplete dislocations only occur in ginglymoid articulations. In these the dislocation is almost always *incomplete*, and very great violence must have operated when the bones are *completely* dislocated. In the elbow the dislocation is partial with respect both to the ulna and radius."

Dr. Hudson fails to show, in his case, the operation of great violence. "A child, two or three years old, falling from a few steps," would, under ordinary circumstances, scarcely fulfill the necessary condition of violence. If the humerus and ulna were the only bones concerned in the articulation of the elbow joint, Dr. Hudson's peculiar construction of complete dislocation would be correct; but, unfortunately for his "New Observation," there is a third bone (radius), whose articular surface (head), he informs us, "is felt in the bend of the arm, occupying the trochlear surface of the humerus, separated from the ulna." It would seem, therefore, that the dislocation is not complete with respect to the radius.

Dr. Hudson further remarks, that "Professor Hamilton may have written the pathology of this mischief with the wood-cut illustrating it before him, instead of the displaced bones, which cut is *obviously* a copy of one in Gross or Fergusson, and that one quite imaginary and erroneous. When *carefully studied*, this belief becomes overbearing; namely, that for the coronoid process of the ulna to rest in the trochlea, and the point of the olecranon on the inner condyle of the humerus, with the arm pointing away from the body, as figured and described by Hamilton, is an *anatomical impossibility*." With all respect to Dr. Hudson's acumen and perspicacity, I suspect that, after "*careful study*" of the pathology, and cut illustrating it, he has failed to discover their true significance. The wood-cut on page 606 of Hamilton's work on Fractures and Dislocations, represents the *posterior aspect* of an inward dislocation of the *left arm*, and not the anterior aspect of the same injury in the right arm, as Dr. Hudson must have supposed, when he asserts that the figure in question exhibits an "anatomical impossibility." Fortunately for the reputation of Professor Hamilton, and equally unfortunate for the "New Observation," the figure as shown above represents the left arm flexed, and the hand pronated and inclined *inward* across the body, the joint presenting to the observer its posterior aspect. In no part of Professor Hamilton's description of this lesion does he describe "the lower arm pointing away from the body," as asserted by Dr. Hudson; on the contrary, he distinctly says, on page 606 of his work on Fractures and Dislocations: "If the dislocation is only inward, the olecranon process can be felt projecting on the inner side and completely concealing the epicondyle; while the head of the radius, having abandoned its socket, may be felt indistinctly in the bend of the arm. The external condyle (epicondyle) is remarkably prominent. The fore-arm is generally more or less flexed, and the hand forcibly pronated. The natural outward deflexion of the fore-arm is lost, or it may be inclined inwards. This phenomenon is explained by the position of the epicondyle, upon which the greater sigmoid cavity now rests, allowing the ulna to overlap a little upon the humerus, rendering the fore-arm actually somewhat shorter along the ulnar margin, although the head of the radius may still occupy the summit of the trochlea." The wood-cut on the same page accurately illustrates the foregoing description as well as the following, given by Dr. Hudson, which is, in its essential points, the same as the above, except as to flexion and pronation, which Dr. Hudson either did not observe, or omits to mention. "The signs of this dislocation (typical?), as presented in our case and in the dead subject under manipulation, were: First, unusual prominence of the outer condyle of the humerus; second, obscuration of the inner condyle; third, pointing of the fore-arm inward diagonally across the body; fourth, head of the radius felt in the bend of the arm with the olecranon prominence removed from the centre to near the inner margin of the arm."

The similarity between Dr. Hudson's symptoms of the lesion, and those given by Professor Hamilton, are too apparent to require comment. Hamilton having added flexion and pronation, and using the terms condyle and epicondyle convertibly, is not Dr. Hudson unwittingly, therefore, demonstrating, in so far as he agrees with Hamilton, fallacious pathology and anatomical impossibilities? As a former pupil of Professor Hamilton, I can not pass, unnoticed, the implied slur upon the character of that truly learned and accomplished surgeon. He who has enjoyed an acquaintance with him will scarcely believe that with his long experience in extensive surgical practice, his own complete anatomical collection and the vast museums of a great metropolis before him, to say naught of his known accuracy and correct anatomical knowledge, he would be reduced to the miserable extremity of writing the pathology of a surgical lesion from a wood-cut borrowed from "Gross or Fergusson, and that one quite imaginary and erroneous." Will Dr. Hudson enlighten us as to the origin of the remaining two hundred and ninety-three wood-cuts that illustrate the incomprehensible pathology of Dr. Hamilton's work on Fractures and Dislocations?

In conclusion, it would seem that Dr. Hudson has failed to convict Professor Hamilton of either anatomical inaccuracies or fallacious pathology, and that his "New Observation" of the pathology and symptomatology of "The Luxated Elbow" is simply a repetition of what had been already clearly and accurately described and figured by Professor Hamilton and others.

Case of Cerebro-Spinal Meningitis.

By D. STEWART SMITH, L. M. C. S. Ed., etc., of Placerville.

On 20th May last I was called to see a fine healthy boy about four years old — nervo-sanguine. Found a white patch on left tonsil, with some constitutional disturbance. In a few days it spread over the right tonsil, soft palate, and pharynx; the glands being also affected. *Diphtheria.* Treatment: Syrupus ferri. iod., with tinc. ferri chlor.; linimentum ammon. mit., to be rubbed over the throat; flannel to be applied. Chlorate potassa as a wash, occasionally; to swallow the last portions. Strong beef soup, milk, brandy and porter, small pieces of ice.

June 7th.—Membrane had disappeared; patient walking round. Did not see the case again until 20th June. Was told he had been out of doors, and feeding and sleeping pretty well; for the last day or two had become "weak on the legs." Speech imperfect; evident paralysis; want of the power of co-ordination; loco-motor ataxia of muscles of lower extremities; very little constitutional disturbance; no pain. Ordered a purgative; rub with lin. ammon. mit., and apply flannel over region of the spine; hot salt water semicupium every night.

June 25th.—No improvement; walking, or rather staggering round. About this time he fell from the top of a fence about three feet high on his head, abrading the skin from the forehead. I was told that he did not appear much hurt at the time of the accident. Treatment continued.

June 27th.—Paralysis of muscles of the neck. Chin has a tendency to rest on the fore part of the chest. Strabismus of left eye; dull expression of countenance more than formerly. Ordered a blister to neck and region of the spine; terebinthine injections per anus, to be repeated; also pulv. jalap. Blister rose well. No marked improvement.

July 4th.—The muscles of deglutition and respiration became affected, and he died in the afternoon. He was only two days entirely confined to bed. All this time the urine was apparently healthy. There was very slight general disturbance.

Was this a case of cerebro-spinal meningitis, terminating in effusion? I think so. Five days before the boy was affected, his sister, a delicate child about seven years old, was attacked by diphtheria, and she ran through the disease favorably in twenty-eight days. Her speech was also slightly affected. Toward the end of the treatment for diphtheria they both complained of acute pain in one and sometimes both ears, after gargling or even swallowing their doses. This wore off after the medicine was discontinued.

I have treated twenty cases of diphtheria in the past five years. Some time ago the disease was prevalent in Coloma. I lost only two in thirteen cases which were entirely in my own charge.

This is the first time I have seen symptoms such as described above supervening on diphtheria. I have been hunting for cases of a similar kind, and have found one reported in October (1869) number of *American Journal of Medical Sciences*, page 480, but no particulars.

Proceedings of the San Francisco Medical Society.

DELIVERY OF THE PLACENTA.—TWO LIGATURES ON THE CORD.

Dr. Favor read a paper on a case of difficult labor, in consequence of the large size of the child, requiring the use of the forceps. The child and mother ultimately did well; the weight of the former was 15¼ lbs.

Dr. Gibbons had one criticism to make on the conduct of the case. This was in reference to the introduction of the hand in the uterus to remove the placenta, unless there were great urgency. The object could be accomplished by traction on the cord with one hand, or hooking the finger in the placenta, a portion of which was almost always in the vagina, while, with the other hand, the uterus was grasped through the abdominal parietes. The introduction of the hand occasioned great pain on account of the supersensibility of the parts. On the other hand, pulling on the cord too much may drag down the uterus. In general, he did not find it necessary to apply two ligatures to the cord. If the bed had not been soiled, he did so to prevent such occurrence; otherwise he tied in but one place.

Dr. Soule asked if Dr. Gibbons did not think it well to tie the cord twice in the case of twins? He had lost one of twins, and the last of triplets, from not doing so.

Dr. Cole said his universal practice was to put his hand into the uterus and remove the placenta. Dr. Gibbons' plan was objectionable: by grasping the abdomen both circular and longitudinal uterine fibres were induced to contract, and delivery was prevented, and pulling on the cord might invert the uterus. He excepted to the statement that hyperesthesia of the soft parts existed. Pressure of the child's head prevented feeling ; it would even induce paralysis of some duration. During the ten minutes while this benumbed condition lasted, the hand was introduced, the os being patulous, and the placenta readily removed. If it should be found adherent, dangerous post-partum hemorrhage might thus be prevented. In nearly twenty-five years of practice, he had adopted this plan and met with no accidents. He applied two ligatures to keep the bed clean and save a second child, should there be one.

Dr. Gibbons said he presumed the danger from traction on the cord was greatly exaggerated. Inversion could not be produced in one case in a thousand. In the majority of cases the placenta was detached and in the vagina, and there was no need of the hand in the uterus. The procedure was meddlesome, and not indicated. As a rule, it was improper. Some obstetricians who, like Dr. Cole, had a small hand, might introduce it with impunity, while many, whose hands were large, would do injury.

Dr. Cole said the vagina would not contain the whole placenta. If the placenta was not in the uterus, of course he did not introduce his hand.

Dr. Morse said he would not have said any thing, did he not believe the practice advised was dangerous. It was practically impossible to introduce the hand before the return of sensibility in the soft parts, on account of necessary attention to the child, and the procedure must be repugnant to the mother. Dr. Cole's plan can not have been long in use, though he had used it twenty-five years. It is only a few years since the impression prevailed that it was improper to forcibly detach the placenta. Dr. Cole's experience was met by that of others who had pursued the opposite plan. In twenty-nine years of practice he had had no serious results; and only two cases of severe post-partum hemorrhage, in both of which the spontaneous expulsion of the placenta immediately followed that of the child. He urged his plan, which was physically right, which was ethically right, and was safe to the parties most concerned. The other plan was objectionable as a rule. Nineteen out of twenty, being adepts, might pursue it without injury, while the twentieth could not. Dr. Gibbons' objection to the plan, on account of the size of the hand, was a good one. He did not believe there was one woman in twenty who could bear the hands which belong to some magnificent physicians and obstetricians, because of pain. He had never introduced his hand without great protestation from the woman; he had, however, waited longer than Dr. Cole allowed. In his practice he had never had a case of inversion; therefore, reasoning as Dr. Cole had done, traction on the cord would not cause inversion. The sensation to the finger, when pulling on the cord, would indicate whether the placenta was detached and would readily come away, or whether it must be removed by the hand. As regarded tying the cord in two places, it was necessary in case of twins, if both children were of the same sex, as Professor Hyrtl had shown that fetuses of the same sex had a common placenta, while those of opposite sexes had different placentas.

Dr. Soule said he would like to hear the experience of all on the points in question, though another subject was awaiting the consideration of the Society. His plan was to remove the placenta at once. The child, on its birth, was handed to the nurse; the hand following the cord was then introduced into the uterus, the placenta grasped and quickly removed. He met with no accidents from the treatment.

Dr. Grover considered the introduction of the hand entirely unnecessary. The placenta could always be reached with two fingers, and if these sufficed, why do more? He strongly objected to Dr. Soule's plan.

Dr. Favor said that theory must fall before fact. It was

said that there was danger in introducing the hand. That was theory. Dr. Cole had pursued the plan for twenty-five years without accident. This was fact. The hand in the uterus will better remove the membranes ; traction on the cord will pull down the womb.

Dr. Bentley believed it best to keep in force the rule that the practice should be left to the judgment of the accoucheur. He was accustomed to remove the placenta as soon as the child was born, and did so by traction on the cord. He felt regret for any one who had not that tactile sense in the fingers which enabled him to tell if the placenta were fixed or not. He greatly objected to the introduction of the hand into the uterus, as a rule, and had never been able to do so early enough to avoid pain. Dr. Cole's objection that the circular uterine fibres will contract, and retain the placenta, seemed untenable. He had in his possession a uterus which, though firmly contracted in the body, had its mouth open. The rule should be to tie the cord twice.

Dr. Haine said if the rule is to tie the cord twice, as Dr. Bentley says, then I have been sinning for thirty-eight years. In but one instance, in several cases of twins, which he had had, did death ensue, and it was apparently due to hemorrhage from the untied cord.

Dr. C. T. Deane said that during the past five years his experience had amounted to nearly five hundred cases. He delivered the placenta as described by Dr. Gibbons. Had introduced his hand but twice, and then in consequence of the breaking of the cord. Had not had a case of post-partum hemorrhage or inversion. He agreed with Dr. Haine in regard to one ligature for the cord. By this plan the placenta disgorged its blood, and was more readily expelled. Had had four cases of twins, and no bad result. In a case of twins, both girls, there were two placentas.

Dr. Morse considered this a singular fact, and opposed to the views of Dr. Hyrtl, whose preparations he had seen.

Dr. Gibbons, Jr., thought the rule had not been properly

stated. It was not that those of the same sex must have but one placenta, but that opposite sexes could not have the same placenta ; while those of the same sex might or might not.

Dr. Morse thought this probably was the rule. If so, Dr. Deane's case was not singular.

Dr. Soule said he had had a case of twins—boy and girl —which, he thought, had but one placenta.

Dr. Holbrook remarked that he could recall three cases of twins, each of the same sex, in which there were two placentas in each case. He agreed with Dr. Bentley in the management of the placenta. He never introduced his hand.

Dr. Gibbons said that, as a delegate to the State Society, he desired to state that the meeting had been a successful one. Though not large, great interest was manifested. A large number of papers were presented, some of much value, and equaling those presented to the National Association. Only one thing occurred at all objectionable, and that was in relation to the election of a member; it occurred through a misunderstanding, and was amicably settled.

Dr. Bentley exhibited several pathological specimens:

1. Aneurism of descending aorta, causing caries of vertebræ. The patient died suddenly.

2. The right lung of a patient, also dying suddenly, showing old cicatrices in upper part, chiefly interesting from the presence of a roughened pleura, illustrating the production of the friction sound.

3. A preparation showing old irreducible hernia with omentocele.

4. Heart and aorta from an old man who died suddenly, aorta and heart-valves diseased, with remarkable thinning of the aorta.

5. Liver with large stone in the gall-bladder.

6. Adenoid tumors removed by Dr. Lane from the neck. During the operation large veins were tied.

H. Gibbons, Jr., Secretary.

Proceedings of the Alameda County Medical Association,

Held in Oakland, November 6, 1871.

Present: Dr. Cushing, President; Drs. Babcock, Bamford, Carr, Holmes, Kittredge, Jno. Le Conte, Jos. Le Conte, Pinkerton, Sherman, Van Wyck.

The minutes of the last meeting were read and approved.

Dr. Bamford read a paper on the treatment of puerperal convulsions, reporting cases to prove the success of venesection, and urging the necessity of prompt and free bleeding in such cases. The Doctor thought that the profession generally abandoned the benefits known to follow the use of the lancet, because of the abuse in its employment in the early days, even to the second half of the present century. He argued its utility in nearly all cases of acute inflammation, but in none was its success more manifest than in the cases under consideration.

A lengthy discussion arose, in which other modes of treatment were reported, and the question was raised as to whether puerperal convulsions were a disease *per se*, or only a complication of convulsions (of whatever nature) occurring at the time of labor.

So many different opinions were advanced, that it was moved and carried that Dr. Sherman be requested to prepare a paper on the subject, giving statistics, authorities, etc., to be presented at next meeting.

Dr. Babcock reported a case of sudden death occurring in tetanic spasms. Nothing was known of the history of the case, excepting that the subject had been drinking hard for two days, and was at the time the Doctor was called under the influence of liquor. The spasms were purely tetanic—not very severe, but frequent. They had lasted for about one hour when professional assistance was called, and immediately succeeding one of them the patient died (about two and a half hours after the supposed first attack) so quietly and suddenly that none present knew when the event occurred. Although at once notified, it was with the greatest difficulty that the acting coroner could be induced to hold an inquest even forty hours afterward; and as he utterly refused to allow an autopsy, on account of the expense to the county, the jury could only find that both the man and the cause of his death were alike unknown! It was Doctor B.'s opinion that the disease was idiopathic tetanus, and the immediate cause of death spasm of the heart; but it might have been a case of suicide or homicide, and the county none the wiser, as far as demonstrated by the farcical inquest.

A verbal invitation was extended to attend the Annual Commencement of the Medical Department, University of the Pacific.

Dr. Jos. Le Conte was appointed to prepare a paper for the consideration of the Association at next meeting.

Adjourned to December 4th, at 7½ P. M.

H. P. Babcock, Secretary.

Vapor of Ammonia in the Treatment of Whooping Cough.—Mr. John Grantham states (*Brit. Med. Journal*, Sept. 16, 1871) that in cases of whooping-cough in the last stage (that is, after the third week) which he has had recently, he has had one ounce of the strongest liquid ammonia put into a gallon of boiling water in an open pan, and the steam kept up by means of half a brick made red-hot throughout and put into the boiling water containing the ammonia, the pan placed in the centre of a room, into which the patients were brought as the ammoniated steam was passing off. "This method was used in the evening, just before bedtime; and it has been so efficacious," he says, "in abating the spasmodic attack, and after three or four days terminating the malady, that I can not overestimate the great value of this mode of inhaling the ammonia as a therapeutic agent in tranquilizing the nervous system in whooping-cough."—*Med. News and Lib.*

Mucilage of Gum Tragacanth.—Rub up one drachm powdered tragacanth with six ounces glycerin, and add ten ounces of water. An excellent mucilage is made at once in this way.

REVIEWS AND NOTICES OF BOOKS.

Essentials of the Principles and Practice of Medicine: A Handbook for Students and Practitioners. By Henry Hartshorne, A.M., M.D., Professor of Hygiene in the University of Pennsylvania; Consulting Physician to the Woman's Hospital of Philadelphia; Professor of Hygiene and Diseases of Children in Woman's Medical College of Pennsylvania, etc., etc. Third edition, thoroughly revised. Philadelphia: Henry C. Lea. 1871. Pp. 487. San Francisco: A. Roman & Co., No. 11 Montgomery street.

We noticed the first edition of this work with much satisfaction. Great pains have been taken, the author informs us, in the preparation of the present edition. It is a genuine *manual*, and contains more good material on its subject than any other book within our knowledge. We do not see the point of the objections made to manuals. On the contrary, they appear to us to be eminently serviceable to both students and practitioners, with the condition in view that they shall not preclude the study of more elaborate works. Though Dr. Hartshorne sets up no special claim to originality, yet there is much original matter in his volume, and there is still more originality displayed in the choice of material, and in the sound judgment which he pronounces on unsettled questions of theory and practice.

St. George's Hospital Reports. Edited by John W. Ogle, M.D., F.R.C.P., and Timothy Holmes, F.R.C.S. Vol. 5. 1870. London: J. & A. Churchill. 1871. Pp. 382. San Francisco: A. Roman & Co.

The value of these reports, of which this is the fifth annual volume, is well known to medical scientists in Europe and America. Among the subjects treated in the present issue are: "Jottings from Clinical Practice," by H. W. Fuller, M.D.; "Strain of the Heart and Great Vessels," by Dr. Clifford Allbutt; "Scarlatina," by Dr. E. Copeman; "Accidental Poisoning," by Dr. C. Paget Blake; "Modern Treatment of Syphilis," by Dr. Venning; "Scrofula," by Dr. Haward; "Recurrent Insanity," by Dr. Blandford: "Distrain of the Heart," by Dr. Reginald Thompson; "Scarlet Fever," by Dr. Barclay; "Diabetic Urine," by Dr. Wadham; Reports on Medicine, Surgery, Ophthalmology, etc., etc.

SKIN DISEASES: Their Description, Pathology, Diagnosis, and Treatment. By Tilbury Fox, M.D., London, M.R.C.P., Fellow of University College; Physician to the Skin Department of University College Hospital. First American from the last London edition. Edited by M. H. Henry, M.D., Surgeon to the New York Dispensary, Department of Venereal and Skin Diseases, etc. New York: Wm. Wood & Co. 1871. Pp. 315. San Francisco: A. Roman & Co.

The importance attached to skin diseases has increased vastly within a few years, and continues to increase from year to year. No explorer in this field has gained a greater and a more deserved celebrity than Tilbury Fox, to whom we are indebted for this, the most complete and the most perspicuous work on the subject, and more particularly on "Vegetable Parasitic Diseases." The "Formulary" is a valuable addition, and so is the "Glossarial Index."

THE PHYSICIAN'S DOSE AND SYMPTOM BOOK, containing the Doses and Uses of all the principal articles of the Materia Medica, Officinal Preparations, Weights and Measures, Abbreviations, Poisons and Antidotes, Index of Diseases and Treatment, etc. By Joseph H. Wythes, A.M., M.D., Late Surgeon United States Volunteers; Author of "the Microscopist;" etc. Tenth edition. Philadelphia: Lindsey & Blakiston. 1871. Pp. 277.

This little work is very useful for reference and for many purposes, as it can be carried in the pocket with convenience.

MEDICAL COMMUNICATIONS OF THE MASSACHUSETTS MEDICAL SOCIETY. Vol. XI. 1871.

The most important paper in this volume is an elaborate essay on Medical Education, delivered at the annual meeting, by Dr. Henry J. Bigelow. It is an original and a valuable production.

OF "ERICHSEN'S SURGERY" 5,370 copies were purchased by Government during the war of the rebellion, and distributed to the medical staff. The author did not get a dollar of the money, the American edition having been "pirated."

AN EMINENT PHYSICIAN of Cincinnati commences a lecture on the Pathology of Hydrophobia: "The body before us, gentlemen, is the corpse of Wm. Bradford, dead of hydrophobia."

EDITORIAL.

Legislation on Medicine.

The Legislature of California will be called on at the present session to enact a number of laws bearing on the public health. The subjects which will probably claim their attention are as follows :

1. The suppression of quackery. On this subject the profession is not united, some of the members believing it the duty of the State to protect the health and lives of citizens from the multitudes of charlatans and nostrums, whilst others regard the task, be it ever so desirable, as too hopeless of success to merit an effort. We may hazard the opinion that quackery is too strongly entrenched behind the newspaper press, and also behind respectable druggists, to be reached by legislation. Whilst lying charlatans can buy up almost the entire newspaper press, including some religious papers, and whilst druggists of respectability transcend their legitimate sphere to vend and advertise infallible cures which they know to be impostures, the curse will remain. In the meanwhile, if legislators, on their own responsibility, are willing to pass laws to protect society from the nuisance, we certainly shall not complain. It is another thing, however, for the medical profession to urge such legislation and expose themselves to the imputation of base and selfish motives.

2. A State health-bill will be called for, to secure a general registration of marriages, births, deaths, and causes of death, and to empower the local authorities everywhere to abate nuisances and guard against the introduction and spread of infectious and other diseases. In this respect California must, sooner or later, follow the example of older States in America and Europe, and fall into line with modern civilization.

3. A health-bill for San Francisco, reorganizing the Board of Health, and restricting its duties, so that the Supervisors shall have control of all matters not strictly pertaining to health and hygiene.

4. It is possible, though not probable, that an application will come from the Board of Supervisors of San Francisco, recommending the passage of a law for the suppression of prostitution. As this is a very important step, involving the question of licens-

ing prostitution, and as it would be manifestly improper to adopt such legislation without the full sanction of public sentiment, it is not to be expected that the Board of Supervisors will act hastily in the matter.

The Social Evil.

Men sprinkle prostitution with rose-water and call it the Social Evil. This is a better title under which to invoke legislation. It keeps persons off the scent. In England, "Contagious Diseases Act" served the same purpose. Such was the title of the law smuggled through Parliament "to improve the health of the Army and Navy." A year or two after its passage people woke up to find they had licensed prostitution in certain districts. Then came opposition and a cry for repeal on the one side, and an effort on the other side to extend the law over the entire kingdom. Associations were organized for both purposes. Opposition has gained ground, and last year six hundred thousand signers protested against the law. The law has been transplanted to America—to St. Louis; nowhere else, as yet. Now comes an effort to apply it to San Francisco. Its friends allege that it has succeeded elsewhere. Its enemies insist that the success is on the surface, and that it has driven the evil out of public view only, and into clandestine retreats, where it is more dangerous to society. Many good people are ranged on both sides. With the enemies of the law, the stumbling-block is the principle of licensing, and thus sanctioning, prostitution. The moral sense of the American people is inflexibly hostile to this principle. They do not believe that the end justifies the means. French and European legislation has schooled many of our citizens of European birth in the opposite faith. Much can be said, and much will be said, on both sides. It is not a subject for hasty legislation. If a plan can be devised to restrict the evil without violating the principles of morality and justice, and thereby sapping the foundations of society, we shall be only too glad to plead for it. But we protest against that one-sided legislation which protects men at the expense of women—which distrains woman of her liberty that she may be made a safe subject for masculine lust—which compels her to submit to examinations and operations in order that she shall not communicate disease to men, and then opens the door of her bedroom to every diseased and beastly lecher, who may enter without examination, without inquiry, without the shadow of restraint. We blush for any professional brother of cultivated conscience and refined morality who would advocate such legislation.

Intermediate Course of Instruction.

An intermediate course of lectures will be given by the Faculty of the Medical Department, University of the Pacific, together with anatomical and clinical demonstrations, commencing on the second Monday of January and continuing till the end of May. There will be from one to two lectures daily, with surgical and practical clinics twice a week at the College Dispensary, and twice a week at the City and County Hospital. Facilities for dissection will be provided. Following is a list of the lecturers and subjects:

Prof. H. Gibbons, Sr.—Insanity and Medical Jurisprudence.

Prof. Lane—The Special Surgery of the Head.

Prof. Cushing—Diseases of Children.

Prof. Ellinwood—Diseases of the Skin.

Prof. Price—Toxicology and Analytic Chemistry.

Prof. H. Gibbons, Jr.—Physical Diagnosis.

Dispensary Clinic—Tuesdays, Thursdays, and Saturdays—by Professors Lane and Ellinwood.

Hospital Clinic—Tuesdays and Saturdays—by Professors Gibbons, Sr., and Bentley.

An important purpose of the Intermediate Course is to afford to students the means of acquiring a practical knowledge of Anatomy and of dissecting, without interfering too much with the regular term.

Professor Bentley will also give, during the recess, a special course of lectures on Pathological Anatomy and Operative Surgery, with copious illustrations.

California Graduates in Medicine.

The commencement exercises of the Medical Department of the University of the Pacific were held on the evening of November 7th, at the Mercantile Library Hall. The Valedictory Address was delivered by Prof. L. C. Lane, and this was followed by an address from W. A. Scott, D.D., which was replete with instructive lessons and sound advice. The Degree was conferred by Rev.

Dr. Sinex, President of the University, on the following gentlemen: Wm. D. Johnston, S. E. Knowles, A. L. Lengfeld, J. Millington—San Francisco; D. Powell, Marysville.

The graduation exercises of Toland Medical College were held in the College building, November 9th. Prof. C. T. Deane delivered the Valedictory and Hon. J. C. Felton, President of the College, conferred the Degree. The Hippocratic oath was administered by the Dean, Prof. R. Beverly Cole. The graduates were as follows: J. E. Hampton; C. A. Kirkpatrick, Redwood City; L. C. Churchill, San Francisco; ——Bailey *(ad eundem)*, Oregon.

Medical Officers.

The following is a list of the medical officers of the United States Navy on duty on the Pacific Coast:

Shore Duty.—Surgeon C. H. Burbank, Navy Yard, Mare Island; Surgeon G. W. Woods, Navy Yard, Mare Island; Assistant Surgeon H. C. Eckstein, Navy Yard, Mare Island; Passed Assistant Surgeon E. B. Bingham, Naval Rendezvous, San Francisco.

In the Squadron.—Fleet Surgeon John M. Brown, Flag Ship *California;* Surgeon W. E. Taylor, U. S. S. *Pensacola;* Surgeon S. D. Kennedy, U. S. S. *Ossipee;* Surgeon F. E. Potter, U. S. S. *Mohican;* Surgeon G. S. Beardsley, U. S. S. *St. Mary's;* Surgeon J. S. Knight, U. S. S. *Saranac;* Passed-Assistant Surgeon G. R. Brush, U. S. S. *Onward;* Passed-Assistant Surgeon E. C. Ver Meulen, U. S. S. *Narragansett;* Passed-Assistant Surgeon J. M. Flint, U. S. S. *Pensacola;* Passed-Assistant Surgeon W. H. Jones, U. S. S. *Pensacola;* Passed-Assistant Surgeon G. S. Culbert, Flag Ship *California;* Assistant Surgeon R. A. Marmion, U. S. S. *Saranac;* Assistant-Surgeon A. M. Owen, U. S. S. *St. Mary's;* Assistant Surgeon J. W. Ross, Flag-ship *California;* Assistant Surgeon J. A. Hawke, U. S. S. *Ossipee.*

American and European Physicians Compared.

It is the custom of many journalists and others of our profession in America to decry American physicians and surgeons, and to make comparisons greatly to their disparagement with those of the old world. But there is no reason to believe that medical men in this country are behind those of Europe in the practical branches, albeit they may possess a smaller amount of learning. Professor Gross, after a visit to Europe, which gave him opportunities of judging, remarks on this subject: "If we compare the results of the practice and operations of American with those of European surgeons, it will be found that they are fully up to the general average, if, indeed, not far in advance. This statement is true alike of our civil and military experience. Where are there better, more enlightened, more able, skillful, or scientific staffs than are to be daily seen in the wards of the hospitals of our cities? Comparisons are odious. In my visits last summer to the hospitals of France, Italy, Austria, Prussia, Holland, Belgium, England, Scotland and Ireland, I saw nothing to induce the belief that the surgeons of these institutions, many of them veterans, whose names are as familiar to the American medical profession as household words, are in any respect superior to the same class of men among us, either in general or professional intelligence, in the art of diagnosis, in therapeutic refinement, or in manual dexterity." Nor is the efficiency of the profession in America denied by our brethren in Europe. Chassaignac, the celebrated French surgeon, declares: "America at this moment wields the surgical sceptre of the world." The fact is, that the American mind has a pliancy, a tact, and an independence, which serve a better purpose in practice than much learning. That our schools have conferred and do confer the degree on many incompetent men, can not be denied. That our standard of medical education ought to be elevated, we all admit. Nevertheless, our schools have but submitted to the necessities of society in America, and conformed to the circumstances of a rapidly increasing and a rapidly extending population, a great part of which is scattered thinly over an immense territory. Let us consider these facts, and cease the excessive use of sackcloth and ashes.

Death after Hypodermic Use of Morphia.

Dr. David Stanton, of Beaver County, Penn., recently elected State Auditor, died suddenly a few weeks ago. "He was suffering from erysipelas," says the account, "and had injected morphia into his arm. Sleep followed, and he never awoke." It is to be regretted that a valuable remedy should be so misapplied as to bring it into disrepute. Some contingency might arise which would justify the hypodermic injection of morphia in erysipelas; but the general rule is decidedly adverse. Other cases have been reported from time to time of death following speedily the same process in various forms of disease. Unfortunately the circumstances are not given with sufficient exactness to furnish a satisfactory explanation, while the unfortunate results have served, at the same time, to frighten practitioners into an entire abandonment of the remedy. We have known the physicians of a whole neighborhood, even of a populous city, permanently deterred from the employment of medicines by subcutaneous injection, by reason of a single fatality resulting from or following it. A full history of all such cases should be preserved and published, to furnish materials for a full and just explanation. When this shall have been done we apprehend there will always appear, either some other cause of death than the injection, or some obvious conditions of the patient which should have forbidden its use.

St. Paul School for Medical Instruction.

This is the title of an educational institution lately organized at St. Paul, Minnesota, with an able corps of lecturers on the various branches of medicine. The object is declared to be "not to represent or take the place of a regular college, but to prepare students for a better understanding of the lectures they will hear in the college course, and to drill them more thoroughly in the elementary branches than can be done in the short time allowed by colleges for instruction," etc. The project, we doubt not, will meet with the universal approval of the profession. If such schools were established in place of some of the regular collegiate institutions which every populous centre in our country is ambitious to put in operation, it would be a great improvement on the present system of grinding out doctors from the raw material with two or three turns of the crank.

A Sensible Witness on Insanity.

There is a certain Dr. J. R. Allen, at Memphis, who has touched a sympathetic cord within us by testifying as follows, when called as an expert in a murder trial in which the plea of insanity was set up: "I have been a practicing physician for nearly thirty years; I have had some experience in cases of insanity, having been ten years medical superintendent of the Kentucky Lunatic

Asylum, and during that time had over two thousand crazy people under my charge; I have heard the hypothetical case read by Mr. Phelan; I am here as an expert, and, before answering this question, I would like to say that the more I have studied the question of insanity the less I understood it, and if you ask me where it begins and where it ends, neither I nor any physician in the world could tell you; in fact, on occasions like this, lawyers make fools of themselves in trying to make asses of doctors."

Counting the Pulse.

Some writers tell us the pulse can not be counted if it is above 150—that it can not be easily counted if above 140. If they mean that this can not be done by counting singly, they may be right. But if they intend to say that it is impossible to ascertain the number of pulsations, they are not right. By counting every second stroke of the pulse there is no difficulty in getting the exact number, even if it be 200 in a minute. By this method, the result of the count must of course be doubled. Even if there were 300 pulsations in a minute, admitting the possibility of so many *distinct* impulses, the number could be ascertained without difficulty by counting every third stroke and multiplying the result by three. Sounds may be counted in like manner—for instance the puffs of a locomotive in rapid motion. It requires but little practice to master the art. The tick of a watch affords a good exercise in sound. Let the watch be held to the ear with one hand, while the finger of the other hand strikes on the table every second or every fourth tick. It will be found easy to enumerate in this way 300 ticks of the watch in a minute.

The Chemistry of Food—so-called.

A thousand fallacies respecting food have been propagated under cover of chemical analysis. The chemist subjects certain substances to analysis, and finding them deficient in some important principle, boldly proclaims them unfit for food, in the face of the fact that they are successfully applied to that use. More than one error of this kind has Liebig made. He is credited with the remark: "Eggs, though nutritious in some respects, can not support life without the addition of other food containing phosphates." This being so, we are tempted to inquire—whence omes the chick, which, in three weeks' incubation, gathers to itself from within the shell the materials of bones and feathers, and of all the tissues which belong to the animal organization?

Traveling in Europe.

Very few of our doctors appreciate the value of a visit to Europe. It is worth more than fifty years' experience at home. To have snuffed the atmosphere of La Charité—to have had the tympanum vibrate sixty seconds with the mellow tones of Virchow, even if they should get no farther into the brain—to have had one benignant smile from the great master at Edinburgh—doubles the circumference of a true American genius, and inflates him with illuminating gas, without the inconvenience of adding a grain to his weight. Henceforth he is a paragon among his home-made fellows, and carries his pre-eminence as conspicuously as a carbuncle on the end of the nose. He goes swaggering in paths professional and unprofessional, always zigzag, detesting grooves. Having seen Paris, he dies.

On the other hand, we have those in the profession who do not know how to take advantage of their European experience, who are content modestly to illustrate its advantages in practice, without strutting and gasconade.

Obituary—Drs. Hubbard and Downer.

We have to record the deaths of two worthy members of the profession, who were among the old settlers of California. Dr. Lorenzo Hubbard, U. S. A., aged 62 years, died at Camp Bidwell, October 3d, 1871. He was a man of considerable literary attainment outside of his profession as well as in it. He wrote the first elaborate article on earthquakes published on this coast, which appeared in one of the early numbers of the PACIFIC MEDICAL AND SURGICAL JOURNAL. Dr. Fenno Downer died in this city on the 24th of November, 1871, aged 69 years. He practiced here in former years, and then moved to Nevada, returning to San Francisco a few months before his death.

A Villainous Quack.

A pamphlet has been extensively distributed through the mails by an impostor who claims to be a member of certain medical societies in Europe, and to have just returned from Europe to San Francisco. He tells the stereotyped story of those lying abortionists that he has consulted with Acton, Aitken, Ricord, and others, and brought from them all the new modes of treatment. To cover a purpose the open avowal of which would send him to San Quentin, where he ought to be, he announces, under the head of Dr. Guizot's Female Monthly Silver-coated Pills, that ladies who suppose themselves *enceinte* should not use them, as a miscarriage would be certain to follow. What is to be done with such wretches?

Glycerin in Leucorrhea.

The remarkable property possessed by glycerin of drawing water from surfaces to which it is applied, makes it applicable as a dressing in many cases. That it arrests suppuration has been known for some time. In leucorrhea, and in certain affections of the mouth and neck of the uterus, it is often highly serviceable. Belladonna or morphia, or both combined, may be joined with it to relieve pain. The most simple and convenient mode of application is by means of a pledget of lint saturated with it. To produce the best results as an exosmotic, it should be anhydrous. An inferior article can not be relied on.

Anesthesia by Hypodermic Injections.

M. Spezza, an Italian physician *(Gaz. Hebdomadaire)*, has employed the hypodermic injection of morphia as a substitute for anesthetic inhalations to prevent the pain of surgical operations. In a case of coxalgia he used this means prior to cauterizing with Vienna paste, and the patient suffered no pain from the application. We know that the most violent pains, from neuralgia and other causes, are relieved speedily by the injection of morphia, and it is but reasonable to infer that the pain of a surgical operation would be prevented by the same agency.

Pedantic Composition.

We sometimes come across writers who put their knowledge of language to bad uses, and who would be capable of doing more good in the world had they never learned any other tongue than the vernacular. Of such is a distinguished physician of London, who lately read a paper before the Royal Medical and Chirurgical Society, combating the doctrine that "dextral pre-eminence is based on conventional agreement, enforced by educational influence, and has no foundation in physical conformation."

Death from Aneurism of the Splenic Artery.

T. Clarkson Taylor, of Wilmington, Delaware, a distinguished preacher in the Society of Friends and teacher in a seminary, died suddenly not long ago, after a brief attack of abdominal pain, which was not considered serious. On examination it was discovered that death had been caused by the rupture of an aneurism of the splenic artery. His health had been good in general, only some slight disturbances having occurred during a period of several months prior to his demise.

An Improper Accusation.

According to the published report of the proceedings of the Board of Health, Dr. Holland, in accounting for the opposition to his bill among physicians, said: "Many see written on the walls a diminution of fees, which would result from the passage of the law, in checking disease." Now we do not believe there is one decent member of the profession in all California who would, on that ground, oppose a law which he considered to be for the public good.

Suppression of Menses from Imperforate Hymen.

Such is the heading of an article in one of our exchanges, contributed by a physician. He should have known better than to write such a heading, and the editor of the journal should have corrected it.

GENERAL SUMMARY.

Failure of Cundurango in England.

All that we hear of the results of the trials given to the cundurango bark furnished by our Government to the Middlesex and St. Bartholomew's Hospitals, through the College of Physicians, confirms the fear that any hope which might have been entertained, of a confirmation of the statement of its utility as a remedy in cancer, must be entirely dismissed. Physiologically, it appears to be practically inert, and its therapeutic effects in the treatment of cancer to be *nil*. It furnishes a slightly bitter extract of feeble character. A detailed therapeutical report will be made by Mr. Hulke, and a careful examination of its physiological action by Dr. Brunton, but this mainly in deference rather to the official sources from which this small supply has been furnished, and to set at rest the excitement caused by the somewhat scandalous claims which have been set up in its favor.—*Brit. Med. Jour.*—*Med. News and Lib.*

Danger from a Solar Eclipse.

A German paper says: "The Elector of Darmstadt was informed of the approach of a total eclipse in 1699, and published the following edict in consequence: 'His Highness, having been informed that on Wednesday morning next, at ten o'clock, a very dangerous eclipse will take place, orders that on the day previous, and a few days afterward, all cattle be kept housed, and to this end ample fodder be provided; the doors and windows of the stalls to be carefully secured, the drinking wells to be covered up, the cellars and garrets guarded so that the bad atmosphere may not obtain lodgment, and thus produce infection, because such eclipses frequently occasion whooping-cough, epilepsy, paralysis, fever, and other diseases, against which every precaution should be observed.'"

Female Medical Students in Moscow.

It is officially stated that the Faculty of Medicine of Moscow, with the full concurrence of the council of the University, have decided to grant to women the right of being present at the educational courses and lectures of the faculty, and of following all the labors of the Medico-chirurgical Academy. The tests of capacity will be precisely the same as for male students.

The Emperor has issued an order to the existing institutions for instructing women in midwifery, and authorizing them to act as surgeons, to vaccinate, and to be employed as chemists.

Death in the Pipe.

A correspondent of the *North British Mail* narrates that not very long ago he paid a visit to an extensive tobacco warehouse, under government locks in a large city, and saw two tobacco dealers examining a lump of foreign-manufactured tobacco, which had been stripped of its box, and which looked like cavendish tobacco of a superior quality. One of the dealers said to the other, "What d'ye think of that?" The other answered, "It looks nice. Where did it come from?" "From New York," replied he. "It's a weed that grows wild. It is not tobacco at all, they tell me." "Does it sell?" asked the other. "It seems to suit the public taste," answered he, "for we sell a good deal of it."—*Good Health.*

Violent Action of Chromic Acid.

The only caustic which approaches in power the chromic acid, is the monohydrous sulphuric acid. It (chromic) acts so energetically on the living animal tissue as to raise the temperature to 125° or 150°. A mouse, plunged into a concentrated solution, is instantly reduced to a cinder, and the ebullition is so violent as to eject a portion of the acid together with the mouse. The use of it as a caustic, therefore, requires much caution.—*Edinburgh Medical Journal.*

Label for Bitters.

The *American Agriculturist*, speaking of California Wine Bitters and other concoctions advertised in the newspapers of this coast, recommends the following label: CAUTION:—Keep the bottles, boxes, or packages in a safe place, where no human being can by any possible mistake swallow any of the stuff.

Sulphur versus Small-pox.

The chief physician of Iceland claims to have smoked out the small-pox, lately imported to that country from France, by means of sulphur, with the aid of sulphurous acid and water drank by the patients. The disease disappeared, and no new cases had occurred for thirty days.

The Oldest Surgeon.

Dr. Josiah L. Stevens, of Castine, Maine, at the age of eighty-eight years, has recently amputated the leg of Alfred Warner, aged seventy-three, on account of a disease of the limb of forty-five years' standing. The result is described as a complete success.

Mortality of Small-pox in Paris.

From July, 1869, to June, 1871, there were 13,614 deaths in Paris from small-pox, of which 1,800 were soldiers. In the civil hospitals there was one death to three cases, and in the military hospitals one in six.

A Malingerer in Bed Twenty-five Years.

Dr. Terrell describes, in the *Virginia Clinical Record*, a case of malingering in a female residing in Hanover County, Virginia, who lay in bed twenty-five years, "expectorating live worms," and taking but little food. She had as nurses two cousins, who appear to have entered into the spirit of the fraud and assisted her. One of them dying, the patient, if patient she was, fell under different treatment, and soon recovered perfectly, her legs being as useful as ever, after twenty-five years of disuse.

Duration of Life of Physicians.

The last issue of Proceedings of the Massachusetts Medical Society gives a list of members who have died in 1870 and 1871, thus far, 37 in number. The ages of 32 are given, averaging 60½ years, the extremes being 28 and 84. This is a much longer tenure of life than common opinion allots to our profession.

Strychnia in Albuminuria.

An Italian physician claims to have cured twelve cases of albuminuria with strychnia. It is best adapted for the scarlatinal form with anasarca.

ITEMS OF NEWS, Etc.

Dr. J. E. Holbrook, formerly Professor of Anatomy in the Medical College of South Carolina, died lately at Norfolk, Mass., of apoplexy. He was the author of a most valuable work on natural history, entitled "North American Herpetology."

Tetanus has been cured in France, in a number of cases, by extremely hot air baths, followed by hypodermic injections of morphia.

Solly, formerly of St. Thomas' Hospital, and distinguished by his writings "On the Human Brain," and other topics, died recently, aged 66.

The Chicago Medical College escaped the late conflagration, but the Rush Medical College did not. The professors of the latter are giving their course of lectures in one of the hospitals.

The deaths by small-pox in Philadelphia, up to November 18th, were about 600.

STATE BOARD OF HEALTH.

Abstract from the Reports of Deaths and their Causes, in the following cities and towns in California, during October, 1871:

Cities and Towns.	Total No. Deaths.	Prevalent Diseases.						Authorities.
		[illegible]	[illegible]	[illegible]	Diphtheria.	[illegible]	[illegible]	
San Francisco	300	12	28	52	2	0	11	S. F. Board of Health.
Sacramento	32	5	1	1	0	0	3	Sac. Board of Health.
Petaluma	7	2	0	1	0	0	2	Dr. G. W. Graves.
Dixon	2	0	1	0	0	0	0	Dr. E. H. Plummer.
Santa Clara								Dr. H. H. Warburton.
Stockton								Stockton Bd. of Health.
Marysville	8	2	1	2	0	0	0	Dr. C. E. Stone.
Placerville	5	0	0	0	0	0	3	Dr. J. A. Kendler.
Auburn								Dr. A. S. Du Bois.
San Diego	11	1	0	5	0	0	0	Co. Med. Society.
San Luis Obispo								Dr. W. W. Hays.
Oroville								Dr. J. M. Vance.
Woodland	0	0	0	0	0	0	0	Dr. A. E. Melarne.
Oakland	11	2	0	1	0	0	0	Dr. T. H. Pinkerton.
Los Angeles	16	2	1	2	0	0	0	Dr. H. S. Orme.
Nevada City								Dr. J. A. Coffin.
Truckee								Dr. Wm. Curless.
St. Helena	2	1	0	0	0	0	1	Dr. J. S. Adams.
San Jose								Dr. J. N. Brown.
Napa City	3	1	0	0	2	0	0	Dr. M. B. Pond.
Cacheville								Dr. F. L. Paramore.
Siskiyou								Dr. E. E. Osburn.
Watsonville								Dr. C. E. Cleveland.
Folsom	1	0	0	0	0	0	0	Dr. L. McGuire.
Bridgeport Township								Dr. G. La Ahey.
Sutter Creek & Amador								Dr. H. M. Fiske.
Monterey								Dr. C. A. Canfield.
Santa Cruz	1	1	1	0	0	0	0	Dr. Geo. Knight.
Vallejo								Dr. J. M. Brown.
Suisun & Fairfield	1	0	1	1	0	0	0	Dr. S. D. Campbell.
Colusa	1	0	0	1	0	0	0	Dr. Luke Robinson.
Trinity County	2	0	0	1	0	0	0	Dr. J. C. Montagne.
Santa Barbara	10	2	1	0	0	0	0	Dr. C. B. Bates.
Redwood City	2	0	0	0	0	0	1	Dr. C. A. Kirkpatrick.
Totals	451	61	37	70	4	0	21	

Abstract from Reports of Births:

Cities and Towns.	Total Births.	Male.	Female.	Still-born.	Live-born.	Authorities.
San Francisco...	85	52	33	27	58	S. F. Board of Health.
Sacramento.....	44	22	22	5	39	Sac. Board of Health.
All other places.	192	105	87	17	175	Various sources.
Total......	321	179	142	49	272	

Remarks.—Notwithstanding we have reached the season of greatest mortality, our record goes to confirm all that was stated last month of the highly favorable condition of the public health which has ruled during the entire year. In Placerville, alone, do we perceive any noteworthy increase of mortality attributable to malarious influences; but our correspondent from Suisun writes, "We are having more typhoid fever in our district than ever known before—not of a very grave form, but of a protracted character; and every case, except one—and that was the first—has relapsed." In San Francisco we discover no evidence, from the mortality report, of such prevalence, but we observe that the number of decedents from diseases of the digestive organs reaches as high as 52—fifty per cent. of which were from cholera infantum. The moral disturbances in Los Angeles seem to have told on the public health; for after deducting 22 deaths by violence, 19 of which were Chinamen, killed during the late riot, there still remains a considerable excess of the average. This excess, however, does not seem to be attributable to any special cause.

THOMAS M. LOGAN, M.D.,
Permanent Secretary State Board of Health.

Puerperal Temperature.—Dr. Henry G. Landis, of Niles, Ohio, gives to the *North-western Med. and Surg. Journal* a record of the temperature of the axilla in 17 cases of labor. The observations were taken at 4 periods—1, during dilatation of the os; 2, within the first hour after delivery; 3, between twelve and twenty-four hours after delivery; 4, three days after delivery. There was an elevation in every case during labor, which was increased in a slight degree subsequently. The average elevation was about two degrees at the first period mentioned, and three degrees at the subsequent times. Considerable difference occurred in the different cases. In two instances an unusually high temperature was followed by copious hemorrhage. In one case the temperature rose to 106 during a fatal puerperal fever.

Frozen Essence of Beef.—Dr. H. B. Hare *(Phila. Med. Times)* found it easy to feed a child, sick with scarlet fever, with frozen essence of beef, when the nutriment was refused in its ordinary form.

Mortality in San Francisco during October, 1871.

BY H. GIBBONS, JR., M.D.

CAUSES OF DEATH.

Alcoholism	2	Dyspepsia	2	Noma	1
Aneurism of Aorta	4	Emphysema	1	Old Age	3
Apoplexy	3	Enteritis	9	Opium	1
Ascites	1	Epilepsy	1	Paralysis	3
Asphyxia	3	Fever, Remittent	4	Peritonitis	3
Atrophia	17	" Typhoid	11	Phthisis	42
Bright's Disease	1	Gangrene of Lungs	1	Pleuritis	1
Bronchitis	3	Gastritis	2	Pneumonitis	12
Cancer of Mesentery	1	Gastro-Enteritis	3	Premature Birth	1
Cholera Infantum	25	Hematemesis	2	Purpura	1
Cholera Morbus	2	Hemoptysis	5	Pyemia	4
Cirrhosis	1	Hemorrhage	1	Rheumatism	2
Congestion of Brain	4	" Bronchial	1	Rupture of Uterus	1
" of Lungs	5	Hepatitis	3	Softening of Brain	1
Convulsions, Infantile	10	Hernia, Strangulated	3	Spina Bifida	1
Croup	3	Hydatids of Liver	1	Stomatitis	1
Cyanosis	1	Hydrocephalus	1	Suffocation	1
Debility, General	5	Inanition	9	Suicide	3
Dentition	3	Indigestion	1	Syncope	1
Diabetes	1	Inflam. of Liver	1	Tabes Mesenterica	2
Diarrhea	5	Injuries, unspecified	2	Tetanus	1
Diphtheria	2	Laryngitis	2	Trismus Nascentium	1
Diseases of Heart	7	Liver, Disease of	1	Ulcerat'n of Intestines	1
" of Lungs	1	Measles	1	Unknown	12
Drowning	3	Meningitis	12	TOTAL	300
Dysentery	6	Metritis	1	Still-births	27

AGES.

Under 1 year	104	From 15 to 20 years	4	From 60 to 70 years	12
From 1 to 2 years	23	From 20 to 30 years	22	From 70 to 80 years	7
From 2 to 5 years	4	From 30 to 40 years	40	From 80 to 90 years	3
From 5 to 10 years	9	From 40 to 50 years	42	Unknown	2
From 10 to 15 years	3	From 50 to 60 years	25		

SEX. — Male, 189; Female, 111. Total, 300.

COLOR. — White, 273; Copper, 24; Black, 3.

NATIVITIES.

California	140	Austria	1	South America	1
Other parts of U. S.	24	Sweden	1	Finland	1
British Amer'n Prov.	5	Spain	1	China	22
Mexico	2	Portugal	1	Australia	2
Central America	1	Italy	3	Azores	1
England	10	Belgium	1	Western Isles	1
Ireland	45	Greece	1	West Indies	1
France	10	Poland	2	Unknown	8
Germany	15				

RECAPITULATION.

Died in City Wards	241	Mount St. Joseph's Infirmary	3
City and County Hospital	16	Ladies' Protection and Relief Sc'y	1
U. S. Marine Hospital	1	Alms House	4
French Hospital	7	Small-pox Hospital	1
German Hospital	1	Casualties	6
St. Mary's Hospital	15	Suicides	3
Italian Hospital	1		

REMARKS.—We report, for October, a considerably larger number of deaths than occurred in the previous month, but a smaller mortality than for the same month a year ago. The deaths in October for six years have been as follows: 1866, 242; 1867, 217; 1868, 334; 1869, 270; 1870, 309; 1871, 300. In September the deaths amounted to 248—showing an increase of 52 for October, the increase being mostly in the following diseases: Inanition, strangulated hernia, aneurism of the aorta, asphyxia, atrophia, cholera infantum, pneumonic affections, and pyemia. The mortality from these diseases was 45 in the former, and 96 in the latter month.

Probably the most striking fact presented by the mortality tables of San Francisco, is the enormous excess of the deaths of foreign adults. In the month under consideration there were ten cases in which the ages and nationality were not known; of the remaining 290 deaths, 147 were under twenty-one years of age, and of these all but 6 were natives of the United States. Of the 143 adults who died, 21 only were natives of the United States, while 122 were foreign-born. Six-sevenths of all the adults who died in October were foreigners! Twice as many Irish-born adults, and as many Chinese, as native adults die every month! It requires no profound investigation to show that the ratio of deaths among the Irish and Chinese at least is largely in excess of that of the native population.

INJECTION OF PUS INTO THE MEDULLA—ABSORPTION.—M. Demarquay, in a report to the Academy of Medicine of Paris (*Gazette Hebdomadaire*), gives the results of injecting various substances into the marrow of the bones of rabbits. When colored water was injected it was immediately absorbed, and found its way into the circulation. In twelve cases he injected from sixty to one hundred and twenty drops of pus with uniform results. All the animals died from purulent infection, after exhibiting the following symptoms: Alteration of the pulse; perceptible indisposition; elevation of temperature from 38 to 39 (Cent.), and in some cases to 41 and 42 degrees. The autopsy revealed phlegmonous inflammation of the side injected; abscesses of the lung, and gangrene in one case; congestion and softening of the liver, spleen, and kidneys; and metastatic abscesses of the liver.

VALEDICTORY ADDRESS

To the Graduating Class of the Medical Department of the University of the Pacific.

BY PROF. L. C. LANE, M.D.

The occasion which your Alma Mater this evening celebrates—the marriage of five of her sons to the profession of their choice—the launching of their barks upon the sea where the great battle of life awaits them—is one of such importance that she would fain ask you for one more audience—ask to speak a few parting words. The young man on the eve of leaving his home, to take part, as an individual, in the struggles of life, often finds long, tedious and prosy, the words which parental caution whispers in his ear, but ere the career of life is finished, his mind runs back to such words, and memory holds fast to them as precious treasures, As your Alma Mater invests you with the battle-cloak and shield, she expects you so to wear them as to bring no dishonor upon the lineage and escutcheons of the old and noble race to which, this night, you are legally wed.

Methinks I hear some of you ask, *how* may we so wear the chlamys and bear the shield, as to satisfy the hopes of the institution which now grants us its highest honors, of the profession with which these honors affiliate us in the future? I will endeavor to answer your question.

First of all, a physician is expected to be an educated gentleman. He is expected to be *educated*, not in the trite meaning of this term, but in a manner universal and encyclopedic in character. Some imagine the physician's attainments to be a kind of seven-toned harp, whose several strings shall ring individually a chemical, anatomical, physiological, obstetrical, therapeutical, surgical, and chemical note; such notes, indeed, his harp should give, clearly and without defect, but his learning should reach much further—it must and does embrace all the objects of nature and their phenomena.

Hence a lifetime is but a short period for such a curriculum. But of this anon.

The physician must be a *gentleman;* nor do I mean this in its modern, ill-used sense; but in its primitive meaning, before conventional usage or affectation had disfigured and perverted the term; when it implied character in which courage was wed to gentleness, heroism to humanity, broad intellectual culture to simplicity, self-respect to a sacred respect for the rights of others; in fact, as the great dramatist has it:

> "A form and combination, indeed,
> Where every god did seem to set his seal,
> To give the world assurance of a man."

The profession to which we introduce you, expects from you earnest work; thorough, untiring and undivided devotion; a fixed resolve, an unflinching purpose to add something to the common treasury of medical knowledge. With a determination like that of Alaric of old, who, when repulsed before the gates of Rome, vowed that either as a victor he would give the land as a heritage to his people or it should give him a grave, you should resolve to give to the future for a heritage at least one new fact; such determined resolution cannot be baffled; sooner or later triumph crowns it; for though Rome gave to Alaric an unknown grave, yet, to his followers, full of inspiration drawn from their leader, it gave a realm. You who are full of hope, of enthusiasm, and of the future, let the great ones of the past inspire you, and never rest till you have added one truth to the public domain of medical science.

One apparently unimportant observation may bring with itself immense results; witness that of Galileo of a swinging lamp in a church at Pisca, his deduction therefrom of the laws of the pendulum, the consequent construction of accurate time-pieces, and finally the chronometer, which, next to the compass, the mariner takes for his guide on the deep. Witness the observation that a frog's legs were convulsed when two different metals were caused to touch its sciatic nerves, thence the construction of the Voltaic pile, thence of a machine which enabled Davy to revolutionize chemistry, and finally gave mankind the means of transmitting thought more rapidly than thought itself; such the gift conferred upon the world by the simple observation of an Italian physician. Science, in return, has immortalized him by giving to one of its most noble sections the name of *Galvanism*. And still again, the apparently trivial observation that the milkmaids in the rural districts of England were comparatively exempt from small-pox, was the first link in the chain of facts which led to the discovery of vaccination, thereby shielding mankind from the mephitic breath of the most cruel of plagues; for as Chalcas the sage,

> "Whose comprehensive view,
> The past, the present and the future knew,"

By his wisdom taught how to appease the plague-god, who, "going forth like Night," breathed death among the Achaian forces before Ilion, so did Jenner, by the magic touch of the lance-point upon the arm, teach his generation to escape this most loathsome disease; and the boon did not, like the services of the sage, expire with his own generation, but will continue to be the inalienable heirloom of all future ages.

The instances cited are enough to show how the slight suggestion of a cause may teem with great results, and as monitors on the highway of time, they inculcate the importance of observing, noting and recording every new fact; for such observation may, like the attractive force which the rubbed amber acquires, or the curve which the swinging lamp makes, become as the germ of a tree which, springing up, bears flowers and fruit, for the cheer and sustenance of generations present and future.

And to *you*, gentlemen, whose years yet rejoice in youth, and whose minds, fertile as an alluvial soil, and warmed by enthusiasm as by a tropical sun, are destined, if properly cultivated, to yield a rich harvest, to *you*, standing face to face with such monitors as incentives, we look with confidence for a kindling in your hearts of an ambition to work and struggle for a place by the side of the great and the worthy of your profession.

In these remarks do not understand me as urging you to seek only for an immortality, and especially would I admonish you not to expect it too early. Young men are often too anxious to leap into the sphere of the immortals. To such I would say, remember Icarus, who vaulted too far aloft on the wings which he himself had made; his pinions were melted by the sun and he tumbled down into the sea; and it is not probable that you would be so fortunate as to have, like him, a sea named for you. Neither would I have your flight too low, lest, Gambetta-like, you might be wounded by an enemy's shot, and, less fortunate than he, your balloon also might be wounded.

But now, if ever you are to do it, is the time to make your resolves, to lay your plans, and to launch yourselves each into an individual orbit, in which, like a planet with permanent momentum, and well-poised motion, you will ever move with an individual identity, undisturbed by any agency internal or external.

In such a character the world looks for something more than a gentleman with educate dintellect. His heart must likewise be educated; and in such a heart the passions and emotions will be found of vigorous development, but thoroughly subdued. For if these be absent then the man might live, and even wear the imperial purple as did the sons of great Theodosius of old, for two or more decades, and yet scarcely leave a trait of personality to which the historian could point. But if the passions are given the ascendant, their unhappy victim is even worse than a planet freighted with internal detonating elements, which, if bursted, leaves monuments of a former existence in surrounding asteroids, while the man, sinking in the vortex of ruin, leaves naught save a dark and charred image in cotemporaneous memory.

For this training and discipline of the emotional nature, your professional career will afford a rich field. The young physician soon learns that he cannot please every one. To some he will find himself personally disagreeable; others dislike to see a young man advancing so rapidly, and such would seem to look upon themselves as having a special mission to throw impediments in his way. Such love to throw his character on the gridiron of criticism, the bars of which have different degrees of temperature, varying from ice-cold, through fever-heat, up to red-hot; the first represents those who say he is a very learned man but we don't think he will make much of a physician; and from the same ice-point comes the wily, left-handed thrust of the old professional brother whose vision is somewhat jaundiced by envy, whose apprehensive ken fears being displaced, who says, he would be a good physician or surgeon if he were not so unlucky in his cases. The second grade of censure is represented by those who have a tolerably well-defined aversion, as shown in the pretty placidly spoken remark that they would not have you to treat their canine. And lastly the red-hot type of censure will appear in the shape of keen, bitter hate, and will come with wasp-like venom in the words, I wouldn't have him to doctor a sick feline for me.

Again, the very nature of the practice of medicine is of a character calculated to develope all the higher moral virtues, those, in fact which distinguish the refined gentlemen from the coarser man. Need I recite the prosperous and adverse endings of human ailments, giving alternate shadow and sunlight to the practice of every physician. Like a pendulum his life vibrates between victory and defeat. The vanity which might arise from the one, runs no risk of extraordinary development, since the envious hand of the latter quickly plucks it up by the roots.

One of the most talented young physicians I ever knew, as one of his earliest operations had a case of ovariotomy; much depended on the result; all the energies of his mind were bent to throw around the patient every circumstance which could favor recovery. Not recovery—but death—came and lifted to the lips of the unfortunate woman his cold chalice as the only reward for her daring. I have never seen disappointment touch more cruelly on the heart of any one, than did the loss of that patient this young physician ; but with that philosophy which springs from a well disciplined mind, he said, "For me perhaps it was better that it failed, for such a triumph at so early a day in my career, might have made me inordinately vain."

Besides the discipline which the practice of medicine, from its inherent nature, will give your minds, the examples of noble character which the sick-bed will present, will be of a nature to widen and lift up the moral sentiment. The battle-field with its wild clash of arms, the roaring cannon, the trampling of cavalry, the sounding drum, the commander's approving eye, and the hope of victory, all conspire to lift the wounded man above his anguish, and, like the hero of Corunna with his left arm nearly torn from his body by a cannon shot and his ribs all crushed, he may die with a smile of triumph on his lips. But it is far different with the wretched consumptive where death is hammering away incessantly, week after week and month after month, ere he makes a successful breach in the vital ramparts, through which he may leap and raise his pale ensign over the citadel of life. Yet through these long days of pain and still longer nights of weariness, there is often presented to the physician's eye a patience and a bravery greater than war can boast.

We may safely assert that there is no profession which requires higher intellectual culture, than the medical ; and this culture must be carried to such proficiency that it can act almost automatically or intuitively. The study of months or even years, is often, in its practical sphere of action, circumscribed to a few moments. Instance, spasm of the glottis, or a foreign body falling into the windpipe, requiring instant performance of tracheotomy. In such a case, how infinitely asunder stand the medical and the legal man; the former has no time to overhaul his tomes to learn whether the statute has changed, whether a recent decision of the Supreme Court will justify him in adopting this or that course, or whether the case may not be adroitly disposed of by a plea of *demurrer*, or whether the client may not be released on a writ of *habeas corpus*, or, worse coming to worst, if the Court may not be induced to grant a stay of proceedings;—I say the medical man has no time for anything of this kind, but his reading must have been done, and every fact so engraven on his memory, that as he runs he may read it. In fact, the young physician, borrowing the words of the greatest of Earth's bards, should thus apostrophize the study of the principles of his profession:

> "Remember thee?
> Yea, from the table of my memory
> I'll wipe away all trivial fond records,
> All saws of books, all forms, all pressures past,
> That youth and observation copied there;
> And thy commandment all alone shall live
> Within the book and volume of my brain,
> Unmixed with baser matter!"

In the practice of law, there is a charm which often fascinates the young man, and more than one medical student have I heard say, that he was sorry he had not studied law. There is, indeed, something captivating to the mind of most persons, in the very manner of conducting legal business. For example a Judge, full of dignity and self-possession, sitting in front of his Court, every eye of which is fixed upon him,

> "With eye severe and beard of formal cut,"

Holds the scales of justice in his hand; a couple of legally indisposed persons, known as plaintiff and defendant, present their cases for treatment, and to aid them detail their complaints, one or more lawyers are arrayed on each side. To see that the scales of justice are impartially poised, twelve men, known as jurymen, are chosen as aids, and after the complaint has been thoroughly illustrated and set forth, these twelve men then pass upon the character and amount of medication proper to be resorted to in the case. Meanwhile a large number of spectators are witnesses of the whole affair, and, as an item last mentioned though not the least in importance, large sums of money have been given or pledged to counsel. But what a contrast when we step from the domain of Law to the practice of Medicine! The physician, especially in the beginning of his career, finds many of his cases summoning him to the squalid haunts of poverty; no convenience—no comfort—but poverty and want, in all their wretched forms, have here found habitation; while disease, a near kinsman to them, has in addition, added its quota to fill up the cup of misery. This is the character of the court where the physician is often called upon to practice his vocation. No Judge here to dignify the scene; no jurymen, perhaps not one spectator, to be a witness of the eventful drama enacted; and for all his work, more arduous than is ever done by advocate before court and jury, not one farthing will ever be received, nor was one expected when the task was undertaken. Nay, more, the physician who undertakes such labor, often does so at extreme personal risk, at the peril of his own life. For example, the great Howard, in his earlier years a merchant, afterwards a student of medicine, spent the remainder of his life in visiting prisons, finally dying in the Crimea while there on a mission to investigate the plague. On his death-bed he asked that no monument save a sun-dial should be placed over his tomb; yet his native land has given him a monument among her worthies, and were it not so, his name would be immortal, since in all cultivated languages the name of Howard is a synonym for benevolence. Before Howard fell a victim to the plague, he had visited all the prisons of Europe except that of Rome and the Bastile; to these two he was denied admittance. The French people, excited to desperation by the heart-sickening tales of poor Latude and others who spent a great part of their lives in the Bastile, razed the latter to the ground. Rome has long since abolished her Inquisitorial dungeons, and the prisons remaining all bear traces of the benevol.nt touch of Howard's spirit.

The case of Howard is but one of a thousand noble hearts, that have thrown themselves into the waves of death, and have gone down while trying to rescue suffering humanity. And if I again refer to the legal profession, it is with no desire of casting a satirical shaft that I ask, where is the advocate who would undertake the case of a criminal, did he know, in defending him, that he drew upon himself as great a risk of being hung as threatened his client.

Again, young gentlemen, there is a great duty which our profession imposes upon each of its members. Let me, in this connection, quote the great George Forster, to whom Humboldt acknowledged that he owed his first impulses to Natural History, and whose name German naturalists are to-day canonizing, though in his life-time, on account of his advocacy of human rights, he was driven from his native land and a price set on his head. George Forster says, writing from exile to his wife:

"I have no home, no fatherland, no more friends; all who were once my friends have forsaken me to form new connections and associations. My misfortune is the work of my principles, not the offspring of my passions. I cannot act otherwise—I would not were it to do over again. Had I been willing to act contrary to my convictions and feelings, I might now have been a member of the Academy at Berlin, with a handsome salary; but to whom then could I sell the shame of having betrayed those principles which I have so often proclaimed." Forster believed in an innate excellence of humanity; he trusted that this would, in the end, gain the ascendancy and render him justice; the future was true to his hope, and one of Germany's leading literary periodicals lately deemed itself honored in giving place to an illustrated engraving of Forster's birth-place.

In an essay on Art, Forster has uttered a sentiment which is so applicable to the physician's career that I cannot forbear giving it to you. He says: "If the recognition of personal merit depended upon others, or were the only reward for which a great artist labors, I doubt then whether a single master-work would ever have been given to us; but like the Divinity himself, self-satisfaction in his own labor must be his chief reward. The artist must find his recompense in this, that in the bronze, the marble, the canvas, or in letters, his own great soul is laid out to view; let him who can, comprehend it there. But if the age be too small, if there be no co-temporary who in the work can discern the artist, in the artist can see the man, and in the man the creative genius, indeed, if the age can produce no heart in which the great work of art can awake a responsive echo, still the stream of time will carry the work along on its bosom, until it meets a kindred soul in which this rapture shall awaken, there to live forever."

He who understands these precious words of this poor exile, driven, for his defence of human rights, from all that he cherished most dearly, can understand how the physician is content to visit the hovel of poverty, to endanger his life at the bedside of pestilence, and to spend days and nights too, in unpaid toil and fatigue, in which limbs, heart and brain are taxed to their utmost; but he who cannot understand such sentiments, or who would scoff and throw stones into this fountain, whence the great, the pure and the good of our profession in all time, have drawn their inspiration, have found their solace, he, I say, should stop and read the words inscribed over the portals of the temple of Medicine: *Este procul profani*—for they were written for him.

To him, likewise, who expects the profession of

Medicine will pour wealth into his coffers, I would say, beware of disappointment. Had the classic epigrammatist lived in our days and scrutinized the purses of the majority of medical men, he would never have written *Galenus dat opes*, unless in irony. This is certainly so in the early career of nearly every medical man, and you, gentlemen, can hardly expect to be exceptions. But still, be not discouraged; patiently work and patiently wait; the harvest, though not a large one, will finally come. There is no more noble sight, no more sublime spectacle, than an honest man earnestly struggling in the line of duty, undismayed by whatever misfortune may overtake him. For as Sue has well said: "Behold a spectacle in which God himself takes delight—a just man struggling against adversity and overcoming it by his courage."

I would not, however, place proverty as one of the aims of your life, nor advise you to endeavor to sacrifice your lives on her altar by way of martyrdom. The Spartan custom of not mourning for those who had fallen on the battle-field, but for those who were so unfortunate as to return home, has much moral sublimity in itself; but the mode of our times of rejoicing with those who have won our victories and have been lucky enough to return home, is probably more consonant with the character of our utilitarian age. You should look to it that your services, when meritorious, be paid for by those who have the means. Between the upright physician and the charlatan there is here a wide gap, which, too often, is not seen by the unwary public, until they are forced to leap it. The quack makes the unsuspecting patient believe that he has some extraordinarily dangerous disease, and when he has thoroughly awakened the fears of his victim, he extorts from him a large fee. I know of no baseness equal to that of obtaining money in this way; highway robbery is more honorable, since it does give its victim a slight chance of defence. The man who will condescend to engage in this species of robbery, has a heart in which every sense of shame has been extinguished, and every feeling of honesty and rectitude burned out by the remorseless and pitiless passion for money. In every city of our land there are scores of men who live thus and go on unscathed in their plundering career, notwithstanding the vaunted protection which our laws claim to furnish to the people. These men may be compared to Satan, as depicted by the fancy of Poe, who built himself a palace in Hell, adorned with every dainty touch of art, with walls

"Of fabulous price and beauty,"

But so cunningly constructed that the very sighs, moans and cries of the damned, as they traversed these walls, were transformed into tones of the most delicious music. And hence I would say to you that even as in Art, it is the form and not the material which commands admiration, so in your professional career, it is not the amount you have gained but rather how you gained it, that will command respect.

But whether your purses, like that of Fortunatus, shall always be well filled, or the scarce, well-worn pence of poverty be your heritage, remains written on a page of the future, and we will wait for the hand of Destiny to turn to it; but the intellectual pleasures which your studies heretofore have brought you, as well as those which your daily professional experience are to bring, will prove a priceless capital which no hand can wrest from you; this is a capital which no fall in stocks can depreciate, no rush upon the banks can lessen in value. The great temple of Natural Science, with its inalienable rights, its privileges and its freedom of thought, is yours. Natural Science, that which embraces universal nature whether organic or inorganic, is the offspring of Medicine. It is here, untrammeled by dogma or shackle of the past, that human intellect developes its highest power and strength. This is the intellectual freedom for which Galileo longed, for which the noble old anatomist Vesalius sighed, who, chased from city to city and from island to island in the Mediterranean, at last died almost of starvation. Vesalius undoubtedly thought it a strange world, where men would cut up and burn up their fellows for the sake of an opinion, and yet, for the sake of suffering humanity, would not allow their bodies to be dissected after they were dead. It was for this same liberty of thought that Michael Servetus sighed, as, bound to the stake, he refused to recant the doctrines contained in his book entitled *Restitutio Christianismi*; it is in one of the chapters of this very book, that he plainly enunciates the circulation of the blood from the right heart, viz: that it goes to the lungs, traverses them, and then returns to the heart; and this was a long time before Harvey's discovery of the systemic circulation. In the Imperial Library at Paris, is the work *Restitutio Christianismi*, bearing the marks of fire on it; for when the Council of Geneva sentenced Servetus to be burned, they ordered his books to be burned likewise; but this volume, more fortunate than its brave old author's body, escaped the flames, and now more venerable than the deciphered hieroglyphics of Egypt and Assyria, and more illustrious than the half-burned parchments of Herculaneum and Pompeii, it still lives, and in it lives the spirit of Michael Servetus, while on its scorched face fall the sunbeams of civil, religious and intellectual liberty for which he died.

But this great charter of intellectual liberty, which, as a symbol of faith, hovers over the altar of Natural Science, does not unloose you from the ties of morality. Those great principles of justice and right, vaguely shadowed forth by Plato as the Beautiful and the Good, by Socrates as the teachings of his *daimon*, and which have been venerated by the great and upright of all ages, must still bo preserved and made the corner-stone of this modern Temple of Freedom. And you, young gentlemen, to whom I have said that in adopting Medicine as your profession you are expected to be educated gentlemen, no less strongly would I impress upon you the necessity of presenting a character tarnished by no immorality. The very spectacle which your profession will daily offer, of what results from allowing immorality to assume the helm, will ever whisper into your ear "shun vice, for it brings poverty, disease, dishonor, and premature death." Nature in her simplicity ushers all upon the threshold of life equal and in a similar manner, yet man, by his perversity, has opened a thousand gateways by which he may escape from life.

Among the aims of a physician none should stand higher than that of a long life. But the engineer who stands by the boiler forgets, in the midst of danger and death, that he too is mortal. But this should not be so; the great hygienic lessons which our practice opens to us should be brought home and used. There is no profession where the power of usefulness is so much augmented with age as ours. Years are required to master its principles. Many more years are required to acquire great aptitude in its practice; and that aptitude, different from knowledge, can never be imparted to others. It is like a treasure that cannot be purchased, nor sold, nor bequeathed. It is a product of individuality, and dies with the man; hence, as long a life as possible is requisite for its exercise. Hippocrates has left us a good example in this respect; he lived to the ripe age of ninety years. Few men, however, could reach that period, but almost all might come much nearer to it than they do. To reach a mature age. much must be done, and still more must be shunned. To run far the horse should have a slight burden; no useless girth or gear should trammel; so we, in like manner, who would run long in life, should cast off as useless baggage, all gnawing cares concerning the future. Ill-humor, like rust, as a source of friction, wears out the mind. Depression of spirits is to be avoided as the worst of evils, while cheerfulness and active occupation will give untiring wings to our spirits.

Three hundred years ago, De Soto and Ponce de Leon came to this continent in quest of gold, and likewise of a fountain of which it was said that those who bathed therein would be restored to youth. The former, after traversing a large portion of the New World, found, as Bancroft says, nothing so remarkable as his burial place. To-day, were De Soto alive, he would know that the fountain of youth is not hidden away among the rhododendrons which adorned the land of the Chicasaws among whom he wandered, nor on the banks of the great river which gave him a grave, but that it is in every man's heart in whom the passions have been kept in control, in whom the moral sentiments have taken deep root, and, having matured, are covered with the white flowers of purity, and in whom the intellect, with wealth gathered from every field of nature, becomes itself a creative power. Such a man, I say, though an octogenarian, has not left youth behind, but has brought it with him. Such a man, greater than earthly king or emperor, has an empire more secure than the Imperial domain of the Cæsars which fell a prey to Goth, Visigoth and Hun; the throne upon which his intellect sits is insulted by no Alaric, scourged by no Attila, while age itself weaves a chaplet of immortal youth and crowns his brow therewith. When Humboldt was visited by Bayard Taylor, he said to the latter, "You have traveled and seen many ruins, and now you look upon one more." "No," replied Taylor, "not a ruin, but a pyramid, and more perfect and enduring than the Parthenon." Hence, as a long life thus affords you ample sphere for cultivating and developing all your higher powers, and bringing to a successful conclusion all your hopes and plans, so it should have high place among your aims. I believe there is much truth in what Emerson says, that no man can die who has yet some high purpose unfinished.

Finally, gentlemen, with such laurels to be gained, with such far-reaching consequences depending on your own exertions, how it behooves you to be well prepared for this great drama of life—a drama which, though of varied acts, can be played but once. An error once made, is made for aye. No prompter stands behind the scenes to impart what you do not know or have forgotten. Fortune, stern, immovable and relentless, looks coldly on each act, allows no mistake to be made. or, if made, with one hand she writes it down to stand forever against you; but, as a word of cheer, the same Fortune holds a crown in her other hand, ready to place it on your brow, if you perform well the eventful acts of this momentous drama.

In conclusion: A sad duty devolves upon me, which, although by no means akin to the matters in which we are this evening engaged, is yet not inappropriate to this hour, viz: paying a tribute to the memory of your late teacher, whom death so prematurely snatched from his profession. And in this matter I will be brief, since the words of sorrow are few and simple, and when they become many and elaborate, they are but a flimsy veil through which the absence of true and heart-felt feeling may be detected.

The late Dr. Isaac Rowell was possessed of a genius great, rare and original; of an intellect brilliant, fertile and inventive; of a heart noble, generous and brave. To the bed-side of the patient he brought a rare amount of practical good sense, which was trammeled by no forms of affected technicality, nor cramped by any inflexible, stereotyped authority. His mind, like a tropical field of boundless luxuriance, now and then found time to wander away from medical themes, and to open up new paths of quaint invention and rare device; had he lived I am sure that future art would have owed to his genius more than one curious invention or discovery. But these wanderings never bore him away from medicine; in behalf of its best and noblest interests his heart ever warmed with the highest enthusiasm; and it was his genius, and his intellect, and his hand, which seconded that kindred master who laid the foundations of the first medical institution on tho Pacific coast, the school which this night enrolls you among its foster sons; nine years ago science and humanity shed their tears over the tomb of the one; to-night our institution brings a chaplet of *immortelles* as a token of remembrance and a badge of grief for the other; and, as one of her servants, she has honored me in allowing me to bring and entwine this simple leaf in the chaplet consecrated to his memory.

PACIFIC
MEDICAL AND SURGICAL JOURNAL.

VOL. V.—JANUARY, 1872.—No. 56.

ORIGINAL COMMUNICATIONS.

Two Cases of Locomotor Ataxia and one of, probably, Cerebral Sclerosis.

Reported by F. H. ENGELS, M. D., City and County Hospital, San Francisco.

CASE 1st. W. P., æt. 35, a native of England, by occupation a sailor, was admitted August 9th, 1870. He is a single man, has always been perfectly healthy and his history in regard to hereditary disease or syphilitic taint gives negative results. Five years ago he had what he terms "a cold," which amongst other symptoms was complicated with severe shooting pains in the lower extremities and strong converging strabismus of right eye. The pains would come on in paroxysms, lasting five minutes, and then disappear. These and the rest of the symptoms lasted for about eight months, when they all gradually disappeared, and he considered himself entirely well, until April, 1870, when he had scurvy, on board a vessel, in Japan. While suffering from this disease he was much exposed to cold and wet, and from this time all the symptoms of his present disease commenced to develop themselves rapidly and severely.

On admission he presents the following symptoms: Decided ptosis and converging strabismus of right eye, contracted pupils, misty and indistinct vision. Hearing good, intellect unaffected; occasional headache referred to the occiput. Heart and lungs perfectly healthy, appetite good, tongue clean, slightly tremulous, bowels exceedingly costive; no pain along the spine on pressure. Bladder slightly incontinent; urine acid, spec. grav. 1024, normal. Sexual desire greatly diminished. Upper extremities normal, the lower extremities being the only ones attacked. Pains of sharp, lancinating character in both feet, commencing in the soles, which are perfectly numb and insensible, shooting upwards towards the knee, especially on the inner surface of the right leg. His gait, even when supported, is extremely unsteady, and agreeing entirely with the definition of ataxic movements. He has to keep his eyes on the ground when walking, and misses his aim by more than a foot—generally towards the right—in trying to put his toe down on a given point. He gets tired very easily, and slightly loses flesh, still there is no perceptible decrease of muscular power. When standing with closed eyes his helplessness becomes even more manifest, as he immediately loses his balance; while any attempt to walk with closed eyes is entirely impossible, for the same reason.

Sensibility, especially on right leg, is considerably diminished, the æsthesiometer showing 4½″ as the nearest distance there for two points to be distinguished.

Under acid. phosphor. dil. gtt. xv. ter die. his general health improved very much; still the cutaneous anesthesia kept on increasing so rapidly that by November 15th, 1870, it had reached the middle of the thigh, and the æsthesiometer was indicating at that place 5″.

With various changes, for the better or worse, the upper margin of the disturbed sensibility finally remained stationary at the upper third of the thighs; the greatest distance of the æsthesiometer remained 5½″ in the vicinity of the knees; and from the middle of January to March 1st, 1871, this condition continued. About two months later the patient had improved considerably; the sensibility was gradually returning in the thighs, the same treatment with phosphoric acid being continued, and only the futile attempts at standing or walking with closed eyes, and the slightly ataxic walk showed the presence of the malady; when all at once a relapse took place, with twitching and cramps of flexor and extensor muscles of lower extremities, more decided strabismus, severe pains, and increased weakness.

The treatment then was changed to the following prescription: R. argent. nitrat. gr. vj.; pulv. opu. gr. v.; extr. nuc. vomic. gr. vj. m. f. pil. No. xxx. S: one night and morning. The effect was almost instantaneous; within a week the state of improvement as present about March 1st had been recovered, and from that time recovery went on gradually but surely, and by November 1st, 1871, he left the Hospital with only a slight numbness of the soles of his feet, and a barely visible weakness in his walk.

Remarkable facts in the course of this case were the complete absence of the peculiar tightening pains around the loins and the entire uselessness of electricity, both the direct and faradaic current, in allaying the muscular spasms. Ophthalmoscopic examination gave negative results.

Case 2d. G. S. æt. 30, a native of Germany and by profession a baker, was admitted November 9th, 1870. His own and the history of his parents reveals no disease of a hereditary or specific kind. He lived nearly seven years in the East Indies and five in Australia, and the only attacks of sickness during that time were Dysentery and acute Rheumatism, each once. Since his arrival in this city, some two years ago, he worked at his trade as baker, which compelled him to sleep in the immediate vicinity of the oven, to get up at any time during the night and to work dressed very scantily of course on account of the excessive heat, and he was consequently exposed to very frequent and sudden changes of temperature.

Since February, 1870, his feet commenced to get numb at the soles; they would easily get tired and were generally weaker, but retained their sensibility to heat and cold.

His condition, November 9th, 1870, was as follows: Heart

and lungs healthy; slight vertigo in the evening; lancinating pains shooting upward from the toes as far as the thighs; peculiar tightening or squeezing feeling around the waist, sometimes extending into the chest. Bowels very constipated; frequent partial retention of urine; appetite fair but losing flesh rapidly. Vision slightly weakened, pupils contracted, especially right, converging strabismus faintly perceptible, no ptosis, no headache. Right side feels always weaker. Feels cold; impossible to stand or walk with closed eyes; even with open eyes has to support himself by a cane, aided by constantly looking at the ground where he is walking. Gait exceedingly ataxic, originating apparently higher up than in the other case. Misses given point with his toes by one to two feet, setting down his feet first to get aim with the toes.

Sexual desire has never been excessive and is not impaired now. The æsthesiometer gives the following figures: Right leg external aspect, 8″, front 4″, internal aspect 6″—up to the knee; above the knee about 3″ all over the thigh. Left leg, external side, 8″, front 3½″, internal side 5″; above the knee 2½″; abdomen 2½″. Chest and upper extremities normal, except the parts supplied by left ulnar nerve which are extremely numb.

Treatment: Acid. phosphor. dil. gtt xv. ter die. Faradaic current to spine and lower extremities.

No improvement was visible in a month, the medicine therefore was changed for increasing doses of Potassii Iodid, commencing with dr.j. per day and reaching oz.ss. in 24 hours, in divided doses, each with gtt. x Tinct. Nuc. Vomic. By February 1st, 1871, no improvement had taken place. Acid phosphor. dil. gtt. xx ter die was recommenced. In fact, the tightening feeling around the waist was gradually reaching higher up into the chest, and kept on ascending until it reached the level of the nipples by February 20th. At the same time diplopia at a distance of three yards appeared. *Pulse* 120, as it had been since admission. Headache and numbness very strong; is unable to leave his bed; nocturnal spasms of flexor muscles of lower extremities very severe; retention of urine. From that time all medicine was stopped except Tinct. Ferii. chlorid. oz. ss. ter die, and Flaxseed tea, but in spite of all care and attention the paralysis of bladder and rectum became complete by June 18th. Ptosis and nightly emissions were also present. As a last resort the same prescription as in the first case, Argenti nitrat. gr. 1-5, Pubv. Opii. ⅛, Extr. Nuc. Vomic. gr. 1-5, in pill twice daily, was ordered, and the same happy result obtained. Within six days the urine commenced to be voided voluntarily—about two quarts the first day! In a few days more the diplopia disappeared and the numbness commenced a retrograde movement from the chest downward. By September 1st he was able to walk around with the aid of a cane, but could not take his eyes off his feet when walking. The same treatment was continued, slowly increasing the dose of Nitrate Silver until a grain was taken daily, and improvement was gradual but exceedingly slow. Occasionally the pills were discontinued for a week in order to avoid discoloration of the skin, but were always resumed as soon as possible. December 1st, 1871. All pains in extremeties and around waist have disappeared; vision as good as ever; general health excellent, except constipation. The only sign of his disease is the gait, which, although greatly improved, is still decidedly ataxic. Sensibility in lower extremities is nearly normal, and he has repeatedly walked a quarter of a mile without being too much fatigued by it.

The most remarkable incident in the case is the constant, great frequency of pulse, varying always from 112 to 120 without the least increase of temperature. Only within the last two months the pulse has gradually descended below 100 and is now about 90, yet nothing abnormal could be detected by ophthalmoscopic examination.

Case 3d. F. S. aet. 31, a native of Denmark, by trade a machinist, was taken sick about September 1st, 1871, with general malaise, chills, headache especially on stooping down, with slight lancinating pains in left side. September 15th, on getting up a sudden attack of vertigo seized him and he fell down but without losing his senses. He returned to bed and on trying to rise in the P. M. he found that he could not walk straight without support. The next day he noticed numbness in the lower extremities up to middle of thigh, and of the arms from the fingers up to the middle of the humerus, combined with prickling sensation in these benumbed parts, inability to walk or stand even with support, and diplopia. At the same time of seeing two objects in the place of one, these objects would appear to move very fast in a circle around him. Drowsiness and severe headache, as if an iron band was encircling his head tighter and tighter, and a peculiar feeling of being shortened by being pushed within himself like a telescope, were prominent symptoms on that day, to which next day—September 17th—were found added paralysis of right side of face, involving the tongue, and causing a great difficulty in speaking. From that day drowsiness and semicoma increased rapidly; he slept nearly all the time and was delirious in the intervals, getting in and out of bed, &c. Of that time and the next following three weeks he has no recollection whatever; even his removal to the Hospital, September 25th, he does not remember at all. On admission, and for eight or ten days after, he was delirious; would get up at night, crawl around on hands and knees and pass urine and feces involuntarily. The delirium was not very active or violent, and after about a week he regained his senses and commenced to improve slowly.

Examination on November 24th, 1871, shewed that the prickling sensation in the lower extremities has disappeared since about November 1st, while the upper extremities are decidedly worse; the formication is very much increased, while the tactile force is so remarkably diminished that his grip resembles in strength that of a child of six or eight years of age. The æsthesiometer gives the following figures: Forearm inside 4″, outside 5½″. Hand palmar $3\frac{1}{2}''$ dorsal: $3''$ fingers, palmar and dorsal aspect $1\frac{1}{2}''$. Lower extremities in strength and sensibility normal.

When he is holding anything in his hand and averts his looks, he is liable to drop the object, and if he does drop it, is not aware by the feeling in his hand that such is the fact. Contact with water suspended all feeling and power of motion. In all these symptoms the right side is principally affected. The impediment in his speech is present yet, and the tongue, though it does not tremble, deviates to the right when protruded. Severe vertigo appears when he stoops down, and the headache although somewhat better is present yet, especially in the occiput. His memory is apparently as good as ever. Pupils widely dilated.

About the middle of November he had a relapse during which all the symptoms were increased, to which was added a difficulty in uttering words or sentences and forming them, although he could find and form them in his mind as well as before, and a singular difficulty appeared in reading long sentences. This relapse is now over and he has commenced slowly to improve again. Diplopia has disappeared and only a slight amaurosis remains. Careful ophthalmoscopic examination revealed nothing abnormal to cause this slight defect of vision but the interesting fact, that a large quantity of pigment is deposited within the meshes of the choroid, leaving the vessels free to run over and between these patches of pigment, which are clearly visible, as well as even one of the venæ vorticosæ. This deposit of pigment in the retina is a peculiarity of very dark complexioned persons reaching its height in negroes, where the pigment forms a uniform dark background of the eye, while here the pigment only appears in large spots of a dark purplish black color. The complexion of our patient warrants this peculiarity as he has dark brown hair, brown eyes, auburn whiskers, and an abundance of dark hair over his body.

His walk is slightly peculiar; he raises his feet higher than natural off the ground, and puts the heel down first;

the same order he observes when requested to touch a given point; he puts the heel down first as near as he can hit the point and finishes with his toes from a shorter distance. Standing and walking with closed eyes is difficult; he loses his balance, staggers and falls toward the right side. He is (involuntarily) inclined to protect himself against losing his balance, by increasing the basis on which he stands and walking in a sailor-like fashion, spreading out his legs, sideways, nearly double the usual distance.

His previous history does not give any points of sufficient importance to claim them as causes for this cerebral disorder, which it evidently is. Three years ago he fell a distance of thirty-five feet, struck arms, chest and head, and was insensible for about five minutes, but without any further consequence. He is neither a habitual drinker nor smoker. Two years ago last April had a chancre on the glans penis, which healed up completely in five or six weeks and was not followed by any secondary symptoms.

The treatment consisted at first in Potass. Iodid. with Bromide in mixture; lately in the Iodide alone, increasing doses, and his recovery seems to be progressing slowly, but with hope of ultimate complete success.

Annual Address before the San Francisco Medical Society.

BY JOHN F. MORSE, M.D.

[The following extract from Dr. Morse's Address presents a vivid picture of the contrast between the old and the new, which our readers will not fail to appreciate.—EDS. P. M. AND S. JOURNAL.]

No page of medical history submitted to inspection, no announcement of discovery, no character thrown with supreme adornment upon the special and popular consideration of the medical mind, no crisis in the affairs of man and society, ever did or ever can fail to arouse the deepest thought and most careful analysis on the part of conscientious and studious medical men. Anything which evokes a new promise, any new arrangement or adjustment of medical principles, any generalizing capacity which integrates new powers, or any circumstances which draw the medical men of the world nearer together and make more practicable new and comprehensive combinations of the thoughts and theories of the grand Brotherhood, are sure of being appreciated by every lover of progress belonging to our Order.

It is this conviction which seems to invite us to a contemplation of some of the signs of the times in which we are living. Never was there a more interesting or wonderful era in the history of the world or the annals of life. The whole universe of man is passing through a metamorphosis so marvelous that it cannot be estimated or expressed by any power of conception or portrayal. And yet, strange, as miraculous, it is but the moving product of human thoughts, the great authors of which, with one lingering exception, have passed away even from the memories of eight-tenths of the changing world. Guttemberg and Faust, Watt, Fulton, Evans and Stephenson, Franklin, Faraday and Morse, are the men who now rule society with forces which may be resisted but can not be overcome, which can not be lost, which the pride and cupidity of man will retain to the last throbbing moment of time.

Emperors and Kings, Popes and Presidents, Priests and people, may struggle against the new dispensation, but they cannot change the assimilating power, nor materially retard the progress of that intercourse and intimate knowledge which are now concentrating the universal minds of the world upon the necessities of accurate knowledge of the defects and necessities of society; the defects and necessities of human governments. These forces, fortunately for man, are really the missionaries of peace, and if ever marked by the phenomena of disorder and calamity, the explanation will be found in man's incapacity to rise above the level of his prejudices and recognise the hand of God gathering together His children, and uniting them by those laws of union, harmony and mutual protection which parental solicitude would suggest and filial reverence commend. Upon our profession these influences are calculated to work out the highest missions of humanity and truth.

The crude and unenlightened medicine which still obtains too generally in the practice of Arabia, Greece and Italy, the almost grotesque medical theories which maintain ascendancy in Asia and Africa, the abstract and metaphysical manipulations of Medical Science in France and Germany, and the science and art of our profession as they are made to commingle in the sterner emulations of practice in Great Britain and America; all of these are being rapidly drawn into one focus, where the sublime lights of truth and universal experience will ultimately codify the laws and promulgate the precepts which a new dispensation has evoked.

To us this closer union, this more familiar and intimate intercourse of nations which steam and electricity have made a necessity to us, this union can be enjoyed in the highest degree; for between no forms of intelligence can there be found quicker or deeper sympathy, kinder or more generous hospitality than are everywhere manifest between intelligent members of the profession. The only introduction one anywhere needs is the declaration of his profession and principles to secure him an amount of attention infinitely gratifying and profitable. In proportion to his passion for science, to his demonstrable familiarity with the great truths of medicine, so is the hospitality which his presence will everywhere enlist.

I do not mean that the great lights of our profession in Europe or America, whose tireless and self-sacrificing toils have crowned them with universal admiration, are likely to stop their labors, to play courtier or host in any process of politeness which consume much time or divert from the lifetime employment of the man and master. But to approach them, shake hands with them, and see them in the houses of their stupendous labors, to witness their methods of teaching and to walk through their wonderful museums of Anatomy, Histology and Pathology, these are the cheerfully accorded, the universal privileges, which to any thirsting mind of medicine are accessible, and almost as free as the air we breathe.

And strange indeed is the contrast which the past and present reveal on the continent of Europe in the conveniences of science and the style of teaching Medicine. I need not have said on the continent of Europe, for even in San Francisco are facilities for teaching and studying medicine so indescribably superior to what were enjoyed in the early days of the old Universities of Bologna and Padua that the contrast is almost ludicrously wonderful. Then the fanati. cism of the age made the dead body of man too sacred to be studied in its oracular and organic relations to science and truth; then the prosecution of Anatomical questions was undertaken almost at the risk of life, and demonstrations made were confined to that external world of observation which the scalpel could unfold, with the incipient and imperfect use of the microscope after its introduction by Malpighi.

Then practical anatomy was sacrilege, and the lessons it taught waked the execrations of the multitude; prosecuted in the same building in which Galileo shocked the religious world with great truths, and where he had the audacity to invent the telescope by way of demonstrating his infamous theories, it came in for the same anathemas, the same spirit which in those times moved only to convict of error or crush with bigotry. Petrarch and Tasso could not redeem the character of the University of Padua, in which it is claimed the first public anatomical demonstrations were made, where Galileo was a teacher of mathematics and Columbus had been a pupil.

Then students could not find a room of huge dimensions, beautifully lighted, warmed and ventilated, almost free from troublesome exhalations, infinitely supplied with mechanical and scientific appliances, where, comfortably seated upon a rush bottomed stool, they could pre-empt the privilege of haggling with indifference or dissecting with devotion a quarter section of dead humanity fresh from the bed of dissolution, and for a mere song. Then indeed, students did not indulge in the luxury of ampitheatres adorned with high-backed seats, perhaps upholstered, in which to sit at ease while the inspiration of divine truth came gleaming and demonstrated from the lips of erudition, the revolving table, the blackboard, or chemist's crucible. Instead of sitting, they entered grotesque terraced standing places which were separated by pale fences so close as to entirely conceal the body, so high as to expose but little more than the head and neck of the student, and with spaces so narrow that a portly man must have been excluded from the common privilege.

Then the circulation was unknown, systems the capricious subjects of conjecture, organs guessed at or perfectly or imperfectly understood as their prominence and use opened the resources of observation and analysis. Then the means of teaching were confined to oral communications, or written transcripts of the facts and theories which learned men promulgated in such ampitheatres to eager students, who, unpunished by impalement, hung with rapture upon the utterances of the crude and primitive hypotheses of medicine. Then, to be a student at all, was to have inherited wonderful pecuniary resources, or to be in possession of a mind so extraordinary as to enlist ample patronage, and the fatigues and dangers of a five hundred mile journey were greater and often required more time than are now demanded in circumnavigating the globe. Then no intuitive faculty, no piercing mind, no soul thirsting after the hidden truths of nature, could escape the grooves and traces of ignorance and superstition. Copernicus was scandalized in the persecutions of his grateful disciple, Galileo, whilst Joshua was vindicated when Urban the VIII made this aged old philosopher publicly declare that his theory of the earth's motion was a LIE! Then the scope of the intellect of man, like the planetary system, was unknown, and its sublime functions utterly and stupidly misconstrued.

Then the Devil had not taught Guttemberg and Faust the final configuration and power of the type; then James Watt had not aroused the indignation of Mrs. Moorhead by his listless dreams over the weird and miraculous powers of steam; then no one prophesied from the lightning's flash the coming of Franklin, and no *a priori* reasoning could have traveled from Watt to Fulton, from Fulton to Faraday, from Faraday to Stephenson and Morse. No medical mind however fertile and sweeping in its perceptive range could have argued from the microscopic exploits of Malpighi, what Virchow, and Bernard, and Pavy, and a thousand others would do with the modern representatives of the crude instrument of Padua. Thoughts startling and sublime, theories grand and inspiring, whether from the brain of Volta or Galvani, of Paracelsus or Hunter, of Kant or Cuvier, were so long in reaching the circumference of society in their days, that we indeed could not appreciate their claims and greatness, until the mind of the new era, disciplined to the speed, and scrutiny, and energy of steam and lightning, had directed attention to their wonderful sagacity, their transcendent powers of intuition.

Now, in the great city of Berlin, hundreds of years younger than Bologna and Padua, one can form some idea of the contrast between then and now. In the Medical University of that city, a student can purchase the right of a seat during a full course of lectures from Professor Virchow for $16.80, and the facilities for hearing and seeing are in complete unison with modern development—seats at a large table, which, though marked by squares and angles, is still so constructed as to allow uninterrupted trains of microscopes to pass from one end to the other on railways exactly adapted to the most convenient and accurate observation.

Here the learned pathologist passes with glowing and

eloquent descriptions of changes which disease portrays upon the general organism and its appearances, to the cellular and molecular transformations from which the morbid processes are evoked that are rendered dangerous and fatal. The theory of the teacher is announced, the general and minute pathology is expressed in the clearest possible phraseology, a field of the diseased structure is adjusted to proper powers of a microscope and started in a railroad track that carries it to the eager eyes of the entire class.

Thus in the same building in which the clinical preceptor generalises the symptomatology of maladies, and applies the best known remedies for the removal of disease, are enjoyed such advantages of necropsy, of dissection and demonstration, as could not have found their way into the dreams of the medical and scientific philosophers of Bologna and Padua.

And there is no dead or sleeping matter in the lecture room of Rudolph Virchow, except that which has been taken from the cadaver for pathological demonstrations. The white haired and venerable professors of Harvard and Yale sandwich themselves with eager complacency in a line of devotees of all ages, all countries, and all capacities, along the common microscopic railroad of modern pathology. The room, the atmosphere, the scene, the subject, teacher and student, make one grand, total, aggregated specialty, where men look, and think, and feel, and speak pathology, until by the intensity of concentration the ultimate elements of death itself become the charmed sources of new hopes and life and intelligence for the world at large.

And the thoughts, the discoveries and theories of men in the new dispensation, have acquired such powers of reproduction, such typological fecundity that, with the prevailing electric affinities of the new rule of intercourse, they are scarcely proclaimed in Paris, Vienna, Berlin, Wurtzburg, Edinburgh or London, before they are acknowledged through all the leading cities and towns of Europe and America.

Man has now some motive beyond posthumous praise for studying out new principles, for making new discoveries, for working into form and use new inventions. Intercommunication, almost momentary and electric, has become a passion of the age; and a man who sets in motion an idea of real consequence is involuntarily carried into the scrutinizing thought-chambers of millions of human minds before the thinking and creative brain can compose itself to sleep. And if peradventure he publish a book, the mail may bring him an elaborate criticism of his work before he has been able to get a copy from the printer for final examination. This is no imaginative speculation. The author of a most exhaustive work on American Inventions and Manufactures, Mr. Bishop, received a letter from Mr. John A. Kennedy of New York, elaborately criticising the same before the author had received his first bound copy. Even now, from hour to hour, our transatlantic cousins report to us the sinking condition of the Prince of Wales. We sometimes think that newspapers and periodicals, telegraphic news associations and reporters, are an inconvenience to society, but they certainly are God-sends to the discoverer, the inventor, the real originative thinker, or the grand integrator of new systems and principles. The speed with which a thought is evolved from the brain is now not lost after it leaves the spirit that has liberated it, but with the aid of Volta, and Faraday, and Morse, it travels with equal facility through air, and earth, and water, until by its omnipotent elasticity and electric diffusion it becomes the accepted property of the world.

THE CHEAPEST MEDICAL SCHOOL.—The Medical College at Keokuk, Iowa, sends out circulars, on the outside of which is printed—"This is the Cheapest Medical School in the Country." So we read in the *Leavenworth Medical Herald.* Such junk-shop advertising is clearly a violation of both the written and unwritten code of ethics, and places the school that is guilty of it nearly on a level with that infamous concern in Philadelphia which sells diplomas like rat-traps. We hope the other medical schools will repudiate the Keokuk concern, by refusing to acknowledge its diplomas.

Clinical Lecture on Primary Syphilis.

By F. F. Maury, M.D., of Jefferson Medical College.

[From the Philadelphia Medical and Surgical Reporter.]

Agreeably to your request, and in place of our usual clinic, I propose, gentlemen, this morning, to give you some practical remarks in reference to the treatment of primary syphilis. In a large city like this you will not find medical men a unit as regards their treatment of this affection in all its stages, but all scientific medical men treat primary syphilis according to the rules I am now about to lay down for your guidance.

Chancre (a local lesion) and bubo constitute primary syphilis. The former may exist without the latter, but the latter must always be preceded by the former. Then again, we may have two varieties of the primary sore, viz: the chancroid, and the true, hard or Hunterian chancre. Certain characteristic features surround either of these conditions, and serve to distinguish them; and, moreover, these sores possess intrinsic differences.

After impure connection a man may suffer either from a chancroid or a chancre—unknown circumstances governing the development of one or the other. In the case of the chancroid, the period of development is more rapid, or, if you please, the stage of incubation is shorter than in the chancre, varying from 5 to 10 or 12 days. As a general rule the chancroid is multiple, the ulcers being the seat of a profuse yellowish or drab-colored discharge, highly auto-inoculable, and the edges of the sores are undermined and serpiginous.

The period of incubation in the chancre is longer, and the sore itself is characterized by great hardness, due to plastic exudation around its base; not because the lymph itself is hard, but because the specific poison intimately blended or mixed with it, makes it hard. Let me call to your mind at this point that induration will follow the cauterization of chancroid. The Hunterian sore, or true chancre, is generally solitary; its discharge, which is scant, is hardly as inoculable as that of the chancroid—certainly not so auto-inoculable.

What do we do then when a patient comes to us suffering from either of these sores? Is it our duty to then and there sit down and speculate upon the unity or duality of the syphilitic poison? No! Be it an abrasion, a crack, a fissure, a soft chancre or a hard, our duty manifestly is to destroy and eradicate it. How—by means of the nitrate of silver or *lapis infernalis?* No! for surely a more infernal stone or remedy could not be brought into use at this stage of the disorder.

Never cauterize a primary specific sore with nitrate of silver; it is not a caustic, but simply a stimulant and an alterant. Use the mineral acids, such as the sulphuric and nitric, and the acid nitrate of mercury. For the chancroid the carbo-sulphuric paste is one of our best caustics; it stops the pus from spreading, and thus prevents auto-inoculation. This paste is made by taking of finely powdered willow charcoal and the strong, fuming, or Nordhausen, sulphuric acid, adding sufficient drops of the latter to reduce the former to the consistence of a paste. It must be made as wanted, for it will not keep; you apply this paste by spreading a quantity, of sufficient surface to cover the sore, upon a piece of lint or old soft muslin. If the chancre is under the foreskin, retract the latter, apply the paste directly upon the sore, and then when the foreskin is drawn back the lint comes between it and the paste, and thus prevents cauterization in a spot where it is not wished. This paste is not allowed to be scraped off, but must remain until it comes away with the eschar, which is generally in about a week.

Another preparation is Canquoin's paste, made by adding together two parts of dry chloride of zinc, four parts of flour, and one part of glycerine. This is rolled into a layer from $\frac{1}{8}$ to $\frac{1}{8}$ of an inch in thickness, and spread upon cloth; and thus when the caustic is applied, as in the previous case, it is prevented from coming in contact with anything but the sore. If the chloride of zinc deliquesces, which it is apt to do, it must be dried again.

These then are the caustics you must use—thorough agents, which do their work well. By cauterizing with nitrate of silver we merely cover up the plague spot, not destroy it, and thus allow our patient to become a subject of syphilis!

If my lecture but succeeds in impressing this one point upon you, you will be well repaid for coming here this morning. Another thing that you must rid your minds of is mercury in connection with primary syphilis. Remember, *you never give mercury with soft chancre, it but makes matters worse.* We give it in cases of hard chancre; not for its specific effect, but to promote, if possible, the absorption of the effused lymph. There are various theories afloat, however, regarding the action of the mercury in these cases. One is that it acts chemically, and destroys the syphilitic poison; another is that it is eliminant, and throws the poison from the system, and a third is that it simply neutralizes the poison.

To show you my precepts put into practice, I have two men before you, lying side by side upon the table, and each the subject of a primary venereal sore. The first case shows a chancroid in its granulating state, after having been touched with the acid nitrate of mercury. The second case is one of inflammatory chancroid, attended with suppurating bubo.

Both of these cases are complicated with long foreskins. There is less liability, however, of these men becoming affected with constitutional syphilis, than if they suffered from hard chancre. These cases where constitutional syphilis does follow the chancroid, may be due to a *mixing of the two varieties of syphilitic poison.* I have arrived at this conclusion after six years of active practice and observation. Particularly have I watched my cases in private practice where the statements of patients are more to be depended on than in the hospital. I have treated cases of chancroid where no constitutional symptoms appeared in forty days—none in six years—and where the birth of perfectly healthy children attested the truth of my deductions.

During the past summer I paid a visit to the Indian Territory, and I find that several of the Indian tribes are almost exterminated by the ravages of syphilis. And you will find that wherever railroads, steamboats and stages go, there you will find gonorrhœa and syphilis. In a small town eighteen months old, and containing about 500 inhabitants, I ascertained there were forty-five prostitutes *and not a doctor!* Forty-three murders had taken place in the town since its settlement. Drovers from as far south as Texas meet in such a place, and desperadoes from everywhere. They have money and spend it with these prostitutes—they receive syphilis in return, and they scatter it broadcast. You will be called upon to treat these cases, and I want you to remember my teachings and treat them right. I was informed that the Comanches, the only tribe that has kept aloof from syphilis, legalize prostitution in the right way—they kill any of their women who have intercourse with the whites.

But to return to my subject: We come finally to the *experimentum crucis* in regard to chancre. Suppose a man presents himself before you with a sore on his penis, and you are unable to determine whether it be specific or non-specific, what will you do? Take a little of the matter on the point of your lancet and inoculate the man in some other portion of his body, not forgetting after doing it to stay on the safe side by cauterizing the original sore. If the latter was not specific, nothing will come from the inoculation; if it was specific you will have erythema on the first day, a papule on the second, a vesicle on the third, a pustule on the fourth, and an open ulcer on the fifth day. If you inoculate from a hard sore, the period of incubation will scarcely be less than three weeks. Now these facts, viz.: the relative period of incubation of hard and soft sores after both impure connection and inoculation, are reciprocally or mutually corroborative. By such means your diagnosis on the one hand is rendered correct, and on the other you take a load off your patient's mind, such that no words can describe. But do not be misled by what I have told you and inoculate those not the subject of the venereal poison, as did poor Auzias Turenne, one of Ricord's *internes*. Turenne in thinking over Jenner's discovery of vaccination, conceived the idea of inoculating everybody with syphilis so as to give them the disorder in a mild form. The matter was brought before the French Academy, and was promptly discarded and discountenanced by that body. Danielson, of Bergen, wound up a series of critical papers by asking Turenne why he did not inoculate himself. To this the latter made no reply; but when he died, two or three years ago, he gave his body to the French Museum, and upon examining it fifty-two ulcers were found upon its surface, where he had inoculated himself. Prof. Bœck practiced what he denominated syphilization for the cure of constitutional syphilis, that is, inoculating and re-inoculating the same individual all over his body, until the specific poison ceases to take effect. This is a disgusting treatment, to say the least of it. I tried it upon two patients in this hospital, one recovered and went away—the other died.

Such, in brief, gentlemen, are some of the landmarks in this great venereal highway. You see that both these men before you have long foreskins, and that you will see in almost every case of syphilis that comes before you. A long foreskin serves to entangle and retain the specific virus, and after a patient has absorbed the poison, complicates the cure. Phymocise, or circumcise, then, all the children you can, and thus decrease their chances of acquiring this disorder. It would not do to circumcise this man with the inflammatory chancroid now, because by so doing we would run every chance of inoculating the whole wound, and thus give him a ring of soft chancre. He must be treated, therefore, as best we can, cleanliness here being emphatically godliness. We will soak the entire penis in tepid water, medicated with permanganate of potassa, or carbolic acid properly diluted, and thus hope to expose the glans. This should be done four or five times daily, for ten minutes each time. Anodynes are often required to allay and prevent morbid erections. No mercury will be given.

Proceedings of the Alameda County Medical Association,

Held at Oakland, December 4, 1871.

Present—Dr. Cushing, President; Drs. Babcock, Bolton, Carr, Hanson, Holmes, Kittredge, Jno. Le Conte, Jos. Le Conte, Pinkerton, Sherman, Van Wyck.

C. H. Allen, M. D., of Centreville, a graduate of the Medical Department University of Vt., class of 1857, was unanimously elected to membership.

Dr. Sherman read a report on Puerperal Eclampsia. The Dr. had read over 1,500 pages from authorities on the subject, and the weight of evidence proved that in over 90 per cent. of all cases on record, albuminuria was detected *prior* to the attack; that in a majority of the remaining 10 per cent. it was discovered *after* the seizure; and that as no other known cause was proven to exist sufficient to account for the convulsions, it might be reasonably concluded that albuminuria was the exciting cause. It was also demonstrated that to confound eclampsia with any other form of convulsion, indicated either a careless examination or false diagnosis. Copious extracts were read from Trousseau, Cazeaux and Elliot to confirm the above conclusions. To controvert some of the views advanced, the Secretary was called on to read from a review in the April number of the American Journal of Medical Sciences. After discussion, the members voted their thanks for the able report.

Dr. Jos. Le Conte read a lengthy and most instructive paper on the "Mutual Relation of Vital and Physical Forces, or the Correlation of Vital Forces and Conservation of Force in Vital Phenomena." By the aid of diagrams, the Dr. explained and illustrated not only the researches of others but his own original investigations.

Dr. Van Wyck called attention to the frequency of criminal abortions and the immunity from punishment enjoyed by those who encourage and practice this business. The Dr. moved the appointment of a committee, who should report at next meeting a Memorial to the Legislature to make a law which would not be a dead letter, as are the present laws. Drs. Van Wyck, Carr and Kittredge were appointed.

Drs. Pinkerton, Sherman and Babcock were constituted a committee to revise the Constitution, By Laws and Fee Table, and report at next meeting.

Notice was given of intention to move the adoption of an amendment to the Constitution, providing for the election instead of the appointment of the Board of Censors.

Dr. Bolton was appointed to prepare a paper for consideration at the next meeting.

Adjourned.

H. P. Babcock, Secretary.

Two Failures of Cundurango.

To the Editors of the Pacific Medical and Surgical Journal:

About September 10th I was consulted by Capt. C., a stout but sallow looking man of 48 years. He had a small tumor situated on the inferior and posterior part of the right Inf. Maxilla, half way between the Symphisis and Angle. It appeared to be firmly attached to the bone, immoveable, and bound down with fascia. On its surface it had that peculiar bluish purple appearance so eminently characteristic of the disease in its early stages. Its size was that of a walnut, hard at its base and indurated in the centre, and on its surface a slight fluctuation. The general aspect of the patient led me at once to suspect cancer. He had a *tallowy*, if I may use such an expression, a very unhealthy look, enhanced by his mode of living; for although wealthy, he had slovenly, dirty habits. He was unmarried, and spent the greater portion of his time in bar rooms, inhaling the fumes of whisky and tobacco in a confined atmosphere—indulging freely in bad liquor. His appetite was good; pulse normal; complained of shooting or darting pains at night when in bed. The treatment at first was Iodine externally and Iod. Potassii with Tonics internally, and afterwards Hydrate of Chloral, and Bromid. Potassii as Anodynes.

Still no treatment appeared to arrest its progress, and it daily increased in size until it occupied the entire sub maxillary space, having the circumference of an ordinary saucer. It became extremely painful and a small puncture on its surface, where fluctuation was felt just under the integument, developed the presence of a sero-purulent fluid with flocula or curdy water. Poultices, Escharotics, Carbolic Acid, and in fact every known remedy were next tried without the slightest effect. Drs. Morse of San Francisco, and Wells of Petaluma, saw him in consultation, and advised the per manganate of potassa, which was used with no better result. The Cundurango was suggested, and with much difficulty obtained at five dollars per ounce, and faithfully administered internally of the same strength as the decoction of cinchona and also freely injected into the cavity of the tumor, but without any change. Daily it became worse, the odor unbearable, and finally exhaustion terminated his sufferings on the 4th of November.

The peculiarities of this case were its rapid and uncontrolable course and the extreme worthlessness of the Cundurango, from which so much was expected by the friends of the patient. This is the second time that I have used it, and I must confess that I cannot speak favorably of it in either case.

The first case was in June last, in Epithelial Cancer of the lip, which I removed twice at the request of the patient. The Cundurango appeared only to increase the virulence of the disease. I take the liberty of sending you these details, to add my humble testimony to the worthlessness of the so-called specific. ALEXANDER J. STEWART, M. R. C. S. L.

Petaluma, December 4, 1871.

Dynamics of Nerve and Muscle.

[SELECTED]

From "Dynamics of Nerve and Muscle." By Charles Bland Radcliffe.

Dr. Radcliffe has long held rather peculiar doctrines. His position entitles him to a hearing, and we may add, the conscientious work he has done, should excuse even those who differ from him to give him full scope. We are not prepared to indorse his views, and just now we have not space to attempt to refute them. We, therefore, beg to report that the present work may be looked upon to some extent as a new edition of a former volume. It presents the author's most recent researches and conclusions on a most interesting subject. We will give him space to tell in his own words what he maintains, and thus we cannot be said not to do justice to him. It thus sums up his views:—

Instead of regarding the state of action in nerve and muscle as a manifestation of vitality, there is indeed, reason to believe that it must be brought under the dominion of physical law in order to be intelligible, and that a different meaning, also based upon pure physics, must be attached to the state of rest.

There is reason to believe that all kinds of electricity act upon the nerve and muscle, not by causing the state of action, but by antagonizing it.

There is reason to believe that "nervous influences" act upon nerve and muscle, not by causing the state of action, but by antagonizing it.

The whole case is simple enough. It would seem, indeed :

(1) That the sheaths of the fibres in nerve and muscle are capable of being charged like Leyden jars, and that during the state of rest they are so charged.

(2) That the sheaths of the fibres in muscle are highly elastic.

(3) That the fibres of muscle are elongated during the state of rest by the charge with which their sheaths are charged, the mutual attraction of the two opposite electri-

cities disposed, Leyden-jar-wise, upon two surfaces of the sheaths, compressing the elastic substances of the sheaths and so causing elongation of the fibre in proportion to the amount of the charge.

(4) That the muscular fibres contract when the state of rest changes for that of action, because the charge which causes the state of elongation during rest is then discharged, and because the discharge leaves the fibres free to return, by virtue of their elasticity simply, from the state of elongation in which they had been previously kept by the charge, and the degree of contraction is proportional to the degree of elongation previously existing.

(5) That the fibres of nerve are not affected in the same way as the fibres of muscle by the charge and discharge of electricity, because the sheaths of the fibres may be wanting in the requisite degree of elasticity.

(6) That the blood antagonizes the state of action in nerve and muscle by helping to keep up the natural electrical charge which antagonizes action.

(7) That "nervous influence" antagonizes the state of action in nerve and muscle by helping to keep up the natural electrical charge which antagonizes action.

(8) The diminished afflux of blood to certain nerve-centres leads to successive action in nerve and muscle by disturbing the electric equilibrium of the nervous system which is maintained during the state of rest, this disturbance causing a partial reversal in the relative position of the two electricities with which the sheaths of the fibres are charged, and so necessitating the discharge which is the basis of the state of action; for by this partial reversal, sheaths of which the charge has become negative at the sides and positive at the ends are brought into juxta-position with sheaths of which the charge remains positive at the sides and negative at the ends—are brought into a relation which necessitates discharge, for discharge must happen when opposite electricities come together.

REVIEWS AND NOTICES OF BOOKS.

THE DRUGGISTS' GENERAL RECEIPT BOOK, comprising a copious Veterinary Formula; with numerous Recipes in Patent and Proprietary Medicines, Druggists' Nostrums, &c.; Perfumery and Cosmetics; Beverages, Dietetic Articles and Condiments; Trade Chemicals, Scientific Processes, and an Appendix of Useful Tables. By Henry Beasley, Author of the "Book of Prescriptions," &c. &c. Seventh American, from the last London Edition. Philadelphia: Lindsay & Blakiston. 1871. Pp. 497. San Francisco: A. L. Bancroft & Co.

The title of the work as given above in full, denotes the nature of its contents. It contains a mass of information not to be found in any other volume, and of great practical value to physicians, druggists, heads of families, and also to every person who owns a horse or cow, or a flock of poultry.

PRACTICAL THERAPEUTICS: considered chiefly with reference to Articles of the Materia Medica. By Edward John Waring, M. D., F. L. S., Member of the Royal College of Physicians, London; Fellow of the Royal College of Surgeons, England; Surgeon (retired) in her Majesty's Indian Army. Second American, from the Third London Edition. Philadelphia: Lindsay & Blakiston. 1871. Pp. 765. San Francisco: A. L. Bancroft & Co.

This work has been for many years regarded as a standard book. Excepting Stille's large work, it embodies more of the essential and practical parts of Materia Medica and Therapeutics than any other treatise in our language. Being a single volume, it is very conveniently handled; and both student and practitioner will find it of great service for daily use and reference.

TRANSACTIONS OF THE AMERICAN OTOLOGICAL SOCIETY. First Annual Meeting: Newport, R. I. 1871.

The proceedings of the Society as here recorded, display a degree of industry and zeal on the part of the members highly creditable to them individually, and reflecting honor on their special vocation.

THE AMERICAN PRACTITIONER: a Monthly Journal of Medicine and Surgery. Edited by David Yandell, M. D., Professor of Clinical Surgery in the University of Louisville, and Theophiles Parvin, M. D., Professor of Medical and Surgical Diseases of Women in the University of Louisville. Published by John P. Morton & Co., Louisville.

Volumes III and IV of this valuable serial are before us, in handsome binding. The excellence of the contents and the exceeding neatness of execution, entitle these volumes to a prominent place in the medical library.

TRANSACTIONS of the Twenty-sixth Annual Meeting of the Ohio State Medical Society, held at Cincinnati, April 4, 5 and 6, 1871. Cincinnati: Bosworth, Chase & Hall. Pp. 351.

A very handsome volume, neatly bound, and containing a number of valuable papers, to which we shall call the attention of our readers in a future number.

A REPORT OF SURGICAL CASES TREATED in the Army of the United States, from 1865 to 1871. Circular No. 3. Surgeon General's Office, War Department.

We regret the necessity there is for deferring till our next issue a notice, somewhat extended, of this invaluable report.

PARTURITION WITHOUT PAIN: A Code of Directions for escaping from the primal curse. By M. L. Holbrook, M. D., Editor of the "Herald of Health." New York: Wood & Holbrook. 1871. Pp. 115. San Francisco: A. Roman & Co.

Although the author of this little volume is in the habit of pushing his views to extremes, yet there is much pleasant and useful information to parents and others contained in its pages. He has convinced himself that all that is necessary to enable a female to escape the pains of labor, is to live on fruit during gestation. His central idea is "the cooling, soothing, and nutritious fruit-diet system."

THE PHYSICIANS' DOSE AND SYMPTOM BOOK; containing the Doses and uses of all the principal articles of the Materia Medica and Officinal Preparations, &c., &c., &c. By Joseph H. Wythes, A. M., M. D. Philadelphia: Lindsay & Blakiston. 1871. San Francisco: A. L. Bancroft & Co.

A pocket manual of 277 pages already noticed by us. That it has reached a tenth edition shows the estimate placed upon it by medical practitioners.

The Physician's Visiting List for 1872. Twenty-first year of its publication. Philadelphia: Lindsay & Blakiston. San Francisco: A. L. Bancroft & Co.

All physicians now-a-days go armed with a "Visiting List."

Text-book of Skin Diseases. By Isidor Neumann, Lecturer on Dermatology in the Imperial University of Vienna. Translated from the Second German Edition, by special permission of the Author. By Alfred Pullar, M. D., Edinburgh, Physician to the East London Hospital for Children. With 67 wood cuts. London: Robert Hardwicke. 1871. Pp. 329. San Francisco: A. L. Bancroft & Co.

The same, translated by Lucius D. Bulkley, A. M., M. D., Surgeon to the New York Dispensary, Venereal and Skin Diseases; Member of the New York Dermatological Society, &c., &c. New York: D. Appleton & Co. 1872. Pp. 467. San Francisco: A. Roman & Co.

Here we have two translations of the same work, an English and an American, each bearing the date of the translator, September, 1871. The purchaser may take his choice. He will find both translations faithfully made, and the wood-cuts and typography equally well executed. The only difference is in the additions made by the American translator, which enlarge the volume, and which refer mainly to the treatment, a branch not much dwelt on in the original. After the recent work of Tilbury Fox, and the other treatises on Cutaneous Diseases published within a year or two, the necessity of a new work might be called in question. But Professor Neumann excels in scientific investigation of the subject, and particularly in the study with the microscope; and his work, therefore, stands alone in some respects, and will be received with satisfaction by the modern student of Dermatology. It illustrates the wonderful advance made in this branch of medical science within the last twenty-five or thirty years.

The Transactions of the American Medical Association. Vol. XXII.

Transactions of the Medical Society of the State of Pennsylvania, at its Twenty-second Annual Session held at Williamsport, June, 1871.

A notice of the contents of these two volumes of transactions is deferred till a future number.

EDITORIAL.

The Money Question—To Subscribers.

We think our subscribers can have no cause to complain that we have dunned them for the last two years. So far from it, we suspect that our indulgent silence on the question of payment has induced some of them to consider us perfectly indifferent on that subject, and perhaps to impress them with the idea that the JOURNAL is published gratuitously. We desire to correct that impression, and to remind those in arrears that they would give us no offense by paying up. Though our terms are "payment in advance," yet we find it impossible to adhere to them without striking from our list a number of worthy men, whom we are loth to part with, and who, we are convinced, will pay up sooner or later. With the present number bills are sent to all in arrears. Meantime we return our cordial thanks to those who have paid in advance, and it gratifies us to be able to say that the number of such is increasing. We have made a singular discovery on this head, namely, that payment in advance adds wonderfully to the interest and value of the JOURNAL in the estimation of those so paying. The consciousness of being in debt for a book one is reading, annoys the sensitive mind and detracts from the interest of the pages. We have some very good friends in this predicament, who will consider us entirely disinterested in advising them to try the experiment of paying up, and thus to augment the gratification they derive from perusing the JOURNAL.

The Social Evil.

It was announced in one of our newspapers, which has taken an interest in manufacturing a public sentiment in favor of legislation to license prostitution, that the Sacramento Medical Society had adopted resolutions favoring such legislation, and that the resolutions and debate would be forwarded to this JOURNAL for publication. Something like a flourish of trumpets accompanied this announcement. But we now learn that the Sacramento Society declines publishing either the resolutions or the debate on them.

Can Chloroform be Used to Facilitate Robbery ?

This question is now exercising the professional mind. It meets with a diversity of responses, the negative preponderating. Not having any practical knowledge of the matter, either subjective or objective, we are not prepared authoritatively to take either side. But we can not escape the impression that if chloroform be cautiously and gradually administered to persons in sound sleep, they would, in many cases, succumb insensibly to its influence; whilst the sudden inhalation of the strong vapor would waken any ordinary sleeper. There are persons whose common sleep is so heavy as almost to equal the coma produced by anesthetic vapors. It would be idle to allege that such individuals could not, by any possibility, be chloroformized without waking. Besides, it would be well to consider, in connection with this enquiry, how easily persons in sleep are overcome with the carbonaceous fumes of a burning house. The victims of a midnight conflagration are commonly found, if there be opportunity for observation, in the attitude of repose; showing that they were suffocated in sleep, before the fire reached their bodies. The effects of burning charcoal in a close apartment may also be taken in consideration.

Expulsion of Dr. Ruppanner.

Our readers are pretty generally aware of the fact that a quarrel has existed for some time between Dr. Sayre and Ruppanner of New York, members of the County Medical Society. The Society feeling called upon to investigate the case, under a charge made against the latter gentleman, was about proceeding to do so, when he sued out an injunction and arrested the proceedings. This interference with the legitimate proceedings was regarded by the society as a flagrant violation of ethics, and the former charge being dropped, the bye-laws were suspended and Dr. Ruppanner unanimously expelled. The action of the New York Medical Society will be sustained by the profession everywhere.

Dr. Bliss—A Warning.

Dr. Bliss had great faith in Cundurango. Like many other medical practitioners, he deceived himself by hasty conclusions.

He was led captive by appearances. This was an error of judgment, for which we may not condemn him. But he did more. He saw money in Cundurango, and came down from the professional curule to speculate in it and to advertise it, quack-like. He lost caste, as he deserved, and as all others will do who shall follow a similar course. And now he finds it expedient to resign his position as lecturer in the Georgetown Medical College, "for the benefit of the College." A good lesson is this for those medical men who may be tempted to estimate the value of professional reputation on a specie basis.

The Percentage System.

A number of practitioners in Canada, as we learn by the Toronto *Pharmaceutical Journal*, are earnestly defending the system of charging double fees to patients by taking toll from the prescriptions, in addition to their regular professional fee. As far as we can read the reasons for so doing, they are, first, that a druggist may properly pay something to those who send him business; second, that it is often good policy to do so, for the purpose of inducing physicians to desist from putting up their own prescriptions; and third, that the abuses arising from the practice are not inseparable from it, but depend on the character of the individuals concerned. All these reasons apply to the pharmacist and not to the physician. Besides, they appeal to one single motive, and that motive the most selfish. On the same principle an arrangement might be made between the doctor and the undertaker, the former purchasing the influence of the latter in procuring business by engaging to turn over to the man of black walnut all his bad jobs. Any abuse of this system would depend on the character of the bargainers, not on the nature of the contract. We doubt whether there can be found anywhere, an intelligent and honorable physician not in the habit of touching the per-centage, who will defend the practice, excepting always that inevitable abnormity who comes in to illustrate human nature by setting all general rules at defiance.

Oxygen Gas in Pulmonary Diseases.

Dr. H. N. Read reports in the N. Y. *Medical Journal* a series of cases of lung disease, in which the inhalation of oxygen diluted with common air was added to other treatment. In some instances great benefit accrued, and in others none. Experiments similar in kind were tried in England by Dr. Beddoes and others nearly a century ago. The Doctor was very sanguine that he had discovered at last a cure for many cases of consumption. But for some reason the practice was abandoned to be revived now as a novelty.

New Treatment of Hydrocele.

The *Gazette Hebdomadaire* of October 13, contains the report of a discussion which took place in the Chirurgical Society of Paris, on a paper presented by M. Monod, describing his method of treating hydrocele and other serous accumulations, by injecting alcohol, either pure or diluted. He first makes a puncture and draws off a drachm or more of the liquid, and then injects the alcohol. The operation is repeated if necessary. By this method he succeeded in curing three cases of hydrocele and a serous cyst of the neck resembling goitre, the injection of a small quantity of alcohol causing the rapid absorption of the entire fluid, without producing inflammation, and without requiring the patients to remain in bed. He suggests the same method for other serous accumulations. It was objected by M. Guerin and others that the plan of M. Monod was not original—that it was but the revival of an old method. But the present method differs from the other in not drawing off the entire fluid, thus avoiding the active symptoms which followed the injections of iodine and other agents as formerly practiced. The difference is certainly a substantial one. The old method had for its purpose the excitation of inflammatory action and the ultimate adhesion of the surfaces of the sac. That of M. Monod proposes only to cause the absorption of the fluid, and in this respect it is not *radical*, technically speaking, however effectual it may be. It would seem that something more is required than mere absorption; for if no permanent change be effected on the secreting serous membrane, a renewal of the dropsy is to be anticipated.

Tenia in a Newly-born Infant.

Dr. Samuel G. Armor, (*N. Y. Medical Journal, December*, 1871), describes a case of this kind, occurring in the Long Island College Hospital. An infant five days old was seized with trismus.

and on the same day, under the operation of calomel and castor oil, began to pass sections of tape worm. Oil of turpentine and oil of fern were subsequently used, and the child recovered after discharging numerous joints of the worm. The mother, who had no symptoms of tenia, was treated with pumpkin seed, two months after her confinement, and passed seventy segments of worm. Dr. Armor is as much perplexed, as he may well be, to ascertain how the animal got into the intestines of the fetus in utero, as was a certain royal personage in regard to the apple in the dumpling.

Cod Oil—Pepsine—Pancreatine.

Every practitioner has been disappointed again and again in the failure to secure any benefit from cod liver oil, in cases presenting the strongest prima facie evidence of the adaptation of remedy to disease. Very often the oil remains unchanged in the stomach, and continues for many hours to rise in the mouth. Here it not only fails to do good, but is positively injurious by retarding digestion and destroying what little appetite the patient may have had. A lack of pepsine may cause this difficulty—the office of pepsine in regard to oily substances being, as far as appears, to dissolve the albuminous cell-wall, leaving the oil to be acted on, after it has passed from the stomach, by the pancreatic secretion. It is easy to replace the deficiency in the gastric juice by the administration of pepsine. But there may be another link in the chain wanting. The fatty granules require to be acted on by the pancreatic secretion in order to perfect a series of processes by which the oil is assimilated and rendered remedial. The pancreatic secretion may be deficient; and here the want may be artificially supplied by the administration of pancreatine. With or without reference to the cod liver oil, those two substances are often very useful in feeble or disturbed digestion. We can not always determine whether the stomach or small intestine is the seat of trouble, or whether both are implicated. If the stomach, pepsine may be the agent required, if the intestines, pancreatine. Experiment alone will settle the question. Often both are at fault, and here the two substances may be employed conjointly. It has been suggested to administer the pepsine first, and in an hour or two the pancreatine, after the pepsine has had time to do its work. But there is often trouble and uncertainty in this plan. There can be no reasonable objection to the inhibition of both together.

Pepsine is well known to the profession, having been in general use for many years. Pancreatine is of more recent introduction, and has not been so extensively employed. We believe it is not properly appreciated. In our hands it has certainly done much good in certain cases of indigestion, or perhaps it would be better to say, of uncertain and irregular digestion. especially in persons of morbid nervous sensibility. It is particularly valuable in feeble digestion attended with occasional diarrhea—cases in which the diarrhea appears to be excited by the accumulation of undigested food, and in which it alternates with constipation or intestinal lentor. Here a tea spoonful of Wine of Pepsine taken immediately before eating, and a tea spoonful of Wine of Pancreatine half an hour or less after eating, will often be followed by the most gratifying results. Under this treatment anorexia will disappear and give place to appetite and enjoyment of food, and regular defecation will be established, so that the annoying exhibition of aperients and astringents may be entirely dispensed with.

The ingenuity of pharmacists has devised a large number of preparations of undoubted excellence, combining not only the two agents above named, but bismuth also, and cinchona, and strychnia. The pancreas of the calf is the common source of supply, the juice being evaporated at a low temperature to a syrupy consistence and then mixed with dextrine and dried. This forms the powder called *pancreatine*, of which the different preparations are made. The principal preparations are Wine of Pancreatine; Elixir of Pancreatine; Syrup of Pancreatine: Troches of Pancreatine; Wine of Pancreatine and Pepsine; Elixir do.; the same with Bismuth; the same with Calisaya; Elixir of Pancreatine and Bismuth; Elixir of Pancreatine, Bismuth and Strychnia; Wine of Pancreatine and Pepsine. Other combinations also have been contrived, all of them possessing the properties belonging to the respective ingredients, and adapted to the most fastidious taste of both physicians and patients. A good preparation in the simple form is the Emulsion, which may be used in the same manner as the powder, as a basis for the various compounds; or it may be used in the simple form, though not pleasant to the palate in this way.*

* We are indebted to James G. Steele & Co., who are among our best pharmacists, for a list of the preparations of pepsine and pancreatine manufactured by them, from which we have made the foregoing selection.

Central Pacific Railroad Hospital.

A notable demonstration of the security of life attainable by adults under proper management, appears in the Report of the Hospital of the Central Pacific Railroad Company, at Sacramento. The employes of the road have access to the Hospital on payment of fifty cents a week. Those who are within reach number about 3,000, a majority of whom are employed in the work-shops at Sacramento, and the remainder on the line of the road as laborers. The whole number of admissions in 1871 was 717, and the number of deaths 11. Three of the dead were brought in moribund from injuries. Deducting these we have 714 cases and 8 deaths, or 1.12 per cent.—a death rate not much above that of adults at large. It certainly speaks well for the medical and hygienic management of the hospital that the lives of the sick and injured inmates were nearly as secure as those of an equal number of individuals out of doors; that is to say, there was scarcely a greater risk of life in being a patient in the hospital than in being outside in the average multitude. The result is the more remarkable in view of the fact that many of the workmen occupy malarious districts. One cannot avoid inferring that their habits of life are generally correct. There is room also to infer the great good resulting from an early resort to treatment; for men who contribute a monthly stipend to entitle them to the privileges of the hospital are likely to be prompt in availing themselves of its benefits, and not to defer the resort to medical aid, as is too often done, until their disease is deeply rooted. The causes of death were as follows: Pneumonitis, 2; hepatitis, 2; congestive fever, 3; typhoid fever, 1; total, 8. It is scarcely fair in this connection to omit the name of Dr. Nixon as the medical attendant.

Contents of the Journal.

Our readers will find the paper of Dr. Ingalls on affections of the spinal cord, to afford an excellent study on this interesting topic. In the investigation of this class of diseases, much advance has been made within a few years.

The extract from the Lecture of Professor Morse exhibits a graphic picture of the contrast between the old and the new in some departments of medicine.

Poison and Antidote.

The best thing of the kind that our eyes have ever beheld, is presented in the two following articles, which appear nearly side by side in the *Pacific Observer*, a religious paper published in San Francisco. We commend the example to other papers which publish the advertisements of Darrin, Doherty, Gibbon, Cohen, Madame Exodius, and so forth. If the editors should say what they think, all these speculators on human credulity and human life would be complimented in terms similar to those meted out to the "Rev. William H. Norton:"

TO THE SUFFERING.—The Rev. William H. Norton, while residing in Brazil as a missionary, discovered in that land of medicines a remedy for Consumption, Scrofula, Sore Throat, Coughs, Colds, Asthma, and Nervous Weakness. This remedy has cured myself after all other medicines had failed. Wishing to benefit the suffering, I will send the receipt for preparing this remedy to all who desire, free of charge. Please send an envelope with your name and addresi on it. Address, Rev. WILLIAM H. NORTON, 676 Broadway, New York City,

CAUTION.—We caution our readers against the advertisement of one Rev. William H. Norton, found in the advertising columns of this paper. The advertisement is one of the vilest swindles ever perpetrated upon the community. In the first place, there is no such man as the Rev. William H. Norton. The name is assumed by a consummate knave and villain, to steal money from the afflicted. You are ready to enquire if a prescription,free of charge, is robbery or stealing? There is the secret. In that pretended benevolence is compounded the quintessence of knavery and villainy. You write to him, enclosing stamped envelope, and he will send you a prescription in such names as nobody ever heard of but himself, which he manufactures for the occasion; you will take that to the druggist to have it filled, and find that he has no such articles. You will ransack town and city in vain to get your benevolent prescription filled; and in despair you will write the Rev. villain that you cannot find such articles as he mentions. Now he has you in the mouth of his net. He will write you immediately, that if you will remit him five or ten dollars, he will send you the medicine. Remit him the money, and by the return mail or express will come a package of some worthless powder;

most usually rotten wood, made bitter with a little gentian or quassia, or a bottle of mean whisky, made bitter with the same articles. You are sold, swindled, outraged, but to attempt to catch the Rev. rogue would be like the Irishman's flea—" 'taint there." You may write to responsible parties in New York, stating your grievances, but they will tell you there is no such man to be found. The name is assumed, and his habitation, if such he has, is in the deepest den of the Five Points. We say to readers, beware! Thousands are swindled out of their hard earnings by such villains. How such advertisements get into newspapers is a mystery.

Liebrich on Chloral Hydrate.

In a recent memoir on this subject, written by the distinguished introducer of the remedy, (*Gazette Hebdomadaire*, Dec. 1,) the conditions of its use are laid down more definitely than they have heretofore been. All cases of insomnia without fever form the basis of its application. For the relief of severe pain, it cannot be depended on, without the addition of opiates. The counter-indications pointed out by Liebrich are as follows:

1. Extended destructive affections of the mucous surfaces of the primæ viæ. Here the remedy, if used, must be much diluted wth mucilage; or it may be thrown in the rectum.

2. Arthritic conditions are unfavorable, unless the blood be first rendered alkaline.

3. In typhus, if given, it should be in small doses.

4. In affections of the circulating apparatus, particularly valvular and other serious troubles of the heart, small doses should be used.

5. Hysteria is often a counter-indication. Here it often increases and fixes the condition of excitement. An inexplicable phenomenon, says Liebrich.

6. Icterus has been regarded as presenting a counter-indication ; but this is doubtful.

The author goes on to say that it should never be given in substance, nor in solution stronger than 20 parts to 100.

It may be mixed in beer, wine, beef tea, and mucilage. He prefers syrup of orange peel. The so-called syrups of chloral-hydrate are solutions in glycerin with sugar. Thin gruel may be employed as a vehicle for an enema. In certain convulsive attacks it may be applied hypodermically. The cigarettes which have been proposed are inadmissible. The best dose for adults is from 30 to 45 grains. Habitual use does not require increase of dose. "Long continued use does not impair the general health. I know persons who have taken it almost daily since its introduction in the same dose and with the same success."

Standing Committees of the California State Medical Society, for the Current Year.

On Practical Medicine, Medical Literature and Hygiene.—Drs. Morse, Oatman, Biggs, Hayes of Los Angeles, Cheney.

On Surgery.—Drs. Nixon, Lane, Franklin, Simpson, Soule.

On Obstetrics.—Drs. Simmons, Scott, Todd, Ferris, Harkness.

On Medical Topography, Meteorology, Endemics and Epidemics.—Drs. Hatch, Hoffman, Brinkerhoff, Cabanis, Pond.

On Indigenous Botany and the Domestic Adulteration of Drugs.—Drs. Bradbury, W. P. Gibbons, Carr, Harvey, Plummer.

On Medical Education.—Drs. J. P. Whitney, Ellinwood, Gibbons, Jr., J. H. Wythe, Le Conte.

On Prize Essays.—Drs. Tyrrell, G. Hewston, Saxe, Taylor. Sherman.

On Publication.—Drs. Logan, Cluness, Grover, Cushing, W. T. Wythe.

Of Arrangements.—Drs. Pinkerton, Cole, Van Wyck, Babcock. Pardee.

Formation of Urea.

Whether Urea is formed in the blood and separated by the kidneys, or formed from its elements in the blood by those glands, is not yet definitively settled. The preponderance of testimony is in favor of the former proposition, which is thought to be confirmed by some recent experiments of a French savan. M. Giehart. But as the experiments involved great disturbance of the functions of the animals on which they were performed. by vivisection and removal of the kidneys, there is still room for the objection that the results may not correspond with the processes which take place in a normal condition of the animals operated on. The question therefore rests undetermined, with the weight of evidence inclining to the theory that urea is formed entirely in the blood, and that the kidneys only drain it out.

Treatment of Chorea by Anesthetic Vapors.

A German practitioner (*Lancet*, Dec., 1871.) cured a case of chorea of one side by the vapor of ether applied to the spine by Richardson's apparatus. A cataleptic condition was induced with suspended consciousness. The application was repeated daily, and the cure was effected in a few days. The same treatment is advised in Tetanus. We do not see in what material respect it differs from the ice-bag treatment of Chapman, which has been for years before the public, and which has undoubtedly proved itself effectual in some instances.

Failure of Calabar Bean in Tetanus.

In the *Philadelphia Medical Times*, Dec. 15, is related a case of Traumatic Tetanus, arising from a pistol shot in the hand, treated in the Episcopal Hospital by Dr. Packard, in which Calabar Bean and Chloral-hydrate were administered without avail. The case appears to have been a fair one as a test of the remedies, and to have enjoyed all the advantages which careful nursing could bestow.

Interesting to Druggists.—An apothecary (*N. Y. Times*, Aug. 4, 1871,) in one of the interior counties of New York, has been sued for damages by the husband of a woman to whom he sold laudanum to be used as a beverage, and the Supreme Court has decided that the suit can be maintained. The plaintiff avers that the apothecary supplied his wife with the narcotic day by day for six months, knowing the use she made of it, and that he was put to great expense in repairing the injury that it occasioned to her bodily and mental health. The case is so similar to that of the liquor-seller supplying liquor to an habitual drunkard, that if the decision of the court is maintained by the Court of Appeals we may expect numerous suits by wives and husbands whose domestic happiness has been ruined by excessive drinking, against the immediate authors of the injury.

Detersive Paste for Removing Grease from Silk—Rub together fine French chalk and lavender, to the consistency of a thin paste, and apply thoroughly to the spots with the fingers; place a sheet of brown or blotting paper above and below the silk; and smooth it with a moderately heated iron. The French chalk may then be removed by brushing.

GENERAL SUMMARY.

Homer on Physic.—Doctress Thetis.

Anesthesia has been traced as far back as the exsection of the rib in the garden; and now comes a writer in the *N. Y. Medical Journal* claiming for Homer a knowledge of the art of embalming. When Patrocles, the friend of Achilles was slain, according to the Iliad, the body was washed and anointed with ointment nine years old, and laid on a bed and covered with fine linen from head to foot; and over all was spread a white mantle. The next day Thetis came and made a *post mortem* injection into the body in order to preserve it, "and then she instilled into it through the nostrils ambrosia and ruby nectar. that his body might be uncorrupted." Thetis would appear to have been the first female physician.

Early Pregnancy.

The *Boston Medical Journal* for December quotes from the *British Medical Journal* a case of child-birth in which conception took place at the age of eleven years and eight a half months. The mother of the girl was epileptic, as well as the girl herself. who appeared to be of feeble mind. She had never menstruated, as far as could be ascertained. Another case is referred to in which delivery took place at the age of eleven years. And a third case is mentioned, reported by Dr. Curtis of Boston, of a girl giving birth to an infant at the age of ten years and eight months.

Bromide Sold for Iodide of Potassium.

Powers & Weightman, the Philadelphia chemists, announce a fraud perpetrated in their name, by the sale of Bromide of Potassium in place of Iodide, which it greatly resembles, but which is much dearer.

Quinia as a Parturifacient.

An Italian physician, referred to in the *London Lancet*, recommends Sulphate of Quinia as a substitute for Ergot in labor. He considers it equal in power to Ergot and much safer.

The Compression Treatment of Aneurism.

It is admitted that the Irish surgeons have succeeded beyond any others in the cure of aneurism by compression. At the last meeting of the British Medical Association, Dr. Macnamara, of Dublin, read a paper on the subject, which is referred to in the *London Lancet* for December, describing accurately the mode of treatment, and attributing the success attending it in Ireland to the following causes: 1, faith in the method; 2, national pride in its success; 3, morning visits of the surgeons to the hospitals; 4, proximity of hospitals to residences of surgeons; 5, removal of all pressure at night; 6, intelligent co-operation of patients; 7, superior physique of patients, who contrast favorably with the plethoric subjects of aneurism met with in England. The following is a brief statement of the method as described by Dr. Macnamara: The patient having been brought into good general health, and being neither anemic nor hyperemic, an elastic compressor is applied to the upper part, say of the femoral artery, a second compressor being arranged some three or four inches lower. The upper instrument is then delicately adjusted, so as to control the artery, and just arrest the pulsation in the sac and no more. A roster of intelligent students is now organized, and to them is entrusted the management of the case. Two are appointed to take charge of the patient for one hour, when they are relieved by two others, and so on during the day, whereby we secure unwearied attention during the period that pressure is kept up; and as in Dublin we visit our hospitals at 9 A.M., the treatment generally commences about that hour, and is continued up to 9 P.M., when all pressure is removed, and the patient is encouraged to take his night's rest undisturbed. Next morning the treatment is resumed, and so on until the cure is perfected.

Ice in the Rectum for Retention of Urine.

Dr. Cazenave, of Bordeaux, (*Journal de Med. et de Chir.*, May, 1871,) says that during twenty years, the following simple expedient has never failed in giving relief in retention of urine. He introduces into the rectum a piece of ice of the form of an elongated oval, and about the size of a chestnut, which he pushes up beyond the sphincters, and renews every two hours. Almost always, in an hour and a half or two hours at longest.

urethral spasm ceases, a certain quantity of urine is passed. and the bladder is emptied without effort by the patient. If in rare and exceptional cases this does not take place, he again introduces pieces of ice into the rectum, and also places broken ice from the anus up to the end of the penis, until the urine flows, which it infallibly does. When there is difficulty in making water, occasioned by prostatic hypertrophy, the good effects of the ice are rather longer in coming on, but almost always are produced. In short, in these circumstances (strictures and prostatic hypertrophies), the sedative effects are so well marked, thanks to the effects of the ice, that the introduction of bougies and sounds into the bladder and urethra is always rendered easy to practiced surgeons, and hardly any pain is felt. In our Chronicle for May we mentioned Dr. Baillie's statement, that ice per rectum was invaluable in the narcosis of chloroform. We have now to add that the same mode of using the same agent has been reported on for retention.—*Med. and Surg. Rep.*

Toxemia from Persistent Use of Chloral Hydrate.

Dr. N. R. Smith of Baltimore, (Boston *Medical and Surgical Journal*) relates two cases of chronic poisoning by chloral hydrate. Among the characteristic symptoms, he mentions erythematous inflammation of the integuments of the fingers, with desquamation and ulceration around the borders of the nails; feebleness of the heart's action, acceleration of the pulse, and in one case, at least, albuminuria and general anasarca. The toxemic effects produced by chloral bear a striking resemblance to those caused by the continuous administration of ergot.

A number of deaths from chloral are reported from various sources. In some instances, a single ordinary dose has produced death. Like chloroform, it seems to be a little uncertain in its action, and in some conditions of the system, a most dangerous medicine. Whether the fatal effects it has sometimes unexpectedly produced are to be ascribed to the drug itself, or to some imperfection in its manufacture, or again to idiosyncrasy or to cardiac weakness on the part of the patient, we cannot as yet positively determine. Till the action of the drug in these exceptional instances is better understood, we shall do well to prescribe it cautiously ourselves, and to discourage its indiscriminate use, as a domestic remedy, for every trifling ailment. —*Detroit Review.*

Carbolic Acid Paper,

Which is now much used for packing fresh meats, for the purpose of preserving them from putrefactive changes, is made by melting five parts of stearine at a gentle heat, and then stirring in thoroughly two parts of carbolic acid, after which five parts of melted paraffine are to be added. The whole is to be well stirred together till it cools, after which it is melted and applied with a brush to the paper in quires, in the same manner in which waxed paper is prepared.—*Druggists' Circular.*

Vesico-Vaginal Fistula.--An Enthusiastic Surgeon.

Professor Boddært, of the University of Ghent, having succeeded perfectly in two operations for vesico-vaginal fistula, performed after the "American method," breaks forth in grateful laudation of Dr. Marion Sims. He is reported in the *Boston Medical Journal* as exclaiming: "Glorious result, a thousand times grander and nobler than the victories of armies, whose triumphs are attained only at the cost of the death of their fellow-men!"

Statistics of Cesarean Operation.

Dr. R. P. Harris furnishes to the *American Journal of Obstetrics* for November, 1871, a valuable paper on the subject of the Cesarean Operation, in which he mentions having traced out 70 operations in the United States, so as to ascertain their history. Of these, 39 recovered—nearly 56 per cent. The greatest number was in Louisiana, and among colored women. The result was more favorable among negroes than whites, owing, as he thinks, to the more speedy resort to the operation.

Ovariotomy in a Child.

A successful case of ovariotomy in a child six years and eight months old, is reported in the *Philadelphia Medical Times*, as having occurred at Higginsport, Ohio.

Death from Corrosive Sublimate Externally Applied.

The *London Lancet* for September reports a case of a child with tinea tonsurans, to whose head was applied an alcoholic solution of corrosiue chloride of mercury, 80 grains to the ounce. Salivation came on severely in thirty hours, and death ensued, apparently from prostration, on the morning of the fifth day.

Reproduction of the Membrana Tympani.

In the proceedings of the American Otological Society a case is narrated illustrating the almost complete reproduction of the membrane of the ear after its annihilation by disease. The power of reproduction of this tissue appears to be fully recognized by scientists.

Mortality of Small-Pox.

The proportionate mortality in Philadelphia for the last eleven years, (*Medical Times,*) has been remarkably uniform from year to year, showing one death in 6.6 cases, or 15 per cent. The whole number of cases in that period was 14,952, and of deaths 2,242.

ITEMS OF NEWS, Etc.

DR. HEADLAND, the author, has been elected to the chair in the Charing-Cross Hospital, made vacant by the death of Dr. Hyde Salter.

A CASE OF GLANDERS in a man, cured by the internal use of carbolic acid, is reported in the proceedings of the Minnesota State Medical Society.

BICHLORIDE OF METHYLENE, the new anesthetic, is reported. by the London *Medical Times and Gazette,* to have killed a patient in Oxford, England.

HELMBOLD, HUMBUG, AND CUNDURANGO, is proposed as the title of a new firm, by the Canadian *Pharmaceutical Journal.*

THE DEATH-RATE in Newcastle, England, was raised during the recent strike from 26 to 40 per thousand.

SIXTY-FIVE EDITORS hath the *Georgia Medical Companion.*

STATE BOARD OF HEALTH.

Abstract from the Reports of Deaths and their Causes in the following cities and towns in California, during November, 1871:

CITIES AND TOWNS.	Total No. Deaths.	PREVALENT DISEASES. Consumption.	Other diseases of Lungs.	Dis. Stomach and Bowels.	Diphtheria.	Scarlatina.	Typho-malarial Fevers.	AUTHORITIES.
San Francisco	238	37	27	7	2	1	14	S. F. B'd of Health
Sacramento	27	9	4	0	1	0	2	Sac. B'd of Health
Petaluma	3	0	0	0	0	0	0	Dr. G. W. Graves.
Dixon	0	0	0	0	0	0	0	Dr. R. H. Plummer
San Clara	6	2	1	0	0		2	Dr. H. H. Warburton
Stockton	12	2	0	1	0	0	1	Stockton Bd Health.
Marysville	16	6	1	1	0	0	3	Dr. C. E. Stone
Placerville	4	1	0	1	0	0	1	Dr. E. A. Kunkler
Auburn	0	0	0	0	0	0	0	Dr. A. S. Du Bois
San Diego	2	1	0	1	0	0	0	Dr. T. C. Stockton
San Luis Obispo	...	...	...	...	...	...	...	Dr. W. W. Hays.
Oroville	...	...	...	...	...	...	...	Dr. J. M. Vance
Woodland	0	0	0	0	0	0	0	Dr. A. B. Mehring
Oakland	8	2	1	0	0	0	0	Dr. T. H. Pinkerton
Los Angeles	29	3	3	1	0	0	0	Dr. H. S. Orme.
Nevada City	...	...	...	...	...	...	...	Dr. J. A. Giffin.
Truckee	3	1	0	0	0	0	0	Dr. Wm. Curless.
St. Helena	...	...	...	...	...	...	...	Dr. J. S. Adams
San Jose	...	...	...	...	...	...	...	Dr. J. N. Brown
Napa City	5	0	1	0	2	1	0	Dr. M. B. Pond.
Cacheville	0	0	0	0	0	0	0	Dr. E. L. [illegible]
Siskiyou	0	0	0	0	0	0	0	Dr. T. T. Cabaniss
Watsonville	...	...	...	...	...	...	...	Dr. C. L. Cleveland
Folsom	0	0	0	0	0	0	0	Dr. L. McGuire
Bridgeport Town'p	...	...	...	...	...	...	...	Dr. J. L. [illegible]
Sutter C'k & Amador	2	0	0	1	0	0	1	Dr. H. M. Fiske.
Monterey	...	...	...	...	...	...	...	Dr. C. A. Canfield
Santa Cruz	4	0	1	1	1	0	0	Dr. Benj. Knight
Vallejo	...	...	...	...	...	...	...	Dr. [illegible] Brown
Suisun & Fairfield	3	0	1	0	0	0	0	Dr. S. D. [illegible]
Colusa	3	0	1	0	0	0	0	Dr. Luke Robinson
Trinity County	2	1	0	0	0	0	0	Dr. J. C. Montague
Santa Barbara	3	2	1	0	0	0	1	Dr. C. B. Bates
Redwood City	2	0	0	0	0	0	1	Dr. Kirkpatrick
Totals	374	63	43	14	5	1	25	

Abstract from Reports of Births.

CITIES AND TOWNS.	Total Births.	Male.	Female.	Still-born.	Live-born.	AUTHORITIES.
San Francisco	47	19	28	8	39	S. F. Board of Health.
Sacramenton	38	18	20	3	35	Sac. Board of Health.
All other places	203	101	102	16	187	Various sources.
Total	288	138	150	27	261	

Remarks.—There have been vague rumors concerning the appearance of small pox in the State, which, after careful inquiry, have been found to have their origin in varicella or chicken pox. The eruptive disorder prevailing to a slight degree in the State of Nevada, has been ascertained to be that form of Varicella, known as "swine pox" in Germany, and confined chiefly to the lower limbs. With this exception, there appears to be no immediate cause for alarm in the public mind, and nothing more, worthy of special comment, at the present time. We will, therefore, appropriate the usual space allotted to us, in this Journal, to a correction of some brief but important omissions in the recent Report of the State Board of Health.

THOMAS M. LOGAN, M. D.,
Permanent Secretary of State Board of Health.

First Biennial Report of the State Board of Health.

Corrections.—At page 59 of the Report, between the 24th and 25th lines, the following words, in italics, were omitted :—*while the ratio of the total number of deaths, per* 1000 *of the population given, is* 18.8; *or.* The omission was not discovered until several hundred copies of the Report were distributed, and before a slip, containing a correction, was inserted. A critical reader would have readily perceived that something was wanting, and doubtless would have supplied, in his own mind, the deficiency. The sentence would have been clearer and more correct, if it had been put thus :—*the ratio of deaths, derived from these data, averages* 13.9 *per* 1000 *of each of the* 24 *localities. while the ratio of the total number of deaths, per* 1000 *of the population given, is* 18.8 *; or, one death to every* 53 *persons.*

Another, but less important omission occurs, at page 56, after the "Table of Mortality of Prevalent Diseases by months ;"—total deaths, 1,807.

Consumption was most fatal in January ;—the deaths being 85.

Consumption was least fatal in May ;—the deaths being 55.

Other lung diseases were most fatal in December and February ;—the deaths in each month being 51.

Other lung diseases were least fatal in June and September ;—the deaths in the former month being 10, and in the latter 16.

Diseases of the stomach and bowels were most fatal in August ;—the deaths being 38.

Diseases of the stomach and bowels were least fatal in April ;—the deaths being 8.

Diphtheria was most fatal in October;—the deaths being 9.

Diphtheria was least fatal in February;—the deaths being 0.

Scarlatina was most fatal in October and November; the deaths in each month being 15.

Scarlatina was least fatal in August;—the deaths being 3.

Typho-malarial fevers were most fatal in November; the deaths being 43.

Typho-malarial fevers were least fatal in April; the deaths being 7.

All prevalent diseases were most fatal in January;—the deaths being 196.

All prevalent diseases were least fatal in April;—the deaths being 114.

Of the balance of deaths, amounting to 3,024, by all the other diseases and accidents to which humanity is liable, and which are almost unavoidable, it is unnecessary to make any comment.

Mortality in San Francisco during November, 1871.

By H. Gibbons Jr., M. D.

CAUSES OF DEATH.

Cause	No.	Cause	No.	Cause	No.
Abscess of Liver	1	Diseases of Heart	8	Liver Disease	1
Aneurism of Aorta	2	Dropsy	4	Meningitis	9
Apoplexy	4	Drowning	2	Metrorrhagia	1
Asthma	1	Dysentery	4	Œdema Glottidis	1
Atrophia	7	Enteritis	3	Old Age	4
Aneurism	1	Epilepsy	3	Paralysis	7
Ascites	4	Eye, Wound of	1	Peritonitis	2
Alcoholism	1	Fever, Remittent	1	Phthisis	37
Bright's Disease	8	Do. Puerperal	1	Pleuritis	1
Bronchitis	3	Do. Scarlet	1	Pneumonitis	16
Burns	1	Do. Typhoid	13	Poisoning	1
Cancer	1	Fracture of Skull	1	Premature Birth	1
Do. of Uterus	1	Do. of Ribs	1	Purpura	1
Cholera Infantum	4	Gangrene of Lungs	1	Salivation	1
Congestion of Brain	6	Gangrene	1	Scrofula	1
Do of Lungs	4	Gastritis	2	Softening of Brain	1
Convulsions Infantile	6	Gunshot Wound	1	Syphilis	4
Croup	2	Hepatitis	2	Tetanus	1
Cirrhosis	2	Hemoptysis	3	Thigh Disease	1
Cerebro Spinal Meningitis	1	Hydrocephalus	3	Ulceration Intestines	2
Debility, General	9	Hydrothorax	1	Unknown	7
Dentition	1	Inanition	5		
Diarrhea	1	Injuries, unspecified	1	TOTAL	238
Diphtheria	2	Jaundice	1	Still-births	8
		Kidney Disease	1		

AGES.

Age	No.	Age	No.	Age	No.
Under 1 year	39	From 15 to 20 years	6	From 60 to 70 years	13
From 1 to 2 years	9	From 20 to 30 years	30	From 70 to 80 years	8
From 2 to 5 years	9	From 30 to 40 years	50	From 80 to 90 years	2
From 5 to 10 years	8	From 40 to 50 years	36	From 90 to 100 years	1
From 10 to 15 years	3	From 50 to 60 years	23	Unknown	1

Sex:—Male, 158; Female, 80.

Color:—White, 212; Copper, 23; Black, 3.

NATIVITIES.

California	65	Scotland	3	Italy	4
Other parts of U. S.	37	Wales	3	China	23
British-Amer'n Prov.	5	France	9	Azores	2
Mexico	3	Germany	18	Norway	2
Central America	1	Austria	1	Unknown	4
England	5	Sweden	2		
Ireland	50	Switzerland	1		

RECAPITULATION.

Died in City Wards	171	Small-Pox Hospital	1
City and County Hospital	31	Casualties	9
U. S. Marine Hospital	1	Italian Hospital	3
French Hospital	2	Alms House	3
German Hospital	2	Mt. St. Joseph's Infirmary	2
St. Mary's Hospital	12	S. F. Lying-in Hospital	1

REMARKS.—The month exhibits a diminution of 62 deaths as compared with October, showing a highly favorable condition of health for November. Eight deaths from Bright's disease is an extraordinary number. A death from Salivation is a remarkable phenomenon. A death from "Thigh Disease" is reported, and one from "Fracture of the Ribs." The preponderance of deaths of the foreign born is even greater than common, being 132, or 30 in excess of those born in the United States. Of the adults 50 were natives of Ireland, and it is reasonable to suppose that 50 of the children were of Irish parentage, making a total of 100 deaths in this nationality. The case of death in the Small Pox Hospital was not from Small Pox. Two deaths from this disease have been reported within the year.

THE NUMBER OF STUDENTS the present winter, in the London schools is 1,468, of whom 468 are new students.

HALF A POUND OF SHOT was swallowed by a man in New York to cure constipation. The result was death.

CHLORAL in the blood is resolved into two substances: Chloroform and formic acid.

CHLORAL HYDRATE is used to cure tooth-ache. It is placed in the cavity of the tooth.

M. NELATON will henceforth reside in England.

PACIFIC

MEDICAL AND SURGICAL JOURNAL.

VOL. V.—FEBRUARY, 1872.—No. 57.

ORIGINAL COMMUNICATIONS.

Mortality Statistics of San Francisco for 1871.

BY HENRY GIBBONS, JR., M. D.

To those who have paid any attention to mortuary statistics, and especially to such as have investigated the subject as regards San Francisco, the accompanying tables will prove of considerable interest. They add additional weight to a conclusion that has generally been held, and which figures have already substantially proved, that few cities, of whatever size, can exceed San Francisco in healthfulness, or at least in their freedom from fatal disorders. The tables presented are the sixth of the series and give a general exhibit of the interesting features of the mortality record for 1871. In the last column of each table will be found the average number of deaths for the five previous years, from 1866 to 1870 inclusive.

On several occasions during the year, in commenting upon the monthly mortality, attention was drawn to the very small number of deaths compared with the population, and to the promise this indicated of a very low annual death-rate. Anticipations then expressed have been fully realized. While the population has certainly not diminished during the year, there has been a diminution of mortality of nearly 400 from that of 1870, and of considerably more from that of 1869 and 1868. The amount however, is about 450 more than for 1867 and 1866, while it falls 129 below the average for the five years.

The census of 1870 makes the population of San Francisco 150,361; our city directory for the same year makes it over 20,000 higher, or 172,750, and the latter is much more likely to be correct, as Mr. Langley, the compiler of the directory, has pointed out many glaring errors in the census, among which is the fact that many hundred names of citizens are not to be found on its rolls. But assuming the census to be correct, our death rate will be only 19.6 per thousand, or one in about 50 inhabitants, while if 172,750 be the proper population it will be but 17.1 per thousand, or one to over 58 inhabitants. It is not the intention in this article to endeavor to point out reasons for the extreme healthfulness of our city. There have been unusual causes, however, operating during the past year. It has been suggested that the necessity for economy has prevented indulgences which frequently lead to disease, especially in children. Besides, may not our immunity be due in a measure to the reaction following the small-pox and kindred disorders, so fatal in 1868 and 1869, just as the thunder storm is said to clear the sky and purify the atmosphere ?

The most gratifying fact which our tables exhibit is the very small mortality (399) from Zymotic diseases. The number is even smaller than in 1866, a very healthy year, when our population was 50,000 less than at present. It is not much more than half the average for the five years, and is only 13.5 per cent. of the mortality for the year. From constitutional diseases, the deaths were 632, somewhat less than, though nearly equal to the average (640.4). They constituted over one-fifth of all deaths. From all local diseases comprised in class IV, there were 1200 deaths, or two-fifths of the total, which is the proportion that usually obtains. There were 382 deaths from developmental diseases (average 250), 136 violent deaths, including suicides—less than 5 per cent.

of the mortality, and 208 deaths from causes insufficiently stated or unknown.

Considering the orders and diseases separately we are struck with the extraordinary immunity from miasmatic disorders. The mortality from these (341) was actually less than for any year since the records have been kept. It was but eleven and a half per cent. of the entire mortality, while in 1867, the healthiest of the preceding years, it exceeded fourteen per cent. and for the five years it averaged nearly twenty-two per cent., about twice as much as for 1871. Of the diseases of this order nearly every one was less fatal than the average. But two deaths from typhus fever were recorded, while the average reaches 26.4. It has been frequently remarked that the deaths stated to be due to typhus fever, were probably all or nearly all from typhoid fever, and evidently during the past year they have been included under the latter term. Although collectively the number of deaths from these diseases was greater than the average, it was much less than during the previous year when it reached 136. We have had little scarlet fever during the year. There were 244 deaths from it in 1869 and 85 in 1870.

The deaths from diarrhea, dysentery and erysipelas were in about the usual ratio; the number from pyemia (17) was precisely the same as the average; on the other hand there were but two deaths from small-pox and two from measles, both these diseases being much more fatal in former years. Again diphtheria, croup and whooping cough were but half as fatal as usual. As might be expected, deaths from constitutional diseases are in more constant ratio to all deaths than those of other classes; their number is much less under the influence of external causes, which indeed may be said of most diseases exclusive of those of Zymotic origin. The mortality from consumption evidently keeps pace with the population, without much reference to the mortality from other diseases. From 25 to 30 for every ten thousand of the population die of consumption each year, but the ratio to all deaths varies from thirteen per cent. (about the average) to seventeen per cent., the proportion for 1871. It may excite surprise that so few deaths from marasmus are reported. Cases formerly classed under this head at the health office are now classed under atrophia, the mortality from which will be seen to be excessive as compared with former years. There were 107 deaths from the two causes, the sum of the averages being 109. Indeed there is so much uncertainty and difference of judgment respecting the application of the terms marasmus, tabes mesenterica, atrophia, inanition, hydrocephalus, tubercular meningitis, and inflammation of the brain, that it is not possible to arrive at any just appreciation of the fatality from each. Considered together there were 316 deaths from these causes, to an average of 326.4. Thus while the greatest variation in regard to them is observed from year to year, we find that it is more apparent than real.

The mortality from diseases of the nervous system in 1871 was somewhat greater than usual, but there were only 118 deaths from convulsions, which is not only less than for three years past, but less than for any of the five previous years excepting 1867.

Forty deaths from aneurism were reported during the year, the average for five years being 39, and the number reaching 53 in 1868. Heart diseases were considerably less fatal than usual; the same may be said of inflammation of the lungs, though the singular fact presents itself that the number of deaths from all diseases of the respiratory organs was precisely the same as the average for five years, or 281. Many, perhaps nearly all of the deaths from hemoptysis should be classed with consumption, but from the data given it is impossible to learn the cause of the hemorrhage, and they are retained in this order.

In regard to diseases of the digestive organs the same fact presents itself as that noted respecting the preceding order. There were just 274 deaths in 1871 and 274 has been the average number since 1866.

Why developmental diseases were apparently more fatal in 1871 than usual was explained when speaking of marasmus. If the excess of deaths from atrophia and inanition, be transferred to other orders where they have heretofore been counted, this excess will entirely disappear, yet it will be observed that old age was the cause of death in an unusual number of cases. Table III shows that 90 deaths occurred above the age of 70 years; this is nearly twice as many as generally obtains.

In former years it was not unusual for the proportion of accidental deaths to reach 7 per cent. of the mortality or even more. The ratio has gradually diminished from year to year, until for 1871 it is less than 5 per cent. The violent deaths for six years have numbered as follows: 1866, 154; 1867, 131; 1868, 146; 1869, 156; 1870, 137; 1871, 136.

It is to be regretted that so many deaths have been reported from unknown causes. This is due, no doubt, to the old difficulty of learning the causes of death among the Chinese. So many "unknown" deaths as 134 in one year is, however much to be regretted. The average has been but 48.8.

Many interesting facts may be gleaned from Table II, the most important of which is the large number of deaths among the foreign born residents. With very few exceptions all under 20 years of age were born in the United States and almost all of them in California. The figures are; deaths under 20 years, native 1097, foreign 48, total 1145; but there were in all 1501 deaths of native born and consequently but 404 of native born over 20 years of age. The remaining adult decedents amounting to 1388 were all foreign born. This indicates of course, a very large foreign population. It would seem to indicate also that the mortality is greater proportionally among them than among our native born residents. In the absence of data in relation to the average ages of the decedents foreign and native, it is impossible to make any conclusive statement. It must be borne in mind, that foreigners have in a large proportion of cases reached middle age before arriving in our country, while much the greater number of those under 30 years of age, were born in the United States. The adult decedents, numbering 1795, constituted nearly three-fifths of the mortality, but the native born (404,) were only 13½ per cent. while the foreign born amounted to 47 per cent. or nearly one half of the total. There were more deaths of adult Irish (440) than of adult natives, more than two-thirds as many adult Chinese (278), and over half as many adult Germans (221). The others were as follows: English, 110; French, 81; Scotch, 31; other Europeans 114; Canadians, etc, 37; Mexicans 27; South Americans, 7; other nationalities 35. The deaths of English, Irish and Germans, were somewhat more numerous than usual, those of Chinese much more so.

Both this table and the succeeding one show the very small mortality among children. Nearly all the deaths of California born were under ten years of age, and we find that the average number of such is 200 more than in 1871. Again while the deaths under one year of age were as many as usual, those between one and five years of age were little more than half as many as common. It may be stated as a rule that about two-fifth of all deaths are of children under 5 years of age, and this is the average in San Francisco, but for 1871 the proportion fell to 32 per cent. Another circumstance it may be well to draw attention to. It is this, that the deaths below the decade from 30 to 40 years were in each instance, except under one year of age, less in 1871 than the average, that they were about the same as the average in that decade, but that in the succeeding decades they progressively increased in number. Thus while under 40 years the deaths numbered 1519 in 1871, to an average of 1841 for the preceding five years, above 40 they amounted to 1438, the average being only 1245.

TABLE I.—CAUSES OF DEATHS.

1871.	January	February	March	April	May	June	July	August	September	October	November	December	TOTAL	Av'rge for 5 Yrs, 1866-70.
CLASS I.—ZYMOTIC DISEASES.														
ORDER 1.—MIASMATIC DISEASES.														
Typhoid Fever	13	8	5	6	4	7	8	10	9	11	13	17	111	77.0
Typhus "	2												2	26.4
Scarlet "	10			2		2		2	1		1		18	91.0
Diarrhea	4			2	4	2	5	3	3	5	1	3	32	27.6
Dysentery	3	3			4		1	3	4	6	4	3	37	40.0
Erysipelas	3			3	1	1		1				1	10	12.8
Small-Pox							2						2	147.4
Diphtheria	4		2	4	1	1	2	1	3	2	2	1	23	83.4
Croup	2	2	2	1	2	2		5	3	3	2	1	25	55.2
Whooping Cough	3	2	5	3	1	1	2	3				2	22	41.4
Measles					1					1			2	21.6
Pyemia (Toxemia)	2	1	2	2		3				4		3	17	17.0
Other Diseases of this Order	1	8	5	1	2	2	4	4	3	6	1	3	40	27.6
ORDER 2.—ENTHETIC DISEASES.														
Syphilis	2	1	2	1	4	1	4	2	1		5	2	25	26.6
Other Diseases of this Order														1.4
ORDER 3.—DIETIC DISEASES.														
Delirium Tremens		1	2		1				1				5	20.6
Alcoholism				4	1			2		2	1	3	13	
Other Diseases of this Order	1	1		3	1	1			1	3	1	2	15	6.6
CLASS II.—CONSTITUTIONAL DISEASES.														
ORDER 1.—DIATHETIC DISEASES.														
Anemia	5					1	1	1	1				9	9.4
Cancer	4	5	5	2	7	3	7	8	3	1	2	2	49	48.2
Other Diseases of this Order	1			1	1					1	1		5	11.6
ORDER 2.—TUBERCULAR DISEASES.														
Consumption	62	41	39	54	38	39	32	41	45	42	37	38	508	393.6
Marasmus			2				1			2		1	6	84.8
Hydrocephalus	4	1	4	5	5	7	1	5	6	1	3	2	42	68.6
Other Diseases of this Order	1	2	2	1			2	2	1		1	1	13	24.2
CLASS IV.—LOCAL DISEASES.														
ORDER 1.—DISEASES OF THE NERVOUS SYSTEM.														
Apoplexy	5	2	5	3	6	1	4	8	6	3	4	7	54	51.6
Epilepsy		1	3		1	2				1	3	1	12	8.0
Inflammation of the Brain	10	12	6	12	11	9	12	8	11	12	9	9	121	103.4
Congestion " "	4	4	4	4	3	5	5	3	6	4	6	4	62	36.0
Cerebro Spinal Meningitis											1		1	3.6
Other Diseases of the Brain		2	4	1	3	1		1	3	1	1	1	18	28.3
Convulsions	12	8	15	11	6	13	12	9	10	10	6	6	118	137.4
Tetanus	2			1		4		1		2	1		11	9.0
Paralysis	4	4	6	4		4	1		7	3	7	3	43	34.0
Other Diseases of this Order		1					1		1				3	4.2
ORDER 4.—DISEASES OF THE ORGANS OF CIRCULATION.														
Aneurism											1	1	2	1.6
" of the Aorta	2	5	3	3	2	4	2	4	2	4	2	4	37	36.0
" of other Vessels							1						1	1.4
Diseases of the Heart	18	13	7	13	6	5	11	10	9	7	8	8	115	131.4
Other Diseases of this Order				1	1							1	3	7.2
ORDER 5.—DISEASES OF THE RESPIRATORY ORGANS.														
Asthma		1	1	1		1		2			1		7	6.0
Bronchitis	3	1	2		2	3	1	2		3	3	3	23	25.4

Table I.—(continued.)

1871.	Jan...	Feb...	March.	April..	May...	June...	July...	Aug...	Sept...	Oct...	Nov...	Dec...	Total.	Av. 5 y's 1866–70.
Laryngitis	1	1	1	...	...	...	...	1	2	2	...	...	8	5.2
Congestion of the Lungs	6	8	4	4	5	1	4	4	2	5	4	3	50	32.2
Inflammation " "	17	22	13	13	6	9	6	11	3	12	16	8	136	172.2
Hemorrhage from "	1	...	1	1	3	...	1	2	6	6	3	2	26	15.4
Other Diseases of this Order	2	3	1	4	2	3	2	1	1	4	4	4	31	24.6
Order 6.—Diseases of the Digestive Organs.														
Cholera Morbus	...	1	...	...	...	...	...	...	...	2	...	...	3	6.4
" Infantum	...	...	...	2	3	6	11	6	14	25	4	2	73	70.4
Diseases of Mouth and Throat	...	...	...	...	...	...	...	1	...	...	...	...	1	8.4
" " Liver	4	5	5	2	5	3	7	1	3	7	7	5	54	53.2
" " Stomach	3	3	3	1	3	1	3	4	7	8	2	6	44	24.6
Enteritis	2	1	5	3	3	2	3	4	6	9	3	3	44	75.0
Other Diseases of the Bowels	...	3	1	1	...	1	1	1	3	4	2	1	18	14.6
Peritonitis	1	4	2	1	1	7	4	3	2	3	2	4	34	23.4
Other Diseases of this Order	...	1	...	...	...	...	...	...	...	2	...	...	3	3.4
Order 7.—Diseases of the Urinary and Genital Organs.														
Diabetes	...	...	...	1	...	...	...	...	1	1	...	...	3	2.4
Bright's Disease	3	3	1	1	2	2	...	...	1	1	8	2	24	28.4
Genital Diseases	1	...	...	...	...	...	...	...	...	...	...	...	1	13.4
Other Diseases of this Order	3	...	1	1	1	...	6	1	1	...	1	3	18	13.8
Order 8.—Diseases of the Bones and Joints	1	...	...	...	...	...	...	...	...	...	...	...	1	2.0
Order 9.—Diseases of the Integumentary System	1	...	...	...	2	1	...	...	...	...	...	3	7	4.4
CLASS V.—DEVELOPMENTAL DISEASES.														
Order 1.—of Children.														
Premature Birth	2	5	9	7	6	3	4	4	1	1	1	3	46	38.8
Cyanosis	3	4	3	...	3	2	2	2	1	1	...	1	22	12.6
Dentition	1	1	...	1	1	3	...	2	4	3	1	...	17	26.4
Other Diseases of this Order	...	2	...	...	...	...	2	...	...	1	...	...	5	12.0
Order 2.—Of Women.														
Child-birth	...	...	...	...	1	...	...	...	...	1	...	...	2	5.4
Puerperal Fever	1	...	1	...	...	1	...	...	...	...	1	...	4	10.4
Other Diseases of this Order	...	2	2	2	1	2	...	2	3	1	1	...	16	2.2
Order 3.—Of Age.														
Old Age	2	1	1	2	2	2	4	3	2	3	4	1	27	17.0
Order 4.—Of Nutrition.														
Atrophy	8	2	8	4	8	10	10	9	12	17	7	6	101	24.2
Inanition	11	3	6	3	7	10	8	10	6	9	5	4	82	45.4
General Debility	6	7	3	3	6	5	4	2	5	5	9	5	60	64.6
CLASS VI.—VIOLENT DEATHS.														
Order 1.—Wounds, Injuries, Accidents.														
Burns and Scalds	1	...	1	2	1	1	2	...	...	...	1	...	9	11.8
Drowning	1	4	1	1	1	...	1	1	2	3	2	5	22	27.6
Fracture of Skull	2	2	...	...	2	1	4	1	...	...	1	...	13	12.8
Gunshot Wounds	3	...	...	2	1	3	2	...	2	...	1	...	14	4.4
Casualties (parts injured not specified)	...	6	...	3	1	1	...	2	1	2	...	2	18	34.4
Poisoning	...	...	...	...	1	...	...	...	...	...	1	...	2	4.2
Other Deaths of this Order	2	2	...	1	3	1	3	2	1	1	3	2	21	14.2
Order 2.—Homicide.														
Infanticide	...	...	...	...	...	...	...	...	...	...	...	...	...	1.8
Murder	...	...	...	...	...	...	...	...	...	...	...	...	...	1.8
Order 3.—Suicide	4	2	1	3	6	3	4	4	3	3	...	4	37	31.0
Deaths, which from Insufficient Diagnosis it is impossible to Classify.														
Asphyxia	...	1	...	...	...	...	...	1	...	3	...	...	5	7.8
Dropsy and Ascites	8	3	4	3	9	2	1	6	2	1	8	6	53	36.8
Hemorrhage	1	1	1	1	1	1	1	...	...	1	...	...	8	3.8
Asthenia	...	...	...	...	...	...	...	...	...	...	...	...	...	9.8
Gangrene	...	...	2	1	...	...	1	1	1	...	1	1	8	6.8
Other Causes	...	...	...	...	...	...	...	...	...	...	...	...	...	3.2
Unknown	9	12	13	9	10	9	7	15	10	13	7	20	134	48.8
Total	298	245	227	232	226	221	230	247	248	300	238	245	2957	3088

Table II.

Sex, Race, Nativity and Locality of Death of Decedents.

1871.	Jan.	Feb.	March.	April.	May.	June.	July.	Aug.	Sept.	Oct.	Nov.	Dec.	TOTAL.	Av. 5 y'rs 1866-70.
Whole number of Deaths	298	245	227	232	226	221	230	247	248	300	238	245	2957	3086.0
SEX.														
Males	197	165	151	151	154	149	149	163	164	189	158	161	1951	1984.8
Females	101	80	76	81	72	72	81	84	84	111	80	84	1006	1101.2
RACE.														
Caucasian	268	219	203	201	198	192	203	203	213	273	212	218	2603	2830.4
Mongolian	29	23	21	21	24	27	22	40	31	24	23	25	310	208.8
African	1	3	3	10	4	2	5	4	4	3	3	2	44	46.8
NATIVITY.														
California	100	77	84	72	81	87	93	79	100	140	65	81	1059	1259.4
Other parts of U. S.	53	49	30	41	37	26	33	42	36	24	37	34	442	556.0
England (and Wales)	16	10	13	10	6	10	5	7	6	10	8	10	111	99.4
Scotland	4	...	3	3	1	1	4	2	4	...	3	6	31	28.4
Ireland	40	40	28	39	39	33	29	29	36	45	50	36	444	395.2
German States	23	17	18	24	15	17	19	21	18	16	19	24	231	216.2
France	8	9	10	6	2	8	6	7	1	10	9	10	86	87.8
Other European Countries	13	11	11	8	9	3	10	12	11	11	9	7	115	87.6
British American Provinces	3	3	1	1	2	4	4	5	4	5	5	2	39	38.0
South America	1	2	1	...	4	...	...	...	...	1	...	...	9	13.8
Mexico	3	3	4	2	1	3	3	1	...	2	3	5	30	34.2
China	30	19	18	21	22	26	21	36	29	22	23	24	291	204.4
Other Countries	4	3	3	5	6	3	2	3	1	6	3	5	44	46.8
Unknown	...	2	3	...	1	...	1	3	2	8	4	1	25	18.8
LOCALITY.														
City Wards	226	175	164	185	176	167	175	191	197	241	171	185	2253	2337.4
City and County Hospital	28	24	22	11	17	16	15	13	15	16	31	19	227	238.4
U. S. Marine Hospital	3	4	2	3	1	3	2	4	2	1	1	2	28	36.4
French Hospital	5	8	7	4	2	5	3	4	3	7	2	4	54	48.8
German Hospital	3	1	2	2	2	3	3	4	3	1	2	3	29	40.4
Italian Hospital	...	...	2	...	1	1	...	...	2	1	3	...	10	...
St. Mary's Hospital	12	6	8	8	3	7	6	7	4	15	12	10	98	94.4
Small-pox Hospital	...	...	...	...	...	...	1	1	...	1	1	1	5	56.8
Alms House	3	2	9	2	1	2	2	2	8	4	3	4	42	...
Other Charities	5	9	8	5	7	8	7	11	5	4	3	4	76	94.0
Casualties	4	14	2	9	10	6	12	6	6	6	9	9	98	108.4
Suicides	9	2	1	3	6	3	4	4	3	3	...	4	37	31.0

Table III.

Ages and Deaths in Different Months.

1871.	Jan.	Feb.	March.	April.	May.	June.	July.	Aug.	Sept.	Oct.	Nov.	Dec.	TOTAL.	Av. 5 y'rs 1866-70.
Under 1 year	57	42	47	43	48	62	68	54	59	104	39	45	668	666.6
From 1 to 2 years	14	13	13	13	12	8	16	12	19	23	9	15	167	251.2
" 2 to 5 "	16	11	12	12	6	9	7	14	10	4	9	9	119	265.2
" 5 to 10 "	11	8	10	4	10	9	2	3	13	3	8	7	94	149.0
" 10 to 15 "	3	7	2	3	5	3	3	3	1	3	3	7	43	48.4
" 15 to 20 "	7	6	4	3	4	4	3	3	3	4	6	7	54	70.4
" 20 to 30 "	53	28	30	29	29	32	25	30	29	22	30	37	374	380.4
" 30 to 40 "	49	47	42	46	43	32	42	48	44	40	50	35	518	519.2
" 40 to 50 "	54	46	37	45	35	34	27	37	36	42	36	46	475	399.8
" 50 to 60 "	13	20	11	15	19	13	16	27	23	25	23	20	231	181.8
" 60 to 70 "	6	12	15	14	7	8	11	6	8	12	13	8	120	86.8
" 70 to 80 "	6	5	3	5	5	5	9	8	2	7	8	7	70	36.0
" 80 to 90 "	2	...	1	...	3	1	1	1	1	3	2	2	17	10.0
" 90 to 100 "	...	...	...	...	...	1	...	1	...	...	1	...	3	2.8
Over 100 "	...	...	...	...	...	...	...	...	...	...	...	...	...	.8
Unknown	1	...	...	...	...	...	...	...	...	2	1	...	4	7.6
Total	298	245	227	232	226	221	230	247	248	300	238	245	2957	3086.0
Still-born	15	21	20	22	21	17	25	20	22	27	8	23	241	254.4

A New Observation on the Luxated Elbow.—Chap. II.

BY A. S. HUDSON, M. D.

Editors Pacific Medical and Surgical Journal:

Please say to Dr. W. S. Thorne, I did not mistake the back view of the cut mentioned in his back-acting criticism; nor do I here offer a drawback on the drawing, nor "go back on the new observation," but hope to hold back a long article.

He supports the misleading error of calling a complete dislocation incomplete, it seems for one reason, namely: when the head of the radius leaves its own articular face and takes the trochlea, which belongs to the ulna; as if a borrowed articular surface equaled a natural one. His quotations from Dunglison and Hamilton redound to my advantage. Thus "Luxation is complete when the bones have entirely lost their natural connection." This is exactly the definition taken in the "New Observation." Now, will Dr. Thorne still say it is a "natural connection" for the radial head to rest against the trochlea? In such a case, has it not completely vacated its natural, and sought an unnatural, niche? Then, if words be endowed with specific meaning, and candor holds the ascendant, can he do any less than to admit the radius to be out of place? If out, how far? Half out or completely so? I re-affirm in the defining language of Dunglison, it "has entirely lost its natural connection" and therefore is a complete luxation.

In displacement inwards, where is the ulna? I showed its greater sigmoid cavity had left the trochlea, and its ridge embraced the internal humeral condyle; and that its lower shaft pointed inwards diagonally across the body. Hamilton says it may incline "slightly inwards," and when Dr. Thorne helps his honored preceptor by adding my description, "across the body," he makes Prof. H. say what he does not say; and contradicts that aged cut on page 606, whose nether part perversely inclines to the left, a contrary direction, that is away from the body. But my critic perverts the inclination "inwards," and says "it is unfortunate for the New Observation" that I mistook it. Really, I am sorry to be obliged to retort on him, and return the same blunt charge on the same question of fact; but the anatomical reader can decide by inspecting the wood cut, Fig. 245, which must prove my opponent has fallen into the essential error he wrongfully put upon me; and also show the frightful gash that cruel cut makes in the bare breast of his logic. Quoting from his preceptor's "symptoms," Dr. Thorne says the "wood cut accurately illustrates the foregoing" as well as the signs of the lesion given in my paper. Now, the facts, unhappily for him, are in reversion. It does not do either. Strange as it may appear, Prof. Hamilton gives two different abnormal positions of the ulna in the same displacement, one of which the cut illustrates and the other it does not; and by quoting the description which did not belong to the venerable cut, and missing the one that did, Dr. Thorne made "the unkindest cut of all." See "Hamilton on fractures and dislocations," page 605, four lines of paragraph on "Pathology; the ridge of the greater sigmoid cavity of the ulna having been driven over the elevated margin of the trochlea, falls down upon the epitrochlea, so as in some sense to embrace it instead of the trochlea." Here is more consistency than science; for the text and the ancient cut agree, to the confusion of practical surgery. They describe an incomplete dislocation of the ulna, if it be possible for such a state of parts to exist on the human elbow. This we deny. His "Fig. 245," portrays a posterior aspect of the arm, and at the same time brings to view the coronoid process, which lingers near its natural site, and the point of the olecranon resting on the condyle makes well nigh a side view of the ulna.

The author says the arm is "pronated," but the cut makes it supinated, since those long ossicles remain parallel; it prone, they would unmistakably cross each other. This we defined an impossible condition of parts, to be found nowhere but in that absurd sketch.

On page 606, paragraph "Symptoms," speaking of the inclination of the arm, Prof. H. says, "this phenomenon is explained by the position of the epicondyle* upon which the greater sigmoid cavity now rests."

Observe! he first says as Pathology, the ridge of the greater sigmoid cavity embraces the *epitrochlea*. On the next page he contradicts the preceding and the poor cut and says, in Symptoms, that cavity embraces, or rests upon the inner *condyle*. It cannot do both at the same time. If the first the lower arm points outwards. If the latter it points inwards. Which do you take? If it occupies one place it does not the other. If on the condyle, then has not the ulna "entirely lost its natural connection," and sought a foreign one its own width away? Here we have Hamilton's definition of complete luxation filled to plethora, which is, "one in which no portions of the articulating surfaces remain in contact." Such is my case. See figure.

ULNA, ON INNER CONDYLE. Posterior View.

Though in error, as we have shown Prof. H. to be, he is not alone; he has good company. Of the incomplete dislocation inwards, as Prof. Gross calls it, "System of Surgery" Vol. 2. page 144, three lines from the bottom, and pointing to the same obsolete diagram of that vexing elbow, he says, "the head of the radius *hitches against the inner condyle*." Look, Dr. Thorne, and ye students of Gross, and see if it does! Then make answer. You see it is no where near either condyle. It is innocently between the two. Then was I not justified in saying "the written pathology of this mischief is simply fallacious and incomprehensible?"

Now, if Dr. Thorne continues to adhere to Hamilton and

I submit to Dr. Thorne, whether it is not unscientific to apply one and the same name to two different objects as Prof. H. applies "epicondyle" to both sides of the lower humerus. The accurate Gray defines them as the "external and internal condyles."

others, in defense of the senile doctrine of incomplete dislocations of the elbow, he elevates only to make conspicuous the awkward status of—Hamilton against Hamilton—with Dr. Thorne to help him.

Formation of Urea.

BY C. B. HOLBROOK, M. D.

Editors of Pacific Medical and Surgical Journal:

In the last number of your valuable journal there is an editorial entitled "The Formation of Urea," which raises the question, as to whether this substance, (urea) is formed in the blood or in the kidneys, and which concludes by affirming that it is not yet definitely settled, the preponderance of evidence, however, being in favor of the first proposition, viz: That it is formed in the blood. That urea is *not formed* in the kidneys, I think, (with all due respect to tne editorial referred to,) is as "definitely settled" as any question in physiology. Indeed, there can be no more question about it, than there is that carbonic acid *is not formed* in the lungs. But, it must be conceded, that the question, in what parts or tissues of the system is urea chiefly formed, (excluding the kidneys) is still unsettled, and sub judice. The recent experiments of Dr. Parkes, (see London *Lancet*, May 20th, 1871), and I may add, they essentially coincide with those of Ranke, Boit and others, tend to prove that urea is formed in the cells of the glandular system; the transformation of albumen into urea taking place mainly in the liver and other intestinal glands. The discovery, (it is but just to state) that urea is formed in the liver, was made by Meissner, and is now being confirmed by others.

E. Cyon, by his experiments, has shown conclusively that blood leaving the liver contains much more urea than when it enters. Pathology also comes to our aid, to prove the urea forming function of the liver, by showing that, in its various lesions of function and organism, there is a diminution of the quantity of urea formed and excreted.

Until the discovery of the urea-forming functions of the liver and other gastro-intestinal glands, by Meissner, modern physiologists maintained that urea could only be formed in the tissues of the muscles and nerves, it being the product of their disintegration. It must be admitted that physiology and pathology unite, to some extent, in support of this theory. But chemistry is rapidly revolutionizing the science of physiology, and the accepted theory of to-day gives place to the more scientific and better one of to-morrow. Within a few years, physiological chemistry has revolutionized our ideas of the functions of the liver, and now that it seems to be clearly proved, that one of the important functions of this organ is the formation of urea, it assumes vastly more importance than ever, from a pathological stand-point; that is, in its relations to practical medicine. May not the complaints and conditions of biliousness be better explained and treated in the light of this discovery?

It is certainly easy to conceive that the common conditions of biliousness may be induced by over-loading and oppressing the system with nitrogenous food which the liver is incapable of transforming into urea. In this discovery may we not find the true explanation of the phenomena of uremia, at all events, a more exact knowledge of the course of pathological events and processes in that grave disorder?

This, to me, is an interesting theme, but fearing that I may trespass upon your valuable space I will not pursue it further.

On the Action of Belladonna upon the Heart and Arteries, and upon the Heart in Pericarditis and Endocarditis.

By David Wooster, M. D.

1. Belladonna is not a hypnotic in any just sense. It does not induce sleep by allaying general nervous irritability, nor by relieving local pain, as a neuralgia, or the pain of a pleurisy, or of a sprain, or of a phlegmon.

2. Belladonna is an excitant in small doses. For example, if five drops of the fluid extract be administered, and two hours later five drops more, in thirty minutes, or less, after the second dose, the pulse will have increased in frequency and tension but diminished in volume. The temperature will have ascended some part of a degree, and sometimes as high as two degrees. The heart will be found to beat with increased emphasis as well as frequency, and if its rhythm was faulty before the doses, this will be found to have improved or become quite regular, the patient will experience a sensation of increased temperature, and perhaps he will find some difficulty in reading a printed page; the letters will appear to "run into each other." This dose will increase the renal excretion, and will not retard peristaltic action of the alimentary canal, but will rather add to this action.

3. Belladonna in small doses doubtless diminishes the caliber of the capillaries and thus relieves peripheral congestion, and perhaps retards or suspends early inflammatory action. Large doses again, in children, will produce a genuine scarlatina of the whole body, attended with delirium and great fear, and often with a sense of choking. Under such doses the child will complain of headache and dizziness, the latter doubtless caused by aberration of vision from dilated irides. Small doses will just as surely produce paleness of the extremities in health, and diminished redness of inflamed surfaces in disease. These two effects are paradoxical in appearance rather than in reality. The drug first stimulates the muscular coat of the vessels to contraction, and this excitation being continued, the sensory nerve filaments at length lose their irritability; that is, fail to appreciate the presence of the drug; and so the vessels not only do not continue to contract, but actually dilate, in consequence of exhausted nerve irritability; and when the drug has been continued to this degree, we have congestion first of the venous and next of the arterial capillaries, and lastly of the whole circulating system; and if the drug be

still continued, total anesthesia follows, and then universal paralysis, in which each individual organ participates, and the sum total is death.

4. But if Belladonna is an excitant to the heart and arteries, and it is so admitted to be, and if it has the same effect applied locally as given internally, and this is admitted, then how can it be recommended in pericarditis and endocarditis? Is it not almost certain that the good effects derived from its employment must be attributed to the remedy in combination with which it has been employed? As spread on blisters applied over the precordia or the joints, given internally with aconite or digitalis, which latter are undoubted cardiac sedatives, and do undoubtedly diminish the frequency and emphasis of the heart beats, and the force, frequency and volume of the pulse?

It is exceedingly difficult to reconcile the known primary excitant action of Belladonna with any antiphlogistic action in the heart affections named above, and the only hope we could have of any beneficial action from it would be in its slight diuretic effect. But this latter would by no means compensate for the nervous restlessness, increased heat, accelerated circulation, vague uneasiness and postponed sleep induced by atropia.

The only conditions of the heart in which atropia would seem to me a probable remedy would be in fatty metamorphosis or in the cardiac debility attending low fevers. It might also be of service in the exhausted condition of the heart in the last hours of endocarditis, when, to hold out any hope of life, cardiac innervation must be prolonged until the amorphous endocardial exudation shall have been so far reabsorbed, as to allow the presence of the blood itself to be appreciated by the sensory filaments of the endocardial lining.

Blisters in the Pneumonia of Infants.

BY GERRARD GEO. TYRRELL, L. R. C. S. I. & K. & Q. C. P. I.

[Read before the Sacramento Society for Medical Improvement.]

In the Dublin quarterly *Journal of Medical Science* for November, 1871, appears an article entitled "Notes of Cases, with Practical Observations," by R. Fitzmaurice, L. K. and Q. C. P. I., in which he advocates as the "sheet anchor" in the pneumonia of infants and children, the practice of blistering; a practice so fraught with danger, that if followed generally by the medical profession, would, in my opinion, increase our bills of infantile mortality to an alarming extent. In view, therefore, of the importance of the subject, and desirous of eliciting upon this question the opinion of the many able American practitioners who compose our Society, I propose making Dr. Fitzmaurice's paper the subject of our discussion this evening. To do this, I shall be obliged to make such extracts as are necessary to place his views before you, together with the cases so treated, both of which I shall do with as great brevity as is compatible with strict justice to him. He says: "The frequent observance of pneumonia in children and infants, and in some cases in which chest symptoms were absent, has led me to conclude that the disease is often mistaken for other ailments, as dentition, remittent fever, worms, and bronchitis, and has caused me to publish the following cases to draw attention to the prevalence of the disease, and the value of blistering as a means of treatment. It seems difficult," says Dr. F., "to diagnose pneumonia in a child from the struggles of the little patient, but by keeping the ear perseveringly to the chest when exhaustion takes place, the hurried breathing facilitates the discovery of *tubular breathing*, the first sign of pneumonia generally discovered in the child, however closely the case may be watched." He then quotes from West, who states, that if the posterior part of the chest is free from a considerable amount of crepitation we may conclude that the infant is not suffering from any serious disease of the lungs. To Dr. Fitzmaurice this remark seems inaccurate, as in his experience hepatized lung is oftener found in other parts of the chest than the posterior, the usual seat in adults, and he then declares that blistering, although abandoned by some practitioners, is, in his opinion, the *sheet anchor* in this disease, and says: "If a blister is put on an infant, left on a suitable time, the part then dressed with mercurial ointment spread on lint, then covered with French wadding, kept on with a few strips of plaster, and not removed for several days, nothing but good will result from it. But if the blisters are cut or pinched, air will enter, a raw surface be exposed, and a troublesome sore probably result." Mercurial ointment, he finds, excludes air more effectually than simple dressing, and no doubt has a resolving effect upon the inflammation. By keeping the child as much as possible upon the healthy side, the bursting of blisters will be avoided; and *all* practitioners will agree with the late Dr. Graves, that all good results will be achieved without opening." From these remarks we may infer the fact, that it is alone from the admission of air that any bad results following blisters may arise, and that air excluded, we may blister with impunity, nay rather that we must blister, if it is as he says, our "sheet anchor." I greatly fear, however, that that anchor will not hold its ground. I shall now epitomize the few cases brought forward by Dr. Fitzmaurice in support of his blistering doctrine: O'Connor, aged 22 months; was feverish, heavy, prostrate, and thirsty. Was treated for teething. Symptoms increasing, was watched closely *for some days*, at the end of which time detected dullness under right clavicle, attended with tubular breathing; blistered immediately, dressed with mercurial ointment and French wadding, and rubbed mercurial ointment into the armpits in the usual manner. Next day the patient seemed lively, tubular breathing replaced by respiratory murmur, and recovery in a few days. He says this child was very ill indeed, and had to be sustained by chicken broth and wine before treatment was directed to the inflamed lung.

Case No. 2, an infant six months old, attended by an apothecary for *some days*, and treated for worms. Found him very ill, lying on his back; belly tympanitic; breathing very hurried, and the case apparently hopeless. Dullness on percussion, and tubular breathing under right clavicle. Gave enema of assafœtida, stuped the abdomen and blistered the lung, dressing it with mercurial ointment. Next day he was much improved, but the pulse continuing high, and respiratory murmur being established over the blistered part; but dullness in the axilla; another blister was immediately put on, and next day respiratory murmur was restored, and the child (Providentially ?) recovered.

Case No. 3 was an infant six weeks old, who was for *some days* brought to the dispensary, and was treated for cough. Getting worse, an examination was made of the chest, and dullness detected, with tubular breathing, in right axilla, and along lower edge of great pectoral muscle. Put on a *large* blister that covered all the dull part, dressing it, as usual, with mercury. Next day respiratory murmur restored, and recovery in a few days.

Case No. 4 was an infant ten months old, who was croupy for *several days*. Had ipecac wine, tartar emetic, and finally a quart of strong decoction of senna, which cured him of the croup; but two days after a catch was noticed in his breathing, and hepatized lung discovered near the base of left scapula. Blistered the part immediately, and mercurialized as usual; with recovery in a few days.

Case No. 5, age not given, was feverish, with pain in side; no signs of pleurisy or pneumonia; leeched the side and gave some aperient medicine. In a few days enteritis set in; for which she was again leeched, stuped, enematized with assafœtida and turpentine, and mercurialized with ointment rubbed into the groins and armpits. Notwithstanding all this heroic treatment, the disease continued unsubdued, when suddenly the abdomen relaxed, the bowels were moved; but the pulse continuing very high, the chest was examined again, when dullness was elicited,

extending from middle of scapula to base of lung. Here there was feeble respiration; blistered immediately, and continued mercurial inunction; dullness nevertheless extended, effusion increased, and the heart was dislocated to right side. The child became so weak as to be unable to move in bed. When, fortunately, the mercurials were stopped, wine and nourishment enjoined, and this, with iodine painted under clavicle, secured her slow recovery.

Case No. 6, was an infant aged 18 months, in whom the blister treatment was not practiced. Although the symptoms were quite as bad as in any of the others, he recovered under tonics and stimulants.

I have now, as briefly as possible, given to you the substance of Dr. Fitzmaurice's paper, together with the cases upon which he founds his experience of the efficacy of blisters in the treatment of the pneumonia of children. It may not be unprofitable to criticise them with brevity. You will observe that five out of the six cases narrated were sick for several days, and treated for anything else than pneumonia, and when this pneumonia was discovered, the application of a blister almost at once miraculously restored the respiratory murmer in the hepatized tissue. Does not the enthusiasm of the author, in the support of this wondrous power ascribed to blisters, carry him irresistibly into the realms of fancy? I must say that from my experience in the pneumonia of infants, I cannot help expressing grave doubts as to the correctness of the diagnosis in the particular cases recorded—and for these reasons: In the first place, all of Dr. F.'s cases were sick for several days before pneumonia was detected. This does not accord with the experience of authors upon the subject, or with my own observation. Pneumonia, I will not deny, may insidiously be superadded to a bronchial catarrh; but when it is, all the symptoms are therewith ushered in. In bronchial catarrh, it is almost impossible to mistake it for remittent fever, worms, or anything else but bronchitis. It is for the incessant hacking cough that the mother seeks our assistance; for as a rule, there is no fever present, and but for the cough, the signs of disease do not present themselves palpably. In pneumonia, on the contrary, the very first onset is fever, and that of such a burning, pungent character, as to be unmistakable; then the moan of pain, the hurried breathing, the suppressed cough, the dilating ala nasi, and the impossibility of a continued suction of the maternal breast, leaves, I think, no doubt as to the true character of the disease, even without auscultation.

My second reason for objecting to Dr. F.'s diagnosis is that in four of his cases he declares that dullness on percussion and tubular breathing existed on the right side in infants ranging from 6 to 18 months old. It is a well known fact that lobar pneumonia, such as was presumed to exist in Dr. F.'s cases, is almost unknown in infants of such tender age as he describes. Vogel acknowledges this fact, because he says: "With the exception of the metastopyemic form occurring in lying-in and foundling hospitals, lobar pneumonia is remarkably rare in the nursling—whereas lobular pneumonia is an extremely frequent affection." Lobular pneumonia being a catarrhal and not a croupous inflammation, we have no true hepatization, and as the probabilities are that these three cases of Dr. F.'s were, from the age of the patients, catarrhal, rather than croupal, the value of his treatment must be lessened.

I must not leave this subject without accounting for the dullness apparent to Dr. F., upon percussing the right side of his little patients, and to do so, will appeal again to Dr. Vogel. Speaking of the difference between the percussion sound of the left and right sides of an infant, he says: "The singular phenomenon just described, namely, the complete dullness posteriorly toward the right side, (explainable by the strong upward abdominal pressure of the liver), causes my confidence to be somewhat shaken in the histories of pneumonia in *small* children that we so frequently find in the text books and journals. I am convinced that attacks of bronchitis, which are in the first days of their existence attended with some fever and dyspnea, are regarded as cases of pneumonia, in consequence of observers not being aware, that the dullness which, under the circumstances described above, appeared on the right side, is a *normal physiological condition:*" and further adds "While in the adult we definitely know the space that is bounded by tracheal respiration, in children this is not the case. In healthy children we hear over the *entire back*, often over the entire thorax, a *loud expiration and a tubular inspiration*, so that, although this condition, when met with in an adult, would make us unhesitatingly affirm an extensive consolidation of the pulmonary tissues, yet it would not in children." "Thus the main conclusion, which in the adult we are able to form from bronchial respiration, is in children lost."

Waiving all objections that might be adduced (from the history of Dr. Fitzmaurice's cases) against his diagnosis, and presuming that they were genuine cases of acute pneumonia, or if not, that in any given case of pneumonia in children or infants Dr. Fitzmaurice would blister, and dress their riven skins with mercurial ointment, and French wadding, the question before us then is: Can we take such treatment as a guide in practice? or is such a course to be pursued in the best interests of our unresisting and already suffering little patients? Most unhesitatingly, Mr. President, I desire to enter my protest against this treatment, both upon scientific and humanitarian grounds. I ask, is it possible for a blister in 24 hours or 48 hours to cause the resolution of an infiltrated and hepatized lung, so that from bronchial breathing and the percussion dullness of solid lung, we can have the clear note and gentle murmur of restored respiration? Where such apparent good effects are noted with complacent satisfaction, and credited to the skill that suggested the blister; a little closer examination, a little more careful auscultation, a better grouping together of all the symptoms, would almost certainly have shown that resolution had already commenced, that destructive metamorphosis had ceased and that if an internal dose of quinia and ammonia had been administered, instead of an outward plaster of cantharides, the recovery would have been a little more speedy without àny of the attending risk. I must confess that I am not a believer in the power of blisters to remove exudation, or hasten absorption in the lung tissue of children; but am a firm believer in their irritating qualities, and their power to do harm. What says Graves of blisters, (not quoted by Dr. Fitzmaurice)? " If allowed to remain upon the skin long enough to produce vesication their effect is to depress the powers of the body, by acting as depletives in proportion to the amount of serum withdrawn from the vessels and so lost to the system. We might indeed as well bleed the patient to the same amount, as the serum of blisters contains almost as much albumen as the blood itself."

Here then is an objection to the application of blisters in young children which is insurmountable. Another effect which we must not fail to recollect is, that blisters when applied to children produce a greater degree of local inflammation than they do in adults, and the shock to the system is more intense; neither are we ever sure that their primary effect may not be followed by ulceration, tetanus, convulsions, gangrene or death. Dr. Fitzmaurice imagines that by keeping the air excluded, and the vesicles uncut, he will prevent any and all casualties from following a blistered surface. Medical history contradicts him. In my own practice, I can recall a case of infantile pneumonia where the earnest solicitation of too officious friends and relatives caused me to depart from my usual practice, and apply a blister to an infant's chest; the child was 18 months old, irritable, uneasy, and oppressed in respiration; the pain caused by this blister, the mother said, almost threw him into convulsions, and when I paid my morning visit my little patient was dying from shock; from that day to this, I have never blistered an infant designedly. Dr. Frey tells me that he can recall a case where he has no doubt, that the irritation of a blister applied to the chest caused the death of the child. Dr. W. C. Roberts, details two cases where children sank under the effects of blisters. Dr. Armstrong says: "I have a great dread of the application of blisters to children on account of the local and constitutional irritation they cause." Dr. Thompson in his materia medica states, that he has seen gangrene and death ensue in an infant from the application of a blister. Dr. North, in his observations on the convulsions of infants, says: "I have frequently seen severe convulsions brought on in consequence of the use of blisters." Dr. Botts writing from Florence, states, that he ordered two small blisters to be applied to the chest of a child suffering from bronchitis; deep ulceration, gangrene and death were the results. Dr. Dickenson says, "If only a simple irritation has been established—a proceeding from which we can recognize none but injurious effects—the nerves supply the route through which it travels. Counter irritation is therefore he thinks more likely to do harm than good, if the nerves are the route through which it acts; for if the irritation be excessive, fatal collapse may ensue, or if less extensive, inflammation, degeneration or vascular alterations of the nerve centre upon which the irritation falls, may result." When we recall to mind the tender cuticle of the infant, the predominance of the spinal over the cerebral system, the general activity of all the vital processes going on in childhood, we need not wonder that the reflex action set up by the shock of rapid vesication, should often exceed the power of the system to bear, and death ensue. Dr. Ross, I believe it is, who claims that a blister acts as a stimulant, and that this influence is excited through continuous and contiguous parenchyma. If that is correct how are we to limit its effects to the exact part to be acted upon, or in trying to combat a local engorgement of tissue, may we not set up a new centre of inflammation in contiguous structures. Dr. Anstie says, that the use of blisters in pneumonia in hope of controlling the inflammation is not only wrong but ludicrous (not for the patient). That being this eminent physician's opinion speaking of adults, is it not a crime to vesicate the nursling at its mother's breast? because we know, or ought to know, that when the local excitement is great, the application of a blister will augment that excitement tenfold, counteract any revulsive action which under other circumstances might possibly be hoped for, increase the internal inflammation and I believe in infants hasten dissolution.

Dr. Smith plainly declares that in infants, blisters are inadmissible. Trousseau is of opinion that when disease is at its height, blisters increase the febrile excitement, and that when it is in a more advanced stage, they are useless. I need not quote any further authorities upon this subject, to sustain my proposition that the blistering of infants or children under two years of age in pneumonia is never necessary; but on the contrary alike unscientific and dangerous, no matter how applied. For years I have abandoned the practice of blistering young children in diseases of the respiratory organs, being well satisfied with the efficacy of the jacket poultice of warm linseed meal; it soothes instead of excites, its grateful warmth and moisture gently woo the sluggish blood to renewed activity, and the infant, fevered and fretted, moaning with oppressed breath and constant pain, drops into a refreshing sleep, and as Chambers says, a "pleasurable calm." Under its influence we have no fear of undue action, no threatening air, without "healing on its wings," to exclude. No depleting serum to guard, lest its escape should bring destruction and perhaps death; no gangrenous sores to heal, or convulsions to combat. No, not these; we hoard the strength of our helpless little patients; with tenderness and care we avail ourselves of all the lessons that Dame Nature is so willing to teach; under her tuition we try to lead danger aside, and not violently disrupt its course, and thus we have, "many a time and oft" the proud satisfaction of restoring to the fond mother's arms, the babe she loved so well, snatched from the very jaws of death by nature's teachings, and by common sense.

I had to-night intended to make a few remarks upon another practice inculcated by Dr. Fitzmaurice, I mean the use of mercury in infants, a practice that he, and other men of his school would do well to abandon. But I find that time will not permit me to enter upon its discussion further than to say, that catarrhal, and croupous pneumonia, both in infants, children, and adults, will get well much quicker and much better without it; it can do no possible good; it is an oxidizer of tissue; a destroyer of vitality; an "irritant weapon" that may kill, while it never cures; a fossil relic of by-gone days, when scientific medicine was in its swaddling clothes, and as Dr. Anstie would say of blisters, it is the "refuge of the destitute, the one haven that seems open in stress of dirty weather." My task is ended, I now invite a free discusston of the views I have advanced, confident that they are in the main correct. If I have made assertions too boldly, ascribe it to my desire to see abolished practices so laden with error, suffering, and death.

On A New Form of Pessary.

By JAMES BLAKE, M. D. San Francisco.

In bringing before the profession a description of a new pessary, I do not propose to enter into any details as to the utility of these instruments in the treatment of uterine disease, as this is, I belive, now pretty generally recognized, although it is but a few years since gentlemen, whose opinions were considered as entitled to some credit, denounced them as worse than useless. This wholesale denunciation of a useful therapeutic agent, is but one instance among the many of that professional quackery by which reputations have been sought to be obtained by the publication of extreme views and startling novelties, on subjects on which subsequent experience has proved their authors to have been lamentably ignorant.

Undoubtedly, we frequently meet with cases in which pessaries have done harm, but in nine cases out of ten this is owing to sufficient care not having been used in selecting an instrument of the proper shape or size, or from its having been left in too long at first, before the tissues of the vagina had become accustomed to the pressure. Occasionally a case is met with, in which no pessary can be worn, the vagina being too sensitive, or its muscles being in a state of spasmodic contraction, as in vaginismus. Many of these cases can, however, by proper treatment, be brought to bear the instrument. When mischief results it is generally owing to inflammation, and even sometimes ulceration being caused by the pessary bearing too strongly on the anterior wall of the vagina.

Now, it is obvious that if instead of being formed of a rigid substance like gutta-percha, the instrument was made of elastic material, so that it would yield, the injurious effects of pressure, particularly of shock-pressure, would to a great extent be prevented. It was these considerations that induced me to endeavor to make a pessary which, whilst it had the form of Hodge's or Hewitt's retro- and ante-version pessaries, should be elastic. Having succeeded in making an instrument which I have been using for the last twelve months, and which I found more suitable than any I had before used, I believe its description and the manner of making it may be useful to the profession. The form I generally use is that of the Hodge or Hewitt pessary, the ends being cut out of sheet brass, and the sides formed of stout watch spring, that known as No. 1 being the most suitable. The necessary curves can be readily given to the spring sides, which are then to be soldered to the ends. The instrument is now to be varnished over well with india rubber varnish, so as to prevent the sheet india-rubber with which it is to be covered from coming in contact with the steel spring, which would otherwise be corroded by the sulphur in the rubber. Strips a little broader than the spring are to be cut from moderately thick sheet india-rubber, and these strips are to be attached to both surfaces of the instrument by varnish. Over this, strips of thin sheet india-rubber are to be wound, the first layer being drawn tight, so as to round somewhat the edges of the thicker strips. These strips should be about a quarter of an inch broad, and must be wound so as to overlap slightly. About three layers will be required, the last one not being drawn very tight, otherwise the india-rubber would be so thinned as to be dissolved by the varnish. They should be laid on as smoothly as possible; the ends should be well stuck down by varnish.

The varnish I use is made from india-rubber dissolved in chloroform, to which is added one-tenth of its bulk of a saturated solution of asphaltum in chloroform, which must be allowed to settle some time before using. About five coats of varnish will be required, but as it dries rapidly, these can be put on in the course of a few hours. The india rubber varnish by itself is acted on by the secretions of the vagina, but by mixing the asphaltum with it the pessary can be worn for months without becoming offensive.

The advantages of the pessary are that it is light, and can easily be made by any medical man, with the assistance of a watchmaker or a tinman, if he has not the instruments for cutting and soldering it himself. This last consideration is of importance, as a pessary, like a splint, has to be adapted to each case in order that the patient should derive from it all the benefit it can afford. Unfortunately there are no stereotyped forms for the vagina any more than for other organs, so that it is impossible in the two or three forms of pessary as usually made, that instruments can be found suited to all cases. The greatest advantage, however, of this pessary is, that it provides for the uterus an elastic support, and thus carries out the principle so elaborately displayed in the natural supports of this organ.

Clinical Lecture on Skin Diseases,

At the College Clinic, Medical Department University of the Pacific.

BY PROF. C. N. ELLINWOOD, January 23d, 1872.

LUPUS.

Gentlemen: Remembering our simple classification of the diseases of the skin, you recognize in this woman an organic disease, *i. e.*, a disease marked by a structural change. Inquiring into the history of the patient, and examining carefully the pathology and general appearances of these ulcerations now healed, we have no difficulty in determing this a strumous disease, of the variety known as lupus, belonging to one of the four classes of organic diseases of the skin defined by uniform causes.

In the outset of our course you will do well to familiarize yourselves with our classification of the skin diseases. Such familiarity will aid you in a methodical study of them, and will aid you too, in making a precise diagnosis in this difficult department of medicine.

All the organic diseases of the skin defined by uniform causes we arrange under four heads, viz:

1. Parasitic affections.
2. Syphilitic affections.
3. Strumous affections.
4. Eruptive fevers.

A careful study of lupus has developed the fact that it is a local manifestation of a constitutional disease—a strumous diathesis, and no matter what variety of lupus you have, it is in every instance dependent upon the same constitutional cause, viz: scrofula. In the older works on Dermatology you will find descriptions of many forms of lupus, words being chosen for their names which are supposed to describe the peculiar character of the local disease, such as lupus serpiginosus, l. non-exedens, l. exedens, l. devorans, etc. These terms indicate the degree of destruction of the tissues merely, and are of no great clinical importance, as it frequently happens, and I may say, generally within my observation, as in this case before you, that you see these several varieties in the different ulcerations in the same case and at the same time. We had here on the cheek a perfect type of the lupus *serpiginosus* as described by Neligan, the cicatrix now marked by a seam in its centre like that of a burn, while the side of the nose was destroyed by the ulceration consuming the integument, subcutaneous cellular tissue and cartilage, furnishing a very destructive type of the disease called lupus *devorans* or l. *vorax.*

We prefer to make but two varieties of the disease, lupus *vulgaris* and lupus *erythematosus.*

Lupus *vulgaris* is the common form and begins with the deposit of tubercular matter in the deep layers of the skin. Its seat is ordinarily the face, sometimes the scalp and very rarely on any other part of the body. Very soon the spot where this new growth occurs becomes a livid red, is raised and a thick crust forms on it, suppuration occurs beneath the crust, and its progress is indolent, undermining the tissues beneath while yet the scab remains. The cicatrix resulting from the healing of such ulcerations is characteristic and which you observe good examples of here.

The other variety, l. erythematosus has quite different habits and appearances which we shall speak of when we have a case to present before you.

Much more important than distinguishing the different varieties of lupus from each other is it to distinguish lupus from other diseases.

What you are most likely to confound it with, are cancerous and syphilitic ulcerations of the skin. The eating character of lupus has caused it to be called by some authors cancroid, but my advice to you is, to avoid those terms which imply a mixing of diseases of any kinds. A thing is either a cancer or it is not, and tne student should not get in the habit of using indefinite terms if he would make a definite diagnosis.

Lupus is distinguishable from cancer in this, that the latter is painful and progresses rapidly and inflames the contiguous lymphatic glands, while the reverse is true of lupus. It is distinguished from syphilis by its seat, the early history of the ulceration and the constitutional symptoms. Lupus appears very rarely in infancy, or for the first time in persons of advanced age; it is a disease of youth and of the prime of life.

This woman, now about fifty, was first attacked by the disease while yet in her prime. From scars upon her legs and the history which she gives of them we know she had scrofulous ulcers during childhood; that the strumous diathesis was manifested early in life; and that at about forty years well marked lupus appeared. It is now nearly a year since she applied to us for relief, and although she improved for the first two months very rapidly yet a relapse supervened, the disease attacked the pharynx, and during its ravages in the throat, she came very near dying from edema of the glottis. The consequence of this complication was a pulmonary inflammation and a profuse bronchorrhea, which debilitated the patient very much and caused extreme emaciation. The *embonpoint* she now presents is due to the persistent use of cod liver oil.

The treatment which this patient has received is that which you will find best adapted to lupus *vulgaris* generally, i. e, constitutionally, cod liver oil and the syrup of iodide of iron, and locally the application to the ulcers of a caustic to destroy the diseased tissue, and afterwards dressing with charpie, wet with one or the other of these solutions: ℞. Hydrarg. Bichlor. gr. vi, Glycerinæ ℥i, Aquæ puræ ℥iii. M. ft. sol.; or, ℞. Potassii Iodidi ʒi, Tinct. Iodinii ʒii, Aquæ puræ ℥x. M. ft. sol.

The caustic which we prefer is the acid nitrate of mercury, and it should be applied with a glass brush, thoroughly, around the edges of the ulcer, (the crust having been removed by forceps,) and if the ulcer is aggressive cauterize its entire surface. Apply the caustic every third day, and after a few hours, apply the dressing as above, and so continue until you have a granulating surface, when you will discontinue the caustic and continue the other dressing.

During the indolent progress of this case I have exhibited many of the drugs which are recommended in such cases, but my opinion is that the treatment which I have just indicated is the only one from which the patient has derived any benefit.

The complications of course received a special treatment, as e. g, the edema glottidis was combated by the inhalation of a tannin spray, but these form no essential part of the treatment of lupus.

The success attained in this case is very satisfactory, considering the extensive ravages which the disease has made and the fact that it is one of the most difficult of all the skin diseases to cure.

Transactions of the Sacramento Society for Medical Improvement.

Discussion on the Treatment of Pneumonia.

Sacramento, Dec. 27th, 1871.

Dr. Hatch, the President in the chair.

Present: Drs. Hatch, Tyrrell, Murphy, Trafton, Simmons, Oatman, Harkness, Montgomery and Nixon.

Dr. Tyrrell read the regular paper of the evening, "On Blisters in the Pneumonia of Infants."

The members being called on for their opinions:

Dr. Montgomery said that he had not heard all the paper read, but agreed with the author so far as he had heard it. Had used blisters in older cases, but never used mercurial ointment as a dressing, and did not think that mercurials should be used in infantile cases.

Dr. Oatman had not for many years applied blisters to infants, but had used them in cases of older persons, as he thought with good effect. He thought the use of mercury positively hurtful. Believed in the nourishing, tonic and stimulating system of treatment, but as the subject of Pneumonia had been thoroughly discussed by the Society some months ago, deemed it unncessary to enter into the discussion ot the subject again on this occasion.

Dr. SIMMONS did not remember that he had ever applied a blister to a child suffering from Pneumonia. Agreed with the author of the paper. The treatment of Pneumonia was so varied that no particular treatment could claim to be the best. Believed much in the expectant plan and thought that nature as a general rule could be relied on. Favored the supporting and tonic treatment.

Dr. TRAFTON agreed fully with the author of the paper. Did not remember that he had ever blistered a patient under five years of age. Believed in poulticing the chest and nourishing and sustaining. Differed radically with the treatment of infantile pneumonia as reported in the cases of Doctor Fitzmaurice.

Dr. MURPHY also agreed with the author of the paper and deprecated the treatment of Dr. Fitzmaurice. Would apply light mustard drafts to the chest, and sustain the system generally. Dr. Flint, in his lectures last winter, recommended the application of the Tinct. Iodine to the chest.

Dr. HARKNESS was much pleased with the paper. Was very skeptical now-a-days in regard to medical dogmas. Blistering should go to the shades with bleeding as a relic of a semi-barbaric age. So far as mercurials were concerned in such cases, considered their use as all wrong. Believed in nourishment, tonics and stimulants. A blister had never been applied to an infant with his consent.

Dr. HATCH said he fully concurred with the views of Dr. Tyrrell. Could not say that he never blistered a case of infantile pneumonia. Was not in favor however of the practice, but on the contrary was opposed to it, and had not blistered a case during the last twenty years. Believed that nature handled such cases very well, and if left alone would generally perform the cure.

Dr. NIXON said he had never blistered a case of infantile

pneumonia, and for many years had given no mercurials in such cases. Thought the society was very unanimous in their views in regard to the treatment of pneumonia. Could well remember the time when a medical man could hardly dare to deprecate the use of mercurials. They entered into nearly every prescription of regular practitioners of some twenty-five or thirty years ago, and to oppose their use was to run the risk of being suspected of irregularity in the profession. Happily that time is past. Dogmas of Medicine are not so powerful now as they once were, and medical men are all the better off for it. Thought Dr. Tyrrell's paper well timed and hoped that a copy of it might reach Dr. Fitzmaurice, whose treatment of infantile pneumonia has been so ably criticised here this evening.

A. B. NIXON, M. D.,
Secretary.

Tartrate of Iron and Potassa in Typhoid Fever.

To the Editors of Pacific Medical and Surgical Journal:

I desire to call your attention to the use of tartrate of iron and potassa in typhoid fever. Having made use of it for several years as a lotion in syphilis, the thought occured to me that it might be used with advantage to modify the ulceration of the intestines in typhoid. I have had several cases in the past year and have prescribed it in all, with the happiest results; the diarrhea, which is usually present in typhoid, being very slight indeed, and in some cases none at all. I have usually prescribed for an adult five grain doses in solution twice a day, increasing the dose in the second and third week to double that quantity.

I noticed a report in the San Francisco papers, that typhoid tever was prevalent, and perhaps the suggestion in this letter may be of service to the profession.

CHARLES H. GORDON, M.D.

MOKELUMNE, CAL. January 8, 1872.

REVIEWS AND NOTICES OF BOOKS.

A TREATISE ON HUMAN PHYSIOLOGY: Designed for the use of Students and Practitioners of medicine. By John C. Dalton, M. D., Professor of Physiology and Hygiene in the College of Physicians and Surgeons, New York; Member of the Academy of Medicine; of the N. Y. Pathological Society; etc. etc. Fifth Edition, revised and enlarged: with 284 Illustrations. Philadelphia: Henry C. Lea. 1871. Pp. 728. San Francisco: A. Roman & Co.

That this work has reached its fifth edition, and that it has been introduced as a text-book in a large number of the best medical schools in America, is ample proof of its great merit. The present edition has been carefully revised by the author, and brought up to the point of advance which has been attained in the rapid progress of physiological research in modern times.

TRANSACTIONS OF THE AMERICAN MEDICAL ASSOCIATION FOR THE YEAR 1871. VOL XXII.

This volume, to which reference was made in the last number of the *Journal*, is for sale by A. Roman & Co.

THE PHYSICIAN'S ANNUAL FOR 1872: A complete Calender and Manual for City and Country Practitioner. By S. W. Butler, M. D., Philadelphia.

Dr. Butler deserves great credit for the industry and enterprise exhibited in this Medical Directory; for such it is. It comprises a Monthly Calender, Hospital Calender of the principal cities of the United States, Chronological Record, a list of Medical Colleges and Institutions, a complete list of Medical Societies in the United States, with form of constitution for Medical Societies, Priced catalogues of Medical Books, Surgical Instruments, etc., besides much other information, not enumerated here, of interest and importance to Physicians. Price 50 cents.

AN INTRODUCTION TO PATHOLOGY AND MORBID ANATOMY. By T. Henry Green, M. D., London; Member Royal College of Physicians; Lecturer on Pathology and Morbid Anatomy at Charing Cross Hospital Medical School, etc. Illustrated by numerous engravings on wood. Philadelphia: Henry C. Lea, 1871. Pp. 260. San Francisco: A. Roman & Co.

Such a work as the above was much needed for the use of Students, the works of Paget, Virchow, and Rokitanski being too elaborate and extensive for profitable use during the ordinary course of medical instruction in our Schools. It is strictly elementary, being designed to give a brief account of the more important morbid processes, in accordance with modern discoveries and doctrines. The author adopts the theory of Beale and others, which regards the cell, in the first instance, to be composed essentially of sarcode or *protoplasm*, about which a membrane or cell wall is gradually formed by retrogressive change.

The Medical Jurisprudence of Insanity: By J. H. Balfour Browne, Esq., of the Middle Temple, Barrister-at-law. London: J. and A. Churchill. San Francisco: Sumner Whitney & Co., Law Publishers. 1871. Pp. 345.

A hurried glance over the pages of this volume leaves us with a high appreciation of its merits. The writer has a philosophic mind and is a deep and accurate thinker. Besides, he brings to his subject illustrations from far and near derived from extensive reading. At the present time, when the subject of medical jurisprudence with especial relation to Insanity has grown to great magnitude, no medical man should venture to stand before a Court as a witness in a case involving the question, without having made it a study; and we know of no treatise so well adapted to that purpose as the one before us.

EDITORIAL.

Climate and Disease.

Individuals who attribute disease to the sensible changes or conditions of climate, will find themselves not a little baffled in attempting to connect the supposed cause and effect during the present winter, in regard to California. Until the middle of December the weather was remarkably dry, with cool north breezes though without severe frost. After the 17th of December the opposite condition of dampness and rain endured for three weeks, with the wind exactly in the opposite quarter. Then again came clear and dry weather. But through these vicissitudes a remarkably uniform and undisturbed condition of the public health was maintained, with the mortality at the minimum point. The old saw—"A green Christmas makes a fat church yard"—was never intended for California. We have had emphatically a green Christmas. The minimum temperature of the winter was 38°, viz: on the mornings of Nov. 30 and Dec. 1. Very few of the most tender plants have been injured by frost in the gardens of San Francisco, and in the ocean climate. Tomato plants, which are among the most sensitive of all vegetables to the action of frost, remain uninjured. In the interior valleys the cold, as usual, has been greater, forming ice, however, only on a few mornings. In the first week of January we collected for a bouquet in a garden at Alameda, flowers of twenty-three different species. Since that time the warm sunshine has brought forth other species.

Passing eastward we find the climate of the interior of the continent quite as extraordinary, but on the extreme of cold, the demonstration of which, as affecting travel on the great rail-road, will not be soon forgotten. On the Atlantic slope also the winter has been rugged, with severe cold at times. In Europe too, it has been exceptionally cold, the winter in Paris having been almost Arctic. In fact, for several years past, climatic disturbances have prevailed to an unusual extent both in Europe and America. That the condition of the general health and the prevalence of epidemics, bear some relations to such climatic aberrations, we can not doubt. But the difficulty is in tracing that relation. It is only by patient and laborious accumulation of exact statistics that the problem can be solved. And here let us remark that this whole question ought to enter much more than it does into the studies of medical men. Every physician should train himself as an observer of meteorological phenomena. The thermometer, the hygrometer, the currents of wind and cloud, should be as familiar to him as the stethescope, the microscope and the speculum. Only in this way can the *medical philosopher* come into being.

The Winter in Paris.

The cold, icy weather of the present winter, has given rise to much bodily injury from falls. Early in January it was computed that at least one thousand persons had required surgical aid on this account, sixty of whom had broken a leg or an arm. Two were known to have died from such injuries.

Collusion between Physicians and Apothecaries.

There may be nothing dishonest or even improper in a treaty of alliance between a practitioner and a druggist, when patients are not made the victims, and when the interchange of good offices is fairly conducted. But when artifice is resorted to, or patients incommoded or taxed, the treaty becomes offensive and censurable. No honorable physician will resort to such tricks to turn a penny. For instance, to write in cypher, which can only be read by an initiated and favored apothecary; or to prescribe certain mixtures the formulas for which are in select hands. We have known a physician whose chirography was so intentionally illegible that but one apothecary could decypher it. And we have known another who had some half dozen favorite prescriptions, mixtures, pills and so forth, to which he gave certain unofficinal names, and which his patients were informed could only be prepared by a certain apothecary. This practice seems to be carried on in some eastern cities. A writer in the Philadelphia Journal of Pharmacy gives two formulas which are often prescribed in New York, and which can be prepared only at certain places. The first is *mistura rhei et sodæ,* of which the following is the formula: ℞. pulv. rhei, sodæ bi-carb., aa ʒij. aquæ menth. pip., ℥iv. M. A table spoonful occasionally, in certain gastric disorders with deficient peristaltic action.

The other is a preparation resembling the "neutral mixture," and often prescribed by German physicians under the name of *potio riveri.* ℞. potass. carb. depur., ʒj;, Acidi citrici, gr. lij, aquæ ℥ij. M. To be taken at a draught.

A New Volume on Pulmonary Consumption.

C. J. B. Williams, M. D., F. R. S., who is well known in the literature of medicine as an able writer on phthisis and other subjects, has just given to the British public a treatise on the Nature, Varieties and Treatment of Pulmonary Consumption, with an Analysis of one thousand cases. A notice of the work in the *Medical Press and Circular,* serves to confirm the impression of its value which the name of the author would create, and to awaken the hope that an American edition will be issued by some of our enterprising eastern publishers.

Medical Experts—Reform Needed.

In the trial of the German physician Schœppe, in Pensylvania, for the murder of a woman, the conviction depended mainly on the testimony of a chemical expert, touching the contents of the stomach of the deceased. In the more recent trial of Mrs. Wharton in Baltimore, charged with the same crime, the same expert being enlisted on the side of the prosecution, his analysis would again have led to conviction, and was on the point of doing so, when, happily for the accused woman, a searching investigation instituted by other chemists proved him incompetent, or at least threw so much doubt on his testimony as to lead to her acquittal. When Schœppe was found guilty, many intelligent persons questioned the chemical testimony on which he was condemned, and it was only through their earnest intercession that his execution has been delayed. Doubtlessly his life will be spared, and even he may be pardoned.

These facts show the propriety of adopting some plan of securing the evidence of experts who are truly competent, and making them officers of the State, and not instruments of the parties litigant. If such fatal errors may occur within the range of a fixed science, how much greater is the risk when the question of insanity is involved, and when the life of the accused rests on the opinion of the witness, rather than on fact? At present, the two parties in a trial both bring their experts to contradict each other. In matters of this kind, circumstances alien to the merits of the question may bias the judgment of honest and capable men and lead to opposite opinions. And when the field is open to the choice of incapable and dishonest "experts," the results are inevitably obstruction of justice, confusion of the jury, and discredit and dishonor to the profession which supplies the so-called experts.

The remedy is obvious. In all important trials, experts should be officers of the State or of the Court, either holding their place for stated terms, as certain chemical experts already do, or appointed *pro re rata*, by the Court. By such means the services of competent men could be procured. As it now is, the necessity of hanging about a court-room hour by hour and day by day, and without compensation, deters many physicians of the best qualified class from serving as witnesses, and leaves one learned profession to be represented in the presence of another and before the public, by the most unlearned of its members. These remarks should derive additional weight from the unusual and increasing number of trials involving the plea of insanity, and in which are involved property of great value, and life, of greater value than property.

Bloodletting in Puerperal Convulsions.

It is a great point in modern practice to descant on the empirical use of the lancet in former days, whilst there is quite as much empiricism in the unqualified disuse of it by modern extremists. In a discussion in the N. Y. Pathological Society (*Medical Record*, January 2.) a member condemned the practice in puerperal convulsions, saying "he believed in chloroform in all cases; it was the first thing he thought of, and he had never found it to disappoint him." Dr. Small referred to the suffused face, bounding pulse and pain inthe head, with incipient paralysis, as denoting a condition not to be permanently relieved by chloroform, but requiring loss of blood. Dr. Briddon had seen a large number of cases of puerperal convulsions, and whenever he had treated them by venesection he had been uniformly successful. His point was to use the remedy early. In some cases when chloroform had been used first, with the effect of arresting the convulsions for a short time, venesection gave permanent relief, speedily restoring consciousness.

A Medical Witness Answers Back.

In the famous Wharton trial which lately took place in Baltimore, the prosecuting attorney, finding that the testimony of Dr. Warren, a witness on behalf of Mrs. Wharton, did not suit his purposes, resorted to the common expedient of badgering the witness, with the following result.

Attorney.—A doctor ought to be able to give an opinion of a disease without making mistakes.

Doctor.—They make as few mistakes as lawyers.

Attorney.—But doctor's mistakes are buried six feet under ground; a lawyer's are not.

Doctor.—No; they are sometimes hung up six feet above ground.

Fee Bill Adopted by the San Francisco Medical Society, and the Society of German Physicians. December 26th, 1871.

For one ordinary Visit...........................	$2 50 to $ 5 00
For one Night Visit, (from 10 P.M. to 7 A. M)...	5 00 to 10 00
For first Consultation..............................	10 00
For each following Consultation.................	5 00

N. B.—Fees for Consultation will be charged by the attending as well as by the consulting Physician.

For Office Advice in ordinary cases.............	2 00 to 5 00
For Special Examinations........................	3 00 to 10 00
For ordinary Obstetrical cases	25 00 to 50 00

For Instrumental and extraordinary cases not less than double fees.

For Vaccination......................................	2 00 to 5 00

Surgical treatment according to custom and agreement.

This Fee Bill is not intended to apply to the practice of specialists or in case of extraordinary services.

The following physicians have agreed to adhere to the foregoing prices:

A. Andrei, A. Aronstein, H. S. Baldwin, A. Barkan, C. M. Bates, Chas. Blach, W. T. Bradbury, A. C. Buffum, C. Burrell, J. Cairns, P. Chamberlin, C. P. Chesley, D. Cohn, R. B. Cole, B. D. Dean, C. T. Deane, T. A. Ehrenburg, K. Favor, J. W. Forrest, W. T. Garwood, W. A. Grover, H. Gibbons, H. Gibbons, Jr., J. Haine, S. R. Harris, J. W. Harville, M. Heinimann, C. B. Holbrook, P. H. Humphrey, W. H. Johnson, H. H. Lehmkuhl, G. H. Malech, A. T. McClure, J. F. Morse, V. Newmark, A. A. O'Neil, C. Precht, J. R. Prevost, V. Polastri, J. Regensburger, J. R. Rice, I. Rivas, A. Rottanzi, Chas. Rowell, J. Scott, W. F. Smith, A. G. Soule, E. Trenkle, C. G. Toland, H. H. Toland, W. L. Twichell, J. D. Whitney, J. P. Whitney, A. Wilhelm, W. G. Wayman.

The Chicago Medical Journals.

Our medical exchanges come from Chicago as of yore, the only difference that we can observe in them since the fire, being an increased display of talent and industry. If our sister city is to be judged by her medical journalism, the great conflagration will very soon be entirely lost in a "renewal of life."

San Francisco Medical Society, Officers for 1872.

This society which has recently had considerable accession to its membership, and in which the interest is continually increasing, elected the following officers at its annual meeting in January.

President, J. F. Morse; First Vice-President, W. T. Bradbury; Second Vice-President, P. Chamberlin; Recording Secretary, Henry Gibbons, Jr.; Corresponding Secretary, W. A. Grover; Treasurer, A. G. Soule; Librarian, J. D. Whitney.

Committee on Admissions—C. B. Holbrook, W. H. Johnson, C. Blach, C. T. Deane, J. Haine.

Committee on Ethics—J. P. Whitney, J. Regensberger, C. Burrell, W. T. Garwood, H. Gibbons.

Committee on Finance—K. Favor, H. S. Baldwin, B. D. Dean.

Committee on Publication—H. Gibbons, Jr., J. R. Prevost, A. G. Soule.

Executive Committee—R. B. Cole, A. C. Buffum, C. M. Bates.

The Social Evil in the Legislature.

We see it stated that a bill is to be introduced, or has been introduced, in the Legislature, to license and regulate prostitution in San Francisco. It is incredible, that when the municipal body representing the city refuse to sanction the proceeding, and when the citizens make no demand for it, the State Legislature will attempt to impose it. It is enough to attempt the introduction of European laws and customs, adverse to the usages and sentiments of the American people, without at the same time invoking the arbitrary authority of the kingly governments of the old world, and ignoring and defying the popular sentiment by enacting a law unasked for by the many and dictated by a few individuals.

The San Francisco Fee Bill.

Physicians desiring a supply of blank bills with the fee-bill attached, as adopted by the Medical Societies of San Francisco, are requested to leave their orders with the Secretary of the County Medical Society, 26 Montgomery street.

Back Numbers of the Journal.

The demand for back numbers has completely exhausted our stock, and we regret our inability to supply even a single set, beyond the last few months.

Thanks to Subscribers.—Articles Crowded Out.

Our thanks are due to the many subscribers who have responded with alacrity to our application for the *quid pro quo*. Their words of cheer and encouragement are particularly grateful to us.

Though the present number of the JOURNAL is somewhat enlarged, yet we have been under the necessity of laying over several communicated articles, besides a variety of selected matter. The following are the principal articles so deferred:

Abdominal Section.—Removal of Cancerous Tumors. By Dr. Reynolds, Yountville, California.

Traumatic Tetanus successfully treated by Calabar Bean and Chloral Hydrate, by Dr. Cushing.

Proceedings and Discussions of the San Francisco Medical Society.

Address to the San Francisco Medical Society. By Dr. Dean, retiring President.

Address to the Alameda Medical Society. By Dr. Cushing, President.

Clinical Lectures at the County Hospital.

Enlargement of the Journal.

With the next volume, which will commence with June, we shall add to the size of the JOURNAL, but to what extent we are not yet prepared to say. Our friends and readers may rest assured that, while we shall not incur the risk of breaking down by costly expansion, we shall give them as much reading as the income of the JOURNAL will warrant.

Report of State Board of Health.

The biennial report of the State Board of Health, made to the Legislature by Dr. Logan, Secretary and Executive officer of the Board, has received favorable notice very generally from the periodical press. It contains a large amount of material of great value for future reference.

GENERAL SUMMARY.

The Glue Bandage for Fractures.

Dr. George Ross, in the *Canada Med. Journal* for Dec. 1871, describes the glue bandage as successfully employed in the Montreal General Hospital. A good article of glue is dissolved in the usual way and a fifth part alcohol added to promote evaporation. The limb is swathed in thin wadding, and a roller of soft muslin applied; the proper adjustment of the fracture having been made, of course. Then a coating of glue is applied by a brush or the hand. A second and a third roller are applied and covered with glue in the same manner. The limb is then swung so that the glue shall dry. In a few hours the outer layers are dry enough to admit of the limb being moved from the swing, if desirable, but forty-eight hours, or longer, is required for thorough drying. "After the lapse of this time," writes Dr. Ross, "the leg is found to be encased in a perfectly-fitting boot, more solid than the thickest sole-leather, and can be moved in any direction without pain. In none of the cases has there been any complaint of pain from the swelling that we might expect to find occur shortly after a fracture has been sustained. On the contrary, the patients have all expressed themselves as feeling extremely comfortable. As soon then as the bandage has completely consolidated, it becomes necessary to split it down the front from one end to the other. Owing to the extreme hardness of the splint, this is a matter of some difficulty, except in the event of one's possessing a pair of powerful properly constructed bandage-pliers; failing this, however, the simplest plan is to slip a very thin piece of wood beneath it, and then cut on this with a sharp, strong knife. Having thus split the bandage from end to end, a number of holes are bored on either side with a brad-awl, and a long tape being passed alternately through these, it is laced up like a lady's corset. The apparatus is then entirely complete, and may remain without being touched until union is perfect. The above description might lead some to suppose that the process was long and tedious, and in consequence objectionable, but our small experience with it in this hospital is such as to make us believe that by reason of its increased comfort to the patient, and of the facts that patients can sooner get up with safety with this than any other form of splint, and that it will never get out of order, and consequently never require re-adjustment, the advantages secured by its employment greatly counterbalance any slight trouble that is necessary to take to ensure its proper application at first.

"At this hospital, the above described method has been put into practice in several cases of simple and compound fracture of the leg, and in all with most satisfactory results. In the majority of cases, the patients were permitted to get up on crutches on the third day from the receipt of the accident. In two, it was thought advisable to make use of a box splint for a few days previous to the application of the bandage on account of considerable swelling and rapid vesication."

Medicinal Use of Alcohol.

An important document has been lately published in England, with the signatures of several hundred of the most distinguished medical gentlemen, with the design of discountenancing the too common prescription of alcohol by physicians, and their habitual dietetic use. We subjoin the "declaration" as found in the *Medical Press and Circular*. The list of signers is headed by Dr. Burrows, President of the Royal College of Physicians and Physician Extraordinary to the Queen. We notice also the familiar names of Paget, Watson, Fergusson, Sieveking, Chambers, Wells, Parkes, Aitken, Barclay, Barnes, Fox, Guy, Greenhalgh, Murchison, Radcliffe, Salter, Williams, Winslow, in fact nearly all the names which illuminate the pages of medical science.

"As it is believed that the inconsiderate prescription of large quantities of alcoholic liquids by medical men for their patients has given rise, in many instances, to the formation of intemperate habits, the undersigned, while unable to abandon the use of alcohol in the treatment of certain cases of disease, are yet of opinion that no medical practitioner should prescribe it without a sense of grave responsibility. They believe that alcohol, in whatever form, should be prescribed with as much care as any powerful drug, and that the directions for its use should be so framed as not to be interpreted as a sanction for the continuance of its use when the occasion is past.

"They are also of opinion that many people immensely exaggerate the value of alcohol as an article of diet, and since no class of men see so much of its ill effects, and possess such power to restrain its abuse, as members of their own profession, they hold that every medical practitioner is bound to exert his utmost influence to inculcate habits of great moderation in the use of alcoholic liquids.

"Being also firmly convinced that the great amount of drinking of alcoholic liquors among the working classes of this country is one of the greatest evils of the day, destroying—more than anything else—the health, happiness, and welfare of those classes, and neutralizing, to a large extent, the great industrial prosperity which Providence has placed within the reach of this nation, the undersigned would gladly support any wise legislation which would tend to restrict, within proper limits, the use of alcoholic beverages, and gradually introduce habits of temperance."

Pills of Sulph. Iron; Creasote; Carbolic Acid.

The *American Journal of Pharmacy* for January, 1872, selects from a French journal the following formulas:

Pills of Sulph. Iron and Carb. Potass.—Take of sulph. iron and carb. potass. each 100 grs.; mix well and add powdered white sugar, 12 grs. Heat the mixture in an iron mortar, with constant trituration, until a sufficient amount of water of crystallization is expelled and a convenient pill mass obtained. These pills keep well, but are slightly hygrometric.

Pills of Creasote.—R. Creasoti, gtt. vj.; Micæ panis, gr. xviij.; Lycopodii, gr. ij.; Mucil. tragac. q. s.—to make twelve pills, each containing half a drop of creasote.

Pills of Carbolic Acid.—℞. Acidi Carbolici, gtt. vj.; Saponis, gr. xviij.; Lycopodii, gr. ij.; Pulv. tragacanth. q. s.—to make twelve pills.

Iodine for Wens of the Scalp.

Dr. Perkins, in the *Georgia Medical Companion*, recommends injecting the encysted tumors which are common on the scalp, with tinct. iodine, by means of the hypodermic syringe. As much of the tincture as possible is thrown into the centre of the tumor, which shrinks away from the surrounding parts in a few days, and may be easily removed.

Vital Statistics of Australia.

The *Australian Medical Journal* reports the death-rate at Victoria as only 17 in 1000. The mortality from phthisis in Melbourne is but little more than half that of the cities of England and America. In a period of 17 years prior to June 1870, sixty of every one hundred interments in Melbourne were of children under ten years.

New Excipient for Pills.

Soluble cream of tartar, made by dissolving bi-tartrate of potash in a solution of borax and evaporating to the consistence of mucilage, (*Am. Jour. of Pharmacy*, Jan. 1872,) is an excellent excipient for making pills of sulphur, chloral hydrate, Dover's powder, nitrate of potassa, chlorate of potassa, etc. A very small quantity of powdered tragacanth is added. The following is the formula for the chloral-hydrate pills: R. Hydrat. chloralis, ʒj.; Mucil. bi-tart. potassæ, gtt. ij.; Pulv. tragac. gr. ij.; M. Ft. pil. xij. Each of these pills contains five grains of chloral. They are to be kept in a bottle, with lycopodium. They preserve their form perfectly and grow harder, while minute crystals of chloral may be seen formed on the surface.

Puncture of Hernial Sac.

Attention has lately been attracted to a method of treating strangulated hernia by puncturing the sac with a fine needle and evacuating a portion of the contents, after which reduction is easily accomplished. There is no escape of air or liquid into the abdomen, and the puncture of the intestine is found to close immediately. The same treatment is habitually resorted to by some practitioners in abdominal tympanites, and also in distension of the bladder from urine when the catheter cannot be passed. A discussion on the subject which took place in the French academy, is minuted in the *Cincinnati Clinic*, for Jan. 6, 1872.

Thirty-two Doctors in one Family.

An English reformer thinks the royal family receive more than their share of medical service. His count runs as follows: "There are three Physicians in Ordinary, three Physicians Extraordinary, one Sergeant Surgeon Extraordinary, two Sergeant Surgeons, three Surgeons Extraordinary, one Physician of the Household, one Surgeon of the Household, one Surgeon Apothecary, two Chemists of the Establishment in Ordinary, one Surgeon Oculist, one Surgeon Dentist, one Dentist in Ordinary, and one other Physician; while the Prince of Wales has for his special benefit, three Honorary Physicians, two Physicians in Ordinary, two Surgeons in Ordinary, one Surgeon Extraordinary, one Chemist in Ordinary, or more—making thirty-two doctors in one family."

Mortality of Phthisis.

In a lecture on this subject by M. Constantine Paul, published recently in the *Gazette des Hopitaux*, he said that the disease represents ten per cent. of the whole mortality in France. At Paris the number rises to 13.4 per cent. ; at Genoa it is 9.7 per cent. ; Naples 8; Rome, 6; Turin, 9; Venice, 8 per cent. To the northward, on the contrary, it increases. In Belgium it is 16 per cent., and in Limburg 21 per cent. In England it appears to be less mortal, the mean mortality being 12 per cent. There is not in England the same difference between town and country as in France. In Germany, the mortality is still greater. From 1839 to 1849, it was at Berlin 17.5 per cent. ; at Frankfort, 25.6, at Hamburg, 21.7, at Vienna, 20 per cent. In certain localities in America it reaches 28 per cent.—*London Press and Circular.*

Traumatic Aneurism from Dislocated Shoulder.

A man fell while drunk and dislocated his shoulder. His fellow workmen twisted it considerably in the attempt to reduce it. He was taken to the Charity Hospital (N. Y.,) and an abscess, as was supposed, was opened, which proved to be an aneurism. He nearly bled to death, but the joint was opened, the bones replaced, a carious portion removed, and the posterior circumflex artery tied. He made a good recovery. The *N. Y. Medical Record*, of January 2, reports the case in full.

Bromide of Potassium in Uremic Convulsions.

Dr. Edwin A. Carpenter, (*Chicago Med. Examiner*,) describes a case of convulsions in a man suffering from general dropsy with hydrothorax, with albuminous urine. Various means were resorted to in vain, including the inhalation of eight ounces of chloroform. Forty grains bromide of potassium was given, and in five hours a copious flow of urine took place. The bromide was repeated several times in smaller doses. No return of convulsion took place after the first dose, and the patient recovered rapidly.

Treatment of Epilepsy.

Brown Sequard employs the following in Epilepsy: ℞. Iod. potassii, ℨj; Bi-carb. potassae, ℈ij; Bromid. potassii, ℨij; Bromidi ammonii, ℨiiss; Infus. columbæ, ℥vj: A tea spoonful before each meal, and three tea spoonfuls at bed time, in water. He uses arsenic to prevent "bromism," [qu ? brominism] combining it in the prescription. Iron, strychnia, and the hypo-phosphites are also administered, and a nutritious diet with abundant outdoor exercise required.

STATE BOARD OF HEALTH.

Abstract from the Reports of Deaths and their Causes in the following cities and towns in California, during December, 1871:

CITIES AND TOWNS.	Total No. Deaths.	PREVALENT DISEASES. Consumption.	Other diseases of Lungs.	Dis. Stomach and Bowels.	Diphtheria	Scarlatina	Typho-malarial Fevers.	AUTHORITIES.
San Francisco......	245	38	22	10	1	0	17	S. F. B'd of Health
Sacramento	24	2	2	0	0	2	1	Sac. B'd of Health
Petaluma	2	0	0	0	0	0	0	Dr. G. W. Graves.
Dixon	1	0	0	0	0	0	0	Dr. R. H. Plummer
Santa Clara.........	6	2	1	1	0	0	2	Dr. H. H. Warburton
Stockton	10	3	2	1	0	1	0	Stockton Bd Health
Marysville..........	9	3	1	0	0	0	1	Dr. C. E. Stone.
Placerville..........	1	0	0	0	0	0	0	Dr. E. A. Kunkler.
Auburn...............	7	2	0	2	0	0	0	Dr. A. S. Du Bois.
San Diego County..	10	2	0	0	0	0	0	Dr. T. C. Stockton.
San Luis Obispo...	...	...	...	...	...	...	...	Dr. W. W. Hays.
Oroville	7	0	5	0	0	0	0	Dr. J. M. Vance.
Woodland...........	1	1	0	0	0	0	0	Dr. A. B. Mehring.
Oakland	4	1	1	0	0	0	0	Dr. T. H. Pinkerton
Los Angeles........	31	5	3	1	0	0	0	Dr. H. S. Orme.
Truckee	2	1	0	0	0	0	0	Dr. Wm. Curless.
St. Helena	1	1	0	0	0	0	0	Dr. J. S. Adams.
Napa City...........	3	1	0	0	0	0	0	Dr. M. B. Pond.
Cacheville	0	0	0	0	0	0	0	Dr. E. L. Parramore
Siskiyou.............	0	0	0	0	0	0	0	Dr. T. T. Cabanis.
Watsonville	...	...	...	...	...	...	...	Dr. C. E. Cleveland
Folsom	0	0	0	0	0	0	0	Dr. L. McGuire.
Bridgeport Town'p	...	...	...	...	...	...	...	Dr. J. L. Asay.
Sut'r C'k & Amador	3	1	0	1	0	0	0	Dr. H. M. Fiske.
Monterey.............	...	...	...	...	...	...	...	Dr. C. A. Canfield.
Santa Cruz..........	4	0	0	0	0	0	0	Dr. C. L. Anderson
Vallejo	...	...	...	...	...	...	...	Dr. J. M. Brown.
Suisun & Fairfield.	0	0	0	0	0	0	0	Dr. S. D. Campbell
Colusa	2	1	0	0	0	0	1	Dr. Luke Robinson
Trinity County......	3	0	0	0	0	1	0	Dr. J. C. Montague
Santa Barbara......	11	2	0	3	0	0	1	Dr. C. B. Bates.
Redwood City	1	1	0	0	0	0	0	Dr. Kirkpatrick.
Totals..............	388	65	37	19	1	4	23	

Abstract from Reports of Births.

CITIES AND TOWNS.	Total Births.	Male.	Female.	Still-born.	Live-born.	AUTHORITIES.
San Francisco..	**114**	**59**	**55**	**23**	**91**	**S. F. Board of Health.**
Sacramento.. ...	**36**	**17**	**19**	**3**	**33**	**Sac. Board of Health.**
All other places	**237**	**129**	**108**	**14**	**223**	**Various sources.**
Total..........	**387**	**205**	**182**	**40**	**347**	

Remarks.—With the exception of Los Angeles, where the mortality has for some time been steadily on the increase, although no special cause for this has been recognized, our table continues to exhibit a most favorable condition of the public health.

It is with regret however, that we now have to announce that small-pox has made its appearance in this State. The facts of the case, which were investigated a short time since, as far as we were able, before public notice was issued from our office, are these. On the 21st December last, Dr. Caldwell, of Marysville, was called to visit professionally, a carpenter in the employ of the Oregon Railroad, who had just arrived from Tehama. On being informed that his disease was small-pox, the patient then stated that a woman with her two children, accompanied by a young man, had recently arrived at Tehama from the East, by rail, and were all ill with the same disease, but that be had had no direct communication with them. Dr. Stone, of the State Board of Health, on being called in consultation, pronounced the case of this carpenter to be confluent small pox, and his unfavorable prognosis was confirmed on the 2nd January, by the death of the patient. Subsequently the attending physician Dr. Caldwell and the nurse were both attacked with the same disease. In the former case the disease assumed the discreet form, and in the latter presented the varioloid variety. Of the patients alluded to, at Tehama, the woman and young man, as I am informed by Dr. Stone, have both died, but the children have recovered. Besides these, there have appeared other cases in Rocklin, and near Antelope, and in Washington opposite Sacramento. In the latter instance, we are informed by the attending physician that the disease has assumed the varioloid form.

Although every precaution has been adopted to prevent the further spread of the infection from these various focal points, yet it is barely possible that we can escape a severe visitation of this loathsome malady. Had the bill, with its sanitary provisions, which has been for some time pending in our Legislature, been passed promptly in accordance with our advice, the disease experience teaches us to dread so much, would never have got the foot-hold it now has in our midst. The topography of California is such, that quarantine regulations, if they are ever to be efficient in preventing contagious diseases, can here be carried out to perfection. We are as completely isolated by land as we are by sea. There is but one gate through which travel enters from beyond our mountain barriers. Therefore quarantine regulations on the line of the railroad among the mountains may be enforced as efficiently as in our one port San Francisco, and thus aid in preventing the introduction of contagious maladies. Connected with quarantine should be health officers, co-operative with the State Board of Health, in every part of the State, to whom ample powers should be given to enforce the laws of hygiene; provided that all regulations should be such as would interfere with commerce and travel only so far as necessary to preserve the public health. Let our Legislators grant these restricted powers to our Boards of Health, and there will be no danger of a repetition of the dreadful scenes caused by the introduction of the Asiatic cholera in 1850, and of the small-pox in 1868.

THOMAS M. LOGAN, M.D.,
Permanent Secretary State Board of Health.

Mortality in San Francisco during December, 1871.

BY H. GIBBONS JR., M. D.

CAUSES OF DEATH.

Abscess	3	Diseases of Heart	8	Liver Disease	1
Do. of Lungs	1	Dropsy	6	Meningitis	9
Alcoholism	3	Drowning	5	Nephritis	1
Angina	1	Dysentery	9	Œdema Glottidis	1
Do. Pectoris	1	Emphysema	1	Old Age	4
Aneurism of Aorta	4	Enteritis	3	Opium Eating	2
Do.	1	Erysipelas	1	Paralysis	2
Apoplexy	4	Epilepsy	1	Peritonitis	4
Atrophia	6	Fever, Typhoid	17	Phthisis	38
Brain, Disease of	1	Fractures	1	Pleuritis	1
Bright's Disease	2	Gangrene	1	Pneumonitis	8
Bronchitis	3	Gastritis	4	Premature Birth	3
Cancer	2	Gastro-Enteritis	1	Pyemia	3
Carbuncle	1	Hemorrhage, Bowels	1	Suffocation	1
Cholera Infantum	2	Hematemesis	1	Suicide	4
Congestion of Brain	4	Hemiplegia	1	Syphilis	2
Do of Lungs	8	Hepatitis	3	Tabes Mesenterica	1
Convulsions	6	Hemoptysis	2	Unknown	20
Croup	1	Hydrocephalus	2	Whooping Cough	2
Cyanosis	1	Hydrothorax	1		
Cystitis	2	Hip-joint disease	1	TOTAL	245
Debility, General	5	Injuries, unspecified	2	Still-births	23
Diarrhea	3	Inanition	4		
Diphtheria	1	Jaundice	1		

AGES.

Under 1 year	45	From 15 to 20 years	7	From 60 to 70 years	8
From 1 to 2 years	15	From 20 to 30 years	37	From 70 to 80 years	7
From 2 to 5 years	9	From 30 to 40 years	35	From 80 to 90 years	2
From 5 to 10 years	7	From 40 to 50 years	46		
From 10 to 15 years	7	From 50 to 60 years	20		

Sex:—Male, 161; Female, 84.

Color:—White, 218; Copper, 25; Black, 2.

NATIVITIES.

California	81	Wales	1	Hungary	1
Other parts of U. S.	34	France	10	Portugal	3
British-Amer'n Prov.	2	Germany	23	Italy	1
Mexico	5	Austria	1	China	24
England	9	Sweden	1	West Indies	1
Ireland	36	Spain	1	Australia	3
Scotland	6	Cape de Verde Isles	1	Unknown	1

RECAPITULATION.

Died in City Wards	185	Small-Pox Hospital	1
City and County Hospital	19	Casualties	9
U. S. Marine Hospital	2	Suicides	4
French Hospital	4	Alms House	4
German Hospital	3	Mt. St. Joseph's Infirmary	2
St. Mary's Hospital	10	S. F. Lying-in Hospital	2

Remarks.—Contrary to expectation, there was scarcely any increase in the mortality for December. It did not reach the figures of either of the three years previous, and was but six in excess of that of 1866. The average for five years is 302, but it must be remembered that in 1868 there were in this month 148 deaths from small-pox alone. The comparatively small number of deaths from consumption and inflammation of the lungs is noticeable. These diseases are usually the cause of more deaths in December than in any other month, and for obvious reasons. The number of deaths from diseases of the heart is unusually small, that from typhoid fever is unusually large. The death noted as occurring in the small-pox hospital was not from small-pox. Considerably over half of the deaths were of foreign born.

Poisoning from Partridge Eating.—A case, not fatal, is narrated in the *Boston Medical and Snrgical Journal*. The bird had a bitter taste.

Transfusion of Blood into the arteries instead of the veins, is recommended and has been successfuly performed in a number of cases. The introduction of air would do no harm, and there is less risk of distending the heart.

The Deaths from Small Pox in Philadelphia, have averaged 30 a day for the last month or two.

PACIFIC

MEDICAL AND SURGICAL JOURNAL.

Vol. V.—MARCH, 1872.—No. 58.

ORIGINAL COMMUNICATIONS.

Abdominal Section—Removal of Cancerous Tumors.

By J. W. B. REYNOLDS, M.D., Yountville, Cal.

Mrs. M. T. W—, æt. 20 y., was confined with her fifth child on the 21st of September last; labor easy and natural; recovery rapid, being up and attending to domestic duties in two weeks. During the last three or four months of pregnancy, had complained of an unpleasant feeling of pain, soreness and tension about the pyloric orifice of the stomach, and thought her feelings were different to those in former pregnancies. A few magnesian laxatives, with four or five grains of bismuth and the same amount of charcoal, three times a day, kept her comparatively comfortable till her confinement.

On the sixth of November she sent for me, and informed me that her abdomen was enlarging, and on making an examination I found the abdomen half full of fluid, and a tumor in the left iliac region about the size of an orange, which seemed attached by a pedicle to the ovary or broad ligament. On palpation it moved or floated freely from one side to the other. There also seemed to be a smaller one on the right, but attached by a shorter pedicle. The general contour of the abdomen seemed but little changed when lying on the back, and on percussion, the flat sound of the fluid was confined to the *anterior* half, while the resonant sound of air was *only heard in the posterior half of the abdomen.* As laid down by the authorities, these were diagnostic signs of encysted dropsy, and I concluded the case was an ovarian unilocular cyst, with a solid tumor, or possibly ascites with fibrous tumors. I told the patient that it was a serious disease, and I was of opinion nothing but an operation would give her a chance for recovery, but as she preferred that I should try the effect of medicine for a while, I did not insist on operating. I kept up pressure by a flannel roller, and gave iodine, biniodide of mercury, digitalis, acetate of potash, and various other diuretics and alteratives, also jalap and cream of tartar, and applied tinct. iodine, ungt. hydrargyri, belladonna and ext. conium externally; but in spite of everything the fluid rapidly accumulated until the 8th of December, when the great difficulty of breathing, (the accumulation of fluid preventing the proper play of the diaphragm) and swelling of the extremities, the increasing emaciation and intense suffering, admonished me of the necessity of tapping. This I did, withdrawing six gallons by measure, when something, probably the omentum, fell against the opening, obstructing the flow. I passed a probe through the tube and held the obstructing body back, but the fluid appeared to be getting thicker and darker, and discharged so slowly, that I thought there was more danger from the prolonged contact of the probe than there would be to withdraw the tube and allow the remainder to drain off gradually. I accordingly withdrew the tube and fastened the bandage (which had been used to keep up pressure), and it continued to flow for four days, discharging about four gallons more. When it stopped, I closed the wound with plaster. No inflammation followed.

For two weeks previous to tapping, the urine had been nearly suppressed, the patient not passing over two or three tablespoonfuls a day. I had used the catheter several times, but found none in the bladder. It contained no albumen. After the pressure of the fluid was removed, the secretion became perfectly natural.

For a week the appetite was excellent, but as soon as the abdomen began to enlarge from re-accumulation of the fluid, this declined. The amount of urine diminished; the bowels became constipated, being hard to start, and when they did act, still more difficult to quiet. The emaciation became rapidly progressive; she now complained a great deal of the stomach, and in answer to the question, "Doctor what can be the matter with my stomach ?" I replied that the symptoms were a good deal like those described in "gastric ulcer." The abdomen was again becoming tense with the effusion, the urine nearly suppressed, and on making a vaginal examination, I had considerable difficulty in reaching the mouth of the womb, on account of bulging in of the anterior vaginal wall. The labia externa were much distended with the fluid. I now told the patient and her friends, that it was useless to try medicines any longer, that she could live but a few days as she was; that another tapping would be followed by a more rapid re-accumulation than the other, in fact she must die unless an operation would save her; that this was dangerous, but it would give her one chance for life, and it could not, at the worst, deprive her of many days. She replied that "she was thoroughly convinced of the truth of what I said, and made up her mind to take the risk if *I* would perform the operation."

I had her then on the use of tonics, which I continued till the 25th, I then gave her a dose of sulphate of magnesia, (as she objected to oil) to clear out the bowels preparatory to the operation on the 27th, knowing from previous experience that it would be at least two days before they became quiet. On the 27th December, (after waiting a week in vain for a clear day) I performed the operation, assisted by Drs. M. B. Pond, and Chas. F. A. Nichell, of Napa City. On making the section (which was the same in all respects as in ovariotomy) down to the peritoneum, I thought it best to remove at least a portion of the fluid, with the trocar, but having no large trocar, I found it was going to keep the patient too long under the anesthetic to draw it off through so small an opening, and satisfied now that the dropsy was intra-peritoneal, I withdrew the tube and enlarged the opening with the knife, and allowed it to run through a three-quarter inch tin tube. In a few minutes it was all withdrawn, and the tumors were visible, one on each side, involving the fallopian tubes near their entire length. But alas! a closer inspection revealed the doom of our poor patient, for the nodulated exterior of the tumors, the light creamy color, interspersed with brownish mahogany looking spots, indicated too truly that the disease was that most malignant and rapidly fatal of all others, *encephaloid.* This discovery made me feel very sad, as it deprived the patient of her last hope. I proceeded, however, to remove the tumors (the pedicles of which were about three inches broad, and only a half or three quarters of an inch long) by passing a sack needle carrying a double carbolized hempen ligature through the centre and tying both ways. The stump was so short that one ligature slipped off, when the blood from an artery which had fed the tumor, as large as a swan's quill, spouted out freely, till my assistant compressed it, and I secured it with a silken ligature. Removing the coagulated blood (about two table-spoonfuls) with the hand, and sponging out the cavity of the pelvis perfectly clean with sponges which had lain all night in water impregnated with sol. of chlorinated soda, we could see interspersed all through the pelvis and over the broad ligaments, specks from the size of a grain of wheat to that of a small bean, of brainy looking matter like the tumors. After all oozing of blood had ceased, I closed the wound with silver wire, (interrupted sutures) applied strips of plaster between, and covered the wound with lint saturated with a solution of carbolic acid, ten grains to the ounce of water. Over this, oiled silk, a flannel compress, and completed the dressing with a flannel roller, when the patient was removed from the table to the bed.

The temperature of the room was 85 to 90 during the operation, and two intelligent ladies, who remained in the room, had, by my directions, the sheets perfectly warm to spread one under and one over the patient as soon as she was ready to be put to bed; a jug of warm water was also put to the feet.

I was much indebted throughout the operation, to the intelligent aid of my assistant, Dr. Pond. And Dr. Nichell, who administered the anesthetic (one part of chloroform by measure, and two of sulphuric ether,) did it so admirably, that after the patient woke she asked her sister-in-law if the operation had been performed; and still apparently not satisfied with her answer in the affirmative, she appealed to me to know if it were really so. On assurance that it was all over, she declared that she did not know that she had ever been removed from the bed. Only about three ounces of the anesthetic was used, though the operation and time lost by the slow running of the fluid, consumed forty-five minutes.

As soon as she was sufficiently awake, I gave her a tea-spoonful of brandy with a table-spoonful of sweet milk, a little sugar, and hot water enough to warm it, and she never had a particle of nausea.

One hour after being put to bed, the pulse was 84, three hours 108, fourteen hours 96; rested well during the night, had a free discharge of urine in the fore-part of the night, and another in the morning, without the least particle of straining. I had cautioned her if she found it would require any effort not to attempt it, but let me use the catheter. From this on she voided it regularly twice a day.

On the fourth day, she felt a desire to evacuate the bowels, when I ordered an injection of two table-spoonfuls castor oil and about a pint of warm water, from which she had two discharges, natural in consistence and color. In fact, there never was a particle of pain, soreness, discharge or swelling about the wound, and by the end of the fifth day it seemed entirely healed. The patient ate well, slept well, was cheerful, and in spite of my cautions, would laugh and talk with friends, though she had been so patient, so brave and resolute, and obedient to my directions throughout her sickness, I could not find it in my heart to deny her the privilege of giving expression to some of the joy she felt at the prospect of recovery.

But on the sixth night, she commenced vomiting, her pulse ran up to 120. I gave lime water, hydrocyanic acid, bismuth, and applied sinapisms, gave brandy and morphia, but the symptoms were only temporarily relieved. Tympanites over the stomach supervened, a dark fetid matter was ejected from the stomach, and finally I noticed that the matter thrown up contained streaks and lumps of a brainy looking substance, similar to that in the interior of the tumors removed; and as there was no tympanites of the abdomen, *which was soft and pliant to the last—nothing whatever that indicated inflammatory action in this portion of the peritoneum*, I concluded that the stomach was also the seat of encephaloid infiltration, or small tumors of this character, which had become disintegrated.

On the morning of the seventh day after the operation, she died. I did not ask the privilege of making a post mortem examination for several reasons. I had remained with the patient from the day of the operation, sleeping little day or night, and administering every dose of medicine myself, and I was in consequence completely worn out. Then there is always some prejudice in the country against mutilating the dead for scientific purposes, and though I know the family had too much good sense to refuse their assent if I had urged it as important, I knew too she was a kind of pet and favorite of a large circle [illegible]ndred and friends, so I concluded not to make the re[illegible]

Perhaps some may think from the rap[illegible]pment o[illegible] the disease, the fast pulse, and great em[illegible] I ought have diagnosed malignant disease, and [illegible] woman without an operation. As to its rapid [illegible]ent it have existed long before the patient was aware of it. Besides, Gross, who is high authority, says, some forms of ovarian cysts are very rapid in their development. By the same authority, the high rate of the pulse may indicate a super-fibrinization of the blood, and I told my assistant before I operated, "that this symptom, with some other circumstances, made it very possible that we might find the tumors fibrous, and the dropsy intraperitoneal."

Both fallopian tubes were so involved with the tumors, that it was necessary to remove both with the malignant growths. I should not apprehend any danger of hematocele from reflex of the menses, in consequence of removal of these tubes, as contended by some writers, except in cases of obstruction in the natural outlet.

The early healing of the incision, the entire absence of all pain, soreness, and swelling, or any other symptoms of peritoneal inflammation in the abdominal or pelvic region; with the healthy, natural action of the kidneys and bladder, warrant the conclusion that had the tumor been benign instead of malignant, Mrs. W. would have recovered from the operation without a bad symptom. And although I had told the lady's friends as soon as I discovered the disease was malignant, that recovery was impossible, yet her progress was so favorable for several days, that, until the disease developed in the stomach, I almost hoped that she was about to prove my prognosis false, and bid defiance to scientific precedent, by getting well anyhow. The tumors weighed one pound and three quarters each, and the fluid withdrawn, thirty-two, making thirty-five and a half pounds altogether.

Dr. Robert Mayne, physician to the Meath Hospital, Dublin, a young man of great promise, died of small-pox after five days' illness.

Dr. Barthelemy Roch, President of the Medical Association of Alais, France, since the year 1854, died lately in the 94th year of his age.

Case of Traumatic Tetanus followed by Recovery:

BY CLINTON CUSHING, M.D., Oakland.

Tetanus is a disease so frightful in its nature, and of which so large a proportion of those who are affected, die, that I embrace the opportunity to place upon record a case in which treatment was followed by a favorable result.

I was called, October 13th, 1871, to take charge of H. S., a boy of 5 years of age, who had sustained a severe injury in the shape of an extensive laceration of the calf of the right leg, the injury involving the deep seated muscles, said injury being produced by the leg being caught in the cog wheels of a horse power.

The leg had been stitched together and dressed when I took charge of the case, and the treatment which I adopted was the internal use of anodynes and the local application of a weak solution of carbolic acid and water with laudanum. At the end of the fourth day quite a large portion of the integument involved in the injury had sloughed away, leaving a healthy granulating surface, an inch and a half in breadth, by four inches in length. I would state here, that the patient had a very sensitive, nervous organization.

Nothing occurred for the following ten days worthy of note, the wound granulating nicely and everything going on satisfactorily. The weather being pleasant, the bed of the patient was allowed to be drawn up to an open window fronting upon the street.

At the end of two weeks from the date of the injury, the patient became very restless and irritable, the tongue coated and the bowels constipated. The mother also stated that he could not open his mouth as well as usual. I ordered a cathartic of calomel and rhubarb, which acted efficiently the following morning.

The next day, it being the 13th from the date of the injury, the "risus sardonicus" was well marked, and the abdominal muscles were contracted and as firm as a board; the patient could open his mouth about half an inch.

I at once prescribed 1-12 grain of the English extract of the calabar bean, and 15 grains of the hydrate of chloral, to be given together every two hours until some relaxation of the abdominal muscles should take place.

The remedies acted well, the muscles became soft, and he could open his mouth an inch after taking the second dose, which was followed by several hours of quiet sleep. Upon awakening, however, general muscular contractions came on, and the whole body became stiff, with slight opisthotonos. The chloral and the bean was repeated, and again with good effect, the second dose controlling the spasms, and producing relaxation. The stomach now became irritable and refused to tolerate the medicine. The pulse was 100, and weak.

I now ordered to be administered by enema, ½ oz. brandy, 1 oz. beef essence, 1-10 gr. morphia, and the same dose of the chloral and the calabar bean as had been administered by the stomach, the above to be repeated every four hours.

Under this treatment the patient steadily improved, and three days after commencing the use of the enemas, he was able to take his nourishment with but little trouble by the stomach, and also a tonic of iron and quinia, but the chloral, the morphia, and the bean, disagreed with his stomach, and had to be used by enema for over three weeks. There was some contraction of the muscles of the jaw for two weeks, and some hardness of the abdominal muscles for over three weeks. As the patient improved there was a longer interval between the enemas, until at the end of three weeks, but two were used in 24 hours. The wound from the first looked healthy and healed rapidly.

During the treatment I stopped the use of the chloral and continued the morphia and bean, but was compelled to again resort to the chloral. I then omitted the morphia, but was compelled to again add it to the other remedies in order to quiet pain and secure sleep.

This combination of remedies has acted so well in my

hands that I should resort to it again in a similar case, with a reasonable hope of a like favorable result.

It may be well to state here that it was fully six weeks from the attack of tetanus before all symptoms of the disease disappeared.

I am disposed to place more confidence in the chloral and morphia, than in the calabar bean, in controlling the disease, notwithstanding the bean has been known, when given alone, to affect favorably the cure of the malady.

Tetanus is divided by writers into acute and chronic; acute, when occurring within a week after the receipt of the injury; these cases nearly all proving fatal. Chronic, when the attack commences over a week or ten days after the receipt of the injury, a considerable proportion of which recover. The greater the length of time which ensues between the injury and the commencement of the disease, the greater the chances of recovery.

In estimating the value of the treatment adopted in this case, it is well to remember that it comes under the head of chronic, or that class of cases in which the tendency to recover is greatest.

It is worthy of note, however, that the remedies controlled the spasms and pain in a satisfactory manner, and whether they exerted a direct curative effect or not, they prevented a vast amount of suffering and pain.

THE WORLD'S FAIR IN VIENNA, in 1873, is to exceed anything in the past. There have been four such exhibitions, the first in London in 1851, occupying 80,000 square meters; the second in Paris in 1855, occupying 100,000 meters; the third in London in 1862, occupying 190,000 meters; and the fourth in Paris in 1867, occupying 440,000 meters. The space allotted to the coming Vienna exhibition is upwards of two million of meters.

FOUR DEATHS A DAY take place in the City of New York, from accidents and violence.

AN EPIDEMIC OF JAUNDICE, prevailed in Paris during the winter months.

Address to the San Francisco Medical Society.

BY BENJ. D. DEAN, M.D., Retiring President.

Delivered January 23d, 1872.

GENTLEMEN :—Another year, filled with its hours of labor and repose, of failure and success, has glided quietly from our possession—another mile-stone has been erected in our cycle of time, and another chapter has been added to the historical record of this Society. And, as we cross the threshold—leaving behind us the old year, and entering hopefully upon the labors of the new year, I have deemed this an appropriate occasion on which to claim your attention for a few moments, while I recall briefly the past success of the Society in behalf of medical science, and offer a few suggestions relative to the aim and character of its future achievements.

In presuming to ask your attention, in accordance with the above intimation, I am fully aware that I am digressing from the course previously taken on similar occasions. Still, I can see no valid objection to such an encroachment on former precedents ; hoping that such a review, brief though it will be, may aid us in some way to win still greater success, as a Society, during the year that now lies just before us. Judging others by myself, we have all found it profitable at times to call to our aid the experience derived from past events ; and what may be advantageous to individuals in this regard, cannot prove an exception with societies, at least to a certain extent.

Without detaining you longer with preliminaries, it is a source of great pleasure to me, on this occasion, to be able to congratulate you, gentlemen, on the high degree of prosperity to which our Society has attained, and for the invigorating influence of harmony which has been manifested on all occasions. Action, guided by such an influence, in whatever field of labor, could not reasonably fail. It certainly has not proved an exception here. The list of our membership is rapidly increasing; thus proving that the efforts of those who were instrumental in organizing this Society, four years ago, have not been in vain. The work then inaugurated by stout hearts and united hands, under many adverse circumstances—prospering from the first—has already become a tower of strength in the ranks of our profession ; and already it merits and receives the plaudits of "well done" from many of the leading minds among medical men here and elsewhere. And still the circle of its influence is extending. The profession is being aroused from its protracted lethargy. Members are beginning to realize more fully in its true light the value of associated action. And I cannot fail to express the hope that the day is not far distant, when every member of our noble profession will feel highly honored by being acknowledged worthy to have his name enrolled as a member of this Society.

During the year twenty-four stated meetings have been held, and at all of these the attendance of members has been sufficient for the transaction of the usual business. This fact alone, considering the interruptions and detentions which are unavoidable in our profession, speaks louder than words of mine in commendation of the zeal and interest which members have continued to manifest in the progress and general prosperity of the organization. With such a fact standing prominently in view, the most casual observer could not really be surprised at the degree of prosperity which it has already attained. This result is in keeping with the laws of cause and effect everywhere. For any work, sustained by such united, persistent efforts, cannot fail to secure positive and satisfactory results. But the good work so faithfully commenced and energetically sustained thus far, must not be allowed to falter now. There can be no good reason to fear such a termination, if we continue to prove true to the high trusts confided to us as medical men. To avoid it, the same deep interest and careful watchfulnes will be required in the present and future years of its duration.

And here let me say that every member, however humble he may estimate his qualifications, has an individual duty to perform. It cannot be done by proxy. If all do not feel confidence in their ability to express freely their opinions on the various questions which may be discussed here, all should feel the vital importance of attending the meetings regularly. The presence of every member would not only be the precursor of great benefit to each, but such a fact would at once begin to develop a greater interest in the welfare of the Society. There are some who, by their presence, seem fully conscious of this fact. Their chairs are rarely ever vacant; even if their attendance is accomplished with some self-denial. It is expected that occasions will occur in the practice of our profession, when engagements will compel our presence elsewhere. But let each member resolve for himself, to make those engagements the exception and not the rule, if possible, for non-attendance. This line of action, if it became general, would be attended by the most beneficial results to the whole membership. "What is worth doing at all, is worth doing well." If we continue to maintain this standard in our relation as members, success will be sure to increase and reward our efforts; and the healthful, fraternizing influence of the Society will extend, until the whole profession shall be made to feel its power, and manifest a desire to share its advantages with us.

Our meetings through the year have been enlivened by able and earnest discussions on medical subjects. These discussions have been instructive, and at all times a proper respect has been manifested for the opinions advanced by all on such occasions. The liberality of sentiment in this regard has been highly commendable, and generously sustains the claims of a learned profession to dignity, unity, and progress.

While speaking of the general character and interest of our meetings, I cannot fail to give suitable recognition to the eminent services of a distinguished member of this

Society, Dr. Bentley, who has rarely failed to occupy the attention of members with his able demonstration of recent pathological specimens, during a portion of each session, through the year. The lucid and scholarly manner in which he has presented their chief points of interest has added great value to our meetings, and furnished many practical thoughts for study and reflection to all in the pursuit of professional knowledge. Deeply appreciating, as I do, the value of such opportunities to witness the progress and results of disease, I feel that I reflect most truly your wishes in giving an expression of appreciation for those valuable services, and in expressing the hope that this important feature of our meetings may long be continued.

From the report of our Treasurer we learn that

THE FINANCES OF THE SOCIETY

are in a very satisfactory condition. On taking this chair, one year ago, I spoke briefly relative to the important influence always exerted by a well-filled treasury towards winning success in any important undertaking. And it is not now my purpose to withdraw from the position then assumed ; for I am more fully impressed with the correctness of the fact that the monetary condition of any institution constitutes the key-note of its success or failure.

Entertaining these views, I feel at liberty to counsel the most rigid economy in the expenditure of money for Society purposes. Not that I am an advocate of holding money without deriving the usual benefit from it, but rather I would be an advocate of holding it for the purpose of realizing greater benefit at a future time. This remark very opportunely prepares the way for me to say that we should not be satisfied with simply paying our current expenses. We should desire to do more than that. We should aim to place our Society on a more permanent basis. In order that such an idea may be more fully realized, we should begin now to anticipate a period in its history when the Society may be the owner of the building in which its meetings shall be held. We should also desire to possess a large and well selected Medical Library. To him who has not given much thought to this idea, the suggestion may seem chimerical. It may appear that we are elevating our mark too high, and that such a desideratum, noble as it would be to possess, is too far beyond our power to reach, or even merit serious consideration. So it is, and ever will be, unless due efforts are made for its accomplishment. But let me remind you, gentlemen, that greater success has been witnessed in the history and development of societies than the above suggestion would contemplate. It is not the result of accident, however, but the reward of long and patient industry, and often self-denial, and far-sightedness, in correctly estimating the results of organized efforts, that may carry their influence and benefits far down the stream of time. If we adopt for our motto "*Labor vincit omnia*," the magnitude of the undertaking may not appear so formidable. On the other hand, if the accepted policy of the Society shall be to spend as it goes, then it would not require the ken of a sage to convince us that the future of our organization will furnish little, if any, encouragement for the realization of such ennobling results. But, in glancing at the many indications of metropolitan grandeur, which lie scattered so profusely in all directions around us, which are sure to be realized in the future growth and development of our city, whose population will yet be numbered by millions ; and remembering our relative and central position towards the whole medical profession of the Pacific coast, and feeling a proper sense of our responsibility in taking early action towards concentrating and vitalizing the great elements which constitute its real power, if you should consider, as I do, that the objects to be attained are more than an equivalent to the gigantic efforts that may be required for their possession, let us begin now to take the first steps towards the enjoyment of such a reality, even if the mutations now unseen in our pathway, should compel us to transmit the great work unfinished to our successors.

From the report of the Librarian, you are informed that the Society already possesses quite a variety of medical publications, which may be considered as a valuable nucleus towards the formation of an extensive and carefully selected Medical Library. The early action taken by the Society, in subscribing for the various home and foreign medical journals, was wise, and in perfect accord with the objects and necessities of our organization. And the recent order by the Society for the further additions to the Library, cannot fail to receive the unanimous and cordial approval of all our members. Thus each one has free access to a large number of recent medical publications, and is thereby able to keep pace with the advancement in the science of medicine, both at home and abroad.

In this hasty review, it is very gratifying to be able to state the fact that general good health has been vouchsafed to our members. No vacancy has occurred in our number by the agency of death.

I refer with pride to the action of the Society in responding so promptly and generously to the call for relief of our professional brothers beyond the mountains, after the fiery ordeal through which they were called to pass. For this demonstration of sympathy in a substantial manner, the Society has received the heartfelt thanks of the recipients.

I will not detain you longer by my remarks on this occasion. But before closing, permit me to return my heartfelt thanks to each of you, for the uniform kindness and forbearance, I have always received at your hands. The pleasant relations I have sustained to you, while occupying this chair during the past year, will never be forgotten by me. Their remembrance will be treasured as among my most sacred recollections. I accepted the trust so generously confided to my care by you, with many misgivings. But, in the discharge of the duties it imposed, I have felt constant support by your courtesy and indulgence. And, again, permit me to thank you all most heartily. In conclusion, let me bespeak for my successor the same generous support.

Report of Two Cases of Placenta Previa.

By HENRY GIBBONS, Jr., M.D.

[Read before the San Francisco Medical Society.]

In the absence of any appointed subject for discussion at the present meeting, I have concluded to present a report of two cases of placenta previa, believing that several points of interest are involved, upon which judgment will differ, and which will give rise to instructive discussion.

On the afternoon of Sunday, January 21st, I received a message from Dr. J. M. Haley, desiring a consultation with my father, or in his absence, with myself. Proceeding at once to the house indicated, my father not being at hand, I found Mrs. M— in labor, with, if I recollect aright, her twelfth child. Two weeks before, she had waked in the night with a profuse uterine hemorrhage, the blood saturating two mattresses, and even soiling the floor beneath. Repeated hemorrhages of smaller amount followed, and on the 20th January the membranes ruptured spontaneously and the waters escaped. At this period Dr. Haley was called, no other physician having been in attendance. The loss of blood continuing through the night; uterine contractions being feeble notwithstanding the completion of gestation; and the probabilities of placenta pervia being strong, though this condition could not be made out by examination, Dr. Haley sent for assistance the morning after his first visit, as above stated.

I found the patient pale and anemic, with feeble and frequent pulse, and feeble and infrequent uterine contractions. Noting these facts, I made a digital examination. The presenting part was barely reached with considerable effort, but the presentation could not be made out. The *os* was dilatable and somewhat dilated; projecting over its left posterior border was felt the edge of the placenta whose detachment had occasioned the hemorrhage. As the hemorrhage was now slight and the contractions were increasing in force, though still by no means strong, we decided to wait, hoping the progress would soon be sufficient to enable us to make out the presentation, which felt firmer than the buttock, but not sufficiently so for the head.

Little or no progress was made in the next two hours. We finally, after some hesitation, fearing the shoulder was at the *os*, gave a medium dose of ergot, which was repeated in perhaps half an hour. These doses seemed to have some effect upon the uterus, and shortly after, by digital examination, firm pressure being made upon the abdomen, I was enabled to make out a shoulder presentation. We decided at once to resort to podalic version. The soft parts being thoroughly relaxed and the patient a multipara, I found no difficulty in accomplishing this. The hand was readily introduced, a knee seized, version accomplished with assistance of manipulation of the abdomen by Dr. Haley, and the child delivered in a very short time. Very little blood was lost. Labor was terminated at once by the removal of the placenta without hemorrhage. The child, which was healthy and well formed, showed no sign of life during version or afterward; no pulsation of the heart could be detected. I did not see the patient afterward, but learned from Dr. Haley, that excepting some hypogastric tenderness, convalescence progressed favorably.

The second case was identical in many of its features with the one just related. In my father's absence, I was sent for by Dr. J. J. Braman, Sunday afternoon, February 4th, to consult in regard to a case seen by my father a day or two before. Mrs. V— was in labor with her first child. She had had a severe flooding a month previously; had frequent smaller hemorrhages subsequent to that time; had become very anemic and prostrate, with weak and frequent pulse. Irregular labor pains had set in two days prior to my visit, but no decided uterine contractions had occurred until the night before. Placenta previa had been diagnosticated, but the presentation had not been made out. The patient had passed the full period of gestation. I found the *os* flaccid and largely dilated ; the edge of the placenta projecting over the left posterior portion of the *os ;* the vertex to the left acetabulum ; the membranes unruptured; and the uterine contractions inefficient. The hemorrhage continuing, though to a small amount, and its speedy cessation being apparently necessary to save life ; moreover, our faith in the ability of nature, even assisted by ergot, to terminate the labor, being inconsiderable, we decided upon version, as in the former case. I had no difficulty in introducing the hand and securing the knee, the membranes being then ruptured, nor in turning the child, but the patient being a primipara, there was some delay in its delivery, and considerable traction was necessary. During the operation, which did not take over half an hour, a large amount of liquor amnii escaped with some force. The placenta was immediately removed from the interior of the uterus, which contracted firmly, all hemorrhage ceasing, and little blood being lost in the process. As a precautionary measure, a dose of ergot was administered shortly after.

The child was of medium size and well formed ; it bore evidences of having been dead for several hours at least. Between half and three quarters of an hour after delivery, I placed my hand upon the abdomen, and found the uterus firmly contracted. The patient expressed herself as feeling quite comfortable ; she had some thirst ; the pulse was weak and frequent, about 120 per minute—that of the left wrist being hardly perceptible, of the right quite distinct. The next morning there was considerable hypogastric pain and tenderness, with tympanites,—flatulence had been annoying prior to the birth of the child. Dr. Braman, who had seen the patient earlier, had directed hot fomentations to the abdomen and a sedative, carminative mixture, which gave some relief. In addition we directed pills of quinine and opium *pro re nata*. Under the combined influence of the pills and fomentations, pain and tenderness speedily subsided, and had almost disappeared by evening. There was then considerable desire for food, some thirst; pulse still feeble, but less so than the day before, and less frequent.

I omitted to mention that a decided febrile attack was said to have occurred in the afternoon; it however left no unfavorable evidences of its having existed. We considered the prospect very favorable and continued the treatment.

Tuesday morning found the patient still improving. She had taken four pills since the evening before, and seven in all; had slept well during the night; was decidedly hungry; felt no pain, and but little hypogastric tenderness, though tympanites still existed. There was a very slight watery discharge from the vagina, but no blood had been seen since delivery. The pulse had not changed from the evening before. We left our patient feeling that recovery was almost assured. Such being the case, it was with considerable surprise that I received an urgent message at 3 o'clock in the afternoon, and hastening to the house, was met by Dr. Brunan with the information that our patient was dead. She had awaked about 2 o'clock from a refreshing sleep, feeling quite comfortable; had shortly after experienced a choking sensation, which increased. The pulse disappeared at both wrists; in fifteen minutes she was dead.

A post-mortem examination was sought, but denied. The cause of death could only be conjectured. I had no opportunity of examining the body after death, but learned that no hemorrhage showed itself externally, and that the *os* was reached with difficulty by digital examination.

The points I desire to call attention to, and which I shall put in the form of questions, are these:

1st. Is it proper to give ergot in placenta previa, before ascertaining the presentation? As a rule I believe not, but under the circumstances as noted in case first, I think it was.

2d. Was the death of the children due to loss of their

own blood, through the detached placentæ, or to impairment of vitality from loss of the mothers' ?

3d. Should the membranes have been ruptured in the second instance, and the case left to nature ? or was version the right thing in the right place ?

4th. Would it have been better to rupture the membranes earlier, if the presentation could have been made out, or otherwise ? My judgment would have been to rupture them as early as possible, being prepared to effect version, if an unfavorable presentation was discovered.

5th. What was the cause of death of the mother ? Was it from concealed hemorrhage, or, as suggested to me by Dr. Chamberlin, from heart-clot, as occurs sometimes in convalescence from diphtheria ?

I was fearful of the sudden formation of heart-clot, following syncope which might have ensued had the patient been allowed to rise, and strictly prohibited any change of position. I learned that the injunction was not disobeyed.

Eucalyptus Globulus.—This tree is being largely cultivated in the south of France, Spain, Algiers, and Corsica. It is a native of Tasmania, where it was of old known to the natives and settlers as a remedy for fever. It prefers a marshy soil, in which it grows to a gigantic height with great rapidity. It dries the soil by the evaporation from its leaves, and shelters it from the sun, thus preventing the generation of marsh miasm. Its wood is as hard as teak. Every part of it is impregnated with a balsamic, oil-of-camphor-like odor ; and besides a notable quantity of astringent matter, it contains a peculiar extractive, which is supposed to contain an alkaloid allied to quinia. At any rate, its efficacy in intermittent and marsh fevers has gained for it in Spain the name of the "fever tree." It is a powerful tonic and diffusible stimulant, does wonders in chronic catarrh and dyspepsia, is an excellent antiseptic application to wounds, and tans the skins of dead animals, giving the fragrance of Russia leather. We can vouch from personal observation for the flourishing condition of the plantations at Hyeres and Nice, where trees from seeds sown in 1859 are said to be now sixty meters [197 feet] high.—*Med. Times and Gaz.* Nov. 11, 1871.—*Med. News and Library.*

A Case of Insertion of the Placenta

ON THE LOWER SEGMENT OF THE UTERUS, WITH PROLAPSUS OF THE CORD AND RETENTION OF THE MEMBRANES.

BY J. BRADFORD COX, M.D., Sonoma, Cal.

Mrs. —, æt. 30; married ten years; pregnant the seventh time; seven children living, having twins three or four years old. Her health has been good since the commencement of her last pregnancy, nine months since. First saw her about six o'clock P. M. She says she has had slight pains since twelve o'clock the night previous; notwithstanding, she has been on her feet most of the time to-day. She says the fetus has been very active, and now "seems to be turning summersaults." The pains are coming about every fifteen minutes, but do not seem to be very effectual. A digital examination shows the *os tincæ* pretty well dilated, and the vertex engaged in the superior strait. The next examination, made an hour and a half or two hours afterward, showed the *os* fully dilated, and a little progress made toward the descent of the vertex. I now ascertained more fully that the presentation was as before stated, and that the position was what is commonly called the first; more properly, however, the left-occipito-iliac-anterior, or the left-occipito-cotyloid of Baudeloque. I ascertained further that the placenta also was engaged in the superior strait, coming down by the side of the head of the fetus, and occupying the right anterior segment of the plane of the superior strait; thus, with the head, filling the other long diameter of the strait not occupied by the occipito-frontal diameter of the fetal head.

I decided not to interfere, but to watch nature's progress, everything else being in a favorable condition.

Descent took place with about the usual rapidity. The membranes or "bag of waters" came down prematurely, and without rupturing were forced beyond the external outlet, and lay there until the head was passing the inferior strait, apparently much elongated, resembling in shape a wine bottle more than the usual ovoid or globular form.

While the fetal head was yet in the excavation, the cord came down and passed the inferior strait, forming a loop of some five or six inches, making ten or twelve inches prolapsed.

As if nature were now about to destroy the fetus, recently so active, the pains diminished in power, and in fact almost ceased entirely; the pulsations in the cord gradually grew less powerful, and soon ceased entirely. Knowing this state of things could not exist long with safety, I replaced the prolapsed cord within the vagina, with one hand (the left), and with the other over the abdomen, at the same time speaking encouragingly to the patient, succeeded in bringing on pains again, and after two or three of these had occurred, a male child was born; without, however, any signs of life. Notwithstanding this almost hopeless condition, by vigorous attempts, persevered in, I succeeded in resuscitating him.

But, after satisfying myself that the child was safe, having requested the husband to keep gentle pressure over the uterus in the meantime, by placing his hand in the proper position, I placed my hand over the uterus and found it contracting very irregularly, presenting a knotty, rough feeling, instead of the round, smooth sensation usual in such cases.

The placenta was delivered in about half an hour. The membranes being examined, I found about half of them had been retained, and could be felt in the vagina. Following them up, I found them pass into the uterus, where they seemed to be firmly adherent. I administered a teaspoonful of fld. ext. ergot, without sensible effect. Waiting one hour, I repeated the dose. In two and a half hours there was still no progress, notwithstanding the pains seemed to have been sufficient. They were now, however, growing less, and I resolved to introduce the hand into the cavity; which I did, and succeeded in detaching the membranes from the left anterior segment of the fundus uteri.

The patient has had no unusual hemorrhage, and is doing well.

Attempted Suicide by taking 10 to 15 grains of Strychnia.

RECOVERY.

Reported by F. H. ENGELS, M.D.

J. W., æt. 41, a robust Irish laborer, was brought to the City and County Hospital at 6:30 P.M., February 2d, 1872. The officer who had him in charge informed the physician on duty that he had taken poison of some kind about 4 P.M., but could give no definite account of the nature or even the immediate effects of the poison, the suspicion wavering between arsenic and strychnia, while the patient stoutly declined to give any information whatever in this respect.

As preliminary to any treatment directed against a particular poison, a strong emetic of sulphate of zinc and pulvis ipecacuanhæ, each ½ drachm, was administered, and a few minutes after taking it the patient was seized with a decidedly tetanic spasm, opisthotonos alone not being present, and settling at once the question as to the kind of poison used. After the emetic had commenced to operate, therefore, its action was encouraged further by the free use of tepid water, ½ pint being given to the patient every 15 minutes, while between times a teaspoonful of the following mixture was given: ℞. Tinct. opii; spir. eth. co. aa ℨiii.; spir. vini gallici ℨx. m.

The stomach was soon thoroughly evacuated; but the convulsions still were extremely violent, and occurred very frequently; always, however, without opisthotonos. The patient perspired copiously; pulse at first 100, full and strong, but slowly getting weaker and less frequent; therefore, at 10 P. M., 5 drops of chloroform and 10 drops of tinct. cannabis indicæ was added to each dose of the previous mixture, the drinks of tepid water still being continued.

This slight alteration seemed to act favorably ; the spasms became less frequent and violent, and finally, by 1 A. M., ceased entirely, at which time treatment was discontinued and the patient declared out of danger. Next morning he felt well, except a tingling and difficulty of moving the lower extremities, and was discharged cured a few days afterwards.

The first portion of the vomited matter was subjected to a careful analysis, and sufficient strychnia discovered to calculate the whole quantity taken at probably 10 to 15 grains, which corresponds with the subsequent confession of the patient, that he had taken "a small pillbox full."

Proceedings of the San Francisco Medical Society.

PATHOLOGICAL SPECIMENS—CANCER—HYPERTROPHY OF HEART, ETC.

January 23, 1872.

Dr. Bentley exhibited several pathological specimens, as follows :

1. Atrophied heart, showing no disease of structure, but resulting from remote disease impairing the vitality.

2. Hypertrophied heart, weighing 3¾ lbs. No disease of valves; hypertrophy dependent upon extensive pericardial adhesions.

3. Hypertrophied heart, similar to the former, but not so large.

4. Large white kidney, from a lady 22 years of age, having ascites and albuminuria.

5. Soft cancer of pyloric extremity of stomach, from a man aged 42 years.

6. Extensive cancer deposits on diaphragm, and involving the liver, stomach, mesentery, etc., from a man aged 63. Three gallons of fluid were found in the abdominal cavity. Cicatrices were found in the apex of the lung, probably following tubercular cavities.

Dr. Holbrook asked if there were any means of diagnosticating pericardial adhesions ?

Dr. Bentley believed not, except by exclusion. Hypertrophy was caused either by valvular disease, by some impediment to the passage of the blood, or by pericardial adhesions. If in a given case of hypertrophy there were no murmurs, it might be inferred that adhesions existed.

Dr. Soule referred to a peculiarity of the beating of the heart in pericardial adhesions, a heaving, lifting motion, which was hard to explain without a case to demonstrate upon. The pulsation was besides intermittent to a considerable extent, while with valvular disease this seldom occurred.

Dr. Holbrook explained that his question had not been understood. It was: Can pericardial adhesion of itself be diagnosticated? He believed not. But when, from long continuance, it produced decided results, as hypertrophy, its existence can be determined.

Dr. Gibbons remarked that the method and reasons for determining adhesions mentioned by Dr. Soule, sounded well, but in the patient from whom the largest heart exhibited by Dr. Bentley was taken, there was decided mitral murmur. Beyond this and the hypertrophy there was no other sign of disease. It seemed the simplest case of hypertrophy he had seen. When first seen, six weeks before death, the distress was great, and was but partially relieved by antispasmodics. The patient obtained most ease by lying with the body reclining at an angle of 45°, the left side of the chest being thrown prominently forward. The patient having the extensive cancer exhibited, had been under his care, and had shown no sign of such disease during life. There had been torpor and constipation of the bowels, poor appetite, but clean tongue, no abdominal tenderness, no demonstrable disease of the liver, no sallow appearance; the ascites was a late symptom, though there had been tympanites; the alvine discharges were normal, there were no pulmonary symptoms, the pulse was feeble, and vomiting occasionally took place; but several times the patient appeared to get better, only to suffer a relapse.

Dr. Soule believed that simple hypertrophy, without valvular disease, might result in murmur, because of insufficient closure of the valves.

Dr. J. P. Whitney thought it feasible to diagnosticate hypertrophy with adhesions. There was a characteristic drawing in of the chest wall with every contraction of the heart, at least when the hypertrophy and adhesions were considerable.

EDITORIAL.

A Very Mean Trick.

A gentleman in St. Louis sends us a puff of Walker's Vinegar Bitters, clipped from a newspaper and headed: "Read what the Pacific Medical Journal says." He desires to know if we ever wrote it. We answer, no. Some years ago, when we had nothing to do with the advertising department of the JOURNAL, an advertisement of the foul concoction was inserted by the then publishers without our knowledge. As soon as we saw it we required its exclusion, and it was excluded. The puff referred to was a part of that advertisement, written by the proprietor of the nostrum, or his agent. And now the vagabond takes what he himself wrote and credits it to the JOURNAL, and circulates it thousands of miles away, where we were not likely to know of its publication. The trick illustrates the manner in which certificates in favor of quacks and quack medicines are procured. It is worthy of note that "Bitters" of different kinds, such as Walker's, Hostetter's, and so forth, are manufactured by the same formula as the certificates of cure.

San Francisco Lying-in Hospital and Foundling Asylum.

Before us is the first printed report of this institution, embracing the period since its organization, in August, 1869. It is intended principally for females who have made the first misstep and are desirous of leading a virtuous life, and for foundling children in general. A large number of our best citizens have interested themselves in its success and contributed liberally towards its expenses. The report states that fifty single women of the class referred to have been received and have given birth to children within the institution, and that only one of the number has failed to maintain a correct course of life. Thirteen have married, with the prospect of making good and useful wives and mothers. Ninety-one children have been received, of which the large proportion of forty-seven have died—a mortality which corresponds with the experience of similar institutions everywhere. There is not in California a charity which better deserves the fostering care of the State than this. It is a necessity of the country and the times. Even granting that the common opinion is true which dooms confirmed prostitutes to hopeless ruin—and we do not grant it—still no one will assert that the class of females taken under protection by this Asylum cannot in general be saved to themselves and to society by proper care. The report, prepared by Dr. Hardy, an old and well-known citizen, holding a highly honorable position in the profession and in the community at large, is an able and convincing document; and had we space, we should like to transfer much of it to our columns. Physicians in different sections of the State, are solicited to further the purposes of humanity by taking pains to commend to this institution such females as are proper subjects of its benevolent design.

Requirements of Candidates for Graduation.

The idea appears to be gaining ground among medical men that the candidate for the Degree of Doctor of Medicine should be examined without reference to the time or mode of his education, and that he should be accorded a Diploma on a satisfactory examination, even though he may not have attended a single lecture. Our neighbors in Canada have been discussing this question, with the view of preventing students from leaving their schools and graduating in the United States. It seems that the Canada schools require a much more extensive curriculum than ours, and that this circumstance, together with the greater clinical advantages furnished by the latter, operates to the disadvantage of the Canada colleges. The editor of the Toronto *Lancet* favors the project, while Dr. Covernton, President of the Ontario College of Physicians and Surgeons, takes the opposite view. Dr. Covernton, however, advances the extraordinary proposition that there should be a Professor of Homeopathy and one of Eclecticism in each regular school, so that students of different proclivities should be attracted, and have their eyes opened to the folly of those systems. The purpose is certainly commendable, and we would propose to Dr. Covernton to go a few steps further in the same direction.

If our neighbors across the St. Lawrence adopt this policy, we will volunteer to supply them from California with occupants for additional chairs: e. g. Dr. Li-po-tai, Professor of Oriental Medicine and Insect Decoctions; Dr. Borchard, Professor of Baunscheidtism; Dr. Darrin, Professor of Lying on of Hands and Lying in general; Dr. Madame Schmidt, Professor of Clairvoyance and Egyptian Darkness, etc., etc.

The Social Evil—Dr. Holland's Bill.

Many persons are anxious lest the bill introduced in the Senate of California by Mr. Wand, should be slipped through by strategy, in defiance of public sentiment as far as expressed. That there are individuals who would accomplish that purpose if it were possible, we do not doubt. The passage of the law would greatly enhance the rental value of a certain class of property in San Francisco; and it would also enable the proprietors of certain houses greatly to increase their revenue by monopolizing trade. Hence, golden arguments are suspected; and the suspicion is justifiable, in view of the pertinacity exhibited in pushing the measure. That some of its advocates have honest motives we do not doubt for a moment. Alarmed by the great extent of licentiousness and disease, some individuals thoughtlessly clutch at any proposed remedy. Others again have had a European experience and have fallen in love with European institutions. Take that class of Europeans and of American travelers in Europe who know everything, and a few excellent Americans who know nothing and go by impulse, and unmarried *miserables*, and married libertines, and you have the head and front of the advocacy of the social evil license. Of the great mass of citizens who acknowledge the obligations of morality and religion, nine tenths are hostile. Among females, the friends of license are among the licentious; whilst virtuous women, almost without exception, shrink from it as by a sacred instinct.

The attempt to obtain legal sanction for gambling is of kindred birth. Both movements belong to the effete and vicious code of the old world. Even in the principal countries of Europe, gambling is now no longer licensed. Whilst the law makers of Europe are abolishing their "hells" as too corrupting for their standard of morals, the attempt is made to transplant the curse to the soil of our young republic. It is not likely such a retrograde movement in civilization would have been made in California but for the precedent which sought license for the other vice. If licensed gambling houses be entitled to the name of "hells," are licensed houses of prostitution less deserving of the appellation? Truly both are *hells;* and we devoutly pray that the Statute Book of California may never be polluted with a legalization of either.

Ancient and Modern Quacks.

In these latter days men boast of progress and improvement. But in the matter of quacks the age has gone backwards. There was once an air of dignity about the quack. He fired high. He held up his head like a man and acted his part with a manly swagger. Nay, he even stood before princes and princesses. Queen Anne had no less than two "sworn occulists," one of whom rose to that dignity from a tailor, the other from a cobbler. She knighted one of them, who became Sir William Reade, and who published a treatise on the eye, which he himself could not read. Of him it was written:

> A tinker first his scene of life began;
> That failing, he set up for cunning-man.
> But wanting luck, puts on a new disguise,
> And now pretends that he can cure your eyes.
> Yet this expect, that like a tinker true,
> Where he repairs one eye he puts out two.

The Loutherbourgs, husband and wife, claimed to have received the gift of healing from the "Lord Jehovah." Parson Atwell cured lords and ladies innumerable with milk and apples. Katerfelto, immortalized by Cowper, traveled in the character of a King of Pain with a large caravan and a lot of black cats.

Modern quacks, how are they fallen! No umbrageous wig, no gold-headed cane, not even a black cat! What was said of the old alchemists may be said of them, with some modification—they begin by lying and end by stealing. They aim at the ignorant and less opulent classes. They gather their knowledge from hospitals in Europe which they never entered, and from masters whom they never saw, except in the capacity of grooms and boot-blacks. With the appetite of the buzzard, they deal in all filth and nastiness. They lend themselves cheaply to the crimes of abortion and infanticide. By the "laying on of hands" they get their hands in the pockets of the credulous. Of the thousand occupations pursued by men, no one involves so much meanness, falsehood, trickery, filthiness, and pocket-picking as that of the advertising quack of the present day.

Poppy and Opium Culture.

In the January number of the *American Journal of Pharmacy* are reported the results of experiments recently made on this subject in Germany, which were highly successful in producing an opium rich in morphia. It was found best to incise the capsules two weeks or longer after flowering, and to make the incisions in the morning, after sunrise. When the juice was collected after flowering and carefully dried, it gave a better article than when left to dry on the plant. The scarifications are best made with a common pen-knife, supplied with a guard to prevent too deep an incision. Very deep incisions injure the head and prevent the perfection of the seeds, while the supply of seeds after proper incisions is greater than when the heads are left undisturbed. This is a matter of importance in regard to the manufacture of oil. A day or two after the first scarifying, the process was repeated, but a third scarification did not pay. The proportion of morphia in the opium was from 10 to 13 per cent., and of course the quality was excellent. The plants were grown three or four inches apart, in two rows six inches apart; a space of two feet was allowed between the pairs of rows. In some instances the soil was sandy and well manured, but the propriety of manuring was questioned. Newly manured soil acts unfavorably on the seed.

It is a matter of surprise that greater attention has not been given to the raising of opium in California. There is no important crop the culture and management of which are so certain and so simple as this. Our agriculturists are prone to concentrate their labor on a single crop, when it is universally conceded that a diversity of products is better policy. We hope to witness numerous experiments in the opium culture the present season.

Tetanus and its Remedies.

The case narrated in this JOURNAL by Prof. Cushing is worthy of note. A case somewhat similar is described in the *American Medical Journal* for October. A man had his great toe crushed by a falling cake of ice. In eight days there was some stiffness of the jaws, and in two weeks from the injury the cramps were severe. Dr. Knox, of Somerville, N. J., who reports the case, did not see the patient till four weeks after the accident, when he was sweating profusely, with jaws firmly locked, tonic spasms of all the voluntary muscles, with exacerbations on the slightest disturbance, or from the slightest current of air. Thirty grains hydrate of chloral every four hours gave speedy relief, and he was discharged cured in ten days.

Dietetics of Disease—Beef Tea.

Within the last thirty or forty years a complete revolution has taken place in the dietetics of disease, by the substitution of nitrogenous for starchy food. Practitioners have followed their leaders implicitly, without inquiry or hesitation, in pouring beef tea into the stomach, whether the patients be young or old, and whether they relish it or not. The idea seems to be that if a given quantity of beef tea can be crowded into the stomach, the strength of the patient must be sustained. Even young children who have always fed on milk, are filled with beef tea when sick. We are glad to see that doubts of the propriety of this plan are starting up, and that farinaceous food seems about to be restored to a place in the sick room. There is needed a wider range of the dietary than modern practice employs. Especially is the practice unsound which restricts young children when sick, as is frequently done, almost entirely to beef tea.

Ergot in Dysentery.

A French physician claims to have succeeded in the treatment of epidemic dysentery by the use of ergot. He gave 7 or 8 grains every four hours, the cure being effected in ordinary cases in two or three days. After a few doses constipation is produced, which lasts three or four days. Ergotin has the same effect.

The Prince of Wales and his Doctors.

The recent illness and recovery of the Prince of Wales appear to have awakened in the people of England a lively interest in the medical profession in general- From the comments made by certain prominent newspapers, one might infer that physicians were until lately regarded as of little worth, and that the illness of a royal patient was necessary to qualify the public to appreciate their merits. Certain it is that medicine and its practitioners have risen greatly in popular estimation since the event referred to.

Innovation not always Improvement.

That our predecessors in medicine were fools—that all old things are follies—that reform means anything modern and new—are points that enter largely into the creed of the present generation of practitioners. But it will do us no harm to enquire if our boasted simplification of medicines is always an improvement. Chemistry has separated the active principles of plants, and added largely to the convenience and comfort of prescriber and patient. Quinia has superseded cinchona and its preparations—morphia has taken the place of opium—and so on, *ad infinitum*. But do we not lose in many instances, by rejecting the compound original for a single, isolated element? Are there not many instances in which we might go back with advantage to the Bark in substance, or its infusion? The same question may be asked in regard to other agents. Again, do we not often sacrifice the interests of our patients to prejudice and popular clamor by giving insufficient doses? For instance, we have known iodide of potassium given for weeks in small doses with no good result, when an increase of the quantity to twenty or thirty grains daily, was followed by immediate benefit. The same may be said of the bromides of potassium and ammonium—of the preparations of colchicum, iron, etc. On these subjects we have positive opinions of our own; but our aim at present is to throw out the hint as a subject of reflection for some of our readers.

Swallowing a Rostrum.

A practitioner of this city—not a "regular," but a recognized exponent of a progressive and reformed system—boasts of having lately cured a patient who had swallowed a "rostrum" every day for three months.

Homeopathy in an Economic Light.

Cundurango is already consigned by the profession to the tomb of the misseltoe. But the homeopaths are discovering extraordinary results from diminutive doses. A tincture is first made, and of this a "decimal attenuation" is prepared—or as the vulgar would say, it is diluted with ten times its quantity of water. Five drops of the dilution are given daily, and cancers are being cured by it. This will kill the speculation in cundurango; for at this rate of administration a single pound of the medicine will cure one thousand patients. Where is Dr. Bliss?

Crotonchloralhydrat as a Narcotic.

Professor Liebreich says that the narcotic effect of crotonchloralhydrat depends on the formation of dichlorallylo in the blood, and that this is analogous in effect to æthylidenchloride.

Deaths.

Dr. EDWARD B. BINGHAM, U. S. N., died suddenly at his residence in Oakland, on the night of February 24th, of "paralysis of the heart." He was a native of Philadelphia, and 29 years of age. He leaves a widow and a young daughter.

Dr. SAMUEL W. BLACKWOOD. late of Sacramento, and a former resident of Alameda County, died October 6th, in Callao, South America, aged about 28 years.

Dr. WM. D. BUCK, of Manchester, N. H., died suddenly January 9th, aged 60 years. He was one of the most prominent medical men in New Hampshire.

Reported Cure by Cundurango.

An advertising sheet styled the "New York Druggist's Price Current," asserts as "a victory over the medical press and the medical profession," the cure of a case of cancer by cundurango. The subject was a lady in New York, whose "left breast had been cut and cauterized by surgeons till patience ceased to be a virtue"—a statement which, of itself, is sufficient to condemn the story as a mere puff of the "Fluid Extract of Cundurango, prepared by Messrs. Bliss, Keane & Co."

Literary Piracy.

Last month we gave a highly complimentary notice of "*The Medical Jurisprudence of Insanity*, by J. H. Balfour Brown, Esq., Barrister"—an English publication. The *Journal of Mental Science* declares that the work is plagiarized from an American book, and that it might almost be called a new edition of Dr. Ray's Treatise on Insanity. We are under the necessity of deferring some comments on this piratical proceeding till our next issue.

Transactions of the California State Medical Society.

We have received from Dr. Logan a copy of the Proceedings of the Annual Meeting at Sacramento in October last. It is a creditable volume of 250 pages, containing a variety of papers, some of which are of value. A further notice of it will appear in the next JOURNAL.

☞ THE ANNUAL REPORT OF THE STATE INSANE ASYLUM will be noticed to some extent in the next number of the JOURNAL.

THE WESTERN LANCET is the title of a new medical monthly published in San Francisco by a "joint stock association," and edited by Drs. Babcock and Treanor, of Oakland, the latter a Professor in Toland Medical College. It is very neatly got up, and, like our own journal, contains some useful reading. Its cheapness—only $3.00 a year—precludes the idea of support by regular subscriptions, and therefore reflects great credit on the enterprise and philanthropy of the stockholders. We are pleased to notice that the *Lancet* does not think it necessary to annihilate our JOURNAL in order to establish itself. There is one remark in its columns which we do not understand, unless it is intended to be personal. It reads as follows: "The winning animal in a donkey race is the last one in. It is the least capable who takes the prize."

"SULPH. MORPHII" is the way it reads in the report of an analysis made in Cincinnati by an "Analytic Chemist."

GENERAL SUMMARY.

Galvanic Treatment of Bed-Sores and Indolent Ulcers.

Dr. Wm. A. Hammond recommends for indolent ulcers and bed-sores, the galvanic treatment as first suggested by Crussel, of St. Petersburgh. He says: "During the last six years I have employed it to a great extent in the treatment of bed-sores caused by diseases of the spinal cord, and with scarcely a failure; indeed, I may say without any failure, except in two cases where deep sinuses had formed, which could not be reached by the apparatus. A thin silver plate—no thicker than a sheet of paper—is cut to the exact size and shape of the bed-sore; a zinc plate of about the same size is connected with the silver plate by fine silver or copper wire six or eight inches in length. The silver plate is then placed in immediate contact with the bed-sore, and the zinc plate on some part of the skin above, a piece of chamois-skin soaked in vinegar intervening. This must be kept moist, or there is little or no action of the battery. Within a few hours the effect is perceptible, and in a day or two the cure is complete in a great majority of cases. In a few instances a longer time is required. I have frequently seen bed-sores three or four inches in diameter, and half an inch deep, heal entirely over in forty-eight hours. Mr. Spencer Wells states that he has often witnessed large ulcers covered with granulations within twenty-four hours, and completely filled up and cicatrization begun in forty-eight hours. During his recent visit to this country I informed him of my experience, and he reiterated his opinion that it was the best of all methods for treating ulcers of indolent character and bed-sores."

Veratrum Viride in Puerperal Convulsions.

D. Colvin, M.D., writes from Clyde, N. Y., January, 1871, to the editor of the *Medical Record*, as follows:

"In reading the proceedings of the New York Pathological Society, I was much pleased to see that the use of the veratrum viride in puerperal convulsions was meeting with much favor. For the past five years I have used it in many cases with better results than from any other course which I had heretofore.

"But a few weeks ago I used it (not in such doses as were

reported by Dr. Eearn to have been given by a homeopathist) in a case of eclampsia, where the consulting physician and myself could distinctly count the pulsations at one hundred and seventy per minute, and where no ameliorations of symptoms could be obtained with the use of chloroform and the other ordinary remedies in use for this grave malady. I gave Squibb's fluid extract, beginning with five drops, and increasing the dose one drop once in two hours until a decided impression was made upon the heart's action. Seven drops, at that interval, were all that was required to sufficiently diminish the pulsations to bring about the desired result.

"I wish to say a word relative to the use of the same remedy in pneumonia. For eight years past I can truly say that, with the exception of an occasional Dover's powder, I have quite exclusively relied upon the veratrum in the treatment of this disease.

"Within the past year I have substituted the chloral hydrate for the Dover's powder, and find it answers a better purpose." *Georgia Medical Companion.*

Action of Chloral Hydrate.

M. Byasson, a French scientist, has presented to the Academy of Sciences of Paris a record of the results of numerous experiments on chloral hydrate, (vid. *American Journal of Pharmacy* for January, 1872,) which tend in some degree to invalidate the views of Liebrich. He finds the hydrate to differ from chloroform in its action, which is peculiar to itself, and is the result of two products into which it is decomposed: chloroform and formic acid. A part of the chloroform formed by the action of the alkaline carbonates of the blood upon the hydrate of chloral is eliminated by the lungs; and a part of the formic acid is found in the urine in the shape of formate of soda. As a practical result of the experiments, the author found that he could distinguish three degrees, produced gradually and successively by increasing doses, but varying in individuals.

(1.) A feebly soporific action and slight sedative effect upon the sensitive nervous system, which may be accompanied by intervals of a peculiar agitation, similar to that produced by some dreams.

(2.) An energetic and powerful soporific action, with diminution of sensibility. Then follows a period of calm slumber of variable duration, but without disturbance to the principal functions of life. By means of successive doses administered when the effects of the previous ones have nearly disappeared, this slumber may be extended during a comparatively long time.

(3.) Anesthetic action, with complete loss of sensibility and muscular power. Death has generally been found to follow when this stage has been reached, in consequence of the inability of the organism to sustain the increasing action of so large a quantity of the drug until its complete transformation and elimination.

Metallic Albuminuria.

By this term certain French writers designate the condition of the renal secretion resulting from the administration of a number of metallic salts. It is found that the introduction into the stomach or veins of cats, rats, and other animals, of the acetates of cadmium, uranium, etc., produces this condition. The same is said of gold, silver, and lead. A paper on this subject was read before the French Academy of Sciences by M. Rabuteau, (*Gaz. Hebdom.*, Dec. 22,) in which also the effects of alkaline chlorides on the urine were minutely described. Those of sodium, potassium and magnesium increased the excretion of urea, stimulated nutrition and elevated the animal heat. But while the chlorides of sodium and ammonium excited the circulation, that of potassium reduced it. Chloride of potassium, therefore, has a double action—as a chloride, it excites nutrition; as a salt of potassium, it reduces the circulation. Its action on nutrition is explained by the augmentation of the quantity and acidity of the gastric secretion, and the increase in the number of red globules in the blood.

Opening of Bubo with Caustic Potash.

Dr. McNamara (*Indian Med. Gazette—N. Y. Med. Gazette*) opens acute bubo by potassa fusa instead of the knife, and thus avoids the tedious process of unhealthy granulation. The bubo is first covered with several layers of sticking plaster, in which a hole is made half the size of the intended opening, and the caustic is then rubbed on the exposed skin. The spot is covered with sticking plaster and an opiate administered. A black eschar is formed, which is removed in a few days by a poultice, leaving a healthy ulcer, which soon heals by the ordinary treatment. Dr. McNamara is very confident that this treatment will always prevent the production of the pale, flabby and unhealthy granulations which are so common in bubo. The patient suffers very little pain from the caustic used in the manner described.

Absinthism and Alcoholism.

Under these heads a series of experiments has been performed by members of the French Academy of Medicine (*Gaz. Hebdomadaire*) to test the effect of alcohol and absinth on the animal system. The results go to show that, while epileptic convulsions are liable to follow the free use of both agents, they supervene much more speedily on the use of absinth. Essence of absinth alone will cause convulsion, whilst those of mint, balm, fennel, etc., produce only a general excitement. When added to alcohol or wine in the form of cordial, absinth appears to develop its toxic action with much force. Its qualities are peculiarly noxious, and the general sentiment is in favor of abolishing it entirely.

Partial Dislocation of Head of Radius.

Dr. Lyell, of Glasgow, quoted in the *Medical Press and Circular*, describes the case of a child whose hand was fully prone and the fore-arm semi-bent, though no displacement of the bones at the elbow could be detected by the touch. He took hold of the child's hand (the right) in his own right hand, and the elbow joint in his left, placing his thumb over the head of the radius, then supinated the hand fully, at the same time extending the fore-arm. In the act of supination he felt a slight jerk, on which the motion of the arm was completely restored. He thinks it not an uncommon accident, though not described in the books.

Rupture of Rectus Femoris Muscle—Recovery.

A man aged 60, was thrown from a wagon and ruptured the tendon of the rectus femoris muscle, close to the patella. The surgeon, Dr. Kelly Addison, fastened the leg to a fixed double-inclined plane, and secured to the upper part of the box an elastic band, which passed around the lower edge of the patella and drew it upward. The apparatus was still further secured by adhesive strips. The patient lay in bed ten weeks, and then walked with a staff. In a year he walked, with the slightest possible halt.—*Canada Lancet*, Dec. 1871.

Trismus Nascentium—Its Cause and Treatment.

Dr. Bailey, of Albany, in an exhaustive essay on this disease read before the New York State Medical Society, (*American Journal of Obstetrics*, Nov. 1871) comes to the conclusion that it is due to irritation of the navel, mostly through neglect of proper dressing, that it is incurable as a general rule, and that prevention is the only security. Cleanliness of both patient and apartment, with mild and soothing applications, must be the main dependence.

Success and Failure in Lithotomy.

The late Mr. Lynn, an English surgeon, cut 25 patients for stone without losing one. He then boasted that he had at last discovered the secret of performing lithotomy with success. Afterwards he declared that the Almighty punished him for his presumption, for he lost the next four cases which he cut. Mr. Liston operated 24 times in succession without a single failure, but lost five of the next thirteen cases.

Tannic Acid in Cancer.

Dr. Wharton, President of the Royal College of Surgeons of Ireland, (*Med. Press and Circular*, Dec. 27, 1871,) recommends tannic acid as a valuable dressing in open cancer. He regards it as possessed of some inherent property by virtue of which it promotes assimilation. It should be liberally applied as a daily dressing.

Chlorate of Potassa in Chronic Dysentery.

Dr. Shackleton, of St. Mary's, Ohio, (*Cincinnati Clinic*) gives 10 grains chlorate of potassa with one fifth of a grain morphia every four hours in chronic dysentery, he says with great success.

Ipecacuanha in Epistaxis.

Dr. John Shrady, of Harlem, N. Y., has successfully exhibited ipecacuanha in several severe cases of epistaxis, especially in the form associated with chronic alcoholism. In one instance, where from a previous experience plugging the posterior nares was strongly objected to, he used vinum ipecacuanhæ in teaspoonful doses until free emesis was produced, with the result of arresting the hemorrhage in fifteen minutes.—*N. Y. Med. Record.*

Treatment of Diabetes.

Dr. G. Moore, of Hastings (*British Med. Journal*), lately read a paper on a case of diabetes of three months' standing. The patient had previously been rigorously dieted. Under a bread-and-milk diet (three pints of the latter daily) and the administration of effervescing salines, with iron, the urine became perfectly free from sugar in a fortnight, and the patient speedily gained flesh and strength. Dr. Moore expressed himself strongly in favor of the free use of milk in such cases.—*N. Y. Medical Record.*

Hydropathy in Typhoid Fever.

In Vienna, sixty patients with ileo-typhoid fever were subjected to the cold water treatment. (*American Med. Journal.*) They were placed in a bath of 60° as often as required to keep the temperature of the body at a natural standard. Twenty-eight per cent. of them died, as against twenty-seven per cent. treated in the ordinary manner.

Effects of Bromide of Potassium.

Dr. Julius Levy, of Berlin, writes that if bromide of potassium in drachm doses, three times daily, is continued for months, a series of boils will be apt to be produced. He says if some preparation of cinchona be given with the bromide, no boils or other evil sequelæ will arise.—*N. Y. Med. Record.*

Process of Embalming.

Alcohol of 90 degrees in which is dissolved a fiftieth part by weight of carbolic acid, is said to form the best liquid to inject for embalming. It penetrates the capillaries much better than when glycerin is employed as a solvent.

Bungling Prescriptions.

There seems to be difference of opinion in regard to the duty of a pharmacist in compounding a physician's prescription; whether he should comply with it in every particular, make immaterial changes in it, or return it to the prescriber.

It frequently happens that a prescription for pills is written containing ingredients that it is impossible to make into a mass that would make pills of a neat and convenient size; or for a solution containing articles that are incompatible, that might prove injurious; or for powders, which, owing to the deliquescent nature of the mixture, it could not be sent to the patient. These prescriptions are often met with in this country, and are frequently a source of much trouble. Is it enough for the pharmacist to throw the entire responsibility upon the physician, and dispense prescriptions regardless of the results arising from it? Let us hear from some of our pharmacists in the State.—*Leavenworth Medical Herald.*

Small-Pox in Utero.

Dr. J. T. Hampton, of this city, has forwarded the following interesting note:

At 10:30 A. M., Sunday, Nov. 12, 1871, I delivered a woman of a child suffering from small-pox. At the time of its birth the disease had reached the vesicular stage, showing that it had passed successfully through the macular and papular stages in utero. On the morning of the fifth day the pustular stage was reached. Up to this time, and until the morning of the tenth day, the child took nourishment and seemed to be doing well. On the morning following it vomited incessantly, blood gushing from its mouth and nose—the same evening it died. The mother was vaccinated successfully six weeks prior to confinement.—*Phila. Med. and Surg. Reporter.*

Treatment of Gonorrhea by Warm Water Injections.

Dr. John O'Reilly (*Am. Practitioner*), in recommending warm water injections in the treatment of gonorrhea, says, that the subjoined conclusions may be drawn from his experience: 1st. That gonorrhea yields to local treatment, and even water injections. 2d. That water injections or medicated lotions owe their efficiency to their frequent application. 3d. That the common small syringe should be done away with in treating this disease, and none used but those throwing a continuous stream. 4th. That large injections, by fully distending the mucous membrane of the urethra, insure a speedier cure than those less copious.—*Canada Lancet.*

A Speedy Cure for Rheumatism.

Dr. R. H. Boyd states that he cures inflammatory rheumatism in from three to seven days by the following method: He gives first a full emetic dose of ant. et potass. tart., and when this has operated, five drops of tinct. opii and five drops tinct. colchici every three or four hours, and a teaspoonful of a half pint mixture, containing dr. iv. potass. acet. every hour. When the patient becomes very hungry, and is quite free from pain, having fasted several days, he allows two teaspoonfuls of milk or one oyster three times a day, increasing the quantity gradually each day.—*Michigan University Medical Journal.*

Poisoning by Strychnia.

Dr. Hazelton reported a case of poisoning by strychnia taken with suicidal intent. The characteristic sypmtoms appeared ten minutes after the ingestion of about two scruples of the poison. The patient was placed under the influence of chloroform, and with some difficulty the stomach tube was introduced and the stomach thoroughly washed out. Two hours after taking the poison, the chance of recovery seemed good, but at the expiration of this time a severe convulsion came on, in which the patient died.—*Boston Medical Journal.*

How to Chose a Doctor.

To have good sense as a doctor, one must have good sense as a man. If your doctor is a nincompoop about other things, you may be sure that he is a ninny as to medicine and surgery. If the doctor's office is untidy and vile to smell of, you may be quite certain that he will come short of giving good counsel as to health and tidiness of body. If he be clumsy in hitching his horse, you may be sure that he is not handy at surgery or midwifery. If he be a great, coarse, blundering fellow,—careless of dress, a two-fisted, farmer-looking man, you may be sure that he will lack perception of those finer symptoms by which a good doctor is guided. If he slanders brother physicians, do not trust him. Good, earnest doctors are too busy to find time to slander their brethren or their rivals. It is all the same with lawyers, ministers and teachers. The truly good and truly great do not detract from the reputation of others, they are generous and magnanimous even to rivals. If your doctor flatters you and humors your lusts and appetites, and helps you out of a bad scrape secretly, without reproof, as if you had done no wrong, distrust him. If you can hire him to do or say what he would not do without hire, beware of him. Good doctors cannot be bought. Your doctor ought not to be a single man. He ought to have a wife and children, and if you see that his wife respects him and his children obey him, that is a very good sign that he may be trusted. If your doctor tells you how to keep well that is a good sign. You come to him with a toothache; he gives you creosote and clove oil for the tooth, and at the same time suggests that you do not wash enough to keep well—that is a good sign. If the children like him, that is a good sign. If you find him reading in his office, that is a good sign, and specially if he be a settled middle-aged man. If you hear him say "I once thought so and so, but I was wrong," that is a good sign. If the doctor is neat and handy in rolling pills and folding powders, that is to his credit as a surgeon. If he understands how to bud roses, graft fruit-trees, mix strawberry pollen for improved berries, cure chicken pip, and tinker a trunk lock, or put a clock in order, all these are so much to his credit. If, further, you love to meet him, the sight of him quickens you, and you are glad to hear him chat; and you know him thus to be a lovable, sympathetic man—he's the man for your doctor, your confidential friend—find him, trust him.—*T. K. Beecher*.

"A Gown and Hood of the Doctor of Medicine" are presented by associations of students or medical men in England to prominent teachers whom they delight to honor.

An Immense Aerolite, weighing 36 tons, has been presented to the Paris Academy of Sciences by the Danish and Swedish Governments.

A Gift of $50,000 has been made to the London Hospital by an anonymous donor.

STATE BOARD OF HEALTH.

Abstract from the Reports of Deaths and their Causes in the following cities and towns in California, during January, 1872:

CITIES AND TOWNS.	Total No. Deaths.	Prevalent Diseases. Consumption.	Other diseases of Lungs.	Dis. Stomach and Bowels.	Diphtheria	Scarlatina	Typho-malarial Fevers.	AUTHORITIES.
San Francisco......	226	48	13	5	1	3	8	S. F. B'd of Health
Sacramento	20	3	4	0	0	0	0	Sac. B'd of Health
Petaluma	5	2	0	0	0	0	0	Dr. G. W. Graves.
Dixon	1	0	0	0	0	0	0	Dr. R. H. Plummer
Santa Clara.........	8	1	1	0	1	0	0	Dr. H. H. Warburton
Stockton	8	1	0	2	0	0	0	Stockton Bd Health
Marysville..........	10	1	1	0	0	0	2	Dr. C. E. Stone.
Placerville..........	3	0	0	0	0	0	0	Dr. E. A. Kunkler.
Auburn...............	6	0	0	0	0	0	0	Dr. A. S. Du Bois.
San Diego County..	5	3	0	0	0	0	0	Dr. T. C. Stockton.
San Luis Obispo...	...	...	...	...	...	...	...	Dr. W. W. Hays.
Oroville	4	2	0	0	0	0	0	Dr. J. M. Vance.
Woodland............	2	1	0	0	0	0	0	Dr. A. B. Mehring.
Oakland	6	0	1	1	0	0	0	Dr. T. H. Pinkerton
Los Angeles.........	17	1	0	1	0	0	0	Dr. H. S. Orme.
Truckee	0	0	0	0	0	0	0	Dr. Wm. Curless.
St. Helena	0	0	0	0	0	0	0	Dr. J. S. Adams.
Napa City............	1	0	0	0	0	0	1	Dr. M. B. Pond.
Cacheville	0	0	0	0	0	0	0	Dr. E. L. Parramore
Siskiyou..............	0	0	0	0	0	0	0	Dr. T. T. Cabanis.
Watsonville	...	...	...	...	...	...	...	Dr. C. E. Cleveland
Folsom	0	0	0	0	0	0	0	Dr. L. McGuire.
Bridgeport Town'p	2	0	0	0	0	0	0	Dr. J. L. Asay.
Sut'r C'k & Amador	0	0	0	0	0	0	0	Dr. H. M. Fiske.
Monterey..............	...	...	...	...	...	...	...	Dr. C. A. Canfield.
Santa Cruz..........	2	2	0	0	0	0	0	Dr. C. L. Anderson
Vallejo	...	...	...	...	...	...	...	Dr. J. M. Brown.
Suisun & Fairfield.	1	0	0	0	0	0	0	Dr. S. D. Campbell
Colusa	0	0	0	0	0	0	0	Dr. Luke Robinson
Trinity County......	4	1	0	0	0	0	0	Dr. J. C. Montagne
Santa Barbara......	5	3	1	1	0	0	0	Dr. C. B. Bates.
Redwood City	1	0	0	0	0	0	0	Dr. Kirkpatrick.
Totals	331	69	21	10	2	3	11	

Abstract from Reports of Births.

CITIES AND TOWNS.	Total Births.	Male.	Female.	Still-born.	Live-born.	AUTHORITIES.
San Francisco..	**97**	**58**	**39**	**22**	**75**	**S. F. Board of Health.**
Sacramento.. ...	**61**	**26**	**35**	**5**	**56**	**Sac. Board of Health.**
All other places	**249**	**136**	**113**	**14**	**235**	**Various sources.**
Total..........	**407**	**220**	**187**	**41**	**366**	

Remarks.—The year opens up with the same favorable state of the public health which has been noted for some time past, and even more favorably than has been before known, as demonstrable by our records. In January, 1871, when we felicitated ourselves as to the low death-rate everywhere, the total mortality was then in San Francisco, 298; in Sacramento, 28; in Stockton, 22; in Marysville, 13, and in Oakland, 12. Compared with these rates, we have now a diminution of 72 deaths in the first named locality, 8 in the second, 14 in the third, 3 in the fourth, 6 in the last; and so on in the same proportion throughout all the minor towns with which we are in correspondence, except Los Angeles. In this latter place, owing to the imperfectness of the records, the causes of many of the deaths are not returned to our office, and of course we are not able to discover the reason of the increased mortality. It in to be hoped that as soon as the present Bill, now pending in the Senate, for the creation of Local Boards of Health, cooperative with the State Board, shall have become a law, measures will be taken to remedy the evils resultant.

Notwithstanding small-pox, as stated in our last month's report, has been introduced into the State, owing to the imperfection of our laws, and the reluctancy with which the people's representatives accord sufficient authority to our Boards of health; still, the prompt action which has been taken to isolate the cases, and to prevent its further propagation, seems thus far to have proved successful. As an instance of the value of these measures, we would state that during the recent epidemic in the smaller cities and towns of New York, where they had no local Boards of Health, nor a State Board, the ravages of the disease were far greater than in Massachusetts, where such Boards exist. Boston has been almost as much exposed as the city of New York, but how different the result? It is true that the last mentioned city has a most efficient local Board, but its action is too limited. The instructions, which were so effective in arresting the progress of the disease in Lowell, Mass., were adopted by the Board at its last meeting, and the press throughout the State is requested to give them as much publicity as possible.

THOMAS M. LOGAN, M.D.,
Permanent Secretary State Board of Health.

Mortality in San Francisco during January, 1872.

By H. Gibbons Jr., M. D.

CAUSES OF DEATH.

Abscess	1	Diseases of Heart	16	Meningitis, Cerebro Spinal	1
Alcoholism	2	Dropsy	3	Metrorrhagia	1
Aneurism of Aorta	3	Drowning	1	Nephritis	1
Do.	2	Dysentery	1	Old Age	2
Apoplexy	4	Enteritis	3	Paralysis	4
Ascites	1	Erysipelas	3	Peritonitis	2
Atrophia	5	Fever, Remittent	1	Phthisis	48
Bowels, Ulceration of	1	Do. Intermittent	5	Pleuritis	1
Bright's Disease	1	Do. Scarlet	3	Pneumonitis	5
Bronchitis	4	Do. Typhoid	8	Poisoning	2
Cancer	1	Fractures	1	Premature Birth	1
Do. of Mesentery	1	Gangrene	1	Pyemia	2
Do. of Uterus	1	Gout	2	Septicemia	1
Childbirth	1	Hemorrhage	1	Softening of Brain	2
Cholera Infantum	1	Hydrocephalus	6	Suicide	3
Congestion of Brain	4	Ileus	1	Syphilis	4
Do of Lungs	2	Injuries, unspecified	1	Tabes Mesenterica	1
Congestive Chill	2	Insanity	1	Uremia	2
Convuls'ns, Infantile	8	Inanition	5	Unknown	10
Do. Puerperal	1	Kidney Disease	2	Whooping Cough	2
Croup	3	Liver, Disease of	1		
Debility, General	3	Do. Hypertrophy	1	TOTAL	226
Dentition	1	Do. Cirrhosis of	2	Still-births	14
Diabetes	1	Laryngitis	1		
Diphtheria	1	Meningitis	6		

AGES.

Under 1 year	28	From 15 to 20 years	7	From 60 to 70 years	10
From 1 to 2 years	11	From 20 to 30 years	31	From 70 to 80 years	5
From 2 to 5 years	10	From 30 to 40 years	44	From 80 to 90 years	5
From 5 to 10 years	6	From 40 to 50 years	45	Unknown	2
From 10 to 15 years	6	From 50 to 60 years	16		

Sex:—Male, 163; Female, 63.

Color:—White, 194; Copper, 28; Black, 4.

NATIVITIES.

California	56	France	8	China	32
Other parts of U. S.	47	Germany	17	Australia	1
British-Amer'n Prov.	1	Austria	1	Azores	1
Mexico	2	Denmark	1	Dalmatia	1
England	3	Sweden	1	Peru	1
Ireland	40	Russia	1	Poland	1
Scotland	5	Switzerland	2	Norway	1
Wales	1	Italy	1	St. Vincent's Island	1

RECAPITULATION.

Died in City Wards	165	Small-Pox Hospital	1
City and County Hospital	19	Casualties	5
U. S. Marine Hospital	1	Suicides	3
French Hospital	4	Alms House	7
German Hospital	5	Mt. St. Joseph's Infirmary	5
St. Mary's Hospital	9	Home of Inebriates	1
Orphan Asylum	1		

Remarks.—The same extraordinary immunity from disease which has been noted for months past continued through January. Not since 1866 have there been fewer deaths in this month than in January, 1872, and not since the records have been kept has there been in any one month so remarkably small a mortality among children under five years of age. While, as has been frequently observed, the rule is that two-fifths of the decedents are children under five years of age, such decedents actually formed but little over one-fifth of the mortality in January. The thought arises, can this be due, in part at least, to a diminished number of births in the past few months? The small number of stillbirths gives color to this idea, but unfortunately we have no facts to decide the question. The record of births is so imperfect as to be useless. Another noticeable fact is the small proportion of female decedents. This generally averages more than half that of the males; in the present instance it is not forty per cent. It will be observed also that the excess of deaths is among the foreign born, nearly one-third being natives of Ireland and China alone. In regard to particular diseases we find that no one cause of death has special prominence. Consumption caused 48 deaths; diseases of the heart, 16; convulsions, 8; meningitis, 6; pneumonia, 5; typhoid fever, 8, &c.; these figures indicating a moderate mortality. As somewhat unusual we note five deaths from aneurism and five from intermittent fever; two from gout, one from insanity, and one from cerebro-spinal meningitis. The deaths in January since 1866 number as follows: 1866, 222; 1867, 226; 1868, 228; 1869, 380; 1870, 263; 1871, 298; 1872, 226.

PACIFIC
MEDICAL AND SURGICAL JOURNAL.

VOL. V.—APRIL, 1872.—No. 59.

ORIGINAL COMMUNICATIONS.

Intussusception and Sudden Death.

CONCUSSION OF BRAIN.

Read before the San Francisco Medical Society, by HENRY GIBBONS, M.D.

Jan. 1, 1872. A. B., female, æt. 2½ years, was attacked suddenly with fever, vomiting, and muscular twitching, threatening convulsions. A quantity of half-chewed raw apple was ejected from the stomach, but the symptoms continuing, I used the warm bath, laxative enemas, fomentations to abdomen, and five grains calomel with about the tenth of a grain of opium. She soon fell asleep, and in due time had several copious fecal discharges of dark, bilious character. A slow improvement took place from day to day, but the fever continued to recur with more or less force, with frequent paroxysms of abdominal pain, a tendency to diarrhea, anorexia and extreme irritability.

After a week or ten days of slow and irregular improvement, an aggravation of symptoms occurred, with alvine discharges of black, coffee-ground matter, highly fetid. The exacerbations were paroxysmal and inclined to tertian. Quinia was administered, with other remedies, and again, in five weeks from the first attack a satisfactory improvement occurred. The appetite became almost voracious, and no traces of disease remained. February 17, attendance ceased.

Feb. 21. I was again summoned hastily, to find the patient suffering with paroxysms of what appeared to be colic, with some vomiting. The bowels had not been freely opened for a day or two. Warm fomentations relieved the pain, and a dose of castor oil was followed by several copious evacuations of a normal character. In the evening she was lively and playful and appeared well.

In the night paroxysms of pain recurred, alternated with retching, small quantities of bile being ejected, yellow at first, then green. Being sent for early next morning, I found her recovering apparently from syncope. In a paroxysm of pain, muscular spasms had occurred, approaching convulsion, for which the warm bath was used. This immediately produced extreme pallor and apparent syncope, which led to her speedy removal from the water. She soon revived, and in half an hour was well enough to take some notice of her playthings. The pulse, however, was slow and somewhat irregular, for the first time. No other symptom of cerebral disorder was present. She gave an occasional brief cry from pain, which she referred to the stomach. This was her condition at 11 A. M., when she was left in charge of the nurse, with instructions, if the pain should recur with severity, to use an enema with 10 drops of laudanum, together with suitable external applications.

In two hours the pain returned. The enema was given, but immediately rejected. She was put in the warm bath, when a spasmodic movement of the muscles occurred, with sudden suffusion of the face, followed by extreme pallor, and death in a few seconds. The eyes were perfectly closed as if in sleep.

The necropsy developed no signs of cardiac or pulmonary disease, but on opening the abdomen the liver was at once perceived to be enlarged and congested, and slightly indurated. Its weight was 1⅜ pounds. The gall bladder contained a small quantity of normal bile. A foot or more below the stomach was an invagination of the intestine, and further on, at intervals of eight or ten inches apart, two others. The length of each invagination was between two and three inches, the upper being tucked into the lower portion, as usual. No adhesions or traces of inflammation existed, though the invaginated intestine was moulded at the point of disappearance, showing compression or strangulation. The stomach and intestinal tract were nearly empty, and were free from disease excepting a patch of injected surface in the ileum, of no special importance. The contents were normal. Other abdominal organs sound. As the congested liver and intussusception revealed sufficiently the pathology of the case, and as it was desirable not to disturb the body more than necessary, the head was not examined.

Perhaps a more thorough examination of this case during life would have detected the enlarged liver. But the little patient was so excessively nervous and so intolerant of handling that, in the absence of the ordinary signs of organic disease of the liver, no other examination of the abdomen was made than by frequent palpation to detect tenderness or tympanites, should any exist.

In the management of the case, during most of the time, Drs. Pigne Dupuytren and Morse were associated with me, and Drs. Andrei and Blach also were called in at the final emergency.

The two features of greatest practical importance here presented are: First, the cause which prolonged the illness and brought on the relapse; and second, the cause of sudden death.

In regard to the first point, the liver appears to have been the only organ liable to suspicion. The black stools, identical in appearance with the ejecta of yellow fever, and the tendency to bilious discharges throughout, naturally led to the inference that the function of that organ was disturbed. But the autopsy shows more than this ; and it may be fair to conclude that it was one of those cases, not very uncommon, in which a diseased liver works stealthily to the production of febrile and other results of a serious character. We know that no viscus is so capable as the liver of concealing its disease and disorganization from ordinary observation. I am inclined to the opinion that fevers associated with hepatic congestion or irritation exhibit a greater degree of periodicity than any other febrile affections not strictly malarious ; in other words, that they most resemble intermittents. To some extent they are amenable to the anti-periodic action of quinia. But as a general rule the efficacy of quinia in arresting periodical fevers is proportionate to the absence of local lesions. Hence, if this remedy fails, or if its effect is transitory, we may infer a lurking source of irritation in the liver, spleen, or other viscus—except sometimes in chronic, habitual intermittents.

As to the immediate cause of death, suspicion in such cases is naturally directed to the heart. A clot might have formed during the syncope, and, being subsequently detached, it might have plugged up the aorta. But dissection revealed no clot, and the valves were perfect. The heart contained fluid blood.

At what period did the invagination take place ? Not in the act of death ; for the invaginated intestine bore the marks of compression, being fitted into the invaginating portion with an abrupt shoulder, like a cork in a bottle. Nor was the obstruction of long standing ; for the bowels had been freely purged sixteen hours before death. During the night and subsequently to the purging, paroxysms of pain came on, alternated with vomiting, or rather retching. It seems probable that the invagination occurred at this time. A tendency to intestinal spasm had marked the case from the beginning. The empty and collapsed condition of the ileum favored the process of intussusception under the spasmodic movements. A degree of strangulation occurring, vomiting was provoked, alternated with paroxysms of pain as in strangulated hernia. The warm bath produced sudden relaxation and syncope, without disengaging the intestine from its displacement. Other sedative applications prolonged the period of relief from spasm. During this period the action of the heart was slow and slightly intermittent, as we observe it in certain cases of obstipation and lead colic. As reaction ensued, the accumulating excitability of a temperament extremely nervous by nature, led to a convulsive paroxysm, which was merged into syncope by the bath—the heart coming to a stand before the respiration ceased.

Many years ago, a case somewhat similar in regard to the mode of death came under my observation. A little girl, aged two years, went to bed apparently in good health, and was seized in the night with a convulsion. In half an hour from the attack I saw her, and while she was still struggling in the fit, placed her in the warm bath. Almost immediately she turned pale, and died before she could be replaced in bed. Dissection showed the whole course of the ileum occupied with lumbricoid worms (ascaris lumbricoides). The worms were of the ordinary size, nearly a foot in length, and were so numerous that three or four lay abreast at any given point. The intestine was invaginated at about a dozen different points. It contained little else than the worms.

At what moment intussusception took place in this instance, and what relation it bore, if any, to the death of the patient, it is difficult to determine. Doubtless the convulsion was due to the irritation of the parasites; and it is probable that volvulus occurred in the act of death, if not after death. But the most interesting point in practice is the effect of the bath. In both cases the warm bath hastened, if indeed it did not determine, the fatal result.

The warm bath is a remedy of great power and value,

especially in children. I am inclined to think it is too much neglected by modern practitioners. The old doctors, whom the present fashion decries as a race of empirics whose range of treatment was limited to the administration of a few heroic drugs, made great account of warm bathing, and enjoined the necessity of always having a supply of hot water on hand in families where there were children. Modern physicians would do well to follow the example of their fathers in this respect. Here in California, where many families allow the kitchen fire to go out even in winter, it is often impossible to procure a bucket of warm water in a case of emergency, even by scouring a whole neighborhood.

But, valuable as it is, the warm bath is not always a safe remedy. Every one has observed its tendency to produce syncope. In all important cases I make it a point to remain during its administration. It is my practice to limit its duration to seven minutes, and always to enjoin the prompt removal of the child from the bath if pallor or other indications of syncope come on.

CONCUSSION OF THE BRAIN.

A lad, aged six years, fell to the ground from a height of twelve or fourteen feet, and was picked up senseless. I saw him in about twenty minutes afterwards, when his condition was as follows: Surface pale and cold; pulse barely perceptible; respiration feeble and very slow; pupils insensible to light, and left one dilated; legs extended in tonic spasm, the great toes drawn forcibly apart from the other toes; occasional spasms of the upper extremities, lasting two or three minutes, attended with vomiting, and followed by a like period of relaxation and repose; muscles of the face not disturbed, and eyes remaining closed. No one had seen him fall, and there were no marks of external injury. Prescribed quiet, and warmth to the surface.

Reaction soon commenced, the surface became warm, and vomiting and spasm nearly ceased. Next morning, sixteen hours after the injury, consciousness was partially restored. The pupils were sensible to light, though there was some strabismus. He fretted occasionally as if from pain, and was able to swallow a little drink, but no food. Inclined to vomit when lying on right side.

From this time onward recovery was gradual and regular. For several days he had considerable fever, but nothing further transpired worthy of note.

REMARKS.—The condition of this patient immediately after the injury, was such as to offer but little hope of recovery. Besides the concussion of the brain, it is evident some injury was inflicted on the spinal cord, in the cervical region, which produced or modified the spasmodic disorder. He complained for some days after restoration to sensibility, of soreness at the back of the neck. I am inclined to think that the vomiting was a good symptom, as it would not have occurred had there been a more extreme lesion of the brain.

Bowel Obstructions and their Treatment.

BY C. B. HOLBROOK, M.D., San Francisco.

I beg leave to report the following cases of bowel obstruction through the medium of your excellent journal, not because they are more interesting than others of their class, but because they are fairly typical and illustrative, and enable me to direct attention to the important subject of bowel obstructions and their *treatment*.

January, 1872, I was hastily summoned to visit professionally a man 28 years old, painter by occupation. The prominent symptoms, which present but an imperfect outline of the clinical features of the case, as I learned them from the attending physician, were as follows: Five days prior to this date the patient was seized with severe pain, at first paroxysmal, like colic, and after a time becoming constant, with frequent aggravations. The pain in the first stages emanated from a fixed point in the right iliac fossa; tenderness, at first not much, but gradually increased, being limited to the side of the pain. After the third day pain and tenderness became more continuous, less paroxysmal, and rapidly extended over the entire abdominal surface. Vomiting was prominent and persistent from the beginning; the matter vomited, after a time, had the odor ot feces and was thought to be stercoraceous.

In this connection, allow me to ask the question: Can real stercoraceous vomiting ever take place in bowel obstructions of any form? In other words, can the contents of the colon ever be ejected from the stomach? This surely can only happen when the obstruction is below the ileo-cœcal valve, which statistics prove is extremely rare. If the ileo-cœcal valve be above the obstruction, and perform its function perfectly, it must effectually prevent the escape of the contents of the large into the small intestine. It follows, therefore, that regurgitation is possible only when both the ileum and cœcum are so much distended as to destroy the function of the valve—an occurrence, I opine, exceedingly rare. In addition to the pain and tenderness of the right iliac region, in the first stages, there was swelling, presenting the appearance of tumor, such as might result from accumulation of ingesta and distention from gas, above the point of obstruction. From the beginning, unyielding constipation, or perhaps more properly termed, obstipation, was a marked feature of the case.

The constitutional symptoms, which to begin with were not prominent, soon began to indicate the existence of a grave malady. The pulse became accelerated, constantly increasing in frequency and feebleness; respiration greatly impeded, and in the advanced stages, thoracic; the temperature reduced, with rapid loss of strength, hiccough, and other symptoms which establish the mode of dying by asthena. These are the leading local and general symptoms, as I have very imperfectly grouped and sketched them.

No autopsy was had in this case, but the diagnosis arrived at was that of invagination seated at the junction of the large and small intestine. In support of this conclusion, I may mention two important diagnostic signs omitted above, viz: constant tenesmus, with frequent discharges of blood and mucus, clearly showing that the large intestine was involved.

Acute peritonitis is not an uncommon event, or incident, of this form of bowel obstruction. In this instance it probably supervened upon the rupture of the intestine, at or near the point of invagination, and was obviously the *immediate* cause of death. The treatment was such as is generally considered applicable in these complaints; it comprised drastic cathartics, such as jalap, gamboge, croton oil, etc., administered at short intervals, with a view to quickly overcome the existing obstruction; medicated enemata were frequently employed for the same purpose, with counter-irritation and hot fomentations alternately applied to the affected parts.

Case 2.—January, 1871. Richard Cotter, 26 years old, boot-maker by occupation, was seized suddenly with colic pain, attended with severe retching and vomiting. These symptoms were thought to be traceable to the eating of can oysters two or three hours before the attack. Accordingly a full dose of castor oil was taken, without, however, affording the coveted relief. Two days after this date I was called to visit him in the night, and found him still retching and vomiting, without colic pain, but instead complaining of a sense of sinking, or dragging, in the epigastrium. At this time there was no swelling or tenderness detectible over any part of the abdominal surface; nor was there tympanites; the bowels had not moved, although they had been persistently vexed by cathartics; the pulse greatly depressed, the temperature reduced considerably below the normal standard, and the respiration much embarrassed and thoracic. The patient was continually throwing himself about in bed and complaining of extreme restlessness and want of sleep.

The following was prescribed: ℞. Bismuthi subnit., ʒss; morph. sulph., gr. iss.; sacch. alb., q. s.; M. ft. chart. v. Sig. Take a powder at once, and repeat after each vomiting. To allay the harrassing thirst, pounded ice was ordered to be held in the mouth, and swallowed in small quantities, with hot fomentations to the abdomen.

On visiting the patient the following morning, I was gratified to learn that he had taken but two of the powders, having vomited only once in the meantime, and slept quietly for nearly four hours. The black draught was ordered to be taken, in divided doses, at intervals, in a little warm beef tea, and aided, at the proper time, by an enema of gruel and beef tea; the ice and fomentations continued as before directed. It was arranged at this time that the patient should be taken charge of by the physician for the Society of which he was a member, and therefore I saw no more of this, to me, interesting case; but learned from my friend, Dr. Chamberlain, who was subsequently called in, that no alvine dejection followed the exhibition of the black draught; the vomiting and retching were attended with all those symptoms that denote approaching dissolution by asthenia. The patient lived four days and a few hours from the date of the attack.

In this, as in the first case, no autopsy was had, and therefore the precise lesion upon which the obstruction hinged, was a matter of inference based upon the clinical phenomena. In the absence of swelling and tenderness in any part of the abdomen, and also of tympanites and other signs indicating peritoneal disturbance, it could hardly have been invagination. Might not a knuckle of the intestine have slipped through the diaphragm or mesentery, and thus become incarcerated? The signs, to my mind, tend strongly to this conclusion.

Case 3.—L. Martin, aged 33 years, drayman, after a hard

day's work (March, '71), was attacked with severe colic pain in the right iliac fossa, with swelling and tenderness, which was soon followed by nausea, vomiting, great thirst, and restlessness, accelerated pulse, coldness of the extremities, and general reduction of temperature. In this condition I found the patient on the morning after the attack, ten or twelve hours having elapsed; during which time he had taken, without medical advice, large doses of castor oil, salts, and various kinds of cathartic pills; all of which were ejected from the stomach almost as quickly as swallowed. These nostrums were taken by the patient under the impression that, to obtain relief from his intense suffering, he must have *open bowels.* Under these circumstances a full anodyne was administered, and bottles of hot water applied to the extremities, and warm fomentations to the seat of the pain. After about four hours, I called to note the effects of the treatment,-and was gratified to learn that the patient had had neither vomiting nor much pain after taking the anodyne; that he had slept nearly one hour, when he awoke and had a full alvine dejection.

In this class of cases, as a rule, the armamentary of domestic remedies (purgative) is exhausted before the physician is called in; and to add to the difficulties of the situation, it is expected by the patient and his friends that he will pursue the line of attack already indicated until *his resources* (purgative) fail, or the *patient* surrenders. Is there not danger sometimes of yielding too much to the predilection or prejudice of patients and friends? It should be remembered that prejudice supplants a desire for knowledge, and is therefore a source of error.

In bowel obstructions, from whatever cause, the prognosis is unfavorable. Cases one and two exemplify this statement. In this connection, it may be worthy of remark, that the differential diagnosis of special forms of obstruction, during life, is simply impossible. Case three illustrates that form of obstruction ending in recovery before permanent incarceration of the bowel had taken place.

But the gravest form of obstruction (invagination) should not be despaired of as utterly hopeless. The all-important question then is (after the diagnosis of permanent incarceration, or strangulation, is well made out), what is the rational treatment of these obstructions? The *mode* of recovery, it would seem, solves this question, and gives us the key to rational treatment. The invaginated portion of intestine sloughs away, and is discharged per anum, the entering and receiving portions becoming adherent, and the perviousness of the intestinal tube being thereby restored.

This is the natural process of recovery. Numerous well authenticated cases are on record in which a large portion of invaginated intestine was thrown off, and recovery followed. The following recorded cases are in point: The case of Dr. Van Buren, reported to the New York Pathological Society; Dr. Peaslee reported a very extraordinary case of intestinal sloughing, followed by complete recovery, in 1865; Dr. Wm. Thompson, of Edinburgh, reported forty-three cases of recovery from strangulated intestine; Dr. Haven reported twelve cases of sloughing of the intestine, and of these ten ended in recovery. This indeed is the only mode of recovery to be looked for, after permanent incarceration of the invaginated intestine has taken place.

Insanity and Disease in California.

By HENRY GIBBONS, M.D.*

PREVALENCE OF INSANITY IN CALIFORNIA—CAUSES.

The prevalence of insanity in California is a subject of frequent notice. In the State Asylum, at Stockton, there are upwards of one thousand patients—a number terribly out of proportion to the means of accommodation, to say nothing of treatment. Every day adds to the number,

* Extract from the Annual Report on Practice of Medicine, &c., in the Transactions of the State Medical Society for 1871.

which increases in a much greater ratio than the general population. It is remarkable how large a proportion of the victims come from the the muscular stratum of society—men and women of coarse nerves, uncultivated and unrefined.

Without dwelling on this painful theme, I will enumerate the principal causes which appear to operate so forcibly among us in dethroning reason.

First—The general character of a people who have left their homes to colonize a distant country. Such persons are not an average of the race. Discontented, restless, enterprising, and ambitious, they combine the elements of character prone to mental aberration.

Second—Absence from home and the want of domestic and family ties, to give repose and relief to body and soul.

Third—Neglect of accustomed religious observances, and failure to cultivate as of old the religious sentiment which would serve as ballast in the storms of life.

Fourth—The want of fixedness—the idea that this is but a temporary home, creating the sensation of being adrift in the world.

Fifth—Nostalgia—longing for the old home, the father land, the scenes of childhood and the objects of early attachment.

Sixth—The eager pursuit of wealth as the chief end of life, and the entire absence of contentment, whether fortune smiles or frowns. Men are miserable unless they are making and hoarding money.

Seventh—Reverses of fortune; alas, how frequent!

Eighth—Absence of all moral restraints to which persons have been amenable in the old and staid communities where they have resided.

Ninth—Constant excitement, keeping up unbending nervous tension.

Tenth—Unbridled indulgence of animal passions.

Eleventh—Self-abuse, incident to excess of male population.

Twelfth—Imaginary diseases, fostered by the advertisements of villainous quacks in the newspapers.

Thirteenth—Practical ignorance of the value of cold water as a beverage.

PREVALENCE OF PHTHISIS IN THE FOREIGN POPULATION.

The excessive mortality among our foreign-born population is worthy of notice. Of all nationalities, the natives of Ireland fare the worst. Pulmonary consumption is more conspicuously prevalent among them. Accustomed in their old home to a diet restricted in quality if not in quantity, one might suppose that transplantation to a land flowing with milk and honey, and the substitution of animal for vegetable food would fortify them against the invasion of tubercular disease. But the reverse appears to be true—and this in spite of the free use of that great prophylactic—whisky!

In no country of the world is the laboring population as well housed, and as well clothed, and as well fed as on the Pacific coast. Nowhere do they so generally own houses and lands, and enjoy the comforts, and even the luxuries of life. The complaint lately made in England by some eminent writers, that the laboring population of Great Britain is underfed, especially the women, has no foundation here. Want of nutrition, whatever agency it may exert elsewhere in the development of tuberculosis, cannot be assigned as a cause of the undue prevalence of phthisis in the Irish population of California. What then is the cause?

RELATIONS OF PHTHISIS TO MODES OF LIFE.

Transplantation of the human animal from barbarism to

civilization, or from simple and rugged habits to a life of comfort and indulgence, appears to enervate the vital force and to favor the development of tubercular and other dyscrasies. The Indians of this coast when taken from their out-door life and placed in houses, under the domestic influence of the superior race, exhibit a proneness to pulmonary disease, and a feeble power of resistance to disease in general. Perhaps the transition from the simple fare and the exposed and toilsome habits of Ireland to the comparative ease and indulgence of their adopted home, has a similar effect on our Irish population. Certain it is that the refinement and luxuries of a high civilization, whilst they protect many individuals, enfeeble the general constitution and deteriorate the stock. Equally certain it is that a change from the ease and luxury of city life to a certain degree of exposure and toil and hardship in the country, tends to counteract the development of phthisis. Suppose that all children of consumptive parents in such a city as San Francisco, or Boston, and all other persons of tubercular tendencies, could be seized by an iron hand at the period of adolescence and dragged into the forest and the mountains, and made to "camp out" and sleep in blankets on the ground, and endure hardships and coarse fare, what, let me ask the reader, would be the result in diminishing the mortality among them from phthisis?

ACCIDENTS OF CHILD-BED AMCNG FOREIGN WOMEN.

Accidents of child-bed are also more frequent among foreign-born women. Such, at least, is the result of my observations during twenty-one years of practice in California. An undue proportion of labors requiring instrumental interference, owing to deformed pelvis and other causes, has been in this class of patients. Deformity of the pelvis I think is most common in European, and particularly German, women.

MORTALITY AMONG CHILDREN.

The mortality is also in excess among the children of foreigners. This is due in great part to sheer carelessness. A majority of American wives study arithmetic in the marriage-bed; and too many of them stand as murderers at the door of their own womb. But foreign women seldom exercise restraint; they multiply and replenish the earth with great industry. But they care less for their offspring after they are born, and suffer many to die from ill management and neglect.

Public attention is frequently called to the great mortality among children, not less than thirty-six or thirty-seven per cent. of the deaths in San Francisco occurring under five years of age. Persons are startled when they learn that so nearly half the children born in the metropolis die so young, and they seek some special cause for the fatality. But it is so in all large cities. In St. Louis, in 1869, a year of unusual health, when the death rate was under nineteen in a thousand, nearly one half the deaths were of children under five years. It should not be overlooked that a season of superior health may swell the infant mortality beyond the due proportion. A comparison of the deaths in children with the entire population, is the only basis for a correct estimate. Judged by this standard, there is nothing remarkable in the infant mortality of our chief city. But the absence among us of infantile diarrhea or cholera infantum, and other affections of the bowels so terribly fatal in summer to young children in the Atlantic cities, ought to reduce the number of deaths of children in California.

ABSENCE OF SUN-STROKE IN CALIFORNIA.

There are two marked differences between the Atlantic cities and those of the Pacific coast, in regard to prevalent diseases and vital statistics as represented in the bills of mortality. One is the comparative immunity which we enjoy from the summer diseases of children, as just referred to, and the other, the absence of sun-stroke. Notwithstanding the intense heat of the interior during the summer months, the thermometer often ranging from ninety to one hundred degrees in the middle of the day for several weeks consecutively, sun-stroke is almost unheard of in California. In both instances the reason will be found in the dryness of the atmosphere, promoting rapid evaporation from the skin, and uniform coolness of the nights, which favors sleep and recuperation. It is the universal testimony that a temperature of one hundred degrees on this coast is more easily sustained than one of eighty-five degrees on the Atlantic side. In the extreme southeastern corner of the State and in the adjacent portion of Arizona, the thermometer is said to rise sometimes as high as one hundred and fifteen or one hundred and twenty degrees. But even this extreme is not incompatible with general health. A physician in feeble health who was stationed at Fort Yuma some years ago, informed me that, during the excessive heat, he was in the habit of sitting every day in the shade of a tree, enveloped in a wet sheet, the evaporation keeping him comfortably cool. The cooling effect of this expedient may be inferred from the fact which I have repeatedly witnessed, that the thermometer will fall from ninety-five degrees in the open air to seventy or seventy-five degrees when the bulb is covered with a wet rag. In the hot, desiccated atmosphere of the interior, the human body bathed in sweat becomes a wet-bulb thermometer, and cools itself by evaporation.

SUPERIOR DIETARY OF OUR POPULATION.

There are few countries in the world, if indeed there be any, capable of furnishing as wholesome a diet as the Pacific slope of North America. This remark holds good as to meats, bread, vegetables and fruit. In the ocean climate, which knows no summer, tainted meat is unknown; and when the sun is in the zenith, your butcher commends his beef because it has been killed several days. In the interior, the dryness of the air renders it antiseptic. By the abundant supply of food and the shortness of winter, if winter it can be called, animals are kept in good condition before slaughter. We seldom hear of epidemic diseases in the farm-yard.

The trichina has been detected in a number of instances in pork. But I am not informed of the occurrence of trichinosis in the human subject in a single case.

THE SUPPLY OF MILK—ITS CHARACTER.

In Atlantic cities, the great mortality among infants is attributed in part to impure milk. The milk supply in California is generally pure and good. It is so, at least, as far as the cow is concerned; but when transported a great distance to market, to San Francisco, for instance, from the country around the bay, it is spoiled, or nearly so, before reaching the consumer, especially when churned in the streets for some hours during distribution. Adulteration is seldom practiced, though dilution with water is not always regarded as a violation of the moral law. Distilleries are not sufficiently numerous to affect the milk supply to any great extent. But it should never be forgotten, that wherever there are distilleries, there will be poisoned milk. The lives of infants so often depend on the wholesomeness of this staple in their diet, that thoughtful and conscientious persons who have them in charge, will never fail to assure themselves that the milk is exempt from this source of contamination.

Dealers in milk are not always destitute of chemica knowledge, which they bring to bear by dissolving a por tion of soda in the liquid, in anticipation of the acetous fermentation, or after that has taken place.

EXCELLENCE OF VEGETABLES AND FRUITS.

Vegetables of all kinds are fresh and perfect almost in every month of the year. Fruits, also, in every variety, are always on hand and in great perfection. The entire absence of the fruit-curculio precludes the presence of worms in any kind of fruit. I have never seen an instance of cholera morbus produced by eating cherries. Visitors from the East are surprised at the impunity with which they may indulge in this delicious fruit. The children of persons owning orchards are permitted to run at large among the cherry trees without apprehension of danger.

SUPERIOR QUALITY OF FLOUR AND BREAD.

There is less of unsound and damaged flour in California than in any other country. Wheat is used almost exclusively, and the mills vie with each other in turning out the finest qualities of flour. Besides, none but the best kinds will command the market. Bakers, in cities and towns, make a sweet and excellent bread. In this respect, the dietary of persons who depend on bakeries, constituting the great mass of the population, cannot be surpassed. In many rural districts, soda and saleratus are used extensively and lavishly in the manufacture of bread, with the effect of neutralizing the gastric acid and promoting indigestion.

WOODEN DWELLINGS—BASEMENTS—NO CROWDING.

Nine-tenths of the people of California live in wooden houses. In our dry and temperate climate, such habitations are not only comfortable but also conducive to health. Many of the better class of dwellings have basements with floors beneath the level of the ground. Such basements should be regarded as unfriendly to health, and especially should they be closed against individuals and families predisposed to pulmonary disorders. The crowded underground life which abounds in large cities elsewhere, is unknown in California. There is no crowding anywhere, except among the Chinese, with whom it is the normal condition.

Mrs. Winslow's Soothing Syrup—A Poison.

By W. F. McNUTT, M.D., San Francisco.

My attention was first called to the baneful effects and the enormous consumption of this nostrum, by an article in the November, '69, number of the *California Medical Gazette*, by Dr. Murray, U. S. A. Dr. Murray had been called to see a child aged six months, apparently in a dying condition from the effects of some narcotic poison. He found that this Soothing Syrup was the only medicine which had been administered, and of it the child had taken two teaspoonfuls within ten hours. There was remaining in the vial from which the two teaspoonfuls had been taken, ten drachms, which yielded, on analysis by a skillful chemist, nearly one grain of morphia and other opium alkaloids to the ounce of syrup. "The specimen of Soothing Syrup analyzed was made by Curtis & Perkins, of New York, who are the only manufacturers."

On the 7th of February, Mrs. W. came into my office with a child five months old in her arms, which, she said, was very sick; that it slept constantly, and would not nurse or move for several days. The child was breathing heavily and its pupils were closely contracted. I asked if the child had been taking opium; she replied that it had taken nothing but soothing syrup. She said that on the 5th, two days before, the child was restless and its bowels costive, and that a neighbor had advised her to give it a teaspoonful of soothing syrup, saying it was excellent to regulate the bowels. (She had previously given the syrup in small doses.) She administered the syrup twice during the day, a teaspoonful each time; the child slept heavily all night, and would not nurse when roused. Not suspecting the syrup had anything to do with its sleeping, she gave on the 6th, at different times, three teaspoonfuls more. The child refused to nurse when roused. On the 7th she gave it another teaspoonful, before bringing it to my office. I told her that the child was poisoned by morphia, of which soothing syrup contained a large quantity. The mother was surprised and alarmed, and had had no idea that there was morphia in soothing syrup.

I ordered brandy and coffee, the bowels to be kept open by injections, and the child to be kept awake as much as possible. The child recovered, but was not able to nurse until the 10th. This is but one of the many instances of poison by this nostrum.

Dr. R. S. Maxwell, my partner, was called to see a child five weeks old, to whom half a teaspoonful of soothing syrup had been given a few hours previous. The child was already past all help, and died in a few hours. No other medicine had been given.

In my own case, the child five months old had taken two teaspoonfuls on the 5th, three on the 6th, and one on the 7th, making six teaspoonfuls from ten o'clock on the 5th until eight A.M. on the 7th; consequently it got over half a grain of morphia in the space of forty-six hours. As susceptible as children are to the influence of opium, it seems almost impossible that the child could have lived. In fact, we know that it could not have lived, had not the tolerance of the poison been induced by previous doses in lesser quantities. We may add that there are very few children at the age of six months, who would not be poisoned to death, were they to take the syrup as directed, (namely: six months old and upwards, one teaspoonful three or four times a day until free from pain,) unless a tolerance of the drug be induced by its previous administration in small doses. The morphia in a teaspoonful of soothing syrup is equal to about twenty drops of laudanum. Here we have thousands of mothers and nurses, ignorant alike of the ingredients and the effects of this deadly nostrum, directed to give a child six months old morphia equal to twenty drops of laudanum, while a physician would not dare to give a child of that age more than three drops.

Dr. Murray, in the article already referred to, says: "I have ascertained that there are about one hundred thousand two-ounce bottles of it sold annually in this city, containing about one hundred and eighty thousand grains of morphia, which are given annually to the babies of this State."

If the babies of this State consume two hundred thousand ounces of soothing syrup, it is but fair to assume that there is seventy-five times that amount used in the whole United States, which would make 15,000,000 ounces of syrup, or about 14,000,000 grains of morphia. Setting aside the direct cost of this nostrum, it would be scarcely possible to estimate the damages which the people of the United States sustain indirectly from its use.

How much the early resort of our youth to tobacco and alcoholic stimulants is due to the previous use of the opium contained in this nostrum is probably not realized. But, that it has much to do with it, any one can believe, who has seen with what avidity the opium eater, when deprived of his opium, will fly to alcohol, ether, hashish, tobacco, or anything that will lull the eternal craving of the appetite for something, other than wholesome food. It would be also impossible to estimate the number of children it sends to the grave before they reach their second year. But that the administration of 14,000,000 grains of morphia annually, to the babies of the United States, by persons ignorant of its effects, must send its thousands, any reasonable person will be inclined to grant. But a still graver question presents itself, namely: How much of the physical disease, of the drunkenness, of the degradation and of the vice, and how many of the weakened intellects, are due to use of the soothing syrup in infancy? Probably enough to make it a wiser Legislature that will prohibit the manufacture of any nostrum for children which contains opium, than the Legislature that passes a prohibitory liquor law for the benefit of its adults.

DR. W. L. ATLEE, reports in the January number of the *American Medical Journal,* his 229th case of Ovariotomy.

Cases of Persistent Hiccough—Treatment.

BY EMORY L. WILLARD, M.D.

Wm. Anderson, aged 34 years, single, native of New Hampshire, a resident of Austin, White Pine, State of Nevada; book-keeper by occupation; plethoric and full habit; light complexion; sanguine temperament. On the 28th day of June, 1869, while at Treasure City, was attacked with pneumonia, and on the 3d day of the attack a persistent hiccough had seized him. At first it was ordinary, and of course little noticed; but on the second day it became distressing. Belladonna and cantharidin plasters were applied to the epigastric region, but with little or no effect. Bismuth and lime water were used, also camphor in powder, to no purpose. The hiccough was becoming more and more distressing, the violent spasms of the diaphragm shaking the body and bed vehemently.

On account of Mr. A.'s other symptoms I did not dare to administer chloroform; but on looking into the rationale of the cause, and believing that the spasmodic action of the diaphragm had become a settled specific action and from a local cause, and believing that an action set up in any manner or by any means as a counter-action, would be the antidote sought for, I administered the salts of white hellebore by inhalation through the nose of the finest powder or dust, after agitation in the stopped bottle, when the spasm ceased, and Mr. A. did not hiccough again. The patient had been afflicted eighty-six hours, and had frequently said that he must die of hiccough, and his haggard and wild look indicated dissolution unless relief should come in time. After relief had come, he rested well the following night, and his pneumonic symptoms became more mild, and a speedy recovery followed.

Case 2.—Mr. John Waldron, of Pinto, Lander county, suffered with hiccough for a considerable length of time before applying for medical aid, when the salt of white hellebore was resorted to with the utmost confidence, and satisfactory results followed. He was cured.

Case 3.—Judge D., of Eureka, Lander county, Nevada, from an intemperate course of life and a debilitated condition of the stomach, as well as from an irregular diet and diminished nourishment, was attacked with hiccough, and had applied to half a dozen "doctors," whose prescriptions were ineffectual, the spasm being in no way changed. I applied by inhalation the salts of "veratria." Nothing could have acted more like a charm. The hiccough stopped as soon as the new action was set up by the remedy.

REVIEWS AND NOTICES OF BOOKS.

PULMONARY CONSUMPTION: Its Nature, Varieties and Treatment. With an Analysis of 1,000 cases to exemplify its duration. By C. J. B. Williams, M.D., F.R.S., Fellow of the Royal College of Physicians; Senior Consulting Physician to the Hospital for Consumption, Brompton, &c.; and Charles Theodore Williams, M.A., M.D., Oxon., Fellow of the Royal College of Physicians; Physician to the Hospital for Consumption, Brompton. Philadelphia: Henry C. Lea. 1872. Pp. 315. San Francisco: A. Roman & Co.

For nearly fifty years has Dr. Williams devoted his best energies to the study and treatment of Pulmonary Consumption. Intent on grasping the whole subject and contemplating it in all its bearings, he has turned and turned the kaleidescope until, if he has not exhausted its combinations, he has observed more of them than any other man living. And when we add, what will strike the reader at once on glancing at the pages of the present volume, that he possesses the very rare talent of ability to pursue a special department without bias towards any single theory, and without contraction of thought towards a narrow channel, the value of his labors here recorded, or at least our estimate of them, is patent. In a brief notice like this it were idle to attempt a description of the varied contents of the volume. In his pathological views, he gives due weight to the different theories of Consumption, and his treatment finds a useful place for a wide range of methods and remedies. The chapters written by his son are not the least valuable portion. We commend the work to the careful perusal of every medical man, with perfect confidence that our estimate of it will be sustained by the profession at large.

ON THE TREATMENT OF PULMONARY CONSUMPTION by Hygiene, Climate, and Medicine, in its connection with modern doctrines. By James Henry Bennett, M.D., Member of the Royal College of Physicians of London; late Obstetric Physician to the Royal Free Hospital; Doctor of Medicine of the University of Paris; &c., &c. Second Edition. New York: D. Appleton & Co. 1872. Pp. 190. San Francisco: A. Roman & Co.

It is remarkable that two books on the same subject should agree so nearly in practical matters as this and the work of Dr. Williams, and still exhibit not a particle of sameness. Dr. Bennett was himself, in early life, a subject of phthisis, from which he recovered. His work is confined mainly to treatment, and if it exhibits any bias or exclusiveness, it is very naturally in favor of the plan by which his own life was saved. It is fortunate for our science that medical practitioners are not exempt from the diseases that afflict their patients; for we owe to this circumstance many of the most valuable monograms that have ever been written. At the same time, it is next to impossible for an author to *clinicize* on his own case without regarding it too exclusively as a type in pathology and treatment. We do not say that Dr. Bennett has done this; but we do say that he has given the world a most valuable and readable little book—one which, while it will be read with increased interest after that of Dr. Williams, itself imparts additional interest to other works on the same topic. We are particularly pleased with his remarks on the alcoholic treatment of phthisis—on the communicability of the disease, and on the subject of marriages of consumptives.

A CLINICAL MANUAL OF THE DISEASES OF THE EAR. By Lawrence Turnbull, M.D., Physician to the Department of the Diseases of the Eye and Ear of Howard Hospital of Philadelphia; Permanent Member and Corresponding Secretary of the Medical Society of the State of Pennsylvania; Author of "Lectures on the Electro-Magnetic Telegraph;" "The Nature, Causes, and Treatment of Nervous Deafness," &c., &c. With a colored lithographic plate and over 100 illustrations on wood. Philadelphia: J. B. Lippincott & Co. 1872. Pp. 486. San Francisco: A. Roman & Co.

Dr. Turnbull was formerly a resident of San Francisco, and was known here as a diligent student, at a period when there was very little study on this coast except on the subject of the precious metals. The present volume embraces a wide range of enquiry and much valuable knowledge, theoretical and practical. Some of the journals, with the too common disposition of Americans to criticise censoriously their own authors, have found fault with its arrangement and some of its details. But we are more disposed to commend it as a compend of the knowledge of the present day on a class of subjects too much overlooked in common practice.

Anæsthesia, Hospitalism, Hermaphroditism, and a Proposal to stamp out Small-Pox and other Contagious Diseases. By Sir J. Y. Simpson, Bart, M.D., D.C., &c., late Professor of Medicine in the University of Edinburgh. Edited by Sir W. G. Simpson, Bart, B.A. New York: D. Appleton & Co. 1872. Pp. 562. San Francisco: A. Roman & Co.

The admirers of Sir James Y. Simpson in America, and they are many, will greet this volume with much satisfaction. With portions of its contents the profession are familiar; but other parts have never before been published. Apart from its intrinsic merits, the name and reputation of the author will command for the work an extensive circulation.

The Principles and Practice of Surgery. By John Ashhurst, Jr., M.D., Surgeon to the Episcopal Hospital; Surgeon to the Children's Hospital, &c. Illustrated by 533 engravings on wood. Philadelphia: Henry C. Lea. Pp. 1011. San Francisco: A. Roman & Co.

This is just the book that was wanted. The splendid and comprehensive treatise of Gross is too voluminous for a text book, which should consist of a single volume. Dr. Ashhurst is well known to the medical world, particularly by his contributions to the *American Journal of the Medical Sciences*. From his own extensive experience, and from the other rich sources at his command, he has collected the materials for the best text book on surgery accessible to the American student.

Medical Thermometry, and Human Temperature. By C. A. Wunderlich, Professor of Clinic at the University of Leipsic, &c., &c.; and Edward Seguin, M.D. New York: William Wood & Co. 1871. Pp. 280. San Francisco: A. H. Bancroft & Co.

The thermometer has now become indispensable in the diagnosis of many disorders, and to Dr. Wunderlich is due, more than to any other person, the credit of developing its application and value. The student will find in this volume nearly everything known to the profession on the subject.

Neuralgia and the Diseases that Resemble it. By Francis E. Anstie, M.D., (Lond.) Fellow of the Royal College of Physicians; Honorary Fellow of King's College, London; Senior Assistant Physician to Westminster Hospital; &c., &c. New York: D. Appleton & Co 1872. Pp. 362. San Francisco: A. Roman & Co.

Dr. Anstie is well known to American Physicians, many of whom swear by him. They like his love of innovation and his original ways of thinking. In this volume he has undertaken the difficult task of separating Neuralgia from various painful diseases with which it has been almost universally confounded. It is a work of great excellence, especially for the reason that it stirs up the mind of the reader and awakens thought. The amplitude and completeness of the index are acknowledged.

Half-Yearly Abstract of the Medical Sciences. Philadelphia: Henry C. Lea. January, 1872.

Braithwaites' Retrospect of Practical Medicine and Surgery. New York: W. A. Townsend. January, 1872.

Half-Yearly Compendium of Medical Science. Philadelphia: S. A. Butler, M.D. January, 1872.

It were highly discreditable to any member of our profession not to be well posted in medical literature, with the facilities at command for gaining information. Here are no less than three half-yearly serials, bringing from all quarters of the globe the treasures of knowledge; all covering the same ground, and yet scarcely crossing each other's path in any instance—a fact which declares the activity of the professional mind the world over, and at the same time the skill and industry which have produced the "Abstract," the "Retrospect," and the "Compendium."

EDITORIAL.

Protection from Suits for Malpractice.

An effort was made to procure from our present Legislature the enactment of a law providing that no suits should be instituted against medical men for malpractice unless the prosecutor first give bonds to indemnify the defendant in case of failure to convict. Such a law appears necessary, not only to protect the physician in the legitimate pursuit of his calling, but to enable diseased and injured persons to obtain proper medical aid, which they cannot now do at all times, for the reason that many practitioners will not undertake cases which may involve them in such suits. In every community there are sordid wretches who are always ready to get up suits of the kind, either for the purpose of avoiding the payment of the bill, or with the more aggressive object of extorting money from the physician or surgeon. In most of these cases the prosecutor is a "poor devil," to whom the service, perhaps laborious, has been rendered without hope or claim of compensation. And there are nearly always, we blush to say it, professional men villainous enough to instigate the prosecution.

For the greater portion of services rendered at unseasonable hours and in emergencies, physicians receive no pay. People who do not expect to pay their doctor are the most ready to call him out of bed at night, even on trivial occasions. The extent to which such impositions are practiced would be incredible to persons outside of the profession. Several years since the writer was called up on a stormy night to visit a sick woman a mile distant; and when he enquired of the messenger why he had come so far, passing by so many doctors, the cool answer was that "all the doctors seem to have the rheumatism to-night." The fact was, they had learned by provoking experience that the patient, who was abundantly able to pay, never paid, and was not likely to be seriously sick. Another individual comes to mind, who kept a wood-yard on Pacific street, and to whom the writer was summoned on account of his having fallen from his cart while drunk. He nearly died from concussion of the brain; and when the bill was presented for the services which had saved his life, he refused payment on the ground that *he* had not sent for any doctor, and that the person who had employed the doctor was responsible! Twenty years have not effaced from the writer's mind the image of that wretched man, nor yet his name, which was Smith—of course. Quite recently an individual holding a prominent position in the city government, while riding furiously down Geary street, at midnight, lost his balance and was picked up senseless. The writer was hurriedly summoned to his relief, and went to the trouble of manipulating his limbs and handling his person, to discover only concussion of the brain and the odor of whisky. And now, when a small bill is sent to him he knows nothing about it! These are specimens such as chequer the whole life of a physician. It is poor satisfaction to record the names of such people on the black list of the Medical Society.

But a much more serious grievance is the custom—for it has become a custom with a certain class of individuals—to endeavor to extort money from the medical attendant by instituting a suit for malpractice. Surgeons are particularly liable to this imposition. The shortening of a leg after fracture, or the stiffness of a joint, or any imperfection, which is most likely after all to be the result of carelessness on the part of the patient, is made the pretext for a suit, in which some starving hyena of the court-room volunteers his legal services for a contingent fee. It is against these flagrant and fraudulent actions that protection is sought; and only that degree of protection which would secure against wanton and malicious prosecutions. Physicians are expected, yes, required, to answer every urgent call. The humanity of their profession as well as public opinion, demands that they do this, paid or unpaid. If a physician refuse to turn out at night to mend a broken head, whether from an accident or a brawl, he will find himself pilloried in the newspapers next morning. And if he *should* respond to the summons, his only compensation may be a prosecution for malpractice, involving loss of time and money, if not of reputation, even though the verdict be in his favor, or the suit be withdrawn as soon as it is ascertained that he will not submit to a black-mail assessment.

Now, let us ask, is it anything more than justice to the members of the profession that they should have some legal protection in such cases ? And do not the interests of society demand the removal of the restraint thus imposed on the exercise of the humane offices of the profession ?

The only argument we have heard against the proposed legislation, is that it would interfere with the rights of the citizen, by depriving the man who has nothing to lose of the power to black-mail with impunity the physician who has been so unfortunate as to save his life.

Danger from the Vapor of Mercury.

That metallic mercury gives off vapor in the air at ordinary temperatures has long been admitted. It is even proved that this takes place at a temperature of 32°. A French scientist, M. Merget, referred to in the California *Scientific Press,* has pursued his experiments on this subject with such enthusiasm as that he "expects to be able to prove" that the vapor which mercury constantly sends forth ascends to the height of 1700 metres, or 1900 feet, at the rate of 200 feet per second. Imagine a surface of quicksilver shooting particles of its substance to a height of the third of a mile with the velocity of a ball fired from a cannon !

Then another class of alleged facts are adduced, and it is asserted that water conveyed in lead pipes carries the metal into the bodies of persons drinking it, where it gradually accumulates and shows its noxious effects—in some cases only after twenty-five or thirty years. As mercury is absorbed and accumulated in the system in the same manner, the logical inference is deduced that it is dangerous to handle mercury, or to inhale the atmosphere exposed to its uncovered surface.

All this sounds well in theory, but is it true in practice? We know that in smelting works and other establishments where metallic vapors are diffused by heat, the most noxious consequences may be suffered by persons exposed to the fumes. But are there any facts tending to prove that such results are possible from the presence of mercury in the ordinary temperature of the atmosphere? At the smelting works at New Almaden the workmen were liable to severe poisoning until pipes were laid to carry the fumes to a distance. Since that time there has been no disease traceable to metallic vapors, and the men whose business it is to bottle the mercury, and who stand constantly over the metal, have never suffered. To say that twenty-five or thirty years is required to test the question of poisoning, is simply to put the whole subject beyond the range of legitimate enquiry. If such latitude be allowed to the argument, we claim that the impregnation of the body with mercurial atoms, whilst so slight as to produce no noxious results, is a prophylactic against many disorders which would otherwise assail the workmen; and that in the aggregate, the effect is salutary and tends to prolong life.

It is not difficult to strain the truths of science so as to extort from them the most absurd deductions. A disposition to do this pervades the medical investigations of our period. It is strikingly exemplified in the exclusive application of the laws of chemistry to the processes of life in health and disease, and to the action of medicines. Experiments and experience are labelled "empiricism" and put to shame; and other results than those directly revealed by the senses are cyphered out by theorem. We are getting altogether too theoretical in the practice of medicine, and too regardless of the plain, blunt truths which crop out on the surface, and which are undervalued because there is no trouble in finding them.

Syphilitic Corpuscles in the Blood.

A letter from Vienna to the Boston *Medical and Surgical Journal* of February 8th, narrates a wonderful discovery made by Dr. Lostorfer and by him communicated publicly in the presence of the writer. The blood of syphilitic patients being placed in slides and laid aside, exhibited on the third day, under the microscope, minute, shining bodies, which grew from day to day till they attained the size of red blood-corpuscles. Their form was rounded, with tapering processes or "sprouts," which continued visible a month. As many as fifty were sometimes visible at once. Dr. Lostorfer had subjected specimens of syphilitic blood together with specimens of healthy blood to

Professors Skoda and Stricker, who invariably detected the difference, thus establishing beyond question the value of the diagnostic sign. "As Dr. Lostorfer ceased speaking a burst of genuine enthusiasm escaped from the assembled physicians, while Professor Skoda rose to greet the hero of the evening as the proclaimer of what was destined to prove one of the most important discoveries of the age." Professor Hebra also confirmed all that had been said.

All this sounds well; and though somewhat sensational, 'tis pity it should not stand as a brilliant triumph of modern science. But Dr. Davis, of the Chicago *Medical Examiner*, whose friends have hitherto credited him with the quality of veneration, most irreverently announces that Professor Salisbury, several years ago, made and proclaimed the same discovery, in a comparatively obscure burgh of Ohio, Cleveland by name; and that another American, Professor Bumstead, found the same organic growth or sprouts in the blood of nurses and others not afflicted with disease, and pronounced them destitute of all significance in relation to syphilis, and the mere products of decomposition. Should this explanation prove true, the Vienna sensation will only add one to the many instances already known, in which enthusiastic scientists have misinterpreted the revelations of the microscope.

Sale of Diplomas.

The great scandal to which the medical schools of America have been subjected for several years past, has at length culminated in a searching inquiry, instituted by the Legislature of Pennsylvania, for the purpose of ferreting out the source of the offense. It must be kept in mind that there are three medical "Universities," so called, in Philadelphia—the University of Pennsylvania, the Philadelphia University, and the American University. The first is the ancient and honored parent of all the medical schools of the land. The second and third are modern enterprises, the titles of which were not chosen with the design of distinguishing them from the first. It was proved before the Committee of the Legislature that the "American University" had sold diplomas shamelessly and promiscuously for twenty-five dollars. The recipient of one of these diplomas testified that he had never attended a course of lectures anywhere. The "Philadelphia University," which has been very generally suspected of selling diplomas, was exonerated, though the Dean rather damaged his own cause by asserting that diplomas had been sold by the University of Pennsylvania. Now that the source of these bogus degrees has been exposed, measures will be taken, we doubt not, to suppress the nuisances.

Value of a Hospital Patient.

The surgeon of one of the Philadelphia Hospitals has received a letter enquiring how much compensation will be given to a patient with Hematocele, if he should come to be "opperated" on. Many years ago it was our good fortune to light upon a person of the same liberal disposition. It was the mother of a child whom we had vaccinated gratuitously. We desired the good woman to keep the crust for us, when she asked with much earnestness, "How much do you give for it, doctor?"

Hemoptysis in Consumptive Patients.

Dr. Condie (*American Medical Journal*, January, 1872) combats the commonly received opinion that bleeding is a predominant symptom in the earlier stages of phthisis. Of 369 cases in his charge, it occurred only in 87—or 24 per cent. He thinks it has no very decided influence, one way or the other, on the character or duration of the disease. The experience of the writer is decidedly confirmatory of the views of Dr. Condie.

Prevalence of Scabies in Paris.

Dr. Louis A. Duhring, in his annual report of the Dispensary for skin diseases in Philadelphia (*Medical Times*) says that there is more scabies in Paris than in any other city in the world. About one-half the diseases of the skin in that city are due to the acarus scabiei. In Philadelphia Eczema takes the lead. Only seven cases of scabies are reported in 425 patients with all kinds of skin diseases.

Castor Oil in Pregnancy and Child-Bed.

Perhaps no medicine is so generally resorted to as an aperient in pregnancy and in child-bed as Castor Oil. And yet it seems to us that it is one of the most unfit agents that can be selected.

Repeatedly have we known labor prematurely induced by a dose of "Oil." We are inclined to think that it would have this effect in a majority of cases if exhibited within a month of full term; or at least that it would bring on pains similar to those of labor, and liable to be mistaken for labor. In fact, the ordinary griping of a dose of oil comes nearer to the pains of labor than the action of most other purgatives. After delivery it is habitually employed to restore the arrested peristaltic action. Here also the result is the restoration of after-pains. So deeply has our experience impressed us with this fact that we never prescribe it in child-bed unless where the patient prefers it to anything else. Nurses are entirely too officious in administering cathartics a day or two after confinement. They do this very generally without the counsel or knowledge of the accoucheur. There is no need of so much haste. An enema may answer the purpose; or laxative food; and where they fail, a small dose of citrate of magnesia, or confection of senna, or anything that will barely establish the normal movement.

Another charge against castor oil is that it irritates the rectum and tends to produce hemorrhoids. Its irritating action on the mucous surface of the lower intestines is acknowledged by authors. This is the probable cause of its tendency to excite uterine pains. And this is the reason also why its operation is followed by constipation—which, by the way, constitutes another formidable objection to its use in the puerperal state.

Bromide of Calcium.

This preparation is beginning to attract considerable attention. It was introduced to the profession by Dr. W. A. Hammond, who attributes any advantages it has over the other bromides to the facility with which its bromine is set free in the stomach. It is a white, crystalline salt, very soluble in water and speedily decomposed in the atmosphere. One hundred grains contain within a fraction of eighty grains bromine. The dose is the same as the other bromides, but it is more pungent and disagreeable. It acts more promptly, and its action as described, appears to place it between bromide of potassium and chloral hydrate. It does not cause acne to the extent of the other bromides. Dr. Hammond recommends it in delirium tremens and in the nervous exhaustion of hysterical women, attended with headache, vertigo and insomnia. It has no advantage in epilepsy, except in young infants. In several cases of insomnia with great excitement, it produced sleep when bromide of potassium had failed. Dr. Hammond advises the following formula: ℞. Calcii bromidi ʒii; syrup. lactophosph. calcis ℥j. M. Sig. A teaspoonful, diluted with water.

Value of Taraxacum—Dandelion Coffee.

We suspect that Taraxacum is not properly appreciated in modern practice, at least in America. In India it is regarded as of great value. A writer in the British *Pharmacist*, quoted by the *American Journal of Pharmacy* for Feb. 1872, speaks of it in these terms: "Medical men admit the value of this preparation, and I know several gentlemen in India who are, by their own admission, kept alive by the daily use of *Taraxacum* coffee. It is fairly entitled to be called a specific for the cure of torpid liver, a complaint from which the majority of Europeans suffer; the fact being made known when they proceed to a cool or hill climate and shiver and shake with cold while the thermometer is at 60° F. only. The sallow complexion of such men, women and children, their languid movements and their enjoyment of heat, all alike proclaim that they are suffering from sluggish action of the liver. The conserve of *Taraxacum* may be made into syrup for use. Horses and valuable dogs, sheep and poultry, all suffer from disease of the liver. A bolus of *Taraxacum* conserve to a horse, and a pill thereof to a fowl, would be most beneficial and act as a curative agent. Rabbits also suffer greatly from liver disease, but if they were supplied with a few (two or four) green *Taraxacum* leaves twice or thrice a week, the mortality of this (hitherto) incurable disease would disappear, and rabbits could then be extensively raised for the market."

To make dandelion coffee the roots are dried, chopped up, and roasted and ground like common coffee. One part of this is mixed with nine parts of true coffee, for table use. The admixture can scarcely be detected by the taste. We may add that the extract of taraxacum may be mixed with coffee in the same way, with good effect. It is admirably suited to certain cases of dyspepsia with torpid liver.

Preserving Vaccine Lymph in Glycerin.

It is probable that the virus of vaccinia can be preserved perfectly and indefinitely in pure, anhydrous glycerin. But if the glycerin be not pure, decomposition may result, and an active and dangerous poison may be generated, such as is developed by allowing powdered crust to stand some time mixed with water. Serious consequences are reported to have followed the use of virus so preserved. Considering the difficulty there is in getting a perfect article of glycerin or in ascertaining its purity, and the very grave results that are liable to follow and that have followed the use of an imperfect article, it is a question whether the attempt to preserve the virus in glycerin should not be entirely abandoned.

Enema of Ipecacuanha in Dysentery.

We have given place to a number of articles at different times, from our correspondents and from other sources, testifying to the value of large doses of ipecacuanha in dysentery. A writer in the *Indian Medical Gazette*, quoted in the *American Medical Journal* for January, advises enemata of ipecacuanha in the same disease, which have succeeded in his experience beyond all other treatment. He injects one drachm in six ounces mucilage three times a day. When used in the early stages it effects a cure in three days, without additional treatment. It strikes us that very few cases of dysentery that have ever fallen under our charge would tolerate a six-ounce enema of anything, unless it may be iced water. But perhaps the dysentery of India differs from ours in this respect.

Discarding the Weight in the Pharmacopeia.

Prof. Redwood and other distinguished pharmaceutists in Great Britain propose to substitute "parts" and measures for weights in the processes of the pharmacopeia. Where "parts" and "measures" occur in the same formula, a measure is the unit of weight whatever that may be. We believe that the British practitioners have pretty generally discarded from their prescriptions the scruple and drachm, expressing the quantity altogether in grains. This method has decided advantages, and we should not regret to see it introduced in America.

Falling off at Harvard.

Since the adoption of the extended curriculum and other innovations by Harvard Medical College, the number of students has been diminished by 105. This naturally deters other schools from following the example, though it reflects the more credit on Harvard to have instituted a salutary reform in teaching which was certain to lessen the class. It is not likely that the loss of students will be permanent.

Reported Cure of Hydrophobia.

In the newspapers appears the statement of a case of hydrophobia which occurred at or near Detroit, and which was treated successfully by the following means: One grain sulph. morph. was injected hypodermically every four hours, and 30 grains castor given at the same intervals. Small quantities of chloroform were also inhaled. Sleep was produced in half an hour, lasting an hour and a half, and finally the convulsions ceased. The patient was wrapped in a woollen blanket wrung out of a warm solution of muriate of ammonia, 20 grains to the ounce; but this was not done till the symptoms began to yield. There was nothing very novel in this treatment, especially as to the morphia and chloroform, which were doubtless the efficient agents, admitting the case to be correctly stated. The castor and the warm fomentation may have aided slightly. But the patient is described as "barking like a dog," seizing the pillows in his teeth and shaking them like a ferocious dog, &c. This part of the story does not add to its credibility. It is matter of surprise that newspapers conducted by intelligent men will continue from time to time to give currency to such statements, whilst physicians everywhere have declared against them as popular errors. Probably one-half the civilized world still believe that men with hydrophobia act the part of rabid dogs, and are frequently relieved from suffering, through professional authority, by pressure between feather beds.

New Gynecological Instruments.

If Smellie, or Baudeloque, or Dewees could revisit the fields of their former labors, nothing would startle them so much as an inspection of the countless instruments devised since their day, to facilitate obstetric practice. A collection of the various patterns of speculums and pessaries would awaken ideas of the machinery of some wonderful cotton-mill, or of implements of modern warfare, rather than of uterine armaments. Nevertheless, the end is not yet. Every month brings us some new conception in this line. The last important accession is pictured in the Boston *Gynecological Journal* for January, by J. Stockton Hough, of Philadelphia. It consists of a self-retaining vaginal, uterine and anal speculum, combined, and "has five blades, two of which are stationary where they are joined to the handle-arms, while the upper blade expands throughout its entire length, and the two lower side-blades are movable in the slots at the extremity of the handle-arms." It is certainly very ingeniously constructed, and has every appearance of a valuable instrument, though trial alone can determine its merits.

California Board of Health.

The Boston *Gynecological Journal* says of the First Biennial Report recently published, that it will be found to bear a favorable comparison, alike as regards the interest of the topics considered, and the ability with which they are discussed, with the similar volumes already published by the State of Massachusetts. The *Journal* is also highly pleased with the steps taken by the National Association to form Boards of Health in other States, as proposed by Dr. Logan at the meeting in San Francisco in May last. A committee for that purpose has been appointed, of which Dr. Logan is chairman, Dr. Stille having withdrawn in his favor.

State Board of Health in Minnesota.

Dr. Merritt, of Red Wing, Minn., writes to us that the Legislature of that State has followed the example of Massachusetts and California, and established a State Board of Health on a similar basis.

District Medical Society.

By favor of Dr. M. B. Pond, we are in receipt of the proceedings of a meeting of physicians of Solano, Napa, Sonoma, and Contra Costa counties, held in Napa on the first of March, for the purpose of forming a District Medical Society. Dr. Frisbie of Vallejo was chosen President ; Drs. Campbell o

Suisun, Stillwagon of Napa, Hudson of Contra Costa, and Allen of Sonoma, Vice-Presidents ; Dr. Pond of Napa, Recording Secretary ; Dr. Vallejo of Vallejo, Corresponding Secretary ; and Drs. Nichell of Napa, and Holbrook of Contra Costa, Censors. Drs. Thomas, Campbell and Pressley were appointed to prepare a Constitution and By-Laws, to be acted on at an adjourned meeting to be held at Vallejo on the 23d of May.

Professional Incidents in Australia.

Our neighbors in Australia are not behind California in the varieties of professional life. A recent number of the Australian *Medical Journal*, published at Melbourne, records three cases. Dr. Miller, of Launceston, "well known as a successful and deservedly respected practitioner," is diversifying the dull life of a doctor by histrionic exercises. "Some time ago he played Baillie Nicol Jarvie, but his last performance is that of Hartmann, the blind violinist, in Tom Taylor's drama of Helping Hands." The other two are sad—"Dr. Owen, surgeon of the ship Patriarch, was found dead in the bush, near Sydney." Dr. Francis Long committed suicide by taking laudanum. "He was only 27 years of age, but had for years been unfortunately the victim of the predominant vice of the colony." The coroner's jury, in their verdict, give it as their opinion that "a stomach pump should be available at all times, and that medical practitioners practising in this locality should possess the same."

National Association—Fare of Delegates—Exhibition, &c.

From Dr. T. M. Logan we have the following communication :

Please mention in your next issue that in my capacity as as Chairman of the Railroad Committee for California, I have made arrangements with Mr. Goodman of the Central Pacific Railroad, for tickets to Omaha at half local rates; and with Mr. Wait of the Chicago and Rock Island Railroad, for tickets at the same rate from Omaha to Chicago, *i. e.*, for Delegates and their wives, to the meeting of the American Medical Association. Dr. Atkinson writes that he has made similar arrangements on the Fort Wayne and Pittsburg and Pennsylvania Central, from Chicago to Philadelphia. If parties should wish to take the route via Niagara Falls, they must give notice beforehand to A. L. Wait, 208 Montgomery street, San Francisco. I would also state that application has been made by me for space for California in the projected Exhibition—but notice must be given of what is proposed to be placed therein. The Exhibition will be modeled after the British plan, and will include choice specimens and samples of whatever is likely to prove interesting through novelty, rarity, and superior character, of drugs, medicines and other remedial appliances, including chemical and pharmaceutical compounds; surgical instruments and implements ; preparations and objects in natural history, comprising human and comparative anatomy, morbid or healthy. Also, models, drawings, paintings, prints and printed works on medical, surgical, and the associate sciences.

New Books.

The following are received from A. L. Bancroft & Co., too late for notice this month :

RINGER'S HANDBOOK OF THERAPEUTICS.
RINDFLESCH'S TEXT-BOOK OF PATHOLOGICAL HISTOLOGY.
BRIGHT'S DISEASES, BY DR. GRAINGER STEWART.
WHARTON P. HOOD, ON BONESETTING.

GENERAL SUMMARY.

The Iodides of Ammonium and Sodium in Syphilis.

Dr. Berkly Hill, in the *British Medical Journal* for December 23, strongly recommends the use of the iodides of sodium and ammonium in syphilis, after the iodide of potassium has failed to produce a good effect. They produce the effect of iodine in many persons who have become nauseated by the potassa salt. Moreover, they contain less alkali per weight of the salt, and their alkali is less deteriorating to the blood than potash. The Doctor reports several cases in support of these statements.—*Detroit Review.*

Vaccination Papers.

In the *British Medical Journal*, December 23, 1871, Dr. T. J. Preston gives a valuable suggestion respecting a new method of lymph preservation. It is certainly portable, very convenient, and, the doctor says, certain in its effects. He paints a sheet of common note paper with the lymph, fresh from the vesicle. The lymph soon dries, and the paper is ready for use. When required, a minute piece may be torn off the sheet, and after being breathed upon slightly, should be stuck upon the freshened surface. If the paper be required to be kept for any length of time, it should, after being charged, be covered with a thin coating of white of egg.—*Detroit Review.*

Function of the Spleen.

M. Mosler, a German scientist referred to in the *Gazette Hebdomadaire* of October 6, 1871, determines as the result of thirty experiments on inferior animals, that the spleen is not essential to life, and that its function is supplied by the lymphatic glands. "The medulla of the bones seems to perform an important supplementary function. It exhibits, long after the extirpation of the spleen, alterations remarkably analogous to those observed in leucemia. The vicarious or supplementary offices of the lymphatic organs, which appear to depend on external circumstances very various in character, are not always completely developed in animals deprived of the spleen ; indeed, for several months after the extirpation or atrophy of the organ, the blood appears altered in composition. There is then some reason for admitting a particular influence of the spleen on the formation of blood, more especially on the genesis of the white and red corpuscles. The spleen does not appear to have any influence on the gastric pancreatic digestion. The abnormal development of appetite in animals divested of the spleen, is not a constant symptom.

Gelseminum in Irritable Bladder.

Dr. W. Scott Hill, of Augusta, Maine, (*American Medical Journal*, January, 1872,) reports five cases of irritable bladder cured by the fluid extract of gelseminum, of which ten to fifteen drops was given three or four times a day. In some cases it was combined with bromide of potassium. The difficulty and pain in micturition were quite severe in two or three of the patients.

A New History of Medicine.

Lindsay and Blakiston of Philadelphia, are about to publish a new work by the late Professor Dunglison, being a History of Medicine from the earliest ages to the commencement of the present century. It will be edited by Dr. Richard J. Dunglison, son of the late professor, and will contain 250 pages. Price to subscribers $2.50. It will be welcomed by the profession every where as a valuable contribution to knowledge.

Examination of Druggists in New York.

In accordance with the law recently enacted, 726 druggists and assistants in the city of New York, presented themselves for examination before the Board, 463 of whom were granted license on the first examination. Of the 263 rejected applicants, 203 had a second examination in three months, all of whom passed. The balance, 60 in number, failed to appear. It is estimated that about 200 persons are engaged in vending drugs in the city without examination and license and of course in violation of law.

Bacteria in the Blood.

Professor Richardson, of Philadelphia, several years ago, in the course of his experiments to determine whether bacteria pass from the stomach into the blood, swallowed four ounces of water which contained, according to his estimate, 27,000,000,000 of these minute organisms. In half an hour he discovered them in abundance in a drop of blood taken from the end of his finger. To swallow at a single gulp twenty times as many vegetable spores as there are human inhabitants on the earth, is but a small exploit for a modern scientist.

Value of Cigar-Stumps.

It is stated that the value of cigar-stumps picked up annually in the streets of Paris and sold to tobacco-manufacturers, is $50,000. We have known them to be gathered up in the streets of San Francisco, for the manufacture of cigarritos.

Value and Safety of Chloral Hydrate.

Dr. C. W. Cram, of Columbus, Ohio, furnishes a paper to the Cincinnati *Clinic*, in defense of the value and safety of chloral hydrate, as employed in the Hospital of the Ohio Penitentiary. In twenty-two months there have been administered to an average of forty-three pa.ients 1662 doses of twenty grains each. The advantages are thus enumerated:

1st. It is prompt in its action, sleep being almost invariably induced in from fifteen to twenty minutes unless the patient has been accustomed to its use.

2d. The sleep it produces is remarkably quiet being very seldom disturbed by dreams or any other form of restlessness.

3rd. Its action is not complicated by those disagreeable attendants that so often follow the preparations of opium, viz.: nausea, constipation and paralysis of the bladder; the former, in some cases, *in anticipation*, strongly contra-indicating the use of any form of this drug.

4th. Its use is not followed by that craving for its continuance which so often attends the administration of the preparations of opium, particularly morphia, producing a multitude of *opium eaters.*

5th. It is safe when given in a proper dose.

Strangulated Hernia Reduced while Standing.

Several writers have lately condemned the supine posture for taxis. Dr. C. C. F. Gay, in the *Buffalo Medical and Surgical Journal* for February, argues at length in favor of the erect and semi-prone positions. He uses this language:

"During the past summer I reduced a femoral hernia, right side, by placing the patient upon her right side, nearly in the semi-prone position, with her thighs flexed upon the body. Seizing hold of the tumor I immediately reduced it without the aid of chloroform, when I had failed with the patient in almost all other positions when she was under the use of chloroform. I am to conclude therefore that the positions heretofore recommended by the books are not always the best positions and that if failures occur in such positions, then it will be wise to resort to the upright, and if need be the semi-prone position, when taxis applied will be made most serviceable and efficient.

"I am quite willing now to advance a step and claim that to reduce hernia, whether inguinal or femoral, by taxis, the semi-prone or upright positions of the patient are always advisable, and I am quite willing to use stronger language, and assert, that the two positions named are the best, and the supine posture the worst for the patient to assume. It is not relaxation, but expansion of the abdominal parietes that we want.

"But yesterday I reduced an inguinal hernia while my patient was standing, after I had made an ineffectual attempt at reduction with my patient lying on his back.

"I will conclude this paper by stating a fact that should be taken into account, when considering the best posture of a patient upon whom taxis is to be employed, a fact too, that has hitherto been overlooked by writers upon this subject. I allude to the fact that all or nearly all persons afflicted with hernia never get down on their backs, but on the contrary stand upright and reduce their own hernias. I shall only add that I shall henceforth believe, and act upon such belief until convicted of error, that the semi-prone and upright postures have a tendency to, if they do not absolutely, dilate the stricture. If this belief has foundation in fact, then the use of taxis will supercede the necessity of the use of the knife in a majority, if not in all the cases of strangulation that may occur."

Concentrated Solution of Tannic Acid.

The following formula is given in the *Pharmacist* (vid. *American Journal of Pharmacy*, February, 1872,) for a concentrated solution of tannic acid: Take of tannic acid, 8 troy ounces; glycerin, 4 troy ounces; strong alcohol, 8 fluid ounces; water, 8 fluid ounces. Mix the alcohol and water; add the tannin, and apply heat until it is dissolved. Filter hot, then add the glycerin and evaporate by a gentle heat until the solution weighs 16 troy ounces.

Suit for Malpractice.

Eight years ago, a Mr. White, of Connecticut, broke both bones of his left leg, just above the ankle. On final recovery there was some shortening and deformity, for which alleged reason he refused to pay his surgeon. Six years after the injury, the latter, Dr. J. C. Jackson, sued for his bill, and at the same time Mr. White sued for malpractice, laying damages at $10,000. The doctor recovered $100 for his services. The other suit was warmly contested, only one medical witness, however, sustaining the plaintiff at all hazards. On his side it was maintained that the fracture box was improper—that greater extension should have been used—that callus never bends when hardened, &c. The physicians and surgeons of Hartford, many of whom were called on by the defense, appear to have been very generally united in maintaining the following positions. We copy from the Philadelphia *Medical Times :*

1. That the evidence was conclusive as to the primary correct setting of the bone, as both Drs. Jackson and Barrows were experienced and thoroughly competent men ; while Dr. Barrows, who asserted that the fracture had been properly reduced, was a most reliable and disinterested observer.

2. That the fracture-box is in very general use, especially for bad oblique and compound fractures of the leg ; is very commonly employed in hospitals, especially in Hartford, and by many surgeons in private practice; and is an instrument, if properly managed, capable of producing the best results.

3. That when Dr. Jackson proposed to rectify the limb about the tenth day, plaintiff refused to have it done, except upon terms endangering his life. Therefore defendant could not be responsible for consequences.

4. That extension was not demanded, and therefore not used, further than laying the leg over an inclined plane of pillows and a box ; that the shortening, being only three-eighths of an inch, and detected by no roughness indicating overriding of the fragments, did not justify traction upon the injured foot.

5. That callus often yields if not fully consolidated, and union cannot be positively assured at a given time ; and that the union might appear firm, yet yield upon too violent use of a limb even after dismissal by the surgeon ; that this yielding might be gradual, and at first imperceptible to a careless observer.

6. That as chloroform had, as testified by Dr. Barrows, produced on its first administration very dangerous symptoms, the surgeons were justified in using their best judgment as to the further employment of anesthetics.

7. That, the deviation of the natural outward bend of the lower part of the tibia being increased only one-fourth of an inch, the lameness could not be very great. This was further proved by plaintiff's having danced all night, and having a gait showing the most trifling lameness.

8. That, plaintiff having left Dr. Jackson before dismissal, defendant was not responsible.

The case was tried before eleven jurors, by consent of the parties ; ten of these were for defendant and one for plaintiff. After being sent out three times by the Judge, an agreement was reached by way of compromise : the verdict being five dollars damages to plaintiff and five dollars costs—a verdict virtually for defendant.

An Act against Empiricism.

The following are the provisions of an act entitled "An act to protect the citizens of Wyoming Territory from empiricism and elevate the standing of the medical profession."

Section first makes it unlawful for any person to practice medicine or surgery in any of its departments, for reward or compensation, who has not attended two courses of instruction in a school of medicine, or who cannot produce a certificate of qualification from some regular medical society.

Section second makes it incumbent upon all persons now practicing medicine or surgery, to file a copy of his or her diploma or certificate with the County Clerk, making oath that they are the identical person named in the diploma or certificate.

Section third provides a penalty for a violation of sections one and two, of a fine of fifty to one hundred dollars for the first offense, and imprisonment in the county jail not less than ten days for the second ; and in no case wherein this act shall have been violated, shall the person so violating receive any compensation for services rendered.

Section fourth exempts dentists and surgeons of the United States from complying with the provisions of this act.

The above act was passed by the late Legislature, signed by the Governor, and is now the law.

Necrology.

Dr. Jonathan Letterman died in San Francisco, March 15, aged 48 years. He entered the Army in 1849, a year after graduating, and in the early years of the Rebellion was Medical Director of the Army of the Potomac. In 1866, having resigned from the service some time previously, he settled in San Francisco, and was shortly thereafter elected Coroner, which office he held until a few months prior to his death. The immediate cause of death was dysentery supervening upon chronic diarrhea, which had existed more or less continuously since a severe fracture of the leg, which occurred early in 1871.

Dr. Carl Precht, a native of Bremen, Germany, died in San Francisco, March 22d, aged 48 years. He had been in practice in this city since 1850.

Dr. James M. Sutton, a native of Philadelphia, died in San Francisco, March 22d, aged 47 years.

Dr. J. Rice, of San Francisco, has lately met with a sad affliction, in the death of his son, a lad of 16 years, resulting from an injury to his foot.

[COMMUNICATED-]

Died, in Nicolaus, Sutter county, February 25th, C. Weston, M.D., late a Surgeon in the Volunteer Service of the Union Army, where he received a wound in the region of the heart while in the discharge of professional duties, from a shell thrown into the hospital. He was born in Charleston, S. C., in May, 1840, and graduated at Jefferson College, Philadelphia, in 1860. The doctor came overland to this State, in search of health, and was measurably successful, in so far regaining his health as to be able to resume the practice of his profession, to which he was ardently attached, and in the active duties of which he continued up to within three days of his death. Conscious of his approaching end, he arranged his business for the event, and suddenly expired in the arms of a friend whom he had requested to raise him up in bed. The doctor leaves a devoted wife to mourn his demise, and the community, while they sympathize with her, also feel their loss in the death of a beloved physician. H.

Dr. CHARLES A. LEE, of New York, died February 14, aged 71 years. Dr. Lee was a remarkable man. No other writer in the United States has contributed more to the literature of the profession. No other individual has exhibited greater industry and energy in the pursuit of his calling. At different times he has held chairs in the medical schools in New York city, in Maine, Massachusetts, Vermont, and in Geneva and Buffalo. For many years he was editor of the New York *Journal of Medicine*, and he contributed largely to other medical journals.

Dr. JOHN FOOTE TROWBRIDGE died at Syracuse, N. Y., February 18th, aged 80 years. He enjoyed a long and honorable career, both in and out of his profession.

The death of Professor T. R. Crosby, of Hanover, New Hampshire, at the age of 56 years, is announced. He died on the first of March, of apoplexy. Dr. Crosby occupied a prominent position in his native State for years. He was for some years Professor in the Agricultural College; edited an agricultural paper; served as surgeon of volunteers during the war; was then Professor of Surgery in the National College, Washington; afterward returned to New Hampshire, and represented his District in the State Legislature.

Dr. GEORGE E. DAY, of St. Andrew's, England, died January 21st, aged 57 years. In many respects Dr. Day bore a very remarkable resemblance to Dr. Lee, who died in New York about the same time. He was a most industrious contributor to medical science, and wrote not only for the English journals but for the Psychological Journal of New York. He is described as one of the most learned men of modern times. His death resulted indirectly from an injury received by falling into a shaft ten years ago whilst on a botanical excursion.

Dr. BAIRD, F.R.S., died January 27th. He was eminent as a scientist and author, and for thirty years was in the Zoological Department of the British Museum.

BROMIDE OF IRON is recommended as nearly a specific in involuntary emissions and spermatorrhea. Three to five grains are given, rubbed up in syrup, three times daily, an hour before or after meals.

STATE BOARD OF HEALTH.

Abstract from the Reports of Deaths and their Causes in the following cities and towns in California, during February, 1872:

CITIES AND TOWNS.	Total No. Deaths.	Prevalent Diseases. Consumption.	Other diseases of Lungs.	Dis. Stomach and Bowels.	Diphtheria	Scarlatina	Typho-malarial Fevers.	AUTHORITIES.
San Francisco......	243	43	26	10	1	3	12	S. F. B'd of Health
Sacramento	26	3	3	2	0	0	0	Sac. B'd of Health
Petaluma	3	1	0	0	0	0	0	Dr. G. W. Graves.
Dixon	1	0	1	0	0	0	0	Dr. R. H. Plummer
San Buenaventura.	1	0	0	1	1	0	0	Dr. C. L. Bard.
Stockton	0	0	0	0	0	0	0	Stockton Bd Health
Marysville...........	4	0	2	0	0	0	0	Dr. C. E. Stone.
Placerville...........	1	1	0	0	0	0	0	Dr. E. A. Kunkler.
Auburn.................	0	0	0	0	0	0	0	Dr. A. S. Du Bois.
San Diego County..	2	1	1	0	0	0	0	Dr. T. C. Stockton.
San Luis Obispo...	...	...	...	...	...	...	...	Dr. W. W. Hays.
Oroville	5	1	1	1	0	0	1	Dr. J. M. Vance.
Woodland...........	5	1	1	0	0	1	0	Dr. A. B. Mehring.
Oakland	16	1	5	1	0	0	0	Dr. T. H. Pinkerton
Los Angeles	24	4	0	3	0	0	3	Dr. H. S. Orme.
Truckee	0	0	0	0	0	0	0	Dr. Wm. Curless.
St. Helena	0	0	0	0	0	0	0	Dr. J. S. Adams.
Napa City...........	1	1	0	0	0	0	0	Dr. M. B. Pond.
Cacheville	...	...	...	...	...	...	...	
Siskiyou.............	0	0	0	0	0	0	0	Dr. T. T. Cabanis.
Watsonville	...	...	...	...	...	...	...	Dr. C. E. Cleveland
Folsom	3	0	1	0	0	0	0	Dr. L. McGuire.
Bridgeport Town'p	0	0	0	0	0	0	0	Dr. J. L. Asay.
Sut'r C'k & Amador	0	0	0	0	0	0	0	Dr. H. M. Fiske.
Monterey............	...	...	...	...	...	...	...	Dr. C. A. Canfield.
Santa Cruz.........	2	1	0	0	0	0	0	Dr. C. L. Anderson
Vallejo	...	...	...	...	...	...	...	
Suisun & Fairfield.	0	0	0	0	0	0	0	Dr. S. D. Campbell
Colusa	1	0	0	0	0	0	0	Dr. Lake Robinson
Trinity County......	2	0	0	0	0	0	0	Dr. J. C. Montague
Santa Barbara......	3	0	1	0	0	0	1	Dr. C. B. Bates.
Redwood City	1	0	1	0	0	0	0	Dr. Kirkpatrick.
Totals	344	58	43	18	1	3	17	

Abstract from Reports of Births.

CITIES AND TOWNS.	Total Births.	Male.	Female.	Still-born.	Live-born.	AUTHORITIES.
San Francisco..	**73**	**33**	**40**	**33**	**40**	**S. F. Board of Health.**
Sacramento.. ...	**28**	**12**	**16**	**2**	**26**	**Sac. Board of Health.**
All other places	**190**	**100**	**90**	**10**	**180**	**Various sources.**
Total..........	**291**	**145**	**146**	**45**	**246**	

REMARKS.—The State continues in the possession of the high sanitary condition that has ruled for some time past. Pneumonia and catarrhal affections have prevailed pretty generally, but of a mild form; also, rheumatism. Several well marked cases of scarlatina have been observed in different points. Small-Pox still continues by frequent importations from other places, but owing to the prompt measures adopted in isolating the cases as soon as discovered, it has not spread. There is now one case in Sacramento, which is quarantined in a tent some two miles from the city. Vaccination has been so general as, probably, to render it impossible for this disease to prevail to any extent during the approaching dry season.

THOS. M. LOGAN, M.D.
Permanent Secretary State Board of Health.

Mortality in San Francisco during February, 1872.

BY H. GIBBONS JR., M. D.

CAUSES OF DEATH.

Abscess	2	Diphtheria	1	Laryngitis	1
Alcoholism	1	Diseases of Heart	12	Liver, Disease of	1
Aneurism of Aorta	2	Dropsy	4	Do. Laceration of.	1
Apoplexy	3	Drowning	1	Meningitis	14
Asthma	3	Dysentery	1	Meningitis, Cerebro Spinal	3
Atrophia	4	Enteritis	6	Murder	1
Bright's Disease	2	Erysipelas	3	Old Age	2
Burns	1	Fever, Remittent	1	Paralysis	5
Cancer	1	Do. Intermittent	2	Peritonitis	6
Do. of Breast	1	Do. Congestive	1	Phthisis	43
Do. of Stomach	1	Do. Scarlet	3	Pleuritis	2
Do. of Uterus	1	Do. Typhoid	7	Pneumonitis	18
Cellular Sclerosis	1	Do. Typhus	1	Premature Birth	2
Chorea	1	Gangrene	1	Suicide	5
Congestion of Brain	1	Gastritis	3	Syphilis	3
Do of Lungs	6	Hemorrhage	1	Toxemia	1
Constipation	1	Hepatitis	4	Tumor	1
Convuls'ns, Infantile	6	Hemoptysis	1	Uterine Disease	1
Do. Puerperal	1	Hydrocephalus	5	Unknown	7
Croup	9	Inanition	7	TOTAL	243
Cyanosis	1	Injuries, unspecified.	2	Still-births	33
Debility, General	9	Jaundice	1		

AGES.

Under 1 year	48	From 15 to 20 years	4	From 60 to 70 years	14
From 1 to 2 years	17	From 20 to 30 years	26	From 70 to 80 years	4
From 2 to 5 years	11	From 30 to 40 years	45	From 80 to 90 years	3
From 5 to 10 years	7	From 40 to 50 years	35	Unknown	1
From 10 to 15 years	4	From 50 to 60 years	24		

SEX:—Male, 158; Female, 85.
COLOR:—White, 210; Copper, 31; Black, 2.

NATIVITIES.

California	86	France	8	Alaska	1
Other parts of U. S.	35	Germany	17	Azores	1
British-Amer'n Prov.	3	Austria	1	Bavaria	1
Mexico	3	Denmark	1	Belgium	1
England	6	Switzerland	2	Greece	1
Ireland	34	Italy	4	Poland	2
Scotland	1	China	28	Norway	1
Wales	1	Australia	1	Unknown	4

RECAPITULATION.

Died in City Wards	187	Casualties	4
City and County Hospital	16	Suicides	5
U. S. Marine Hospital	2	Alms House	2
French Hospital	5	Mt. St. Joseph's Asylum	7
German Hospital	5	Italian Hospital	4
St. Mary's Hospital	4	S. F. Female Hospital	2

Remarks.—Little of interest is to be said in relation to the report herewith presented. Although the mortality of February was materially greater than that of January, notwithstanding the former was two days the shorter month, it by no means indicates an unhealthy condition of our city. While there has undoubtedly been some increase of sickness, not the slightest evidence of epidemic tendency exists. We hear of the ravages of small-pox in the larger Eastern cities and even on the lines of the railroad near our borders, but it has not showed itself among us, nor is it likely to. In looking into the causes of the increased mortality of February, we will find this increase confined to a very few diseases. From pneumonitis alone there were eleven more deaths in February; from croup, enteritis, meningitis, peritonitis, and general debility there were twenty-five more. The number of still-births (33) reported is very large. Among the unusual causes of death we notice, murder, cerebro-spinal meningitis, chorea, constipation, and schlerosis telæ cellulosæ, the latter an infant nine days old. It will be observed that the deaths of children under five years of age was largely in excess of the number for January, which, however, was extraordinarily small in that month. If the fact could be ascertained we would probably find that many more births took place in February than January. In the aggregate, the deaths in public institutions were unusually small, excepting, perhaps, Mount St. Joseph's Infirmary—a home for young children. The deaths in February for some years past were: 1866, 199; 1867, 201· 1868, 209; 1869, 267; 1870, 254; 1871, 245.

ITEMS OF NEWS, Etc.

TELEGRAPHIC SURGERY.—When Vallandigham lay dying of a gun-shot wound in the abdomen, it is said that Marion Sims sent a telegram to his attending surgeons to cut down upon and ligate the bleeding vessels.

WHOOPING COUGH is now to be cured by *compressed air*. Dr. Sardahl, of Stockholm, reports 102 cases rapidly cured by this treatment.

A DR. N. E. CUSHING, in Brownsville, Ga., gives public notice to saloon-keepers that he is an inebriate, and if they sell him liquor they will be prosecuted under the law in such cases made and provided.

"INFUS. EJUSDEM" wrote a New York doctor in a prescription, immediately beneath "Tinc. gentian. comp." Whereupon a number of apothecaries were sorely vexed, not finding the tincture of ejusdem on their shelves, nor yet in the Dispensatory.

FEMALES constitute one-tenth of the matriculants at the University of Zurich, Switzerland.

COLLODION TEETH are manufactured in England, having the hardness of bone and ivory.

A GRAND REUNION of the Alumni of Jefferson Medical College is to be held during the meeting of the National Association.

TWENTY-FIVE MILLION of dollars has been appropriated by the city of Birmingham, Eng., to establish a system of sewerage.

☞ DR. SIMMONS of Sacramento having declined the appointment of Chairman of the Committee on Obstetrics of the State Medical Society, the President of the Society has appointed Dr. Ira E. Oatman in his stead.

PACIFIC

MEDICAL AND SURGICAL JOURNAL.

Vol. V.—MAY, 1872.—No. 60.

ORIGINAL COMMUNICATIONS.

Hypertrophy of Heart and Pericardial Adhesions.

By J. BRADFORD COX, M.D., Sonoma, Cal.

After a careful perusal of the "Report of Meetings of the S. F. Medical Society," in the *Western Lancet* for February; also having the Journal for March before me, in which the proceedings of the same Society, for the same date (January 23d), are published; my inability to reconcile discrepancies in the two reports is my apology for again offering a communication.

The report in the *Lancet* would make one of the members of the Society say that he believed a diagnosis impossible in a case of hypertrophy of the heart. (See page 123.) The Society then engaged in the discussion of another subject, viz : that of druggists re-filling prescriptions without orders.

What I wish to say is this : That such an assertion, made and not refuted, while the subject was yet under discussion, does not speak volumes for the skill of the medical profession of this coast.

We country practitioners look upon the discussions in the leading Medical Societies as something to be highly prized; as one of the many sources from which to draw for

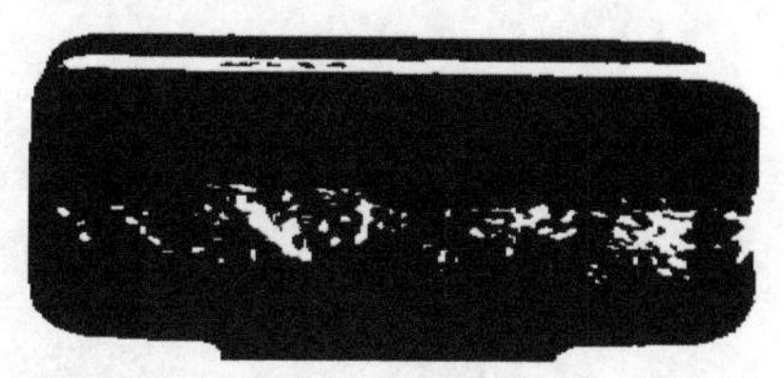

information in the various departments of our noble profession. I have too much respect and reverence for the skill of the members of the "San Francisco Medical Society" to think that they could not—most of them at least—make a correct diagnosis in hypertrophy of the heart, in either of its two principal forms. I must, therefore, hold the *Lancet* responsible for an error in its representation of the status of the profession on this coast.

Should the number of this periodical to which I have referred, reach the hands of some of the critics of the profession in the East, I fear they would not be flattered with the progress we are making in percussion and auscultation.

But, to revert to the *facts* in the case. The Journal, page 462, says the member to whom I have already alluded, "explained that his question had not been understood. It was—can pericardial adhesion of itself be diagnosticated? He believed not. But when from long continuance it produced decided results, as hypertrophy, its existence can be determined."

First a few words in regard to hypertrophy, and then to the question above.

Aitken's description is—"an abnormal increase in the muscular substance of the heart." This agrees with the meaning of the two Greek words from which it is derived, and will exclude many cases of supposed hypertrophy, in which there is simply a dilatation of the cavities of the heart, without any perceptible change in the muscular structure of the organ; it being neither increased nor diminished—neither hypertrophied nor atrophied.

Since the investigations of Cruveilhier, and more recently those of Budd, we are justified in excluding also the so-called concentric hypertrophy, except as a congenital malformation.

This leaves us with—1st. Simple Hypertrophy, or cases in which there is an increase in the muscular substance, without any perceptible change in the size of the cavities. 2d. Hypertrophy with Dilatation, or cases in which there is in addition to the increase in the muscular substance a dilatation or enlargement of the cavities.

Cases in which there is simply an enlargement of the size of the organ, without increase or decrease in the muscular substance, should be called simply *dilatation*, and should be excluded from discussions on either hypertrophy or atrophy.

In regard to a diagnosis of hypertrophy, all will admit that without physical exploration we would almost always fail; but with it, the task is an easy one; one that, with even an ordinary knowledge of percussion alone, we can decide with some degree of certainty. And when we bring to our assistance the auxiliaries, inspection, mensuration, palpation and auscultation, the diagnosis is rendered quite easy.

True, there are some diseases from which it must be differentiated. Perhaps the one most likely to deceive us is pericarditis with effusion. In this we have the precordial space or triangle enlarged, the flatness extending beyond the left nipple in some cases, and where the effusion is not excessive the flatness does not extend higher than in cases of hypertrophy; the heart sounds are weakened; the first sound is short and valvular like the second; there is absence of organic murmurs if valvular lesions do not exist, which signs are the same in both diseases; that is, in one form of hypertrophy, viz: hypertrophy with dilatation, and in pericarditis with effusion. In some cases of the latter the characteristic "pericardial friction murmur" (according to Flint) disappears, and could we go no further, we might stop here and say we were unable to decide. But we will not stop here. Let us see what can be developed by palpation. Placing the hand on the chest—in one case we feel the intercostal depressions pushed out, and motionless; the impulse of the heart lost, or if appreciable, raised to the fourth or third intercostal space. In the other case we feel a heaving movement of the precordia, the heart's impulse is felt in the intercostal spaces above the apex beat with more or less power, while the apex beat itself is lowered from the fifth intercostal space, to the sixth, seventh, or eighth, according to the degree of hypertrophy, and often removed from its normal situation, one, two, or three inches to the left.

The general health with the history of the case should also be closely observed; and if properly interrogated will throw light on the diagnosis.

But to return to the other question—: "Can pericardial adhesion of itself be diagnosticated?"

I am not prepared to say with the member who propounded the question that "I believe not;" but *will* say that I consider it a more difficult task than the diagnosis of hypertrophy.

In this instance I should depend more upon the history of the case than any other points that could be brought to bear in the decision. For I think the experience of the profession has been, and the teachings of pathology show, that without pericarditis, adhesions are not likely to occur; (may I not say *never* occur?) and the symptoms attending a case of pericarditis are sufficiently well marked. I might add that the signs as contra-distinguished from symptoms are pathognomonic.

Therefore unless we could ascertain that the patient had at sometime during life had an attack of pericarditis, I should not hesitate in saying that pericardial adhesions did not exist.

However when we find them post mortem it is difficult to learn the history of the case.

So far as physical exploration gives light on this difficult subject I have been unable to find anything very definite. The heart is said to beat irregularly; but it beats irregularly from other causes; therefore we cannot always say that in a given case it is due to this or that cause.

There is a view of the question which I have not seen discussed in any of my medical works, but which I am inclined to think will throw light upon it when properly investigated. It is this: when the adhesion exists to an extent sufficient to interfere with the symmetrical contractions of the muscular fibres of the heart, which, I fancy, it would in almost any case where it existed at all, the contractions and relaxations not taking place in that smoothly gliding manner that is usual where there is no impediment whatever, I cannot refrain from thinking that in such cases the sphygmograph would show by its delicate tracing that a contraction or relaxation was not steady as it should be. Therefore if we could exclude valvular lesions, aneurisms, etc., which could be done by physical exploration, we might diagnose pericardial adhesion. This would be rendered almost certain if we could trace it back to an attack of pericarditis.

I am inclined to believe there is not the intimate relation existing between hypertrophy of the heart and pericardial adhesions that some of the members of the society seemed to think there was. I do not think they stand in the same relation of cause and effect. Prof. Flint in his Practice of Medicine, says: "The mechanism of the production of hypertrophy of the heart is long-continued, augmented power of the heart's action." With this view of the origin of hypertrophy I fancy we must look beyond pericardial adhesion for an explanation. This we find in the various valvular lesions to which the organ is subject. In fact, the same author says, that "Enlargement of the heart in the great majority of cases proceeds from valvular lesions, and the latter, sooner or later, in the great majority of cases, give rise to cardiac enlargement." Here we have the best authority in the profession on the subject. I have already said enough in regard to the origin of pericardial adhesions.

The specimens brought before the society, and which gave rise to the discussion, had before death a decided mitral murmur. It is not stated however whether it was mitral regurgitant or mitral obstructive—or either of these. Prof. Fliut says, in his Compendium of Percussion and

Auscultation, and he also teaches his private classes in Bellevue Hospital, that a mitral murmur, beginning with the first sound of the heart, does not always denote mitral regurgitation. Such a murmur may be distinguished as a mitral systolic, or an intra-ventricular murmur. Bear in mind that this is the peculiar murmur heard in endocarditis. He also says and teaches, in regard to the mitral obstructive murmur, that it does not denote mitral lesions, in all cases, when it is associated with aortic regurgitant lesions. Waiving the point then as to which of these murmurs the one in question might have been, we may conclude that by whatever mechanism the said murmur was produced, we have, in the act of its production, a sufficient cause for long-continued, augmented power of the heart's action; hence a sufficient cause for the hypertrophy.

The probable history of the specimen was that at some time during the life of the subject from which it was taken, there was pericarditis with endocarditis—not an uncommon occurrence—or, technically, endo-pericarditis. That the result of the pericarditis was the pericardial adhesion. That the endocarditis by influence over the heart's action, it being morbidly excited, beating with an abnormal force, and continuing for a sufficient length of time, inaugurated the process of hypertrophy, which perhaps continued until death.

The murmur of endocarditis, the mitral systolic or intra-ventricular, is generally permanent, and is the one which was heard before death. It generally remains after all trace of the inflammation has disappeared; notwithstanding the inflammation may not have resulted from valvular lesion.

Prof. Flint has known such a murmur to continue for several years after recovery and then disappear.

New Mode of Operating for Radical Cure of Varicocele.

BY H. B. DAVISON M.D., San Francisco.

There is a surgical disease that many persons are suffering from, of the existence of which they are ignorant. I allude to *varicocele* of the spermatic cord.

The medical examinations of the military surgeons show that nearly one person in every ten was rejected on account of that lesion. I believe that it occurs oftener as a congenital defect, than brought on by external causes.

No matter whether it exist congenitally or otherwise, it is always a source of great discomfort and suffering to the person so afflicted, physically and mentally, and if not treated palliatively by astringent lotions or the suspensory bandage, or radically by ligating the vein, atrophy of the testicle sooner or later occurs, and a corresponding loss of sexual power.

Formerly, ligation of the veins was held to be fraught with danger, but more modern operations have shown the danger to be imaginary.

The so called "subcutaneous" ligation of the spermatic vein for the cure of varicocele is not strictly a subcutaneous operation. The scrotum is perforated through both walls, and the ligation is generally performed on the patient standing, or in a semi-recumbent position, which will cause the varicose veins to become distended. When the ligation is completed there remains a plug, or clot of blood, shut off or excluded from the circulation, which acts as an extraneous body, and greatly increases the resulting inflammation of the testicle and its coverings.

It must be conceded that the danger arising from *phlebitis* will be greater in proportion to the length of time that the ligature is allowed to remain, which usually is from six to ten days, before the enclosed vein is separated.

The method which I have adopted, and have successfully performed in all cases operated on, may be briefly described as follows:

The patient is placed in the recumbent position, and an anesthetic administered, or not, at the option of patient and surgeon. The varicose veins are separated from the arteries and vas deferens; the testicle held up that the veins may be emptied of all blood, so that, when ligated, no plug of blood remains between the point of ligation and the body of the testicle.

The next step in the operation will be to pass a steel or silver needle, *curved* so that it will form a little more than a half circle, armed with a strong silk ligature, well waxed, through but *one* fold of the scrotum *under* the vein to be ligated.

Pass the needle in, and manipulate it through the walls of the scrotum, draw down far enough so as to draw in some of the ligature, then guide the point of the needle (which must not be sharp, for fear of wounding some of the vessels,) *up and over* the vein, and seek to make its exit from the orifice of entrance, which will not be difficult with a little gentle manipulation.

Draw through sufficient of the ligature to pass through the two holes of the silver or ivory button. Tie down with a double loop, which may be tightened again in from twelve to twenty hours.

The patient may be given a mixture of chloral hydrate and elixir of opium and left in the recumbent position with sorbefacient application to the scrotum, which should be supported by a folded towel placed beneath.

In from ten to sixteen hours the inflammation will have been sufficient to cause a plug of plastic lymph to obliterate the ligated vein, and the ligature can be removed with safety in from two to three days.

The better way to remove the ligature is to untie the loop and cut off one end close to the scrotum, then by gentle traction on the remaining portion of the ligature, it will come away without cutting through the vein, which is unnecessary and only adds to the danger of phlebitis and retards recovery.

By the above mode of operating, I claim three great advantages over any other means yet known to profession:

First, by perforating only one wall of the scrotum, less pain, less inflammation and less risk of adhesion of the wounded sac and spermatic cord.

Second, by placing the patient in a recumbent posture when the operation is being performed, so that no blood may be enclosed in that portion of the vein cut off from the circulation, the resultant inflammation will be much less and the testicle will not swell so much, and absorption will be accomplished in much less time.

Third, by removing the ligature before it cuts through the vein the risk of *phlebitis* is lessened and the patient is enabled to resume his ordinary duties much sooner.

Those who have been operated on have no return of the disease, and it would require a very close examination of the parts to discover that any operation had been performed. In one case the patient had been wearing a suspensory bandage for over twenty years, and the left testicle was much *atrophied*. It is now about sixteen months since the operation, and the testicle has regained its normal size, and the patient has a corresponding increase of sexual power.

Nutrition of the Human Body.

With some Suggestions How to Regulate it in the Prevention and Cure of Disease.

[Read before the Sacramento Society for Medical Improvement, January 18, 1872.]

By AUGUSTUS TRAFTON, M.D.

The subject which I have selected for this evening's discussion, is the Nutrition of the Human Body, the great function to which all others are subservient. In its widest sense it properly embraces all the processes concerned in producing and maintaining the condition known as life. In this short paper it would be impossible to discuss all the various means by which the physiological decay of the various fluids and solids is counterbalanced by the continuous appropriation of new material. We know that in a state of health the body is always changing in every part. The tissues of the lungs, heart, brain, skin, muscles, nerves, bones and ligaments, all are being gradually changed into effete matter which is carried out of the organism by the several emunctories; and, at the same time, certain other organs are quite as busily engaged in preparing new material to be assimilated by the various tissues of the body. This continual change in the particles of matter forming the human body is necessary to, and is an inevitable condition of, life. This process may be accelerated or retarded by climacteric and climatic changes, by mental or bodily exercise, by various conditions of disease, and by the quantity and quality of the alimentary substances taken as food.

The nervous system is no doubt responsible for the correct performance of many of the functions of organs concerned in normal nutrition, and is likewise chargeable with many of the vagaries of abnormal or imperfect nutrition. But it is not so certain that nervous influence is actually necessary to nutrition in some of the tissues, for Virchow has declared "that secretion and nutrition, both normal and abnormal, can be carried on without the influence of the vascular and nervous system." On the other hand, Brown Sequard describes secretory, nutritive, incito-secretory and incito-nutritive nerves, and says: "They are the antagonists, in many respects, of the vaso motor nerves; the latter producing contraction of the blood-vessels, thus diminishing the supply of blood to a part, in consequence of which the various vital properties, the secretions and animal heat, are diminished; whereas the nutritive and secretory nerves occasion a dilatation of the blood-vessels, thus favoring the phenomena that tend to increased circulation, animal heat, and consequently increased nutrition." Sequard says "that these nerves can produce inflammation, suppuration and ulceration by a reflex action." Virchow says: "More recent observations have gradually done away with the whole class of the so-called neuro-paralytical inflammations." Thus these great masters seem to differ in regard to the influence of the nervous system on nutritive processes. However this may be, no one, I suppose, will object to the proposition that the nervous system *does influence* both secretion and nutrition in a variety of ways. I can see nothing wrong in making the nervous system subservient to purposes of nutrition as far as it can be satisfactorily demonstrated.

With regard to the vascular system, the same difficulty occurs. We know that nutrition does take place in extra vascular tissues as well as in those in which vessels are known to exist. I think it reasonable to suppose that the changes of structure in the arterial system—(which are susceptible of demonstration so far as the capillaries)—are continued still further, the investing membrane of the final capillaries changing into connective tissue, in which the ultimate cells are imbedded; the reticulated connective tissue anastomosing with the finer capillaries, lymphatics and cells, forming a most delicate system of communication through which the nutritive juices are conveyed to the ultimate cells. We might also account for a nervous influence, an "excitation or irritation," which, according to Virchow, is exerted in the cells and cell contents. It would only be necessary to suppose the connective tissue a conducting material for nervous influence, to conduct that influence from the ultimate filaments or "Paccinian bodies" to the ultimate cells, thus furnishing a *reason* for the "irritation" said to exist in the cells and thus *influencing* nutrition in the most extreme parts of the body. Austin Flint, Jr., says: "The nature of the main forces involved in nutrition, be it in a highly organized part like the brain or muscles, or a tissue called extra vascular, like the cartilages or nails, is *unknown*." If we know *little* with regard to some of the modes by which nutrition is influenced, we *still* know more than we do of *what it is* that causes the organs of a living animal to change into effete matter incapable of farther serving a useful purpose in the animal economy, or what it is which confers on the organism the power of assimilation and self regeneration, when aliment, which has undergone the necessary changes, is, under proper conditions, presented to them.

These great questions are beyond the reach of the physiologist of the present day; they are mysteries of which the human mind can scarcely comprehend the immensity. We know that nutrition cannot be arrested for any considerable time without producing fatal consequences. Either the lack of assimilation, or retention in the body of the secretions, would produce disease and death. Thus we are made aware of the vast importance of studying the phenomena of nutrition, and the best methods of controlling and regulating them.

With regard to the human animal, we might say the *first act of nutrition*, when a new being is first formed, is a fecundating copulation. The ovum, which a moment before possessed no vital power, is now vivified; it soon begins to appropriate material from the maternal organism: a sort of change of material, protein or plasma, into the rudimentary nerves and blood-vessels which are to be instrumental in still further nourishing the embryo. The various substances necessary for the further development of the fetus are now supplied through the vascular prolongations of the fetus which are constantly bathed in the maternal blood as it circulates through the placenta. A sufficient amount of oxygen is supplied along with the other nutritive material, and circulation, secretion and excretion are normally performed by the fetus up to the close of gestation.

After the birth of the child other means of support become necessary. Respiration, alimentation and digestion are added to the other functions, and all the processes concerned in general nutrition are fully inaugurated, to be continued under favorable circumstances to the end of the "three score and ten" years allotted as the duration of human life. Many and varied will be the influences brought to bear on the individual during his journey through life. The various ills of childhood will scarcely be safely passed before the influence of puberty and manhood affect still further the nutrition of the system. Then follows a period of a few years in which the antagonizing forces of assimilation and physiological decay are nearly equal. This contest goes on for a longer or shorter time until the assimilative powers begin to weaken, more fuel is required to keep the temperature of the body at the normal standard than can be supplied, the nervous system—the vascular system—the glandular system—all become weakened in their action, until at last the human machine ceases to go, and life is extinct.

I have now defined and described the process of nutrition, with some of the forces which seem to influence it. It remains for me to show in what way we may benefit our patients by an intimate knowledge of the forces regulating the phenomena attending this indispensable process of nutrition. Our duties in this respect sometimes commence *before* the birth of our patient, (if you will allow me to consider the fetus in utero a patient.) Physicians are often consulted as to the best means to enable the fetus to maintain its position in the gravid uterus until the completion of the full term of gestation. A solution of the problem will often be found by inquiring into the habits of the mother. Perhaps some of the functions connected with the nutrition of the ovum will be found imperfectly performed. For instance: an insufficient or an over abundant supply of the nitrogenized articles of food may be taken; the clothing may be inappropriate in many ways; the exercise may be less, or more, than should be taken; or it may be of an improper kind—all these acts of the mother have a physiological and direct bearing on the nutrition of the fetus—our yet unborn patient.

After the birth of the patient our duties are more plainly indicated, and consist in regulating the surroundings of the child. As respiration is one of the first requirements, a well ventilated nursery is a necessity. And as the action of the skin has been considered a necessary adjunct to respiration, if not a part of the process, *cleanliness* must be insisted upon. Alimentation is next to respiration in importance, and often tasks the ingenuity of the practitioner—(in cases where the feeding is artificial)—to the utmost, to prescribe a proper diet for the little patient. Sometimes the nutriment furnished is lacking in quantity or quality. This may necessitate a chemical inquiry into the constituents of the milk; after which the intelligent practitioner, guided by a positive knowledge of the ingredients of the lacteal fluid, will be able in most cases to supply the deficiency.

Digestion, another of the processes necessary to the normal performance of nutrition, may be at fault and will demand prompt attention. This may be interfered with in various ways. As Austin Flint, Jr., has included "Prehension of food, mastication and deglutition" in his chapter on digestion, it will not be considered out of the way to remind the physician that some physical condition of the buccal cavity and fauces, which can be remedied by surgical interference, may stand in the way of nutrition by preventing haustion in the infant, or proper mastication by the child or adult. The proper method of removing such impediments to nutrition will be suggested by the nature of the case. Sometimes a division of the frenum linguæ, or an operation for palatal fissure, may be required; and in case of adults an examination of the teeth will sometimes reveal the main cause of the indigestion of the patient.

TO BE CONCLUDED IN NEXT NUMBER.

Eucalyptus — Its Medicinal Virtues.

BY DAVID WOOSTER, M. D., San Francisco.

I wish to call your attention to the effects of fluid extract of Eucaliptus. I have now used some gallons of this extract during a period of eight months in the U. S. Marine Hospital, and am surprised at its uniform and reliable effects in affections for which it is suitable. It is a diuretic of rare virtue, and may be administered when most of the diuretics now in common use are inadmissible. It is an aromatic tonic, and has notable restorative effects in low states of the system, as in typhoid fever, typhoid diarrhea and dysentery.

In vesical catarrh it alone cures. In spasmodic stricture it relieves with great promptness. In all affections of the mucous membranes its beneficial action is remarkable. We have treated many cases of acute gonorrhea with no other remedy. Per contra, in syphilis it is useless except as an alterative.

It has no anti-periodic action. It relieves headache apparently as the saline diuretics do, by its diuretic action.

As an external application in chronic ulcers, it has great value.

It does not impair, but rather improves the appetite. It is to be hoped the profession will try it more generally. I have now used it in some hundreds of cases. Dr. Coleman, formerly of Stockton, now in this city, first called my attention to its virtues, and I have used the fluid extract of his manufacture. Indeed I believe it has not yet been manufactured by any other party.

Bromide of Potassium in Poisoning by Strychnia.

By C. B. BATES, M. D., Santa Barbara.

On the morning of April 3d, I was called in great haste to J. D.,, aged 22, who had poisoned himself with strychnia. It seems that from some unexplained reason he had determined upon self-destruction, and after making a coffin which I discovered hidden beneath the bed, had taken about 10 grs. of strychnia. His stomach was empty at the time, having had nothing but a cup of tea for breakfast. Upon my arrival, about half an hour afterwards, I found him in a most violent tetanic convulsion, and at once forced him to swallow a dose of tartar emetic and ipecac; then I sent for a stomach pump, but before the return of the messenger the emetic had commenced to. operate. Its action was kept up for some time by the administration of copious draughts of warm water and mustard and water until the stomach was thoroughly evacuated. During the whole of this time convulsions were recurring every few minutes, and as I was satisfied there could now be no more of the poison remaining in the stomach, I gave him one grain of sulphate of morphia with about forty of bromide of potassium. Soon the paroxysms decreased in violence, and the intervals of rest became longer. The bromide of potassium in doses of forty grains was repeated every hour until he had taken half an ounce, when he was out of danger, and all that remained of the muscular spasm was an occasional jerking of the muscles of the lower jaw.

I learned afterwards that an aunt, on his father's side, and two brothers had attempted suicide—one of the latter successfully; so that the tendency to suicide in his case would appear to be hereditary.

Necrosis of the Tibia.

BY E. W. KING M.D., Ukiah, Mendocino County.

E. McD—, male, about ten years of age, of strumous habit, came under my care about the middle of June 1870; having been confined to his bed for months with disease of the right tibia.

At the time the case came under my care the boy was considerably emaciated. Appetite capricious, but no evidence of any disease except in the leg. At a point about three inches below the lower border of the patella, the bone was exposed, and its surface denuded of periosteum for perhaps an inch and a half along its anterior surface, and an inch wide. The exposed surface was evidently dead bone.

About half way from this point to the ankle joint were three or four openings dicharging pus and sanious matter, through which diseased bone could be felt with the probe, and through which small particles of bone had been discharged at different times.

The amount of pus discharged daily through the upper and lower openings was quite large. The former history of the case was the ordinary history of acute necrosis.

The boy was put on quinine and iron with laxatives, a generous diet and plenty of fresh air, under which he rapidly improved in flesh and strength. As soon as he was able to use them, crutches were given him and he was directed to take as much exercise in the open air as was consistent with his strength. In about three months he was so far improved in general condition as to go all around the place on his crutches, and he appeared robust and healthy.

Sept. 16th—The diseased bone appears to be separated from the healthy. With the assistance of Dr. W. C. Alban of this place, a portion of the tibia was removed, 4 3-4 inches in length, commencing just below the tubercle and running downward.

After the operation, an examination of the bone revealed the fact that the whole circumference of the shaft of the tibia, two and a half inches in length, had been removed.

An examination of the leg showed that a new bone had been in process of formation for sometime between the periosteum and the diseased bone. This had partially lifted the diseased portion out of its bed and had already united the upper and lower portions of the tibia, and was making an effort to fill up the gap made by the removal of the diseased portion. This space filled very rapidly.

An extract from my note book, Oct. 16, just one month after the operation, will show its progress.

"New bone is forming in place of the old, and although the space is not entirely filled, the bone is sufficiently strong to support the weight of the body in walking." This boy continued to improve steadily until he was well, and now that several months have passed, he still remains in good health, the leg appearing to be as strong as ever.

Diagnosis of Adherent Pericardium,

And Rejection of Concentric Hypertrophy as a Cardiac Disease.

By EDWIN BENTLEY, M.D.

[Read before the San Francisco Medical Society, April 9, 1872.]

It will be remembered by some of you, that a few weeks ago I presented to the Society specimens of adherent pericardium and hypertrophy of heart, and in connection with them I made a few extemporaneous remarks, at the conclusion of which I was asked to give some symptoms of adherent pericardium, by which it might be recognized during the life time of the patient. In this I failed to satisfy either my interrogator or myself. Several distinguished gentlemen of the Society followed, with like success (at least so far as I was concerned). At a subsequent meeting a second specimen of adherent pericardium was presented, and in as much as it had been distinguished during the treatment, or as nearly so as this condition ever is, I felt a special interest in calling up the previous specimen which had been exhibited. But in this I did not succeed, from the inadvertence of the gentleman to whom I referred, but who has since very kindly favored the Society with a more elaborate and extended detail of the matter than I anticipated. This has had the effect to stimulate in me an inquiring disposition, in regard to the literature of the two conditions in question, lest I should find myself a teacher of false doctrines, an exponent of pathological conditions not in harmony with the acknowledged authorities of the age, or in keeping with the accepted revelations of the cadaver. For I hold now as ever that while symptoms are oftentimes unreliable, ambiguous and deceptive, making medicine the uncertain art that it is confessed to be, anatomy and pathology have a right, which we all admit, in their high aspiration to attain to the position of exact, certain and demonstrable sciences. I will, therefore, with the permission of the Society, endeavor this evening to sustain the position that I first assumed; not so much, however, by arguments or observations of my own, as by the opinions of observers of acknowledged ability.

In determining, then, a case of *adherent pericardium*, many things deserve to be taken into consideration. The history of the case should receive attention, since for thirty years and more, articular rheumatism, renal diseases, albuminuria, &c., have been regarded as concomitants of *pericarditis*, by such men as Pit cair Dundas, Wells, Latham, and Elliotson. According to Dr. Fuller, it is more likely to occur in young subjects, when it is frequently associated with pleuritis or pleuro-pneumonia. Dr. Chambers found it in pyemia in the proportion of 18 in 135 cases. He also observed it in cases of scarlet fever, scurvy, and continued fevers. When found in infancy, he observed the patient to have a sharp, shrieking cry, like what is heard in acute meningitis. Dr. Flint, whom we all know as an unyielding and persistent observer, and who would insist on the ability of physical signs to correctly interpret as much of the internal workings of the great vital organs as any man living, says of adherent pericardium, "Whatever evidence is available must be derived from physical signs," and then adds this forcible qualification: "The diagnosis cannot always be made with accuracy." "It is more marked, when in addition to pericardial adhesions there exists firm adhesion of the exterior of the pericardium to the parietes of the chest." When the heart is not covered by the lungs, we are told that the apex beat is frequently suppressed. But, it is added, it must be remembered that it is suppressed also in other diseases and in healthy persons. When the apex beat is felt between the fourth and fifth ribs, it is significant of adherent pericardium; but successive movements in different intercostal spaces, presenting an appearance of undulations, can hardly be considered as a sign of adhesions if enlargements exist.

A jogging or tumbling motion of the heart, as perceived by the hand when placed over the precordial region, was considered by Dr. Hope as a distinctive sign. In regard to this symptom, however, Dr. Flint says: "Tranquil regularity of the heart's movements is perfectly compatible with universal and close adhesions." Louis, in his once famous work on phthisis (page 51), reports two instances of adhesions of the pericardium; in one the patient experienced "great palpitation, and the pulse was exceedingly irregular." In the other no such features are recorded.

Laennec (third London edition, p. 677), alike the pathologist as specialist—and to the former may well be attributed his wonderful success as a rational expounder of physical signs in its early days—after narrating the principal signs, adds: "I must repeat, however, that we must not accord too implicit confidence to these signs, even when they coexist, for pericarditis may assuredly exist without them, and they without pericarditis." Lancisci and Vieussens consider it as frequently causing palpitations; Meckel, as rendering the pulse exceedingly small; Senac, as producing frequent faintings. Corvisart makes three forms, one the result of pericarditis proper; the second of rheumatic origin; the third without causation being assigned. The classification of Corvisart I simply refer to as believing it to be a natural one; that is, adhesion may be the result of simple inflammatory action; it may be the result of rheumatic diathesis, or it may depend on causes not clearly demonstrable.

Laennec again says: "I have understood that an English physician—Dr. Sanders—has announced, as an infallible sign of adhesion of the pericardium to the heart, the existence of a hollow during each systole of the organ, in the epigastrium, immediately below the left false ribs." The same observation has been attributed to Dr. Heim, of Berlin. And this is the symptom which I have understood as having been referred to in this Society with considerable emphasis, as a diagnostic symptom, if not absolutely pathognomonic. Let me give Laennec's expression of this old symptom full fifty years ago—and I venerate it none the less for its age: "During the last two years I have sought in vain to verify this observation among my patients who presented any disorder of the circulation; and in none of them have I found the epigastric depression, although several had this very adhesion of the pericardium." The dimpling of the epigastrium which takes place with the ventricular systole, Dr. Hope says, "we have searched for attentively in several cases of adhesion, but have not been able to detect it in any degree which could constitute a sign." No one, I trust, will doubt the opportunity or assiduity of this authority. To interpret this symptom Laennec has added the observation of a philosophic mind, as true in this case as in the case of the stethoscope, when by putting his ear at the end of the log, he heard magnified, the sound made at the other end. "For I think this could not take place unless the stomach, by adhering both to the diaphragm and the abdominal parietes, formed the medium of retraction." Skoda, in his first edition, says: "No symptoms are discoverable through percussion or auscultation, which can be ascribed to adhesion of the heart and pericardium." And while denying the force of the abrupt jogging or tumbling motion in the pericardiac region, which has been described here, as an inexpressible sense of commotion, and not accepting the extinction of the second sound of the heart, on which Aran so persuasively dwells, he asserts that "the most trustworthy sign is this: the drawing up of the apex during contraction of the ventricles, with depression of the intercostal spaces." This view of the question is in a measure accepted by Dr. Flint, who leaves what he asserts to be the only way of making out the diagnosis by percussion and auscultation, and says: "Inspection furnishes the most distinctive sign, viz: Retraction of the intercostal spaces, and depression of the epigastrium at the left of the xiphoid cartilage, occurring synchronously with the ventricular systole." He explains his position by this theory: The drawing in is due to the attachment of the base of the pericardium to the cordiform tendon of the diaphragm. The intercostal spaces are drawn in when the ventricles contract, and are most marked when the pericardium is attached to the parietes of the chest. Walshe associates this dimpling only with pleuritic adhesions, and this is the sentiment embraced in my original remarks, and corresponds most fully with my observations in this direction. Dr. Flint condenses the following signs: The area of precordial dullness remaining unaltered in different positions of the body; not affected by deep inspirations; apex beat suppressed, or raised above the normal position; retraction of one or more of the precordial spaces; depression of the epigastrium synchronously with ventricular systole. And he concludes with this graphic truth on which I insist, and to which I respectfully invite your attention: "All these signs may be wanting in pericardial adhesions, and are never marked unless pleuritic adhesions exist also."

Dunglison, in the third volume of his Cyclopedia, observes that rheumatic pericarditis frequently terminates in an adhesion of the pericardium. Lancisci, Vieussens, Meckel, Senac, and Corvisart, are of the opinion that in complete and intimate adhesions, the patient cannot live in a state of health. A very different opinion, however, has been formed by Laennec and Bertin. The former has opened a large number of subjects so affected, that had never complained of any derangement of the respiration or circulation. Hence he very naturally infers that they do not interfere with those functions. Dr. Hope says he has never examined a case of adhesions without finding enlargement of the heart also; this enlargement being due to the embarrassed actions of the heart which the adhesions produce. Bennett (p. 524) has observed complete adhesion of the pericardium, without any symptoms during life. This fact I have corroborated by a large number of cases of death from accident or violence, both among citizens and soldiers. Dr. Wood, in his "Theory and Practice," remarks that the most reliable symptom is the unchanged dullness; but that there is no sign by which it can be certainly recognized. The eccentric Dr. John Elliotson, long Professor of Principles and Practice at the University College, London, says adhesions may exist without previous evidence of inflammation. In this view or opinion he is sustained by Bertin, and Baillie, who, so early as 1799, first published the relations of pericarditis to arthritis. Dr. John A. Swett, long the physician of the New York City Hospital, and finally Professor of Institutes in the University of the City of New York, and whose ability as a faithful and zealous student of thoracic diseases none have ever doubted, thus records : "Pericardial adhesions give rise to symptoms which cannot, so far as I know, be distinguished from those of enlargement of the heart." According to Fredreick, there is a peculiarity about the veins of the neck, in adherent pericardium, viz : When the sternum, after having been drawn down by the systolic movement, springs back again with the diastole, creating an expansion of the chest, and the veins collapse.

Finally, gentlemen, without wearying you with a further detail, I will conclude this part of my paper, by expressing my views of adherent pericardium, in the words of a man whose pre-eminence as a diagnostician will be universally accepted. I scarcely need to say that I allude to Da Costa, of Philadelphia, from whose work on diagnosis I make this quotation : "There are no general symptoms that prove a pericarditis to exist. There are symptoms by which we may infer that pericarditis is present—but there are none which absolutely belong to it, and would prevent it from being overlooked."

I now pass to a brief consideration of concentric hypertrophy. At the beginning of the present century, when cardiac diseases had commenced to be studied with the enthusiasm which Laennec had thrown around all the affections of the thoracic viscera, we find Bertin dividing hypertrophy of the heart into simple eccentric and concentric hypertrophy. With the latter we have only now to deal. It is called by Wood hypertrophy with contraction, or concentric hypertrophy of Bertin ; a condition which might be owing to vigorous contraction at the time of death or immediately afterwards. In support of this opinion, the facts are adduced that a similar diminution has been observed in criminals after execution, and that the contracted cavity has been dilated with the finger. *Wood*, II–176. Niemeyer says concentric hypertrophy is exceedingly rare, insomuch that its very existence has been doubted by Cruveilhier. Rokitansky and Bamberger speak of its being very rare, and only allow it as an increase in bulk of the primitive muscular fibres; which position is denied by Fœrster, who has never been able to demonstrate the thickening of them. Jones and Sieveking make three forms, apparently from usage, or compliment to Bertin, for the former immediately adds: "The last variety, referring to concentric hypertrophy, has no existence as a morbid condition, but is, according to the showing of Drs. Budd and Cruveilhier, a post-mortem effect only—an evidence simply of the powerful tonic contraction of a robust heart, found in all persons decapitated by the guillotine. And in all concentric hypertrophied hearts, the ventricle may be easily dilated by the finger, or dilates itself when the rigor mortis goes off." Tanner, in the late edition of his Practice, says: Concentric hypertrophy is now believed only to occur as a congenital malformation, and never as the consequence of disease. (Fifth ed., p. 593.) Flint says, p. 310: Enlargement of the heart, with or without valvular lesion, is of two kinds. 1st. Enlargement due to abnormal growth or hypertrophy; 2d. Enlargement due to dilatation; thus making only two forms. Sir Thomas Watson, whom all regard as a scholar and philosopher, speaks thus: "The semblance of concentric hypertrophy is most common in the left ventricle, and depends upon the ventricle being nearly empty at the time of death, and upon the corpse being examined while the heart is contracted by the rigor mortis. The fallacious appearance is accordingly noticed in cases where, from the manner of dying, the left ventricle, or the entire heart, contains but little blood, and where, from the muscular power not having been previously exhausted, the rigor mortis is of long duration. Concentric hypertrophy could answer no mechanical purpose; nor could its formation be accounted for on mechanical principles.

Let us conclude, without elaboration, with this paragraph from the modern orthodox text of Aitken: "The existence of concentric hypertrophy is now disbelieved, except as a congenital mal-formation, it having been proved that no such form of hypertrophy exists as the result of disease. Practically, therefore, the physician has to deal with the diagnosis and treatment of simple hypertrophy, hypertrophy with dilatation of one or more of the cavities, and simple dilatation with or without attenuation of the walls of the cavities." In the light of these brief and hasty references, which cover an extended field, I trust it will be clearly perceived by all, that concentric hypertrophy has not been recognized as a result of disease, since Cruveilhier first demonstrated its real nature.

Two Cases of Hemiplegia—Necropsy.

[Read before the Sacramento Society for Medical Improvement, February 20, 1872.]

By F. A. WHITE, M. D.

The subject for discussion this evening will embrace a few points in the pathology of certain nervous affections. I do not propose to enter minutely into the subject, but shall confine myself chiefly to the consideration of two cases which I had the opportunity of examining in the dead house of the County Hospital.

Case 1.—J. S. admitted into the Hospital Jan. 2, 1871. Age, 51; laborer, of very intemperate habits; gave a history of primary syphilis, followed by secondary skin eruptions. When admitted he stated that he had had several epileptic convulsions. There was no paralysis at the time of admission. There was obstinate vomiting which I considered to be due to disease in the brain. Bromides were given in large doses without any apparent effect. Then the constitutional treatment of syphilis was tried.

In February the patient began to fail. Had slight hemiplegia of left side. The left side of the face was expressionless, and the left arm hung loosely by the side. There was no dimness of vision nor difficulty in deglutition. He had frequent attacks of epileptic fits, which grew worse and more obstinate. Bromides were utterly useless. About the middle of May the patient presented symptoms of very grave cerebral disease. He failed rapidly; was at times delirious; had to be restrained in bed to prevent violence to himself and others. He would fall out of bed if not watched constantly. He seemed to have lost sensation completely and had no power of co-ordinating muscular motion. He was unable to take food in any considerable quantity. Finally death came to his relief, May 22, 1871.

I made a post mortem examination the following morning, and found very extensive disease of the brain. On the surface, or rather in the cortical substance of the cerebrum, there were very large nodules, as large as a pigeon's egg, of hardened tissue. On the surface of the cerebellum there was also evidence of pathological changes. Making a section of the cerebrum, I found spots of softening very marked in the middle lobe of the right hemisphere. In the ventricles of the brain there were patches of morbid matter resembling albumen or gelatin. The optic thalamus was apparently very slightly softened.

Case 2.—J. F. Age 57; laborer; admitted May 22, 1871. This patient denied ever having had syphilis, but had suffered from rheumatism several times.

I examined the case with Dr. Donaldson, and we readily made out the diagnosis as being hemiplegia of the left side. He complained of difficulty in deglutition; the voice faltered; there was a slight dimness of vision; the facial palsy was very marked. The treatment availed nothing in this case; he grew worse from day to day, and August 4th, '71, he died. I made a post mortem examination the following day, and found the middle lobe of the right hemisphere very much softened and almost purulent. There was considerable effusion in the ventricles. The optic thalamus and corpora striata were both diseased. The two ganglia are so closely connected that any considerable lesion of the one will soon extend to the other.

It will be observed that in the first case, while there was very extensive disease of the brain, it was confined chiefly to the cortical substance. In the second case the optic thalami and corpora striata were seriously affected. The optic thalami in the first case were slightly affected. In the second, the corpora striata were very considerably diseased, together with some change in the optic thalami.

These two cases illustrate tolerably well what Dr. DaCosta says, viz.: "We may reasonably conclude the morbid forces to have affected the corpus striatum if motion be seriously impaired, or to have attacked the optic thalamus if there be paralysis of sensation."

Proceedings of the Sacramento Society for Medical Improvement.

The Society met, pursuant to adjournment, at the office of Dr. White, Feb. 20, 1872, with Dr. Hatch, the President, in the chair. Present: Drs. White, Trafton, Hatch, Nelson, Harkness, Simmons, Wythe, Taylor, Murphy, Montgomery and Nixon.

A communication was read from Dr. Wm. F. Smith, of San Francisco, requesting the reports of the transactions of this Society for publication in the *Western Lancet.* The Secretary was instructed to notify Dr. Smith that according to a resolution adopted by the Society some two years ago, the transactions were to be furnished to the PACIFIC MEDICAL AND SURGICAL JOURNAL; and that, for the present, they will continue to be forwarded to that journal only.

Dr. White read the regular paper of the evening, which brought into view the Pathology of certain nervous diseases. The paper was confined to two cases, which he had examined in the dead house of the County Hospital. [See the preceding article published in this JOURNAL.]

Dr. Taylor being called on, said he had no remarks to make, but considered the cases reported as quite interesting and instructive.

Dr. Nelson asked if the first case had any disease of the lungs.—Was answered that the lungs had not been examined.

Dr. Trafton thought that the tubercular deposits were sufficient to account for the epileptic convulsions.

Dr. Wythe coincided in opinion with Dr. Trafton.

Dr. Simmons said that in regard to the first case, the morbid growths were undoubtedly the result of syphilis. These morbid growths were sometimes found in the liver as well as in the brain.

Dr. Hatch believed the first case was one of syphilitic epilepsy, and that such cases were generally fatal.

Dr. Simmons offered a resolution for the appointment by the Chair, of a committee of three, with reference to the establishlishment of a City Dispensary for the benefit of the indigent poor of Sacramento.

After some discussion, the resolution was adopted, and the President appointed Drs. Simmons, Trafton and Cluness on said Committee.

A. B. Nixon, M. D.,
Secretary.

Extracts from the Proceedings of the San Francisco Medical Society.

February 13, 1872.

Dr. Bentley exhibited the following pathological specimens:

1. The encephalon of a man 48 years of age, of regular and sober habits. Having been exposed to the fumes of lead in a manufactory for four hours, the man became comatose, lost all consciousness and muscular power. In two weeks he had in a great measure recovered; there remained no general or local paralysis, except with regard to speech. At this time, when supposed to be convalescent, a noise was heard in his room early one morning, and he was found on the floor, unconscious. He died eleven hours afterward, comatose.

The encephalon showed general extravasation of blood, especially in the fissure of Sylvius, on the left side, in which region many observers locate the faculty of speech. This extravasation was evidently the cause of the primary symptoms, from which partial recovery had taken place. There was, in addition, extravasation into the fourth ventricle and at the base of the brain, which immediately preceded, and was the cause of death. The aorta in its upper portion was atheromatous; in its lower portion calcareous; the kidneys were granular, with wasting of the cortical portion from the deposition of innumerable cysts.

2. Kidney, showing large abscess. This was the only lesion, except congestion of the brain, found. The subject was a stranger.

3. Lung showing cicatrices and concretions in its apex, from healing of old vomicæ.

4. Liver showing atrophy as a result of peritonitis.

5. Heart hypertrophied, and with pericardium adherent at apex.

This case was examined within 20 hours of death, yet the kidneys, liver, spleen, &c., were in a state of decomposition. The heart lesion had been diagnosticated by Dr. Soule, that is the adherent pericardium. There was no valvular lesion, no atheroma, no displacement. The tremulous action, insisted on by Dr. Soule as a diagnostic, was present.

Dr. Bentley doubted the correctness of the statement made by Dr. J. P. Whitney at the previous meeting, that in hypertrophy and adhesion, especially if considerable, there was a characteristic drawing in of the chest wall with every contraction of the heart. A study of the anatomy of the parts would not confirm this idea. Unless pleuritic adhesion also existed, such contraction could not take place.

6. The last specimen was a liver, whose left lobe constituted almost the entire organ, the right lobe being very diminutive.

Dr. Soule said that the case just mentioned by Dr. Bentley was the one he spoke of at the last meeting when discussing the symptoms of adherent pericardium. He had never been able to detect any valvular lesions, but the heart's action was exceedingly intermittent and irregular, and there was that peculiar heaving motion of the chest which induced him to diagnosticate adherent pericardium, which the autopsy had verified. He had been fortunate in tracing the progress of pericarditis in several cases in the City and County Hospital. The friction sound first heard at the apex, was heard higher and higher up at each subsequent examination, at the same time disappearing successively at the points below, until it disappeared altogether. Months after, an autopsy revealed adherent pericardium.

Dr. Holbrook, remarking that *he* had raised the question of the diagnosis of adherent pericardium, said that, notwithstanding Dr. Soule's case, he believed there were cases that could not be diagnosticated. Recession of the interspaces was not pathognomonic; it occurred in capillary bronchitis, and also in pleurisy, and besides did not occur in adherent pericardium, unless there were also pleuritic adhesions, as shown by Dr. Bentley.

Dr. Soule said he had never found lumbricoides in California born children, though he had seen them in children coming from the East.

Dr. J. P. Whitney remarked that he had seen numbers, and Dr. Bates that he had had a case the day before.

FEBRUARY 27, 1872.

Dr. Bentley exhibited a liver with large abscess in the right lobe, which contained 62 oz. of pus. He knew nothing of the history of the case, but ventured to say that it was what is called tropical abscess, and that the patient had been a resident of the tropics. There was a marked distinction between tropical and pyemic abscess; with the latter there was no chance of recovery—in other cases recovery may take place. Some authorities claimed that a connection existed between tropical abscess and other forms of malarial disease, as dysentery; but one writer found no abscess in 17 cases of dysentery, another found 51 cases of abscess in 204 cases of dysentery—possibly only a coincidence.

Dr. Regensberger said that the patient from whom the liver came had been his. He entered the hospital with pleurisy and effusion to the third rib on the right side. Enlargement of the liver then developed itself. He was positive that the abscess was pyemic. The effusion in the right pleural cavity was so great that the lung was greatly compressed—carnified: there was effusion in the pericardium; no peritonitis. The patient had pyemic chills.

Dr. Bentley's second specimen was a hypertrophied heart, which, with the membranes, weighed over 4 lbs. The patient, a mulatto, was admitted to City and County Hospital two weeks prior to his death, with extensive anasarca, great oppression in breathing and that peculiar commotion in the cardiac region said to be diagnostic of adherent pericardium. There was, of course, great dullness, but no valvular lesions or displacement, and no adhesion of pericardium. Dr. Bentley thought the specimen would be a good evidence that there were no diagnostic symptoms of adherent pericardium. In the same case were found hobnail liver and granular kidney, albuminuria having been present during life.

The third specimen consisted of two atrophied kidneys, the smallest he had ever found in an adult. No albuminuria existed at the time of death.

The fourth specimen was the uterus and appendages, showing fallopian pregnancy, from a lady aged forty years, the mother of two or three children. She had had many physicians whom she had discharged successively, as they did not agree with her that she was pregnant. She had finally fallen on the floor, fainting. On reviving, feeling that she was about to die, she requested that an examination be made. The thorax and its organs were healthy; on opening the abdomen clots of blood were detected floating near the ovary, when it was supposed that an aneurism had ruptured. The tumor in the right fallopian tube being then discovered, it was found that the blood had escaped from rupture of a distended artery, and that there was tubal pregnancy.

MARCH 12, 1872.

Dr. Whitney referred to his proposition at the previous meeting to offer some remarks upon the diagnosis of pericardial adhesions. Perhaps the subject was of little practical importance, but it was one in which had arisen a difference of interpretation, and of this he desired to speak. It had been said by one of the ablest of philosophers that "Reason is the harmonization of thoughts with things." He liked the definition, and spoke of the attempts made to harmonize ideas with what is learned from observation, and believed that often more was learned from mistakes in diagnosis than in cases where examination proved their correctness. He had been greatly interested in Dr. Bentley's demonstrations. Conditions were shown to which Dr. Bentley gave his interpretation, and he had no fault to find with him for doing so, but claimed a like privilege for himself. Dr. Bentley had exhibited, two months ago, enormously hypertrophied hearts having adherent pericardii. He had stated that pericardial adhesion could not, of itself be diagnosticated, and that there was an anatomical reason why retraction in the cardiac region with every contraction of the heart, was not characteristic. To this he would oppose two cases which he had observed, in which there was no edema or dropsy, but emaciation, and in which there was noticeable over the region of cardiac dullness, which was extensive, a peculiar retraction of the intercostal spaces with every systole. He had inferred from this fact that pericardial adhesions existed, and in both cases autopsy verified the inference. He would defend this inference and take issue with Dr. Bentley on this point as well as upon another statement that concentric hypertrophy does not exist. He believed it did, and that there was physical reason for it. If effusion takes place between the two serous surfaces and becomes organized, the heart is limited in ability to work; it labors under difficulty, is fixed to the walls of the chest; does not move freely; hence the law of hypertrophy. Now we know another law. When lymph is effused on serous surfaces, and becomes organized, the next step is contraction and the formation of firm ligaments. What would be the inference in such a case? The action of the heart is interfered with and hypertrophy results. What if the pericardium be so thickened that the heart cannot dilate, and more power be required? The hypertrophy must arise at the expense of the cavity—hence concentric hypertrophy. Dr. Whitney then stated the following propositions:

1st. That a largely hypertrophied and firmly adherent heart in a case in which the intercostal spaces can be observed, may naturally be expected, during ventricular systole, to retract.

2d. That concentric hypertrophy does exist.

In support of the latter proposition, he read from Mayo's Outlines of Pathology, which recognized three forms of hypertrophy: first, without alteration of the cavity; second, with dilatation of the cavity; and third, with contraction of the cavity.

Also from Aitken, who writes that concentric hypertrophy sometimes takes place, the cavity contracting to the size of an unshelled almond only.

Also from Watson, who was Mayo's associate, and reasoned against the concentric form, being almost the only writer, so far as he recollected, who took this side of the question. Watson stated that concentric hypertrophy never occurred except as a congenital malformation. But on further examination Dr. Whitney read from Watson the statement that Cruveilhier was the first to reject the idea of concentric hypertrophy.

Dr. Holbrook desired to take issue upon one point only, i. e., the harmony between lesions and their outward exhibitions. If, for example, the lesion be cardiac, the outward exhibition would take a widely different course in different individuals. A knowledge of the cardiac lesion would have little to do with the treatment. The kidneys, the lungs, the brain or the liver might be prominently affected, and the treatment would be directed to such organ; it was not settled by the anatomical condition, but by the clinical aspect of the case. Diseases developed according to the relative weakness or strength of parts—their vulnerability. From a practical stand-point the pathological specimens were of very little value, for nothing was known of the history of the cases. The tendency was to look too much for post-mortem appearances, and not to the clinical history. Locomotor Ataxy, or as it was formerly called Tabes Dorsalis, was another illustration of the value of clinical observation. If a man had darting pain in the back, staggering gait, was unable to walk in the dark, &c., we knew he had Tabes, though we might not say that the posterior grey columns of the cord were degenerated without post-mortem examination.

Dr. Holbrook concluded by reiterating his former remark that pericardial adhesion, of itself, could not be diagnosticated, and he thought that all authors agreed on this point. The adhesion might be inferred, not diagnosticated.

Dr. Gibbons expressed surprise at what Dr. Holbrook had said. There was a time when his last remark might have been applied to very many subjects which now were clear. Were the remark correct, no chance for improvement would be left, and he was far from believing that pericardial adhesions could never be diagnosticated.

Dr. Holbrook asks, "What has therapeutics to do with anatomical lesions? What can we do with anatomical lesions?" In some diseases of the lungs we can reach the disease by giving force to the system to overcome it. Did we not, then, reach the lesion by therapeutics? He took issue with the

Doctor in regard to the treatment of organic derangements produced by heart disease. We did not treat the symptoms only, but directed our remedies to the heart. We did not treat the brain if it became diseased as a result of heart lesion. The treatment of diseases by symptoms was the homeopathic doctrine.

Dr. Gibbons concluded by objecting strongly to the idea that the morbid specimens presented there were valueless.

Dr. Holbrook replied that his remarks had been misapprehended. He wished to say that there was danger of physicians magnifying anatomical lesions at the expense of clinical study.

Dr. Bates said, Is not an autopsy a proof of our diagnosis? Do we not otherwise grope in the dark? From an autopsy we gain important facts, which are valuable even though little previous knowledge be obtained. He did not agree with the gentleman that the specimens here presented were of little value.

Dr. Baldwin expressed much gratification for the privilege of examining the specimens. They were valuable without histories. We often practiced on supposition, and confidence was increased when circumstances permitted a verification of the diagnosis.

Dr. J. P. Whitney remarked that he hoped no member understood him to underrate Dr. Bentley. It was proper for every man to judge for himself. Neither Dr. Bentley, nor Watson, nor any one else had a right to reason for us. Dr. Bentley had exhibited exceedingly interesting specimens, which he believed to be exceedingly valuable without even a scrap of history. The hepatic abscess exhibited on a previous occasion, was a case in point. Without any knowledge of the history, Dr. Bentley had confidently believed it to be tropical abscess, and that the patient had resided in the tropics. Dr. Regensberger, however, who had treated the case, said he had not resided in the tropics, and that the abscess was pyemic.

Dr. Whitney said he was inclined to believe that large hepatic abscesses were often pyemic. As was shown, they frequently arose in cases of dysentery. Pus corpuscles gaining entrance to the veins, found their way to the liver, causing multiple abscesses, which finally coalesced, forming a large one. Referring to the value of pathological specimens, he said we should avail ourselves of every opportunity to make post-mortem examinations. He did not agree with the previous speakers in regard to the relationship of symptoms and lesions to therapeutics. It was said we did not treat lesions. He thought with Alison, that we treat the tendency to death in a majority of cases. It was undoubtedly true that lesions can be removed by treatment. The effused lymph in syphilitic iritis is caused by lesion, which mercury removes.

Dr. Holbrook explained that he had no intention to disparage Dr. Bentley's anatomical exhibitions; he hoped he had not been understood to do so.

Dr. Gibbons said he had never been able to see anything in the remark that "we treat the tendency to death." It was not true. In nine-tenths of the cases there was no tendency to death. This position was illustrated by reference to different diseases, as diarrhea.

Dr. Whitney said he was surprised to hear there was no tendency to death in diarrhea, that killed so many younglings, and verged into cholera. Treating light or fanciful cases was not practicing medicine.

Dr. Holbrook asked if there was not a tendency to death in cancer, tuberculosis, aneurism, and if the treatment were not directed to this tendency.

Dr. Baldwin thought Dr. Gibbons had not been understood. He had not denied that some diseases tend to death.

Dr. Smith thought that a remark in Tanner's Practice gave the best explanation of Alison's idea. In speaking of typhoid fever, the patient is compared to a ship, the physician to a pilot; the pilot does not attempt to quell the storm, but to guide his vessel safely through it.

Dr. Gibbons claimed that in nineteen-twentieths of the cases a physician was called upon to treat, the idea of death did not enter his head. So far as cancer and similar diseases were concerned, no attempt was made to treat the tendency to death. Treatment was directed only to easing the patient. There was no practical significance in the expression.

REVIEWS AND NOTICES OF BOOKS.

A Text-Book of Pathological Histology: An Introduction to the Study of Pathological Anatomy. By Dr. Edward Rindfleisch, Professor of Pathological Anatomy in Bohn. Translated from the second German edition, with permission of the author, by William G. Cloman, M. D., assisted by F. T. Miles, M.D., Prof. of Anatomy, Univ. of Maryland: with 208 illustrations. Pp. 695. Philadelphia: Lindsay & Blakiston. 1872. San Francisco: A. L. Bancroft & Co.

Pathological Anatomy is but a "young science," and already comes a new book on it. Yesterday we had Billroth, the day before Virchow, and to-day Rindfleisch. Virchow is antiquated so soon. Billroth is mainly surgical. The present volume covers the whole field. In many respects pathological doctrines are as unfixed thus far as women's fashions. Our author himself refers to his present views on new pathological formations as entirely different from those enunciated in the first edition of his work. "There has not been left one stone upon another," he says. Nevertheless, the studies now in progress are so eminently practical that they cannot fail soon to establish fixed principles .The microscope is everything in this day. "This Book," says Rindfleisch, "originated more at the microscope than at the writing table." It is in fact a condensation of numberless microscopic observations. The translation, however, we are sorry to say, is very imperfect—so full of German idioms and forms of expression as greatly to obscure the sense. But a good translation of a German scientific work is a most difficult task to accomplish.

A Hand-Book of Therapeutics. By Sidney Ringer, M. D., Professor of Therapeutics in University College; Physician to University College Hospital. New York: William Wood & Co. San Francisco: A. L. Bancroft & Co. Pp. 483.

This work, which has been of high repute in England since its first publication, now appears for the first time from the American press. It confines itself to the action of medicines on the body, describing the effects in the following order: the skin, mouth, stomach, intestines, blood, the urinary organs; and finally their elimination from the system. It is a condensed and valuable record of the modus operandi of medicines, according to the most recent views.

A PRACTICAL TREATISE ON THE DISEASES OF WOMEN. By T. Gaillard Thomas, M. D., Prof. of Obstetrics and Diseases of Women and Children in the College of Physicians and Surgeons, New York; Physician to the Roosevelt Hospital, N. Y.; Attending Surgeon to the N. Y. State Women's Hospital, &c., &c. Third edition, enlarged and thoroughly revised, with 246 illustrations. Philadelphia: Henry C. Lea. 1872. Pp. 784. San Francisco: A. L. Bancroft & Co.

As far as we know, but one opinion has ever been pronounced by the profession on the former editions of this work; and there is not the slightest danger that the superior excellence ascribed to it will be damaged by the present edition, which is enlarged and modified in correspondence with the advances of gynecological science. The work of Dr. Thomas has become indispensable to American practitioners. A single drawback in practice will be felt by the majority of them, on account of the prevailing use of the cylindrical speculum; as Dr. Thomas, with modern pioneers generally in this department, employs the Sims speculum, and his examinations and processes are all described in connection with the use of this form of instrument.

A PRACTICAL TREATISE ON BRIGHT'S DISEASES OF THE KIDNEYS. By T. Granger Stewart, M. D., L. R. S. E., Fellow of the Royal College of Physicians, Lecturer on Clinical Medicine, &c., &c. Second edition. New York: William Wood & Co. 1871. San Francisco: A. L. Bancroft & Co. Pp. 334.

Though much has been written, and well written, on this subject, yet the theme is far from being exhausted. The present volume stands high as authority in Great Britain, and has received the warmest commendation from the press and from medical men generally. On the subject of Waxy Degeneration of the Kidneys, it is especially luminous. The illustrations of microscopic appearances are not to be surpassed.

ON BONE-SETTING (so-called), and its Relation to the Treatment of Joints Crippled by Injury, Rheumatism, &c., &c. By

P. Hood, M. D., M. R. C. S. London and New York: Macmillan & Co. 1871. Pp. 156. San Francisco: A. L. Bancroft & Co. Price $1.

The natural bone-setters are a variety of the human race that one meets with in various parts of the world—ignorant people who fancy that they possess a *gift* in the direction of their specialty, and who, by long usage and dexterous manipulation, succeed just often enough to make an impression on the human mind. This volume explains the methods by which they sometimes hit their mark, and is useful to surgeons in showing how tact and manipulation may often be substituted for main force in the reduction of dislocations and some other processes of surgery.

Medical Thermometry, and Human Temperature. By C. A. Wunderlich, Professor of Clinic at the University of Leipsig, &c., &c., and Edward Seguin, M. D. New York; Wm. Wood & Co. San Francisco: A. L. Bancroft & Co.

This important little volume has already been noticed in the pages of the Journal.

Plain Talk about Insanity: Its Causes, Forms, Symptoms, and the Treatment of Mental Diseases. With Remarks on Hospitals and Asylums, and the Medico-legal Aspects of Insanity. By T. W. Ingham, M. D., late of the Boston Hospital for the Insane. Boston: Alex. Moore. 1872. Pp. 97. San Francisco: Libby & Swett, No. 11 New Montgomery street.

Persons outside of the profession, who would gain a general view of the subject of insanity with but little reading or study, cannot do better than get this book. It is designed for popular reading, and is well adapted for the purpose.

Animal and Vegetable Parasites of the Human Skin. By B. Joy Jeffries, A. M., M. D., Fellow of the Mass. Med. Society; Member of the American Ophthalmological Society; Ophthalmic Surgeon to various Public Institutions, &c., &c. Boston: Alex. Moore. 1872. Pp. 102. San Francisco: Libby & Sweet.

The information comprised in this little book ought to be

known to every intelligent person. It will prove not only very useful, but highly interesting to every non-professional reader, and for this class it appears to be chiefly intended.

Small-Pox: The Predisposing Conditions and their Prevention. By Dr. Carl Both. Boston: Alex. Moore. 1872. San Francisco: Libby & Swett. Price 25 cts.

Insanity and Insane Asylums.—Report of E. T. Wilkins, M. D, Commissioner in Lunacy for the State of California. Made to His Excellency H. H. Haight, Governor, Dec. 2, 1871.

In performing the duties of his position, Dr. Wilkins visited 149 Insane Asylums in Europe and America, collecting from them statistical and other information, the leading points of which are condensed in this Report. The Report, containing 340 pages besides numerous diagrams, covers a wide field of enquiry, embracing nearly every consideration that lies within the range of the subject. It will be found very useful for reference, especially in regard to the various plans for the construction of Asylums, which are elaborately described and illustrated.

EDITORIAL.

Contents—End of the Volume.

Our present number is largely occupied by discussions on Pericardial Adhesion and Hypertrophy of Heart. We will pay the compliment to our subscribers to believe that very few of them will fail to appreciate the ability exhibited in the investigation of these topics.

To the Index attached to the closing number of the volume, we refer with some pride, as a proof that our year's labor has covered no small field of medical science, and has returned to the friends of the Journal an equivalent for their money.

Reports of State Board of Health.

During the absence of Dr. Logan, Secretary of the Board, who has gone to the meeting of the National Association in

Philadelphia, the publication of the monthly mortuary reports will be suspended. Meanwhile, the physicians in the several localities who make the returns, are requested to procure and preserve the records with care, so that the series shall not be broken.

State Boards of Health Recommended.

Governor Geary, of Pennsylvania, recommends to the Legislature the formation of a State Board of Health, on a plan similar to that of Massachusetts and of California, which were the first States to organize such Boards. The Governor was a member of the first Board of Health constituted on the Pacific coast. This was during the prevalence of cholera in San Francisco in 1850. We opine that before many years shall have passed by, nearly every State in the Union will have its State Board of Health.

Warm Bath in Insanity, and in Burns.

Dr. Wilkins, in his *Report* to the California Legislature, on Insanity, refers to the warm bath as a favorite treatment in Italy and in some parts of Holland and France. He often saw a dozen patients in one bath-room with their heads alone in sight, the bathing tub being covered except a hole for the head. There they usually remain from one to three hours, in some instances six to eight hours, and occasionally for days at a time. Dr. Gudden, of Zurich, kept a man thus immersed for five days, on account of a high state of excitement connected with bed-sores. The patient is represented to have slept well during a portion of the time, and to have been cured of the sores. No exhaustion or ill consequences followed. A case is related of a man scalded by steam, and not insane, who was placed by Hebra in a tepid bath and kept there for three weeks, until a new cuticle had formed over the entire surface. This patient recovered without inconvenience. The water was kept at the temperature most agreeable to the patient. Thus employed it is said to relieve effectually the extreme pain from the burns.

Hypodermic Injection of Ergotin in Hemoptysis.

Dr. C. Currie Ritchie, of Manchester, Eng., quoted in the

Practitioner, has had remarkable success in the treatment of pulmonary hemorrhage by this means. Reflecting on the action of ergot in contracting the muscular fibres, and thus lessening the calibre of the bloodvessels and diminishing the volume of blood, and taking in view its therapeutic action in aneurism, he inferred that it would be a powerful agent in producing hemostasis and arresting hemorrhage. In eight cases of hemoptysis he used the injection with uniform success, the blood ceasing to flow after a few minutes. The solution employed consisted of three grains of ergotin dissolved in equal parts of glycerin and rectified spirits. Very little local irritation was produced by it, though the solution in distilled water proved highly irritating.

Departed Heroes.

An extraordinary number of the great men in our Profession have gone to their long homes within the past twelve months. We have now to add to the list Professors Samuel Jackson and Samuel Henry Dickson, of Philadelphia; and Zina Pitcher, of Detroit. Professor Jackson had attained the ripe age of 85, with the full enjoyment of his faculties. Professor Pitcher died on the same day (April 5), at the age of 75. He was the principal founder of the University of Michigan, and his name has been identified with Medicine for many years. Professor Dickson died March 31st, from aortic aneurism, at the age of 74. As a student, a writer, and a lecturer, he distinguished himself through a long life.

When Dr. Jackson was entering on his long and honored career as an instructor, the senior editor of this Journal, then a student, attended a course of lectures given by him as Professor of Materia Medica in the Philadelphia College of Pharmacy, and also his first lecture in the University of Pennsylvania, to which he was promoted in the year 1828 as an adjunct of Professor Chapman. From the start he was highly popular with the class; for though possessed of no oratorical grace, and with a poor utterance, his enthusiasm gave charms to his lectures and always fixed the attention of the students. He had the singular defect of inability to pronounce the terminal g of the present participle; and none of his old students will ever forget the emphasis which he always gave to the expression frequently occurring in his lectures on physiology—"*livin beins.*" Dr. Jackson was also a favorite with the students from his social manners and the personal interest which he always exhibited towards them.

A Point in Ethics.

It is quite possible to violate the spirit of our code by inconsiderate efforts to enforce its letter. This is done not unfrequently by hasty exposures of supposed professional delinquencies. A rumor of misconduct on the part of a brother flies through the air and strikes the tympanum of some over-zealous and self-appointed medical policeman, who forthwith rushes into the court-room of the Medical Society or of the medical press, with accusation and condemnation. On enquiry the charge may prove entirely baseless; and though our code has no special provision against the promulgator, yet he should not be allowed to escape without censure, on the strength of his innocent credulity. Even if there be some ground for complaint, a hasty appeal to the public, or to the profession through a public channel, is neither gentlemanly nor fraternal. The spirit of our code is embodied in the Gospel law, which requires private labor for the purpose of reconciling difficulties, and which authorizes public exposure only when other means have failed. And if this course be proper in the case of real offenses, how much more so when the imputed error rests only on hearsay or suspicion!

These thoughts have been suggested at different times by the appearance in medical journals of statements censuring members of the profession by name for publishing, or suffering to be published in the newspapers, accounts of their cases or operations. In several instances the editors or correspondents of journals have attacked in this way their brethren in the profession, assuming that the parties attacked were at least cognizant of the publications in question, when the result showed that they had nothing whatever to do with the affair. The haste with which such exposures are made implies a fondness for this kind of work, and proves that there are men prominent in the profession who would much rather wield the sword of the law to cut off a brother's head, than extend to him the hand of friendship. Some very estimable men—with this fault excepted—belong to the class referred to. They make troublesome members of a medical society, and give rise to trouble generally. They know but one mode of treatment for offenders, and that is by epispastic discipline. They practice homeopathy in this, barring the impotent doses, and treat irritation by irritation. How much better it would be for them to cherish an opposite disposition—to seek out good traits instead of bad—to aim at saving by conservative treatment rather than rush into hasty amputations.

Small-Pox on the Railroad—Barbarity and Philanthropy.

In the days of Howard, physicians who attended the prisons of England stipulated that they should be under no obligation to visit them on the outbreak of any pestilential disease. And yet even then our profession claimed to be philanthropic. Such philanthropy would not pass current now-a-days. The world would pronounce it barbarity. But the same world claims for itself the right to exercise greater barbarity. The dread of pestilence dehumanizes the mass of mankind. It brings out the selfish phase of human nature without even a veil of gauze to cover its naked brutality. A passenger on a railway train is attacked with small-pox, and the fact is telegraphed to the point of destination. Consternation seizes the people, and measures are immediately taken to shut out the sufferer from the city. The protection of the community appears to demand this, and public officials may be right in their action. But the total disregard of the welfare of the victim is not creditable to Christian civilization. It is not much better than the policy of savage tribes who kill off their aged and infirm members to rid themselves of a burthen. Where is the "Good Samaritan" when pestilence approaches on the railway? Not outside of the medical profession, we should judge. Society at large appears to consider its obligation to humanity discharged by interposing a Board of Health, or Health Officer, or some other professional defense. And here, thank God, our profession never shirks its duty. Physicians, like other men, are liable to contract disease. They have families, too. They have no charmed life—no mysterious prophylactic—no means of averting the plague except what they freely impart to the world. And yet the world requires them to take the post of danger and stand between it and the angel of death ; while it cares not to bestow on them reward or honor. In every land men educated to medicine are governed by the same divine code. They are soldiers of their country, always ready, without a second thought, to throw themselves into the front rank for her defense against pestilence—the forlorn hope, if need be, to ward off the shafts of destruction from their fellow-men. Who is not proud to be numbered in the ranks of such a profession !

Benjamin Rush and Henry Holland—A Contrast.

It is related of Sir Henry Holland, M.D., that very early in life he determined never to allow himself to be so engrossed by his medical practice as to prevent his spending two months of each year in travel, and that he carried out this resolution through a career of fifty years. His purpose was to secure for himself long life, health, and happiness. A striking contrast was presented in the case of Dr. Benjamin Rush, of whom we were once informed by an aged physician who had been his student, that in the latter portion of his long life, he boasted that for thirty years he had not spent a single night outside of the city of Philadelphia. The example of the latter is more creditable to the philanthropic character of the profession, though love of self may have been a leading motive with both.

Death of Mrs. Dr. Price.

Our colleague of the Medical College of the Pacific, Professor Thomas Price, has encountered the great affliction of the loss by death of his young and estimable wife. She died of phthisis on the 27th of April, aged 27 years.

The noted Indian Chief and Physician, Dr. Peter Wilson, died recently at his home on the Cataraugus Reservation, N. Y. He was a son of Red Jacket and a well educated man, and highly useful to his tribe. His Indian name was Ha-da-gess, or One-who-heals-the-sick.

GENERAL SUMMARY.

Eczema Cured by Vaccination.

Dr. Lawrence Tait, in the *British Medical Journal*, describes two cases of inveterate eczema in children, which were completely cured by vaccination, the disease disappearing entirely in a few weeks. In both cases vaccination was deferred a long time for fear of doing mischief by it—so extensive and severe was the cutaneous affection.

Black Urine from Carbolic Acid.

The long continued internal use of carbolic acid has been observed in some cases to darken the urine, so that in mass it looks black. Analysis by German chemists has not explained the phenomenon satisfactorily.

Physician Senators.

Four Italian physicians have been chosen to be Senators of the New Kingdom. They are Professors Stanilaus, Cannizzaro, and Maggiorani, of Rome, and Porta, of Padua. In the face of the example which has been set by her continental nations, it is incomprehensible why Britain should withhold from her distinguished children in the Profession of Medicine, the only distinction which can be said to be at all adequate to their deserts. Alive to the want of medical legislative ability in the House of Commons, the Government is about to create the office of Minister of Public Health, yet it refuses to reward the services which the public so gratefully recognize, and to strengthen the scientific power of the House of Lords by advancing Sir William Jenner to a well-merited peerage.—*Med. Press & Circular.*

Pruritus of the Face as a Precursor of Small-Pox.

Professor Crespi, of Bologna, says that a few moments' observation of patients who are in the incubative stage of small-pox will prove that they always suffer from an unpleasant sensation of itching about the face, especially on the forehead and chin. He has thus been able to diagnose small-pox in the earliest stages, and he believes the symptoms will be found to be uniform.—*Med. Press & Circular.*

Nitrite of Amyl and Chinese Samshu.

Dr. F. Porter Smith writes to the *Practitioner* for January, with reference to "the effect of nitrite of amyl" in causing flushing of the face, that Chinese "samshu," (*i. e.* thrice distilled,) or native corn brandy, produces upon the people a remarkable reddening of the eyes and whole head, with a very evanescent excitement. This is due to the presence of fusel-oil, (amyl alcohol,) and has exercised no small influence upon the drinking habits of the Chinese. The suffusion of the head and face immediately proclaims the fact of having drunk wine. The smell of the spirit, depending upon propylic and butyric as well as amylic compounds, acts as another tell-tale. Very strong and cheap spirit is easily obtainable in China, and may be used in the preparation of tinctures, due allowance being made for the presence of the amyl compound, which the Chinese distillers never remove by rectification. It acts like the salutary stink of gas, in giving timely warning of its near neighborhood. Why remove fusel-oil from British brandy?—*Med. Press & Circular.*

Atomized Turpentine-Water in Chronic Bronchitis and Consumption.

Dr. S. Goodwin, of Victoria, Texas, writes us that he has lately been using turpentine-water, inhaled by means of an atomizer, with signal advantage in cases of chronic bronchitis and consumption, where there was copious expectoration of either mucus or pus, with hemorrhage or violent cough. The turpentine-water is prepared from spirits of turpentine by magnesia, in the same way that aromatic waters are commonly prepared by druggists.—*Med. News—New Remedies.*

Ice in Acute Rheumatism.

Prof. Esmarch, in a communication to the Berlin Med. Society, related instances of the great benefit which he had derived from the continuous application of ice to joints affected with acute rheumatism. The general temperature becomes lowered, the pain abated, and course of the disease abbreviated to an extent procurable by no other means. So far from fearing the induction of cerebral affection by repelling the articular inflammation—the *phrenopathia rheumatica* being here, as in typhus, dependent upon increased temperature—ice is especially indicated for its prevention and removal.—*Med. Times and Gazette—New Remedics.*

Lupus Exedens of Twenty Years' Standing Cured by Large Doses of Iodide of Potassium.

Mr. Gay (London *Lancet*, Dec 9, 1871) details a case in which the disease had steadily progressed for 20 years, eating away the greater portion of the maxilla and the nasal bone and cartilage on the left side. There was no syphilitic basis whatever, but cicatrization commenced in a very short time after the exhibition of half a drachm of iodide of potassium three times a day, and was nearly completed at time of report.—*New Remedies.*

Mortality in San Francisco during March, 1872.

BY H. GIBBONS JR., M. D.

CAUSES OF DEATH.

Anemia	2	Dentition	2	Intussusception	1
Angina Pectoris	2	Diabetes	1	Jaundice	2
Aneurism	1	Diphtheria	1	Meningitis	11
Aneurism of Aorta	2	Diseases of Heart	13	Old Age	2
Apoplexy	6	Dropsy	2	Paralysis	1
Asthma	2	Dysentery	2	Peritonitis	5
Atrophia	3	Enteritis	3	Phthisis	53
Bright's Disease	4	Erysipelas	3	Pleuritis	1
Bronchitis	5	Fever, Intermittent	6	Pneumonitis	19
Cancer	2	Do. Scarlet	3	Premature Birth	2
Do. of Bowels	1	Do. Typhoid	7	Poisoning	2
Do. of Uterus	1	Do. Typhus	2	Purpura	1
Congest'n of Stomach	1	Gastritis	2	Pyemia	4
Congestion of Brain	2	Hepatitis	1	Rheumatism	1
Do of Lungs	3	Hemoptysis	1	Suicide	2
Convulsions, Puerp'l	1	Hemorrhage	1	Syphilis	2
Do Infantile	10	Hydrocephalus	3	Tabes Mesenterica	1
Croup	3	Inanition	11	Unknown	16
Cystitis	2	Influenza	1	Whooping Cough	3
Debility, General	3	Injuries, unspecified	6	Still-births	31
TOTAL					256

AGES.

Under 1 year	61	From 15 to 20 years	6	From 60 to 70 years	7
From 1 to 2 years	18	From 20 to 30 years	37	From 70 to 80 years	6
From 2 to 5 years	7	From 30 to 40 years	31	From 80 to 90 years	
From 5 to 10 years	4	From 40 to 50 years	49	Unknown	
From 10 to 15 years	5	From 50 to 60 years	25		

SEX:—Male, 175; Female, 81.

COLOR:—White, 215; Copper, 40; Black, 1.

NATIVITIES.

California	89	Scotland	2	China	38
Other parts of U. S.	43	France	5	Azores	1
British-Amer'n Prov.	2	Germany	18	East Indies	1
Mexico	3	Sweden	3	Isle of Man	1
Chile	2	Russia	1	Poland	2
England	9	Switzerland	1	Norway	1
Ireland	37	Italy	1		

RECAPITULATION.

Died in City Wards	202	Casualties	6
City and County Hospital	12	Suicides	3
U. S. Marine Hospital	1	Alms House	3
French Hospital	4	Mt. St. Joseph's Asylum	11
German Hospital	3	Industrial School	1
St. Mary's Hospital	7	S. F. Female Hospital	2
Small-Pox Hospital	1		

REMARKS.—The average mortality in March, for six years past, is about 231. This is but little less than that of the present month, which is notably small for a city of 180,000 inhabitants. The number of deaths from consumption and other lung diseases, (particularly pneumonia,) is markedly in excess of that which usually obtains. On the other hand, no deaths whatever have taken place from cholera infantum, alcoholism, diarrhea, drowning, softening of the brain, etc. Six deaths are recorded from intermittent fever. The question arises —Is such a fever competent to produce death? If intermittent fever did exist, may not death have been due to some intercurrent affection? We confess to very grave doubts as to the *possibility* of simple intermittent, in San Francisco, terminating fatally, and believe that, as in the case of typhus, some other disease should have the discredit of the deaths. It will be seen that congestion of the stomach is given as the cause of death in one instance. The number of stillbirths continues large, but the mortality of young children has been small—barely over a third of the total. Nearly a third of the deaths occurred in persons between 30 and 50 years of age; and between a third and a fourth were natives of China and Ireland. The death in the Small-Pox Hospital was not from small-pox.

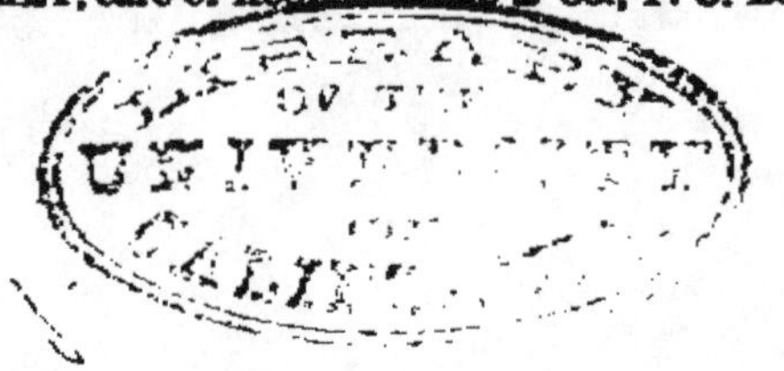

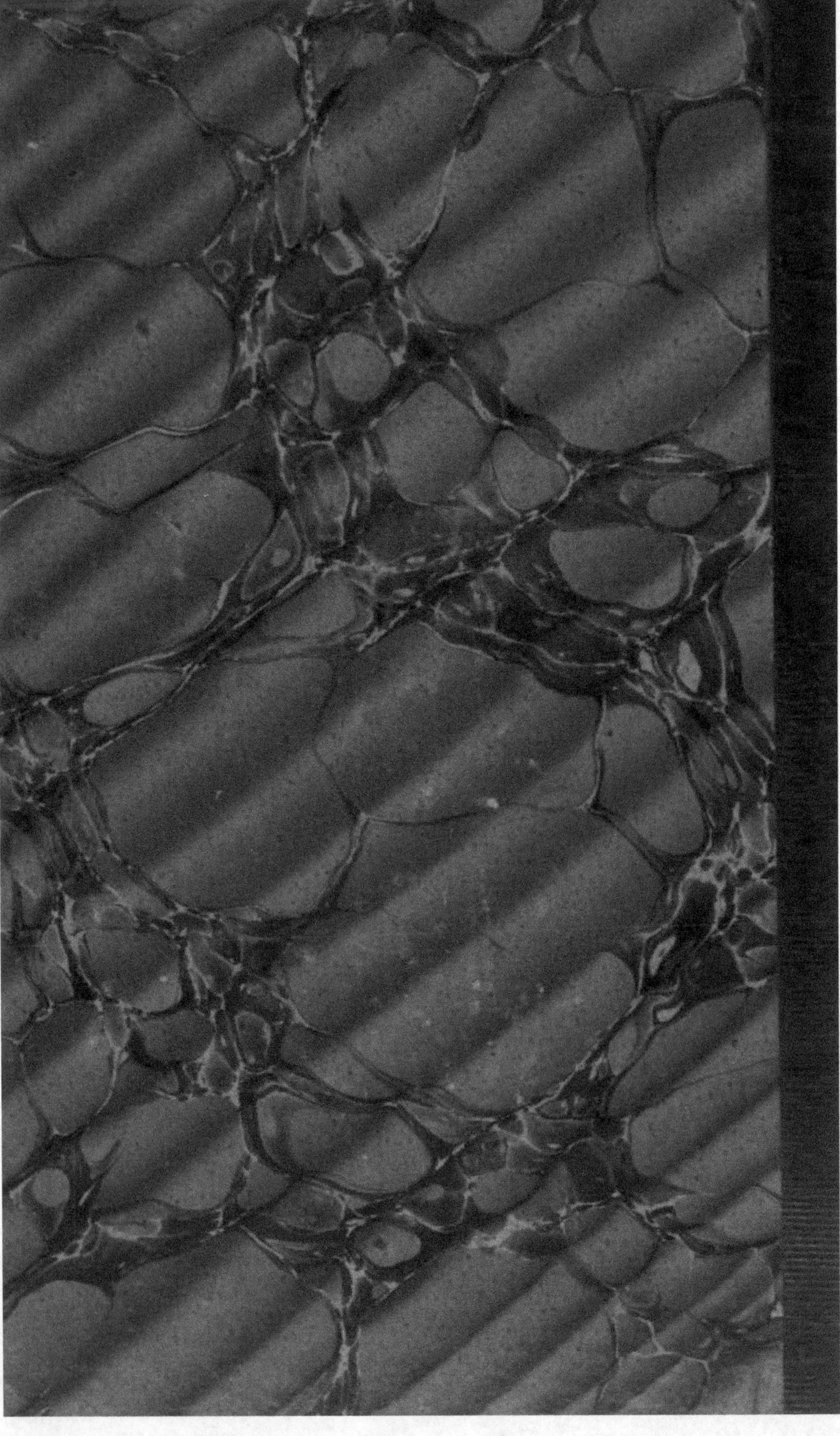